Freedom and the Construc

VOLUME II

Free Persons and Free States

Freedom, today perceived simply as a human right, was a continually contested idea in the early modern period. In *Freedom and the Construction of Europe* an international group of scholars explores the richness, diversity and complexity of thinking about freedom in the shaping of modernity. Volume I examines debates about religious and constitutional liberties, as well as discussing tensions between free will and divine omnipotence across a continent of proliferating religious denominations. Volume II considers free persons and free states, examining differing views about freedom of thought and action and their relations to conceptions of citizenship. Debates about freedom have been fundamental to the construction of modern Europe, but represent a part of our intellectual heritage that is rarely examined in depth. These volumes provide materials for thinking in fresh ways not merely about the concept of freedom, but about how it has come to be understood in our own time.

QUENTIN SKINNER is Barber Beaumont Professor of the Humanities at Queen Mary, University of London. His publications include *The Foundations of Modern Political Thought* (2 vols., 1978), *Reason and Rhetoric in the Philosophy of Hobbes* (1996), *Liberty before Liberalism* (1998), *Visions of Politics* (3 vols., 2002) and *Hobbes and Republican Liberty* (2008).

MARTIN VAN GELDEREN was Professor of European Intellectual History at the European University Institute from 2003 until 2012 and has just become director of the Lichtenberg Kolleg, the Göttingen Institute for Advanced Studies in the Humanities and Social Sciences. He is currently completing a monograph *Rembrandt, Grotius and Manasseh: Visuality and Religious Toleration.*

Freedom and the Construction of Europe

VOLUME II

Free Persons and Free States

Edited by Quentin Skinner

and Martin van Gelderen

Cambridge
University Press

CAMBRIDGE
UNIVERSITY PRESS

University Printing House, Cambridge CB2 8BS, United Kingdom

One Liberty Plaza, 20th Floor, New York, NY 10006, USA

477 Williamstown Road, Port Melbourne, VIC 3207, Australia

314-321, 3rd Floor, Plot 3, Splendor Forum, Jasola District Centre, New Delhi - 110025, India

79 Anson Road, #06-04/06, Singapore 079906

Cambridge University Press is part of the University of Cambridge.

It furthers the University's mission by disseminating knowledge in the pursuit of education, learning and research at the highest international levels of excellence.

www.cambridge.org
Information on this title: www.cambridge.org/9781108817783

First published 2013
First paperback edition 2020

A catalogue record for this publication is available from the British Library

Library of Congress Cataloging in Publication data
Freedom and the construction of Europe : religious and constitutional liberties / edited by Quentin Skinner and Martin van Gelderen.
p. cm.
Includes bibliographical references and index.
ISBN 978-1-107-03307-8
1. Liberty – Europe. 2. Civil rights – Europe. I. Skinner, Quentin.
II. Gelderen, Martin van
JC599.E85F74 2013
323.094 – dc23 2012027491

ISBN 978-1-107-03307-8 Hardback
ISBN 978-1-107-03184-5 Hardback (2 vol set)
ISBN 978-1-108-81778-3 Paperback

Contents of Volume 1

Part II Liberty and liberties in constitutional thought

Contents of Volume II

Acknowledgements

While we were editing our earlier volumes on *Republicanism: A Shared European Heritage* (van Gelderen and Skinner 2002) we came to see that there was a need for a work of comparable scope devoted to the theory and practice of religious and political liberty in early modern Europe. With this idea in mind, we held a meeting in 2004 with Annabel Brett, Richard Fisher and Iain Hampsher-Monk at which we agreed on the topics that such a study would need to encompass and drew up a preliminary table of contents. Following the model of our earlier volumes on Republicanism, we also agreed that the best way to bring together the latest research on the subject would be to hold a series of conferences out of which a book might eventually emerge.

We recognised that such a project would require large-scale funding, but this problem was solved when Quentin Skinner was awarded a Balzan Prize in 2006. After some discussion, the Balzan Foundation generously agreed to the following scheme: that we should assemble an international group of younger scholars, preferably at the post-doctoral stage of their careers; that they should be invited to attend a series of conferences at which their work would be presented and discussed; and that their conference papers should subsequently be revised and extended with a view to turning them into a book.

The project was advertised in the summer of 2007. After sifting a large number of applications we appointed twenty-eight members of a core group, all of whom delivered papers at a series of four conferences held at the European University Institute between July 2008 and September 2009. We also invited a number of senior scholars to speak at one or other of these meetings, and we are especially grateful to those who not only joined us but agreed to turn their papers into publishable texts.

We owe an overwhelming debt to the Balzan Foundation for welcoming our proposal and providing us with such munificent support. Above all we should like to thank Salvatore Veca, Chairman of the Balzan General Prize Committee, for his unfailing interest and warm encouragement. A special word of thanks is additionally owed to Suzanne Werder, Secretary to the Prize Committee, for her invaluable guidance about administrative matters at every stage.

We are also deeply grateful to the European University Institute. By providing Martin van Gelderen with a 'seed-money' grant, the Institute originally set our project in motion, enabling us to hold our preliminary meeting and sketch the contours of our work. Subsequently the Institute placed us yet more deeply in its debt by permitting us to make use of the spectacular facilities at the Villa Schifanoia in San Domenico di Fiesole for our conferences. We want to express our particular thanks to the then President, Yves Mény, who generously supplied us with additional funding and showed such a friendly interest in our work.

The division of editorial labour between us has been as follows. Martin van Gelderen took responsibility for organising the series of conferences. He wishes to express his appreciation to Sergio Amadei and Nikki Koniordis for much indispensable practical help. Quentin Skinner edited the conference papers and negotiated with Cambridge University Press. After the reports of the Press's referees were received, Quentin Skinner re-edited the revised chapters to produce the final version of our text. He wishes to acknowledge the extensive help he received from Tommaso Giordani, who ensured that the chapters were submitted in uniform style, and who created, edited and checked the bibliographies.

We should like to pay tribute to the exceptional helpfulness of the Press's anonymous referees. One in particular gave us detailed comments on each individual chapter, and our whole project greatly benefited from the criticisms we received. We also need to express our warm thanks to our contributors for their forbearance and co-operation in revising – and in some cases extensively rewriting – their texts in the light of the referees' reports.

We cannot speak too highly of the advice and assistance we have received from Cambridge University Press, and especially from Richard Fisher as our editor. He involved himself in our project from its inception, and gave us much wise counsel about how to shape and develop our work. Shortly before these volumes went into production he was appointed Managing Director of the Press. But he nevertheless continued, in spite of endless calls on his time, to oversee our project with his habitual generosity and effectiveness.

We should also like to thank Lucy Rhymer for much helpful and enthusiastic guidance in the final stages of production. As these volumes go to press, it is a pleasure to add our thanks to Sarah Roberts, our production editor, who saw them through to publication with unfailing patience and efficiency, and to Frances Brown, our copy-editor, who worked her way through our large and complex text with tireless dedication and meticulousness.

QUENTIN SKINNER
MARTIN VAN GELDEREN

Notes on contributors

CATHERINE BALLÉRIAUX is a Ph.D. student in history at the University of Auckland, New Zealand. Her thesis, 'Reformation Strategies: Conversion, Civility, and Utopia in Missionary Writings about the New World, c. 1610–1690', compares French, English and Spanish missions to the native peoples of America.

ANNABEL BRETT is Reader in History at the University of Cambridge and a Fellow of Gonville and Caius College, Cambridge. She is the author of *Liberty, Right and Nature: Individual Rights in Later Scholastic Thought* (1997) and *Changes of State: Nature and the Limits of the City in Early Modern Natural Law* (2011).

THEODORE CHRISTOV is Assistant Professor of History at the George Washington University in Washington, DC. He previously taught political theory at Northwestern University. He has published articles on Hobbes and international thought, on Vattel and the liberal state, and on the history of the early modern idea of Europe.

JOHN COFFEY is Professor of Early Modern History at the University of Leicester. His books include *Persecution and Toleration in Protestant England, 1558–1689* (2000) and *Exodus and Liberation: Deliverance Politics from John Calvin to Martin Luther King* (forthcoming 2013). He co-edited *The Cambridge Companion to Puritanism* (2008).

MICHAEL COOK is the Class of 1943 University Professor of Near Eastern Studies at Princeton University. Before going to Princeton in 1986 he taught for twenty years at the School of Oriental and African Studies, University of London. His books include *The Koran: A Very Short Introduction* (2000); *Commanding Right and Forbidding Wrong in Islamic Thought* (2000); *A Brief History of the Human Race* (2003); and *Studies in the Origins of Early Islamic Culture and Tradition* (2004).

ROSANNA COX is Lecturer in Early Modern Literature at the University of Kent. Her publications include articles on ideas of liberty in Milton's *Samson*

Agonistes, on republican diplomacy and on early modern marriage. She is currently completing a monograph on Milton and citizenship.

HANNAH DAWSON is Senior Lecturer in the History of Ideas at the University of Edinburgh. She is the author of *Locke, Language and Early Modern Philosophy* (2007), and is currently editing Locke's *Disputations on the Law of Nature* for the Clarendon Edition of the Works of John Locke.

SERENA FERENTE is Lecturer at King's College London. She works on the social and political history of late-medieval and Renaissance Italy. Her latest projects focus on the passions in the political languages of late-medieval Europe, and on the role of gender in debates about sovereignty.

FONNA FORMAN is Associate Professor of Political Science and Co-Director of the Center on Global Justice at the University of California, San Diego. She is the author of *Adam Smith and the Circles of Sympathy* (2010), and has work forthcoming on contemporary global justice theory and on ideas of exile and escape in eighteenth-century cosmopolitan thought. She edits the *Adam Smith Review*.

FELICITY GREEN is a Chancellor's Fellow in History at the University of Edinburgh. Previously she was the holder of a Junior Research Fellowship in History at Trinity College, Cambridge. She is the author of *Montaigne and the Life of Freedom* (2012).

TOMASZ GROMELSKI is a Research Fellow at Wolfson College, Oxford. He was formerly at the Institute for Human Sciences in Vienna and at the European University Institute. Research interests and publications focus on political thought and political culture in early modern Poland-Lithuania, and on the social history of Tudor England.

POLLY HA is Lecturer in Early Modern British History at the University of East Anglia. She is the author of *English Presbyterianism, 1590–1640* (2011) and co-editor, with Patrick Collinson, of *The Reception of Continental Reformation in Britain* (2011). She is currently working on a critical edition of sources relating to pre-revolutionary Puritanism.

LENA HALLDENIUS is Professor of Human Rights at Lund University. She is a Life Member of Clare Hall, Cambridge, and former Torgny Segerstedt Pro Futura Fellow at Uppsala University. Her writings include a monograph on liberalism and articles on the concept of freedom and the political thought of Locke, Hobbes and Wollstonecraft.

IAIN HAMPSHER-MONK is Professor of Political Theory at the University of Exeter. He is the author of *A History of Modern Political Thought* (1992), and co-editor of *History of Concepts: Comparative Perspectives* (1998) and *The History of Political Thought in National Context* (2001). He jointly edits the journal *History of Political Thought*.

Jaska Kainulainen currently holds a post-doctoral research position in the Department of History at the University of Helsinki. His research focuses on Paolo Sarpi, on whom he has published articles in *Beiträge zur Romanistik* and in *European Review of History*.

Thomas Kaufmann is Professor of Church History in the Faculty of Theology at the University of Göttingen and Vice-president of the Academy of Sciences. His publications include *Universität und lutherische Konfessionalisierung* (1997), *Dreißigjähriger Krieg und Westfälischer Friede* (1998), *Türckenbüchlein* (2008), *Geschichte der Reformation* (2nd edn, 2010) and *Luthers Judenschriften* (2011).

Lovro Kunčević is a researcher at the Institute for Historical Sciences of HAZU in Dubrovnik. He has published on political thought and identity discourses of early modern Dubrovnik, and is currently completing, with Gábor Kármán, a book on the European tributary states of the Ottoman Empire in the sixteenth and seventeenth centuries.

Daniel Lee is Assistant Professor of Political Science at the University of Toronto. He was previously a member of the Society of Fellows at Columbia University. His research has appeared in *Journal of the History of Ideas*, *History of Political Thought*, *Review of Politics* and *Politica Antica*, and he has contributed a chapter to the forthcoming volume *Hobbes and the Law*.

Avi Lifschitz is Lecturer in European History at University College London. Currently he is a Fellow at the Wissenschaftskolleg zu Berlin. He is the author of *Language and Enlightenment: The Berlin Debates of the Eighteenth Century* (2012), and co-editor of *Epicurus in the Enlightenment* (2009).

Thomas Maissen has been full Professor of Modern History at the University of Heidelberg since 2004. He is the author of *Die Geburt der Republic: Staatsverständnis und Repräsentation in der frühneuzeitlichen Eidgenossenschaft* (2006); *The Republican Alternative: The Netherlands and Switzerland Compared* (2008, with A. Holenstein and M. Prak) and *Die Geschichte der Schweiz* (2010).

Reidar Maliks is a Postdoctoral Fellow in Philosophy at the University of Oslo, having previously taught at Columbia, Harvard and Oxford. His book *Kant's Politics in Context* is forthcoming.

Sarah Mortimer is University Lecturer and Official Student and Tutor in History at Christ Church, Oxford. Her first book, *Reason and Religion in the English Revolution* (2010), won the Forkosch Prize and she has recently co-edited, with John Robertson, a volume of essays on *The Intellectual Consequences of Religious Heterodoxy* (2012).

Eric Nelson is Professor of Government at Harvard University. He is the author of *The Greek Tradition in Republican Thought* (2004) and *The Hebrew Republic: Jewish Sources and the Transformation of European Political Thought* (2010). He has also edited Hobbes's translations of the *Iliad* and the *Odyssey* for the Clarendon Edition of the Works of Thomas Hobbes (2008).

MARTINA REUTER is docent of Philosophy at the University of Helsinki and Lecturer in Gender Studies at the University of Jyväskylä. With Sara Heinämaa she has edited *Psychology and Philosophy: Inquiries into the Soul from Late Scholasticism to Contemporary Thought* (2009).

ALEXANDER SCHMIDT is a junior Professor of Intellectual History at the Friedrich Schiller University, Jena. He is the author of *Vaterlandsliebe und Religionskonflikt: Politische Diskurse im Alten Reich 1555–1648* (2007). His articles have appeared in *The Historical Journal*, *History of Political Thought*, *Modern Intellectual History*, *Francia* and elsewhere.

FREYA SIERHUIS is a Research Fellow in the Department of English Literature at the Ludwig-Maximilians-Universität in Munich, where she is working on a monograph on Fulke Greville. She has published on Calvinism and Arminianism, revenge tragedy and the biblical drama of Joost van den Vondel.

QUENTIN SKINNER is Barber Beaumont Professor of the Humanities at Queen Mary, University of London. His publications include *The Foundations of Modern Political Thought* (2 vols., 1978), *Reason and Rhetoric in the Philosophy of Hobbes* (1996), *Liberty before Liberalism* (1998), *Visions of Politics* (3 vols., 2002) and *Hobbes and Republican Liberty* (2008).

PETER STACEY is Assistant Professor of History at UCLA and the author of *Roman Monarchy and the Renaissance Prince* (2007). He is currently writing a book about Machiavelli's theory of the state.

TIMOTHY STANTON is Senior Lecturer in Politics at the University of York. He has been Beinecke Fellow at Yale University (2008) and Balzan-Skinner Fellow at the University of Cambridge (2011). He is currently completing a critical edition of John Locke's unpublished 'Defence of Nonconformity' (1681–2).

ANTTI TAHVANAINEN received his Ph.D. from the University of Helsinki, and is the author of *Rhetoric and Public Speech in English Republicanism, 1642–1681* (2012). He has published articles on John Milton and James Harrington.

MARTIN VAN GELDEREN was Professor of European Intellectual History at the European University Institute from 2003 until 2012 and has just become director of the Lichtenberg Kolleg, the Göttingen Institute for Advanced Studies in the humanities and social sciences. He is currently completing a monograph *Rembrandt, Grotius and Manasseh: Visuality and Religious Toleration*.

MÁRTON ZÁSZKALICZKY is a Ph.D. candidate in the History Department of the Central European University, Budapest. His dissertation is entitled 'Protestant Political Theology and Corporate Constitutionalism in 16th–17th century Hungary'. With Balázs Trencsényi he co-edited the volume *Whose Love of Which Country? Composite States, National Histories and Patriotic Discourses in Early Modern East Central Europe* (2010).

Introduction

Quentin Skinner

During the period surveyed in this second volume, two connected claims about the nature of free persons and free states enjoyed widespread acceptance.[1] One concerned the character of human freedom itself. A broad array of writers discussed in the chapters that follow – ranging from Montaigne to the Levellers, from John Milton to Mary Wollstonecraft – were in essential agreement about what it means to speak of being in possession of one's liberty. They all invoke a distinction that had been central to the law of persons ever since its formulation in the *Digest* of Roman law in late antiquity. According to the *Digest*, what it means to be a *liber homo* or 'freeman' is not to be a slave, and hence not to be *in aliena potestate*, in the power of another person and hence at their mercy.[2] Picking up this distinction, the authors I have cited accept that freedom can be defined as absence of dependence upon the will of anyone else. Freedom is taken to consist, in other words, in the absence of arbitrary power.

Of no less importance is the fact that in speaking of 'freemen' these writers take themselves to be putting forward not merely a legal definition of civil liberty but an ideal of citizenship. This ideal was eventually encapsulated in a set of phrases that have never ceased to figure in the stories we tell about the significance of our autonomy and independence. To be a freeman is held to be equivalent to being 'your own man', not beholden to a patron or master, not the creature of anyone else. A freeman is therefore someone to be reckoned with, someone who can look you in the eye, who can reason and negotiate on terms of equality without feeling any need to doff the cap or bend the knee. As a result, freemen are said to enjoy the respect – and

1. In outlining these claims I draw on Skinner 2009b.
2. *Digest of Justinian* 1985: 1.5.3, vol. 1, 15; 1.6.1, vol. 1, 18.

the self-respect – that comes of being known to speak frankly and behave without fear or favour, acting solely as reason and conscience dictate.

The contrast is always with the figure of the slave. If you are condemned to live in dependence on the goodwill of a *dominus*, then you will be able to act only by the grace of your master, only with his implicit permission, which can be withdrawn with impunity at any time. But to say that all your actions are performed as a matter of grace is to acknowledge that none of them can ever be performed as a matter of right. As the *Digest* expresses the point, your predicament is that you are unable to act *sui iuris*, because you are wholly restricted to acting as your *dominus* is willing to allow.[3] One implication is said to be that this kind of servitude can hardly fail to induce servility. Confronting a master with the power to act as he may choose, it is almost inevitable that slaves will resort to slavish self-censorship. Not knowing what may happen to them, and desperate to avoid their master's rage, they will be sure to behave in appeasing and ingratiating ways.

The other and connected claim put forward by the exponents of this line of thought concerned the nature of the legal and institutional arrangements under which the ideal of freedom as absence of dependence can be realised. They agree that, just as it is possible to live and act freely if and only if you are a freeman, it is possible to live and act as a freeman if and only if you live in what they like to describe as a 'free state'. Discussing the freedom of states, they employ the term in the same way as they do when speaking about individual liberty. To describe a civil association as free is to say that it is capable of acting according to its own will – that is, according to the general will of its citizens – as a result of not living in dependence on the will of anyone other than the citizen-body as a whole. Here their argument stands in strong contrast with that of the classical utilitarians who rose to prominence in the course of the Enlightenment. For David Hume, and later for William Paley and Jeremy Bentham, civil laws are inevitably the enemies of individual liberty because their imposition involves the use of force or the threat of it. But according to the writers I am considering, any civil law which I help to enact, and to which I agree to submit myself, can be construed as an expression of my will rather than a restriction upon it, and must therefore be compatible with my liberty.

There are said to be two distinct ways in which it is possible for a body politic to lose the capacity to act according to its will and thereby lose its standing as a free state. One is when the power of the state falls under the

3. *Digest of Justinian* 1985: 1.6.1, p. 18.

control of anyone other than the sovereign body of the citizens, whether the usurping agent be a monarch, an oligarchy or a ruling class. The other possibility is that the state may fall into a condition of dependence upon the will of another state, whether as the result of conquest, colonisation or any other process that has the effect of bypassing the will of its citizens as the source of law. When either of these disasters occurs, those who are excluded from giving their consent to the laws by which they are governed find themselves reduced to living in dependence on the will of those who have arrogated the power to legislate. But to live in such circumstances is what it means to live in servitude. Hence the claim that, unless you live in a free state, you will find yourself bereft of individual liberty.

This commitment makes the writers I am considering sound like democrats, and it is certainly true that they think of sovereignty within free states as ultimately lying with the citizen-body as a whole. Generally, however, they modify this commitment in two ways. First, they espouse the cause of popular sovereignty largely for instrumental purposes, treating it less as an ideal in itself than as the only possible means of securing the cherished value of liberty as absence of dependence. Secondly, when they declare that civil laws must express the general will of the people, they usually add that the people must be prepared to allow their sovereignty to be exercised by some form of representative government. They concede that, if our representatives can plausibly claim not merely to be speaking in our name but to be safeguarding our values and interests, it remains appropriate to think of ourselves as living in a free state.

Addressing these connected themes, several of the following chapters concentrate on the claim that it is possible to live as a free person only in a free state. In Chapter 10 Reidar Maliks examines Kant's classic formulation of the argument itself, while other chapters consider the nature of the institutions and safeguards needed to uphold the ideal of freedom thus understood. In Chapter 9 Theodore Christov discusses Vattel's contention that civil liberty can be promoted by commerce between states, while Antti Tahvanainen, writing in Chapter 7 about seventeenth-century England, stresses the importance attached to elections and even to secret ballots by the radical thinkers of the time. Similarly focusing on England, Iain Hampsher-Monk adds in Chapter 6 that the freedom of freemen was additionally held to depend on their membership of the kinds of corporations that could help to uphold their rights.

A number of other chapters focus on the underlying vision of civil liberty as independence from the arbitrary will of others. In Chapter 12 Lena

Helldenius explores Mary Wollstonecraft's reading of the implications of this commitment. If you are controlled by someone else's will, Wollstonecraft argues, then strictly speaking you cannot be said to be capable of moral action at all. As long as you live in subjection to a master, your actions can never be the product simply of your own will and desires; they will always be the product in part of what your *dominus* is willing to permit. As Avi Lifschitz reminds us in Chapter 5, Rousseau traced the origin of this form of servitude to the act of instituting the state itself. But as he goes on to show, Rousseau's account of the state of nature as a condition of freedom was powerfully contested by Moses Mendelssohn, who insisted on interpeting our alleged natural liberty as a species of enslavement.

Felicity Green and Rosanna Cox pursue further implications of the basic contrast between freedom and dependence. Examining the case of Montaigne, Green argues in Chapter 2 that his call to reclaim ownership over ourselves was his practical response to the problems of being a citizen in a war-torn world. For Montaigne, public service was a form of servitude, making us into slaves by encouraging us to engage with events over which we have no control. Montaigne's retreat to his estates represented an exile of the will, an inward refuge and a means to transform himself into a free man beholden only to himself. A comparable ideal of freedom, Rosanna Cox shows in Chapter 8, underlay John Milton's view of family life, and in turn affected his anti-monarchical propaganda as well as his tracts on divorce. Milton sees free consent as the only moral basis for family as well as public life, arguing that marriage between incompatible partners, no less than subjection to monarchical power, amounts to an intolerable form of servitude.

Although the ideal of freedom I have been sketching was crucial to the self-image of European citizens in the early modern period, we must be careful not to over-estimate its significance. One exaggeration to which many writers fell prey was that of supposing their opposition to the enslaving effects of arbitrary power to be a peculiarly European value. But as Michael Cook shows in Chapter 15, the story is more nuanced and complicated. Although the concept of freedom as independence undoubtedly played a less prominent role in the traditions of the major non-European civilisations, we find considerable overlap in the case of Islam. The early Islamic polity was remembered not merely as egalitarian in its outlook but as strongly opposed to the exercise of arbitrary power.

As several other chapters indicate, we also need to recognise that, even in early modern Europe, the idea of freedom as independence was far from universally endorsed. Some writers denied that freedom is anything to do with having the status of freemen who are not subject to others. Thomas Hobbes was the first to put forward a rival definition, and he was followed by the classical utilitarians, including Jeremy Bentham and William Paley. Freedom, as Hobbes defines it in *Leviathan*, is simply the absence of 'externall Impediments of motion'; we are rendered unfree not by living in conditions of dependence, but only by being interfered with in the exercise of our powers.[4] Still more radically, others doubted whether the ideal of freedom should be construed in negative terms at all, whether as absence of independence or merely as absence of interference. Catherine Ballériaux shows in Chapter 13 that many religious and especially missionary writers continued to insist that the pursuit of freedom should be envisaged not as a quest for autonomy, but as an attempt to establish harmony between God's nature and man's will. Finally, we need to take note of a more secularised version of the claim that freedom consists in the realisation of our powers, a version that came to prominence in the course of the Enlightenment. In Chapter 14 Fonna Forman uncovers its presence among the cosmopolitan thinkers of the period, while in Chapter 11 Alexander Schmidt isolates a similar ideal among a number of German thinkers of the late eighteenth century and beyond.

So far I have been speaking about rival understandings of the concept of free action. But many philosophers of the early modern period were more interested in questions about the freedom of the will and the inner freedom of the mind. Martina Reuter focuses in Chapter 4 on Descartes' examination of the free-will controversy, arguing that his defence of the equal capacity of human beings to reason derives from his account of the will and its capacity to judge freely. As Reuter shows, this commitment helps to explain how Descartes came to endorse, in his own idiom, the well-established theological belief that 'the mind has no sex'. In Chapter 1 Annabel Brett considers a specific implication of the idea of free will associated with the Jesuit philosophers of the early modern period. Francisco Suárez argued that one of the powers of the human will consists in its ability to generate 'moral entities', including not just property and jurisdiction but freedom itself, which Suárez construed as a power over our own actions susceptible of being alienated just like any other piece of property. With Pufendorf's discussion of *entia moralia* in his *De iure naturae et gentium*, as Brett illustrates, this analysis eventually entered the Protestant tradition as well.

While those who meditated on freedom of mind often differed in outlook from those who focused on freedom of action, they shared a fundamental

4. Hobbes 1996: ch. 21, 145.

interest in the attainment of inner-directedness and self-mastery. We need finally to note, however, that a number of early modern writers rejected all such ideals of autonomy, treating them as nothing better than fictions designed to deceive ourselves. As Freya Sierhius shows in Chapter 3, such writers were generally led to this conclusion by way of espousing a distinctively neo-Stoic conception of reflection and self-scrutiny. For these writers, among whom Justus Lipsius was the most prominent, the possibility of freedom depends on our capacity to use our reason to control our passions, thereby preventing our liberty from degenerating into mere licence. Faced with this demand, however, many responded that the enslaving power of passion is so overwhelming that any sustained commitment to rational purposes is sure to fail. The project of self-mastery was rejected as a psychological impossibility.

Modern European conceptions of freedom and citizenship have largely been fashioned out of the traditions I have been surveying, so that each strand of thought examined in the chapters that follow can be shown to have left some mark on our contemporary world. At the same time, however, we find that the contours and complexities of these inherited patterns of argument have been flattened and simplified. We hear little nowadays about freedom as independence,[5] and even less about freedom as a project of self-realisation based on self-mastery. We largely identify the possession of liberty with nothing more than an absence of interference with our desires. But as the following chapters richly illustrate, this commitment has involved an abridgement and arguably an impoverishment of our intellectual heritage. This being so, a reading of the following chapters can hardly fail to have at least two salutary effects. One is to supply us with a comprehensive understanding of the intellectual materials out of which we have constructed our contemporary world of individual liberty and rights. The other is to provide us with a means of reflecting on whether some of the materials discarded along the way may not be worth picking up and reusing to produce a better edifice.

5. But this may be changing. For efforts to reinsert this conception into contemporary political theory see Pettit 1997, Skinner 1998, Laborde and Maynor 2008, Lovett 2010.

Part 1

Free persons and freedom of action

1

Human freedom and Jesuit moral theology

ANNABEL BRETT

It is well known that Jesuit theologians of the late sixteenth and early seventeenth centuries defended, against their theological rivals (Calvinists, Lutherans, and their fellow-Catholic Dominicans), a strenuous conception of the natural freedom of the human will. In this chapter we are concerned not so much with the theological controversy but with the implications of this conception of intrinsic human liberty for freedom in the economic and political domains. As we shall see, it underpinned a particular understanding of the moral world, that is, the world in which human beings do not simply act or not act with a freedom that is natural to them of their essence as such, but are additionally involved in a series of relationships (for example, of property, of contract, of subjection to jurisdiction) which alter the moral quality (the goodness or badness) of those same free actions. The moral metaphysics they developed to support this world allowed Jesuit theologians an enormous subtlety and flexibility in analysing the increasingly complicated commercial transactions of early modern capitalism as well as the demands and limits of political obligation, with the overall end of guiding and protecting the conscience of economic agents and political subjects. As we shall see further, however, for some of its exponents this sophisticated metaphysical toolkit did not come without its own danger, that of making the moral world purely self-referential and losing its connection with natural good and evil.

It is a common feature of late scholastic action theory that the freedom of any external action (in scholastic terminology, an *actus imperatus*, for example taking a walk) is dependent on the freedom of the precedent act of will (an *actus elicitus*, in this case the choice to take a walk).[1] It is central to this view that the human will is, of its nature, free to act or not act, although

1. Pink 2003.

certain circumstances may intervene to compromise or even negate this freedom. The free operation of the will, together with the activity of reason in presenting to the will the good which it may or may not choose, gives a human being command or mastery, *dominium*, over his own actions. This latter idea goes back to Aquinas and was inherited by the Jesuits through the mediation of their sixteenth-century Dominican predecessors, in particular, perhaps, Domingo de Soto, whose treatise *On Justice and Right* fundamentally influenced Luis de Molina and other later Jesuits. On this conception, to have *dominium* over one's own actions just is to be able to act freely. It is what differentiates the human freedom of a man walking down a road from the animal unfreedom of (say) a cow, which, although it may appear to be doing the same thing, has no command over whether it walks down the road or not. It is this internal self-command or *dominium* of human beings which allows them to have *dominium* as an external relation both to goods and to other persons.[2] Thus, the spheres of both economics and politics are premised upon the understanding of a human being as a free being in this strong sense of a self-commander.

In the course of the sixteenth century, the issue of the alienability of liberty – in particular, the alienation involved in voluntary slavery – put a certain pressure on this inherited language of human freedom. Soto conceded that a human being may, in the most extreme of circumstances (that is, for the sake of life itself), sell himself into slavery. It is possible because liberty, as a case of *dominium*, is alienable just as is all *dominium*.[3] This concession assimilates liberty to *dominium* in the sense of property, and the implication was pursued by Molina, who explicitly argued that a human being is the owner (*dominus*) of his own liberty.[4] During the late sixteenth and early seventeenth centuries, the idea that human beings have ownership of their liberty became a central tenet of Jesuit moral theology. It influenced both their casuistry of conscience, supporting an assumption of the moral freedom of individuals to act as they chose in cases of doubt, and their understanding of freedom of contract in the economic sphere.[5] Nevertheless, it demanded a refinement in the inherited terminology. The liberty that is like any other piece of property and can be alienated as such cannot be the same as the intrinsic liberty of the human being that differentiates him from an animal such as a cow. In the case of voluntary slavery, it is alienated by a free act of will and the slave remains a human being, intrinsically capable of acting

2. Tierney 2006; Seelmann 2007.
3. Soto 1566: lib. IV, q. 2, a. 2.
4. Molina 1614: tract. II, disp. 30, n. 14; Kaufmann 2007: 219–20.
5. Schüssler 2006; 2007; Decock 2009a.

freely. The question arises, therefore, of what kind of entity or 'being' – the scholastic term is *ens* – this alienable liberty is. The answer is that it is an *ens morale*, a 'moral being', part of the moral world in which all economic and political activity is situated. It is not distinctive as such, but one of a number of everyday phenomena such as the price of goods that are regulated by law or the obligations we incur when we make a contract. In the first part of this chapter, I want to look at how this world of 'moral being' was constructed on the basis of the intrinsic liberty of the human will in the work of the Jesuit philosopher Francisco Suárez.

Suárez's gift for systematisation meant that his work on metaphysics, the *Disputationes metaphysicae* of 1597, and on law and rights, the *De legibus* of 1612, came to form an indispensable point of reference not only for Catholic, but also for Protestant academic philosophers all over Europe. But in order to understand his thought on moral being, we need to go back to some of the earlier and less well-known work belonging to his period at the Collegio Romano between 1581 and 1585, where he commented on the moral sections of Thomas Aquinas's *Summa theologiae*, that is, the *Prima secundae* and the *Secunda secundae*. The work that mainly concerns us here is the *Tractatus quinque in primam secundae Sancti Thomae*, first published in 1628. The third of these tractates is entitled 'On the goodness and badness of human actions' (*De bonitate et malitia humanorum actuum*), and one of the issues it tackles is that of the status of moral being in relation to two other kinds of being, *ens reale* ('real being') and *ens rationis* ('being of reason'). In the scholastic understanding, 'real being' is the kind that exists outside and independent of what we would call the mind; 'being of reason', by contrast, exists only in the mind or as a result of the operations of the mind. Increasingly, this distinction was glossed by Jesuit philosophers as one between *ens physicum*, 'physical being', and *ens fictum*, 'fictive being', or being that is fabricated by the mind. The question, then, was whether the moral world is purely mind-dependent, or whether it has some relation to reality; and, if so, what. Not for the last time, Suárez's target here was his fellow-Jesuit Gabriel Vásquez, although the prompt for Vásquez's ideas seems to have been that *enfant terrible* of the Dominican Order Melchor Cano, who had reportedly asserted in his usual uncompromising fashion that 'the goodness of virtue, and moral goodness in general, is a being of reason'.[6] Gabriel Vásquez had argued that the morality of an act consists in the relation of agreement or disagreement with rational nature, which is a relation of reason, not a

6. Gemmeke 1965: 11–13.

real relation, although he stressed that this relation of reason nevertheless has a real foundation in the real circumstances of that act. Still, in positing morality as a relation of reason, he essentially revived the late medieval nominalist perspective of William of Ockham, who had posited that the range of things that the scholastics commonly call *ens morale* – things like a sign, or the price of a thing – are constituted by a relation of reason.[7]

Suárez developed his opposing thesis in the *De bonitate et malitia*, which itself takes off from the conclusions of the second tractate in the series, 'On the voluntary and the involuntary'. A major theoretical effort of this second tractate is to establish the distinction between the voluntary and the free. An act can be perfectly voluntary which is nonetheless necessitated, and therefore not free. The classic example of this throughout the Jesuit scholastic is the love of God on the part of the saints in heaven. This act is perfectly voluntary as it is an act of the will that proceeds from perfect cognition (imperfect cognition makes an action less voluntary). But it is nevertheless not free, because the saints cannot *not* love God. Freedom demands perfect indifference: that even when all the conditions necessary for an act are in place, the individual is still free to do or not to do.

Coming now to the third tractate, it begins by asking what human acts count as moral acts. The first opinion it considers is 'that a moral act is the same as an act that is properly and perfectly human, or perfectly voluntary'; and this, Suárez goes on, 'appears to be the view of Saint Thomas in the *Prima secundae* . . . because he always poses the question in terms of the human act, an appellation that he runs together with the appellation "moral": and this can be briefly argued, because any act, by the very fact that it is a human act, is capable of rectitude and honesty (*honestas*), and its contrary defect: therefore, by this very fact, it is a moral act'.[8] The second opinion is 'that a moral act adds something on top of a human act, viz. liberty-in-act (*actualis libertas*): for we said before that liberty does not belong to the rationale of a human act as such, because an act can proceed from full deliberation and the faculty of reason and will, without freedom'.[9] It will be no surprise to learn that Suárez, while always respectful of the first opinion, nevertheless goes for the second (for which in his usual fashion he finds some support in Aquinas). A moral act is by definition a free act, and it cannot be found in children, the mad, or animals, which do what they do naturally or necessarily, and therefore cannot be worthy of praise or blame. Suárez further does not

7. Kobusch 1993: 56. 8. Suárez 1856: disp. 1, sect. 1, n. 3.
9. Suárez 1856: disp. 1, sect. 1, n. 4.

hesitate to say that the love of the saints in heaven for God is, for the very same reason, not a moral act.

Having established that moral being depends upon freedom, Suárez proceeds to ask: 'What, in a moral act of this kind, is that being moral (*esse morale*)?'[10] There is no doubt that the substance of the act of the will is 'something physical and natural'. But with regard to 'its formal denomination or the form from which the act is denominated moral . . . it is very obscure what it is.'[11] Suárez goes on to give various reasons why it cannot be purely *ens rationis*. 'First of all, it cannot be a being of reason properly so-called, because this being moral is in the things themselves, without the intellect making up anything (*nihil fingente*) or making any comparison (*comparante*). Again, this being moral is the root of real properties, like value, etc., but a being of reason cannot confer anything real. Furthermore, it cannot be an extrinsic denomination taken from some other thing: in the first place, because this kind of denomination differs scarcely at all from a being of reason, because since it is not in the thing itself that is denominated, it appears that it can only come into being as the result of the intellect comparing one thing to another.'[12] But on the other hand, Suárez goes on, it cannot be any real being – physical or natural – intrinsic to the act either. So we have a problem.

Suárez again rejects what he takes to be Aquinas's answer, i.e., that 'the morality of an act of the will is its intrinsic and essential being-ness (*entitas*), so that this being is not said to be moral because it is not also natural and physical, but because it is such a being which of its nature comes into being from a rational will . . . such an act of its nature involves a real relationship to its principle, which is the reason and the will, and to its object which is presented to it by reason: but out of the force of this relationship it is a moral act'.[13] This will not do, because what it describes is really nothing other than the natural and physical being of an act of the will; but its *morality* cannot result solely from that kind of being, because (as we have established) there could be such an act which is nonetheless not a moral act. So the formal rationale of morality must lie elsewhere. In a complex and extended sequence of reasoning, Suárez further rejects Vásquez's solution, that morality is a relation to rational nature – or to right reason, as Suárez glosses, which is not quite the same thing.[14] His own solution, which has something of the air of being the best we can do, places morality in the distinctive mode of emanation that an act of the will can have: 'Being moral, in an act of the will,

10. Suárez 1856: disp. 1, sect. 2. 11. Suárez 1856: disp. 1, sect. 2, n. 1.
12. Suárez 1856: disp. 1, sect. 2, n. 1. 13. Suárez 1856: disp. 1, sect. 2, n. 2.
14. Suárez 1856: disp. 1, sect. 2, nn. 7–14.

adds nothing to its entity and substance other than the mode of a certain kind of emanation from, or of moral dependence upon, reason adverting [to an object] and the will operating freely. This assertion can be proved first of all from a sufficient enumeration, because, supposing what we have excluded, nothing else can be thought of.'[15] Secondly, this mode 'is not anything that physically or intrinsically inheres in a moral act, but, in the case of an external act, it represents a denomination from the free act of the will; and in the act of the will itself, it represents, beyond a physical emanation from the will, a denomination taken from reason in its directive capacity, and the will acting from its full power in such a way as that it could also not act'.[16] It has to be, therefore, what the scholastics call an 'extrinsic denomination', that is, a name that is applied, as a result of the operation of reason, on the basis of something extrinsic to the object itself.

According to Suárez, now addressing the initial arguments, this denomination avoids being altogether extrinsic, at least *to the agent*, 'because with respect to the agent this entire denomination is taken from potencies, or acts that are intrinsic to him'.[17] The denomination *is* extrinsic, however, to the *act* of the will, because it is taken not from the act itself but from the potentials of the reason and the will. But – and this is a position repeated elsewhere in Suárez's work – an extrinsic denomination is not necessarily an *ens rationis*, a fiction.[18] It can be something real in the things themselves, depending on a real relationship between the thing denominated and the thing from which that denomination is taken; and so it is in the case of morality. And on this basis, he goes on,

> we deny that this denomination, explained in these terms, is not sufficient to produce moral effects, because it is clear that in human affairs this kind of denomination is much esteemed and valued with regard to moral effects; for *dominium*, jurisdiction and the like do not add any physical entities to things, but moral faculties produced by the free consent of the will. And the ground for this is that men are governed by reason, and in the estimation of reason the ordering of things in order to the will and human freedom, and to the will of a superior, has great weight; particularly since, this denomination not being altogether extrinsic to the actor, it is not surprising that it can lead to praise, value, and other effects.[19]

15. Suárez 1856: disp. 1, sect. 2, n. 15.   16. Suárez 1856: disp. 1, sect. 2, n. 16.
17. Suárez 1856: disp. 1, sect. 2, n. 19 *ad fin.*: *cum praesens denominatio non sit omnino extrinseca operanti.*
18. Doyle 1984: 128.   19. Suárez 1856: disp. 1, sect. 2, n. 19.

Importantly, then, it is not purely the relationship of the phenomenon to a free act of the will that makes it a 'moral' phenomenon, with moral effects; it is also the work of practical reason in valuing a denomination made upon that basis.

We are now, finally, arriving at the solution to the question with which we started, the nature of liberty as the kind of *dominium* that is alienable like any other property. We see now that *dominium* in this sense is an *ens morale*, a 'moral being', different from the *dominium* over our own actions that is intrinsically involved in acting freely. In his lectures on the *Secunda secundae*, *De iustitia et iure*, from the same period, Suárez made this distinction clear. Here he separated out two things: on the one hand the '*dominium*, as a physical thing' that I have over my own actions, which 'consists in the intrinsic faculty of acting freely'; on the other, the '*dominium* [of those actions] in a moral sense, or right'.[20] The former is inalienable, the latter is not. In the later *De legibus*, Suárez developed the equation between the second kind of *dominium* and right in its subjective sense as something belonging to the individual. *Ius* in the sense of 'right', rather than 'law', 'is properly called a certain moral faculty, which each has either with regard to his own thing or something which is due to him';[21] again, '*ius* sometimes signifies law, sometimes the *dominium* or quasi-*dominium* of a certain thing'.[22] Human liberty, then, is a moral right, and for Suárez as for others among his Jesuit contemporaries we possess it unless we explicitly alienate it or some explicit obligation can be demonstrated that takes it away.[23]

Returning to the *De bonitate et malitia*, Suárez went on to make the ontological status of these moral phenomena clearer in the third section. Here he distinguishes within *entia moralia* or 'moral beings'. Some of them are physical things which are moral by denomination: for example, an act of the will itself, but also something like a reward, which is a physical thing but has moral being *as a reward* from its relation to a free act of the will, from which the denomination is taken.[24] But some things are moral 'entitatively and substantially', with regard to their entire being, and in this category he includes 'the obligation that arises from a promise, *dominium* which is transferred at the will of the owner, the bond of matrimony, the value of a thing which arises from a law determining its

20. Suárez ed. Giers 1958, [q. 12]. 21. Suárez 1971–81: lib. I, cap. 2, n. 5.
22. Suárez 1971–81: lib. II, cap. 14, n. 16.
23. Suárez 1971–81: lib. II, cap. 14, nn. 18–19; cf. Schüssler 2007: 264–72.
24. Suárez 1856: disp. I, sect. 3, nn. 4–5.

price'.[25] Such *entia moralia* are destroyed in the same way that they come into being, i.e. by extrinsic denomination: 'just as these beings are said to be through their relation to human apprehension, which can change its moral judgement on what is to be done: thus by parity of reasoning, they are destroyed by their relation to the same estimation of prudent men, when . . . right reasoning apprehends that some moral mutation has happened in the object . . . just as the value, or price of a thing lasts while the law determining it is in place, but when it is revoked . . . the value is taken away'.[26] Another example is the destruction of an obligation through the remission of a promise. But if it is purely through their relation to human apprehension that such things have their being – which is *moral* being – then why are they not simply *entia rationis*, beings of reason? Suárez only clears this up later in the *Metaphysical Disputations* of 1597, where he says that 'even if these denominations, taken as inherent or intrinsic, are beings of reason, nevertheless as they are in themselves, they are truly denominations taken from real forms, even if these are extrinsic'.[27] Thus, my being obliged – which is a moral being, of course – is an extrinsic denomination taken from an act of my will or someone else's, which is a real thing to which my being obliged has a real relation; but understood intrinsically or inherently as my obligation, it is a being of reason.[28]

In sum, Suárez distinguished the being of moral entities from that of real entities while still insisting on the connection between the moral and the physical worlds. For some, this is his distinctive achievement over and against later moral theorists such as Kant.[29] But I want to move on now to a strand of Jesuit thinking that is heavily critical of this position. It denies the intermediate ontological status of moral entities, somewhere between

25. Suárez 1856: disp. 1, sect. 3, n. 4. These kinds of *entia moralia* have some kind of foundation in a physical thing, which is the source of their being denominated as such, but do not have any physical being in themselves: *ibid.* n. 5.
26. Suárez 1856: disp. 1, sect. 3 n. 6. Late scholastic economic theory distinguished between 'natural price', which is a function of 'common estimation' (*communis aestimatio*), and 'legal price', which is fixed by law (de Roover 1971: 70; Gómez Camacho 1998: 521–36; Chafuen 2003: 82–90; Decock 2009b: 61–2). In Suárez's handling, *aestimatio* has a place in creating the latter price as well, with the caveat that this must be the *aestimatio* of the prudent (late scholastic economics recognised that human passions can affect the *communis aestimatio* and thus the natural price).
27. Quoted in Knebel 2000: 501–2 n. 76. As Knebel explains, what reason does is to transform an extrinsic denomination into an intrinsic denomination: *ibid.*, 501.
28. Suárez in fact concedes something of this in the *De bonitate et malitia* itself, when he admits that 'from this relationship between things' – sc. the real relation from which the extrinsic denomination 'moral' is taken – 'the intellect assumes a foundation either to impose names, or to confect relations of reason; and perhaps those who call this kind of being a being of reason mean nothing other than this': *De bonitate et malitia*, disp. 1, sect. 2, n. 19.
29. Elorduy 1943–45: 158–9.

ens reale and *ens rationis*, while still not suggesting that the moral world is a pure fiction.[30] The nominalist metaphysics of Pedro Hurtado de Mendoza (1578–1641) gave a sharp impulse to this critique. In his *Universa philosophia* of 1624, Hurtado de Mendoza insisted that 'there is no moral being which is not real being, if that moral being has its being independently of the intellect'.[31] This position is reflected in the work of the major mid-century Spanish theologian, Juan de Lugo, who taught at Valladolid and Salamanca and then at the Collegio Romano before being made cardinal in 1643. Lugo is best known today for his place in the history of economic thought. However, underlying his conclusions in the domain of economics, as a branch of moral theology, was an innovative account of the moral entities which constitute the object of that domain. Lugo held that moral being contradistinguished against real or physical being 'is properly nothing'.[32] As we shall see, this committed him to a fundamental re-examination of the entire moral universe.

Lugo's juridical work, *De iustitia et iure*, was strongly influenced by Molina's work of the same title. However, he supplemented Molina's account of rights and obligations with an extensive discussion of the real nature of these 'moral effects', one that he developed originally in the context of discussing the justice of relations between man and God in his work on the incarnation, *De incarnatione*, published in 1633. The basic argument of Disputation III of this work, which asks 'Whether the incarnation was necessary in the rigour of justice to make satisfaction for the sins of men', is that, even after the works of Christ, God could not have been obliged, in strict justice, not to demand any further satisfaction for the sins of man.[33] The reason for this is that, if God were so obliged, this would mean that he would commit *iniuria* - violation of right - if he were to do so, thus entailing that either Christ, or men, had a right against God. But if this were the case, God could not be said to be perfectly and fully *dominus* of everything in the

30. Knebel 2000: 496–7.
31. Hurtado de Mendoza 1624: fo. 950 (*Metaphysica*, disp. XIX, sect. 2, subsect. 5, para. 51). For Hurtado de Mendoza's nominalism on the question of universals, see Caruso 1979; cf. Knebel 2000: 496 n. 49.
32. Knebel 2000: 497 n. 49.
33. Lugo 1633: disp. III, sect. 1, n. 1. Lugo stresses that this is different from the position (with which he agrees) that Christ's satisfaction extinguishes God's right to punish man further: for in this case, 'it is understood that God cannot, in justice, exact anything further for the sin, not because man had any right in justice against God, but because God does not have a title in justice against man; so that if God punished man, he would not act unjustly in the sense of contrary to the right of man, but he would act unjustly in the sense of without a title in justice to punish, and in consequence against the rule that dictates that an innocent is not to be punished'.

universe, because there would be some actions that he could not, in justice, perform; whereas it is of the rationale of *dominium* that the *dominus* can do anything he likes with regard to the thing or things of which he has *dominium* without violating the right of anyone else. This is so even though, of course, physically God could still do anything he wanted. But God's *dominium* being a moral as well as a physical thing, mere physical power does not prove the relevant point. If God is to remain perfectly *dominus* of everything in a moral sense, a creature cannot have a right against him.[34]

Up to this point, Lugo has been using the familiar language of 'moral faculty' to describe *dominium*: 'full *dominium* is the moral faculty of using one's own thing without violating the right of anyone else in every case'.[35] But as a result of facing the usual battery of objections to any scholastic position, he offers a further definition that establishes a new language of right. Thus, he admits his debt to Molina in defining *dominium*, and right more generally, in a negative sense – that is, with reference to the violation of right that a person does *not* commit in using his own thing or what he has a right to.[36] But, as his opponent argues, violation of right cannot be explained without circularity except with reference to an independent conception of right. So what *is* it? 'It seems that this right, which is the object of commutative justice, and which is set down as the genus in the definition of *dominium*, is nothing other in its conception that a kind of moral preferment (*praelatio*), by which this man is morally preferred to others in the use of this thing by reason of the peculiar connection that the thing has with him.'[37] For example, if someone catches a wild animal, then that animal has a peculiar connection with that person on account of having been caught by him, and this gives the person moral preferment over everyone else in the use of that animal. Lugo stresses that 'this moral preferment must be founded in the peculiar connection of the thing itself. For moral preferment founded on any other title does not found the right of justice'. He elaborates upon the point in his later *De iustitia et iure*: the *praelatio* of an ecclesiastical superior – a prelate, precisely – or any other superior is not a case of right or *dominium*. Right is a preferment in *use*: 'because on account of the peculiar connection that this thing has with a person, it ought entirely to be referred and ordained to his own utility'. But the connection that a prelate or superior has with the actions of his subjects is to their utility, not his. This is the difference between a subject and a slave,

34. Lugo 1633: disp. III, sect. 1, nn. 5, 6, and 11; sect. 2, n. 38.
35. Lugo 1633: disp. III, sect. 1, n. 6.
36. Lugo 1633: disp. III, sect. 2, n. 41.
37. Lugo 1633: disp. III, sect. 2, n. 42; briefly discussed in Carpintero Benítez 2003: 372.

as indeed Aristotle had said.[38] The latter is an object of commutative justice or exchange, the former is not.

In both works, Lugo stresses that the 'peculiar connection' that founds right is a *real* connection, which he further glosses as a 'physical connection'. In the *De iustitia et iure* he lists catching, finding and making. So what of someone who has acquired *dominium* of a thing by sale or gift? Here he says that 'even if the person who receives the gift, or who buys it, is not the maker or the finder of that thing; nevertheless he represents the person of the first giver, or seller, who had had some real connection with that thing, and who transfers his right to the recipient or buyer, with the will that he should be preferred to others in the use of that thing in the same way as the giver or seller himself... which, in moral estimation, is to have that connection just as if he himself had made or found the thing'.[39] In the *De incarnatione*, this point is still made in the context of arguing that God cannot acquire any obligation towards his creatures, nor they any right against him; but since he is talking about God's *dominium* over human beings, not things, he discusses another 'real connection' that founds *dominium*: capture of another human being in a just war. Since this is, for human beings, the only real connection that founds *dominium* over other human beings, any contract of servitude has to be regulated by our understanding of that connection. So 'a man who hands himself over to another as a slave wills that he should henceforth be his master just as he would have been had he captured him in war. And a master manumitting a slave wills that he should henceforth be as if he had never been captured.'[40] All transfers of right by contract have to be referred, by moral equivalence, to the capacity that human beings have to acquire *dominium* in other, and real, ways. 'So that no contract can give a right to anything for which there is no capacity by some other means.'[41] In the case of voluntary servitude, this functions as a precise limit on the rights of the master: 'therefore man cannot, through contract, hand himself over to another as a slave in such a way that the master can mutilate, kill, gravely wound him, etc., at will without any right of defending himself, which belongs to the slave by natural law; because man could not ever acquire such a right over another man in any other way'.[42] In the case of relations between man and God, since there is no real way that a man could ever acquire a right against God, and similarly no real way that God could ever be obliged to a man, we cannot understand that there has been any pact or contract whereby

38. Lugo 1646: disp. 1, sect. 1. 39. Lugo 1646: disp. 1, sect. 1.
40. Lugo 1633: disp. III, sect. 2, n. 50. 41. Lugo 1633: disp. III, sect. 2, n. 50.
42. Lugo 1633: disp. III, sect. 2, n. 51.

God, through the works of Christ, is obliged to man in such a way that man has a right against him.

So, then, we have established that God can never violate any right of man. Can a man violate a right of God's? Yes, Lugo says, but this is only very rarely the case – against Suárez, who had held that every sin violates God's right in some way, for which man is obliged in justice to make satisfaction.[43] Lugo holds that most sins are not violations of right but acts of disobedience or some other vice. Nevertheless, in arguing that there are still some cases in which man does violate God's right, he faces the following objection: to violate a right is to do something against the will of the right-holder. But we can never act against God's will, since everything happens at God's will, and this includes our own actions.[44] Whatever we do, then, is what God wills us to do. If one replies that when we sin, we indeed act against God's commanding will, this is not to the point: because this will to command or oblige us relates to jurisdiction, not *dominium*. *Dominium* is not a will to oblige, but a will for the things (in this case the actions) themselves that are the object of *dominium*. *This* is the will that we contravene when we violate right. And so the objection holds, because God, precisely, wills all our actions.

Lugo's response is to deny that this is what constitutes the distinction between *dominium* and jurisdiction. For, he explains, it is not necessarily the case that the will of the *dominus* terminates or has its object in the things or actions themselves of which he is *dominus*: for 'we can easily consider, in the case of one who has *dominium* of property, a will that does not terminate directly in the thing that is his own, but in obliging his slave or his debtor by title of justice; and as long as that will lasts, injustice will be done by the debtor, even if the creditor does not have any absolute will for the thing that he exacts.'[45] Thus, to take an example, I may not, as a matter of fact, actually want the book I have lent you; but I do want you to be obliged to give it back. And as long as that will lasts, I have *dominium* in the book and you cannot keep it forever without injustice to me. In the later *De iustitia et iure*, Lugo refers back to this point in explaining why animals cannot have any right or any *dominium*. He avoids the standard Thomist answer, given by both Soto and Molina, that because animals do not have *dominium* of their own actions, therefore they cannot have *dominium* of anything else. This answer directly refers *dominium* back to the human capacity of free will, the perfect indifference which means that my act is subject to me alone, not determined

43. Lugo 1633: disp. III, sect. 3, n. 54.
44. Lugo 1633: disp. III, sect. 4, n. 67 [recte 68].
45. Lugo 1633: disp. III, sect. 4, n. 74.

by anything else. But, although such a conception of freedom is still at the root of Lugo's conception of human agency, it is not the proximate reason for animals' lack of *dominium*. Rather, the reason is that 'he alone suffers violation of right, who suffers it against his will . . . not the will by which he wills the thing that is his own, but the will by which he wills to retain the right to that thing, or to oblige others not to take it away . . . But animals cannot have such a will, because they cannot recognise moral obligation or wrong.'[46] Thus, going back to the *De incarnatione*, *dominium* and jurisdiction are parallel phenomena, because in both cases what is apparently willed is not the thing itself – my book, or an action of my slave, or an action of my subject – but an obligation, either upon a subject, or upon a slave, or upon a debtor.[47]

Now, that a legislator in legislating must will not the action itself, but an obligation on subjects to perform that action, is a position that is already clear in Suárez's *De legibus*.[48] The obligation of a law is a *moral effect* and it arises only from this specific will of the prince. But the problem lies precisely in this notion of an obligation, which seems to be completely reflexive: it appears to be the *object* of the will of the superior, but is constituted by nothing other than that very same will. It is here that Lugo makes his nominalist commitments clear as he has not done up until this point.

> For if you prescind from the thing itself that is commanded [which is not the relevant object of the will, as we have seen] you will not easily find anything . . . else distinct from the will itself, which could be the object of that will. For to say, that the object of the will is some moral thing, viz. the obligation (in the passive sense) that results in the subordinate: this, I say, does not seem to satisfy, because that moral thing is in reality that thing, by which the subordinate is formally obliged; and this, in reality, is that same will of the superior – or you must give some other physical thing. *For every moral right must be resolved into something physical*, which is called moral just because it is equivalent to that other thing in order to certain effects.

And the same goes for an owner: 'if you say that the owner, through that will, wills to retain the right that he has to such-and-such a thing; for straightaway

46. Lugo 1646: disp. 3, sect. 1. In the *De incarnatione*, Lugo gives another example in a different moral matter, marriage. Thus, the Virgin Mary, when she married Joseph, did not in fact have any will for the mutual use of each other's body that matrimony entails. Her will was purely to give her husband the right to it, in other words, to make it licit as a matter of justice. Lugo 1633: disp. III, sect. 5, n. 85.
47. Lugo 1633: disp. III, sect. 5, n. 77.
48. Suárez 1971–81: lib. I, cap. 4, nn. 8–9.

I ask, what *is* that retention of right, that the owner wills, and you will not find anything adequately distinct from that will itself, or its intimation'.[49]

In answer to this dilemma, Lugo draws upon a solution that he developed in his work on penitence, concerning the forgiveness or absolution of sins. Here, the forgiving will does not effectively will the forgiveness, because that would be to will itself. But it is as if someone were to say: 'I would wish (*ego vellem*), as far as in me lies, that from the past offence or violation of right there should not result to me any further right against you.'[50] Similarly in the transfer of *dominium* through gift, the giver would wish, as far as in him lies, that the thing given should have the same connection with the recipient as it previously did with himself as the giver; and the superior binding a subject to something would wish, as far as in him lies, to render that thing impossible to him in the genus of morals, that is, morally wrong. In all these cases, the will is of itself ineffective – *vellem*, 'I would wish', not 'I will' – but it comes to have the effective force of absolution, or of transferring *dominium*, or of creating an obligation, from the moral estimation of practical reason in the concrete form of 'prudent men'. It is this that makes the will to bind, to forgive, to give, etc., effective, and thereby constitutes a remission or a transfer or an obligation. Now the objection to this is that the ineffective will falls into the same trap as positing an initial effective will. For example, the will of the superior is not to make a particular thing wrong for a subject with any kind of wrongness, but precisely with the wrongness of being contrary to an obligation; and not any kind of obligation, but the obligation not to do that thing which effectively results from the very will of that superior. And therefore this will too is reflexive on itself.[51]

Lugo's answer is the most interesting part of this whole discussion. The will of the superior does not have its own obligation, that is, itself, for an object, but a different kind of obligation, in willing which it effectively imposes a true moral obligation in the estimation of prudent men. Thinking about what this other obligation might be involves going back to human nature: understanding, by the light of natural reason, that it is decent or fitting – *decet* – for men to live a political life and to follow the counsel and warnings of those whom nature itself has constituted as their leaders, either by age, or paternity, or learning, or some other natural title. The decency of doing so is not enough to constitute an obligation, for example on the son to obey the father. But suppose the father were to say: 'I would wish,

49. Lugo 1633: disp. III, sect. 5, n. 78, emphasis mine.
50. Lugo 1633: disp. III, sect. 5, n. 87.
51. Lugo 1633: disp. III, sect. 5, n. 89.

as far as in me lies, to render that decency obligatory, i.e. that it should be wrong for my son to depart from this my counsel, just as it is wrong to depart from other objects to which natural law binds.' This will of the father does not have for its object the obligation itself that arises from the will, but another obligation which is at that moment impossible, that is, an obligation of natural decency. It is impossible because of itself natural decency is *not* obligatory. But the natural connection between the father and the son is enough for prudent men to judge that, when once such a will is in place, the son is truly obliged; because 'nature itself as if accepts that ineffective will of the father, and makes it effective in effectively obliging the son on account of the desire of the father'.[52] What men do in setting up a *political* superior is to establish a political title or authority which is morally equivalent to or supplies, in the estimation of the prudent, the natural title of the father or wise man.[53] Just as, in transferring *dominium*, we are supplying by moral equivalence, in the estimation of practical reason, the natural or physical connection that the original owner has with what is his own.[54]

Lugo's solution was criticised by his fellow-Jesuit, Rodrigo de Arriaga, a theologian and philosopher of comparable eminence who studied originally at Valladolid, but moved to Bohemia in 1625 following the restoration of Catholicism and taught at the University of Prague for the rest of his life. Arriaga shared Lugo's position on moral entities: 'all morality must necessarily have something physical for its primary foundation. For there are no intermediate entities between real or physical entities and entities of reason that are fictive, which without doubt do not constitute morality; and therefore all morality ultimately reduces to physical good and evil.'[55] He expressly applied the same principle to the question that had puzzled Lugo, that is, what is the object of the prince's legislative will? 'You will reply, that that will has for its object obligation, i.e., that a subject is bound to do that thing. But against, because I ask, what *is* that being bound or that obligation?'[56] 'This difficulty', he goes on, 'is truly great on our principles that deny intermediate moral entities distinct from real and fictive entities; because, supposing the command, no other real and positive being is laid down, distinct from itself,

52. Lugo 1633: disp. III, sect. 5, n. 90. 53. Lugo 1633: disp. III, sect. 5, n. 96.

54. There is an implicit premise here, which Lugo does not articulate, and that is that catching a fish, say, constitutes natural title, i.e. a *natural* 'preferment' with regard to other people who might want to get their hands on that fish. For the cases to be parallel, as Lugo wants in this section, 'nature itself' must accept the ineffective will of the original catcher and make it effective in obliging others to keep off the fish.

55. Arriaga 1644: disp. IV, sect. 1, subsect. 2. 56. Arriaga 1644: disp. II, sect. 2, n. 6.

which could be assigned as the object of that volition.'[57] And don't tell me, he says, that the object of the law is the absence of moral liberty to do otherwise, because that is precisely the same as an obligation, and solves nothing.[58]

However, Lugo's solution is the wrong one, something that we can both argue theoretically and, conclusively, illustrate from practice.[59] No king ever wishes that there could be in his subjects some 'chimerical' obligation, and then thinks of himself as having caused a genuine moral obligation by ineffectively willing the chimerical one. But if kings are completely unaware of this chimerical obligation that they are willing, they cannot possibly be willing it. You may reply that in the king's saying that it is his will, as far as in him lies, to make such-and-such a thing obligatory just like other natural obligations, he *is* thereby willing the chimerical obligation.[60] But, Arriaga counters, the legislator is not doing this: he is willing a different kind of obligation, one which he himself can cause, even if it is in some sense similar to a natural obligation. And we can demonstrate this absolutely with the following point: let us suppose that nature does *not* dictate that anything is illicit, that everything is indifferent, and the only principle we have is that there must be some moderator or regulator in the commonwealth whom all obey. In this case, there *are* no natural obligations, something similar to which could be the object of the legislator's ineffective will; and the legislator could only command by saying 'I want you to do this.' But this is in fact exactly what he does now, and the force of legislation – the creation of the moral effect of obligation – arises from this alone. Thus Arriaga's own solution is to say that the legislator's command 'does not have anything for its object except the external act that it commands, and it does not have an obligation for its object; rather the will is itself the obligation'.[61] The legislator's command is not the same as the effective will for that external act, since, on Arriaga's principles as well as Lugo's, willing that something be obligatory is not the same as willing the thing itself. But it *is* a special kind of volition for an action, which we experience in ourselves when we say, 'I bid you do such-and-such.' And this has of itself obligatory force, if everything else is in place. 'Neither', he declares, 'do I see what else we are bound to explain in this point.'[62]

In some sense, Arriaga's down-to-earth critique of Lugo's elaborate moral machinery has to be right. But in criticising the doubling of decency and obligation that he accurately summarises as Lugo's solution in handling

57. Arriaga 1644: disp. 11, sect. 2, n. 7. 58. Arriaga 1644: disp. 11, sect. 3, n. 10.
59. Arriaga 1644: disp. 11, sect. 3, n. 27, s.v. *Tertia*. 60. Arriaga 1644: disp. 11, sect. 3, n. 28.
61. Arriaga 1644: disp. 11, sect. 5, n. 31. 62. Arriaga 1644: disp. 11, sect. 5, n. 33.

not just the obligation to obey the law, but all other moral effects, such as *dominium*, he misses all the force of Lugo's idea. What Lugo is saying is that we cannot think about moral phenomena independently of some original real or physical connections between things that do not do anything in themselves, but which nature or the light of natural reason take to be the basis for preferring some people over others with regard to some particular actions. If I don't understand the decency of following a parent's counsel, and if I don't understand the decency of keeping my hands off a fish, say, if someone else has caught it; and if I don't feel the force of the genuine obligation that nature itself creates on these bases; then I am not going to understand political subjection or any kind or property relations, nor are we collectively going to be able to create such institutions. Contrary to Arriaga, if it really were the case that nothing were naturally illicit, then the sovereign *could not*, in fact, legislate.

An interesting parallel to the positions of Lugo and Arriaga can be found in the work of the Protestant natural law theorist Samuel Pufendorf. As Hannah Dawson shows in her contribution to these volumes, Pufendorf shared a broadly late scholastic understanding of human freedom rooted in a will that is not merely spontaneous but indifferent. Equally, he accepted the distinction between the moral and the natural, and the existence of specifically moral as opposed to natural entities. But, in addition to compromising that distinction in the way that Dawson describes, he also insisted in a positive way that moral obligation, and the consequent moral quality of actions as morally good or bad, cannot be entirely detached from considerations of what is naturally good or evil to human beings as natural, and naturally social, beings.[63] Natural good is as it were a 'handle' for rational creatures in thinking about moral good. The spectre that then looms, however, is that the specific kind of obligation that is *moral* obligation becomes redundant, concomitantly with the Hobbesian and Humean rejection of a theory of free action that depends on the freedom of the act of the will. When these are gone, so is moral goodness itself as a distinctive kind of goodness, and with it the entire metaphysics of moral entities. That is not to say, however, that nothing remains of this complex moral world, nor of the free agents that lie at its heart. Late scholastic writers on economics are widely hailed as the founders of modern economic liberalism, while the Jesuit casuistry of the human subject as the owner of his liberty has as much claim to be the origin

63. For this point and the following see Pink 2009; my thanks to Tom Pink both for directing me to this article and for a helpful discussion of the overall argument.

of libertarian theories of morality and politics as anything to be found in the work of Locke.[64] But the distinctive force of the Jesuit conception lies in its insistence on the continuing role of moral prudence as the necessary complement to the free operation of the human will, which does not create its moral effects independently of the judgement of practical reason. In this, whatever their metaphysical differences, Lugo and Suárez concurred.

64. As argued in Schüssler 2007: 281–2.

2

Freedom and self-possession: The case of Montaigne's *Essais*

FELICITY GREEN

I

In April 1570, Montaigne sold his office as a counsellor to the *parlement* of Bordeaux, a position he had held for the past decade. The following year, he commemorated this decision by having a Latin inscription painted on the wall of a little room adjacent to his library:

> In the year of Christ 1571, at the age of thirty-eight, on the last day of February, anniversary of his birth, Michel de Montaigne – long wearied of the servitude of the court and of public charges, and yearning to hide himself, while still whole, in the bosom of the learned Virgins, where in calm and freedom from all cares (if the fates permit it) he will complete what little remains of his life now more than half run out – has consecrated this seat, this sweet ancestral refuge, to his liberty, tranquillity and leisure.[1]

In this inscription, Montaigne cast his resignation from public office as a vindication of his liberty, freeing him, on the approach of old age and death, from a lifelong condition of *servitium* or slavery. By dedicating his ancestral home to 'libertati suae, tranquillitatique et otio', he sought not only to celebrate the beginning of a new life, timed to coincide with the anniversary of his birth, but to set forth for himself a certain way of living and dying, by dedicating *himself* to the performance of a particular philosophical persona: that of a man in full possession of his freedom.

The need to preserve ourselves from slavery, by living for the sake of that which is properly our own, represents a central area of questioning and concern in the *Essais* – the collection of philosophical 'soundings' or

1. Montaigne 2007: 1315. The translation given here is based on Frame 1965: 115.

'trials' of judgement that Montaigne began writing in the year following the sale of his office, and that he continued to revise and expand over a period of two decades until his death in 1592.[2] This important dimension of the text remains largely occluded, however, in prevailing accounts of his project, which continues to be understood largely from the vantage-point of modern modes of self-awareness, as an exercise in individual self-expression and psychological introspection.

The *Essais*, as Montaigne makes clear on numerous occasions, are designed to be read not merely as a compendium of moral and philosophical reflections, but as an attempt at *self*-study. Montaigne is himself the 'matter' of his book, his object in writing being to 'give knowledge not of things, but of [himself]'.[3] At the heart of this project is a call for a symbolic retreat from the world into the obscurity and seclusion of one's own home, library or *arriereboutique* – spaces in which it is possible to live for or belong to oneself (*estre à soy*).[4]

This foregrounding of the self resonates strongly with modern readers. Montaigne's declared aim as a writer – 'to be seen in my own simple and natural fashion, without study or artifice' – strikes a particular chord with our own culture's suspicion towards the visible, legible self and its power to alienate and displace our innermost, private identity even as it seeks to express it.[5] The subjectivity of the *Essais*, according to this interpretation, emerges at a point of perceived friction between artificial and authentic layers of conduct and self-understanding – as a struggle for self-definition and self-presence in a world of duplicitous appearances and masks.[6]

This approach fails to account, however, for a crucial dimension of Montaigne's self-portrait: the fact that the 'ruling form' that he claims to discover in himself is specifically that of a *free* self.[7] In *On presumption*, for example, Montaigne describes himself as 'extremely idle, extremely free, both by nature and by art'. His actions succeed only when moved by his 'pure and free will', he has 'a soul free and all its own', and he has had 'until this hour

2. All references to the *Essais* are by book, chapter and page number to the edition prepared by Jean Balsamo, Michel Magnien and Catherine Magnien-Simonin, which is based on the 1595 text (Montaigne 2007). Donald Frame's version (Montaigne 1958) has provided the starting-point for my own translations of Montaigne into English.

3. 'To the Reader': 27; II.10: 428. 4. I.38: 246; III.3: 870. 5. 'To the Reader': 27.

6. See for example Starobinski 1985: 94: 'When I turn my affection upon myself, eager as I may be to possess the truth about myself, isn't artifice incorporated into each of my acts and each of my perceptions? Hasn't appearance – that cause of all great change – insinuated its evil effects between me and myself?' See also Martin 1997: 1135: '[The *Essais*] gave poignant expression to a widely-felt need, in the age of the court, to find certain spaces – in one's own room, or library, or friendships, or writings – to provide a comparatively honest or sincere account of oneself and of one's feelings.'

7. III.2: 851.

neither forced governor nor master'.[8] In *On vanity*, similarly, he identifies 'idleness and freedom (*la franchise*)' as his 'very favourite qualities' – an assertion mirrored later on in the same chapter by the claim that 'liberty (*la liberté*) and idleness' are his 'ruling qualities'.[9]

To be free, as these quotations suggest, is to have one's own will – a 'pure et libre volonté' – as opposed to being subject to a master. We must tread carefully in public life, Montaigne urges, because it removes us from ourselves – not in the sense that it exposes us to the distorting gaze of others, but because it turns us into slaves, by rendering us dependent on the favour of others and by encouraging us to live for the sake of that which lies beyond our powers. Liberty here consists in self-possession, understood both as the absence of personal subjection to the will of others and as an internal disposition of the mind, achieved by turning one's attention and one's will back towards oneself.

II

Montaigne's alignment of *libertas* with *tranquillitas* and *otium* links the 1571 inscription to a long-standing tradition of humanist reflection on the ethics of public engagement and service. Like Thomas More, like Justus Lipsius, the author of the *Essais* draws upon the resources of ancient Stoicism in order not merely to set retreat against engagement, but to explore the possibility of their reconciliation.[10] As Freya Sierhuis observes in Chapter 3 in this volume, however, Montaigne's project of self-examination and self-regulation is far removed from Lipsius's rigorous equation of freedom with subjection to divine reason.[11] What Montaigne offers to his readers is a highly personal, tentative exercise in moral thinking, couched in a discourse of human frailty, vulnerability and self-protection: 'I have nothing of my own except myself', he writes in *On vanity*, 'and even there my possession is partly lacking and borrowed'.[12]

As is now widely acknowledged, the essayist's retirement from the *parlement* did not commit him to a life of leisure and contemplation.[13] As well as a double term of office as mayor of Bordeaux from 1581 to 1585, Montaigne

8. II.17: 680–1. 9. III.9: 1014, 1038.
10. On More's distinctive contribution to humanist debates about *otium* and *negotium* see Skinner 2002b and Parrish 1997; on the emergence in England of a 'Lipsian paradigm' in service of political engagement rather than resignation see McCrea 1997.
11. See Chapter 3 in this volume, pp. 46–64. 12. III.9: 1013.
13. See Hoffmann 1998 and Fontana 2008.

held appointments as *gentilhomme de la chambre* to both Henri III and Henri de Navarre, serving as an intermediary and negotiator between opposing parties in the wars of religion then ravaging France.[14] This continuing public career, however, would only have given greater urgency to the difficulty highlighted in the 1571 inscription: can freedom be achieved even in the midst of public servitude?

Montaigne readily admits that his duty is to serve the common good: 'both my word and my faith, are, like the rest, part of this common body: their best effect, is public service: I take that for granted'.[15] His liberty and idleness, however, are 'qualities diametrically contrary' to the 'service of public dealings', a profession with which he declares himself to be 'disgusted'.[16] *Oysiveté* in Montaigne's usage, it should be stressed, refers not so much to inactivity or irresponsibility, but rather to a profound aversion to care (*soing*, *soucy*, *solicitude*), testifying to his deep concern to protect his will and his mind from pressure and perturbation. He is, he insists, 'easy and ready for any man's need', but only as long as they ask of him 'nothing involving business and care', for he has 'declared war to the death against all care'.[17] By pairing freedom with idleness, however, Montaigne shifts attention away from the dignity of *otium* to the ambivalent humility of laziness and negligence. *Oysiveté* is a highly problematic category, as is made clear in the short chapter that bears that name.[18] Having 'retired to [his] home' in order to allow his *esprit* 'to entertain itself and stay and settle itself in itself', Montaigne finds that, far from inducing inward peace and contentment, this 'full idleness' only serves to increase his inconstancy and agitation, engendering countless 'chimeras and fantastic monsters' in his mind.[19] True tranquillity, in this perspective, is to be sought not through the repudiation of action and occupation, but through a process of measured engagement and judicious self-regulation.

Montaigne's retreat is accordingly to be thought of not as a wholesale withdrawal from public society and service, but as an exile of the will – a transformation of the conditions of his involvement with the world.

> If, at times, I have been pushed into handling affairs foreign to me, I have promised to take them in hand, not in lung or liver; to take charge of them, not to incorporate them; to take care of them, yes; to be impassioned about them, never.[20]

14. Frame 1965: 223–45, 266–88. 15. III.1: 837. 16. III.9: 1038. 17. III.9: 1015.
18. On the ambivalence of *otium* in Renaissance culture more generally see Vickers 1990.
19. I.8: 54–5. 20. III.10: 1049.

The focus of Montaigne's endeavours, as he expresses it in the title of the chapter from which this passage is extracted, is 'mesnager sa volonté' – an attempt to husband or economise his will, to dispose of it with the same circumspection and thrift that one might exercise in managing one's household (*mesnage*). His aim is to preserve an affective distance, to establish a refuge within his mind, in order to protect himself from the twin tempests of violent passion and anxiety within his soul, and fortune and opinion in the world.

> I do not want a man to refuse, to the charges he takes on, attention, steps, words, and sweat and blood if need be:
> *To die for dear friends,*
> *Or for my country, I do not fear.*
> But this is by way of loan and accidentally: The mind holding itself ever in repose and health, not without action, but without vexation, without passion.[21]

Far from precluding a public career, Montaigne's suspicion towards engagement is here a precondition for it: 'I have been able to engage in public duties without leaving myself (*sans me despartir de moy*) and to give myself to others without removing myself from myself (*sans m'oster à moy*).'[22]

This contrastive and emphatic use of the pronoun 'moy' is characteristic of the language that Montaigne uses to articulate what we would now call 'the self'. As Terence Cave has shown, Montaigne does not write about *le soi* or *le moi*, understood as an abstract or reified entity, or as a concept in philosophy requiring elucidation and justification.[23] This use of 'self' as a substantive noun is only to be found, in French, from the second half of the seventeenth century – notably in Pascal's retort to Montaigne: 'le moi est haïssable'.[24] Montaigne, by contrast, always uses 'moy' in its standard, pronominal form, as a reflexive rather than ontological signifier. His subject, as announced in his prefatory address to the reader, is not 'the self' but simply *himself*: 'it is myself that I portray (*c'est moy que je peins*)', 'I am myself the matter of my book (*je suis moy-mesmes la matiere de mon livre*).'[25]

Insofar as Montaigne can be said to be writing about 'self' at all, his efforts focus on the need to distinguish all that is properly 'moy' or 'à moy' ('myself', 'my own') from all that is not – on the need to engage ourselves to ourselves, by distancing ourselves from all that is not us. His 'moy' is defined in opposition to 'les autres' or 'le monde', its location designated by images

21. III.10: 1052. The quotation is from Horace, *Odes*, IV.ix: 51–2. 22. III.10: 1053.
23. Cave 1999: 111–27. 24. Pascal 1963: fragment 597. 25. 'To the Reader': 27.

of circular or centripetal motion. As he explains in *On presumption*: 'the world always look straight ahead; as for me, I turn my gaze inward (*je replie ma veue au dedans*), I fix it there and keep it busy. Everyone looks in front of him; as for me, I look inside of me (*moy je regarde dans moy*): I have no business but with myself.'[26]

This practice of contraction and reflection allows Montaigne to protect, contain and appropriate himself. We must seize hold of and reclaim ownership over ourselves, he urges, by separating ourselves from that which is alien to us and binding ourselves only to ourselves:

> Let us break free from these violent traps, which engage us elsewhere, and distance us from ourselves. We must unknot these so powerful obligations and, from now on, love this or that but marry nothing but ourselves. That is to say, let the rest be ours, but not joined and glued to us in such a way that it cannot be pulled apart without flaying us, and tearing away some piece of ourselves. The greatest thing in the world is to know how to belong to yourself (*sçavoir estre à soy*).[27]

This distinction between that which is ours and that which is not provides the foundation for a striking rhetoric of self-possession. 'Few things touch me', he claims in *On managing the will*, 'or, to put it better, have a hold over me', for 'it is right that things should touch us, as long as they do not possess us'. He opposes himself 'with all [his] strength' to those affections which 'distract' him from himself and 'attach [him] elsewhere', arguing that 'we must lend ourselves to others, and give ourselves only to ourselves'. Other men 'give themselves for hire': their 'faculties' are not 'for them, but for those to whom they would enslave themselves'. Montaigne, by contrast, maintains that 'we must husband the liberty of our soul, and mortgage it only on just occasions. Which are in very small number, if we judge sanely.'[28]

III

This emphasis on self-possession has led some scholars to identify Montaigne with 'a liberal politics of the individual, based on recognising a man as having a property in himself and therefore self-owned'.[29] The *arriereboutique*, according to this view, represents a rigorously private sphere, defined in opposition to the encroachments of other individuals and of the state.

26. II.17: 697. 27. I.38: 246. 28. III.10: 1048–9.
29. Jordan 2003: 432. For similar claims see Keohane 1977 and Schaefer 1990: 315–21.

This interpretation strikes me as profoundly mistaken. Coercion and constraint are both presented as deeply antipathetic to Montaigne's free nature. However, it is dependency – the fact of having a master, of living at the mercy of someone or something other than ourselves – that constitutes the deepest and most basic affront to Montaigne's freedom. To this extent, the *Essais* may be said to partake of what Quentin Skinner and Philip Pettit have described as a 'neo-Roman' (or 'republican') conception of liberty, 'in which the antonym is not interference as such but rather . . . domination', defined as 'subjection to an arbitrary power of interference on the part of another – a *dominus* or master – even another who chooses not actually to exercise that power'.[30]

Montaigne's polemic against the jurisprudence of his times, in *On experience*, leads him to reflect that the mere sight of a prison, even from the outside, is intolerable to him:

> I am so sick for liberty that if anyone should forbid me access to some corner of the Indies, I should live distinctly less comfortably . . . All my little prudence in these civil wars in which we are now involved is employed to keep them from interrupting my liberty of coming and going.[31]

In *On vanity*, meanwhile, the image of a man who is physically jostled and restrained by the crowds that surround him is offered as a vivid analogy for the obstacles and snares imposed by public life:

> He who walks in the crowd must step aside, keep his elbows in, step back or advance, even leave the straight way, according to what he encounters. He must live not so much according to himself as according to others, not according to what he proposes to himself but according to what others propose to him, according to the time, according to the men, according to the business.[32]

This emphasis on unencumbered movement, on having space in which to manoeuvre, echoes Montaigne's claim, earlier in the chapter, that 'the bond of an obligation' is a 'cruel stranglehold for one who likes to give his liberty elbow-room in all directions'.[33] The idea of free movement is indeed fundamental to the chapter as a whole, which offers an extended apology for his

30. Pettit 2002: 340. See also Pettit 1997; Skinner 2002a; 2008a.
31. III.13: 1119. 32. III.9: 1037. 33. III.9: 1014.

restless appetite for travel and for the wandering motion of his own text: 'my style, and my mind, alike go a-roaming'.[34]

This antipathy towards confinement is paralleled by an equally visceral hatred of compulsion. In *On the education of children*, Montaigne writes that his childhood education was conducted in such a way as to train his mind 'in all gentleness and liberty, without rigour and constraint'.[35] This 'mild, free fashion, exempt from rigorous subjection', he complains in *On presumption*, has taught him to chafe against all manner of prescription and command, making him 'soft and useless for serving others, and no good to anyone but [himself]'.[36]

There is no doubt, then, that Montaigne takes the fact of being fettered or forced to be an infringement of his liberty. The dominant emphasis of the *Essais*, however, falls not on captivity or compulsion as impediments to free action, but on dependency as a source of slavery. This order of priorities becomes clear if we return to *On vanity*. The 'cruel stranglehold' suffered by the man who wishes 'to give his liberty elbow-room in all directions', when read in the context of the passage as a whole, turns out to refer not to a limit imposed on his power to act, but to a state of subjection, an alienation suffered by the will.

The quotation occurs in the context of an extended deploration of the uncertainty experienced by Montaigne as a result of the civil wars. His house, we are told, 'has always been free, very accessible and at any one's service'. It has therefore won 'considerable popular affection', and has thus far remained miraculously 'virgin of blood and pillage' amid so much local disturbance and unrest. Yet Montaigne is deeply troubled by the fact that he owes this continuing escape not to 'the protection of the laws' but to the good will of other men:

> As things stand, I live more than half by others' favour, which is a harsh obligation. I do not want to owe my safety either to the kindness and goodness of the great, who approve of my obedience to the laws and my liberty, or to the easy ways of my predecessors and myself.[37]

The term *obligation* here signifies both a claim on Montaigne's gratitude (he is obliged to those more powerful men on whom he relies for his protection) and an affront to his freedom: to live *de la faveur d'autruy*, to owe one's safety to others, is to be bound, to be reduced to subjection.

34. III.9: 1041. 35. I.25: 181. 36. II.17: 681–2. 37. III.9: 1010–11.

This account of the civil wars as a state of intolerable dependency provides the starting-point for a wider discussion of 'the science of benefaction and gratitude'.[38]

> I hold that we should live by right and authority, not by reward or grace. How many gallant men have preferred to lose their life than to owe it! I shun to submit myself to all manner of obligation. But especially, to that which binds me by a debt of honour. I find nothing so dear, as that which is given to me: and for which, my will remains mortgaged (*hypothéquée*) by the title of ingratitude: and I more willingly receive offices, that are for sale. Rightly so, I think: For the latter, I give only money: For the others I give myself.[39]

Our freedom is eroded, Montaigne suggests, whenever favours are bestowed on us, for we are always in debt to, and under the control of, those who have benefited us: 'as giving is an ambitious quality and a prerogative, so is accepting a quality of submission'. Those whom he sees 'so readily making use of one and all and engaging themselves to them' would not do so 'if they relished', as he does, 'the sweetness of a pure liberty, and if they weighed the bond of an obligation as much as a wise man should'.[40] The word *engageure* (bond) here takes on its full connotations, as a form of subjugation and expropriation – placing us quite literally *en gage*, on pledge, as if we had mortgaged and pawned ourselves out to others.

Montaigne's concern is not to obtain greater latitude for the unimpeded fulfilment of his personal preferences and wishes, but to teach his soul 'to be contented with itself and manfully to do without the comforts that come to it from outside, when fate so ordains'.[41] All that he owes, he owes 'simply to the common and natural obligations'. He has not allowed himself to be bought, to become a bondsman: '*the gifts of the powerful are to me unknown*. Princes give me plenty if they take nothing from me, and do me enough good when they do me no harm.'[42]

Slavery is here identified with arbitrariness – with that condition of radical uncertainty and insecurity that results from living at the mercy of the mere will (or *arbitrium*) of another. Montaigne takes care, accordingly, to distinguish service or subjection (which consist in reasoned submission to lawful authority) from servitude (which stems from dependency on the personal whim and favour of another). In *On the education of children*, in particular, he

38. III.9: 1013. 39. III.9: 1011. 40. III.9: 1014. 41. III.9: 1013.
42. III.9: 1013. The quotation is adapted from Virgil, *Aeneid*, XII, 519–20.

lists, among 'the most profitable lessons of philosophy' which a young man is to be taught, 'the difference between . . . servitude and subjection, licence and liberty'.[43]

The significance of this elliptical remark is made clear a few pages earlier by a late addition inserted into an existing discussion of the conduct to be adopted 'in discourse and contestation'. A young gentleman, he argues in the original version of the chapter, should be taught to obey the commands of truth rather than those of any man, for that is what it means to judge freely. He must learn 'above all to surrender and throw down his arms before truth as soon as he perceives it, whether it be found in the hands of his opponents, or in himself through reconsideration'. He shall be neither 'set in a chair to say a prescribed role', nor 'pledged to any cause, except by the fact that he approves it'; he shall not be 'of that trade, where one sells for ready cash the liberty to repent and reconsider'.[44]

It is at this point, in the final version of the text, that Montaigne inserts a quotation from Cicero's *Academica priora* (II.3.8), followed by an explanation of the difference between being a servant of one's prince and being a 'pure Courtier':

> *Nor is he forced by any necessity to defend everything that has been prescribed and commanded.* If his tutor is of my humour, he will form his will to be a very loyal servant of his Prince, and a very affectionate, and very courageous one: but he will cool in him any desire to attach himself to that prince otherwise than by public duty. Besides several disadvantages, which harm our liberty, by these private obligations, the judgement of a man who is hired and bought, is either less whole and less free, or tainted with imprudence and ingratitude. A pure Courtier can have neither lawful power (*loy*) nor will, to speak and think otherwise than favourably of a master, who among so many thousands of other subjects, has chosen him to nourish and raise up with his own hand. This favour and utility corrupt his freedom, not without some reason, and dazzle him. Therefore we habitually find the language of those people different from any other language, in a state, and little to be trusted in such matters.[45]

Instead of being bound by 'public duty' alone, the courtier is 'attached' to his prince through 'private obligations': he is personally in his debt, since he owes him his position, his power and his possessions. His liberty is compromised and corrupted: he has been 'hired and bought (*gagé et achetté*)'; he no longer

43. I.25: 165. 44. I.25: 160. 45. I.25: 160–1.

belongs to himself. The consequence of this is that the courtier cannot judge or speak freely: his language cannot be trusted. He has alienated his liberty to repent and reconsider; he surrenders not to the truth, but to the demands of his uncertain and dependent condition.

Why is the courtier 'forced', as Montaigne has it, 'to defend everything that has been prescribed and commanded'? In the first place, he is 'dazzled' and flattered by the favour shown to him, his judgement clouded by gratitude and wonder at the prince's power: he does not, Montaigne suspects, have the 'will' (*volonté*) to do anything other than please. Even more importantly, he has no authority, no right (*loy*), to speak or think openly, even if he wanted to. It is not merely that the courtier owes it to the prince to show gratitude for his favour. In addition, it would be imprudent for him to say anything that might displease the man who is, as Montaigne makes clear, not only his prince but his 'master'.

In what we have come to think of as the liberal tradition, freedom is a predicate of actions: we are free if and only if we are able to act in accordance with our wishes, without hindrance or coercion. Montaigne, by contrast, describes freedom as his favourite or ruling *quality*, defining the kind of man that he wants and takes himself to be. This characterisation of liberty as a property of Montaigne's person shifts attention away from his capacity to perform, or refrain from, specific actions, towards a consideration of his own status as an agent, and in particular of his standing in relation to other men. For Montaigne as for the neo-Roman tradition, liberty names the condition of the man who acts, thinks and speaks independently, by virtue of the fact that he has no master: indeed, it is a condition of being an agent or person in the first place, as opposed to another man's creature, instrument or property.

This understanding of liberty as a condition of personhood and independent agency is essentially juridical in origin and character. To be a slave, according to the Roman law of persons, is to be subject to another's will, to be under the power of a master (*in potestate dominorum*, *in dominio alieno* or *in alieno iure*). The free man, by contrast, has his own will: he is able to act *sui iuris* ('in his own right'), being responsible for his conduct to no one but himself.[46] To own yourself or to have property in yourself, from this perspective, is simply to be 'your own man, your own person, not a mere creature of someone else', 'to be able to act independently of the arbitrary will of anyone else'.[47]

46. Mommsen and Krueger 1985: I.5–6: 15–19. 47. Skinner 2006: 164–5.

This juridical account of freedom as a status of persons has come to be associated with a very particular set of political commitments. Skinner has always emphasised, to be sure, that there is nothing exclusively *republican* about the claim that liberty consists in non-domination. The crux of the neo-Roman account lies instead, he argues, in an attack on the presence of arbitrary power within the commonwealth. On this view, however, the freedom of the individual can be secured only through participation in a self-determining polity: the legal state of self-ownership is the distinctive property of the citizen.[48]

Montaigne's version of non-domination, by contrast, is ethical rather than constitutional in orientation. Even if it were possible to read his work as a contribution to political theory, in violation of his insistence that he studies no subject but himself, one would find that he has relatively little to say about government, except to condemn the vanity of political philosophy, to present himself as a loyal subject of the French monarchy, and to distance himself from all efforts to challenge or reform the existing constitution of the state.[49] The way to liberty, according to the *Essais*, lies not in a constitution that protects citizens from domination, but in a practice of inward retreat allowing us to disentangle ourselves, both physically and mentally, from our public servitude.

In Montaigne's hands, accordingly, the juridical terminology of neo-Roman liberty unites with the moral language of Stoic freedom. In *On physiognomy*, for example, we read that 'true freedom consists in having power over oneself for everything', a declaration to which Montaigne adds a sentence from Seneca's *Letters to Lucilius* (110.34): 'he is most powerful who is in his own power (*qui se habet in potestate*)'.[50] Slavery – and Montaigne is here quoting from Cicero's *Stoic paradoxes*, 35 – is 'the obedience of a broken and abject soul, lacking its own will (*arbitrio carentis suo*)'.[51]

When Montaigne appeals for us to 'bring back unto ourselves, and unto our ease, our thoughts and our intentions', he echoes Seneca's assertion that the wise man, faced with adversity, will 'return into himself and be with himself (*in se reconditur, secum est*)'.[52] When he urges us to 'sequester ourselves and repossess ourselves (*se . . . sequestrer et r'avoir de soy*)', or when he writes of the soul that 'we must bring it back and withdraw it into itself (*ramener et retirer en soy*)', his language mimics the *Letters*' injunction to Lucilius: 'retreat into yourself (*recede in te ipsum*), as far as you can'. When he calls

48. Skinner 2008b: ix. 49. See for example III.9: 1001–2, 1040. 50. III.12: 1092.
51. III.9: 998. 52. I.38: 246. Cf. Seneca 1989: I.9.16: 52.

upon us to own ourselves – to 'lend ourselves to others, but give ourselves only to ourselves' – he appropriates to himself Seneca's claim that he does not 'surrender himself to his affairs, but only lends himself to them . . . giving himself to his friends without removing himself from himself'.[53]

Freedom, in this perspective, is a matter of psychological as well as forensic independence, grounded in self-knowledge and self-care as well as self-jurisdiction. Self-possession here entails both knowing how to own ourselves by shunning all that renders us dependent upon, and subject to, the power of others, and knowing how to live for ourselves by understanding what it is that we owe to ourselves.

IV

This analysis of Montaigne's critique of public life and society has thus far focused on the vicissitudes of personal obligation and dependency, and on the dangers of becoming someone else's client and creature – that is, on the 'servitude of the courts' mentioned in his commemorative inscription. But Montaigne is also deeply preoccupied by the problem of public office and its ability to remove us from ourselves. It is to this second aspect of public slavery that I should now like to turn.

The problem with 'public charges', as Montaigne terms them in his inscription, is that they may require us to forfeit our conscience and virtue in the name of public necessity. Vice, cruelty and treachery, detestable as they may be, are both integral to human nature and unavoidable in politics: as he explains in *On the useful and the honourable*, 'the public welfare requires that a man betray, and lie, and massacre'. Montaigne refuses to surrender himself in this way: 'let us resign this commission to other more obedient and flexible men', he contends, 'to more vigorous and less fearful citizens who sacrifice their honour and conscience just as the ancients sacrificed their lives in order to save their country'.[54] His assertion, in *On presumption*, that his liberty has made him 'soft and useless for serving others' takes on a fresh significance in this context. He cannot be put to *use*, both in the sense that he has nothing to contribute to public utility, and in the sense that he cannot bear to be used as an instrument: he cannot be made fit for a political universe ruled by expediency rather than honesty.

To 'prostitute one's conscience' for the sake of the commonwealth, Montaigne argues, is to consent to slavery.[55] Socrates, Pythagoras and Diogenes,

53. I.38: 243, 244. Cf. Seneca 1989: I.7.8:34; I.62.1–2: 426, 428.
54. III.1: 830. 55. III.1: 839.

for all their greatness, were 'too enslaved to reverence for the laws, to authorise and support which true virtue has to give up much of its original vigour'.[56] Of the hangman who was ordered to deflower Sejanus' daughter, since virgins could not be executed under Roman law, he writes that 'not only his hand, but even his soul, is a slave to public convenience'.[57] In all his dealings with princes, accordingly, he makes clear that his own freedom must come first:

> I do not want to be considered either so affectionate or so loyal a servant, as to be found fit to betray anyone. He who is unfaithful to himself, is excusably so to his master. But these are Princes, who do not accept men by halves and scorn limited and conditional services. There is no remedy: I freely tell them my limits: for a slave, I must be to reason alone, and I can barely even do that properly. And they too are wrong, to expect from a free man, such subjection to their service, and such obligation, as they do from a man, that they have made and bought: or whose fortune depends particularly and expressly on their own.[58]

Montaigne here draws once more on the now familiar contrast between the free man and the man who has been bought. It is hard not to see this passage, however, as a response and correction to the 'very affectionate' and 'very loyal' subject described in *On the education of children*. Princes may be 'wrong' to treat him as if he were their creature and yet, Montaigne here suggests, it is in their nature to disdain the 'limited and conditional services' provided by free men. There is 'no remedy', moreover, to this state of affairs: all that Montaigne can do is to stand his ground, and to allow his 'services' to be scorned.

Montaigne's 'limits' are here determined not merely by the need to preserve his independence, by avoiding all 'private obligations' to his prince, but by the obligation of loyalty and fidelity that attaches him to his own self. This concern to distinguish those obligations that we owe to the commonwealth from those that we owe to ourselves is central to *On managing the will*:

> Most of our occupations are farcical, *The whole world is acting a part* [Petronius]. We must play our role duly, but as the role of a borrowed personage. Masks and appearances must not be made into a real essence, nor that which is alien into that which is proper.[59]

This account of the world as a theatre in which the essential and the accidental, 'le propre' and 'l'estranger', are characteristically confused – in which

56. III.1: 836. 57. III.1: 839. 58. III.1: 834. 59. III.10: 1057.

our public roles are mistaken for ourselves – has typically been interpreted as evidence of Montaigne's alleged appeal to a deep, interior self, torn between the demands of prudent dissimulation and those of sincerity, and incommensurable with our artificial social roles. To describe our public charges as masks (or as *personae*), however, is not so much to indict social life for its inauthenticity, or even for its hypocrisy, as it is to offer a subversive rewriting of a widespread, humanist ethics of public office, as articulated most influentially by Cicero in *De officiis*.[60] Montaigne continues:

> I see some who transform and transubstantiate themselves into as many new figures, and new beings, as they undertake charges: and who make themselves prelates down to their liver and guts: and drag their office with them right into their privy. I cannot teach them to distinguish between hats doffed to them and those doffed to their commission, or their retinue, or their mule. *They give themselves so much over to fortune that they forget their own nature* [Quintus Curtius]. The Mayor and Montaigne have always been two, by a very clear separation.[61]

From the perspective of *De officiis*, virtue is an essentially public quality, realised in visible, outward expression and inseparably connected to the performance of duties (*officia*) identified with our social roles. A man's identity lies in the performance of his *personae* – as father, son, friend, patron, citizen, magistrate and so on. But for Montaigne, I am *not* exhausted by my offices: there is an all-important difference between the world of our public charges and that of 'real essences', a clear and evident distinction between the mayor of Bordeaux and Michel de Montaigne.

Montaigne's point is not that we should simply abandon our public duties: we 'must play our role duly'. But I must not give *myself* up to these parts: they are borrowed ('emprunté'), alien ('estranger'): they belong to someone or something other than myself; they are under the sway of fortune, not nature. We must learn to act for ourselves, to own our actions by performing our part, by distinguishing our true offices from those that properly belong to others. Even in the performance of our borrowed roles, we must remember that we are acting on behalf of another – and that our true contentment and our true role lie elsewhere.

> I have enough to do to order and arrange the domestic pressures that oppress my entrails and veins, without giving myself the trouble of adding extraneous pressures to them; I am enough involved in my

60. This point is also made by Baldwin 2001. 61. III.10: 1057.

> essential, proper, and natural affairs, without inviting in foreign ones. Those who know how much they owe to themselves, and for how many duties they are obligated to themselves, find that nature has given them in this a commission full enough and not at all idle.[62]

To be free in this context is to assume responsibility for ourselves as independent moral agents. As Montaigne makes clear in *On repentance*, the point of 'living a private life, on show only to ourselves' is to 'establish a pattern within, as a touchstone for our actions', by learning to accept no one but oneself as the arbiter of one's performance:

> Any man can play his part in the play, and represent an honourable person (*personnage*) on the stage: but within, and in one's breast (*au dedans, et en sa poictrine*), where everything is permissible, where everything is hidden, to be ordered there (*y estre reglé*), that's the point. The next step to that is to be so in our own house, in our ordinary actions, for which we render account to no one, where nothing is studied or artificial.[63]

Montaigne is here distinguishing those moral qualities that can truly be accounted our own, because they are practised for their own sake, in secret, rather than for ostentation, from all those attributes that are merely imputed to us by opinion and reputation. Our 'real essence' is to be found 'within', not in the sense that our true identity is to be sought beyond the alienating gaze of others, but because our conduct in public life provides a doubtful guide to the true condition of our soul.

Solitude and privacy are here required not in order to provide space for the expression of our true feelings or individuality, but so that we may preserve our mind and our will at liberty. As Montaigne expresses it in *On three kinds of association*:

> The solitude that I love, and that I preach, is principally, nothing but leading my affections, and my thoughts, back to myself: restraining and shortening, not my steps, but my desires and my care, abandoning foreign solicitude, and mortally fleeing from servitude, and obligation: and not so much the press of people, as the press of business.[64]

The figurative space of the library, like that of the *arriereboutique*, provides a closeted, private refuge in which one can hide oneself, dispensing with all artifice and ceremony in order to seek company and conversation only

62. III.10: 1049. 63. III.2: 848–9. 64. III.3: 864.

with oneself: 'wretched to my mind is the man who has nowhere in his home where he can be his own (*estre à soy*): where he can pay court to himself privately: where he can hide'. This state of seclusion, however, is represented as a condition of dominion and liberty, rather than as a locus of introspective self-discovery. Freedom, to this extent, is intimately tied to freehold: the free man can do without the material rewards of princely service; he is not in the employ of any other man; he lives in a state of leisure and enjoys authority over his own household. Montaigne's tower library is his 'siège', his throne or seat: 'I try to make my dominion (*domination*) over it pure . . . Everywhere else, my authority is merely verbal: in essence confused.'[65] To withdraw from the world, from the 'servitude of the court and of public charges', is to remove oneself from the temptations of dependency, by withdrawing our will into ourselves – into that room at the back of the shop that is 'toute nostre, toute franche', entirely ours and entirely free, in which we may 'establish our true liberty and our principal retreat and solitude'.[66]

V

Before drawing this chapter to a close, I should like to raise and respond to a possible objection to the argument that I have so far laid out. If, as I have claimed, independence and not sincerity provides the key to Montaigne's preoccupation with 'self', then what are we to make of his insistence that the *Essais* are a 'book of good faith', and that he is 'hungry to make himself known, little caring to how many, provided it be truthfully'?[67] Should this commitment to undisguised self-revelation not be taken to imply that authentic self-expression and self-presence *are*, after all, at the core of his project?

Deceit, hypocrisy and art are, it is true, forcefully denounced by Montaigne as symptoms of an epidemic of false self-presentation and self-delusion. It is crucial, however, that we see just what is at stake in this critique. Despite his deep concern with the immorality of lies, his desire to promote a sincere civility based on friendship and equity, and his heightened awareness of the disparity between appearance and reality, Montaigne indicts art, not as evidence of inauthenticity, but as an expression of servility. His rhetoric of openness and naturalness, purged of all false glosses and accretions, is inseparable from, and subordinate to, his identification of himself as a free man.

65. III.3: 870.   66. I.38: 245.   67. 'To the Reader': 27; III.5: 888.

The *Essais* are adamant in their condemnation of lying as a fundamental betrayal of human sociability and a perversion of language and communication. As Montaigne argues in *On liars*, 'we are men, and hold together, only by our word. If we recognised the horror and the gravity of lying, we would persecute it with fire more justly than other crimes.'[68] To lie is to corrupt speech, to render meaningful communication impossible. As he puts it in *On giving the lie*, 'mutual understanding is brought about solely by way of words', as 'the only instrument by means of which our wills and thoughts communicate'. He who 'falsifies' his *parolle* 'betrays human society', for 'if it fails us, we have no more hold on each other, no more knowledge of each other', and 'if it deceives us, it breaks up all our relations and dissolves all the bonds of our polity'.[69]

The problem with dissimulation, however, lies not in its inherent artifice or bad faith, but in its fraudulence, as a debasement of the currency we use to judge the morals of men: 'our truth of nowadays is not what is, but what others can be convinced of; just as we call "money" not only that which is legal, but also any counterfeit that will pass'. False speech, in this sense, 'enfolds cowardice and faintness of heart', there being no 'more obvious cowardice' than 'to deny our own word' and, 'worse yet, to deny what we know'.[70] The man who dissimulates and hides himself is guilty not of insincerity, but of moral turpitude and weakness.

The courtier, as we have seen, is condemned to flattering and ingratiating himself with his master, contorting himself into whatever posture shall best please the man who holds him in his power. But nor is he able, as a consequence, to judge or speak freely about himself. As Montaigne writes in *On presumption*:

> It is a craven and servile humour to disguise ourselves and hide under a mask, and not to dare to show ourselves as we are . . . A generous heart should not belie its thoughts; it wants to reveal itself even to its inmost depths.[71]

This connection between freedom and frankness is then reaffirmed through an appeal both to Aristotle, who 'considered it the function of magnanimity to hate and love openly, to judge, to speak with complete frankness, and to have no regard for the approbation or reprobation of others in comparison with truth', and to Apollonius, who 'said that it was for slaves to lie, and for free men to speak truth'.[72]

68. I.9: 58. 69. II.18: 705–6. 70. II.18: 705. 71. II.17: 685. 72. II.17: 686.

Montaigne's unabashed examination and exposition of himself in the *Essais*, is, from this perspective, a final testament to his liberty. As he maintains in *On the art of conversation*:

> Not to dare to speak roundly of oneself shows some lack of heart: A stout and lofty judgement which judges sanely and surely, uses its own examples on all occasions as well as others, and testifies as frankly about itself as about a third party: We must pass over these common rules of civility in favour of truth, and liberty. I dare not only to speak of myself, but to speak only of myself.[73]

The image that the text contains, I contend, is offered not as the intimate trace of an elusive, authentic self, but as the bold imprint and index of Montaigne's moral preoccupations and sensibility – a register of that which he can truly count his own. His book, in other words, represents him as he truly is – but as a witness of his moral character as a free man, not as an expression (sincere or otherwise) of his innermost psychological being.

73. III.8: 988.

3

Autonomy and inner freedom: Lipsius and the revival of Stoicism

Freya Sierhuis

I

Perhaps in reaction to the surge of studies that followed Stephen Greenblatt's influential *Renaissance Self-fashioning* in examining the performative nature of Renaissance notions of identity, early modern intellectual and literary historians have recently taken a renewed interest in the dimensions of inwardness, inner freedom and moral autonomy, the existence of which at least the cruder variety of new historicist and cultural materialist studies had denied. Some of these studies have broached new subjects in studying Renaissance concepts of selfhood and identity, such as the relation between embodiment and selfhood, or the impact of the Reformation on notions of human subjectivity, while others have focused on the literary and discursive practices constitutive of the early modern self, such as the sonnet, the autobiography, the essay and the soliloquy. Still others have focused on the self's philosophical moorings, in the moral-psychological theories of passions and affect, or on the currents that provided the two main vocabularies of selfhood in the early modern period: Augustinianism and Stoicism.

It is in this last debate that this chapter seeks to position itself. It attempts to establish what kind of notion of self the neo-Stoic philosophy of Justus Lipsius posits, and what it means for this self to be free or autonomous. The emphasis on neo-Stoicism's ethic of obedience that has for a long time characterised the historiography of Lipsius, in particular through the work of Gerhard Oestreich, has dimmed our eyes to the fact that liberty, the freedom attained by the individual by submitting to reason, is in effect the cornerstone of neo-Stoic psychology and ethics.[1] While it is true that this notion of liberty as freedom from passion and a willing submission to providence had a long

1. Justly emphasised in Lagrée 1999: 91.

history, stretching from the medieval translations of Boethius *De consolatione philosophiae*, Petrarch's *De remediis utriusque fortunae* and the translations of Seneca and Epictetus by an earlier generation of humanists, the neo-Stoicism of Justus Lipsius can be distinguished from its precursors by its larger scope and ambitions, and its attempt at systematisation. As Jan Papy has rightly pointed out, Lipsius scholarship has been hampered by an overemphasis on the *De constantia* and the *Politicorum seu civilis doctrinae libri sex*, and a relative neglect of Lipsius's doxographical works, the *Manuductio ad Stoicorum philosophia* and the *Physiologia Stoicorum*.[2] In underestimating the extent to which Lipsius's ethics and his political thought are rooted in a monist neo-Stoic physics encompassing the natural world as well as the human soul, the extent to which Lipsius envisaged the different components of his project as part of a larger whole has been insufficiently recognised. While Lipsius is concerned to carve out a space in which the individual subject is fully free and beyond the reach of fortune or tyrannical power, the language in which he articulates this notion of liberty is itself, as I shall explain, derived from the domain of politics, being figured on the opposition between freedom and servitude, self-mastery and slavish submission, between the acquisition and the loss of power and autonomy. It is exactly this side of neo-Stoic philosophy, I claim, that generates most interest in the English response to Lipsius, and marks out that particular variety of English neo-Stoicism which left its imprint on early modern English culture in the period stretching from that of Philip Sidney to that of John Milton and Thomas Hobbes.

II

Taking stock of the wider ramifications of Lipsius's project for the restoration of a new form of Stoic philosophy inevitably forces us to rethink the notion of neo-Stoicism as a philosophy of moral self-preservation. Self-preservation, in this reading, entails a separation between public and private ethics, and the imperative for individuals to obey the laws, custom and public religion of the country in which they are born. This reading, in which Lipsius and Montaigne are often juxtaposed, sees the main contribution of this phase of late humanist culture to moral philosophy in its elaboration of a notion of an interior domain – captured in Montaigne's image of the *arrière-boutique* – separated from the domain of public life and its demands, while its political ethic of dutiful but dispassionate service is seen as a transitional phase between

2. Papy 2004: 48–9.

the Ciceronian political ethics of sixteenth-century humanism, and the new theories of sovereignty of the seventeenth century.[3]

At first sight, Lipsius and Montaigne do indeed seem to share a concern for the need to balance duty with detachment. In *De constantia*, Lipsius attacked the notion of love of the fatherland in order to redefine the duties of the citizen. While we owe loyalty, obedience and service to the state in which we are born, it is inaccurate as well as inappropriate to describe these obligations as *pietas*, a duty we owe to our parents and to God alone. While we should, if necessary, be prepared to lay down our life for the common welfare, we should nevertheless do so in an emotionally disengaged way.[4] In a similar manner, Montaigne argued that one should accept the charges of public life with 'the mind holding itself ever in repose and health, not without action, but without vexation, without passion' (cited by Green in Chapter 2, p. 31, above). Felicity Green argues that Montaigne's unease about being 'distracted' from himself by engaging oneself to external things, and his insistence on protecting his freedom by refusing to be indebted, obligated, or in any way owned by someone else, stem from a deeply felt need to keep his will and judgement free, a position that is incompatible with living at the mercy of the will of another. Montaigne wants, under all circumstances, to be his own master. This ideal of rational self-mastery bears a distinct resemblance to that of Lipsius. The rhetoric of self-possession which Green traces in Montaigne's work can be heard in Lipsius's work as well, and both employ the spatial metaphors of the self (re)turning to itself, dwelling with or entering into itself, derived from Roman Stoicism.[5]

Yet the differences between the two authors are at least as striking as the similarities. When Montaigne argues that he can offer princes only 'limited and conditional services' as he can only be a slave to reason 'and I can barely even do that properly', one feels that Lipsius would only partially concur (cited at p. 40 above). For Lipsius, the 'self' is always free as long as it acts in accordance to right reason, and has mastery over the passions that arise from false judgements about the true value of external goods. From this perspective, spiritual servitude, or 'oppression of the mind', is a mirage, a fiction based on a lack of proper understanding of what the soul is:

> He seemeth unto mee to knowe neither himself, nor the celestial nature of the mind, which thinketh it may be oppressed, or constrained. For no outward force can ever make thee to will what

3. For this interpretation, see Keohane 1985; Tuck 1993. 4. Lipsius 1595: I.xi
5. Foucault 1984: 61.

> thou will not; or to believe what thou beleevest not. A man may have power upon this bonde or fetter of the minde, but not over the mind itself. A tyrant hath power to loose it from the body, but not to unloose the nature therof. Such things as bee pure, everlasting, and of fierie nature, set naught at all by external and violent handling.

The 'thing of fierie nature' refers to the rational part of the mind of man as a spark of the divine fire, a notion to which Lipsius would return in greater detail in the *Manuductio* and the *Physiologia*. Viewed from this transcendent perspective, the return to the self is only a preparatory first step in aligning the mind with the cosmic reason which governs the world. The description of the retreat into the garden as a metaphor for the philosophical approach to life is significant here. Within the composition of the *De constantia*, it marks the transition from book I, which is concerned with Langius's attempt to cure Lipsius's distressed state of mind by demonstrating to him how the passions arise from our mistaken opinion of things, to book II, which argues that what from our limited viewpoint may appear as evils or calamities are not evil, when viewed from the perspective of providence, destiny and the natural order of the universe. The dual turn which the retreat into the garden entails – the return towards the self, and the outward, and upward movement – allows us to appreciate the dual nature of Lipsius's understanding of inner liberty.

The assumption of a correspondence between the rational soul and divine reason would have probably struck Montaigne as exactly the kind of philosophical vanity he lambasted in the *Apologie pour Raymond Sebond*. Montaigne, who claimed that 'ces humeurs transcencendants' inspire him with a fear like that of vertiginous heights, nevertheless advances a penetrating criticism of the idea of a comprehensible cosmos.[6] We have, he argues, no communication with being: not only does our own constantly changing view and position prevent such a universal perspective; the things themselves have no stable or fixed essence:

> Finalement, il n'y a aucune constante existence, ny de nostre estre, ny de celuy des objects. Et nous, et nostre jugement, et toutes choses mortelles, vont coulant et roulant sans cesse. Ainsi il ne se peut establir rien de certain de l'un à l'autre, et le jugeant et le jugé estans en continuelle mutation et branle.[7]

There is no real point of contact between this position and Lipsius's neo-Stoic identification of man's essential self with his reason. Lipsius seeks to

6. Montaigne 1962: III.xiii, 1096. 7. Montaigne 1962: II.xii, 586.

identify reason as man's fixed and immutable core, and make it the linchpin of his notion of inner liberty. To this extent, Lipsius is not interested in selfhood as some kind ineffable individuality; his notion of the self is, although subjective, at the same time universal and objective.[8]

III

Due perhaps to the moral-philosophical slant of much of sixteenth-century neo-Stoicism, with its emphasis on *orthopraxis* over *orthodoxia*, Lipsius's contribution to the history of early modern ideas has been viewed in terms of ethics and political prudence, while his role as author of the first systematic account of Stoic physics and cosmology, and thereby his influence on the development of seventeenth-century natural theology, has been largely overlooked.[9]

This omission is curious, seeing that Lipsius himself asserted that an ethics not grounded in natural philosophy stands without any foundation. The question of how one performs one's office in life according to what is good and just cannot be answered if one does not know what the Good is.[10] Lipsius explains the need for methodical and intellectual coherence through the metaphor of the tree of philosophy, in which the relations between first principles, general rules and individual precepts are compared to that of root, trunk and branches.[11] Even though the *De constantia* already contained an exposition of the nature of the soul, and of the relation between God, Providence, destiny and fate, it is nowhere near as methodical and exhaustive as its treatment in the *Physiologia Stoicorum*. That Lipsius devoted the later years of his life to the systematisation of those elements of Stoicism that had made his *De constantia* controversial among Catholics, Calvinists and free will theologians such as Coornhert alike gives us a sense of the scope and ambition of Lipsius's endeavour.

Before we turn to Lipsius's discussion of human freedom, we ought first to understand his account of man's position in this hierarchically ordered cosmos, and the restrictions this places on his liberty. The fundamental link connecting Lipsius's anthropology and physics is his distinctive interpretation of the Stoic definition of the highest Good as living according to nature.

8. It is a difference which distinguishes what Christopher Gill has termed the subjective-individualist and the objective-participant approaches to the self in Hellenistic philosophy. Gill criticises Richard Sorabji's emphasis on individual selfhood: Gill 2006: xv, cf. Sorabji 2000.

9. Lagrée 1994: 52, 56.

10. Lipsius 1604b: II, xii, 93–4.

11. Lipsius 1604b: II, xii, 95.

Proceeding in a way typical of the *Physiologia* and the *Manuductio* in combining doxography with critical evaluation, he gives the different definitions of Zeno, Cleanthes, Chrysippus, Seneca and others[12] to argue that living consistently, according to nature and according to virtue, ultimately means the same thing, and that this life according to reason is to obey God. Positing the different positions as a series of consecutives (*Virtus rationem sequitur, haec naturam, ista Deum*),[13] he joins the imperative of *naturam sequere* directly to Seneca's *Deo parere libertas est.*[14] Through a last-resort appeal to Plato and Pythagoras, he defines this obedience to God, nature, reason and virtue as *Deo assimilatio.*[15] While, as we shall see in the following, he naturalises theology, he also reinserts ethics into the sphere of religion.

For a closer examination, however, of the link between nature, reason, God and man, we need to turn from the *Manuductio* to the *Physiologia*. Dissertationes V to XI of the first book define the nature and attributes of God. Lipsius here examines the Stoic definitions of God as *natura communis*, *ignis artificalis*, or as the reason or soul of the world.[16] He emphasises that this creative fire is equivalent to what Seneca called *incorporalis Ratio ingentium operum artifex.*[17] This fire infuses all things, and it is this fire which maintains and sustains all that is created.[18] Lipsius does not, like Tertullian, attempt to identify the Stoic λογος with Christ as the Λογος. Instead of trying to establish identity, he argues for similarity, attempting to aim if not for harmony then at least for consensus, showing how the notion of the *rationes seminales* that emanate from the divine fire are in line with Plato's theory of ideas,[19] and how similar notions can be found in Heraclitus, Homer and Hermes Trismegistus.[20] Proposing a metaphorical interpretation of the Stoic divine fire, he adduces the biblical examples of God appearing to Moses in the burning bush, the fiery column leading the Israelites through the desert, and the Holy Ghost descending upon the Apostles in tongues of fire, to conclude that, although one cannot say 'God is fire', the Stoics had grasped a fundamental trait of the divine nature.[21]

Despite this caveat, Lipsius's definition of the soul in the *Manuductio* and the theory of the rational soul as a part of the universal *ratio* make one doubt whether his natural theology can ultimately be fitted into a Christian framework without friction. For while Lipsius's God is certainly not immanent in creation, he is not altogether transcendent either.[22] The rational part of

12. Lipsius 1604b: II, xiv –xviii. 13. Lipsius 1604b: II, xviii, 108.
14. Lipsius 1604b: II, xvi, 104. 15. Lipsius 1604b: II, xix, 113. 16. Lipsius 1604a: I, v, 12.
17. Lipsius 1604a: I, v, 12. 18. Lipsius 1604a: I, v, 12–13. 19. Lipsius 1604a: I, v, 13.
20. Lipsius 1604a: I, v, 13. 21. Lipsius 1604a: I, v, 14. 22. Lagrée 1994: 55–6.

man and divine reason are different in degree and in excellence, but are not ontologically distinct. *Ratio*, reason, is thus both the link between God and man, and the ordering principle that ensures the stability and intelligibility of the cosmos. Lipsius's natural theology is here as interesting in what it explains, namely the divine origin of the soul, as for what it leaves out: the Fall, man's natural depravity and the need for grace. Despite Lipsius's pious avowal in the introduction of the second Latin edition of the *De constantia* that the value of ancient philosophy lies in its role as the handmaiden of theology, the first principles of neo-Stoic philosophy appear to make the role of revealed religion redundant. In a revealing passage in *dissertatio* XVI of the first book of the *Manuductio* the imagery of the divine fire is taken up again to argue that God before the advent of Christ, who is Wisdom himself, had already dispensed these sparks of wisdom to disperse the mists of vice and error.[23]

The rationalism that links Lipsius's physics, natural theology and ethics sets the parameters within which human and divine freedom of action operate. While Lipsius makes sure to avoid fatalism by making fate the executive, so to say, of Providence, the notion of Providence itself is fundamentally altered. God's Providence is an ordering and sustaining principle, which governs the universe in all, even in what seems contingent. It is rational, everlasting and immutable. God does not intervene in the natural order of creation through miracles, a possibility which the *De constantia* had still explicitly allowed.[24] Likewise, God does not feel pity, nor does He repent.[25] At first sight, Lipsius's rejection of miracles appears hard to reconcile with the publication, in the same period as the *Physiologia*, of two devotional tracts on miracles of the Holy Virgin of Halle and Scherpenheuvel. Yet it should not be forgotten that these works were written at the request of the archdukes Albert and Isabella, who in 1595 had appointed Lipsius as royal historiographer, and had a lot to gain by being able to present the leading humanist of the day as a devout Counter-Reformation Catholic. Lipsius, it is well known, was a spiritualist, with ties to Hendrick Niclaes's Family of Love, but his spiritualism, unlike that, for example, of the toleration thinker Coornhert, had always been allied with religious conformism and an emphasis on the need for religious uniformity.[26]

More important for Lipsius's Christian-Stoic project is his commitment to the claim that a Stoic notion of Providence does not do away with human

23. Lipsius 1604b: I, xvi, 53. 24. Lipsius 1604a; 48; 1595: 113. 25. Lipsius 1604a: I, xvii, 529.
26. Roth and Stayer 2007: 146. There is, however, no consensus on the issue, and Lipsius's religious beliefs continue to stimulate controversy, see Kraye and Stone 2000: 96.

freedom. Providence works through secondary causes, to create a sphere in which human beings act with a certain measure of autonomy. Lipsius here uses the well-known metaphor of the passengers on a ship who, even though they cannot change its course, are free to perform whatever action they wish while travelling.[27]

Within a universe in which everything flows directly from God, man is therefore able to exercise his free will. Yet the notion of the freedom of the will should here be understood as depending upon the ordering of the mind, rather than, as both Catholics and Protestants would maintain, upon the inclination of the will towards or away from God. As Lagrée has correctly observed, Lipsius's neo-Stoic Providence is cosmological rather than salvational, rational and abstract.[28] Reason is the only link between man and the Deity; nowhere does Lipsius speak of the love of God for man, while the love of man for God must in this scheme of things by necessity be a form of *amor Dei intellectualis*.[29]

Human liberty, then, is realised as freedom through obedience. The first step on the path towards liberty is achieved by the individual's taking command over himself, by taking control over the volitions of his mind. The *hegemonikon*, or the ruling part of the mind, either can be governed by passion, (παθος, *perturbatio*) which is caused by false value-judgements, which in turn can develop into veritable diseases of the soul when not corrected,[30] or can learn to acquire self-mastery by refusing to give assent to these judgements, and ordering itself according to right reason. This, then, is the essence of human liberty: man is free when the ruling part of his mind is untrammelled by passion. In a remarkable intrusion of the language of Roman law into the domain of moral psychology, this state of freedom is defined as the mind being *sui iuris*.[31] Conversely, when the individual has fallen prey to passion, he has fallen into a state of voluntary servitude: 'The principall and souveraigne part hath let fal the Scepter, and is become so vile and abject that it willinglie serveth his own servants.'[32] Liberty, likewise, is defined through metaphors of self-rule and political power:

> To obey [reason] is to bear rule, and to be subject thereunto is to have the souveraigntie in all human affaires. Whoso obeyeth her is lord of all lusts & rebellious affections: whoso hath this thred of Theseus may passe without straying through all the labyrinths of this life.[33]

27. Lipsius 1604a: I, xix, 543. 28. Lagrée 1994: 68–9. 29. Lagrée 1994: 78.
30. Lipsius 1604b: III, vii.
31. Lipsius 1604a: III, xix, 186. On the neo-Roman concept of liberty, see Skinner 1998.
32. Lipsius 1595: 4. 33. Lipsius 1595: 11–12.

The uncompromising nature of Lipsius's rejection of the passions is yet another trait which sets his philosophy apart from other contemporary forms of neo-Stoicism. Unlike most other neo-Stoic authors, who advocate the tempering rather than the eradication of the passions, Lipsius insists that *apatheia*, rather than *metriopatheia*, is the only desirable state of mind.[34] It is because of the stringency of Lipsius's logic that he is able to cut to the root of the problem faced by the individual whose strength of mind falters when confronted with the horrors of civil war. In what is undoubtedly the *De constantia*'s most forceful claim, a twofold attack on the two main arguments against imperturbability, love of country and fellow-feeling, Lipsius demonstrates that both are false values, arising from erroneous judgements, which need to be corrected before the individual can fulfil his or her proper role as a citizen. The argument for *apatheia* is systematised in the *Manuductio* which rehearses and answers the Platonic, Aristotelian and Academic objections on the naturalness of the passions, and their necessity in attaining virtue, and offers a condensed summary of the Stoic response.[35]

It is this stringency which allows Lipsius to examine and endorse the famous Stoic paradoxes, while qualifying or rejecting only those that are most clearly incompatible with Christianity. Here, however, it is important to bear in mind the distance separating the sage from the *proficiens*, the man striving, but not yet in possession of perfect wisdom. Constancy can perhaps be described as the virtue of the *proficiens*, while only the *sapiens* possesses complete imperturbability and impassability, never straying from his self and possessing true and lasting felicity and peace of mind. Here too we detect a movement akin to the one described earlier concerning the converging of ethics and theology. For while Lipsius gives a Christianising slant to some of the paradoxes, the account of the sage's impassivity and self-sufficiency patterns the condition of the sage on that of God. Thus, with regard to the third paradox (*Sapientem sibi parem, & in gaudio semper esse*), Lipsius adduces, next to a host of Stoic sources, the authority of St Ambrose, which effectively elides the difference between Stoic *gaudium* and Christian beatitude.[36] The sage is also said to be self-sufficient, and this notion is expressed in the vocabulary of existing within and for oneself (*secum morari, secum consistere*) a state which, as Lipsius agrees with Seneca, approximates the condition of the Deity.[37]

34. Lipsius 1604b: III, vii, 151–60. 35. Lipsius 1604b: III, vii, 151–60.
36. Lipsius 1604b: III, v, 148. Cf. III, vi, 151. 37. Lipsius 1604b: III, x, 166.

This parallelism should not of course be pursued too far. On the question whether the sage feels pity, Lipsius admits that the Stoic view has been challenged by the Church Fathers, even though he subtly leaves open the possibility that their opinion is perhaps less offensive than it has been made out to be.[38] The condemnation of the Stoic approval of suicide is unequivocal. The paradox which claims the sage to be equal to God equally stands in need of qualification.[39] The sage is said to carry God within him, rather than to be equal with him. Yet the distance which separate man's rational mind from divine *ratio* is, despite the lip service Lipsius occasionally pays to the need for divine assistance, one of degree and pre-eminence.

While Lipsius thus tones down certain aspects of the rationalism of the ancient Stoa, his systematising drive elsewhere reinforces it in unexpected ways. While man's rational mind is not without limits, for the workings of Providence will remain unfathomable to man, it does enable him to order his mind according to universal *ratio*, to live according to reason and virtue, and to approximate to an understanding of the Deity. It was, as I shall next attempt to show, exactly this notion of the autonomy of the rational mind, its ideal of human liberty and empowerment, and the correspondence between human and divine *ratio*, with which some of Lipsius's most perceptive readers took issue.

IV

To the extent that Lipsius was the propagator of Seneca and Tacitus, the two authors of the silver Latinate whose style and ideas would dominate the literary and intellectual culture of late Renaissance and Baroque Europe, his influence extended throughout Europe, from Poland to England and from the Dutch Republic to Catholic Spain. His *De constantia* sparked off a vogue for similar treatises counselling the individual in *publicis malis*, of which that of Du Vair is merely the best known, while the influence of the *Politica* has been claimed for authors as different as Grotius and Gabriel Naudé. Yet while neo-Stoicism can be viewed as a pan-European phenomenon, its distinct form and impact were determined by the particularities of the different political and literary cultures into which it was received. Gerhard Oestreich's influential thesis that neo-Stoicism furnished the ideological armour of the emergent absolutist states of early modern Europe therefore needs to be approached

38. Lipsius 1604b: III, xix, 192. 39. Lipsius 1604b: III, xiv, 177–80, 179.

with considerable caution.[40] Only in France and Spain can a close and lasting alliance between neo-Stoicism and the crown actually be demonstrated. In England, as John Salmon has convincingly argued, neo-Stoicism often bore the characteristics of a philosophy of opposition, taken up by those out of favour at court or opposed to royal policy.[41] Salmon demonstrated a particular interest in neo-Stoicism among the poets and literati associated with the circle of Sidney and the Earl of Essex, and in the Jacobean period, with those courtiers and scholars dismayed at the perceived favouritism and corruption of the court of James I. By looking at the occurrence of Lipsian ideas in the work of Philip Sidney and Fulke Greville, this chapter follows recent developments in Lipsius scholarship, exemplified by the classic study of Mark Morford, in focusing on the personal, literary and political ties between individuals in different and changing positions in relation to the centres of power, rather than a somewhat abstract notion of 'intellectuals in service of the state', on which Oestreich's analysis depended.[42]

By the end of the 1580s, the English soil was certainly well prepared for the reception of Lipsius's neo-Stoic project. Familiarity with Seneca and Stoic philosophy had grown through the vernacular translations of Seneca and Epictetus of the mid sixteenth century, and the work of Lipsius and his followers likewise rapidly found its way to a wider audience. In the domain of moral and political philosophy, neo-Stoicism often entered into an alliance with that other, newly fashionable literary form, the essay, as in the work of William Cornwallis, Anthony Stafford and Francis Bacon. The philosophy as well as the dramatic works of Seneca had an explosive impact on the English theatre, from the closet drama of Daniel and Greville to the plays of Kyd, Marston, Chapman and Jonson.

A strong counter-reaction to Lipsian neo-Stoicism can be found in the moral-psychological and religious literature of the period. Against Stoicism's unitary view of the mind, authors like Robert Burton and Thomas Wright maintained the conventional division of the soul into an irascible and concupiscible part, stressing that the passions were both natural and impossible to eradicate, and that they could, if used correctly, be conducive to virtue. As Monserrat has noted, it was this understanding of the soul as divided into parts and faculties that prevented the Stoic idea of passion as error from finding acceptance.[43] As Edward Reynolds put it poignantly, Stoicism 'goeth

40. See Oestreich 1982 and 1989. 41. Salmon 1991: 169–188.
42. Morford 1991. See also Enenkel and Heesakkers 1997; Laureys 1998; Tournoy *et al.* 1999.
43. Monserrat 1984: 84.

about to give unto Man an absolute government over himself, [it] leaveth scarce any thing in him which he may command and govern'.[44]

From this spectrum of attitudes towards neo-Stoicism and its particular conception of human liberty, the role of the Sidney–Greville circle needs to be singled out for particular attention. One reason is that, with Sidney and Greville, we can trace a direct and continuous exchange between English culture and continental neo-Stoicism. During his stay at Leiden with his uncle Leicester, Sidney met Lipsius, who dedicated a treatise on the pronunciation of Latin to him. Shortly before his death, Sidney attempted to persuade the scholar to accept a position in England, an occasion lost through Lipsius's apparent reluctance to move, and Sidney's untimely end.[45] Lipsius also befriended members of Sidney's circle, such as Edward Dyer and Daniel Rogers. The interest in Seneca and Tacitus which Lipsius's work had generated, and the connections between English literary culture and Continental humanism, thus stretched from the later decades of Elizabeth's reign into the Stuart era, when Fulke Greville appointed the young Dutch Tacitus scholar Isaac Dorislaus to his newly founded chair of history at Cambridge in 1623.[46]

A further and more important reason is that, in their attempts to make a neo-Stoic ethic applicable to a life in service of the public good, we discover the most searching analysis of the question of neo-Stoic moral autonomy. In his analysis of the *Old Arcadia*, Blair Worden has compellingly argued how 'lovers and subjects . . . are subjected to a dependency incompatible with true liberty, the liberty within'.[47] My emphasis differs from Worden's in foregrounding how, in the *Arcadia*, the idea of moral autonomy, what Worden termed 'Sidney's philosophy of self-reliance', is simultaneously invoked and questioned, before showing how Greville moves from this position to a more fundamental critique of the idea of the mind being, ever, *sui iuris*.

Many passages in Sidney's *The Defence of Poesie* appear optimistic about man's natural capacities and his in-born urge to follow nature, reason and virtue. He holds it for true that 'where reason hath so much over-mastered passion, as that the mind has a free desire to doo well, the inward light each minde hath in itself, is as good as a Philosophers booke, since in Nature we know it is well, to do well, and what is well, and what is evil (. . .)'.[48] While Sidney places the poet over the philosopher, he is careful not to sever, but rather

44. Monserrat 1984: 85.
45. On the personal contacts between Lipsius and Sidney, see van Dorsten 1986: 22–3; Worden 1996: 256–7.
46. On the uses of Tacitus in Stuart England, see Smuts 1994: 21–43 and Salmon 1991.
47. Worden 1996: 340. 48. Sidney 1962: 19.

strengthens, the link between poetry and philosophy. While the *Defence*'s most striking innovation, the lifting of 'fiction' to the status of higher, universal truth, exalts the standing of the poet, it concurrently depreciates the value of factual truth. While the poet's fiction contains universal truth, allied with the power to delight and to move, the mere factual truth of the poor historian seems to assume the function that Stoic philosophy awarded to opinion: 'But the Historie being captivated to the trueth of a foolish world, is many times a terror from well-doing and an encouragement to unbridled wickedness.'[49] Poetry, on the other hand, 'sets virtue out in her best cullors, making Fortune her well-wayting handmaid',[50] as the poet can 'frame his example to that which is most reasonable, be it in warlike, politike, or private matters'.[51]

It seems likely that the poetics outlined in the *Defence* caused Sidney to undertake the revision of the *Arcadia*. That the *New Arcadia* allowed for such a reading is shown by Greville's *Life of Sidney* which claims that Sidney intended to depict the 'exact picture in every posture in the mind of any man', teaching how to 'set a good countenance upon all the discountenances of adversity, and a stay upon the exorbitant smilings of chance'.[52]

Despite such Stoic echoes, the *New Arcadia* hardly provides a less troubled didactic exemplarity than the *Old Arcadia*. In the *Old Arcadia* perfect reason and virtue are embodied in King Euarchus whose authority restores Arcadia from chaos and civil war to order, order which is however effected by the just but merciless condemnation of the princes and princesses, whose deaths can only be forestalled by the miraculous return of Basilius. In the *New Arcadia*, too, the conflict between reason and passion is never resolved, as the stichomythia between Reason and Passion that forms the second Eclogues of book II suggests; a temporary armed truce that precludes true resolution is the most that can be attained in this life.[53]

Indeed, love, the driving force of plot and episodic narrative in both the *Old* and the *New Arcadia*, is never free of such conflicts either. Even the novel's heroes, whose devotion to their ladies is cast in the idiom of noble and ennobling Neoplatonic love, are liable to fall prey to love's more anarchic impulses of desire and violence which trouble the *Arcadia* as they do *Astrophil and Stella*.[54] Musidorus, overtaken by desire, nearly rapes his beloved Pamela, while Amphialus, who virtuously rejects his mother's advice to rape the captive Philoclea, is brought from love-possession to murderous demonic

49. Sidney 1962: 18. 50. Sidney 1962: 18. 51. Sidney 1962: 17. 52. Greville 1986b: 11.
53. Sidney 1963: 339–40; for this passage, see McCoy 1979: 47–51.
54. McCoy 1979: 69–109. Compare however Worden 1996: 297–319.

possession, slaughtering those who 'came to take away Philoclea'.[55] None of the protagonists of the Arcadia are, needless to say, *sui iuris*. Selfless service to the virtuous, inaccessible Lady is, more often than not, described in terms of servitude, courtly love as arbitrary tyranny. Yet this is a voluntary servitude, from which the heroes cannot and will not depart, and from which indeed, as Amphialus's agony illustrates, only death promises delivery.

The last chapters of book III of the *New Arcadia*, which have sometimes been interpreted as the trial by fire from which the protagonists emerge purified, with exemplary Stoic constancy, suggest that the moral autonomy which the heroines here claim in the face of Cecropia's tyrannical power is linked to a notion of selfhood that has its foundation in love, not reason. It cannot be denied that the princesses, Philoclea and Pamela, demonstrate admirable patience and constancy during their increasingly unbearable captivity. Whether the princes attain a similar moral fortitude, however, is very much to be doubted. When Pyrocles/Zelmane sees what he believes to be the head of the executed Philoclea, he falls into a stupor of sorrow. Philoclea, who is of course not dead, visits him, playing the Stoic to assuage his grief, reminding him that excessive sorrow is neither manly nor fitting because death is natural and those for whom we grieve do not suffer anymore. 'O woman's philosophy, childish follie', is the reply of Pyrocles, who, literally blinded by grief, only recognises his beloved when he has leapt up to hit her.[56] The mock-execution, the climax of the sisters' ordeal, opens up a dilemma of considerable moral and emotional complexity that forestalls any attempt to see their decision as unequivocally laudable. Both Pamela and Philoclea are confronted with the same choice: to marry Amphialus or to see the other die. Both, believing or surmising that the other would do as they would do, refuse to yield. Yet when Cecropia uses Pyrocles/Zelmane to attempt to persuade Philoclea to save her own life, the tortuous syntax of Philoclea's answer betrays something of her troubled state of mind:

> And why should I do all this? To live, O Pamela, sister Pamela, why should I live? Only for thy sake Pyrocles I would live: but to thee I know too well I shall not live; and if not to thee, hath thy love so base allay, my Pyrocles, as to wish me live? . . . No, my Pyrocles; and for that I doo thanke thee, and in my soule thanke thee; for I confesse the love of thee is herein my chiefest virtue. Trouble me not therefore, deare Pyrocles, nor double my death by tormenting my resolution: Since I cannot live with thee, I will dye for thee.[57]

55. Sidney 1963: 388. 56. Sidney 1963: 486–7. 57. Sidney 1963: 481.

Apart from the fact that Philoclea's readiness to die for love entails that she is also willing to sacrifice her sister's life, it will be clear that her constancy in love has fundamentally nothing to do with neo-Stoic constancy.[58]

In the *Arcadia* Sidney seems to wish for that leeway for love which a more analytic mind like Greville would be unwilling to grant. One can position Greville's work in that current of turn-of the-century literature that accomplishes what Christopher Tilmouth in his excellent *Passion's Triumph over Reason: A History of the Moral Imagination from Spenser to Rochester* has called the fracturing of familiar terms: the challenging of the moral orthodoxies of the period, including the imperative of reason's sovereignty over the passions, and the definition of virtue as constancy.[59] In his tragedy *Alaham* Greville performs a far more incisive anatomy of the idea of virtuous constancy than Sidney was willing or, perhaps, able to do, by examining the hidden motives of the apparently flawlessly virtuous Caelica. Her eagerness to embrace martyrdom is deconstructed by the chorus of evil spirits in truly Augustinian manner as stemming from love of reputation rather than true obedience.[60] As in the literature examined by Tilmouth, Greville's plays problematise ideas about rational governance by depicting human nature in Tacitean terms, as essentially passionate, driven by fear, desire and ambition, and by showing reason's myriad delusions and self-deceptions. This does not mean, however, that Greville sees no value at all in an ethic of moral self-reliance. In the *Life of the Renowned Sir Philip Sidney*, Sidney is emphatically described as 'standing alone', a position associated with freedom of thought and speech, and with laying claim to an inalienable individual liberty.[61]

To understand what value Greville finds in such an attitude of Stoic self-possession, we need to turn to the text in which he engages most extensively with the neo-Stoic idea of inner liberty: the *Letter to an Honourable Lady*. This treatise poses as a letter of consolation for a gentlewoman who is mistreated by a cruel and unfaithful husband, yet in this guise it offers a way for any subject – Greville explicitly draws the analogy between political and domestic subjection[62] – to maintain, even in the most dire condition of unfreedom, a stance of moral integrity and liberty.[63]

58. Sidney 1963: 481. 59. Tilmouth 2007: 114–56. 60. Greville 2008: 373, vss. 57–8.
61. Greville 1986: 39. 62. Greville 1986b: 154.
63. My analysis here differs from Worden's, who emphasises the difficulty for the women of the *Arcadia* to 'stand on their own virtue', a conclusion which is not borne out by the actions of the female protagonists, Pamela and Philoclea, who, on the whole, make their suitors look fickle and feeble in comparison. See Worden 1996: 344.

Greville identifies the first cause of the lady's predicament as the decline of the original equality between husband and wife, resulting in 'the affected absoluteness of a husbands power'.[64] The authority her husband possesses over her is not natural, but is given by custom, law and ultimately force. Yet he warns her not to be mistaken into believing that she can with any hope of success try to vindicate her right against him. The 'juries of common opinion', as he says, 'will always look upon law, rather than equity, custom, rather than nature, and strength, rather than right'.[65] Thinking that such subordination is unjust, and that her moral superiority over her husband in love, chastity and piety entitle her to equality, she will merely demonstrate a logical error in failing to distinguish different types of virtues, different types of rights.[66] Having no serious chance of legal redress, and even less chance of winning back her husband's affection, she should accept her fate and abstain from engaging in battles she cannot win. Rather, she should turn her powers inwards, and, like a tree in winter accepting the loss of leaves, draw her 'sap' down to her roots.[67]

Critics have often stressed the fact that Greville, even though he acknowledges the subordination of women to be institutional and not natural, nevertheless takes a 'conservative' position in insisting that obedience belongs to a wife's estate. But a hackneyed opposition between 'radical' principles and 'conservative' conclusions wholly misses the point of the analysis of the nature of authority and true liberty that Greville is trying to make. Authority, Greville emphasises, is nothing but *A commandinge power, which hath relation to the obedience of inferiors*.[68] Neither the origin of nor the difference between supreme and subaltern power, he adds grimly, make a difference here. The fundamental point is that those who resist authority in the name of liberty are more likely to lose a more fundamental form of freedom: 'Since in obedience we need overcome but one (our selfe I meane) where in these other contentions, we must serve many masters, worshippe equals, flatter inferiors, and trust in strangers'.[69]

This, however, is a radically different plea for the dissociation of political and inner liberty than we find in Lipsius. Seeing the arbitrary nature of political and domestic power, Greville challenges the notion that we can enter into this fundamentally contingent world without hazarding our freedom of mind. For Lipsius the twin passions of hope and fear are the main stumbling blocks of the mind which, once conquered, will allow the individual to face

64. Greville 1986b: 140.
65. Greville 1986b: 159.
66. Greville 1986b: 165.
67. Greville 1986b: 159.
68. Greville 1986b: 164.
69. Greville 1986b: 165.

all circumstances with equanimity. For Greville, who does not share Lipsius's optimism about the rational ordering of the world, such an idea is a mirage. Irrationality and force inhere in the nature of things, and fear and hope, 'two craftie spies of power', are the instruments of tyranny that bind the mind to the external world.[70]

The lady's real challenge, therefore, is not merely to take on an attitude of patient obedience, but to recognise that her misfortune, when seen for what it is, will open the path to liberty. In a loving marriage, her affections would have remained centred on her husband. Her actual situation, as Greville repeatedly reminds her, will allow her to 'draw her powers to herself', and she will thus 'be set at libertie to spread as farre as the limits of nature, or grace can possiblie be extended'.[71] Having attained freedom, she will be able to set her mind to 'new Ideas, larger ends, nobler ways'. Instead of one man, she has a whole world to win. Although this progress of the well-disposed mind may have a Stoic ring to it, it is ultimately antithetical to the alignment of the rational mind to universal *ratio* that Lipsius proposes. In rising to larger ends and nobler ways, she will come to understand that there is ultimately no real difference between trying to win one person and trying to win a world. Only a radical form of dissociation from the world will lead to true liberty, and will allow the mind to direct itself towards God, where it will find unity, infinity and eternity.[72]

V

Within the complex of languages for expressing selfhood and subjectivity available to the early modern period, neo-Stoicism offered the most consistent attempt to articulate a notion of individual liberty, and within the neo-Stoic movement Lipsius's effort to graft an ethic of inner liberty unto a neo-Stoic physics and natural theology was undoubtedly the most forceful attempt to defend it against the critique levelled at it by theologians and exponents of traditional faculty-psychology-based ethics. Far more than providing a philosophy of moral self-preservation, Lipsius strove to define a notion of inner liberty as that of the mind being *sui iuris*. This notion of inner liberty was defined through a dialectic of freedom and obedience, self-mastery and submission: freedom is achieved by subjecting the passions and ordering the mind according to universal reason, by taking command over one's own powers, and subjecting oneself to God, the only form of obedience

70. Greville 1986b: 158. 71. Greville 1986b: 173. 72. Greville 1986b: 176.

which entails true freedom. While the two aspects of this notion of inner liberty are, as I have attempted to show, impossible to separate from each other, it is the first, rather than the second, that has attracted attention from scholars.

The attraction of Lipsius's philosophy of liberty through dutiful obedience has been demonstrated for an entire generation of statesmen and literati, and it extended well into the seventeenth century. Yet the very first authors who engaged with Lipsius's legacy problematised, rather than endorsed, the notion of inner liberty it posited. They asserted the validity of its ethical imperative, while questioning the moral-psychological and theological assumptions on which it was based, leaving their protagonists in a virtual double bind, enjoined to pursue something they will never be able to achieve. *Psychomachia*, rather than constancy, is the near-permanent condition of Sidney's protagonists, as their tenuous hold on reason is exposed, time and again, by the inroads made by passion, as well as their own errors of judgement.

Other authors would continue this scrutiny of the neo-Stoic ideal of moral autonomy and the notion of reason on which it was based. Shakespeare's *Julius Caesar* problematises the notion of the autonomy and sufficiency of human reason, questioning the equation of virtue with reason, showing how even the most noble mind is not free from the errors of deception and self-deception.[73] *Hamlet* and *King Lear* challenge the idea of a correspondence between human reason and divine *ratio*, entertaining the possibility of a providence which is radically arbitrary, inscrutable and, possibly, malign.

Few works, however, reached as stark a conclusion as Greville's *Letter to an Honourable Lady*, which places its heroine, and by implication any person living in a condition of subjection, in a world in which the connection between human reason and divine *ratio* is severed, a world of false appearances and destructive passions, violent and radically contingent. The only form of human liberty lies in the severing of the mind from everything that binds it to the external world. Greville then proceeds to turn neo-Stoicism against itself, arguing that from this minimal position of liberty one will be able to see that all ideas of human autonomy are a mirage. Here, the return to the self only serves to enable its ultimate annihilation.

The problem of human reason, and thereby that of human moral autonomy, was one that would continue to occupy the authors and philosophers

73. See the analysis of the play in Tilmouth 2007: 115–30.

of the seventeenth century. As I have tried to argue, the idea of individual liberty as the autonomy of reason acted as a catalyst for intense speculation about the human condition. The lasting importance of Lipsius's notion of inner liberty, then, should perhaps be seen in this light, rather than in terms of influence.

4

Freedom of the will as a basis of equality: Descartes, Princess Elisabeth and Poullain de la Barre

MARTINA REUTER

On 6 October 1642 René Descartes wrote to his friend Alphonse Pollot, a gentleman-in-waiting to the Prince of Orange, that he would be more than happy to discuss philosophical matters with the Princess Elisabeth, since he set 'far more store by her judgment than by that of those learned doctors whose rule is to accept the truth of Aristotle's views rather than the evidence of reason'.[1] Descartes did sincerely believe that his philosophy was best accessible to women and other laypeople, who were not polluted by the prejudices of scholastic learning.[2]

By now several historians of philosophy have shown the impact that Descartes's philosophy had on seventeenth-century discussions about the equality and freedom of women.[3] Commentators agree that Descartes's distinction between the mind and the body strengthened and gave a new metaphysical foundation to the old theological claim that 'the mind has no sex'. But much less attention has been paid to *how* Descartes's conception of the mind contributes to equality and freedom. In what sense are all Cartesian minds free and equal? I shall argue that, in order to grasp the full egalitarian potential of Descartes's philosophy, we must focus on his conception of the will and its radical freedom. His philosophy cannot be properly understood without taking into account the profound distinction he makes between two different kinds of thought: the actions and the passions of the mind. It is generally agreed that Descartes belongs to the voluntarist tradition,[4] but there has not been much scholarly discussion of how his voluntarism is connected with his claim that all humans have an equal capacity to use their reason.

1. Descartes 1991: 215. 2. Descartes 1985: 151.
3. See Harth 1992; O'Neill 1999; Perry 1999; Wartenberg 1999; Broad 2002; Stuurman 2004.
4. See for example James 1997: 196–200; Schneewind 1998: 184–93; Alanen 2003: 208–57.

I first look at how Descartes articulates his conception of the will in an epistemological context, examining what Descartes actually means when he claims at the beginning of *Discourse on the Method* that reason is 'naturally equal in all men'. Next I focus on the correspondence between Descartes and the Princess Elisabeth, in which they discuss the role of the will in the realm of practical life. Finally I examine some aspects of François Poullain de la Barre's Cartesian feminism. I argue that, contrary to what recent commentators have assumed,[5] Poullain did not adopt Descartes's conception of the free will, even though in many other respects he made a detailed and ingenious interpretation of Descartes's philosophical thought and developed this interpretation into explicit arguments on behalf of equality between the sexes.

I

At the beginning of his *Discourse on the Method*, Descartes claims that 'the power of judging well and of distinguishing the true from the false – which is what we properly call "good sense" or "reason" – is naturally equal in all men'. He continues by emphasising that 'it is not enough to have a good mind; the main thing is to apply it well'.[6] Descartes distinguishes between capacities of the mind such as a quick wit, a sharp and distinct imagination and a prompt memory, which all show great individual variation, and reason, which 'exists whole and complete in each of us'.[7] He acknowledges that people have different (inborn) intellectual capacities, but these differences do not affect their ability to use their reason. It is especially important to note that by 'reason' Descartes here means 'the power of judging well'.[8]

A judgement, according to Descartes, combines a perception and an act of the will. In the *Principles of Philosophy* he defines judging explicitly in relation to our two general modes of thought: perception, or operations of the intellect, and operations of the will. Perception includes several apparently different modes of thought, such as sensory experience, imagination and pure understanding, whereas willing consists of modes such as assertion, denial and doubt.[9] After separating perception and willing, Descartes describes how judging involves both intellect and will. He writes:

5. Welch 2002: 130; Stuurman 2004: 213. 6. Descartes 1985: 111. 7. Descartes 1985: 112.
8. Descartes 1985: 111.
9. Descartes 1985: 204. See also the *Meditations*, Descartes 1984: 19, and *Passions of the Soul*, Descartes 1985: 335–6.

> In order to make a judgment, the intellect is of course required since, in the case of something which we do not in any way perceive, there is no judgment we can make. But the will is also required so that, once something is perceived in some manner, our assent may then be given.

Descartes's prime interest is to show how error is possible despite the perfect and infinite nature of God. Humans are able to err because the 'scope of the will is wider than the intellect'. Descartes emphasises that the perceptions of the intellect always remain limited and tied to the objects presented to it. The will, on the other hand, can 'in a certain sense be called infinite'.[10] This infinity means that humans are able to assent in cases that transcend what our finite intellect can perceive. This ability makes error possible. Descartes emphasises that falling into error is 'a defect in the way we act, not a defect in our nature'.[11] Our ability to act voluntarily allows us to err, but is simultaneously the 'supreme perfection of man', which makes us responsible for our judgements and allows us *not* to err, as far as we assent only to what we perceive clearly and distinctly.[12] By giving us a free will God has made our nature as perfect as possible. The use of this perfected capacity is our own responsibility, the ultimate ground on which we can be praised or blamed.

Descartes studied at the Jesuit College of La Flèche from 1607 to 1615. It comes as no surprise that his conception of the will is in many respects influenced by the Jesuit discussions examined by Annabel Brett (Chapter 1 above). There has been some scholarly discussion on whether Descartes thinks that the free will allows humans to judge against what they clearly and distinctly perceive to be true or good.[13] Does the infinity of the will mean that the will can act against our better knowledge? There is one indication that Descartes held this radical view. In a letter from 1645, probably addressed to the Jesuit Denis Mesland, he writes that 'it is always open to us to hold back from pursuing a clearly known good or from admitting a clearly perceived truth, provided we consider it a good thing to demonstrate the freedom of the will by so doing'. This passage is not very conclusive. Descartes continues by arguing that freedom consists in a facility of determining ourselves and that it is easier to determine oneself if one has good reasons to do so. Therefore 'we can always act more freely in those cases in which we see much more good than evil than in those cases which are called . . . indifferent'.[14]

If we compare Descartes's remarks with Suárez's position presented by Brett, we can see that Suárez's distinction between the voluntary and the

10. Descartes 1985: 204. 11. Descartes 1985: 205. 12. Descartes 1985: 205, 207.
13. See Marshall 1998: 38 n. 4, 148 n.1. 14. Descartes 1991: 245.

free, though not explicitly adopted by Descartes, clarifies what Descartes is trying to express. Descartes's understanding of a free act in the latter quotation resembles Suárez's definition of a voluntary act, which becomes more voluntary when it proceeds from a more perfect cognition. When Descartes emphasises our ability to hold back from pursuing a clearly known good, on the other hand, he is referring to the freedom of the will in Suárez's sense of a free act, which requires indifference and by which an individual is always free to do or not to do, even when the conditions for an act are settled.[15] Descartes claims explicitly that we are freer when we act according to what Suárez calls a voluntary act than when we act according to Suárez's free act, requiring indifference. It can perhaps be claimed that Descartes's conception of the freedom of the will is in this respect less novel and less radical than Suárez's conception. Descartes acknowledged the possibility of acting against better knowledge and attributed this possibility to the infinity of the will, but he did not consider this capacity to reveal the true meaning of freedom. It is our acting according to reason which separates freedom from mere arbitrary chance. Like the neo-Stoic Justus Lipsius before him, Descartes saw no difficulty in combining his idea of the free will with divine providence,[16] which again suggests that he held a rather traditional view of freedom as acting according to the good.

Descartes's discussion of judgement in the *Principles* illuminates what he meant when he claims in the *Discourse* that reason, or the power of judging well, is equal in all humans. Ultimately it is the perfected, infinite and indivisible will, the capacity to assert or deny, which secures that all humans share an equal capacity to distinguish the true from the false and avoid error. This equality allows for the fact that people's intellectual capacities as well as their education and practice in thinking may be unequally distributed. The intellect, with its inborn and acquired capacities, is in any case finite, 'extremely limited',[17] compared to our infinite will. Intellectual capacities affect how *much* finite knowledge we may have about different things, but not how certain our knowledge is. Certainty consists in asserting only what we clearly and distinctly perceive and ultimately depends on the supreme perfection of our nature, that is, our will, not on our finite intellect.

15. See Chapter 1 of this volume, pp. 11–16.
16. See for example *Principles*, part 1, § 41, Descartes 1985: 206, and letter to Elisabeth, 6 October 1645, in Shapiro 1997: pp. 120–2. For Lipsius's position, see Chapter 3 in this volume and Schneewind 1998: 172–5.
17. Descartes 1985: 204.

Descartes nowhere explicitly claims that women and men have an equal capacity to reason, but it is evident that women are included among 'all men', when he discusses the equal distribution of reason at the beginning of the *Discourse*. He emphasises that equally shared reason distinguishes men from animals and not including women would thus have meant regarding them as soulless animals. Descartes's correspondence with Princess Elisabeth, lasting from 1643 until his death in Stockholm in 1650, gives plenty of evidence for his high regard at least for this woman's power of judgement. The case of Elisabeth shows that Descartes regarded women not only as equal to men, but also as capable of exceptional intellectual capacities.

Descartes praises Elisabeth's capacities in a dedicatory letter that prefaces *Principles of Philosophy*. Dedicatory acts of this sort usually implied a plea for patronage. Elisabeth was a poor refugee, but she was respected for her learning, and was known as someone occasionally engaged in university politics.[18] We cannot exclude the possibility that Descartes had some ulterior motive when he decided to dedicate the *Principles* to Elisabeth, especially since he intended this work to be used as a university textbook.[19] But when we read the preface in the context of Descartes's and Elisabeth's private correspondence, we are easily convinced that his praise cannot be explained solely in such terms.

The dedicatory letter is interesting for several reasons. Descartes's praise of Elisabeth's intellectual abilities is directly related to the distinction between the perceptions of the intellect and the dispositions of the will. He writes that there are 'two prerequisites for . . . wisdom . . . namely the perception of the intellect and the disposition of the will' and continues by emphasising that 'whereas what depends on the will is within the capacity of everyone, there are some people who possess far sharper intellectual vision than others'. Elisabeth belongs among those few who combine a firm will with an unusually sharp intelligence, capable of mastering metaphysics as well as geometry. The dedicatory letter is also interesting because Descartes shows his awareness of how circumstances restrict women's possibilities of developing their intellects. He praises Elisabeth for the fact that 'neither the diversions of the Court nor the customary education that so often condemns young ladies to ignorance' has prevented her from developing her capacities.[20]

18. See Shapiro 2007: 12–13.
19. See letter to Mersenne, 31 December 1640, Descartes 1991: 167.
20. Descartes 1985: 191–2.

II

According to Descartes, the freedom of the will makes humans responsible for their epistemological judgements as well as their moral acts. The question of morality enters Descartes's correspondence with Elisabeth when they decide to read Seneca's *De vita beata*.[21] Rather than discussing it in detail, they use the book as a platform to develop their own positions. What follows is Descartes's most elaborate attempt to spell out his moral thought. He distinguishes himself from Seneca's Stoic ethics on two major points: when he claims that the passions are not bad in themselves, and that morality is not entirely based on reason. Descartes writes:

> For the rest, all sorts of desires are not incompatible with true happiness; only those that are accompanied by impatience and sadness are. It is also not necessary that our reason never be mistaken. It suffices that our conscience testifies that we have never lacked resolution and virtue to execute all the things that we have judged to be the best. Thus, virtue alone is sufficient to render us content in this life.

Here it remains an open question, though, exactly what role Descartes attributes to reason. There is a tension between the above bracketing of its importance and his claim a few lines later, where he writes that 'on the other hand, the right use of reason, giving us a true knowledge of the good, prevents virtue from being false'.[22] As we saw in the previous section, Descartes held the view that acting in accordance with reason is necessary in order for the will to be free rather than just arbitrary. Thus, on the one hand, Descartes claims that virtue ultimately depends on resolution, that is the firmness of one's will, and on the other he claims that the right use of reason is necessary in order for the will to be either virtuous or free. Elisabeth is not convinced by Descartes's description of virtue and especially questions his claim that virtue defined in this way would be sufficient for contentment. She writes:

> I do not yet know how to rid myself of the doubt that one can arrive at the true happiness of which you speak without the assistance of that which does not depend absolutely on the will. For there are diseases that destroy altogether the power of reasoning and by consequence that of enjoying a satisfaction of reason.[23]

21. For further discussions of the correspondence and its philosophical content, see Shapiro 1999a; 2007: 1–51; Wartenberg 1999; Reuter 1999; 2000: 33–9; Broad 2002: 15–34; Alanen 2004.
22. Shapiro 2007: 99.
23. Shapiro 2007: 100.

Descartes tries to tackle the problems raised by Elisabeth's objections in several letters written during the autumn of 1645. He admits that there are bodily conditions that may take away the power of reasoning and even that 'often a bodily indisposition prevents the will from being free'. He emphasises that 'what I have said generally of all men should be extended only to those who have free use of their reason . . . we are able to be absolutely responsible for ourselves only so long as we are in our power'. The prospect of not being in one's power is more dreadful than death. Descartes writes that '[n]o fear is more upsetting to [the soul] than that of being joined to a body that entirely takes away its freedom'.[24] We should note that this revised view presents a slightly less equal view on the power of reason than in the *Discourse*, where Descartes does not acknowledge the possibility of bodily limitations. On the contrary, when he discusses the specifically human capacity to express one's thoughts in speech, he claims that 'there are no men so dull-witted or stupid – and this includes even madmen – that they are incapable of arranging various words together'.[25]

It seems evident that Elisabeth made Descartes more aware of the fact that bodily circumstances may affect how good a use we can make of our mental capacities, even the capacities regarded as equal in all humans. Elisabeth was hesitant concerning her mind's possibility to tranquilise bodily disturbances according to the Stoic-like therapy Descartes recommended to her, and refers to the fact that she has 'a body imbued with a large part of the weaknesses of my sex'.[26] Descartes does not comment on Elisabeth's sex in the correspondence, but his mechanistic physiology and anatomy denies that there can be any specifically female weaknesses. In the posthumously published *Description of the Human Body*, he argues that even conception does not require any significant sexual difference. Descartes claims that there does not have to be any difference between the seed provided by the male and the female, since 'just as we can observe how old dough can make new dough swell . . . so we can easily agree that the seeds of the two sexes, when mixed together, serve as yeast to one another'.[27] Even if bodily circumstances do affect the use of the will, Descartes's explanatory framework would not allow that these affections vary according to sex. But his concession that there are some bodily disturbances that do affect the will opens a more fundamental problem of how it is possible that the body sometimes takes away the freedom of the will, even though it normally does not affect it. How severe must

24. Shapiro 2007: 107. 25. Descartes 1985: 140. 26. Shapiro 2007: 88.
27. Descartes 1998: 187; for a discussion of the egalitarian potential of Descartes's physiology and anatomy, see Reuter 1999 and 2002.

bodily disturbances be in order to limit the freedom of the will? Descartes does not seem to be fully aware of this problem.

Descartes was unable to give a satisfactory explanation of the extent to which bodily conditions do affect the use of mental capacities, but he was more successful in developing his view on how virtue depends respectively on the will and reason. In a letter to Elisabeth dated 6 October 1645 he defines sovereign good as consisting in the exercise of virtue, which is the same thing as 'the possession of all the goods whose acquisition depends on our free will'. Descartes specifies that in order to act virtuously one must act resolutely and judge as well as possible under the reigning circumstances. He writes:

> [O]ne has no reason to repent when one has done what one judges to be the best at the time that one had to be resolved to act, even if afterward, in rethinking the matter with more leisure, one judges that one was wrong. But one would sooner repent if one had done something against one's conscience, even if one discovered afterward that one did better than one would have thought. For we are responsible only for our thoughts, and human nature is such that we do not know everything or always judge so well off the cuff as when we have a lot of time to deliberate.[28]

As we saw above, Descartes emphasised the finitude of human knowledge. In an epistemological context this means that we must assent only to the limited range of things we are able to perceive clearly and distinctly. But in the practical context of moral decision making we cannot withdraw from action whenever we lack certainty. To tackle this problem, Descartes distinguished between metaphysical and moral certainty. Metaphysical certainty can be reached only in an epistemological context, when we have the luxury of assenting only to clear and distinct perceptions, whereas moral certainty is 'certainty which is sufficient to regulate our behaviour, or which measures up to the certainty we have on matters relating to the conduct of life which we never normally doubt, though we know that it is possible, absolutely speaking, that they may be false'.[29]

It is moral certainty that must guide practical action. We must judge as well as possible, but since knowledge is finite and practical circumstances limit the time we have to deliberate, we have to accept the fact that we are prone to commit mistakes. Descartes's emphasis on the fact that we often err when circumstances force us to act is a direct answer to a previous letter from

28. Shapiro 2007: 116. 29. Descartes 1985: 289.

Elisabeth, where she argues that in order to be able to make choices, which we do not have to repent afterwards, we must know all the options perfectly and in order to do this 'one would need to possess an infinite science'.[30] Descartes replies that we certainly do not have infinite knowledge, but we do not need it in order not to regret our actions, because repentance should truly depend only on our conscience, that is, on the conviction that we have done our best. Doing our best relies on our will in two ways: first, the will is responsible for making a judgement on how to act, and second, the will answers for the resoluteness of our action. We are never able to have completely certain knowledge of practical matters and we cannot predict the outcome of our actions. Therefore virtue must ultimately depend on our will, which we control and for which we are thus responsible. On the other hand, Descartes does not claim that *only* resoluteness matters. Virtue requires that we must use both our intellect and our will in order to judge as well as possible.[31]

Descartes rejects the idea that virtue is based on the perfection of moral knowledge, but he does not give up the ideal of perfection. His position can be understood only if we realise that he is attributing perfection primarily to the actions of the will, not to the perceptions of the intellect. The will is, as we saw above, the 'supreme perfection of man'.[32] In a letter to Queen Christina, Descartes goes as far as to claim that the 'free will is in itself the noblest thing we can have, since it makes us in a way equal to God'.[33] It is the infinity of the will which makes it Godlike; by being infinite the will cannot be more perfect than it is, and it is thereby the only human capacity which equals God's perfection. Virtue is all about carrying the responsibility that this infinite capacity gives us.

III

In his correspondence with Elisabeth, Descartes repeatedly claims that virtue is sufficient to make humans content, but he does not spell out how this is supposed to happen until the third part of the *Passions of the Soul*. His theory is based on a distinction between six primitive passions. Wonder (*l'admiration*) is the first and has a specific cognitive importance 'since it makes us disposed

30. Shapiro 2007: 110.
31. For a discussion of the relation between resolution and judgement in Descartes's moral thought, see Marshall 1998: 72–82. Marshall also gives a detailed account of Descartes's view on the nature of the true values that should guide our moral judgements (117–47).
32. Descartes 1985: 205. 33. Descartes 1991: 326.

to acquire scientific knowledge'.[34] Wonder is dispassionate in the sense that, contrary to other passions, it does not contain an evaluation of whether a thing is useful or harmful; when we wonder, we do not evaluate a thing in relation to its utility. Still, this does not mean that wonder is completely value-neutral. It does contain an element of admiration. We are especially inclined to wonder at infinite things.

In the third part of his treatise, Descartes examines the specific passion of generosity.[35] Generosity is raised by the wonder we experience when we are confronted with the infinite freedom of our will. It shares the dispassionate nature of wonder and consists in a legitimate and dispassionate self-esteem, a true self-knowledge. He describes generosity in the following words:

> Thus, I believe that true generosity, which causes a person's self-esteem to be as great as it may legitimately be, has only two components. The first consists in his knowing that nothing truly belongs to him but this freedom to dispose his volitions, and that he ought to be praised or blamed for no other reason than his using this freedom well or badly. The second consists in his feeling within himself a firm and constant resolution to use it well – that is, never to lack the will to undertake and carry out whatever he judges to be best. To do that is to pursue virtue in a perfect manner.[36]

Here it is evident that Descartes does not give up the idea of achieving perfect virtue, even though he is explicit about the impossibility of achieving perfect knowledge.

Descartes continues by arguing that virtuous actions of the mind make us content because they are simultaneously pleasurable passions. He claims that, when we will, we simultaneously perceive that we are willing.[37] Actions of the soul produce passions, which he calls internal emotions, because they are produced by the soul itself.[38] When he discusses how generosity may be acquired, he claims that virtuous thoughts 'may be produced by the soul alone; but it often happens that some movement of the spirits strengthen them, and in this case they are both actions of virtue and at the same time passions of the soul'. These virtuous passions of the soul are pleasurable. They produce a legitimate self-esteem, which makes us feel content and strengthens our habit of having virtuous thoughts. Descartes draws the conclusion

34. Descartes 1985: 355.
35. On Cartesian generosity, see also Marshall 1998: 150–66; Shapiro 1999b; Alanen 2003: 251–4.
36. Descartes 1985: 384. 37. Descartes 1985: 335.
38. Descartes 1985: 381. For a discussion of internal emotions, see James 1997: 196–200.

that 'if we occupy ourselves frequently in considering the nature of free will and the many advantages which proceed from a firm resolution to make good use of it . . . we may arouse the passion of generosity in ourselves and then acquire the virtue'. The passion of generosity strengthens our disposition to act virtuously. In the same way as wonder is the first of the passions, generosity is 'a key to all the other virtues', which provides a contentment that helps to calm our minds and thus to judge as well as possible under reigning circumstances.[39] In his correspondence with Elisabeth, Descartes seems to claim that calming the mind also affects bodily disturbances.[40]

When Descartes claims that virtue is both necessary and sufficient for contentment he is following a Stoic line of thought, but departing from a Stoic understanding of the nature of virtue.[41] It is evident from their correspondence that Elisabeth was unwilling to accept Descartes's view of virtue as ultimately based on the freedom of the will. Her reluctance may partly have been related to her Calvinist upbringing. Discussing the differences between Elisabeth's and Descartes's views, Lisa Shapiro suggests that Elisabeth comes close to a classical Stoic position, according to which virtue consists in 'a fully developed or *perfected* capacity of reason, that is, complete knowledge' whereas Descartes holds a neo-Stoic position, according to which 'virtue consists in our *perfecting* our reason'.[42] Thus for Elisabeth, virtue and the contentment it gives is either completely achieved or lacking, whereas for Descartes virtue and contentment are achievable in degrees. Shapiro's interpretation illuminates the fact that virtue does not, according to Descartes, require perfect knowledge, but overlooks the role of the will as the ultimate foundation of virtue and the contentment achieved through it.[43] The main difference between Elisabeth's and Descartes's positions is rather that Descartes shifts focus from the perfection of knowledge and reason to the perfect nature of the will.

Descartes's analysis of generosity constitutes his ultimate attempt to answer Elisabeth's worry that repentance destroys the possibility of contentment. The self-knowledge and legitimate self-esteem, which is essential to generosity, prevents us from feeling ungrounded repentance. When

39. Descartes 1985: 387–8. 40. See Shapiro 2007: 87–8 and 92.
41. For a description of the Stoic view about the necessary and sufficient relation between virtue and contentment, see Long 2003: 391.
42. Shapiro 2007: 47. See also Freya Sierhuis's discussion of the difference between the sage or *sapiens* and the *proficiens* in Chapter 3.
43. It is odd that Shapiro overlooks Descartes's view on the perfect nature of the will in her discussion of the correspondence, since she has previously given an excellent account of it (Shapiro 1999b: 252–9).

Descartes describes how humans may become virtuous by acquiring generosity, he is describing a gradual process achieved step by step.[44] But he seems to conceive the contentment achieved through generosity as complete, rather than graded, in the sense that when we feel truly content, nothing can be added or taken away. This completeness must be understood in relation to the indivisible nature of the will. The freedom of the will is, according to Descartes, absolute and not achieved in degrees, even though we may gradually learn how to strengthen our resolution. We feel contentment when we cognitively as well as emotionally realise the true nature of our free will. Since the object of this feeling, the will, is complete, the feeling becomes complete. Either we understand the true nature of our will and feel content, or we do not.

Freya Sierhuis shows in Chapter 3 how the neo-Stoic Lipsius identifies the essential self with reason. Descartes, as we have seen, identifies the essential self with the will. Since contentment is ultimately tied to a perfection of what is most truly oneself, Stoic contentment depends on the perfection of reason, whereas Descartes claims that the perfection of our free will makes us feel content.[45] Descartes position differs from the position of Lipsius and classical Stoicism also by its attempt to regulate rather than overcome the passions. Descartes takes up the neo-Stoic ideal of constancy, discussed by Sierhuis, but he reformulates it as a constancy of the will that does not stand in necessary conflict with the passions. The passion of generosity does on the contrary play a crucial role in strengthening our resolution and thus achieving virtue. Here we may note that Descartes's emphasis on the will, in its departure from Stoicism, shows quite a lot of affinity with Michel de Montaigne's view on self-possession, examined by Felicity Green (Chapter 2 above).

Stoicism, in its classical as well as early modern forms, embodies explicitly egalitarian intentions, expressed especially by the attempt to make virtue independent of wealth, power and other material circumstances. Descartes's egalitarianism does not break with the Stoic tradition, but rather radicalises it. He seems to have an explicitly egalitarian motive to make virtue and contentment ultimately dependent on the will, which is, as he writes in the *Principles*, 'within the capacity of everyone'.[46] As we have seen, Descartes held that people have different intellectual capacities and that these are always limited by the general circumstance of human finitude. He seems to think that the perceptions of the intellect and the knowledge

44. Descartes 1985: 387–8.
45. For Descartes's relation to Stoicism, see also Marshall 1998: 97.
46. Descartes 1985: 191.

based on these perceptions are less equally distributed and more strongly tied to circumstances than acts of the will. Since the freedom of the will is equally at everyone's disposal, perfect Cartesian virtue is more equally distributed than a virtue which depends on moral luck or is based on perfect knowledge.[47]

Descartes genuinely attempts to make the perfection of virtue and the contentment earned by virtue equally available to all, men and women, low and high born. His attempt was not successful in all its details. As we saw above, he admits that there are cases when the soul is 'joined to a body that entirely takes away its freedom'.[48] This means that the will is not completely independent of material circumstances. Descartes was not able to spell out what consequences the fact that the body in some cases affects the will has for his general view of the will as completely free and thus perfect. We must also note that Cartesian equality based on the freedom of the will is an individual, moral and by its very nature apolitical kind of equality. Descartes's focus on the will limits his perspective to the decision to act, whereas a political perspective has to take the actual act and its consequences into consideration. As Lisa Shapiro has pointed out, some of Elisabeth's hesitancy can be related to the fact that her perspective was that of a potential ruler.[49] From her point of view, Descartes's disregard of consequences may have seemed politically naïve.[50] Perceived from a political viewpoint, equality necessarily includes the question of equal circumstances. When I now turn to Poullain de la Barre's discussions of the equality between the sexes, it will be a political turn exactly in the sense that Poullain focuses more on the relation between capacities and circumstances than Descartes himself did.

IV

In *On the Equality of the Two Sexes* (1673) Poullain writes:

> Since there seems not to be any greater difference between the minds of the two sexes, we can say that the difference does not lie there. It is rather the constitution of the body, but particularly education, religious observance, and the effects of our environment which are the natural and perceptible causes of all the many differences between people.[51]

47. For a discussion of Aristotelian moral luck in the context of Descartes's and Elisabeth's correspondence, see Shapiro 2007: 45; see also Marshall 1998: 66, 112 and 157–8.
48. Shapiro 2007: 107. 49. Shapiro 2007: 49. 50. See especially Shapiro 2007: 110.
51. Poullain 2002: 82.

Poullain was acutely aware that differences in circumstances have consequences for the course of people's lives. His main focus was on women, but he compared the situation of women to that of other underprivileged groups such as peasants.[52] Between the years 1673 and 1675, when he had recently quitted his theological studies at the Sorbonne, Poullain published three treatises on the woman question: *On the Equality of the Two Sexes*, *On the Education of Ladies* (1674) and the rhetorical *On the Excellence of Men* (1675). Especially the first two treatises adopt and develop Descartes's philosophy in great detail: Poullain follows the method of doubt and extends its application from a purely epistemological context to social and cultural prejudices;[53] he uses the notion of clear and distinct ideas to define true knowledge[54] and emphasises the unity of the sciences;[55] he grounds virtue firmly in self-knowledge[56] and emphasises that, since bodies are mechanical entities, there are no significant qualitative differences between male and female bodies;[57] and finally, he draws the feminist consequences of Cartesian dualism and the independence it secures the mind.[58]

On the Education of Ladies includes a reading-list, which tells us that Poullain was acquainted with all available works by Descartes. He also recommends the works of influential Cartesians, such as Louis de La Forge and Jacques Rohault, and works by critical members of the Cartesian tradition, such as Antoine Arnauld and Pierre Nicole, whose *Logic of Port Royal* is mentioned.[59] The student who wants to develop her or his reason in an appropriate manner should, according to Poullain, start by adopting the right method of thinking, which meant studying the elements of geometry and the French language. Poullain perceives morality as the final and most important science and concludes his reading-list by recommending 'the first volume of [Descartes's] letters to the Queen of Sweden and to the Princess of Bohemia . . . . You will realize from these letters that he didn't consider women incapable of the highest sciences.'[60] Poullain refers to the first volume of Claude Clerselier's three-volume edition of Descartes's letters, which was generally considered to be Descartes's major work on moral philosophy.

52. See Poullain 2002: 60. 53. Poullain 2002: 49–50 and 175–7.
54. Poullain 2002: 49–50, 85–6, 91, 242 and 286. 55. Poullain 2002: 85, 96 and 208.
56. Poullain 2002: 79, 83, 92, 157, 210–25 and 230.
57. Poullain 2002: 53, 83 and 105; cf. Descartes 1998 187. For a discussion of how Descartes's anatomical and physiological writings influenced Poullain's conception of equality, see Stuurman 2004: 100–9.
58. Poullain 2002: 82.
59. Poullain 2002: 237–8. For a discussion of Rohault's and La Forge's Cartesianism and its influence on Poullain, see Stuurman 2004: 43–4, 70, 90–1, 146, 197 and 298.
60. Poullain 2002: 237–8, cf. 240.

This edition does not include Elisabeth's letters to Descartes, which were not published before 1879.

I will now focus on Poullain's conception of mental capacities and discuss the main similarities and differences between his and Descartes's views. In *On the Equality of the Two Sexes*, Poullain writes that 'it is only the use of the mind which should be considered when we discuss the differences between individuals.'[61] These words closely resemble Descartes's opening of *Discourse on the Method*.[62] Poullain's position also resembles Descartes's when he emphasises the role of judgement. He writes that the 'greatest advantage that we can expect of learning is to be able to discern and to judge between what is true and evident and what is false and obscure'.[63]

Poullain's most detailed discussion of the mind and its capacities is found in *On the Education of Ladies*. This book consists of five discussions between two young ladies, a young man and a tutor. In the fourth conversation, the tutor Stasimachus lists five operations of the mind: sensation, imagining, remembering, judgement and reasoning. The description of judgement resembles Descartes's definition of judgement as composed of a perception and an act of the will. Poullain writes:

> Judgment, which is the second operation of the mind presupposing the first, is an action by means of which we attribute to a thing what we recognize as relevant to it, or we separate from it what we recognize as not relevant to it.[64]

'Second' means second in relation to sensation, imagining and remembering, which are simple non-composed operations. Despite clear resemblances there are profound differences between Descartes's and Poullain's descriptions of our basic mental operations. The most apparent is the lack of the will in Poullain's list. Further, Descartes wants to bring all modes of thinking or operations of the mind under two general headings, perception and volition,[65] whereas Poullain's list lacks this kind of classification. Poullain does not make an explicit distinction between the actions and passions of the mind. Finally, Poullain separates judgement and reasoning whereas Descartes generally treats them as synonyms. According to Poullain, we reason when 'we form a third judgment on the other two'.[66] He seems to mean that reasoning is a judgment concerning the truth or falsity of a sensation, imagining or remembering. Poullain's account lacks Descartes's explicit analysis of judgement as composed of a perception and a volition,

61. Poullain 2002: 72. 62. Descartes 1985: 111. 63. Poullain 2002: 64.
64. Poullain 2002: 216. 65. Descartes 1985: 204. 66. Poullain 2002: 216.

but he seems to follow Descartes's basic intuition about its composed nature. Poullain's claim that judgement is an action, by which we attribute or separate, implies an element of volition, even though it is not spelled out in terms of an act of the will. Correspondingly the claim that judgement is 'second' and presupposes a first operation implies that it acts upon a sensation, imagining or memory, which plays the same role as perceptions in Descartes's definition.

The absence of the will as an aspect of judgement is explicit in another passage, where Poullain denies the role of the will in reasoning. He writes that 'it is not our will but our reason that attaches our intelligence to a viewpoint, the intelligence should always be ready to detach itself when reason dictates it'.[67] This is a truly anti-Cartesian formulation, where Poullain seems to have completely missed Descartes's point that the assent or dissent necessary for judgement is, by its very nature, an act of the will.

The role of the will is mentioned, but remains unexplored when Poullain describes the specific nature of the mind. The will is included in *On the Excellence of Men*, where Poullain characterises the mind as 'the principle of knowing and willing'.[68] The situation is different in *On the Education of Ladies*, where the mind is defined as three capacities: the capacity of thought, which is identified with 'getting understanding by various means'; the capacity of 'defining itself according to its understanding'; and the capacity of 'provoking the body to react in different ways'.[69] Here volitions are not included among the capacities of the mind, even though they seem to be presupposed by the mind's capacity to provoke bodily action. Poullain's focus is throughout on the union of mind and body and the nature of the mind is discussed from this perspective. In *On the Equality of the Two Sexes*, he emphasises that feelings, passions, and the will – which is here explicitly mentioned – maintain the union between the mind and the body.[70] In *On the Education of Ladies*, he claims first that 'all the actions of the mind . . . depend on the participation of the body' and some pages later less rigorously that 'one almost never acts without the other'.[71] The first claim explicitly contradicts Descartes's distinction between the actions and the passions of the mind, according to which passions depend on the body whereas volitions do not.[72] It is interesting to note that Poullain's conception of the interdependence between mind and body resembles Elisabeth's position (even though he did not have access to her letters).

67. Poullain 2002: 190. 68. Poullain 2002: 309. 69. Poullain 2002: 215.
70. Poullain 2002: 82. 71. Poullain 2002: 213, 223. 72. Descartes 1985: 335.

Most often Poullain seems to conceive the role of the will as motivational. He emphasises, for example, the importance of having 'a firm, constant will to understand things'.[73] Poullain's conception of the will does not have – or only dimly has – the cognitive role of assenting versus dissenting that is so essential to Descartes's conception of the infinite will as the basis for human perfection. Nor does he adopt Descartes's claim that the will is equally distributed, whereas intellectual capacities may differ. Like Descartes and the Stoic tradition, Poullain emphasises that only what belongs to the mind is entirely up to us,[74] but he does not adopt Descartes's voluntarist claim that it is ultimately the will that is most our own.

Like Descartes, Poullain claims that humans are created equal in perfection. But whereas Descartes identifies equal perfection with the will, Poullain writes 'a man is perfect if he possesses all the attributes he needs, according to divine law, for producing and receiving the effects for which he is destined'.[75] This perfection includes body as well as mind and to be imperfect means that one has more or fewer parts than one needs, or some indisposition that keeps one from one's goal. Descartes's example of a soul 'joined to a body that entirely takes away its freedom'[76] would fit Poullain's description of imperfection. We are created, according to Poullain, with two dominant desires, corresponding to the principal needs of mind and body. We desire what is necessary for the preservation of our body and we desire 'knowledge that can contribute to the perfecting of the mind'.[77] Since Poullain does not acknowledge the role of the will in judgment, his conception of perfect knowledge is different from Descartes's. According to Descartes, we have as perfect knowledge as possible when we assent only to what is clearly and distinctly perceived. The will is ultimately responsible. Poullain claims that we know things perfectly when 'we know them with all the certainty that we have been able to acquire'.[78] Acquiring perfect knowledge is the sole responsibility of reason: a few lines later comes the above quoted passage where Poullain denies that will plays any role in attaching our intelligence to a viewpoint.

Despite Poullain's emphasis on reason rather than the will, there are many similarities between his and Descartes's conceptions of virtue. According to Poullain, virtue 'consists for the most part in the firm and steadfast resolve to do what one thinks best, depending on the different situations.'[79] Like Descartes, he emphasises that the success of our virtuous attempts do not

73. Poullain 2002: 173, cf. 84. 74. Poullain 2002: 223, 230. 75. Poullain 2002: 102.
76. Shapiro 2007: 107. 77. Poullain 2002: 197, translation modified.
78. Poullain 2002: 190. 79. Poullain 2002: 108.

depend completely on us. Therefore we must focus on what is in our power: 'one should be self-sufficient and act with absolute assurance when one has taken necessary measures, insofar as occasion, experience, and capacity allow'.[80] Poullain is also aware 'that our mind is limited by the brevity of life, which does not give us time to examine the infinite number of things, manners, circumstances, and incidents that exist in nature and in society'.[81] His conclusion, that we must act as wisely and firmly as possible under given circumstances, comes very close to Descartes's view.

Self-knowledge is the cornerstone of Poullain's conception of virtue. He argues explicitly against the claim, presented by La Rochefoucauld in his *Maxims*, that man is necessarily hidden from himself.[82] From Poullain's focus on the mind – body union it follows that self-knowledge is to a great extent concerned with knowledge of how the body affects the mind.[83] Like Descartes in his analysis of generosity, Poullain emphasises that the contentment provided by virtue depends on self-knowledge. In order to find happiness in the practice of virtue we have to pay attention to what we are doing. Poullain writes that the satisfaction produced by virtue 'comes from the fact that virtue is not a simple speculation about the good we are obliged to seek but an effective desire that springs from our conviction. We cannot practise virtue with willing hearts (*avec plaisir*) without feeling some emotion.'[84] There is no mention of the will here, but 'effective desire' fits into the motivational role that Poullain assigns to the will. Again like Descartes, Poullain seems to think that our determined desire to act virtuously gives rise to joyful emotion, but since he lacks Descartes's detailed analysis of the relations between the actions and passions of the mind, he does not have much to say about *how* this happens. The connection between self-knowledge and contentment is also more diffuse in Poullain's account than in Descartes's, where self-knowledge culminates in the insight that true perfection consists in the infinite will and this insight gives rise to the feeling of generosity.

Like the Stoics, Montaigne and Descartes, Poullain emphasises that it is not pleasure, honours or riches, but 'inner freedom which is the main component of our felicity'.[85] Poullain is sometimes more Stoic than Descartes in his formulations, as when he writes that a 'slave of Algiers, while overtly doing the bidding of a master, can still keep his internal freedom intact'.[86]

80. Poullain 2002: 191. 81. Poullain 2002: 234.
82. Poullain 2002: 211; for a discussion of Poullain's critique of La Rochefoucault, see Welch 2002: 133.
83. See e.g. Poullain 2002: 78–80, 209 and 213–15; see also Stuurman 2004: 112.
84. Poullain 2002: 92; 1984: 73. 85. Poullain 2002: 230. 86. Poullain 2002: 182.

Contrary to Descartes, Poullain claims that our inner freedom consists in our reason, not our will. In *On the Education of Ladies*, Stasimachus explains that, when he speaks about freedom, he does not mean the 'rash permissiveness' of the libertines, but 'enlightened freedom based on love of truth'.[87] Far more than Descartes, Poullain showed a political awareness of how unequal circumstances condition people's lives. In *On the Equality of the Sexes* he argues that circumstances should be changed and all professions opened to women.[88] But when Poullain discusses education he focuses on how learning strengthens the inner freedom of reason. When Stasimachus, Sophia, Eulalia and Timander part company at the end of their last conversation, they decide to meet soon again 'to celebrate together the freedom of the mind'.[89] At this point Poullain is not a more political thinker than Descartes.

We may now conclude. Descartes's conception of the absolute freedom of the will pointed at an important sense in which all humans can be conceived as equals. His view was in some respects overtly optimistic and his account of the extent to which the body did affect the will remained unsatisfactory. Elisabeth's and Poullain's emphasis on the interdependence between the mind and the body was in many respects more realistic than Descartes's focus on the will. But I want to claim that Elisabeth's and Poullain's inability or unwillingness to grasp Descartes's account of the will in its full scope meant that they remained unable to understand a significant aspect of what it means to say that all humans are free.

87. Poullain 2002: 147. 88. E.g. Poullain 2002: 96–9. 89. Poullain 2002: 251.

5

Language as a means and an obstacle to freedom: the case of Moses Mendelssohn

AVI LIFSCHITZ

I

Could human beings have made the perplexing transition from nature to culture on their own, without direct divine intervention? If so, how could they have possibly transformed a bestial existence into a fully fledged civilisation on a markedly different level from the rest of the animal kingdom? Though this question has attracted much reflection ever since antiquity, the Enlightenment is usually portrayed as the heyday of anthropological inquiries into origins, producing a plethora of natural histories of mankind and the earth, speculations over the emergence of political institutions, and different accounts of the progress of language.[1] In all these domains, a crucial transition was depicted from a rudimentary condition termed 'nature' to a man-made sphere of artifice, deliberately crafted by human beings. The challenge was to clarify how such a qualitative change in all aspects of human existence could have occurred throughout history without any supernatural intervention.

This theoretical difficulty was particularly highlighted in accounts of the emergence of language, seen in the naturalistic account of human evolution as a prerequisite for conventional agreements and political life. Language was usually treated as one of the most evident indicators of the deep chasm between the bestial and the human, or between the natural and the civilised. This view was shared, for example, by Descartes and Hobbes, despite their

Different parts of this chapter were read at the European University Institute in Florence in 2008 and at Haifa University in 2010. I am grateful to the conveners of these events – Quentin Skinner, Martin van Gelderen, Fania Oz-Salzberger and Thomas Maissen – and to the participants for invaluable suggestions. Important comments have also been provided by Gideon Freudenthal, Andrea Schatz and Alexander Schmidt.

1. See, among others, Duchet 1971; Rossi 1984; Zedelmaier 2003; Pross 1987; 2006.

manifest disagreement on most other aspects of the human mind.[2] The transition from nature to civilisation entailed a complete overhaul of the mechanisms of communication: from natural cries and gestures, or the sounds commonly referred to as animal language, to the deliberate employment of arbitrary signs denoting abstract entities. This artificial idiom was regarded as uniquely human in the sense that it facilitated a whole range of pursuits beyond mere subsistence, especially thinking in general terms, representing the self to others and negotiating the creation of collective human associations. The necessity of artificial signs for all these activities may account for the serious engagement of eighteenth-century authors with the origin of language and its cognitive and social functions. Their fascination with language did not stem only from the need to account for the origins of an indispensable tool of communication; the emergence of speech also mirrored the evolution of political institutions, economic structures and the arts, particularly in its emphasis on the difficult transition from the natural to the artificial.

Recent attempts to shed more light on the significant links between language, epistemology and politics in Hobbes's and Locke's works have resulted in fresh interpretations of their thought.[3] Here I would like to explore a similar rapport between language, nature and freedom in the philosophy of one of the pivotal authors of the German and Jewish Enlightenments, Moses Mendelssohn, by examining two of his works: the response to Rousseau appended to his early translation of the *Discours sur l'origine et les fondemens de l'inégalité parmi les hommes* (*Discourse on the Origin and Foundations of Inequality among Men*, 1755), published in 1756, and *Jerusalem, oder Über religiöse Macht und Judentum* (*Jerusalem, or On Religious Power and Judaism*) of 1783. As in the case of other early modern authors, research on Mendelssohn has tended to treat his works on language separately from his political philosophy.[4] Moreover, *Jerusalem* has been largely analysed against the background of earlier interpretations of divine revelation and Mosaic

2. 'Discours de la méthode' (1637), ch. 5, in Descartes 1953: 164–7; Hobbes 1996: ch. 3, 23. On the eighteenth-century scene more generally see Aarsleff 1982; Lifschitz 2012a; 2012b.
3. Dawson 2007; Pettit 2008.
4. On Mendelssoh's political thought see Rotenstreich 1966; Guttmann 1981; Albrecht 1982; Altmann 1982a, 1982b; Arkush 1994: ch. 4, 6–7; Harvey 1998; Goetschel 2007. For language in Mendelssohn's hermeneutics see Sorkin 1996. Thorough discussions of Mendelssohn's philosophy of language, if not clearly linking it to his political theory, are Engel 1994; Ricken 2000; Schatz 2009; Pollok 2010: 355–89, as well as Engel's introductions to volumes v.1 and vi.2 of the *Jubiläumsaugsgabe* of Mendelssohn's works (Mendelssohn 1929–). Insightful suggestions about script, ceremonies and observance in *Jerusalem* have been offered in Eisen 1990; Funkenstein 1993: 222–9, Hilfrich 2000; Goetschel 2004: 160–6; Sorkin 2008: 202–6, albeit with scant reference to the larger context of Enlightenment theories of language.

legislation by Jewish rationalists such as Maimonides and Spinoza. This chapter, by contrast, emphasises Mendelssohn's sustained engagement with contemporary works on the emergence of human society and speech.

Read with alertness to Enlightenment discussions of language and freedom, Mendelsson's early and late views of language may open up new perspectives on his thought. Such a reading could explain, for example, Mendelssohn's uncompromising critique of religious oaths, creeds and formulae of confessional union. While grounded in a theory of a transition from incomplete to complete rights and duties, Mendelssohn's stance was also linked to a shift of focus in his theory of language. From a largely naturalistic account of the evolution of language in 1756, Mendelssohn turned towards a two-pronged theory strictly distinguishing between, on the one hand, speech and gesticular action – seen in 1783 as natural and almost innate – and, on the other, written characters, famously identified in *Jerusalem* as generating idolatry. This account of language had direct implications not only in the religious sphere but in the political one as well. Language became, for Mendelssohn, the principal device enabling the emergence of civil liberty, while at the same time jeopardising individual freedom of conscience. Mendelssohn's views of the social and cognitive functions of language may also account for his nuanced portrayal of the transition from natural freedom (in the state of nature) to political freedom (in civil society). On this point, Mendelssohn remained consistently opposed to the views of some of his contemporaries such as Jean-Jacques Rousseau.

II

In order to have a clearer overview of Mendelssohn's early views about the emergence of language and political society, I shall briefly outline the main points to which he responded in 1756. Methodology was one of the most significant points in the *Discours sur l'inégalité*, as Rousseau emphasised in its exordium. The aim was not to trace an actual process but to delineate a hypothetical one, 'better suited to elucidate the Nature of things than to show their genuine origin, and comparable to those [conditional reasonings] our Physicists daily make regarding the formation of the World'.[5] As Rousseau noted in the same paragraph, established religion might sanction a particular version of the origins of inequality, grounded in God's will, just as it would adhere to the biblical account of the creation of the universe. However,

5. Rousseau 1997b: 132.

Rousseau granted himself the same licence to pursue the evolution of human beings as that assumed by physicists making hypotheses about the creation of the universe. Maintaining a healthy distance from the biblical account, natural philosophers claimed to speculate only on the basis of 'the nature of man and of the Beings that surround him, about what Mankind might have become if it had remained abandoned to itself' (132). This phrase is one of the keys to Rousseau's conjectural account of human evolution, as well as to similar Enlightenment narratives. Though providence may have had a hand in the contingent, actual history of the world, 'mankind abandoned to itself' signalled the potential (or essential) course of things without the optional intervention of God, this or that political agent, and the odd natural disaster.[6] It was a conjectural account, albeit one tracing the unfolding of essence and nature as opposed to history seen as the record of contingency.

This may help us to understand Rousseau's main argument against his predecessors who had speculated on a state of nature. In his eyes, they had not gone far enough in their quest for the natural, still ascribing to humans in the state of nature many of their socially developed characteristics. Rousseau followed seventeenth-century authors such as Hobbes in describing civil society as an unnatural (though perhaps inevitable) human condition: an arrangement constructed artificially by human beings interacting with one another. Despite his diatribe against the earlier uses of the term 'natural law', Rousseau too tried to derive the fundamental principles of conduct from the essential and natural human constitution, famously arriving at the conclusion that only 'two principles prior to reason' speak to human beings 'immediately with the voice of nature': self-preservation and pity, the latter defined as 'a natural repugnance to see any sentient Being, and especially any being like ourselves, perish or suffer' (127). To these two principles Rousseau later added perfectibility, a faculty enabling the improvement of one's condition with the help of circumstances (141). What perplexed most of Rousseau's eighteenth-century readers was the instinctive or bestial character of his man of nature, mute in the absence of language and devoid of reflection and self-consciousness. This condition was crowned by natural man's self-sufficient isolation and lack of any dependence on others, which accounted for both his natural freedom and his silence. The point was clearly and consistently

6. It recurred, for example, in the 1771 prize question on the origin of language at the Berlin Academy (a contest won by Herder): 'En supposant *les hommes abandonés à leurs facultés naturelles*, sont-ils en état d'inventer le langage? Et par quels moyens parviendront-ils d'eux-mêmes à cette invention?' (Harnack 1900: II, 307; emphasis mine).

argued by Rousseau, to the exclusion of familial life and domestic interaction in the state of nature.

The *Discours sur l'inégalité* highlighted some of the most acute issues preoccupying the authors of contemporary conjectural histories. On the one hand, Rousseau claimed that the succession of events would have always occurred in the same manner, give or take a few insignificant modifications. On the other, it was not entirely clear why the qualitative transition from nature to artifice must have taken place, and whether its projection over a vast expanse of time could explain such an extreme shift from 'repose and freedom' to civil society, whose interpersonal relations and their consequences 'have no true foundation in Nature' (186–7). It was Rousseau himself who cast serious doubt on this transition, when exploring in depth the origin of language in the first part of the *Discours*.

Examining the naturalistic account offered by Condillac, Rousseau identified three challenges. First, the 'immense distance' between the 'pure state of nature' and a condition in which humans were in need of language (146), a problem which he set aside in order to consider what he saw as two greater difficulties: consent and abstraction. The substitution of arbitrary sounds for natural cries and gestures could have hardly occurred accidentally or as an unforeseen response to needs, as described by earlier authors from Lucretius to Condillac.[7] The conventional character of human language would have required common consent, an all but impossible act in the absence of speech, especially as 'this unanimous agreement must have been motivated' (147). Finally, Rousseau wondered how human beings with no reflective reason could have invented conventional signs for abstract, non-physical notions. This could only be the result of thinking in general terms – for which, however, artificial signs would have already been required (148–9). Critically, Rousseau concluded his examination of the origin of language by admitting he was 'frightened by the increasing difficulties and convinced of the almost demonstrated impossibility that Languages could have arisen and been established by purely human means' (149). This acknowledgement seems to undermine his entire edifice. If the transition from a linguistic state of nature to a socially based language had been impossible, or if convention in words could not have emerged among motivated agents, how would the same transition have occurred in the political sphere? If language had not been established 'by purely human means', the same conclusion might apply to the emergence of conventionally constructed political institutions.

7. Cf. Lucretius 1975: bock v, lines 1028–90, pp. 458–63; Condillac 2001: part 2, ch. 1, 113–19.

III

Gotthold Ephraim Lessing and Moses Mendelssohn pondered these questions seriously when discussing Rousseau's *Discours sur l'inégalité* in Berlin immediately after its publication. Lessing encouraged his close friend to translate the work into German and comment on it, a task which Mendelssohn promptly accomplished. This first translation of Rousseau's *Discours sur l'inégalité* into German was published in Berlin in January 1756, concluding with Mendelssohn's comments in a *Letter to Lessing* (*Sendschreiben an den Herrn Magister Lessing in Leipzig*) in which Mendelssohn summarised the issues that the two had discussed over the previous summer.[8] This was the occasion for Mendelssohn's first sustained engagement with language and its origins, an enduring interest that would culminate in his *Jerusalem* of 1783. Rousseau's problematisation of the naturalistic account of the evolution of language received the closest analysis in these comments; as Mendelssohn wrote, he and Lessing 'discussed this difficult matter very frequently'.[9]

Mendelssohn employed several ideas from the arsenal of contemporary sensualist philosophy in the defence of the natural evolution of language, for 'it is not necessary to insult God with an invention that is so detrimental according to Rousseau' (108). His main strategy was to link the emergence of artificial signs to the human capacity for associative thinking. Just as Mendelssohn was vividly reminded of Lessing each time he searched in vain for his friend in the garden where they used to meet, human beings had the natural faculty to connect ideas that had been perceived together due to proximity in space, time or causal relations. This association of ideas could have been mastered by natural man ('a savage', as Mendelssohn called him throughout his comments) and its limited traces could be found even in animals. In this way, man in the state of nature could have encountered a sheep surrounded by flowers in a meadow. The sound of bleating could initially be used to refer only to its source, the sheep, but in some people's minds it might also summon the entire original setting. Gradually, they would leave out the middle link in this associative chain to refer by the sheep's bleating directly to the flowers. As bleating had a merely arbitrary relation to flowers, depending on circumstances rather than inherent in nature, Mendelssohn claimed that this process demonstrated how natural

8. See Rousseau 1756; the Letter to Lessing is reproduced in Mendelssohn 1929–, II: 81–109. On the early collaboration between the young authors see Altmann 1973: 36–50, Goldenbaum 2000; Bourel 2004: 109–19.
9. Mendelssohn 1929–: II, 104.

sounds could be transformed into arbitrary ones by exclusively human means (105–8).

This account was meant to elucidate the emergence of symbols with no natural link to the objects they signified, but Mendelssohn seems to have largely ignored the deeper problems that haunted Rousseau. He did not refer to the mutual assurance required for any consensual agreement, so that it was not clear how conventional signification could have emerged if human beings initially referred by bleating to the different objects and emotions they associated individually with sheep. (To the extent that the sheep's bleating could be associated with flowers, it might as well have denoted the meadow, rain or a momentary feeling of frustration.) Moreover, Mendelssohn did not thoroughly consider Rousseau's question about the necessity and purpose of language for human beings who had never hitherto spoken. Rousseau's discussion of the length of time required to generate the smallest modification seemed to Mendelssohn 'insignificant' (109). Towards the end of the *Sendschreiben* Mendelssohn insisted that a large temporal sweep and human inventiveness could explain the natural transformation of a mere plaything (*Spielwerk*) into a fully fledged language.

In this vindication of the natural evolution of language one can detect motives and strategies similar to those employed by Mendelssohn in his comments on Rousseau's notions of freedom and the state of nature. In both areas Mendelssohn refused to acknowledge the acuteness of what Rousseau had underlined as a challenging conundrum, the incommensurability of the natural and the artificial. Rousseau's readers had to recognise how the mind and the passions 'change in Nature' between these two human conditions,[10] and his examination of language highlighted the problematic assumption that one could explain by slow evolution the shift from the pre-civil to the political or from the self-sufficiently silent to the socially communicative. Mendelssohn, by contrast, assumed that the capacity for associative thinking and artificial naming had always existed in human beings. According to his account, this dormant capacity only had to be activated by certain circumstances and given sufficient scope to develop. Unlike Rousseau's two incompatible human natures, the difference between the state of nature and civilised existence was not categorical in Mendelssohn's eyes.

On this point, Mendelssohn referred to Rousseau's own argument that man in the state of nature walked upright, despite the evidence from infants and feral children.[11] Mendelssohn disputed what he saw as Rousseau's

10. Rousseau 1997b: 186. 11. Rousseau 1997b: 134, 190–2.

equation between the original and the natural: man in his supposedly original condition would have been similar to infants crawling on all fours with their accordingly limited rights and duties. But this posture (and its parallel social obligations) was in no way natural to human beings only because it could be found at their point of origin. The natural features distinguishing mankind from the animal kingdom should be abstracted from grown up, physically and mentally sound human beings (91–2).

When confronting Rousseau's account of the rudimentary mental and ethical capacities of human beings in the state of nature, Mendelssohn also rejected the use of this condition as a heuristic space opposed to civil society. Trying to vindicate some of Rousseau's abused predecessors, Mendelssohn pointed out that the term 'law of nature' had borne different meanings throughout history. Earlier writers on natural law had correctly examined mankind as it was, equipped with all its powers in the 'state of perfection to which he [man] had elevated himself after a long effort' (92). Any alternative view would reduce human beings to the level of cattle, establishing a law of nature suitable only for beasts. Rousseau's precursors merely extricated man from society, which for Mendelssohn meant not the postulation of a completely pre-civil condition but the abstraction of humanity from any contingent duties to which it might have subjected itself at particular times and places. The aim was to reach what was 'just (*rechtmäßig*) in and for itself': natural law, according to Mendelssohn in 1756, was nothing other than 'the laws of justice that flow from our essential organisation (*Beschaffenheit*), and which cannot be modified even if all nations on earth united themselves against it' (92).[12]

This view of natural law as an eternally valid set of basic rules for conduct, reflecting what is eternally good or just, was common to various early modern authors. But Mendelssohn was especially indebted to Gottfried Wilhelm Leibniz's critique of Samuel Pufendorf's voluntarism.[13] In the first part of his comments on the *Discours sur l'inégalité*, Mendelssohn recast Rousseau's vocabulary in a Leibnizian mould, suggesting that Rousseau had neither adequately understood nor properly defined his terms. Pity and perfectibility, basic properties of man in the state of nature according to Rousseau, were two such terms; freedom, another.

12. On the interrelations of reason and freedom in earlier accounts of natural law, see Hannah Dawson's chapter in these volumes.
13. 'Opinion on the Principles of Pufendorf' (1706) in Leibniz 1988: 64–75. This critique was translated and discussed by Jean Barbeyrac in his translation of Pufendorf's *De officio hominis*; see Mendelssohn's claim in 1759 that the view that there was no law of conduct without a lawgiver had been 'long ago refuted' (Mendelssohn 1929–: v.1, 113).

Pity, Mendelssohn explained, was not a fundamental human emotion but rather one derived from love, and love itself was grounded in a striving for perfection, order and beauty. Pleasure guided human will, but it could be found only in perfect images of the good and the beautiful. Where human beings saw perfection they naturally wished it to increase, which accounted for the pleasure they took in their beloved's self-improvement. When they perceived a lack of perfection in others, they experienced displeasure which they called pity. In this manner, Mendelssohn argued, even if one robbed natural man of everything we consider human, he would still be inspired by pity derived from love. This alone would prompt him to strive for his own perfection, inextricably linked to his peers' well-being and self-realisation. Therefore, the 'smallest seed of humanity, the pitiful emotion which Rousseau must have allowed to the savage, put us on track to restore him to all his rights and let him extract himself from the bestial state' (88). Perfectibility too was interpreted by Mendelssohn as evidence that Rousseau could not avoid some of the tenets of Leibnizian philosophy. Mendelssohn regarded perfectibility as the striving to perfect oneself, which could not be realised merely through material improvement. 'If nature endowed us with the capacity to make ourselves more perfect, it must have equally concealed in our essence [an ability] to raise all our faculties up to the most complete harmony' (89).[14]

Seen from this perspective, it is perhaps unsurprising that Mendelssohn employed an argument reminiscent of Leibniz's *Theodicée* (1710) as his overarching explanation of the indisputable ills of modern society, evoked so vividly by Rousseau. Mendelssohn did not completely deny Rousseau's assertion that social evolution and the expansion of mutual dependence had some detrimental consequences. However, he interpreted it as an unavoidable aspect of divine creation, the realisation of a possible world. Evil existed in human society just as it existed metaphysically in the universe, due to God's choice to turn some imperfect potentialities – whose nature did not depend on his will – into actual existence. This decision, on the whole, must be seen in a positive light. Since God opted for creation, he certainly chose the best option among the potentialities, and evil in this world must be outweighed by the good. What applied to God, Mendelssohn claimed, was true in human beings as well. The unfolding of our potential capacities in society was an extension of our being or essence (*Daseyn*), which elevated us on to a higher

14. Lessing tried to correct his friend's interpretation of Rousseau's perfectibility in a letter of 21 January 1756 (Mendelssohn 1929–: XI, 33–5).

level of actuality. The fuller a being's reality, the higher the degree of evil it had to endure as part of its capacity to achieve a greater good. The evils of political society were therefore inherent in human beings' natural inclination to live with one another and perfect themselves. Within the larger framework good triumphs over evil, or else human beings would never have been created (87–8).[15]

Mendelssohn was also at cross purposes with Rousseau about human freedom, troubled by the latter's depiction of modern societies as all too many variations on the theme of enslavement and political bondage. Quite the opposite, Mendelssohn argued: it was the alleged freedom of the state of nature that qualified, if adequately understood, as slavery. The blind pursuit of instincts in a bestial manner was merely the 'impertinence of unbound lawlessness', which even Rousseau would consider, according to Mendelssohn, as contrary to human freedom. Real freedom was 'a condition in which we are not inhibited by any external compulsion in the satisfaction of our real needs in an innocent way' (100). To modern ears this may echo a classic liberal or 'negative' notion of liberty, but Mendelssohn's emphasis here was on the 'satisfaction of real needs' which practically entailed the fulfilment of duties in the individual and the social realms. Mendelssohn acknowledged only two alternative applications of the notion of freedom. Individually it could express itself as 'the capacity of a mind to act according to deliberate motives', yet this could not apply to a creature with no insight, general ideas and self-consciousness. The second potential reference of the term was communal, the republican freedom identified with ancient Rome, and which he saw as 'an external political condition after which all wise men strive, and without which the life of the most patient man would hardly be tolerable' (99).[16] This too, Mendelssohn noted, could hardly be related to Rousseau's pre-social state of nature, where no sustained interpersonal relations existed.

As in his account of the emergence of conventional signs, we see Mendelssohn resorting here to innate human capacities in response to Rousseau's problematisation of naturalistic accounts of the transition from the natural to the artificial. However, if on the linguistic front Mendelssohn tried to portray a diachronic picture of the evolution of abstract ideas and their signification, in the ethical realm he postulated what he saw as basic human traits and capacities existing universally and eternally. The state of nature was a particular instance where these capacities were dormant, in a

15. Cf. Leibniz 1712: 131–5, 524–6.
16. On contemporary meanings of republican freedom see Skinner 1998 and Van Gelderen and Skinner 2002.

similar manner to individual infancy. Mendelssohn's comments may therefore constitute a rejection not only of a particular account of the state of nature but of an entire genre tracing social evolution from barbarism to civilisation. In Mendelssohn's eyes, the basic human traits had always been the same; what made us peculiarly human could not be abstracted in thought experiments. As Rousseau had criticised Pufendorf for assuming one could sell one's freedom – an essential human quality – as if it were a commodity,[17] Mendelssohn pointed out that the same objection applied to the alienation of reflective reason in Rousseau's own account of the state of nature (98). This point would be enhanced in Mendelssohn's *Jerusalem*, his philosophical elaboration of the relationship between state and religion. An examination of this work would provide further insights into Mendelssohn's aversion to the explanation of civic freedom or human language by reference to a single foundational agreement.

IV

One of the central points in Mendelssohn's *Jerusalem* was his insistence on the futility of religious oaths. This may be comprehensible given that such oaths were often prerequisites for assuming public office (as in the case of university chairs). However, Mendelssohn went further, insisting that doctrinal oaths were inadmissible not only in civil institutions but also within religious associations themselves. This claim was part of his decisive attack on the self-arrogation of earthly rewards and punishments by established religions; in 1782 he had already argued that ancient Judaism could not have included the right of ban or exclusion.[18] The publication of *Jerusalem* in 1783 was prompted by August Friedrich Cranz's pamphlet of the previous year claiming that, by denying his own religion the right to banish heretics, Mendelssohn had departed from one of its time-honoured principles.[19] In

17. Rousseau 1997b: 179.
18. In a preface to the German translation of Menasseh Ben Israel's seventeenth-century plea for the re-admission of the Jews to England, *Vindiciae Judaeorum* (London, 1656): *Manasseh Ben Israel Rettung der Juden aus dem Englischen übersetzt nebst einer Vorrede von Moses Mendelssohn* (Berlin and Stettin 1782), in Mendelssohn 1929–: VIII, 3–25. This was a contribution to the debate following the publication of Christian Wilhelm Dohm's *Über die bürgerliche Verbesserung der Juden* (Berlin, 1781). More on the Jewish controversies surrounding the writing of *Jerusalem* can be found in Feiner 2003: chs. 4–7.
19. August Freidrich Cranz, *Das Forschen nach Licht und Recht in einem Schreiben an Herrn Moses Mendelssohn auf Veranlassung seiner merkwürdigen Vorrede zu Manasseh Ben Israel* (Berlin, 1782) in Mendelssohn 1929–, VIII: 75–92. See Mendelssohn 1983 for a thoroughly annotated English edition of *Jerusalem*.

refuting this view, Mendelssohn adopted a twofold strategy. On the broader philosophical arena he wished to demonstrate that no social contract could have endowed religious institutions with the right to property and the exercise of coercive measures upon their own members. This argument was linked to Mendelssohn's view that rights over persons and goods did not depend on beliefs and opinions, only on public conduct. On a more specific level, Mendelssohn argued that penalties or rewards were never linked in ancient Judaism to belief and doctrine.[20] On both platforms, the function and evolution of language played a pivotal role.

In the first part of *Jerusalem* Mendelssohn introduced into his discussion of the state of nature and civil society a distinction that had not formed part of his response to Rousseau in 1756: the difference between complete (*vollkommen*) and incomplete (*unvollkommen*) rights and duties.[21] In the state of nature, according to Mendelssohn, all duties and rights were merely incomplete or imperfect: no one had enforceable or complete rights to others' benevolence or any similar duty to help them. In this condition one had only rights and duties of omission, such as not injuring one's peers and preventing others from injuring oneself. Natural freedom or independence amounted to the absence of any positive obligation to anyone and an incomplete duty (or right) of persons to settle cases of collision between their own and others' claims to benevolence and resources.

Although it may sound somewhat similar to Rousseau's account of freedom in the state of nature, this was no freedom of indifference. Within Mendelssohn's framework, where every right corresponded to a duty, the right to settle parallel claims was essentially a duty of conscience, *Gewissenspflicht*.[22] This point signals a major difference between Mendelssohn and Rousseau: for Mendelssohn, as we have seen, the laws of nature were eternally valid and the state of nature encompassed various moral duties and rights, however incomplete in character. Indeed, this was Mendelssohn's main criticism of Hobbes in *Jerusalem*: if human beings had not been bound in the state of nature by any inherent sense of duty, they would never have been able to form agreements and contracts for which an understanding of

20. On the Erastian background of Mendelssohn's defence of Judaism, see Eric Nelson's contribution, vol. I, Chapter 6.
21. This distinction had already appeared in a shorter essay of 1781, 'Von vollkommenen und unvollkommenen Rechten und Pflichten' (Mendelssohn 1929–: III.1, 280–2). Mendelssohn's most immediate source was probably a translation of Adam Ferguson's *Institutes of Moral Philosophy* (1769) by Christian Garve (1772); see the footnote in Mendelssohn 1929–: VIII, 123–4 and Altmann 1982a: 180. But see also this distinction in Pufendorf 1703: I.7.7, 63.
22. Mendelssohn 1929–: VIII, 120–1.

mutual obligation was required (106–7). For Mendelssohn, natural freedom meant incomplete social duties, not the instinctive pursuit of self-interest.

Mendelssohn employed here the terms 'state of nature' and 'social contract' in a similar manner to his use of 'natural law' in his comments on Rousseau. Like the laws of nature, in *Jerusalem* the state of nature was not so much an inaccessible point of departure as a perpetual condition out of which human beings emerged spontaneously at all times and places. All of us had to realise eventually that happiness and self-perfection implied much more than egotism and lawlessness. Human beings could not become perfect without mutual assistance, or active and passive interaction with their peers. Self-improvement, for Mendelssohn, necessarily entailed benevolence and the control of self-seeking emotions (116). All human beings could, therefore, feel an urge for co-operation that prompted agreement on certain issues, backed by a natural sense of duties and rights. This impulse was responsible for the formation of small interpersonal contracts, from marriage (inspired by the desire for reproduction) to other settlements transforming incomplete rights into complete ones through 'sufficiently intelligible signs' (122–3). Human beings thus used language to enter into contracts in order to expand their scope of action for self-perfection; solitary existence would not have allowed them to pursue effectively their happiness and betterment.[23]

Within this framework, a social contract – or the incessant, never-ending contracting of duties and rights through language – could only transform the incomplete duties existing in the state of nature into complete duties, enforceable and coercible within civil society. This point is of the utmost significance for Mendelssohn's argument about religious associations. Human beings could settle the collision of their incomplete rights and duties towards one another by agreements and contracts, but this was not applicable to the relationship between them and God. God did not require human assistance, nor did he possess incomplete rights in conflict with those of human beings; in this case, there could have been no contract at all. Where no incomplete duties or rights had existed, Mendelssohn argued, complete duties and rights could not have been produced *ex nihilo* by a social contract. Therefore, civil society (or the state) could lay claim to complete rights over its members, based on the same members' incomplete natural duties towards one another. Established religion, by contrast, could have never acquired any complete

23. Cf. the juxtaposition of natural sociability, rights and duties in Wolff 1756: 2.1 §210–25 and 2.3 §270–2, where the establishment of civil society had a more foundational and irrevocable character.

rights enforceable by violence, penalties or remuneration. The only tool in its arsenal was persuasion through reason and compassion (126–8).

Having criticised Rousseau in 1756 for assuming too broad a gap between nature and civilisation, Mendelssohn attempted in *Jerusalem* to heal this fracture. He accomplished the task by depicting the social contract as comprised of minute and myriad verbal agreements among independent agents at different times and places, not a constitutive moment at which rights and duties were established together by all members of a group or transferred from them to a sovereign. The transition from a state of nature to civil society, as Alexander Altmann has suggested, was projected in *Jerusalem* from society as a whole on to the individual level, becoming a psychological trajectory to be traversed by each member of society as a rite of passage from childish self-centredness to mental adulthood.[24] This reading may be further corroborated by Mendelssohn's critique of Lessing's essay *Die Erziehung des Menschengeschlechts* (*The Education of Mankind*, published partly in 1777 and fully in 1780). Contrary to his close friend's vision of the moral progress of humanity towards a religion of autonomy and reason, Mendelssohn pointed out that humanity as a whole always oscillates between progress and decline, never moving forward without retracing its steps. 'Progress is for the individual man', Mendelssohn explained, and mankind did not mature from childhood to old age throughout history; such an upward progress was not necessary for the vindication of God's providence (162–3).[25] Mendelssohn's denial of a cumulative civilising process highlighted his emphasis on the shift from nature to artifice as an individually experienced transition rather than a social change shrouded in the mists of prehistory. Unlike divine legislation, agreements modifying the scope of natural freedom had to be psychologically reaffirmed in different ages and circumstances, once individuals grasped the natural link between self-perfection and benevolence.

The second part of *Jerusalem* developed a similar argument about Judaism. Mendelssohn's main point was that the faith of his forefathers was perfectly compatible with the tenets of the Enlightenment's natural religion (the existence of God, providence and the immortality of the soul), usually regarded as universally accessible to all human beings. The revelation at Sinai contained, according to Mendelssohn, only ceremonial law or particular precepts for everyday action, not propositions necessary for salvation and happiness. God gave the ancient Israelites historical truths – facts and

24. Altmann 1982b: 48–9.
25. For the contemporary background of Mendelssohn's theory of history see Berghahn 2001: 68–119.

events that must be taken on faith – rather than eternal truths, universally accessible to reason due to their internal coherence or following observation (156–60). The sanctions attached to the revealed law never addressed matters of belief, only ceremonial actions. Such punitive measures were necessary as long as God was lawgiver and king of the Hebrew nation; once the civil bonds of the state were dissolved through foreign occupation, religious transgressions ceased to be crimes against the state and Judaism was turned from a theocracy into a religion (193–6).[26]

Mendelssohn did not, however, merely portray ancient Judaism as an impeccably natural religion augmented by a revealed ceremonial law. One of the most distinctive features of *Jerusalem* is his account of human language, which may serve as a link between the political theory of the first part of the treatise and the defence of the Jewish faith in the second. Throughout *Jerusalem* Mendelssohn emphasised that eternal truths, necessary for salvation and happiness, were revealed to all humanity through 'nature and thing' (*Natur und Sache*) – the structure of the universe and human constitution, open to any enquiring mind. On the other hand, historical truths could be revealed through 'words and script' (*Worte und Schrift*), written characters comprehensible to a particular group of people at a certain time and place (157–60; 191–3). Consequently, unlike the ceremonial law, Jewish beliefs and doctrines were not written down in ancient times. According to Mendelssohn, the tenets of belief were transmitted through lively spiritual conversation and oral exchange, not via rote learning or scripted instructions. This initially applied to the revealed law as well; it was forbidden to record in writing more than the fundamental points inscribed by Moses. The ceremonial law was a 'living script stimulating mind and heart' to be observed and imitated by its students, a set of meaningful actions which were the occasion for further reflection and edification.[27]

The depiction of Jewish ceremonial law as a form of social action that had to be experienced rather than read flowed from Mendelssohn's critical stance towards the print revolution, and more generally towards the transition from spoken language to written characters. The increased circulation of printed books, Mendelssohn argued, entirely transformed man: one learned about human nature and the universe from printed books rather than from direct

26. On the engagement of early modern thinkers with Josephus's view of the ancient Jewish state as a theocracy, see Nelson 2010 and vol. I, Chapter 6.
27. The particularly oral and animated character of ancient Hebrew was emphasised by Mendelssohn also in 'Or la-Netivah', the Hebrew introduction to his annotated edition of the Pentateuch (Mendelssohn 1929–: XIV, 213–18).

experience and interaction. Academic teaching, religious preaching and even leisurely entertainment were all mediated via the printed word in silent absorption or public declamation. 'All is dead letter; nowhere is the spirit of living conversation to be found', Mendelssohn lamented; 'man has almost lost his worth to other men' (169–70). One did not have to seek the wise man as long as one could get hold of his printed works, and conversation became strictly utilitarian. Drawing on contemporary theories about the origin of articulate discourse in a 'language of action', a melodious idiom of sounds and gestures reflecting the primordial energies of the human mind, Mendelssohn argued that before the rise of script 'men were more necessary to one another; instruction was more closely related to life, contemplation better linked to conduct' (170).[28] In the same manner that print fragmented the unity of human life in modern times, written characters had caused much harm in antiquity by giving rise to idolatry. The initial use of the images of objects or their outlines generated confusion between sign and signified, and the mixed hieroglyphic representation of different items only exacerbated the situation by promoting animal worship.

Against the background of this near-universal idolatry and the detrimental effects of written characters, God chose the descendants of Abraham as his nation, an example for others in its adherence to the concepts of pure natural religion. Mendelssohn noted, however, that God could not have turned the fugitives from Egypt into such a nation by consigning pure ideas to written or inscribed characters. Images and hieroglyphs prompted idolatry and superstition, while alphabetical script divided theory and practice by making human reflection too rarefied. Actions, by contrast, were ephemeral, so that there was no risk of their misinterpretation for idolatrous purposes; they also encouraged social exchange, conversation and mutual imitation. The tenets of Judaism were therefore linked to everyday activities and rituals, each having its value in prompting further reflection. Transitory action replaced permanent signs as the vehicle of moral ideas, and as a result 'teaching and life, wisdom and action, speculation and social interaction were linked together most tightly' (185).

But such an idyllic situation was not to last, and the ancient Jews lapsed periodically into idolatry. However, the lesson of this account of writing, idolatry and revelation was clear to Mendelssohn: written words mutilated concepts by freezing active, changing ideas within the artificial permanence

28. See, for example, Warburton 1742: 2.4.4, 81–95, and Condillac 2001: 2.1.1–4, 114–37. On the impact of William Warburton's theory of the origin of language and script, see Cherpack 1955; Assmann 1997: 96–115; Lifschitz 2009: 216–18.

of immutable figures. As explained earlier in *Jerusalem*, 'words and script' were not only particular in the sense of being limited to distinct groups of speakers, readers and receivers of revelation. Contrary to 'nature and thing', legible universally by human reason, 'word and script' forced living ideas into the Procrustean bed of unchanging forms. While nature could be interpreted differently albeit correctly by members of various communities throughout history, written letters imposed one generation's conceptual gridlock on all posterity. This insight enhanced Mendelssohn's condemnation of contemporary projects for confessional unification. Pointing out that such schemes, supposedly based on the shared concepts of natural religion, were diametrically opposed to toleration of the other and the different, Mendelssohn added that the minimal doctrine agreed upon would be a meaningless formula. Each community would attach different senses to its words, ensuing in universal hypocrisy (202).

This conviction echoes the end of the first part of *Jerusalem*, where Mendelssohn sharply criticised religious oaths. These were portrayed, not unlike the formulae of religious union at the end of the second section, as empty words. As Mendelssohn argued, oaths could be taken only about evidence of the external senses: events and objects which people saw, heard, received or relinquished. Convictions and beliefs were, however, a very different case. Rarely did one mould one's thoughts into words and signs in the manner of another, and people regularly designated different ideas by the same word. Moreover, internal perceptions were so subtle and elusive that one could seldom express precisely what one felt or thought by way of written signs. Therefore, requiring candidates for office – be it clerical or civil – to swear allegiance to standard articles of faith amounted to violating their conscience. One presented them with expressions of refined metaphysical views, clothed in a particular language centuries ago, while expecting the wholehearted approval of active, thinking agents. The uttered words, Mendelssohn claimed, would be mere noise without meaning. Written formulae could never reflect individual belief in all its distinctiveness and living force (131–7).

V

In the *Sendschreiben* of 1756 Mendelssohn wrestled with the problematic emergence of articulate language as depicted in Rousseau's *Discours sur l'inégalité*, where it mirrored the incommensurability between a bestial state of nature and the institutions of civil society. A similar challenge concerning language and political life engaged Mendelssohn in 1783, when the critical question was how to preserve freedom and creativity in both spheres. Mendelssohn's account of the evolution of society and script indicated a double-edged relationship between language and freedom. While language enabled the perpetual construction of civic freedom, its written form could seriously curtail individual liberty of conscience, a kind of freedom best preserved beyond the reach of church and state.

The first part of *Jerusalem* illustrated how natural freedom was transformed into civil liberty through a series of linguistic performances such as marriage, property transactions and other mutual agreements. These all involved the transformation of incomplete rights into complete ones through 'sufficiently intelligible signs'.[29] Language was thus a key instrument in the transition from nature to civil society, which was for Mendelssohn a spontaneous personal itinerary with positive outcomes. In contrast, written characters had pernicious implications in the realm of individual beliefs and thoughts, where freedom was unaffected by the ongoing small-scale agreements. Any attempt to force convictions into written creeds, oaths and formulae of confessional union would disfigure individual beliefs, incorrigibly constraining human freedom. This principle is particularly manifest in Mendelssohn's account of ancient Judaism and its ceremonial law, where immutable characters were eschewed and replaced by living actions and oral exchange.

Mendelssohn's mature view of language and freedom elaborated his 1756 argument against Rousseau: the conviction that linguistic representation, even in the guise of general terms, is a natural human capacity. Rousseau's conundrum concerning the shift from natural signs to artificial words was transferred by Mendelssohn in 1783 to another difficult change, from audible sounds to written characters. This became the transition which, in Mendelssohn's eyes, might have required 'more than common human powers'.[30] Spoken language was portrayed in *Jerusalem* as a natural human capacity, a supple and adjustable instrument of social intercourse and the positive limitation of natural freedom. Writing, in contrast, solidified language and ideas to the point of ossification, dividing too dichotomously the spheres of speculative thought and social action. Against this background it may be easier to understand the link between language

29. While analysing Mendelssohn's account of the emergence of language and script, Ricken (2000) does not refer to the role of language in the creation of a political sphere in the first part of *Jerusalem*.
30. Mendelssohn 1929–: VIII, 174.

and freedom according to Mendelssohn. His aversion to oaths and creeds, written testimonies of belief requiring compulsory allegiance, echoed his reluctance to imagine a constitutive moment or contract in which rights and duties were transferred *en masse* from citizens to sovereign. On both fronts, agreements and contracts required self-motivated consent and autonomous conviction on the contractors' part rather than empty words crafted for them by remote ancestors at some point of origin.

Part II

Free citizens and the state

6

Liberty and citizenship in early modern English political discourse

Iain Hampsher-Monk

I

This chapter draws together two bodies of literature, one in the history of political ideas, specifically in the history of the recovery of republican discourse, and one in social and political history, exploring the structure, practice and extent of early modern office-holding. In doing so it not only gestures at the recently influential German genre of conceptual history (*Begriffsgeschichte*) but respects F. W. Maitland's injunction that in considering these matters the historian should 'neglect neither English life nor Italian thought'.[1]

A distinctive claim of conceptual history is that practices, as well as discourse, periphrasis and lexical markers, can demarcate and bear the historical subject, i.e. the concept, under investigation. 'Political liberty' and 'citizenship' can each be construed as lexical markers and as social practices. But the reason for treating them together is not just that both therefore offer the opportunity to examine the discourse–practice relationship but also the intimate ways in which their practice, meanings and lexical markers have been mutually entangled in English history.

Whilst the practices we associate with citizenship were surprisingly widespread in early modern England, the use of the word 'citizen' was highly restricted. 'Citizen' was used in a largely specific and institutionally descriptive sense and even there the preferred English locution was often 'freeman'. What both citizen and freemen possessed were liberties, and they possessed

Many thanks to Quentin Skinner for orchestrating the wonderful group of young scholars, and for all their comments. Thanks too to Wyger Velema and the Dutch Conceptual History group to whom a version of this was presented, and to Jonathan Scott, Terence Ball, Quentin Skinner again as editor, and Cambridge University Press's anonymous referees for their comments.

1. Maitland 1898: vi.

those liberties in consequence of membership of some institutional body.[2] One was not *presumed* free unless one possessed some such membership. One particular early modern locution is revealing of this. Men (it was usually but not exclusively men) were said to be free of – meaning by virtue of – the corporations of which they were members. By contrast, in modern usage, the locution 'free of' is used to designate not what *endows* one with freedom but what it is that might have *impeded* one's enjoyment of it. In modernity, freedom has become a universal, ascriptive property of individuals, and not a contingent possession that they might or might not enjoy; there is now, accordingly, no point in rehearsing how one might have come to posses it. In the countryside too, liberty was a privilege; individuals, like cities, could be free in the sense of possessing privileged exemption from otherwise universal obligations, or possessing tenures that did not involve personal service, by contrast with 'base tenures' as they came to be called.[3] In England – and perhaps in Europe generally – we have moved from a conception of *freedoms* as specific, institutionally defined and derived, and so contingent, to a conception of freedom as inclusive, and indeed universal and ascriptive. The conceptual history of 'freedom', I suggest, tracks that of 'citizen', in moving from being a specific and institutionally linked description to playing a universal and ascriptive role.

I proceed by taking three snapshots, one around 1600, one during the English Civil War, and another in the 1790s.

II

The earliest recorded uses of the term 'citizen' in England (1314 – citizenship is a much later coinage)[4] refer, as in many European vernaculars, to the inhabitants of a city, and more especially those possessing the rights, privileges or freedoms of the corporation of that city. Whilst the distinction between cities and towns was ecclesiastical (cities possessed cathedrals), on a purely secular level towns too characteristically possessed a charter granting liberties or freedoms from feudal obligations, such as the right to hold a market, and rights of assembly and to benefit from educational and other foundations associated with the town. Those rights were guarded and exercised by the aldermen or burgesses appointed or elected under the charter,

2. This is true of town corporations, and of trades or craft guilds.
3. For the medieval background to such 'freedoms' and the argument that political liberty of action (as opposed to merely free legal status) derives essentially from such privilege, see Harding 1980.
4. *OED* 'citizen'.

and although only freemen of cities were technically 'citizens', in both city and town such individuals might describe themselves as 'freemen'. In all but the most oligarchic charters, a wider group of 'freemen' also enjoyed franchises, rights and privileges – freedoms, we might say, which could include the right to stand for election, or to elect or review the acts of those who could. Such 'freemen' commonly contested their 'freedoms' with the local oligarchy. Even those below such exalted positions enjoyed some freedoms; for by living in a town one largely escaped the web of feudal obligations characteristically incurred by living in the manorial countryside. The existence of wide (and narrow) denotations of 'citizen' – to refer to office-holders in as well as inhabitants of urban centres – thus had some reflection in real life, and there was sense in lumping the two categories together. Indeed one longstanding conceptual opposition in English was between a 'citizen' (or townsman) and a 'countryman'. A curious feature (for moderns) of this tying of citizenship to cities was that those most likely to be fully active agents of the national political community (lords, knights of the shire or county representatives and their 40 shillings electors – conceptually citizens in the modern sense) were most unlikely to be lexically designated 'citizens'.

However, as indicated above, there was competition as to how to designate those who enjoyed these corporate and urban privileges. A more English way of expressing this status was to call them 'freeman' of London, or Exeter, or wherever; and 'freeman' too had this double meaning of being entitled to hold office but also of being 'free of' the feudal nexus. There were thus, at this point, two locutions in which to express what was one undoubted meaning of the concept of citizenship: the possession of the freedoms resulting from urban or corporate membership. Our two lexical markers here overlap in designating the activity we might conceptually identify as that of a citizen but it was the term freeman that was more commonly deployed. Part of our story must be to outline how the term 'citizen' came to map onto its concept.

In the late 1980s Patrick Collinson published the seminal article 'The Monarchical Republic of Queen Elizabeth I'. The argument, and indeed its imagery, recalled Montesquieu's famous claim that in England a 'republic was disguised as a monarchy'.[5] In England, claimed Collinson, 'citizens were concealed within subjects'. Collinson thereby not only developed his predecessor Geoffry Elton's criticism of the idea of 'Tudor Despotism', but, more germane to our concerns, questioned J. G. A. Pocock's assertion that the idea of 'civic society as a . . . republic of equal citizens' was 'something

5. Montesquieu 1989: v, 19, 70.

not to be found in England and [as yet] scarce imagined there, prior to 1642'.[6] Pocock had been a champion of the recovery of a republican narrative in the English – and British – Civil Wars, and Collinson's argument seemed to some to open up the possibility of a 'republican' vision going back sixty years, and hinted at an answer to the puzzle as to why and how full blown republican aspirations could have emerged with such celerity in the 1640s.

Collinson's initial case rested on the interpretation of two social phenomena at different ends of the social scale. The 'republic' of Elizabeth's privy councillors and MPs comprised individuals who had benefited from enough of a civic, renaissance education to imagine themselves as virtuous citizens contributing not to a realm or a kingdom but to a commonwealth – the neologism although dating from the later fifteenth, becoming famously widespread in the sixteenth century.[7] Not only did they so conceive of themselves; they acted accordingly. In the Bond of Association of 1584, they pledged themselves, by the authority 'residing in the body politic', to exclude from the throne anyone (including an otherwise legitimate successor) who might be the beneficiary of a violent act against the Queen. Even more strikingly, a bill introduced by Lord Burghley provided for interim rule by the Privy Council and their choice of successor, in the event of Elizabeth's sudden death, a move that has provoked irresistible proleptic parallels with the events of 1688.[8] Clearly, major actors at the state level conceived of themselves in civic mode, as citizens – highly aristocratic citizens it is true but citizens nonetheless, and ones with strikingly extensive freedom of political action.[9]

Collinson's second sketch was at the other end of the social spectrum. It provided a view of the village of Swallowfield, Wiltshire; a village – like many – without gentry, where the local administration devolved fully on the common people. In such villages, 'countless' English subjects, with very modest incomes and no knowledge of Cicero, spoke in public meetings, voted on local issues, raised and disposed of local taxes, and believed themselves to have the standing and prerogatives to 'do so'.[10] Collinson thus pointed us to practice at two levels in Tudor society where identifiably free and 'civic' activity was going on; activity which, at least in one case, was self-consciously identified as such.

6. Cited in McDiarmid 2007: 2. 7. *OED* 'Commonwealth'. 8. Guy 2002.
9. For a discussion of the way the bond of association betokens a 'radical dimension' to Elizabethan political thought, see Stephen Alford in Burgess and Festenstein 2007, pp. 17–36.
10. Adapted from Shagan 2007: 19.

A second seminal article took up this theme: Mark Goldie's 'The Unacknowledged Republic: Office-holding in Early Modern England'.[11] Goldie massively extended the evidential base of office-holding. State office-holders were few (the court employed only 1,200 people) and confined to a narrow elite. Yet Goldie demonstrated, beyond Westminster, throughout early modern England, how widespread office-holding was, providing examples of brickmakers, tanners, bakers and soap-boilers (a proverbially lowly occupation). At the lowest, parish level, he estimated there were 50,000 office-holders at any one time. This, with rotation, implied that over any fifteen-year period half the adult male population would have held office. This figure is more than confirmed by detailed local studies, one of which found that one in three householders in London's Cornhill ward held office in any one year.[12] Office-holding could be seriously burdensome – records of complaints and excuses abound – but it could clearly stimulate wider political reflection and engagement. Nehemiah Wellington, a London puritan carpenter and freeman of the city, juryman and churchwarden, left 2,600 pages of records and reflections on the relationship between his religious and political duties and loyalties.

These two works are complemented by others[13] which have thickened our sense of the texture of civic language and sensibilities in the period, and which sometimes appeal (as Collinson was careful not to) to continuities between the civic self-image of the court elite of the 1580s and the 'country' republicanism emerging in the later 1640s. These flesh out claims of a submerged and 'unacknowledged' republic in late sixteenth- and seventeenth-century English culture, where the 'concept' of citizenship was collectively held as a combination of practice and literary and discursive resources.

The emergence of claims to full-blown republican liberty during the English Civil war and Interregnum has always been something of a historical puzzle. Where did they come from? And how could they make headway? The answer could now be argued to lie in the neoclassical literary culture of the English renaissance where classical Roman literature reprised its oft-performed historical role of importing a civic content under the guise of formal and stylistic models. But congruent with such elite, discursive or literary civic awareness were the practices of a huge body of middling and even quite lowly sorts of people. Many elements of the concept of citizenship were in place here: the practice of the self-reliant decision-making community, at both national and local level; the idea of the responsible 'citizen'; the

11. Goldie 2001. 12. Archer 1991: 163. 13. E.g. Peltonen 1995; Norbrook 1988.

idea and practice of specific rights, privileges and liberties pertaining to the occupancy of a particular political status.

However, three differences between the discourse and the practice of office-holders stand out. Firstly, the latter were often much more lowly than the idealised classical citizen, for it was at the very local level that office-holding was most widespread. Secondly, and again contrary to the secular way in which early modern citizenship has been recovered and theorised, that most local and widespread level was an ecclesiastical and only secondarily a civil unit of administration – the parish. The final point to make about the unacknowledged and monarchical republic was its unacknowledgedness. Lowly office-holders – unless members of the urban corporations of cities – did not describe themselves as citizens at all.

III

This disconnect between the vocabulary and practice of citizenship is exposed by the difficulty early modern commentators had in applying the classical vocabulary to the prevailing practice, revealing how uncomfortably language and practice, institutions and their lexical markers, related at the time.

Sir Thomas Smith was ideally equipped to bridge the worlds of classical discourse and vernacular practice: a classical scholar and first Regius Professor of Civil Law at Cambridge, he was also a JP, an MP and Secretary of State to both Edward VI and Elizabeth. His *De republica Anglorum*, subtitled 'A discourse on the commonwealth of England', was written in English whilst Smith was ambassador in France between 1562 and 1563, and circulated widely in manuscript. After Smith's death it was revised and published posthumously by an unknown editor in 1583.[14] Historians have divided over how much credence to give to Smith's account.[15] But further editions were published in 1584, 1589, 1594, 1601 and 1609, and a Latin translation published in 1610 was republished three times by mid-century. There is thus considerable evidence as to its popularity, as well as its invocation as an authority.[16] My concern here is with the way it reveals

14. Smith 1982. Smith possessed a very substantial collection of ninety volumes of Latin and Greek texts (now in Queens' College, Cambridge).
15. Withington 2001: 247.
16. Smith 1982: Appendix 1, 'The Printed Editions'; for Smith being invoked as an authority, Introduction, 5ff.

the extraordinary tensions between classical terminology and vernacular practice, and the relationship between each of these and liberty.

Smith opens by rehearsing Aristotle's tripartite classification of 'three most simple kindes, or fashions of government', monarchy, aristocracy and democracy, accepted by 'they that have written heretofore of Common wealthes', and of 'another division of each of the three into two: good and just . . . evill and unjust', with a warning that in practice these are often to be found mixed.[17] However, despite this classical opening, in which Smith shows off his Greek, the bulk of the book is concerned with the hugely gothic issue of status, and his conception of the polity and of politics is highly juridical, since the whole of books II and III are concerned with judicial structures and processes.

In several passages Smith addresses the concept of citizenship and its relationship to freedom. At I.16 he considers the 'parts and persons of the commonwealth' as households and families, villages and towns, and freemen 'as subjects and citizens[18] of the commonwealth', as opposed to 'bondmen who can beare no rule nor jurisdiction over freemen [and are] but instruments and the goods and possessions of others'. However, he goes on to observe that this distinction is not quite the one he wants to highlight, which is between 'them that beare office' and those 'that beare none: the first are called magistrates, the second private men'. But then, reviewing the practice of the Romans, Greeks and French, he notes that 'we in England divide our men commonly into foure sortes, gentlemen, citizens, yeomen artificers, and labourers'.[19] In his discussion of the nobility, knights and squires – who 'have the greatest charge and doings in the commonwealth' – Smith continually seeks to establish parallels within the Roman social order.[20] Having briefly dealt with 'Citizens and Burgesses . . . as officers within the cities and burrowes'[21] he then turns his attention to the yeomen. Yeomen are 'freemen borne English, [who] may dispend of his owne free lande in yerely revenue to the summe of xl. s[hillings] sterling [the qualification for the franchise in the counties]'. They 'confess themselves to be no gentlemen . . . and yet they have a certaine preheminence and more estimation than labourers and artificers, and commonly live welthilie'. Such upwardly mobile people, by working and trading hard, 'come to such wealth that they are able to buy the lands of unthriftie gentlemen',[22] send their sons to university, and leave

17. Smith 1982: 49, 50, 52.
18. The (to civic sensibilities) somewhat oxymoronic 'subject and citizen' is quite conventional. See the pervasive early Stuart epithet 'freeborn subect'. Foxley 2004: 851.
19. Smith 1982: 64–5. 20. Smith 1982: 17, 18. 21. Smith 1982: 73. 22. Smith 1982: 74.

them enough to make them gentlemen. Yeoman was 'next to gentleman' and was to be distinguished from the 'husbandmen labourers' and the 'lowest and rascall sort of people'. Slipping briefly into classical mode Smith recalls that these yeomen were what 'Cato called the *Aratores*, and the *optimos* [*sic*] *cives in Republica*', and that Aristotle too had good things to say about this quiescent middling sort who 'tende their own businesse, come not to meddle in publike matters and judgments but when they are called, and glad when they are delivered thereof'.[23] However, they are the backbone of the army: English archers and footsoldiers generally playing the most successful part against the French.

Smith now seems to have reached the limit of the politically active inhabitants. For the next chapter is headed 'Of the fourth sort of men which doe not rule', who are immediately identified with the Roman *proletarii*. They are labourers and artificers – tailors, shoemakers, carpenters, brickmakers and bricklayers – but also merchants and traders who have no freehold land. Such people 'have no voice or authoritie in our common wealth, and no account is made of them but onelie to be ruled not to rule others'.[24] However this claim to their exclusion from ruling and being ruled by turn, the classic Aristotelian characterisation of citizenship, is curiously almost immediately contravened.

For Smith continues, 'Yet they be not altogether neglected. For in cities and corporate towns, for default of yeomen, enquests and juries are impaneled of such manner of people. And in villages theyme commonly made Churchwardens, alecunners, and . . . constables which office toucheth more the common wealth and at the first was not implied upon such lowe and base persons.'[25]

Despite the distinct tone of regret with which Smith reports the need for recourse to these 'mean and rascall' persons, he is quite clear that they *do* hold office, a fact that militates against his earlier clear division between those who do and do not 'beare office' on the basis of status. Might all of these people be said to share in some sense in citizenship?

One group clearly does not; that is treated in the chapter 'Of Bondage and Bondmen'.[26] Again a classical analysis segues into a feudal background to modernity. Justinian's code recognises two forms of bondmen: the classical slave, taken in war, or bought or born into bondage, and the emerging serf of the late classical *latifundia*, who 'appeareth in *Justinians* time . . . bond not

23. Smith 1982: 75–6. 24. Smith 1982: 76. 25. Smith 1982: 77.
26. Smith 1982: ch. 8.

to thc person but to the mannor or place'. English law actually recognises both categories, but of the first Smith 'never knewe any in the realme in my time'. The influence of Christianity led men 'to have conscience to hold in captivity and such extreme bondage him whom they must acknowledge to be his brother' and so they were all manumitted; and of the second there were so few 'that it is not almost worth the speaking'.[27]

As if anticipating an objection, Smith recognises that villein or servile tenure might be said to continue this status. But 'to consider more deeply' he points out that in fact *no* land in England is technically held freely (allodially), since 'all lande, even that which is called most free lande, hath a bondage annexed unto to it . . . [and] doth bring a certain kind of servitude to the possessor. For no man holdeth land simply free in Englande; [except the King] all others holde their land in fee, that is upon a faithe or trust, and some service to be done to another.' If such a form of tenure rendered the tenant unfree, even the lords and knights of the shire would be servile, a position he is understandably loth to concede.[28]

Smith's account maps interestingly onto the arguments used by Collinson and Goldie. His admitted facts – which agree with theirs – about the lowly status of office-holders, continually tend to disconcert the classically influenced categorical distinctions he initially makes between rulers and ruled, servile and free. Similarly the pervasively feudal character of land tenure seems to threaten to preclude the independence required to identify the classical citizen with the early modern knight or esquire. More generally he struggles to apply his classical conceptual categories to his contemporary social and political world.[29] But nowhere does he assert the language of citizenship or identify citizens, except as office-holders in cities: 'citizens and burgesses [are] such as not onely be free and received as officers within the cities, but also be of some substance to beare the charges'. They serve only 'in their cities' and 'in the shires [countryside] they be of none accompt, save only in the common assembly of the realm to make lawes which is called the Parliament'.[30]

IV

During the English Civil War the potentialities in the concepts and the terms 'citizen' and 'liberty' were exploited to the full by a flowering of

27. Smith 1982: 136, 130. 28. Smith 1982: 138.
29. Cf. Peltonen 2002: 87: 'Smith had no difficulties in combining monarchy and citizenship.'
30. Smith 1982: 73.

classical republican thought, paradigmatically with James Harrington, whose republican experience included not only a careful reading of Machiavelli but military service in the Netherlands and travel in the vestigially republican landscape of Italy. Despite the excitement Harrington and others generated amongst historians of political ideas, the failure of republicanism as a practical project suggests that the concept of citizenship on classical lines, as a category applicable at the level of the national state, struck no chord. Moreover, despite the regicide, it is not clear that a story about the gradual coincidence of discourse and practice explains the emergence of interregnum republicanism. In the view of several commentators there is no pervasive concept of republican liberty or attendant active citizenship which is performing any orchestrating role in the 1640s, or even (except very marginally) in the 1650s.[31] As late as 1643 Henry Marten MP had been sent to the tower (by the House of Commons itself!) for suggesting that kings were unnecessary. The regicides did not 'use the language of civic republicanism' or 'execute the king in order to change the constitution'.[32] The rebels evaded the constitutional question until after the act, and even then did not introduce a republican constitution, but 'merely eliminated those aspects of the old constitution against which they had turned or which had got in their way',[33] a feature of the regime distinctly if embarrassingly signalled for a while by the existence of the Rump Parliament. Moreover real republicans, such as Harrington, inveighed against the 'kingless rule' by a parliamentary oligarchy who appeared ignorant, or wilfully heedless, of the principles under which alone liberty and freedom might flourish. Republican or not, the regimes of the interregnum – unsurprisingly given their increasing isolation – placed little emphasis on active citizenship as an essential feature of constitutional arrangements. But then neither did Harrington, who required, even of his commons, only that they vote, and not debate.[34]

One group that did stress political activism was the Levellers. Yet it has proved difficult to cast them as writers – or actors – of a classical republican script for the English Civil War. There is scant evidence in their writings (prior to their enforced withdrawal from politics in 1649) of any awareness of Renaissance or even classical sources or of the political uses to which they could be put, or, in their blunt or – as in the case of whispering William

31. Worden 1995; Scott 1992. Milton and Nedham are conceded to be exceptions by Scott (2004: 233–43).
32. Worden 2002: 315.
33. Worden 2002: 317.
34. Harrington 1977a: 274, 336. For this view of Harrington see the discussion by Scott in Van Gelderen and Skinner 2002: 71ff.

Walwyn – sometimes Bunyanesque prose, of the rhetorical skills so praised and exemplified by classical republican writers.[35] Yet the Levellers unswervingly championed an impeccably republican agenda over the fifteen years of their existence. In one of their last tracts, published in the dying days of the Commonwealth, they summarised their position in four strikingly phrased fundamental principles:

1 'The government of *England* ought to be by Laws and not by Men.' And to this end judges should not hold office at the pleasure of political rulers.
2 The Levellers asserted the constituent and continuing legislative authority of the people, and the priority of the common good as an aim of legislation: 'all lawes, levies of Monies, War and Peace, ought to be made by the peoples deputies in parliament, to be chosen by them successively at certain periods of time, and that no Council table Orders or Ordinances or Court Proclamations'. They denied the legality of any law, regulation or authority not issuing from the legislative assembly of the people.
3 Equality before the law: 'That every man of what Quallity or Condition Place or Office whatsoer ought to be equally subject to the Laws.'
4 Citizen militia, and no mercenaries: 'the People ought to be formed into such a constant Military posture, by and under the commands of their Parliament that by their own strength they may be able to compel every man to be subject to the Laws and to defend their Country from forrainers and inforce right and Justice', since 'no government can stand without the force of arms'.[36]

Moreover, the Levellers, unlike many commonly cited republicans, propounded an activist view of citizenship: getting 'the people' involved in petitioning, subscribing and agreeing was a major, and at times the only, strategy available to them. The construction of a free, constitutionalist and self-governing republic (with or without a chief magistrate) was not, they insisted, 'our worke only, but every man's conscience must look to itselfe, and not dream out more seasons and opportunities'.[37] It was not only at the Republic's birth that activism was required; they made it clear that, although forfeitable through delinquency (royalism) or, for some, dependency (poverty), there was at least an initial presumption that all must participate in the choosing of the legislature.

35. But for the most sustained attempt see now Glover 1999.
36. 'The principles and maxims . . . of those that are commonly called Levellers' [1659] in Levellers 2003: v, 426ff.
37. Agreement of the Free People of England (1649) in Sharpe 1998: 168–9.

Withholding the epithet republican from the Levellers is understandable given that, however republican the practices they sought to promote, they did not do so in terms of the language of classical – or any other – self-identified republicanism. Indeed it is extraordinary how they manage to conduct long reflections on the importance of self-governance in communities, the active defence of rights, the unreliability of mercenaries and the presence of an indigenous soldiery, exemplified not only in England but in Rome, Turkey and the Netherlands, without once reaching for the vocabulary of citizenship, which they reserved for the technical sense of members of, or electors of, a city or town corporation. So, for example, 'England's new chains discovered' (1649) which was described as being 'Presented . . . by Lieutenant Colonel John Lilburne and diverse other citizens of London and borough of Southwark'.

Careful readings of possible counter-examples reveal them not to be so. 'The remonstrance of many thousand citizens' (1646), addressing as it does a national complaint to Parliament, might be thought to imply a national conception of citizenship. But the full title is 'The remonstrance of many thousand citizens *and other freeborn people of England . . .* ', revealing that citizens were, for them, a discrete group amongst the freeborn, and not co-extensive with them, and not, therefore, with the possession of liberty. In contrast to many petitions which were from citizens, country-wide petitions and agreements were from the people – 'many Thousands', 'diverse well affected people in and about the City of LONDON', 'many thousands of well affected people',[38] 'the freeborn people of England' – and were addressed to 'countrymen and fellow commoners'. Their 'Agreements of the People' were 'Agreements of the free people of England'.

So although Levellers often equated 'citizen' with 'freeman' in the technical sense to refer to a member of, or elector in, a civic corporation, they never, as far as I can find, extended the use of 'citizen' in the way they did 'freeman' – in a rhetorically innovative and ideologically redescriptive move – to argue that all Englishmen were citizens. Their extension of 'freeman' was a melding together of the universality of freemen, in the sense that all were now freed from feudal obligations, with the specific and institutional freedoms of freemen in the narrow sense of the rights acquired through corporation membership. Through such rhetoric, as Rachel Foxley shows, Lilburne made the phrase 'free-born Englishman' into a shorthand for an emerging concept of citizenship'.[39] But he did not attach the word 'citizen' to it.

38. 'Gold tried in the fire', Walwyn in Levellers 2003: II, 222, 232, 234.

39. Foxley 2004: 251.

At times, indeed, they seem scrupulous in avoiding the temptation to do so. Wildman's late 'London's liberties' (1650) asserted the rights of the citizens of London to elect their officers, aldermen, lord mayor, etc. When arguing from within positive law or institutions, Wildman uses the term 'citizen' interchangeably with 'free-man', a legal status. When he argues – although ultimately conceding not to press his case on these grounds – in general terms, he uses the term 'people'. Thus the aim of the petition was 'to have the ancient right of the Citizens of London restored to them'; again, 'I humbly propose no other end but to enforce the petition of the free men of this city.' But he buttressed his claim to be recovering ancient right with a more general and abstract claim based on common and natural right which informs 'the very first principles of just Government'. And here he drops the term citizen, referring instead to 'the people', whose 'just subjection under government, ought to proceed from consent. [Office-holders] are but trustees for the good of the people. The original of all just power under God proceeds from the people.' He then switches back to the specific case of London, the liberties of the citizens of which 'appear more ancient than any charter of the city that's visible to us'.[40]

The Levellers were, and saw themselves as, exponents of a continuous, if always threatened, autochthonous political tradition of liberty which owed more to common law and the freeman–villein polarity, which, with the demise of villeinage, left all free.[41] These principles, they claimed, laid them open to no charges of novelty or inconsistency, 'the same fundamentals of Government having been claimed by our Ancestors as their right, for many hundred years'.[42]

It was a freedom that they presented as pervading the physical terrain of England – to the extent, Lilburne claimed (evidently with Harrison's case in mind) that even a slave, should he set foot on English soil, would cease to be a slave. Not to be a slave was admittedly not yet, in most discourses, to be a citizen, but the Levellers insisted that, being *free*, all inhabitants had a right to the political privileges that undoubtedly protected specific freedoms where they had already existed – foremost amongst which was the vote. As Rainsborough, the soldiers' representative at the extraordinarily preserved

40. Wildman 1650 [repr. 1972].
41. Levellers demanded the 'abolition of base [i.e. insecure or service-based] tenures' (e.g. *The Foundations of Freedom or An Agreement of the People* [1648] in Levellers 2003, IV), the latter being the original distinction between free and villein. This suggests that although villeinage may have been strictly an empty category, in practice it was still a preoccupation.
42. *The Leveller* (1659) in Levellers 2003: v, 429.

debates held in Putney church in 1647, famously put it when asked by the bullying Ireton why non-property owners should have a vote:

> For really I think that the poorest he that is in England hath a life to live as the greatest he, and therefore . . . every man that is to live under a government ought first by his own consent to put himself under that government; and I do think that the poorest man in England is not at all bound in a strict sense to that government that he has not had a voice to put himself under.[43]

This right was not merely, for the Levellers, a right of individual self-protection (although it was that). It was informed by a sense of the common, collective good. Where they give concessions on the extent of citizenship they are worried by the strength of the power relations that might force 'some men to give their voices [votes] to their friends, landords or the richest, weighing men's merits by the pound or the acre'. So Lilburne warns people to 'be careful in their elections, to have an eye apon the publick and chuse such as have appeared most eminent and active in the Establishment of Love and Freedom'.[44]

The Levellers used the ambiguity of 'free man' to link the undoubted sense in which, with the passing of villeinage, all were freemen to the much more exclusive sense in which being a freeman of a corporation endowed one with certain privileges – such as political participation. Yet the seamlessness of such liberty is continually fragmented by their claims and aspirations to specific and plural freedoms, rights, liberties, privileges and immunities, leading to the suspicion that however much 'Lilburne . . . remodels freedoms into a more unified conception', nevertheless 'freedom was seen by the Levellers as a composite'.[45]

V

In the first part of the eighteenth century, opportunities for urban office-holding increased dramatically. There was expansion in the numbers of charity boards, hospital and poor-relief trusts, and educational, mutual and friendly societies of one kind and another, as well as canal, turnpike and highway, pavement and street-lighting trusts, all emerging as voluntary associations managed by unpaid local committee members. Whilst not yet technically part of the state apparatus, they were undoubtedly civic, in the sense

43. Sharp 1998: 103. 44. Lilburne 1659: 9, and *in extenso* Hampsher-Monk 1976.
45. Foxley 2004: 857, endorsing Wende 1974.

of relating to the management of the needs and activities of the *civitas* or city. Jonathan Barry has coined the term 'bourgeois collectivism' as a way of challenging the notion of the archetypical bourgeois as individualist and self rather than socially focused.[46] This work can be seen as an extension of the Goldie thesis – that it is in the practice of office-holding that we should look for an understanding of the concept of citizenship. Philip Withington has made the case explicitly:

> England's towns and boroughs underwent two 'renaissances' over the course of the period: a 'civic renaissance' and the better-known 'urban renaissance'. The former was fashioned in the sixteenth century; however, its legacy continued to inform political thought and practice over 150 years later. Similarly, although the latter is generally associated with 'the long eighteenth century', its attributes can be traced to at least the Elizabethan era.[47]

Yet the very diversity of these new opportunities must surely provoke reconsideration of their relationship to citizenship. Citizenship is a status that overrides others, in the same way that, as Aristotle states, the political association overrides other associations.[48] Citizenship is what all the members of a polity have in common with each other, indeed what gives them a common to have. Whilst the practice of office-holding in these voluntary associations looks like the kind of thing citizens do, and when done in pursuit of the city's increasingly divergent needs might indeed be called 'civic', their very diversity and particularity surely militates against the equality and uniformity presupposed by the bond of citizenship. The possession of 'citizenship *skills*', that is, does not entail the possession of a shared civic identity. The relationship of associational skills to political freedom and citizenship itself might be thought to depend on exactly where and for what purpose those skills were deployed.

Another aspect of this second urban renaissance reflects its tenuously political character. It has been described as urban rather than civic. With corporations becoming more oligarchic, and many towns modelling the 'urban' on the new West End of London and on Bath, urban renewal (like the arts-led renewal programmes of the late twentieth century) was not linked to any specific political traditions, or citizenship roles. Although urban renaissance occurred within cities, it was largely dominated by landed elites, rentiers and mobile professionals whose uneasy relationship with local citizens begins to be chronicled in the social novels of the time. Jonathan Barry writes:

46. Barry 1994. 47. Withington 2001: 239. 48. Aristotle 1996, 1252a.

> To participate, townspeople had to cast off their old civic particularism and dissociate themselves from the culture of their fellow townsfolk. Although a whole new world of association for leisure and cultural purposes developed, the associations involved were restricted to those who could afford to aspire to the values and life-styles of a refined elite.[49]

The opening up of the eighteenth-century public sphere promoted associational diversity, a leisure and luxury sector, commercial opportunities, and a multiplicity of communities of concern and interest. In England, the increasing toleration of different devotional communities cut across the old parishes; and the professionalisation of the army gradually replaced the local militias and their associational forms, subverting two important organisational dimensions of citizenship. This diversity looked congruent with the kind of modern citizen appropriate for Constant's modern liberty: fragmented and in competition with the salience of traditional offices and militating against the dominance of the individual's civic identity which was a part not only of the classical model and meaning of citizenship, but also of an indigenous tradition of freedom attached to widespread and institutional community – but nationally articulated – office-holding.

This associational diversification, much remarked on by Scottish Enlightenment thinkers, ushered in a new understanding of the tension between monarchy and liberty, recognising the possibility, indeed the desirability, of the free, limited and commercial monarchy. How then was one to describe its inhabitants? Adam Smith normally reserves 'citizens' for his discussion of the politically active members of classical Greece and Rome.[50] When talking of his contemporary Britain he refers to 'the people' or sometimes – I think revealingly – the collective 'the public'. But his usage is very context sensitive, that is, sensitive to his argumentative rather than the descriptive context, and he seems happy to use 'citizen' in quasi-judicial situations. For example in talking of gradations of social condition in Britain he refers to 'particular classes of citizens'.[51] In the *Lectures on Jurisprudence* his discussion of access to citizenship compares Athens, Rome and modern republics with England and other modern European monarchies, and the term citizen seems comfortable to him in discussing this legal position. But he uses 'subject' and 'citizen' interchangeably. For example in discussing 'Whether the sovereign may be guilty of crimes against the subjects' he finds himself having to discuss 'who are the subjects?' Here he immediately substitutes 'citizen' for

49. Barry 1994: 87. 50. Smith 1976: 556, 774ff. 51. Smith 1976: 21.

'subject'. He points out that in smaller countries – where citizenship entitles one to particular privileges – 'being descended from one who is a citizen' tends to be the rule. In countries of large population (such as England) '[place of] Birth determines citizenship'. There are, he concludes, 'two foundations of citizenship in all countries; in the larger ones birth, in the smaller ones having one's father a citizen.' But this conclusion is as true for subjects of monarchies as for members of republican regimes.[52] And in the report of the 1766 version he concludes the same discussion of being a citizen and how one acquires citizenship with the words 'Having thus considered who are properly the subjects of a state.'[53] 'Citizen' carries no distinctive animus and the distinction between it and 'subject' dissolves into a civically amorphous 'member' of a state.

The late eighteenth century saw a number of campaigns for parliamentary reform invoking 'liberty'.[54] One strand of this took up the claim that the rights claimed by charter in the boroughs 'should rightfully have been the perquisite of every freeborn Englishman'.[55] Amongst some of these, the invocation of the epithet 'citizen' began to acquire a truly political character. Amongst the first to do this was historian and radical pamphleteer Catherine Macaulay. Moreover, she glosses 'citizen' in a way that exposes how the term has cut loose from its longstanding institutional attachment: 'Citizens (that is men who have a just regard for the rights of nature, for the general happiness of the human species, and for the happiness of their countrymen in particular)'.[56]

The 1790s saw a campaign for political liberty already foreshadowed by these movements and by the religious dissenters' campaign against their legal disabilities.[57] Joseph Priestley explicitly linked religious and political liberty. Given the disabilities imposed on dissenters for their religion, he argued, 'it was hardly possible that we should be other than friends to the civil liberty of our fellow citizens'. Rights more generally, Paine argued, in what we now recognise as a classic neo-Roman statement, 'could only be preserved by giving each person an equal right in the exercise of power; for to deprive a man of the right to vote reduces him to the status of a slave', since 'slavery consists in being subject to the will of another, and he that has not a vote in the election of representatives is in this case'. The right to vote was 'the primary right by which all other rights are protected'.[58]

52. Smith 1978: 306ff. 53. Smith 1978: 433. 54. Christie 1962; Black 1963.
55. Sweet 1998: 96. 56. Macaulay 1775: 13–14. 57. On the 1790s see Goodwin 1979.
58. Paine 1945: II, 579.

Such arguments play a role in the history of the discourse in which is embedded the history of the *concept* of citizenship and its complex relationship with liberty – still at this stage being conceived of as a discrete number of rights. I have tried to point to the distinctive histories enjoyed by the word 'citizen', political liberty, and the concept of citizenship as embodied in institutional practice. It is only in the 1790s, on the street as it were, that theory, social history and the word citizen finally come together as never before. However infused with the concept, Paine's *Rights of Man* barely mentions the term 'citizen'. Yet, in the political conflict within which that work was situated it comes to assume an agency of its own.

The political reform associations active in the wake of French events constituted the most focused expression of political agency from the unenfranchised since the English Civil War. The most famous of these was the London Corresponding Society. The LCS sought constitutional and franchise reform, reviving elements of the Leveller programme – universal (male) suffrage and annual parliaments, and a decidedly active conception of citizenship – but unlike the Levellers they explicitly linked the term 'citizen' to this programme.

The Society published addresses and appeals, and records of its minutes and correspondence with other societies within and beyond the kingdom.[59] In the absence of political rights themselves and with the decline in the number of offices of political self-government in the sprawling new urban spaces, the political association enabled ordinary men, and sometimes women too, to construct for themselves a forum in which they could be free in the civic sense of practising and exhibiting political activity – and hold office. The Society's internal minutes and correspondence were conducted and recorded with a self-conscious concern for appropriate procedures that endows them with the kind of portentous self-importance of a British Trades Union Congress *c.* 1980. But such formality was important in evading charges of unruliness, in matching the gravitas of their political masters, and most of all of in enacting their political maturity and earnestness. Nor was it only a formal imitation of parliamentary (or perhaps Conventional) procedures; it was a demonstration of their capacity to replace it by supplanting a corrupt parliament through a national convention of corresponding societies.[60]

The invocation of the term 'citizen' was the epitome of such civic self-invention. It was not immediate: early publications were addressed

59. London Corresponding Society 2002; Thale 1983.
60. Gerald 1793. On the invocation of such 'conventions' see Parssinen 1973.

to 'the inhabitants of Great Britain', 'Friends and fellow Countrymen', 'Frenchmen!' (to the National Convention), 'Fellow Countrymen!', the 'Nation at Large'. However, towards the end of 1792, the salutation 'Citizen!' starts to figure prominently in the forms of address prescribed for the conduct of meetings, admission of members, etc. It was clearly a self-conscious programme – and not without opposition. The minutes of the General Committee record the objection of some divisions to the introduction of the word 'citizen'. In other cases more radical divisions had struck out 'Mr' or 'Sir' and replaced them by 'fellow citizen'.[61] An active civic identity was, through such vocabulary, to be inscribed on the passive subject. The Society's public addresses appeal to a shared 'duty to preserve inviolate the liberty of his fellow citizens', reminding readers that it is 'no less the right than the duty of every citizen to keep a watchful eye on the Government of his country' and to ensure that private interest is not substituted for Public Advantage'.[62]

In the repressive atmosphere of the mid 1790s – and with the increasingly republican example of France – 'citizen' became a loaded and subversive term. By 1794 and the first treason trials of reformers following the National Convention in Edinburgh, the LCS was insistently addressing their pamphlets simply to 'Citizens!!' (at the head of each paragraph).[63] Authorities and radicals alike knew that uttering the very word was a speech-act of clearly political import: a brazenly subversive consciousness-raising device, but one for which radicals could scarcely be prosecuted. The *Tribune* records how the court official sent to arrest Thelwall and others for examination before the Privy Council 'flew into a rage' when they referred to each other by the title 'citizen'.[64] In the 1790s the word 'citizen' did not merely re-emerge as a distinctive way of referring to active political agency, its very use was that agency.[65]

It is not merely the meeting, associating and agitating that is important here, but the ostentatious publication of their having done so in records, minutes, proceedings and so on, which constitute effectively a new political genre – albeit one with social roots as far back as the *Spectator* itself. Their communicating the fact of their associative activity was dramaturgical – seeking to embolden and elicit similar actions and associations elsewhere –

61. Thale 1983: 77.
62. *The London Corresponding Society's Addresses and Resolutions*, April 1792, in London Corresponding Society 2002: 78.
63. See Thelwall 1995: 88ff. where almost every paragraph begins: 'Citizens!'.
64. Thelwall 1795: 4 April.
65. Correlatively, oligarchical councils such as Liverpool's denounced (longstanding) reassertions of right by freemen citizens as 'Jacobinical'. Sweet 1998: 108.

and the proliferation of corresponding societies across the country shows their success in doing so. Corresponding societies, as well as asserting a concept of citizenship, invented a space in which to rehearse it. They aspired to insert both within the state. Although they never succeeded, in their attempt they brought together, unequivocally, and for the first time in English history, the concept of active citizenship as a practice and condition of liberty, ascribed extensively to members of the state and not merely to those of a town or city – and the very word *citizen* itself.

VI

The 'citizen', or 'freeman', was originally an office-holder within a civic or occupational corporation, in virtue of which he acquired certain freedoms. But the English citizen, unlike his Aristotelian or Ciceronian counterpart, was not conceived of as entering a realm of freedom by virtue of his office-holding; rather the freedoms he enjoyed were specific freedoms, privileges (commonly described as such), exemptions from the presumptive and widespread constraints endured by non-freemen. Further, the freedoms they possessed were those required to discharge the duties of their office. Freedom was a range of discretion related to office.

If this is right, then any temptation – which a conceptual history approach suggests – to yoke the practice-base of early modern office-holding to the presence of a discursive conception of classical citizenship as a realm of freedom and a definitive quality of persons needs reining in considerably. For what office brought to the office-holder was not freedom as a quality of his person, but particular freedoms as a consequence of his role.

This brief survey suggests that a similar trajectory was described by the history of the concepts of both citizenship and liberty. The universalisation of the concept of citizenship from denoting those possessing particular roles and responsibilities in corporate bodies, to anyone (or at least any male one) seems to be paralleled by the way liberty moves from connoting particular liberties entailed by the possession of office, to connoting an abstract and universal liberty connected with an abstract and universalised concept of the person. The treatment of the early modern claim that freedoms were 'chartered' reflected this shift. The Brady controversy between Whigs and Tories over the collective and immemorial or royal origins of representative institutions was repeated at local level; at the national level it gave rise to ideologically charged histories, but locally to local corporations.[66] Tom Paine's

66. Sweet 1998: 105 lists many such histories.

famous rejection of chartered freedoms as exemptions from a presumed structure of subordination was a redeployment of the ancient constitutionalist presumption, pointing out as he did that they created the subordination of the unprivileged: 'it is a perversion of terms to say, that a charter gives rights. It operates by a contrary effect, that of taking rights away. Rights are inherently in all the inhabitants; but charters . . . leave the right by exclusion in the hands of a few.'[67] T. B. Oldfield's influential *History of the Boroughs* agreed, since the franchise had originally extended to all householders; the 'granting' of charters purporting to create that right were 'political injuries against the whole body of boroughs unchartered, that had an equal claim'.[68]

This presumption of universal liberty is not, however, an incremental change in the *concept* of liberty, but a gestalt-like reversal. The change is not merely to universalise the class of (initially male) persons in possession of particular liberties, but to move from liberties as a description of particular positive, legally (or customarily) defined permissions to a specific range of actions, to liberty as an ascription of a presumptive right of action. Whilst the concept of liberty as a legal condition – in opposition to slavery or villeinage – became, as the latter conditions ceased to exist, something universally claimed; the liberties personally enjoyed by individuals were still commonly related to specific offices or roles.

The idea that early modern liberties were office-dependent is not a particularly new one.[69] But the extent to which this constrains and limits the *concept* of liberty available is not always acknowledged. It can still seem possible to conceive of early modern actors with access to a concept of unconstrained personal liberty, of which liberty of office can be thought of as granting, as it were, small parcels or *quanta*. Accumulating enough of these, it might be thought, could create a *plenum* of liberty in the modern sense. Such, after all, was the process by which the emperor had acquired his.

But that this is not, at least initially, the case, is clear from the evident and interminable casuistry as to how we should understand the 'freedom' of the one individual who, it might be thought, had accumulated all the available parcels of liberty – namely the absolute monarch. For the distinction between monarchy and tyranny – retained by all but one of even the most absolutist theorists of monarchy – is surely unsustainable without a conception that freedoms, even all of them put together, are there to discharge duties and not to evade constraints. The exception, of course, is Hobbes, and it is no accident that for Hobbes liberty is not distinctively human (in either the

67. Paine 1969: 242. 68. Oldfield 1792: 111. 69. Condren 2006: ch. 3 *passim*.

classical or the Renaissance sense) at all, and certainly not conceptually tied to the *telos* of office. Rather it is the persistence of nature into the artificial world of politics; and significantly, Hobbes's sovereign is the one individual who retains this natural liberty. If this is right, the effrontery with which Hobbes entitles Chapter xxx of *Leviathan*, '*Of the* OFFICE *of the Sovereign Representative*', is one of his more startling rhetorical coups, quite on a par with (and not unrelated to) his rhetorical re-description of liberty as the absence of external impediment.[70]

If office-dependent liberties were not parcels of natural freedom, how are they to be conceived? One of those who has pressed most insistently their distinctiveness has been Conal Condren. He claims that although:

> liberties of office could be as strenuously defended as are liberties now . . . the very terms through which liberty of office was delineated and defended takes us to a world of semantic and conceptual relationships rather alien to our own patterns of political discourse.[71]

In such a world the antonym of subordination was not liberty but licence. Not, as Hobbes might have put it, that 'licence was merely liberty misliked', but because licence was dislocated from the structures of moral purpose within which human life and liberties were to be conducted. Crucial to that alien world was the perception not merely that liberty was a (partial and specific) exemption from a structure of authority, but that it was embedded in and held by authority of one (or a body) to whom one was properly subordinate. For early moderns – even though slavery and villeinage had gone – 'No man . . . [was] without office, no aspect of life without rule.'[72] As a result, their concept of liberty, far from being incompatible with subordination and authority, presupposed it. For whilst the liberties one enjoyed in one's office did indeed offer a degree of discretion in performing the tasks incumbent on it, the possession and scope of those liberties was established and delineated by, and could only be vindicated by, a higher authority within which that office, its purpose and necessary discretions were nested. The pursuit of liberty beyond such scope – what Condren calls the 'Luciferic case' – was wicked, licentious and anarchic.

Now it is true that in early modern England ultimately – and in some cases proximately – the higher authority was God; and failing a church that could authoritatively claim to speak in his name, an appeal to vindicate liberty could only be made in prayer, or, as Locke finally acknowledged,

70. I am grateful to Tim Stanton for raising Hobbes's use of the term 'office' here as a problem.
71. Condren 1997: 461. 72. Condren 2006: 54 citing Bohun 1684.

through the contingencies of physical resistance, which, it was hoped, would be providentially superintended. It is at this point – at the end of Locke's second *Treatise* – that we reach, *de facto*, if not quite yet *de iure*, the modern concept of liberty as the presumption in favour of self-legitimating action.

7

Free elections and freedom of speech in English republican thought

ANTTI TAHVANAINEN

I

When Parliament in May 1649 declared England to be 'a Commonwealth and Free State', one effect was to raise with new urgency a number of practical questions about republican theories of government. This chapter will focus on two issues that particularly came to the fore: the role of elections and the significance of freedom of speech. During the 1650s a variety of claims were made about the electoral process and its role in the institutions of popular government. However, elections and their procedures, such as secret voting, have been somewhat neglected as topics of historical study. Partly this may be due to their current almost self-evident status: even when scholars point to the contests about elections in the early modern period, they seem to be taken by surprise by contemporaries' 'reluctance to come to terms with integral parts of the electoral process'.[1] Similarly, much of the scholarship on classical republicanism has emphasised the role of *studia humanitatis*, and rhetoric especially, in creating the virtuous citizens needed to maintain a well-working republic, with less interest shown in the institutional workings of such republics.

For early modern English republicanism, this emphasis has been recently questioned with the claim that the traditional republican emphasis on education was deliberately abandoned in favour of an emphasis on institutional arrangements.[2] However, there are a number of reasons for questioning this argument. First, it is very difficult to find evidence of any republican arguing against, or explicitly disowning, the value of education. Secondly, the relative dearth of writing about education does not necessarily translate into a changed perspective on its value. Thirdly, despite the variety of views on

1. Hirst 1975: 16. For election as selection, see Kishlansky 1986. 2. Rahe 1994: 259.

political institutions, references to education are remarkably similar. The value of learning was a commonplace of the time, shared by political writers across the board, who did not necessarily perceive education and institutional arrangements as alternatives.

Another commonplace in republican theories of the time was the role of natural law. There is much less scholarly interest in this aspect, possibly for historiographical reasons. In the history of political thought, there has been a longstanding tendency to bifurcate early modern political theorists into liberals, following an ontology of natural law and individual rights, and into republicans as participatory collectivists.[3] This dichotomy seems to have more to do with our contemporary ideological divisions than with the historical record. Viewed in context, there is an argument from expediency to explain the frequent use of natural law arguments: as the defenders of the new republic could not easily put forward arguments from custom and tradition to justify the new political situation, it was more reasonable to argue from the perspective of natural law. For reasons that will become apparent, it also played a much more important role than education in helping to understand the variety of institutional arrangements at the time.

We may begin with John Milton's theories on popular government. Unlike his contemporaries, Milton neglected the role of institutions in most of his writings. It has thus been argued that Milton was an 'antiformalist', someone for whom the very idea of dealing with forms of government was to invite dogma into political life. According to this view, Milton was above all a believer in the liberating power of education, freedom from within – thus, 'anti-form'.[4] Nevertheless, this interpretation needs to be qualified, since Milton did write about republican institutions at the end of the 1650s. As to what his preferred form of government involved, it can be concisely described as republicanism in the Isocratean tradition,[5] a form of government where the 'fittest' rule. This meant those chosen not for their inherited status, but for their moral and intellectual capacities.[6] In the second edition of *The Readie and Easie Way*, Milton insisted that the establishment of popular assemblies had always led to a 'licentious and unbridl'd democratie'. Other than asserting the theoretical right of the people to overthrow a government if it became tyrannical, Milton had little time for 'popular remedies' – which included rotation of offices and elections.[7]

3. Pocock 1975. 4. Davis 1993: 265–88. 5. Nelson 2001: 214.
6. For a thorough description of the 'fittest', see Chapter 8, Rosanna Cox in this volume.
7. Milton 1953–82b: VII, 437–40.

It is also unlikely that Milton's choices solely reflected the difficult situation of early 1660, when the risk of monarchy being reinstated through popular elections was topical. Already in his *Eikonoklastes* of 1649, Milton had referred to frequent elections as an ancient liberty, the removal of which amounted to tyranny on the king's part.[8] Nevertheless, while other republicans were willing to advance arguments as to why frequent elections were beneficial, Milton had nothing to say on this point. Accordingly, in Milton's *Readie and Easie Way*, the choice of the fittest is made not through a popular election, but through a series of elections, where those of 'better breeding' choose among the even better sort in several rounds.[9]

It is possible to dismiss Milton's approach simply by arguing that he is not interested in elections since he is an elitist and not a democrat. While undoubtedly accurate, this view is unfruitful, due to the fact that as terms elitism and meritocracy are quite difficult to distinguish from one another – they have a fairly paradiastolic character. It is plausible to argue that to a large extent every form of representative democracy aims at some kind of elite rule, and in the seventeenth-century context this was certainly the case.[10] Consider the case of John Streater, possibly the most popularly oriented republican of the period: according to Streater, a government 'by the better sort of the people, without respect of Nobility or Riches at their constituting' is defined as '*Democratical Government*'.[11] However, these 'better sort' had limited terms in office and were directly elected.

Elitism as such cannot be the only explanation of Milton's attitude. A stronger argument is his claim that elections, rather than being an exercise in liberty, are a grave threat to it. In *The Readie and Easie Way* he claimed that it is better 'that a less number compel a greater to retain their liberty', than 'a greater number, for the pleasure of their own baseness, compel a less most injuriously to be their fellow slaves'.[12] Anything risking a loss of republican liberty would be a risk not worth taking. Nevertheless, this seems to be incompatible with the theory of republicanism as a form of government. If liberty means living in a state of non-domination in a self-governing society (that is, a society where all who are affected by decisions have a say in them), how can that freedom be lost by the very act of establishing a state of popular sovereignty? It cannot, if we assume that all decisions should be made by majority rule. The crucial question is the source of authority: what is the basis of legitimate power in a republic?

8. Milton 1953–82a: III, 408. 9. Milton 1953–82a: VII, 442–4. 10. Manin 1997.
11. Streater 1654: I, 6. 12. Milton 1953–82a: VII, 455.

In Milton's case, it is quite clear that any argument relying on *vox populi vox Dei* as an answer was to be rejected. The voice of God is the voice of right reason and natural law. Milton defended the idea that representatives are chosen on their worth as befits their *dignitas*: through careful selection, not through the popularity contest of elections.[13] There would be no need for vote-counting, since in properly conducted popular councils reason, and not political ambitions, would sway decisions.[14] Allowing people a say in their own affairs was simply not as important as the common good as seen from the viewpoint of reason and natural law. Promoting any system of government, or institutions thereof that might prioritise the quiet peace or legitimacy of the majority, in favour of reason, truth and natural law, would simply be wrong.

In considering the arguments against majority rule, the works of another official propagandist of the new republic, John Hall of Durham, are no less pertinent. Hall's line of argument is similar to Milton's: against monarchical rule, he argued in *Grounds and Reasons of Monarchy* that better solutions to 'Civill matters' would be found 'in a number of choice experienced heads'. And although he referred to a royal coronation, Hall's dismissive remarks are indicative of his views on the authority gained through elections in general:

> As for that formall election and stipulation, who sees not what a vain and ridiculous cheat it is, they coming with swords in their hands to demand the Scepter of a weak and stupid multitude that appears onely to gaze upon the Ceremonies, and whose refusal were ineffectual; but it is a gracious piece of the Caball of *Tyrannie* to deceive the People with Shadows, Fantasmes, and names of Liberty.[15]

Two years later Hall defended Oliver Cromwell's dissolution of parliament and subsequent assumption of power in *A Letter written to a Gentleman*. Again, the similarities with Milton are apparent in Hall's argument for preserving liberty through a state of exception, since 'though *multitude of Counsellors* is strength and safety, yet in *distemper'd* and turning States it is weaknesse and *distraction*'. Hall argued for expediency and did not hesitate to engage in a rhetorical redescription, as 'if you will say that the *Liberty* of the *People* by this meanes is *stifled*, I must tell you again, it is only *suspended*'. The popular liberty was 'a Sword taken out of a *Mad* Mans hand, till he recover his *senses*'. A 'Rationall Man' would not expect 'a *Liberty* of choosing a *Representative*' in such a situation.[16]

13. More on Miltonic meritocracy based on *dignitas* and *auctoritas*, see Cox, Chapter 8.
14. Milton 1953–82a: VII, 414, 427. 15. Hall 1651: 19, 35. 16. Hall 1653a: 12, 15–16.

Hall's most important text for understanding the sources of republican authority is the tellingly entitled *A Stop to the Mad Multitude*. Hall sets 'the Representative of the people' against democracy – contrary to the 'Vulgar Error' of a traditional view that saw them as 'convertible'. Hall concedes that authority would be legitimate in a 'true Democracy', where 'every man whatsoever' has 'a free vote and suffrage' in choosing the government, whose members may be altered 'according to the will and pleasure of the people', and – most importantly – where 'nothing must be done without the joint and mutual consent of all'. None of these things held true in the representative system in force in England, where less than 1 per cent of the population could vote in elections, where the representatives sat indefinitely, and where 'the Majority of voices is sufficient' for elections and legislation.

Hall asserts that although he seems 'to give the Praecedency to Democracy', he does not want to 'derogate from the honour of our old Parliamentary Government'. For practical reasons, true democracy is impossible in 'so great and populous a place as *England*', even if it was feasible in ancient Greek city-states and 'many free Cities, and Cantons at this day, which do still conserve their Liberty by a Democracy'. Representative government does not have the inherent legitimacy of democratic authority, since democracy is not 'established upon power'. According to Hall, representative government relied fundamentally upon force: 'What reason is there, that ninety nine should be forced to take Lawes from an hundred? Is it not from this presumption, that an hundred is like to beat ninety nine?' Thus in principle representative government could not be any more legitimate an authority than rule by a beneficial 'Lord Protector' such as Oliver Cromwell.[17]

What were then the theoretical sources of authority, if democracy was impossible and parliamentary government had been found wanting? There were two directions to take, one of which involved more popular measures, such as voting. This Hall found utterly abominable: 'if Prerogative be once prostituted to the licentious liberty of the giddy Multitude, it will be an hard matter to restore Authority to its due Majesty, and to recall the People to their wonted Obedience, and sobriety'. Outside true democracy, popular measures would only lead to licence. A better option was to rely on the 'choice experienced heads', who would utilise 'that excellent way of judging according to right reason'. The role of the governors was to do what was right for the common good, not what was popular: 'to be forestalled with popular

17. Hall 1653b: 18–19.

opinion, an Error will soon gain as good a reputation . . . as the greatest, and most Demonstrative truth'.[18]

Hall's *A Stop to the Mad Multitude* was written against a text called *Grand Politick Informer* by John Streater. Although that text is no longer extant (it was suppressed), enough of Streater's other works remain to give us a sense of how more popular republican institutions were conceptualised at the time. Like Milton and Hall, Streater founded his political theory on natural law. In *A glympse of that jewel, judicial, just preserving libertie* (1653), he noted that 'All Law and Government originally ariseth from the Law of Nature'.[19] Nevertheless, from the same premises Streater ended up with a very different theory of republican government. Accordingly, he did not receive any remuneration from Cromwell's government, only several jail sentences due to his unrelenting vitriol against Cromwell's rule.

Streater's main ideas can be found in his *Observations, Historical, Political, and Philosophical, Upon Aristotles first Book of Government*. Streater's conception of a free individual and a free state are similar to Hall's 'true democracy', yet he considered representative government to have legitimate authority as well. Everyone should be consulted about 'the good of Societie', and 'if the body be too large to meet in Councel together', then 'all free people ought to be in [Councel] by their Representatives'.[20] The authority of laws can be derived through representation, or to put it in negative terms: 'That is not Law, that is imposed upon a people, when neither they, nor those deputed by their lawful election, have given their consent thereunto.'[21]

Authority is thus derived from consent, which for Streater depends on extreme sensitivity to any use of force or influence, however benign. Consent has to be gained without force, threats of force or being 'over-awed', and even without being 'invited [to] be expecting reward, or fearing displeasure'.[22] These caveats applied to government decision-making as well as individual electoral choices. This is still a republican form of liberty, but one taken to an individualistic extreme. As such, it would seem to be in contradiction with a view of republican polity as one of politically active, virtuous citizens in pursuit of honour gained by the *vita activa*. As Streater's argument shows, however, the ideal of positive participation is not necessarily useful in explaining seventeenth-century English republicanism. Streater is less concerned with political participation than with avoiding dependence on the will of others.

18. Hall 1653b: 24, 30. 19. Streater 1653: 8. 20. Streater 1654: VII, 52.
21. Streater 1654: X, 75. 22. Streater 1654: VIII, 58; X, 75.

Accordingly, Streater's institutional arrangements reflect his great mistrust of 'those in power', who are soon seduced 'by their minions and flatterers'.[23] His aim is to insure that such lust and fallibility are channelled to positive ends. If legislators were not held accountable, if there were no separation of powers, if laws did not check those in power, everyone would be a slave (either to others or to their own lusts), which was in the interest of neither the state nor any individual citizen.[24] The maintenance of popular liberty was possible 'when several intrests are incorporated into the one publick interest'.[25] This same appeal to self-interest was argued in defence of elections and the rotation of offices: without them those in power 'make not laws for the society, but for themselves, and in favour of their interest'.[26]

The role of the self-interested individual thus plays a central part in Streater's republicanism, and is likewise essential to understanding the institutional theories of his fellow republican James Harrington. There is a strand of scholarship that perceives the notion of private interests as antithetical to virtue, so that any talk of interests can be interpreted as a desertion of the republican cause.[27] Similarly, liberal theorists have seen interests as a step towards broader democracy by giving everyone a stake through their legitimate interests.[28] However, the mid seventeenth century saw many republicans interpreting the role of private interests as a guarantee of the supremacy of virtuous politics and the public interest in the republican mode.

In James Harrington's *Oceana*, 'reason of state' equalled 'the interest (or error, as was said by Solomon) of the ruler or rulers'. The point here was not to argue against reason of state simply because it could promote monarchical interest or had monarchical connotations: reason of state could also signify the error of the people.[29] This point has created confusion among scholars, and Harrington's conceptualisation has been seen as inconsistent, his theory as confused.[30] To shed light into this confused state, we need to take into account the moral dilemmas caused by the uninhibited use of the language of interests, in the manner of reason of state theorists. Despite their currency and superficial novelty, the topics of national interest and reason of state were considered within the framework of expediency and moral good, might versus right. In the early modern context, this dispute can be described as the conflict between *honestas* and *utilitas*,[31] and it concerned both political theory[32] and rhetoric.[33]

23. Streater 1654: VII, 52. 24. Streater 1654: XI, 83. 25. Streater 1654: V, 35.
26. Streater 1654: VII, 53. 27. See e.g. Scott 1993: 139–63. 28. Holmes 1990: 284–5.
29. Harrington 1977a: 171. 30. For example, see Gunn 1969: ch. 4.
31. For an overview see Condren 1994. 32. Mautner 2005.
33. Concerning the proper ends of deliberative rhetoric: Cox 1997.

Following Stoic examples, Harrington defined government '*de jure*, or according to ancient prudence' as 'an art whereby a civil society of men is instituted and preserved upon the foundation of common right or interest'.[34] This last 'or' has caused difficulties. It has become a commonplace in the scholarly literature to assert that Harrington equated right, reason, interest and law. In the Stoic approach this is not completely impossible, but few Stoics would have approved of the simple view that whatever brings utility equals good, yet this is what Harrington's line on 'reason is nothing but interest' would seem to indicate.[35]

However, if we look at Harrington's assertion in its narrow context, it does not seem reasonable to conclude that he was promoting an amoral approach. In the 'Epistle Dedicatory' to the *Elements of Law*, Thomas Hobbes had argued 'that they who have written of justice and policy in general do all invade each other, and themselves, with contradiction'. This was because they relied on a dogmatic kind of learning, relying on earlier authority, thus causing 'truth and the interest of men' to collide. Therefore everything could be disputed 'because it compareth men, and meddleth with their right and profit; in which as oft as reason is against a man, so oft will a man be against reason'.[36]

Harrington quoted this line with insouciant recognition that it 'is thought to be a shrewd saying,[37] *but will do no harm*' (my italics). No harm, since not all interests were alike or similar in value – 'for be it so that reason is nothing but interest, there be divers interests, and so divers reasons'. The most important interest, or reason, is of course the common good: 'There is a common right, law of nature, or interest of the whole, which is more excellent, and so acknowledged unto be by the agents themselves, than the right or interest of the parts only'.[38]

Harrington's argument about the nature of the common interest started from the following quotation from Grotius: '*tho it may be truly said that the creatures are naturally carry'd forth to their proper utility or profit, that ought not to be taken in too general a sense; seeing divers of them abstain from their own profit, either in regard of those of the same kind, or at least of their young*'. Harrington used this Stoic idea of *oikeiosis* to emphasise his point that, although self-interest was an acknowledged force in society, it did not lead to the conclusion that everyone should aim only at utility and profit. Even animals could do that

34. Harrington 1977a: 161. 35. Harrington 1977a: 171. 36. Hobbes 1999: 19.
37. This reference, 'And as often as reason is against a man, so often will a man be against reason', in *Oceana*, was missed by the editor, who noted only their italicisation, 'as if H had meant them to be read as a quotation' with 'a Hobbesian flavour': Harrington 1977a: 171n.
38. Harrington 1977a: 171.

much, and sociable individuals could certainly pursue other than purely and immediately self-serving ends.

Given that it was possible to think of other interest than one's own, anyone willing to reflect could also realise that not all private interests universally increase the common interest. In his later works, Harrington elucidated with various examples the existence of 'a common interest of mankind distinct from the parts taken severally'. The reason he gave was that he was expecting his ideas to be controversial since they promised 'more for the people than has bin perform'd by the stoics'. To give a few of his examples: even though thieving may be in the private interest, it can hardly be in the common interest. Or, to be free and not enslaved is a 'common and natural interest' that cannot be reconciled with an individual interest to own slaves.[39]

Harrington's assumption was that people capable of such reflection could be allowed to give their consent through elections. Harrington's elections were a means to aggregate not voters' private interests, but rather their views on the common interest. This set his theory apart from might-makes-right theories new and old, from Hobbes all the way to 'his furious master Carneades'. Thus, against Hobbes, Harrington could seemingly concede a point, while promoting his own: 'if reason be nothing else but interest, and the interest of mankind be the right interest, then the reason of mankind must be right reason'.[40]

Through his appeal to *oikeiosis*, Harrington was thus able to bring together a natural law ideal of right reason with the ideal of popular government. Such a conception of consensual authority would not fall prey to the claims that uneducated masses would not care for the common good, thus needing to be ruled by a technocracy. This conception also allowed him to bypass the claim, familiar from John Hall, that majority rule essentially involved rule by force. Since people were able to look beyond themselves, they would consent to majority decisions in the same way as to anything requiring certainty: 'that which appeared unto the most, is most authentick. And what can you desire more of certainty in a government, than all that certainty which can be had in the world?'[41] Harrington remained adamant in this view even in 1659. Whereas even John Streater in *Government described* argued against allowing free elections that might restore monarchy, Harrington maintained that elections could be allowed since eventually people would see that their true interest lay in a republican form of government.[42]

39. Harrington 1977a: 415, 718. 40. Harrington 1977a: 171–2. 41. Harrington 1977a: 720.
42. Streater 1659a: 17–18; Streater 1659b: 8; Harrington 1977a: 745.

Harrington presented several historical systems of voting – though not always accurately – to argue for the authority of his system of rotation of offices and voting. His version was ultimately based largely on the Venetian system of ballots, which meant among other things secret voting.[43] Although electoral privacy has since become the norm, at the time it was yet another contentious issue for the protagonists of republicanism as a theory of government. From classical authors to modern theorists, a persistent argument has been that the purpose of elections is to make each individual vote for the choice they see as most conducive to the public interest, and there is less chance of this happening in secret voting.[44] Yet Harrington argued for electoral privacy precisely from his understanding of republican liberty: 'the election or suffrage of the people is freest' when done in secret.

Harrington followed Streater in a very individualistic conception of liberty. In the case of voting, there were to be no favours, coercion or intimidation, to 'impair a man's liberty'.[45] Equally, before a vote of approval in the lower chamber of the parliament 'there be no laying of heads together, conventicles or canvassing to carry on or oppose anything', based on the view that then 'all may be done in a free and open way'.[46] As befitted a classical republican, Harrington quoted from Cicero's *Oratio pro Plancio* (6:16), how secret voting was 'a welcome constitution' to the Roman people, as it 'increased the freedom of their judgment'.[47] Anyone accepting bribes would in effect sell his own liberty, and open voting would only allow those skilled in manipulation, bribery or canvassing to exert dominion over others. These problems bring us to our second topic, freedom of speech.

II

If we were to approach free speech simply as a question of a right to free expression, it would become readily apparent that Harrington showed very little interest in such a right in his works. Much of Harrington's writings were ripostes to other authors, but as such they concerned argument at hand, and lacked the common commentary about scandalous publications and whether they should be allowed. Indeed, the only instance where Harrington talked of anything resembling freedom of expression can be found in *Oceana*, in reference to poets and theatres:

43. On the history of electoral secrecy see Buchstein 2000.
44. A recent contribution is by Brennan and Pettit 1990.
45. Harrington 1977a: 180.
46. Harrington 1977a: 281.
47. Harrington 1977a: 180.

> These things among us are sure enough to be censured, but by such only as do not know the nature of a commonwealth; for to tell men that they are free, and yet to curb the genius of a people in a lawful recreation unto which they are naturally inclined, is to tell a tale of a tub.[48]

Certainly, this view of freedom as a lawful recreation, which should not be arbitrarily curbed, fits within the framework of republican liberty. Nevertheless, it is doubtful whether Harrington meant this to be a paean to free expression alone, since the context of poets and theatres has more to do with public morals and the role of women – poets and prostitutes both engage in what comes naturally, effects of which are, to an extent, a matter for policy, but not the most pressing one.[49] The perspective of free speech as a right to freedom of expression is thus very limited, since the priority issue for Harrington and his contemporaries was the role of political rhetoric in free speech.

Harrington included in *Oceana* a conversation between a character tellingly called Epimonus de Garrula, who makes the claim that there was no need for secret voting in parliament, since the debate was conducted as 'sober conversation; a man might know and be known, shew his parts, and improve 'em'. This was related to an argument for promoting purportedly straight-talking, honest conversation as a method of parliamentary debate, as opposed to the use of rhetoric in politics. Garrula claims that this kind of conversation is much superior to the ideal debate of classical rhetoric, as it 'flowed forth into language that... is far better than Tully's; or let anybody but translate one of his orations and speak it in the house, and see if everybody do not laugh at him'.[50]

The response of Lord Archon, the legislator-governor of Oceana, was to point out how 'is it not a strange thing that [the ballot boxes] should be thrown first into the fire by a fair gamester?' It was precisely those skilled in manipulation who stood to gain most from open voting. It made sense for them to feign frankness and plain talk. And even more importantly, in the end it did not even matter whether the anti-rhetorical argument for open truth was made honestly or not, since the dangers involved were not removed. There would always be those 'that are not able to withstand the brow of an enemy, and others that make nothing of this, are less proof against that of a friend'. To ensure a 'fair vote', freely done, open voting was not an option.[51]

48. Harrington 1977a: 354. 49. Harrington 1977a: 355. 50. Harrington 1977a: 242.
51. Harrington 1977a: 244.

Harrington's mistrust of feigned *parrhesia* was a commonplace worry in the seventeenth century, and one which has recently received growing scholarly attention.[52] Undoubtedly this was a period of great anxiety about the ambiguities of language,[53] and this anxiety has been seen as an explanation for the rise of reason of state theory, through the replacement of most symbolic forms of speech. According to this interpretation, interests represented the unconcealed truth, independent from the forms of speech, thus making interest theory a form of rhetoric-free political theory.[54]

From the point of view of freedom of speech, the essential underlying difficulty lay in the nature of *vita activa*: how to present forms of political action that would rely on speech, and yet somehow be arhetorical. This problem was already present in many classical texts, for example in the views presented by Cicero concerning counsel in the *De oratore*. Against the view that societies were founded on the efforts of eloquent men in gathering and convincing the people to renounce their old ways and unite in the pursuit of common good, the character of Scaevola argued that they were 'convinced by the reasoning of the wise' rather than 'snared by the speeches of the eloquent'. For Scaevola, Romulus was an example of someone who founded a commonwealth by 'good counsel and singular wisdom' rather than through eloquence.

Scaevola's role was that of an interlocutor whose views are refuted: his definitions were artificial, as content could not be separated from the form.[55] Nevertheless, this goes to show that, as a paradiastolic trope, the distinction has a long history. The opponents use deceitful rhetoric, flatter, have hidden agendas, whereas proponents give plain, honest, transparent advice. Of course, the proponents could be accused in turn of false frankness.[56] While most of this is obvious for anyone who has ever witnessed political campaigns, it is imperative to notice its presence in academic scholarship as well. Large swathes of scholarly studies transpose our contemporary positions to the seventeenth century: depending on the scholar's own political position, anti-defamation and libel laws are perceived as either methods of repressive state control or as legitimate answers to hate speech. Correspondingly, texts against immorality or in favour of free speech are presented as either educating or manipulating their readers.[57] This is repeated in relation to rhetoric,

52. Colclough 2005 and Richards 2003. 53. For a recent study see Dawson 2007.
54. Luhmann 2000: 101. For a useful recent overview of interest theory, see Malcolm 2007: 92–123.
55. Cicero 1942: ch. 1, 36–8.
56. The intricacies of this issue have even given birth to a whole genre of literature on how to tell a flatterer from a friend.
57. Shuger 2006.

where – ironically enough – it is essentially a reuse of early modern rhetorical techniques: supportable parts are truthful, unsupportable mere rhetoric.[58]

In view of the inherent difficulties of the topics of free speech and rhetoric, that clearly risk turning the study of political thought into mere propaganda, it would undoubtedly be most fruitful to have a methodology that could transcend these problems. While waiting for that, however, there are few points that can be made. One is the historical context of moving from dissent to establishment. Before the establishment of the English republic, the republican position was fairly straightforward: the claim was one of oppressed freemen resisting with brave rhetoric tyrannical monarchs and their flattering courtiers. Having gained power, the republicans had to deal with the same 'flatterers', who would still argue against the republic, but could now claim the mantle of dissenters. And in addition, opposing strands of republicanisms came often in conflict, leading to different solutions by different authors. The second point concerns critical interpretation. During this period, opposing works could both claim to be without rhetoric while being blatantly rhetorical, and claim to represent the public interest. For the early modern readers this was a well-known tactic and it was accordingly common to point it out in any further writings on the topic. It is doubtful whether there are any good reasons for modern scholars to read the same works any less critically.

The last and most important point is the difference between free speech as a rhetorical approach and as a right. The seventeenth century is undoubtedly an unfailing source for anyone looking for eloquent references to free speech as an inalienable right, and the period was certainly an important stage in the development towards such a conception. Nevertheless, free speech was not necessarily perceived as a right. Especially not as a relativist right, which would have instantly been blamed as licence, not liberty. Appeal could be and was made to classical principles for listening to both sides of an argument, and rhetoric as a school subject trained pupils in arguing *in utramque partem*. Yet this mildly sceptical approach should not be confused with the liberal belief in the inherent value of various opinions and the right to air them without official repression. The republican idea of liberty obviously gave strong arguments against the dangers of self-censorship and the instrumental value of holding rulers accountable, but this is not the same as the liberal right to free speech – which does not necessitate a republican form of government.

58. Mitchell 2004.

A case in point is John Milton's approach. His *Areopagitica* (1644) is still considered a canonical defence of free speech. On its title page Milton asserts as 'true liberty, when freeborn men/Having to advise the public may speak free'. Yet left without further restrictions, such free speech would not easily stand the test of liberty as non-domination. From classical literature we can easily find a certain high-ranking Roman trained in Greek philosophy professing 'that in a free country there should be free speech and free thought'.[59] This man, who in addition professed many claims for free speech along the lines of those found in *Areopagitica*, was Tiberius – the bête noire of any classical republican. Which goes to show how freedom of speech within an arbitrary government is, in essence, a cruel joke.

From this point we can consider the argument in *Areopagitica* for preventing pre-censorship, as opposed to banning books afterwards. This is a topic which could give rise to accusations of inconsistency on Milton's part, but looked at from the perspective of the rule of law, there is nothing inherently unfree in accepting censorship based on accepted and non-arbitrary legislation.[60] Yet there remains a republican argument against the dangers of self-censorship: if one is free to publish whatsoever, but can be held accountable for publishing things that the republic does not approve of, would this not encourage everyone to write non-threatening texts? Which would be an essentially slavish approach, one to be avoided. This argument would be valid if one were to accept that there are many truths and that all opinions are of equal value. For Milton, they were not. It needs to be emphasised that Milton's idea of the public sphere is fundamentally different from our relatively recent conception of 'the marketplace of ideas'. This formulation would have been abhorrent to Milton. Truth cannot be a question of voting – it is not a popularity contest.[61] Milton aims to find the right reason, and it and contradicting arguments cannot both be true. In *Areopagitica*, differing arguments need to be sifted in the public arena, but when truth will out, it means that those who are lying or spreading false claims should pay the price. Milton does not want to repress this battle – most of his career is ample testament to that – but the purpose of the struggle is consequential, not valuable for its own sake.

The pursuit of truth and right reason is fundamentally important to understanding the nature of Milton's republicanism, which is supported by the strong premium Milton puts on the value of strong individual 'worthies' willing to stand by the truth, no matter if the world should fall around them,

59. Suetonius 1913: 28. 60. Dzelzainis 2000: 151–8. 61. Milton 1953–82, VII: 414.

as the Horatian adage very popular at the time went.[62] Indeed, where would be the virtue of saying whatever you please, without being willing to stand behind your words? Choosing evil, yet getting off scot-free? That would be licence, which would not reward the honest nor punish the wicked. This is the essential division between the perpetrators of the public debate, false dissemblers and virtuous orators – just to give two examples from a legion of names in Milton's texts. This is a division that Milton presents over and over again in his texts: presbyters, royalists, are called to the task for pursuing falsehoods in their attempts to expurgate the newfound liberty. The issue here is not the renunciation of rhetoric. Milton presents a choice not between truth and rhetoric, but between truth and falsehood: rhetoric can ameliorate truth and help in its propagation, and – unfortunately – give strength to the sophisms of the enemies.

Milton's eagerness to engage in the battle of ideas was shared by most republicans in deed, if not always in words. John Hall's *A Stop to the Mad Multitude* is again a telling example, as it was written against a text that was suppressed, yet one which was extensively reproduced in his own rebuttal of it. At the same time, Hall's stated intentions are far from encouraging for the idea of free speech: 'Of all the many evils which this untoward Age is guilty of, I find none greater, nor more dangerous, than the idle and wanton liberty of the Press.' Obviously the qualification 'idle and wanton' designates a licentious type of liberty, which by definition cannot be true liberty. Hall shared Milton's contempt for 'shallow apprehensions', 'wild fancies' and 'impudence' of writers with diverging views on politics. Yet unlike Milton, Hall advocated a retreat to the 'private sphere'. He did so somewhat unconvincingly, since at the same time he was 'engaged to endeavour at least to set a stop to the easily deluded multitude'.[63] Nevertheless, Hall abstained from making any explicit arguments on the merit of free speech as such: *concordia discors*, tolerance through scepticism, preventing social unrest through 'venting of ill spirits'. Arguments such as these were used by many other republicans – officially employed or not.

The last republican approach to free speech to be considered probably has most affinities with our current positive beliefs. However, when presenting such 'winning arguments', there is all the more reason to guard against merely transposing our present understanding to the seventeenth-century frame of reference. In John Streater's case we can see an appealingly liberal approach

62. On the qualities of the 'worthies', see Cox, Chapter 8 below. 63. Hall 1653b: 2.

to free speech, yet one that was very pragmatic and aware of the difficulties with licence. To begin with, Streater saw free speech as 'natural for all men', as 'Man is a rational Creature, and hath power and is able to judge truly, and aright of all causes and things.' Accordingly, it was the 'Law of nature which ordained speech', the liberty of which 'none ought to be deprived of'. Nevertheless, this did not mean that it was an uninhibited liberty, as there was a caveat: 'provided that it extend not to scandal, and that what is said is spoken with wisdom, gravity, and constancie'.

At the same time, uninhibited and arbitrary censorship was also unacceptable. Even if unimplemented, it risked causing self-censorship – or causing the degeneration of noble speech into servile praise, as the classic Tacitean argument went. When 'a people dare to do no other then flatter and lye, they will flatter and lye'. This insidious effect has close connections with Streater's individualistic conception of liberty as not being 'over-awed' and 'free from fear'. From a pragmatic point of view, the effects of such censorship would mainly be counterproductive, since 'when people are forbid to say that those in power are unjust, they think that they are the more unjust'. Similarly free speech was argued from 'the greatest advantage' to be gained: 'benefit the freedom of Speech will bring to a Commonwealth, and that it is chiefly to detect Injustice and Oppression'. Obviously censorship would only result in shooting the messenger rather than solving the problems, as 'if people have not cause to speak evil of those in power, they will not speak evill of them'.[64]

All these things, together with a plethora of other arguments, paint an impressive picture of the detrimental effects of arbitrary censorship and the political benefits to be gained from free speech. Nevertheless, it did not take away the problems involved with uninhibited free speech and rhetorical ambiguity. Having published such arguments in an issue of the *Observations*, Streater devoted much of the next issue to the abusers of rhetoric and free speech. Whereas his earlier picture had rested much on a view of the natural goodness of people and suspicion of those in power, Streater now adds further caveats to free speech based on the admission of 'those that intend evil, or are of an evil minde'. Such people include demagogues, for whom 'the pretence of publike good is the onely way to carry on a designe for a particular interest', and false prophets, who would induce the people 'to expect happiness in another world, rather then Liberty in this'. For Streater,

64. Streater 1654, VII: 58–62.

'discipline' was justified in such cases, but if unfounded or arbitrary, 'it preserveth not people, but instead thereof brings them into perfect servitude'.[65]

To shed further light on the foundations of Streater's pragmatic approach to free speech, it is useful to consider free speech in relation to forms of government other than republican ones. Streater associates free speech with resistance to tyrants, who 'debar a man of that noble priviledge of Liberty of speech', which is 'his right by nature'. At the same time, he also claims that an absolute monarch would 'be free to permit the liberty of speech', if he ruled well.[66] Considering his strong advocacy of republicanism, this might seem odd on first reading. According to Streater, 'free Commonwealth, is to put a difference between the Legislative power, the Executive power, and judicial power: if either two or all three are joyned in one, it is no other then a tyranny'.[67] If by definition an absolute monarch, even a benevolent one, inherently wields tyrannous power leading to a loss of liberty, how could liberty of speech even exist under such a ruler? The crux of the matter is that, despite the connections and compatibility between republican liberty and free speech, they are not quite the same thing. Republican liberty is a question of status, whereas rights and privileges can be either granted or taken, or, if natural, protected or limited by authorities of any kind.[68]

III

As I hope my study has shown, the relationship between rights, democracy, law and liberty was by no means simple in seventeenth-century republican thought. Republican liberty could trump free speech as a right (natural or customary), natural law arguments did not lead into inescapable condition of democracy, nor was democracy a necessary condition of free speech. We find theorists of republican liberty who could not abide the idea of republican self-government, but celebrate free speech, and so forth. Of course, many of these approaches still exist in modern political practice: can an unelected body have legitimate authority; are arms-length organisations the only way to ensure that particular national interests do not destroy the greater common good; what would be the optimal circumstances for open deliberation and

65. Streater 1654, IX: 70. 66. Streater 1654, VIII: 59–60. 67. Streater 1654, XI: 83.

68. A point not lost to Tacitus: the oft-quoted, 'sentire quae velis et quae sentias dicere licet' was, after all, 'rara temporum felicitate' – i.e., a chance, subject to lucky circumstances: Tacitus 1925: ch. 1.1.

voting? I make no claim that the study of seventeenth-century republicanism can give us any new answers to those particular problems. But for understanding our own conditions of liberty in relation to freedom of speech and modes of government, perhaps this attempt to open up the complex web of these matters in the seventeenth century may help us to reflect on our current understanding of the same matters.

8

John Milton's free citizens and the politics of the family

ROSANNA COX

In *The Tenure of Kings and Magistrates* (1649), Milton offers a stark and uncompromising definition of liberty:

> No man who knows aught, can be so stupid to deny that all men naturally were borne free, being the image and resemblance of God himself, and were by privilege above all the creatures, born to command and not to obey.[1]

Interpreting natural law and its manifestation in social contract theory, Milton's argument harmonises with those offered by Parliament to counter Royalist claims that the laws of the land invested sovereignty in the king, whilst Parliament figured as a mere body of counsel. Propounding the key parliamentary argument of *salus populi suprema lex*, in his *Observations* (1642), Henry Parker had located parliament's power in the social contract: although people elect governors because they are social by nature, 'power is but secondary and derivative in Princes, the fountaine and efficient cause is the people'.[2] The development of social contract theory in the period preceding the civil wars is most often associated with the advocates of popular or parliamentary rights, but it was also an important strand of Royalist argument. For both supporters of the king and their opponents, the social contract and its terms, conditions and principles lay at the heart of the debate about England's ancient constitution, the liberty of the people, and the rights and responsibilities of monarch and subjects.[3] Whilst supporters of Charles I

1. Milton 1931–8: v, 8. All future references will be to this edition, unless otherwise stated, and will appear in the text.
2. Parker 1642: 2. See Sanderson 1989: 13.
3. See Sommerville 1999, for a summary of the constitutional debates; see also Burgess 1992; Cromartie 1999; Kahn 2004.

most commonly drew on doctrines of divine and patriarchal right and turned to designation theory to vindicate claims of absolutism, some turned to the social contract to mount a defence of sovereignty on the basis that the people had ceded their authority to the original monarch and, under the terms of this inviolable contract, remained subject to him and his heirs irrevocably.[4] In response to Henry Parker's argument that, as the people had yielded power and authority, so they could take it back, Sir John Spelman replied: 'I should rather think if Regall power were originally conveyed from the people, they by conveying it over have divested themselves of it.'[5]

For Milton, the limits of sovereign power are clear, as are the rights and duties of the citizen. He deploys Parker's argument (and the Levellers' development of the radical potential implicit in it), claiming that the king must be understood as a servant of the people, bound to their service by the vows made at his coronation:

> It follows, that to say Kings are accountable to none but God, is the ouerturning of all law and government... for if the King feare not God... we hold then our lives and estates, by the tenure of his meer grace and mercy, as from a God, not a mortal Magistrate, a position that none but Court Parasites or men besotted would maintain. (v, 11–12)

In making himself answerable only to God, a king heretically assumes the powers of God and renders himself a tyrant and his people slaves. A magistrate, as Milton constructs him, cannot 'hold our lives and estates by the tenure of his mere grace and mercy', since it is contrary to 'all law and government' to imperil or, crucially, to threaten to imperil the independence of the people. Authority is vested in kings and magistrates 'in trust from the people' and, in consequence, they could and should be held accountable by the people in whom 'the power yet remaines fundamentally' for it 'cannot be taken from them, without a violation of thir natural birthright'. He goes on to argue that, according to the terms of the social contract, it is the 'liberty and right of free born Men' to depose their governor as they see fit (v, 8–14).

As he presents his version of the liberty and rights of the people here, Milton appears to be a fully fledged populist. However, as many of Milton's opponents, including Filmer, were quick to point out, when Milton spoke

4. See Sommerville 1999: 9–37. In *De jure belli ac pacis* (1625), Hugo Grotius had argued that a free people might, voluntarily and without reservations, divest themselves permanently of their liberty and independence to a sovereign; in his *Leviathan* (1651), Thomas Hobbes famously develops this idea to argue for unlimited sovereign power on the basis of the social contract.
5. Spelman 1642: 9.

of the people, he often had a much smaller and more select body of men in mind.[6] Indeed, as Milton lays out the terms of liberty, government and the political franchise, he is careful to distinguish between those who are fit to govern and be part of the political process and those who are unfit: 'fitness' being key to understanding Milton's evocation of ideal communities of citizens and, of course, readers.[7] In the first edition of *The Tenure*, Milton insists on distinguishing 'those Worthies who are the soule of' the republican 'enterprize' from 'the throng . . . of Vulgar and irrational men' who stood in their way (v, 3). The crucial decision then, as to whether or not a magistrate is a tyrant, should be left to the 'uprighter sort in whom faction least hath prevaild above the Law of nature and right reason, to judge as they find cause', and not to the people as a whole or even their representatives (v, 7). Indeed, Milton had little confidence in or political use for the multitude; his growing distrust of the people's ability to exercise rational judgement in political matters goes some way to explaining his failure to endorse popular elections.[8] Contemptuous of both 'the blockish vulgar' and his 'inconstant, irrational' and immoral political opponents, he also denies Roman Catholics, Presbyterians and atheists a share in liberty, against whom he is vitriolic in his condemnation (v, 64, 309).[9] It is, rather, 'the choisest and the learnedest', a select band of mature, rational, classically educated, godly and manly men to whom he ascribes the duty of political reformation and the responsibility for political action (III.2, 378).[10] That these ideal citizens might resemble Milton himself (or an idealised version of himself) is hardly surprising.

So who is fit and who is not to be 'upright', to govern? Can men make themselves fit for Milton's ideal state and community? The answers lie in a consideration of Milton's understanding of dependence and independence, of liberty and slavery, of the qualities and virtues (as well as the challenges and constraints) of citizenship. Milton's abiding belief in the power of rational thought, judicious reading and persuasive writing to create, shape and make fit a community of citizens is nowhere more evident than in his evocation and validation of the godly, rational and classically educated individual who confronts the irrational impediments of customary authority in the divorce and anti-monarchical tracts.[11] As the opening of *The Tenure* so clearly states,

6. Filmer, *The Originall of Government* (1652) in Filmer 1991: 199; see Rahe 2008: 109–10.
7. See Tahvanainen, Chapter 7 above. 8. See Tahvanainen, Chapter 7 above.
9. On the limits of toleration in Milton's thought see, for example, Achinstein and Sauer 2007.
10. See Rahe 2008: 109. 11. See Hausknecht 2005: 20.

> If men within themselves would be govern'd by reason, and not generally give up thir understanding to a double tyrannie, of Custom from without, and blind affections within, they would discerne better, what it is to favour and uphold the Tyrant of a Nation. (v, 1)

The capacity for self-government is rooted in both inner moral and spiritual regeneration and outer political transformation: as Milton makes clear in the *Readie and Easie Way* (1660), it is a free commonwealth which is 'the noblest, the manliest, the equallest, the justest government' (vi, 119).[12]

We see these ideas at work in Milton's writings from the early 1640s onwards. It is a reading of Roman law and the classical historians of ancient Rome which colours his thinking and provides him with a powerful vocabulary with which to articulate conceptions of civil and fundamental liberty (this is especially evident in *Eikonoklastes* (1649) and *The Tenure*). But in his divorce and anti-monarchical tracts, Milton's conceptions of civil liberty are most clearly framed by a politics and vocabulary of *masculine* or manly independence. Manliness, as Milton treats it throughout his works, is about being made potent, in terms of desire not for women or for power, but for liberty and for active civic endeavour.[13] Associated with mature reason and judicious political activism, manliness is a civic virtue to be both drawn upon and realised in the fight for liberty. It is also a marker of differentiation between those citizens who are worthy of governance and those who are not. Manhood, in its 'fidelity and ripeness', is about self-governance and independence, about mastery of the self; not all men are manly, not all men reach manhood (iv, 324). However, all men should be independent; since this is the only way that liberty can be achieved and secured.

The terms of liberty are, for Milton, unquestionably rooted in classical and neo-Roman (or republican) conceptions of freedom and unfreedom (and independence and dependence), as Quentin Skinner has argued.[14] As Milton comments in his Commonplace Book, which provides the notes for much of his work and thought during the 1640s, if we want to see 'what Lawyers declare concerning liberty', we should turn to the discussion of freedom and

12. Milton makes a similar point at the opening of *The Doctrine and Discipline of Divorce*, in which he demands that men reject the twin dangers and sever the unholy alliance of 'Custome and Error' (iii.2, 367–8).
13. Hausknecht describes such a process as being 'transformed by desire' although such phrasing suggests a lack of rational control, which is, I think, crucial to Milton's thinking about manliness and potency (Hausknecht 2005: 20).
14. See Skinner 2002a; see also Dzelzainis 1995; 2007; Cox 2007; 2010a. On the use of neo-Roman and classical ideas of liberty in the 1640s, see also Skinner 1998; 2002b; 2008.

servitude in the *Digest* of Justinian.[15] According to the *Digest* of Justinian and the *Institutes* of Gaius and Justinian, all men are naturally born free, a sentiment that, as we have seen, Milton echoes in *The Tenure*. This he makes central to his claim that it is indispensable that we should live in free states. To be free, according to Milton and following Roman law, is essentially to be independent, not to be subject to or dependent upon the arbitrary will of anyone else.[16] It is thus to be in a position to act in one's own right, and not to be the dependent, servant or creature of anyone else. In Roman law, this idea of 'natural freedom' is inevitably limited by legal constraints enshrined by the law of personal status and the law of nations, both of which insist on the distinction between those who are in their own power (*sui iuris*) and those who are subject to the power of another (*alieni iuris*).[17] Those who are *alieni iuri* are slaves, who are continually subject to the will of their master, and children, who are continually subject to the will of their father until he dies – although they are freed from guardianship (*tutela*) when they reach an age at which it is judged that they are able to reason independently.[18] The association of mature manhood and independence is confirmed in the organisation of the Roman household and instituted in law. Although women are *sui iuris* in terms of the laws of nature and nations, they cannot be so termed according to the law of persons because they are, in the household or *familia*, 'subjected to the power of one person', *patria potestas*, who has mastery over the entire household and all persons within it.[19] Virtually all free women were under one of the following three types of legal authority in early Roman law: *patria potestas* ('paternal power'); *manus* ('subjugation to a husband's legal power'); or *tutela* ('guardianship') for those not under *potestas* or *manus*. A woman never became a *paterfamilias*; she did not exercise *potestas* over any other person, though if her *paterfamilias* were dead, she would be *sui iuris*. In the domestic sphere male status was a matter of power resting both on control over other family members and

15. Milton 1953–82: I, 410, 470.
16. For Roman law, the primary sources are, above all, the writings of the early imperial jurists, dating from approximately 31 BC to AD 235. The most important texts, and those referred to by Milton, are Justinian's *Digest* (a collection of edited excerpts from other legal writings), *Institutiones* (an elementary textbook) and *Codex* (a collection of rescripts), along with Gaius' *Institutiones*. The definitions of liberty and slavery are given at the opening of the *Digest*: 'Summa itaque diuisio de iure personarum haec est, quod omnes homines aut liberi sunt aut servi . . . Et libertas quidem est, ex qua etiam liberi vocantur, naturalis facultas eius quod cuique facere libet, nisi si quid aut vi aut iure prohibitur' (Justinian 1985: 1:1:5, 15).
17. Justinian 1995: 1:1:16, 17.
18. Justinian 1985: 1:1:16, 18.
19. Frier and McGinn 2004: 18–20. The Law of Persons does not permit women to be the head of households, except in cases where there is no senior man (see Justinian 1995, 1:1:6, 18).

on mastery and independence of the self. Milton's texts (particularly the divorce and anti-monarchical tracts) test these classical ideas of dependence, independence and *virtus* in locating the terms of liberty in the relationship between the household and the state and, more specifically, in the figure of the householder/citizen.

The analogy between family and state had a long and distinguished history in political philosophy before 1640, although the terms of the relation between the domestic and the political were disputed. Whilst Plato conflated the roles of king, statesman and householder, Aristotle claimed a crucial distinction between families and kingdoms and between fathers and ruler. This difference lay in the separation of household (*oikos*) from polity (*polis*); the government of the household was both of slaves and of free individuals, whilst government of the state was only of free persons.[20] Cicero believed that the family lay at the foundation (or 'seedbed') of the state, 'seminarium rei publicae'.[21] At the beginning of the seventeenth century, Puritan handbooks in wide circulation, such as Dod and Cleaver's *Godlie Forme of Householde Government* (1612), 'enthroned the father as sovereign in the household'.[22] As the Protestant writer and clergyman William Gouge describes it in his analysis of the godly household:

> An household as it were a little common-wealth, by the good government whereof, God's glory may be advanced . . . There are two sorts in every perfect family: (1) the governors; (2) those that must be ruled.[23]

Jean Bodin meanwhile argues that the commonwealth is reliant upon the proper ordering of the family unit:

> Familie is the right government of many subjects or persons under the obedience of one and the same head of the family; and of such things as are unto them proper. The second part of the definition of a Commonweale by us set downe, concerneth a Familie, which is the true seminarie and beginning of every Commonweale, as also a principall member thereof.[24]

In establishing his absolutist credentials, James I had reinforced the importance of patriarchal theory in his *Trew law of free monarchies* (1598), using the metaphor of benevolent fatherhood, but also claiming literally to become father of the people upon his coronation:

20. Aristotle 1996: I, 11–15. 21. Cicero 1991: I, 54, 23. 22. Ng 2007: 2.
23. Gouge 1622: 323. See also Dod and Cleaver 1612. 24. Bodin 1606: 8.

> By the Law of Nature, the King becomes a Naturall Father to all his Lieges at his Coronation: And as the father by his fatherly duty is bound to care for the nourishing, education, and virtuous government of his children; even so is the king bound to care for all his subjects.[25]

But it is Robert Filmer's *Patriarcha*, written in the period before the civil wars, but finally published in the context of the Exclusion Crisis in 1680, which has come to be seen as the definitive statement of absolutist political patriarchalism, as responses by Locke, Tyrell and Sidney brought Filmer and his text to a new and much wider audience. Filmer made explicit and literal the link between fatherhood and sovereignty, consolidating monarchical and paternal power by tracing sovereignty back to the first father, Adam, in an unbroken succession: the authority of Adam was manifested in his having been 'the father, king and lord over his family . . . [to whom a] son, a subject, and a servant or slave, were one and the same thing at first'.[26] Whilst patriarchal theorists tended to focus on the hierarchical relations of fathers and sons, 'fathers are, at one and the same time, husbands'.[27] As Filmer makes clear, Adam's political right stems initially from his right as a husband over Eve: 'if Adam was to become a father, Eve had to become a mother. In other words *sex-right or conjugal right must necessarily precede the right of fatherhood*'.[28] The exercise of conjugal power in the household, by extension, thus provided an equally significant analogy for monarchical rule: King James I, in a speech to Parliament in 1604, the second year of his reign, used the marital metaphor to establish an inviolable, intimate and assuredly hierarchical relationship between himself and his subjects: 'I am the Husband, and all the whole Isle is my lawfull Wife.'[29]

Such absolutist theories of political obligation, which rely on a view of godly household government as predicated upon the rule of fathers over sons and husbands over wives, and stressing rigid authoritarianism, seem at odds with ideas of companionate marriage and affective relations between husband and wife, parents and children. And yet, in many accounts of the godly household, the ideal relations between husband and wife were at once hierarchical and cast as a mutually beneficial partnership, with women and men playing complementary, and equally important roles, as nature

25. Cited by Schochet 1975: 87.
26. Filmer, *Observations Upon Aristotle's Politiques* (1652) in Filmer 1991: 237. On Filmer's theories of political obligation and the history and forms of patriarchalism in the period, see Schochet 1975; Jordan 1993; Sommerville 1999.
27. Brennan and Pateman 1979: 185.
28. Pateman 1988: 87 (emphasis in original).
29. King James I and VI 1994: 136.

intended.[30] As Thomas Smith puts it in chapter 11 of his *De republica anglorum* (1583):

> So nature hath forged ech part to his office, the man sterne, strong, bould, adventerous, negligent of his beautie, and spending. The woman weake, fearefull, faire, curious of her bewtie and saving. Eche of them excelling other in wit and wisedome to conduct those thinges which appertaine to their office, and therefore where their wisedome doth excell, therein it is reason that ech dothe governe. And without this societie of man, and woman, the kinde of man coulde not long endure . . . Which to maintaine for his part God hath given to the man greater wit, bigger strength, and more courage to compell the woman to obey by reason or force, and to the woman bewtie, faire countenaunce, and sweete wordes to make the man to obey her againe for love. Thus ech obeyeth and commaundeth other, and they two togeather rule the house.[31]

The patriarchal view of marriage derived from St Paul's Epistle to the Ephesians is central to the Protestant idea of the relations between men and women and the wider significance of the domestic life:

> 5:22 Wives, submit yourselves unto your own husbands, as unto the Lord.
>
> 5:23 For the husband is the head of the wife, even as Christ is the head of the church: and he is the saviour of the body.
>
> 5:24 Therefore as the church is subject unto Christ, so let the wives be to their own husbands in every thing.
>
> 5:25 Husbands, love your wives, even as Christ also loved the church, and gave himself for it.

Protestant reformers took this Pauline notion of marriage to stress the duties of both women *and* men in marriage: thus women should yield to their husbands, but men must cherish their wives. A husband's conjugal power is assured, but he must always take care to show moderation and restraint in exercising his domestic authority; the conduct books warned against domestic tyranny since it was liable to destabilise the household and lead to rebellion and revolt.[32] It was in and through reciprocity, responsibility, mutual

30. The depiction of the family as rigidly hierarchical of Stone (1977) has been challenged by Houlbrooke (1984), amongst others, who argues that relations between family members were often more affectionate than Stone allows.

31. Smith 1583: 11–12. 32. Gouge 1622: 396–7; see also Capp 2004: 69–126.

dependence and esteem, exclusivity and spiritual accord that marriage could truly be the image of Christ's relationship with the church. But the godly household must nevertheless have at its head the man, made first in God's image, and most naturally given to be the wiser.

It took John Locke's dismantling of patriachalism as a theory of absolutist political obligation in the *Two Treatises* (1699) to break the analogy between family and state. Targeting Filmer, Locke drew crucial distinctions between public and private and political and domestic authority, thereby separating what he terms paternal power from political power; for Locke, father and ruler are 'things inconsistent' and, whilst a man might have absolute authority over his wife, children and servants in the household, this does not make him supreme ruler in the public sphere.[33] Locke makes explicit the 'inherent dilemma' in patriarchalism and thereby explodes the myth that structures of authority are homologous throughout society:

> For if kings are fathers, fathers cannot be patriarchs. If fathers are patriarchs at home, kings cannot be patriarchs on their thrones. Patriarchal kings and patriarchal fathers are a contradiction in terms. The patriarchalist therefore walks a tightrope. On the one hand he wants to emphasize sovereignty in kings and obedience in subjects, but on the other hand he has to preserve the father's property and freedom.[34]

During the generation before this decisive intervention, however, relations of authority and dependence were scrutinised, debated and re-fashioned as political (and, for Milton, personal) exigencies demanded; the analogy between family and state was shaped and re-moulded for various political ends and in various polemical contexts. For both opponents and supporters of the king, the marriage contract and relations within the household proved to be a powerful analogue for the social contract. For royalists, the marriage contract was an ideal exemplar for the contract between king and subjects, in that both parties freely consented to a contract, which established a relationship of authority and dependence, hierarchical and immutable. Whether or not each party fulfilled his or her marital duties or violated God's ordinances concerning marriage, the relationship between husband and wife remained

33. In his *Leviathan* (1651), Hobbes demonstrates an awareness of the contradictions in the family–state analogy; he uses the analogy but also questions its usefulness, see, for example, Hobbes 1991: 142.
34. Hinton 1967: 294; see also Ng 2007: 222–5; Schochet 1975: 243–67; Hindess 1996: ch. 3. However, whilst Locke insists on a 'voluntary Compact between Man and Woman' as the genesis of the original society, he nevertheless accepts 'that there is a natural foundation for a wife's subjection' (Pateman 1988: 93).

sacrosanct, and resistance (or divorce) could never be justified or alter that relationship. Similarly, the people might freely have consented to establish a monarchy, but the monarch's power once instituted was as permanent and unalterable as that of the husband. Consent once given could not be withdrawn. Royalist writers such as Henry Ferne and Dudley Digges sought to marshal evidence from a variety of sources including Scripture and conduct books to make the case that the people's subjection to the king was as fixed as a wife's subjection to her husband:

> The Jewes could have made this plea, grounded in the nature of a Covenant, the breach of which (though instituted by God betweene King and People, Deut. 17.) was no dispensation for them to Rebell, as was evidenced formerly.... So there is a contract between Husband and Wife, the violation of which on the man's part doth not bereave him of his dominion over the woman. I confesse, a great obligation lyes upon Kings.... And if they abuse their power, God's punishment will be as high as their ingratitude.[35]

Arguments that Parliament held in trust some reserved power with which to hold the monarch to account and to invalidate the contract between him and the people were dismissed as both seditious and ridiculous by Ferne.[36] For both Digges and Ferne, men had willingly consented to the civil compact and had therefore renounced their natural freedom: as Ferne explained it, 'many things which are altogether in our disposing before we part with them, are not afterward in our power to recall'.[37]

In countering these definitions, republican and parliamentarian writers were required to re-think customary ideas about marriage and domestic relations, to disrupt and undermine their opponents' premises. Accepted ideas about hierarchy and the indissolubility of the marriage contract came under scrutiny as the occasion demanded – as did the terms of the familial analogy itself.[38] As Parker argued in responses to Royalist deployments of the family metaphor:

> The father is more worthy than the son in nature, and the son is wholly debtor to the father, and can by no merit transcend his dutie, nor challenge any thing as due from his father... Yet this holds not in the relation between King and Subject, for its more due in policie, and more strictly to be chalenged, that the King should make happy the People, than the People make glorious the King.[39]

35. Digges 1644: 112–13, cited by Shanley 1979: 81.
36. See Ferne 1643a; and Digges 1644.
37. Ferne 1643b: 19, cited by Shanley 1979: 81–2.
38. See Shanley 1979: 80.
39. Parker 1642: 184–5.

In using the marriage contract analogically, however, parliamentarians and republican writers exposed and were exposed to the ideological tensions and volatility of the metaphor: in attempting to provide evidence of limitations to a king's power over his subjects and justifications for resistance, pamphleteers were forced to consider possible limitations to a husband's dominance over his wife and the corresponding rights of women to resist coercive husbands and end their marriages.[40] Such a radical re-visioning of conjugal power (and concomitant extension of the rights argument to women) constituted a step too far for many, resulting in inconsistent and contradictory arguments about the status of men and women in the household.[41] Such debates, moreover, conducted between men in the public sphere, tended to obscure women's active involvement in contemporary political events, as well as the reality of social practice. Although conduct books, marriage treatises and pamphlets of the period proscribed women's activity in the public sphere and stressed their submission to patriarchal authority in the home, women often had more authority than has been acknowledged, given the high number of widowed women and orphaned children.[42] Moreover, during the 1640s, scores of women petitioned Parliament, demanding their voices be heard and acknowledged in the political process, and female members of radical Protestant sects preached in public.[43] Far from being immured from public view and activity and subjected to patriarchal oppression, many women defied any simple separation of 'public' and 'private' spheres, as social practice diverged from the ideal principles of womanly conduct as determined by writers like Dod, Cleaver and Gouge.[44] In debating the terms of liberty, however, and tussling over the familial metaphor, supporters of the king and parliamentarians alike depended on the idea that men and women were, as Milton famously puts it in *Paradise Lost*, 'Not equal, as their sex not equal seemed': as Aristotle had argued, a woman's virtue lay in subordination to a man and was justified in nature, *aretē hyperetikē*.[45]

For Milton, the stakes could not have been higher in wresting control of the language and terms of the debate about political and familial obligation: committed to republican liberty and to making the case for a free commonwealth, Milton was also, by virtue of his own disastrous marriage, convinced

40. Palmer 1643: 35–6. On analogical thinking in this period, see Sharpe 1989.
41. See Shanley 1979: 85; Kahn 2004: 58–79; Shaffer 2004: 54.
42. See Ezell 1987: 18.
43. See Stone 1977: 225–6. On the political status and public interventions of Leveller women see Hughes 1995: 162–88; see also Achinstein 1994.
44. See for example, Ezell 1987: ch. 2; Amussen 1998.
45. Milton 2007: book IV, line 296; Aristotle 1996: book I; see Jordan 1993: 312. On the portrayal of marriage in *Paradise Lost* see, for example, Turner 1994 and Luxon 2004.

that the liberty of divorce was a fundamental constituent of true liberty. Milton's own first marriage was notoriously unhappy. In 1642, at the age of 34, he married the 17-year-old Mary Powell, daughter of one of his father's debtors; they were almost immediately estranged as she went back to Oxford and to her family. It was at this stage that Milton re-directed his energies from campaigning against the bishops in his anti-prelatical tracts, to arguing for a reformation of divorce laws and for incompatibility to be included as grounds for divorce, alongside grounds such as sexual offences, impotence, physical cruelty and consanguinity.[46] Despite an eventual reconciliation, the effects of this separation upon the newlywed Milton were undoubtedly momentous: the personal and the political coalesced to powerful rhetorical effect in the divorce and anti-monarchical tracts.

Milton locates the liberty of men as rooted in the household, couching the liberty of the people in terms of household (and indeed land) management: A nation, he says, 'has only ridiculous and painted freedom, fit to coz'n babies', if

> wanting that power which is the root and sourse of all liberty, to dispose and *œconomize* in the Land which God hath giv'n them as Maisters of Family in thir own house and free inheritance. Without which natural and essential power of a free Nation, though bearing high thir heads, they can in due esteem be thought no better than slaves and vassals born, in the tenure and occupation of another inheriting Lord. (v, 40)

The *OED* cites Milton's as the first use of *œconomize*, meaning 'to act as governor of a household', but this passage is also significant for the competing definitions of freedom and servitude, of independence and dependence which Milton accesses to make his point about liberty, the state and the household. Milton here references classical ideas of liberty and slavery, likening dependent and hamstrung heads of households to unfree babies and implying that the fact of living in dependence on the goodwill of others is enough to reduce men to servitude. But, as Fenton points out, he also references common law arguments, invoking '*vassalage* for its suggestion of atavism, back-stepping towards feudal obligation and subjugation of individual liberty'.[47] It is to the head of household, 'the maister of the family', that Milton turns his attention in his attempts to shape a republic of citizens. Individual liberty is dependent upon self-directed management of the household and its dependents

46. See Campbell and Corns 2008: 150–75. 47. Fenton 2003: 154.

and property; the self-esteem gained through the exercise of such authority is crucial to promoting civic activity.[48]

Throughout his works, and as a particular focus of his divorce tracts, Milton seeks to restore self-esteem, potency and independence to men in their households: such freedom allows men to bear 'high their heads' and thereby maximise their potential for active citizenship.[49] As he argues in *Tetrachordon* (1645), 'nothing now adayes is more degenerately forgott'n, then the true dignity of man, almost in every respect, but especially in this prime institution of Matrimony, wherin his native pre-eminece [*sic*] ought most to shine' (IV, 74). Milton considers the relationship between companionate marriage and Pauline patriarchalism and finds that, whilst there may be exceptions to such a rule, the man is likely to prove the wiser and therefore has ultimate jurisdiction and sway over the household, which becomes his territory and estate:

> But *St. Paul* ends the controversie by explaining that the woman is not primarily and immediatly the image of God, but in reference to the man . . . Neverthelesse man is not to hold her as a servant, but receives her into a part of that empire which God proclaims him to, though not equally, yet largely, as his own image and glory: for it is no small glory to him, that a creature so like him, should be made subject to him. Not but that particular exceptions may have place, if she exceed her husband in prudence and dexterity, and he contentedly yeeld, for then a superior and more naturall law comes in, that the wiser should govern the lesse wise, whether male or female. (IV, 76–7)

The exceptions that Milton permits mark a significant departure from the conventional wisdom of Stuart marriage advice manuals; his treatment of household organisation asks important questions of customary assumptions and insists that reason must determine fitness to lead and govern. Milton's ideal household then is, at least in theory, a meritocracy. However, Milton continually retreats from this radical re-visioning of the household and reverts to a familiar understanding of masculine identity. The dignity and self-esteem of man in his household depends upon a hierarchy that places woman as 'subject' to him. And yet, at the same time, this manly self-assurance

48. On the relationship between male status and property and self-sufficiency in the period see Shepherd 2000.
49. Milton's conception of male dignity and its relation to self-esteem should be understood in the context of the Roman traditions of *dignitas* and *auctoritas*, of reputation, status and ethos, rather than in the Kantian sense of unalienable intrinsic human worth; I am grateful to Antti Tahvanainen for this point.

should also derive from a man's recognition of the glorious virtues of his wife, as it could *not* do from mastery over a servant. Milton's 'exceptions' which allow a woman to rule over a man if she surpasses him 'in prudence and dexterity' depend absolutely on the complacent agreement of her husband who, even if he delegates responsibility for household management to his wife, nevertheless remains the ultimate authority in the household.

And so Milton turns to St Paul to suggest that an unhappy marriage causes and is simultaneously caused by a subversion of the natural and proper hierarchy of the household:

> What an injury is it after wedlock not to be belov'd, what to be slighted, what to be contended with in point of house-rule who shall be the head, not for any parity of wisdome, for that were something reasonable, but out of a female pride. *I suffer not* saith S. Paul, *the woman to usurp authority over the man.* (III.2, 475)

This idea of marriage as companionate, but which positions men as the heads of their households, is central to Milton's view of the relations between the sexes and lies behind the four tracts he wrote on divorce in the 1640s.[50] Although he claims that his proposals for divorce are 'TO THE GOOD OF BOTH SEXES', as set up on the title page of the tract, marriage and divorce are generally understood throughout as for the benefit of men and, more specifically, central to their psychological well-being.[51] Marriage is there to provide a 'solace', a 'fit help', a 'consort' to a man who would otherwise be 'solitary' and 'lonely'. In a faulty marriage, it is the woman who is usually responsible for the fault: 'the bashfull mutenes of a virgin may', Milton claims, with his own experience in mind, 'oft-times hide all the unlivelines and naturall sloth which is really unfit for conversation'. Men who are forced to endure such misery are portrayed as having been 'train'd by a deceitfull bate into a snare of misery' (III.2, 395, 399, 382, 405). And yet, despite the impassioned and polemical language and the 'spurre self-concernment', which it betrays (III.2, 371), Milton's personal commitment to the reformation of divorce legislation is, at the same time, a commitment to liberty. In fact, as Milton writes in 1654 in the *Defensio secunda*, the right to end an emotionally and spiritually barren marriage was a primary constituent of domestic liberty, which was itself an integral part of 'real and substantial liberty' (VIII, 131).

50. For an overview of Milton's portrayal of marriage in the divorce tracts, and in *Paradise Lost* and *Samson Agonistes*, see Cox 2010b.
51. On Milton's views on the rights of women to divorce, see Biberman 1999.

In his writings on marriage and divorce, ideas of manliness and effeminacy, liberty and slavery, and independence and dependence are at the heart of Milton's arguments. In the subtitle to the first and second editions of *The Doctrine and Discipline of Divorce*, Milton claims that divorce can replace the current bondage of canon law with 'Christian Freedom', provided the Westminster Assembly and Parliament (to whom the book is addressed) are prepared to reconsider what constitutes 'the tenure and free-hold of mankind' and the rights and liberties of men (III.2, 375). Marriage, as Milton states clearly, not only is the bedrock of family relations, but simultaneously is the basis of civil society in that it institutes the relations between fathers, sons and brothers, that is, between male citizens. The household is the arena and training ground in and upon which men can prepare both themselves and their sons for civic activity. Whilst Milton insists on the contractual, rather than sacramental nature of marriage, it is nevertheless more than a private arrangement between consenting partners and thus must be recognised for 'its public and societal components; it enables both civil society as well as religious community'.[52] For Milton domestic 'œconomy' is simultaneously both *analogous* and *homologous to* government and is *a part of* government: the family or household unit epitomises in microcosm the hierarchy of the state, and the way it should (and should not) be governed. Men who do not have mastery in their households, who are not *sui iuris*, will be faulty citizens and make correspondingly faulty political decisions:

> For no effect of tyranny can sit more heavy on the Common-wealth, then this houshold unhappines on the family. And farewell all hope of true Reformation in the state, while such an evill as this lies undiscern'd or unregarded in the house. On the redresse wherof depends, not only the spiritfull and orderly life of our grown men, but the willing, and carefull education of our children. (III.2, 375)

The tyranny that prevents men's household agency thereby nullifies their civic agency. Men who have not the spiritual and emotional ballast of happy marriage are useless to society; 'unserviceable and spiritlesse to the Common-wealth' (III.2, 501): dysfunctional marriage 'degenerates and disorders the best spirits, leavs them to unsettl'd imaginations, and degraded hopes, careles of themselvs, their houshold and their friends, unactive to all public service, dead to the Common-wealth' (IV, 129). The subversion of the proper hierarchy in the home, which is often attributed to a 'bad wife' (III.2, 475),

52. Ng 2007: 166.

combined with a forced submission to tyrannous laws, which prevent a severing of the dysfunctional relationship, is construed as directly related to, and even responsible for, failure to reform the state. The inability of men to legislate in their own households does not simply render them unfree, it also has a devastating effect upon their self-esteem, masculine identity and potential for acts of civic greatness. Husbands who, as Milton describes them, and with an unambiguous reference to Samson, 'grind at the mill of an undelighted and servil copulation', are enslaved but are also slavish; through 'Custome and Error' they become habituated to a life of servitude and lack the requisite manly civic potency to shake off their shackles (III.2, 367–8).

In *The Tenure*, Milton ridicules the Presbyterians who had recently refused to accept the right of Parliament to put the king on trial as 'slaves within doors' (V, 1). Rather than being 'govern'd by reason', these men are, according to Milton, governed both by passion and by their wives at home: their failure properly to enact their conjugal power in the domestic sphere, to assert the correct hierarchy of man over woman (and, simultaneously, of reason over passion), means that they are *alieni iuri* – under the power of another, and therefore enslaved. They suffer from what Milton terms in *Paradise Lost*, 'effeminate slackness' – a charge that is levelled at Adam's disordered relations with Eve and his failure to control his passion for her.[53] In *Eikonoklastes*, Milton argues that the king himself is as emasculated as many of his subjects, with even more disastrous ramifications:

> Examples are not farr to seek, how great a mischeif and dishonour hath befall'n to Nations under the Goverment of effeminate and Uxorious Magistrates. Who being themselves govern'd and overswaid at home under a Feminine usurpation, cannot but be farr short of spirit and autority without dores, to govern a whole Nation. (V, 139)

Here Milton suggests not only that Charles I and his counsellors have failed to assert themselves as masters of their households and have thus been emasculated by their wives, but that their passions have led them into voluntary servitude: they are both 'effeminate' or unmanly and 'uxorious'; that is, they luxuriate wantonly in their perverted marital relations. Milton's proposition that the relationship between Charles I and Henrietta-Maria was dysfunctional due to an inversion of traditional gender hierarchies was not a novel charge during this period.[54] Here, Milton makes his case against the royal household and the court using notions of freedom and servitude, related to

53. Milton 2007: book XI, line 634.
54. See, for example, the Royalist *Parliament of Women* 1646 and Neville 1647.

and informed by neo-Roman legal arguments and the writings of the Roman historians: 'Those *alieni iuris* were in the power of some other person. Those *sui iuris* were independent and not under the power of another: they must therefore be heads of families (*patresfamilias*).'[55] The accusations which Milton levels at the supporters of the king (and the king himself) is that they are enslaved because they fail to act as heads of their households or *patresfamilias*; they are not independent (*sui iuris*), but are in their wives' power. Moreover, in succumbing to passion (and thereby abandoning reason), they have proved themselves incapable of rational self-rule and are thus unqualified to rule the people.

Milton's denunciations of Charles I and his ministers as both tyrannical and effeminate derive from a variety of classical sources. According to histories of the fall of Rome – which profoundly influenced Milton's thinking about the effects of living under tyranny, and inspired his belief that the emerging commonwealth would be 'another *Rome* in the west' – tyranny revealed itself in effeminacy (VI, 118). In Sallust's *Bellum Catilinae*, for example, effeminacy is shown to be both a cause and a consequence of the loss of *virtus* and moral debasement of Rome and is linked with the pursuit of luxury.[56] The privileging of sexual over civic interests, rather than enhancing masculinity, actually nullifies it: 'Nay more, the passion which arose for lewdness, gluttony, and the other attendants of luxury was equally strong; men played the woman.'[57] For Sallust, and for Milton, *virtus* is the quality which exemplifies a *vir*, a man.[58] Challenges to *virtus* are thus also necessarily challenges to masculinity, and are therefore effeminising. The reckless abandonment of civic endeavour in favour of *luxuria* is shown by Sallust to be a movement from manliness to effeminacy, as men become women and women become men through their pursuit of sexual pleasure. Sallust is here suggesting not only the practice of homosexuality as evidence for waning morals, but also that passivity is inherent in a society which has discarded *virtus* in favour of *luxuria*, and that manliness is a quality of the mind rather than the body. For Milton 'true manliness' lies both in judgement and in

55. Harris 1899: 37. Whilst in the time of Gaius being in the state of *alieni iuri* (i.e. in the right or power of another) was divided into two further parts – *in manu*, or in subjection to a husband, and *in mancipio*, or in bondage – the Laws of Justinian recognised only freedom (*sui iuris*, or the state of being able to act in your own right) and unfreedom (*alieni iuri* or the state of being subject to the right of another).
56. On the place of *virtus* and its relation to liberty in the republican tradition, see Pocock 1975; Skinner 2002a.
57. Sallust 1920: XII, 22. On ideas of manliness and effeminacy in Sallust, see Weiden Boyd 1987.
58. See Hausknecht 2005: 19–33 and Cox 2010a. On the relationship of manliness and *virtus* in the Roman republic, see McDonnell 2006.

rational mastery of the self and not, as we might expect, in sexual activity with women. Those like the king, who fail to assert themselves in their households and who abandon themselves to the sensuous pleasures of feasting and revelry, to sexual gratification and to an uxorious reliance on their wives, are to be despised as passive, effeminate and unmanly, as voluntary slaves.[59]

The radical political ramifications of these arguments are clear, as are the analogies upon which they depend. The king and his ministers cannot rule the state because they are unable to master their own households; they are not truly manly men and are thus not suitable to rule. Their effeminacy is a consequence of an unwary submission to passion and concomitant abandonment of reason; their behaviour sets a terrible example to their people. In Milton's reconfiguration of the marital relationship as a covenant or contract between two people, rather than a sacrament – a bond instituted for the good of (the) man – the dissolution of the relationship should be permitted if the relationship had failed in its purpose. Milton's arguments about marriage and divorce provide a model and a powerful analogy for contesting the king's relationship with the state, and possible ways of severing it. As Milton writes in *The Doctrine and Discipline of Divorce*: 'He who marries, intends as little to conspire his own ruine, as he that swears Allegiance: and as a whole people is in proportion to an ill Government, so is one man to an ill mariage' (III.2, 374). In making his case for divorce, Milton borrows extensively from natural law theories and from Parliament's use of natural law arguments in arguing for the social contract between the people and their governors; in demonstrating the intimate ideological relationship between the household and the state, Milton argues that, just as the marital relationship between the governors and the governed in the household should not be indissoluble, neither should that between king and subject in the state.[60] The continuation of tyrannical rule, like the continuation of an unhappy or 'unmeet' marriage, makes an idol of the outward ceremony of the contract, thereby elevating the agreement above the good of the people involved:

> So when it shall be found by their apparent unfitnesse, that their continuing to be man and wife is against the glory of God and their mutuall happinesse, it may assure them that God never joyn'd them; who hath reveal'd his gracious will not to set the ordinance above the man for whom it was ordain'd. (III.2, 424)

59. On Milton's denunciations of luxury, see also Knoppers 2010.
60. On Milton's use of natural law arguments and social contract theory, see Ernest Sirluck, 'Introduction' in Milton 1952–83, II: 153–8; Kahn 2004: 196–207.

Household freedom, and the ability to determine his own happiness in marriage, lies at the heart of a man's liberty in that it is integral to, and emblematic of, the exercise of rational self-rule, citizenship and thus to securing a flourishing commonwealth.

In both his divorce and regicide tracts, then, Milton establishes a distinctively republican analogy between household and state in order to contest royalist, patriarchalist arguments and customary defences of the king as a father of the nation. Milton's attempts to refute presentations of Charles I as a benign father-king involve a re-imagining of the king both as a tyrannous patriarch whose sway over the lives of his children-subjects renders them slaves and as an effeminate, unmanly slave himself. In the *Readie and Easie Way*, Milton castigates those who would submit to the tyranny of the rule of a monarch, after all that had gone before:

> And what madness is it, for them who might manage nobly their own affairs themselves, sluggishly and weakly to devolve all on a single person; and more like boyes under age then men; to committ all to his patronage and disposal, who neither can performe what he undertakes, and yet for undertaking it, though royally paid, will not be thir servant, but thir lord? how unmanly must it needs be, to count such a one the breath of our nostrils, to hang all our felicity on him, all our safetie, our well-being, for which if we were aught els but sluggards or babies, we need depend on none but God and our own counsels, our own active vertue and industrie. (VI, 122)

Not only are those who 'devolve' responsibility for their lives to a monarch 'unmanly' in that they are emasculated and effeminised, they are also cast as having failed to attain the state of mature manhood – they are mere 'boyes under age' or even 'babies'. This state of immaturity, engendered through disordered service to an incapable proxy, prevents citizens from enacting their own *virtus*, which is a condition of liberty and a signifier of maturity. In entrusting the management of their affairs to such an individual, the people demonstrate a lack of reason and render themselves infantile, incapable of active, muscular citizenship.[61] In Milton's republican version of the household, he claims authority for men not on the basis of fatherhood, but on the basis of virtuous and potent *manhood*. This is, I think, a moment when Milton's version of republican liberty diverges from his Roman law sources as part of his polemical agenda. Whilst Roman law insists on the

61. See Cox 2010a: 15; Dzelzainis 2007: 57–67.

power of the father, on *patria potestas*, in the household, Milton is determined to reconfigure the household such that it is the truly manly man (the *vir virtutis*) rather than the father to whom power most properly belongs. Milton denies the king and his ministers their masculine authority rather than their patriarchal authority and thereby reconfigures the terms of the debate. In this way, 'Milton gives family metaphors republican meanings to counter the king's portrait of family relations.'[62] Instead of the image of the 'royal father-god'[63] and the people as his children, Milton idealises *husbands* as manly citizens, and marriages that enable an independent and potent community of citizens who can set about the task of constitutional reform with the necessary vigour, industry and purpose. It is in mastery of the household estate, in the proper ordering of the hierarchy of man over woman, and in mastery of the self that true citizens can assert their liberty and become active participants in the emerging commonwealth. And yet, in this distinctive formulation of the family, Milton distinguishes between mastery based on virtuous superiority and tyranny based upon arbitrary and customary conditions; his husbands are rational, virtuous, upright and manly citizens rather than tyrannous patriarchs.

For Milton, liberty and civic virtue are inextricably linked and both are gendered as male.[64] But what, then, are the ramifications of such thinking for the rights and liberties of women? In a key passage in *Tetrachordon*, Milton's deep and abiding belief in justice and liberty extends to women's rights in the household: 'The law is to tender the liberty and human dignity of them that live under the Law, whether it bee the mans right above the woman, or the womans just appeal against wrong, and servitude'; an 'enthrallment' to one with whom it is impossible to be companionable is 'the ignoblest, and the lowest slavery that a human shape can bee put to' (IV, 121). Justice, rational debate and the charitable application of law liberate people from bondage; women have the potential to be as deserving of such an emancipation as men. This is where, perhaps, we might begin to think of Milton's critique of customary forms of household and political arrangements as seeming to allow a partial advance in thinking surrounding women's rights in the family and in political society.[65] However, whilst Milton is prepared to acknowledge women's claim to liberty and dignity in marriage, he pulls back from

62. Ng 2007: 59. 63. Cable 1995: 150.

64. Gina Hausknecht suggests that whilst liberty is, for Milton, gendered, it is not sexed; that is, it is available to all who have a claim on it, regardless of sex. However, Milton consistently pulls back from this position, reinforcing the links between liberty and civic activity and manliness; see also Woods 1998.

65. See Schaffer 2004.

an unequivocal endorsement of women's rights since his notion of male self-esteem and civic vigour is dependent upon traditional gender hierarchies and, crucially, the language and values associated with such hierarchies. The true purpose of marriage, as Milton sees it, is the role it plays in preparing a man for civic action and in promoting and safeguarding his autonomy, independence and rational masculine identity. Milton's validation of companionate marriage does not concern men and women forging a bond to sally forth together in emotional and civic unity; it lies in promoting the right circumstances for men to be manly, independent and politically active in shaping the emergent commonwealth. And it is a notion of manliness or masculinity which is hard to pin down precisely because Milton employs it with typical strategic slipperiness: to be manly is synonymous throughout Milton's texts with 'doing the right thing', for example, reading like a man, divorcing like a man, ruling like a man, rejecting custom like a man and so on. At times these ideas of manliness are articulated through classical discourses and with specific associations with classical ideas of liberty; at other times these definitions recede or are bent and shaped to a particular polemical purpose. But in all cases being manly means being active and such activity is profoundly dependent on thinking like a man, and indeed *thinking like Milton*. And so the kind of manliness being promoted in the first instance is that not of the body, but of the mind. The right state of mind is absolutely crucial to any undertaking, a condition of doing the right thing, of gaining and realising political power and civic potency. For Milton, 'native liberty' is synonymous with 'true manliness'; it is in the exercise of legitimate authority, and the ability to distinguish the limits and conditions attached to it, that the people can show and fashion themselves fit to be both free and manly.

9

Vattel's Rousseau: *ius gentium* and the natural liberty of states

THEODORE CHRISTOV

I

Central to early modern discourses on the idea of freedom was the proper relationship between the law of nature, *ius naturale*, and the law of nations, *ius gentium*. The former dictated an active pursuit of a state's preservation in maintaining its natural liberty, while the latter demanded a commitment to a wider humanity in observing international law. This relationship was far from straightforward and, throughout the seventeenth century – from Grotius through Hobbes to Pufendorf – it followed a rather torturous and uneven course, marked by an inherent tension between liberty as independence and obligation as interdependence. At the heart of that tension lay the residue left by Hobbes's unresolved question of whether the construction of a civil state domestically could indeed bring an end to the state of war internationally. Some of Hobbes's earliest critics attacked his reductionist account of the conversion of interests into rights and the grim consequence of its extension to the international sphere.[1] None of those critics, however, attempted to relate systematically the conclusions of Hobbes's natural condition among individuals to that among states, in their capacity as sovereigns among other sovereigns.

It was this failure of the natural jurisprudence tradition that so profoundly affected Kant and led him to indict its main protagonists – Grotius, Pufendorf and Vattel – as 'sorry comforters', who 'have been cited in justification of war, though their code, philosophically or diplomatically formulated, has not and cannot have the least legal force'.[2] Despite a general tendency to regard Kant as the first major thinker to have engaged methodically with the application of Hobbes's conclusions to the international domain, this essay

1. Parkin 2007. 2. Kant 1970: 103.

will suggest that it was his predecessor Emer de Vattel, the last of the 'sorry comforters', who made great efforts to reconcile the relationship between the law of nature and the law of nations. He did so not so much as a direct critic of Hobbes, as had become customary, but rather as a critic of Rousseau, himself one of the most insightful readers of Hobbes in the eighteenth century. While acknowledging that Hobbes, the 'master', was 'the first who gave a distinct though imperfect idea of the law of nations', Vattel quickly departed from his political philosophy. The maxims of the law of nature and those of the law of nations are not identical, as Hobbes had supposed, but must suffer a 'necessary change'.[3] The law of nations required a separate treatment from the law of nature, and it was to Rousseau and contemporary voices of Swiss liberty, rather than to the more distant Hobbes, that Vattel turned for intellectual inspiration.

From the context of mid-eighteenth-century Swiss debates on the natural liberty of small states and the commercial liberty of imperial powers, this chapter will trace two distinct – and ultimately irreconcilable – approaches to accommodating the liberty of states and obedience to the law of nations within an emerging modern European political system.[4] Throughout his writings on war, drafted in the mid-1750s, Rousseau struggled to overcome his own scepticism, but in the end remained trapped in his pessimism about international peace: a permanent state of international war is the price to pay for maintaining states' liberty. It was Vattel, his Swiss contemporary in Neuchâtel, who provided an alternative – and more enduring – vision to Rousseau's deep-seated pessimism, and one that was sensitive to the new political arrangements in Europe at the time. Vattel's solution lay in a profound disagreement with Rousseau over the constitution and character of the state of nature, which had served as a model for conceptualising international relations at least since Grotius.[5] The absence of a Rousseauian *volonté générale* among sovereigns, similar to that among civil men, did not preclude the possibility for adherence to the law of nations. For Vattel such adherence was derived from reciprocal voluntary relationships, in which states enter through *traités publics*, and such public treaties had no strict equivalent at the level of individual men. The liberty of states was not a product of a union of wills, as Rousseau would have it, but emerged from the interaction of rival societies based in pragmatic-driven sociability. The first part of this chapter, correspondingly, will explore Rousseau's state of war, followed by Vattel's critique of it – tacit or express – and show that

3. Vattel 2008a: 8. 4. Whatmore 2009. 5. Tuck 1999.

Vattel's conception of international relations is best situated as a rejoinder to Rousseau's pessimism and the prospects for international peace. The second part will then engage Vattel's description of modern Europe as his model for international sociability, held in equilibrium through commercial relations in maintaining states' natural liberty. The conclusion will remark on the uniquely Swiss nature of these early modern debates and their relevance for present-day transformations of the European Union in invigorating a culture of freedom and democracy.

II

At the heart of Rousseau's reflections on the place of war in the human condition lies a profound sceptical challenge to Hobbes's own project of overcoming scepticism: if international war is a fact, as no observer in the eighteenth century would deny, then the institution of a Leviathan not only does not end the state of nature but reinforces it. While the Hobbesian state emerges in response to the calamities of the natural condition and solves conflict between private individuals, it simultaneously creates an *international* state of nature, where states themselves now become enemies. The Leviathan may save us from ourselves, but it cannot save us from other Leviathans, and, in *Émile*, Rousseau would even ask rhetorically whether for this reason 'it would not be better to have no civil society than to have several... Is it not this partial and incomplete association which is the cause of tyranny and war?'[6] Despite our pretence that civil society clothes the nakedness of human aggression, for Rousseau it places us in a double predicament and leaves men exposed to the evils of *both* the state of nature and international war. There is an obvious difficulty here for any perceptive reader of Rousseau: if the law of nature makes it imperative that we each follow our fundamental moral duty in leading ourselves out of the state of nature, why would we then, as associated members of the *corps politique*, still find ourselves in a true state of war, where the number of atrocities is even greater 'than had been committed in the state of Nature for centuries together over the entire face of the earth'?[7] Does Rousseau provide any real solution to this dilemma, or does his sceptical challenge to Hobbes remain unanswered?

The tragedy of modern politics, as Rousseau writes in his unfinished manuscript on *The State of War*, revealed itself as a 'manifest contradiction' in the constitution of the human race: the very solution to natural

6. Rousseau 1915: II, 96. 7. Rousseau 1997b: 174.

inconveniences in the creation of a civil state domestically became simultaneously the source for perpetual conflict internationally.[8] As citizens we live in the social order of a civil state, but 'as nations each enjoys the liberty of nature'.[9] Subject to 'the evils of both without gaining the security of either', we are constantly thrown in a 'continual vacillation [which] makes our situation worse than if these distinctions were unknown'. The 'true origin of our calamities' stems from the 'double condition in which we find ourselves': because the law of nature 'addresses itself to the heart of individuals', whereas the laws of nations are based on the 'utility of the one who submits to them' and thus remain 'only [as] illusions that are more tenuous even than the notion of natural law', we 'have put ourselves in the worst possible position'.[10] There is little, if any, hope of reconciling the law of nature with the law of nations. The principle of the former is derived from a desire to transform the particular will of each individual in order to achieve the *union sacrée* of the 'body politic.' It is inscribed on human reason and emanates from the depths of our hearts. The law of nature speaks to *us*, perhaps even more powerfully than our own reason, whereas it is *we* who speak the law of nations, for it is men who dictate its principles. The law of nations is law not in a proper sense, deriving its force from the natural precepts inscribed in the human heart. It is law only in a secondary sense, where 'force alone' directs the law, appearing 'as law to its own citizens and *raison d'état* to foreigners'. Rather than being upheld in order to establish international justice in the absence of a *volonté générale* among sovereigns, the law of nations is respected only to the extent that it 'confirm[s] one's own self-interest' and becomes merely an excuse for the perpetration of violence.[11]

It all goes back to 'the error of Hobbes', of course, whose 'horrible system' and 'absurd doctrine' extolled the state of war as most natural to man. His 'insane system of a natural war of every man against every man' constructed a false foundation for establishing the origins of natural jurisprudence.[12] Rousseau attacked that very foundation not by naïvely denouncing the Hobbesian system, as many of Hobbes's contemporaries had done, but by engaging in a thoroughgoing reconsideration of it. Despite his claim to depart significantly from Hobbes in his description of the character of the state of war in its belligerent posture, Rousseau turned out more Hobbesian than he himself would ever have wished to acknowledge. He did so in order to express deep sympathy for the problem of securing liberty, rather than

8. Rousseau 1990: 186.
9. Rousseau would later restate the same position, almost word for word, in book v of his *Émile*.
10. Rousseau 1990: 186. 11. Rousseau 1990: 186. 12. Rousseau 1990: 186.

seeking to side with the solution of that problem as proposed by 'one of the greatest geniuses that ever lived'. But even if both agreed that we need to examine the condition of natural man, they disagreed on how to characterise *ab initio* the relations between its agents. Rousseau's natural man was devoid of any kind of social interaction, which would have struck Hobbes as inconceivable, if not even irrelevant, for the 'multitude of passions' – such as competition, diffidence and glory – clearly operates within the state of nature.[13] Rousseau's isolated individual, 'naturally peaceful and shy', rather than immediately exposed to the dangers of war, as Hobbes would have him, remains unperturbed by the passions. '[H]onor, self-interest, prejudice, and vengeance' all emerge only 'by force of habit and experience' and 'after having associated with one man'.[14] But apart from this radical isolationism in Rousseau's initial construct, there is little divergence in the rest of their accounts of the growth of human conflict and emergence of warfare.

For Rousseau, as for Hobbes, the depiction of natural man is much less an account of the personal qualities of private individuals under duress of basic survival than an attempt to create a model of social values that would be one resource for analysing the international state system. He uses men's radical unsociability in their individual autonomy and experience of natural liberty in order to make a point about the context out of which states' propensity for war emerges. In an important way, Rousseau's narrative about natural men is not a story about private individuals naturally inclined to peace and between whom no war could ever take place (after all, men become soldiers only after having associated as citizens). Rather, it is an argument about how public persons, formed as artificial beings with a singular will and brought into existence by the social compact, wage lawful war amongst themselves. The question is not what establishes war as an advantageous affair of the one who wages it, but what renders it legitimate.

Rousseau had already stated this question in one compelling form when he examined the origin of inequality in his *Second Discourse*. In his insistence that we must not to confuse 'savage man with the men we have before our eyes', he wished not only to distinguish himself from Hobbes, but also to refute prevalent arguments that inherent unsociability can generate societal cohesion: 'It would be absurd to suppose', he insisted in his *Essay on the Origin of Language*, 'that the means of uniting them [can be] derived from the cause of their separation'.[15] Radical unsociability would come to characterise natural man and become the hallmark of the *Second Discourse*, which Rousseau

13. Hobbes 1991: 88. 14. Rousseau 1990: 188. 15. Rousseau 1997b: 138; 1966: 11–12.

completed in 1754, the same year he was editing the works of Abbé Saint-Pierre and already engaged in thinking about the possibility for international peace. Just two months after the *Second Discourse*'s first publication (May 1755 in Amsterdam) Vattel published a critical review of it in *Journal Helvétique*,[16] denouncing the 'new book from Mr. Rousseau', which 'is causing a stir in the world'.[17] The criticism is direct and unapologetic: 'the same genius', who reduced 'the Sciences and the Arts to a level below that of uselessness' now 'clothed his paradoxes in so much artistry and so much elegance that he had them crowned by an Academy'.[18]

Rousseau's portrayal of natural man, Vattel writes, reduces him to a brute animal, if not even 'more stupid than various species of animals'. His natural man is incapable of 'thoughtful awareness of self' and hence deprived of perfectibility: 'The entire bliss of Mr. Rousseau's natural men seems to come down to idleness and apathy.' Awareness of oneself presupposes the natural duty to care for one's own preservation. It also implies a disposition for human interaction, which only 'society' and 'communication between men' can achieve. By removing 'perfectibility' as an essential attribute of human nature, Rousseau in effect denies 'the principle of sociability, from which Grotius and other great writers have deduced all Natural Law'. It is not sufficient for men to come together as a group, for 'beavers, bees, ants and other animals' are similarly predisposed to form groupings, and some of them even 'have a kind of language of their own'. It is also necessary to explain the products of their association. Through the use of language – which developed naturally, first through 'abstractions' and then through 'halting words' – men have removed themselves from their original condition to a superior state. For Vattel language is what makes men truly human by declaring their presence to others not by 'sounds of sadness' or a 'cry for scolding', as brute animals do, but through reasoned intelligibility in 'communication between men' in order to 'perfect their reason and knowledge'.[19]

The problem with Rousseau's inability to explain the 'simple and natural origins of language' runs much deeper than just being an ignorant observation – albeit disguised in 'beguiling eloquence' and 'taste for paradox' – about the brutish solitude of humanity.[20] His denial of a sociable disposition, which

16. Vattel, *Reflexions sur le Discours de M. JJ Rousseau touchant l'origine de l'inégalité parmi les hommes* (*Journal Helvétique*, Neuchâtel: August 1755). It was republished in his *Mélanges de littérature, de morale et de politique* (Neuchâtel, 1760).

17. Vattel 2008b: 97.

18. Vattel here refers to Rousseau's *First Discourse on the Arts and Science*, which had won him the prize of the Dijon Academy.

19. Vattel 2008b: 97 and 99.

20. Vattel 2008b: 97 and 98.

for Vattel is innate and stems naturally from our moral composition, deprives us of the medium to pursue our most basic inclination, that of self-love. As he explains in one of his earliest essays,[21] self-love 'causes us to desire and seek for our happiness or the perfection of our condition . . . of our soul, the well-being of our body, and the prosperity of our fortune'.[22] The origin of self-love, 'the first principle of all obligation, and in particular of the obligation to keep natural law', lies both in the feebleness of the human condition, and in the drive to improve our nature only with the assistance of others.[23] The instinctual formation of social groups out of security-seekers is driven as much by a desire 'to band together to make a stand against violence' as by the recognition that our happiness lies in 'our well-being, our expediency, our advantage'.[24] On this reading, sociability is not based on Aristotle's notion of *koinonia* and a recognition of a fellow-feeling in the natural pursuit of a *summum bonum*. Rather, it follows the dictates of right reason coupled with self-interest in the pursuit of utility. The source of sociability lies within the laws of nature, 'whose rationale is found in the essence and nature of man, and of things in general'.[25] It stems from our obligation to them even in the absence of any external punitive superior, introducing common justice, or a single *volonté générale*, establishing our unity. It is this obligation to oneself primarily, in the attainment of the highest degree of one's happiness, and to others only secondarily, that requires men to enter into 'communication and commerce with each other'.[26]

Vattel's solution to the asceticism of Rousseau's natural man was the conflation of man's inherent propensity for self-preservation and his capacity to procure it only in association with others. What Rousseau had failed to notice is that our natural inclination for perfection is inseparable from our duty to care for the self in common with others: men advance sociability not out of considerations for enhancing general benevolence, but merely for the sake of channelling cooperation to secure their safety and proper advantage. Cooperation through enlightened sociability was the key to solving the fundamental moral question of maintaining peace and freedom, and Vattel used the international state system as the model that best described these

21. Emer de Vattel, *Essai sur le fondement du droit naturel, et sur le premier principe de l'obligation où se trouvent tous les hommes, d'en observer les lois* [1746], in *Loisir philosophique, ou pièces diverses de philosophie, de morale, et d'amusement* (Geneva: G. Conrad Walther, 1747). Prior to completing his *Law of Nations* in 1757, which is the work that made him famous, Vattel had published an elaborate defence of the philosophical system of Leibniz (1740–41) as well as essays on self-love and friendship, all throughout the 1740s.

22. Vattel 2008a: 753. 23. Vattel 2008a: 754. 24. Vattel 2008b: 99. 25. Vattel 2008a: 747.

26. Vattel 2008a: 15.

moral relations. States, as public persons, were, above all, communicators, who, even in the absence of any superior authority, tend to generate a degree of reciprocal compliance in their relations. Cooperation was the intended consequence of their communication.

Communication between nations, for Vattel, builds mutual trust and enhances international cooperation, where 'bodies politic' enter into voluntary contractual relationships with a view to increasing public welfare and fulfilling a natural obligation 'imposed upon them by humanity'. The most prudent nations endeavour to procure these advantages by entering into treaties and alliances with other states while 'respecting their own private affairs'.[27] Treaties 'can only be made by the superior powers, by sovereigns who contract in the name of the state', and for this reason they are called 'public treaties' (*traités publics*), since they are made by the public authority of states.[28] Unlike the contracting members of Rousseau's *contrat social*, who need a *volonté générale* to hold them as one and indivisible, the contracting parties to international agreements possess no general will, but they all share 'equality in dignity' as a condition of their sovereignty.[29] Small republics and powerful kingdoms stand on an equal footing with regard to their capacity as agents in the international domain, and are considered, like Hobbes's pre-civil men, naturally equal.[30] Their equality is based on a reciprocal rendering of duties in a mutual respect for observing the clauses of their alliance and honoring their agreements. 'A dwarf is as much a man as a giant [is]', Vattel insists (being a citizen of a small and potentially vulnerable Swiss canton), and power or weakness produces no difference with respect to the practice of their sovereignty and independence.[31] States are moral persons endowed with an understanding and a will of their own, and susceptible of obligations and rights according to the laws of nature.

The acts and judgements of the moral person, who resides in the public authority of the state, are to be considered only in relation to the coalitions and alliances of which it is a part. While there is no superior authority representative of the will of all nations, the alliances amongst them circumscribe an identifiable range of conduct. Vattel suggests not that states form a single international entity, modelled after the unity of civic bodies, but that we can

27. Vattel 2008a: 338. 28. Vattel 2008a: 338. 29. Vattel 2008a: 348.

30. Around the same time, Adam Ferguson similarly insisted on equality of states by asserting that the small republics of Europe should not be regarded, in the face of imperial powers, as 'shrubs, under the shade of a taller wood, choked by the neighborhood of more powerful states' (Ferguson 1995: 61).

31. Vattel 2008a: 75.

think of inter-state conduct as occurring within a kind of a *system* of reciprocal compliance and relatively stable interactions.[32] Alliances and coalitions tend to minimise the scope for conflict and alleviate mutual fears. They act as an incentive that constrains the international system and facilitates communication. States are moral persons because they are fundamentally communicative, and this means that they recognise that the pursuit of their interest would require cooperation with other states.

To assume in the manner of Rousseau that, just as individual men are the only agents in the natural condition, so sovereign states are the only actors in international affairs, is in effect to deny the existence of secondary associations (civil societies being primary associations). Communication between states gives rise to various forms of association between them that in no way forfeits their natural liberty. It is 'a union of interests', operating within the laws of nature, that regulates such associations, where 'the difference of religion is a thing absolutely foreign' to them: Christians and Muhammedans may contract alliances, not as professing their religion but as equally subject to the laws of nations.[33] Apart from differences in religion, Vattel is keener to insist that difference in power is also irrelevant to the conditions of an alliance: even a potentially unequal alliance between the mighty French and the much less powerful Swiss can be counterbalanced by 'the valour of the Swiss troops' and thus 'preserve the equilibrium' between them.[34] The prominence of secondary associations – whether defence groups or economic alliances – suggests that a complete equivalence between the interpersonal and international state of nature disregards how the pursuit of common interest could bring rival states together in transcending national boundaries.

In opening up the possibility for transnational associations, Vattel drew attention as much to the independence of states as to their interdependence, where reciprocal duty compliance contributed to international peace and cooperation. Promise keeping, mutual trust and good faith among nations constitute the very foundation upon which international justice is established. Even enemies make 'obligatory' promises and observe a level of trust in their mutual engagement, which allows them to determine the means for the resolution of their conflict. In the absence of a common superior to adjudicate pretensions between bodies politic, faith in treaties is 'to be held sacred and inviolable between the nations of the earth', and becomes

32. Standard interpretations of Vattel in the international relations literature have, misleadingly, placed him squarely within the Realist tradition, see Walzer 1977: 63.

33. Vattel 2008a: 512 and 342. 34. Vattel 2008a: 350.

the only means of establishing common rules of conduct.[35] The observance of *fides* in mutual agreements is held sacred, for its practice is a reciprocal acknowledgement of the rights of free and independent states. The framers of the early American republic, in particular, took to heart this aspect of Vattel's argument and sought to extend its validity in the transatlantic context precisely when the emergence of the United States provided Vattel's theory with most fertile ground for the creation of a new nation.[36]

Faith in treaties, however, functions differently at the interpersonal and international level. In the natural condition of mankind, as Hobbes had put it, 'covenants, without the sword, are but words, and of no strength to secure a man at all'.[37] In that condition, a superior is needed not to ensure the observance of such covenants (Hobbes does recognise their existence – weak and unstable as they may be – even in the state of nature), but to remove the fear of non-performance and, more importantly, to guarantee their validity. At the international level, however, treaties between states are, for Vattel, 'no better than empty words, if nations do not consider them as respectable engagements'.[38] The emphasis here is not on a superior Leviathan-like authority validating contractual relations. Rather, states themselves need to exercise prudential judgement and, in a way, each acts as an authority unto itself.[39] It is in this act of consideration and self-authoring that states are in fact most free. Their capacity for judgement is best exercised when they consider that their transgressing of faith constitutes a violation of nothing less than their own liberty, 'the soul of abilities and industry'.[40] The natural liberty of states may partly be secured through their general observance to the laws of nature (and here Rousseau and Vattel would be in agreement), but it is also partly safeguarded through their interaction with other states, as being part of – what Vattel would call – the 'great society of mankind'.[41]

Our obligations under the laws of nature are, for Vattel, partially derived from the 'end of the natural human society established among men', and the gulf between the partial associations of civil society and the natural society of mankind is not as vast as Rousseau had supposed.[42] The austerity of the Spartan model, through its simplicity, civic religion and lack of extreme individualism, is, for Vattel, just one possible – though ultimately not

35. Vattel 2008a: 387.
36. Armitage 2011: 16–18. On Vattel's considerable influence on the early American Republic, see Lang 1985.
37. Hobbes 1991: 117.
38. Vattel 2008a: 387.
39. For a critique of this aspect of Vattel's argument, see Onuf 1998.
40. Vattel 2008a: 127.
41. Vattel 2008a: 387.
42. Vattel 2008a: 6.

viable – way of preserving the liberty and independence of small polities. (This was especially true in the case of the highly distinct cantons loosely federated in the Swiss republic.[43]) But the Rousseauian model of Spartan virtuousness, as much as it curbs the passions of self-interest, can in no way respond to the political demands of emerging commercial republics. Vattel was at pains to preserve the benefits of valour, pride and patriotism of the unique Swiss heritage, while at the same time he ridiculed Rousseau for his idealism for small polities and distanced himself by asserting that we 'are bound to cultivate' the 'universal society of the human race'.[44]

Far from idealising Vattel as a benevolent universalist, my intention here is to point to his profound disagreement with Rousseau on how states best secure their natural liberty and independence. The claim here is that it is the legacy of Vattel's pragmatic aspiration for a balance between the local and the international by contrast with Rousseau's model of austere localism that continues to animate current debates on the construction of Europe. The remainder of this chapter will thus consider Vattel's attempt to pacify the international order in the specific context of the diplomatic practice of public treaties between sovereigns and the political economy of reformed commercial relations in the eighteenth century. Vattel's new Europe, of small republics and imperial powers alike, held the promise of maintaining their natural liberty through an equilibrium of commercial and power relations. It is the legacy of this Europe, further evolved over the last two and a half centuries, that we have come to anticipate in the political project of the European Union today.

III

The formation of any 'private association' by 'unit[ing] in civil society' does not exempt us from performing our 'duties towards the rest of mankind', and in fact, in Vattel's mind, it strengthens our obligations imposed 'by human nature'. As citizens of a particular *civitas*, with an authority to give commands, prescribe laws and exercise compulsion over those who refuse to obey, men are subject to civil laws, while also retaining their duty to promote the general happiness of mankind, and 'cannot liberate themselves from the obligation by any convention'.[45] If it is the authoritative nature of the state that serves as the fountain of *ius civile* and hence justifies our obedience to it,

43. For eighteenth-century Swiss reforms, see Kapossy 2006.
44. Vattel 2008a: 72.
45. Vattel 2008a: 72.

what would be the corresponding equivalent to the fount of *ius gentium* in the international domain?

While it is clear that a state's authority does not supersede our obligation to the general laws of humanity, but in fact bolsters it, it is much less clear whether we should look for a similar kind of authority beyond the state. Allowing for a 'natural society between nations', Vattel adamantly repudiated any notion of a universal republic 'by nature', or a supreme state, established on the same principle of authority as in a civil state, although he was much in favour of Europe as 'a kind of a republic' (*une espèce de République*).[46] Like Hobbes, who had denounced the idea that a global Leviathan is a logical extension embracing all *civitates*, Vattel asserted that a *civitas maxima*, of the kind that his immediate predecessor Christian Wolff had promoted,[47] was unnecessary, and in fact detrimental, to 'the peaceable enjoyment of that liberty which belongs to it [a state] by nature'.[48] Given that sovereign states 'are much more capable of supplying all their wants than individual men are', and do not require the same kind of mutual assistance, the idea of a supreme state is subversive of their natural liberty, which no higher authority can presume to direct.[49] In introducing a distinction between a natural society of men (whose origin lies in a commonly recognisable humanity) and a global republic of nations (with the authority of a civil institution on a grand scale), Vattel eases the tension which had so troubled Rousseau: that between the demands of partial association, the local, and obedience to duties to humanity, the global. Men may be bound in a common society by nature without being domestically contracted under the artifice of a regulative public authority.

The possibility of obeying the laws of nations without undermining the particular laws of our state emerges within a distinctly moral framework, where states themselves are considered as moral persons, 'possessed of an understanding, volition, and strength' peculiar to themselves.[50] The morality of states, however, is limited to the mutual recognition of their duties and obligations to one another, rather than constitutive of a thick prescription for promoting virtuous citizenry. While Vattel would have been just as comfortable with Rousseau's characterisation of states as moral persons, he would have quickly rejected his position that in a condition of international conflict our domestic security is best ensured through 'zeal and glory' for

46. Vattel 2008a: 14 and 496.
47. Christian Wolff had advanced the argument for *civitas maxima* in his *Ius gentium methodo scientifica petractatum* (1749) and *Institutiones juris naturae et gentium* (1750).
48. Vattel 2008a: 15. 49. Vattel 2008a: 262. 50. Vattel 2008a: 73.

the fatherland,[51] as the case of Poland allegedly illustrated.[52] The maintenance of the social compact, for Rousseau, should be closely safeguarded by 'a patriotism enlightened by experience', which alone can cement ties of equality and freedom in defence against the state of war.[53] *L'amour de la patrie* can act as a bulwark not only against foreign aggression, but also in the face of so many internal divisions, making it hard, in the first place, for patriotism to 'arise in the midst of so many other passions that stifle it'.[54] Love of the fatherland, 'a hundred times more lively and delightful than the love of a mistress' and 'the most heroic of all the passions', as Rousseau tells us, is the most effectively intoxicating instrument of turning self-seeking men into law-abiding citizens.[55] In his recommendations to the governments of Corsica and Poland (the only two European nations that had not yet been corrupted despite their experience of foreign aggression), Rousseau seeks to establish the conditions for a 'patriotic zeal', which alone would be capable of developing 'the principle of national character'.[56]

But the more the practice of patriotic ardour transforms self-interested residents into virtuous citizens by denaturing them, the more they need to be reminded why their love of the fatherland distinguishes them from foreigners, and it is here that Vattel is troubled by Rousseau's departure from basic internationalist sentiments and cosmopolitan values. If fatherland carried the same meaning and significance for all equally, citizens and foreigners alike, Rousseau had insisted, then it would be an empty word worthy of derision. For who can possibly object, he asked, that we do in fact feel closer to our fellow-citizens, merely 'through the habit of seeing one another, and the common interest' that unites us, than we feel to those with whom we share no physical space or common heritage?[57] Physical proximity to one another and the occupation of the same space, Rousseau reasoned, bring out the distinctiveness of a people in their morals, habits and practices in directing and continually reinforcing the general will.

Clearly, the circles of commiseration and sympathy cannot expand indefinitely to embrace all equally and 'must in some way be constricted and compressed in order to be activated'.[58] The more they expand geographically to encompass other people and areas, Rousseau warns us, the more 'the sentiment of humanity dissipates and weakens as it spreads to the whole

51. Vattel distinguished between 'the glory of arms' to satisfy ambition and 'true glory', which is 'the prize for the *good* use made of it' in defending one's fatherland, in his *Dialogue between Peter the Great and Charles XII of Sweden on the Glory of Conquerors* (1760), see Vatel 2008b: 80 and 81.
52. Rousseau 1997a: 249. 53. Rousseau 1997a: 216. 54. Rousseau 1997a: 21.
55. Rousseau 1997a: 16. 56. Rousseau 1991: 161 and 150. 57. Rousseau 1997a: 16.
58. Rousseau 1997a: 15.

earth' until the idea of a general society of humankind completely vanishes and remains as a mere chimera in the systems of philosophers. It is hardly surprising 'that we cannot be as touched by the calamities of Tartary or Japan as we are by those of a European people', or even as by our next-door European neighbours.[59] Rousseau's larger point, though, is that the problem with certain 'cosmopolitan souls' – such as the ardent European federalist Saint-Pierre – is that they strive to appeal to sentiments of humanity in order to derive our duties as citizens.[60] But what kind of sentiments are those, he asks in his *Geneva Manuscript*, if no such humanity can possibly be imagined, let alone experienced, for 'the word *mankind* offers the mind only a purely collective idea which does not assume any real unity among the individuals who constitute it'.[61] How can one simultaneously subscribe to a system that embraces all the values of a single human community, and yet belong as a citizen to a specific *polis* with a distinct form of civility? To resolve the paradox, either we must admit that 'we conceive of the general society in terms of our particular societies', for men must become citizens first before they can be called men properly, or we must plainly contradict ourselves, as 'supposed cosmopolites' do, who, in 'justifying their love of fatherland by their love of mankind, boast of loving everyone so that they might have the right to love no one'.[62] Precisely by embracing the values common to all humanity, 'cosmopolitan souls' lack any. It would be even more absurd to claim, on Rousseau's grounds, that the state has a responsibility to cultivate duties to humanity, and hence enhance obligation to other states, so that it may then use its authority to direct our private interests into a general will.

Rousseau's state may be best suited to denature man and give him the tools to carry the *moi* into the common unity, but as a political institution it clearly fails to equip its citizens with the capacity to carry out their duties to humanity. It belongs to the 'state, and its rulers', Vattel emphasises, 'to fulfill the duties of humanity toward strangers', for the obedience that citizens owe to their state is merely an extension of their general duty to humanity and 'a necessary consequence of the wise and rational love' they owe to themselves.[63] While it is within the purview of the authority of the state to instil civic virtue – and Vattel is clearly in agreement with Rousseau on this point – it must also seek to cultivate 'offices of humanity' in contributing to the perfection of other states. The inwardly oriented Rousseauian state may purge its citizens of the passions of self-interest and invigorate their political

59. Rousseau 1997a: 16. 60. Rousseau 1997b: 174. 61. Rousseau 1997a: 155.
62. Rousseau 1997a: 155 and 158. 63. Vattel 2008a: 73.

virtues, but instead of making them feel part of a greater whole, it localises their experience of liberty and limits their sentiments of humanity. The consequences of Rousseau's 'localised' liberty for the relations between states were rather dramatic: his political bodies emphasised self-sufficiency and independence instead of openness and interdependence. Vattel's solution to this seemingly irreconcilable paradox was simple. The general guiding principle of foreign politics was communication, and commerce provided the medium for that exchange to take place. In the case of modern Europe, specifically, relations between states were further regulated by an artifice – a humanly enforced equilibrium of political forces – which took the form of a jealously guarded balance of power.

As a citizen of a small republic, surrounded by imperial powers, Vattel was sensitive to survival strategies that would allow republics to preserve their liberty in the post-Utrecht states-system. He rejected a union of European states, of the kind proposed by Saint-Pierre's *Project for Perpetual Peace*, for it would give licence to aspiring monarchs to establish a universal monarchy in 'delivering up all Europe to servitude'.[64] The fantasies of Saint-Pierre would undermine the precarious achievements of the common system of states, established at Utrecht, and now held together by treaties. A union of monarchies, or even a single hegemonic power, such as France, would be particularly dangerous to the noble aspirations of *ius gentium*, which had taken the place of the fanaticism of the Wars of Religion and the ambitions for imperial expansion. Vigilance characterised the new system of order and liberty, where 'nations [need to] be watchful and alert in repressing that growing power', threatening their common security.[65] Small republics could combine their forces in the formation of leagues and confederations against powerful states. War would not be eliminated, Vattel insists, but it would no longer be an instrument in ambitious pursuits of *raison d'état* and would become merely auxiliary to solving conflict. Necessity and expediency, rather than mere advantage or greed, would dictate shifts in the distribution of power. States would continually check on each other and seek to counterbalance a rising hegemon to ensure that the distribution of international power among variously positioned units – small or large – remains relatively stable.

Such a balance was not chimerical – as Kant would later claim, deriding it as a 'pure illusion' – but could be said to describe quite accurately the relations between states 'at present pursued by the sovereigns of Europe'.[66] The emergence of a power equilibrium was inevitable, for it underscored the

64. Vattel 2008a: 73. 65. Vattel 2008a: 495. 66. Kant 1970: 92; Vattel 2008a: 497.

specificity of the European states-system and the common political destiny that its members shared. It arose as mutually advantageous in tending to produce joint action that only a common threat could generate. The members of the system, however, were not giving up their liberty by joining their forces with others. Each nation remained a 'mistress of her own actions' as long as it recognised that the preservation of its liberty demanded a willingness to defend it militarily in overcoming a potential hegemon.[67] It was liberty, rather than foreign aggression or aggrandisement, that determined the point of equilibrium in international power.

For Vattel it was neither the antiquated self-protectionist ambitions of France, seeking to dominate the continent, nor the cunning of Spain, allying out of convenience, that could exercise a constructive role in Europe's balance of power. It was England that held the unique position of 'holding the political balance' and acting as the guarantor of international security.[68] Part of England's special status in influencing power balancing was geography – situated on an island, she had a more objective vantage point for judging the Continent's political dynamic. And as a maritime power, England's 'formidable fleets' exercised a positive influence 'without alarming any state on the score of its liberty' since it had 'cured [itself] of the rage of conquest'.[69] England was the patroness of small republics in protecting them from large hegemons, and saw herself as the fulcrum of Europe's power relations. In large part, England was able to achieve this pre-eminence because 'of all modern states' she was 'most distinguished' in promoting foreign trade. What England had perceived was how effective commerce could become in regulating the affairs between rival states, for 'it is chiefly commerce that places in her hand the balance of Europe'.[70] Commerce, rather than naked reason of state, was the engine of power balancing.

The political economy of commercial states had transformed Europe from 'a confused heap of detached pieces . . . very little concerned with the fate of the others' to 'a kind of republic', whose 'common interest' led them to 'unite for the maintenance of order and liberty'.[71] In this balanced system of states, whose natural liberty and independence were the preconditions for their capacity to engage in commerce, communication and exchange brought previous rivals into a common security project. The system could operate on the condition that it was wilfully practised and its principles of respect and reciprocity existed subjectively in the conscience of each of

67. Vattel 2008a: 75. 68. Vattel 2008a: 497. 69. Vattel 2008a: 497.
70. Vattel 2008a: 131. 71. Vattel 2008a: 496.

its members, equally benefiting from its maintenance. This self-regulatory balancing opened a novel way of conceptualising international affairs: it was indeed possible to construct an inter-state order with some level of constancy and predictability. The novelty of Vattel's modern understanding of the balance of power lay in linking it to what J. G. A. Pocock has called the 'enlightened narrative' of Europe, one that had 'outgrown barbarism, fanaticism, and conquest . . . communicated everywhere by commerce'.[72] This was the new Europe of commerce and civilisation in progressing from the instability of ancient constitutions to the order and liberty of modern states. The restructuring of the international arena from hegemonic impulses to a balanced multipolar system in effect transformed the Old Continent into a confederation of independent states held together by treaties. States could no longer afford to view the rise of ambitious potentates with 'an eye of indifference', nor 'remain quiet spectators of the rapid increase of her power'.[73] Their natural liberty and shared experience called them to act in concert and united them 'into a political system, an integral body' against the common fear of universal monarchy.[74]

The practice of *ius gentium*, with its adherence to established norms in the post-Utrecht era, was based in a system of international relations that itself gave the definition of 'Europe'. Vattel's new 'Europe' was not Voltaire's *la grande République* of a 'Christian Europe, give or take Russia . . . all [states] having the same basic religion, though divided into various sects'.[75] A common Christian heritage is not what laid the foundation for a balanced Europe (though it may certainly have contributed to its maintenance[76]). The definition of 'Europe' was derived from a general recognition that international balancing, with its adjudication of rights and duties, can alone protect the liberty of diverse states, small and large alike. 'Europe', so defined – as a single political universe, whose centre of gravity was anchored in order and liberty – was essentially an equilibrium of international power. Despite disagreements over the natural frontiers of where Europe begins or ends, Vattel's 'Europe' was an enlightened community of states whose progressive commercial relations drew them closer together. His endorsement of Europe as 'a kind of republic' was one that combined the traditions of European thought on *ius gentium* with the particular circumstances of diplomatic practice in the mid eighteenth century. It was a new Europe of treaties and settlements that effectively functioned as 'constitutions' for Europe.

72. Pagden 2002: 64. 73. Vattel 2008a: 495. 74. Vattel 2008a: 496. 75. Voltaire 1966: 40.
76. Vattel acknowledged that it was the common threat from the Ottoman Empire that united rival Christian sects, see Vattel 2008a: 475.

These new inter-state arrangements did not produce an organised political union – not at least for two centuries after Vattel – because of the strict configuration of domestic sovereignty. But they did establish a common political culture of order and liberty among right-minded states, whose progressive commercial interaction emphasised the utility of cooperation. Albeit precarious and short lived, this brief period of about four decades – between the Seven Years War and the Napoleonic Empire – marked the beginning of what would turn out to be a long and bumpy road towards pooling sovereignty and designing peace as a common political project for Europe. Vattel's insight that modern Europe could be transformed from a battleground of competing imperial ideologies into an equilibrium of power balanced in liberty was not an inherently moral argument with a prescriptive purpose. It was primarily a practical proposal, workable under the specific circumstances of commercial progress and economic advancement. As a practical proposal, it did not rely on Condorcet's brotherhood of 'the enlightened nations of Europe' whose task was to 'civilise' non-European people, waiting to become 'friends and pupils' of their European 'brothers'.[77] Nor did it extoll Constant's 'living association of European people'.[78] Vattel had recognised Rousseau's deep tension between the natural liberty of states and their commitment to the law of nations, and his proposal remained firmly grounded in the reality of a workable international political order. States still needed to maintain armies, even if, for some, neutrality was their foreign policy objective. Militarism would never disappear from a future European political order (for liberty had to be protected and defended, if necessary), but it would be transformed from a force for expansion into a resort to security.

Near the end of the eighteenth century Friedrich Schiller remarked that 'the society of European states seems to have been transformed into one large family', but, as he was quick to observe, it was not the principle of familial love holding it together. Instead, 'peace is now kept by an ever-armoured war, and the self-love of one state makes it a guardian of the other's wealth'.[79] Schiller's characterisation could be said to describe aptly Vattel's idea of Europe, with the addition that such a 'large family' of states had a further duty to establish similar ties of mutual reciprocity with nations beyond Europe. The extension of that argument, however, would be developed systematically only after Vattel, in Kant's sketch of *Perpetual Peace*, laying the groundwork for a 'cosmopolitan right' in moving from older imperial

77. Condorcet 1955: 180 and 177. 78. Constance 1988: 73. 79. Kosseleck 1998: 46.

structures to a pacific federative model.[80] Kant's idea of Europe is generally taken to be prophetic and far ahead of its own time, in serving as a model – if only a condition of future time – for the development of the modern European Union. But the story of the place of liberty in the construction of Europe, despite its Prussian – and later, Franco-German – origins, has much deeper roots, recognisable in early modern Swiss quests for order and security, and, perhaps, going as far back as the Swiss confederation in the thirteenth century. As this chapter has shown, Rousseau and Vattel were, above all, citizens of Swiss republics, and despite their differing approaches to the preservation of the liberty of states, their arguments illustrate the distinctiveness of their Alpine origins. That distinctiveness continues to animate contemporary debates on the nature of the European Union today and raises serious questions about the practice of citizenship, as Europeans – particularly in Brussels – continue to clamour for more liberty in an expanded union.

IV

It is a peculiar fact that in the heart of the modern European Union is nested a country which is not a member. Largely perceived as intentionally isolationist, intensely democratic and fiercely neutral, Switzerland remains an oddity and represents a real anomaly in the landscape of European politics today. Its prominent absence from the structures of the most promising political project in Europe provides some of the richest context for thinking about the relationship between the liberty of states and international law. Switzerland's reluctance to join the European Union reflects the long history of that tension, as explored here through the thought of Rousseau and Vattel.

Contemporary Swiss debates (advanced primarily in the German-speaking cantons), depicting European Union membership as an unacceptable compromise with their country's direct democracy and experience of freedom, echo Rousseau's defence of the local over any larger community. The transformation of men into citizens is partly invigorated by the immediacy of physical space and the feeling of proximity to one another. Citizens need to be constantly reminded of the precariousness of liberty. As long as they can *directly* defend themselves and their liberty – through a referendum rather than representation – they are truly masters of their own political destiny. Rival debates (made mainly in the French-speaking cantons) place

80. Kant 1970: 105.

their hope, instead, in a reformed Switzerland that regards membership in the European Union as an opportunity rather than a threat to its liberty. With their insistence that Switzerland could enjoy the advantages of a closer European integration without compromising civic freedom, defenders of Swiss membership are Vattelian at heart. They see the treaty-based nature of the European Union as a partnership of sovereignty committed to the self-determination of the state, not its submergence.

The political reality of Switzerland today is more complicated than a reductive binary between a Rousseauan-inspired resistance to further European integration and a Vattelian-inspired defence of membership may suggest. The relations between Switzerland and the European Union are framed around bilateral treaties that form the core of their policy of cooperation. This approach ensures that popular support is exercised at regularly convened referenda. It allows the Swiss to express a collective will and preserve the rigidity of their sovereignty. Every major bilateral agreement must be put to a popular vote: even a referendum decided that Switzerland should join the United Nations as a full member in 2002, making it the only country ever to have joined on the basis of a popular vote. No other modern country has come closer to the experience of direct democracy in conducting its foreign affairs, where the citizens themselves decide what kind of international treaties and agreements it should endorse. Even though it is not a member of the European Union (its accession application has remained open since 1992, when a canton-wide referendum rejected membership in the European Economic Area), Switzerland is, in many ways, a virtual member. As a member of the European Free Trade Association, it already applies much of European Union law, contributes to its budget, and is even a member of the passport-free Schengen area.

At a time when the European Union is expanding geographically and deepening its integration, Switzerland – with its rich political thought – seems to constitute a real anomaly amongst its neighbours. But in fact, the country remains a test for the conscience of Europe. The European Union may have replaced old forms of absolutism across the continent with a single international agreement – the Treaty of Lisbon – that protects the liberty of its citizens, but it has yet to invigorate the democratic spirit, which alone has the capacity to turn men into citizens, as Rousseau reminds us. We must not mistake liberty protection – as enshrined in the European Union's seemingly endless documents – for political freedom itself. The institutions of liberty only guarantee the opportunity to exercise that liberty, but they do not of themselves bring forth the spirit of liberty. They do not give citizens the opportunity of being European and acting as Europeans. The Union must pass from a delegates' representation to a citizens' democracy, and it is here that the case of Switzerland proves to be most instructive.

It might seem ironic that the liberty of states – so ardently defended, in different ways, by two Swiss contemporaries, Rousseau and Vattel – remains one of Switzerland's legacies to a more unified and integrated modern Europe, while it has not been part of it, at least not formally in the last fifty years. When Churchill spoke of the 'tragedy of Europe' amidst the ravages of the Second World War, he could find hope and inspiration only in the Swiss experience of liberty. What would be the remedy to 'make all Europe, or the greater part of it', he asked in a speech delivered at Zurich University in 1946, 'as free and happy as Switzerland is today'?[81] If Europeans would be wise enough to pool their strength and 'recreate the European family', he instructed, they 'would as if by a miracle transform the whole scene' of devastation into lasting peace. Switzerland provided an enduring model for how to structure the liberty of a new post-war Europe that both valued international autonomy and prized general solidarity. That lesson of liberty is far from having been learnt, let alone accomplished, but one thing is certain. The simultaneous presence and absence of the Alpine lands in the heart of Europe serves as a constant reminder of what we may have lost in an enlarged union, but more importantly, what is to be gained from the long legacy of Swiss liberty.

81. Winston Churchill, Speech at the University of Zurich, 19 September 1946.

10

The state of freedom: Kant and his conservative critics

REIDAR MALIKS

I

At the height of the French Revolution a debate about freedom took place in Germany.[1] The concept had been central in public discourse for decades, but the discussion gained urgency due to the Terror, which led most German writers to turn against the Revolution and its principles. Conservatives like Justus Möser (1720–94) and progressives like Immanuel Kant (1724–1804) agreed about the significance of freedom but they understood different things by it, and were divided in particular over whether freedom implies equality. Conservatives worried that the egalitarian concept of freedom was responsible for the excesses of the French Revolution, and mounted a defence of the old regime by prescribing severe limits on freedom and, in some cases, dusting off the concept of the old German liberties, where freedom was understood in the plural, in reality representing unequal privileges among social ranks.[2] Progressives, who were often inspired by Rousseau, defended the modern concept of freedom based on the rights of man and the universalistic ideals of the Enlightenment. Both parties disagreed on how freedom ought to be implemented politically. Conservatives levelled a critique against the progressive desire to transform reality according to principles of freedom, and thereby not just dismantling the old regime but risking anarchy.

A few years before these events, in 1785, Kant had published *Groundwork for the Metaphysics of Morals*, where he provided a moral theory resting on the idea of a free will, which became immensely influential.[3] It was not clear, however, what that theory would imply for the organisation of society,

I am grateful to Theodore Christov, Leif Maliks, Mark Philp, Véronique Pouillard, T. J. Reed, Alexander Schmidt and Quentin Skinner for comments on an earlier version of this chapter.

1. Schlumbohm 1975; Klippel 1976; Vierhaus 1967.
2. Schmidt 2006; Klinger 2006.
3. Kant 1911. Translations are from Kant 1996, except Kant 1922b which are from Kant 1999.

because it was primarily a theory of personal conscience and not of political conduct. Although Kant had lectured on natural law for years, his writings on the subject were limited. Some of his students took the initiative to compose their own Kantian tracts on politics,[4] others wrote to ask for his opinion,[5] and eventually, in September 1793, he published the essay 'On the Common Saying: That May Be Correct in Theory, but It Is of No Use in Practice', his first sustained theory of justice. In this essay Kant sided unequivocally with the progressive cause and argued for an egalitarian conception of civil liberty. But he left many questions unanswered. He failed to explain why persons who have the capacity to be morally autonomous in the sense of having a free will must also have a right to civil liberty. And, despite the title, he said little about how to implement theory in practice. The *Theory and Practice* essay became the centre of the discussion and was criticised from all sides. This chapter will focus on the conservative critics Friedrich von Gentz (1764–1832) and August Wilhelm Rehberg (1756–1836), in addition to Justus Möser. They claimed that Kant's basic principles of freedom do not have egalitarian consequences and actually support key institutions of the old regime, in particular hereditary nobility.

Kant's debate with his conservative critics has not received much attention, perhaps because, except in the case of Möser, he never formally answered them. Those who have written on the debate have therefore focused on the critics rather than on Kant's response.[6] Others have tried to show that Kant was really responding to canonical writers like Hobbes.[7] But there is good textual evidence that much of what Kant wrote in the years to follow was prompted by and intended as answers to his conservative critics, and that, as a result, he developed his political thought in two directions. First, he attempted to show why exactly someone committed to his view of a free person must also be committed to a republican constitution. Second, he developed a pragmatic view on the implementation of theory in practice, showing how civil liberty can be instituted gradually rather than as it happened in France. In the first part of this chapter I present the debate on freedom and Kant's contribution to it; next, I show how conservatives reacted to Kant's intervention; finally I show how Kant subsequently developed his initial ideas in order to counter his critics.

4. See Chapter 11 of this volume.
5. See letters from Heinrich Jung-Stilling, 1 March 1789, in Kant 1922b: 7–9 and from Johann Gottfried Kiesewetter, 15 June 1793, 1922b: 436.
6. Henrich 1967; Vogel 1972; Stolleis 1972; Beiser 1992; Knudsen 1986.
7. Riley 2007; Williams 2003.

II

The French Revolution put political transformation on the agenda in the German states. In 1789 the Revolution had been extremely well received in Germany, and was hailed by many as the triumph of the philosophy of the Enlightenment.[8] Gentz's statement from a letter to Christian Garve in December 1790 was not untypical:

> The revolution constitutes the first practical triumph of philosophy, the first example in the history of the world of the construction of government upon the principles of an orderly, rationally-constructed system.[9]

But as the Revolution reached its radical phase German intellectuals turned against it. Gentz came under the influence of Edmund Burke and cooled on the principles of liberty that he had once defended. He now warned about the 'fanaticism of freedom', the fervent belief in a limitless liberty to do as one pleases, which he had seen unfold during the Revolution.[10] This led to scepticism about theorists in general: 'the philosopher creates systems; the rabble forges murderous weapons from them'.[11]

Conservatives did not abandon the principle of liberty, however, but either defended a liberty severely curtailed by the state, as Gentz did, or else reached for the traditional view of freedom of the old estate society (*Ständestaat*).[12] Möser defended the traditional inegalitarian conventions of the old German *Reich* where freedom was understood in the plural and not taken to be a basic feature of the human condition. No one should be called simply free because everyone serves someone: a general who does not stand in the ranks of soldiers is not free *as such* because he serves elsewhere in a different way. Even the prince serves and Möser wrote that the prince is therefore as little free as the common man.[13] One should only speak of freedom as exemption from an obligation or a general burden that others must carry. Freedoms therefore come in a wide array of rights, privileges and immunities distributed unequally according to status in the social pyramid.[14]

Defenders of egalitarian principles of freedom had reason to worry, because their ideals were seen as connected to the Revolution. Natural rights theories, like Gottfried Achenwall's, had been dominant in Germany. Achenwall (1719–72) described humans as naturally free, equal and independent

8. Gooch 1966; Aris 1936; Valjavec 1951; Vierhaus 1967. 9. Cited in Epstein 1966: 436.
10. Gentz 1991: 405–6. 11. Quoted in Vogel 1972: 90, my translation.
12. Schlumbohm 1975: 41; Klinger 2006: 451. 13. Möser 1944: 68. 14. Klinger 2006: 449.

of the command of others.[15] When entering the civil state men give up some of their natural freedom and take on obligations; their civil liberty is defined by the rule of law established by civic authority.[16] Natural rights theory was easy to combine with Rousseau's principles, which had had a remarkable influence in Germany. Under his influence, thinkers had, before the Revolution, not merely called for civil freedom but also, like Johann Michael Afsprung (1748–1808), for political freedom, the right of citizens 'to a voice in determining legislation'.[17]

The debate on freedom had immense importance for the question of the justice of hereditary privileges.[18] On Möser's view, these were perfectly compatible with liberty, whereas they were excluded on the egalitarian natural rights view. This was a question of particular importance in Kant's and Gentz's Prussia, where the nobility during the eighteenth century had gained an increasingly powerful position in the bureaucracy, economy and military.[19] Likewise, in Rehberg's Hanover the nobility had never been quite subdued by the monarch,[20] and in Möser's Osnabruck the late medieval *Ständestaat* remained largely in place.[21] The parties to the debate could not know it at the time, but the strength of the German nobility (which was characterised by its anti-democratic views) would come to shape decisively the course of German history over the next century.[22]

Although Kant's debt to Rousseau and Achenwall was obvious, his concept of personal autonomy from 1785 was not a direct argument in this debate because he had not explained its implications for politics. There was no theory of individual rights; his main concern was with the categorical imperative as the test for duties of individuals in abstraction from society. The idea of transcendental freedom might easily be seen as apolitical. It is in principle possible to have a free will even within states that fail to provide civil liberties; personal autonomy does not depend on whether one lives in a monarchy, an aristocracy or a democracy.[23] Someone who only knew Kant's theory of inner freedom might have expected him in the political domain to settle for patient stoicism. But when he published *Theory and Practice* in *Berlinische Monatsschrift* in 1793 he unequivocally sided with the modern concept of a right to equal liberty.

15. Achenwall 1763: §§ 106, 219. 16. Achenwall 1763: § 107.
17. Afsprung quoted in Bödeker 2002: 37. 18. On that debate, see Schultze 1925.
19. Hans Rosenberg named the period Prussia's 'age of noble reaction'. See Rosenberg 1966: 70, 181. Also Berdahl 1988: 78; Wilson 2004: 243, 332.
20. Epstein 1966: 547. 21. Knudsen 1986: 1ff. 22. Berdahl 1988: 3ff; Sheehan 1989: 504ff.
23. On Kant's concepts of internal and external freedom, see Uleman 2004.

Theory and Practice is framed as a polemic against a 'worthy gentleman' who disparages theories and systems. Some have conjectured that Burke,[24] Gentz[25] or Möser[26] was on Kant's mind, but the evidence is inconclusive and it might equally well have been a synthesis of them. Suggestively, however, Möser had published a piece in *Berlinische Monatsschrift* in 1791 where he wrote that the 'scholarly theory (*Buchtheorie*) of the rights of man' had led the Revolution in France astray and that society should instead be guided by 'common practice'.[27] Kant's essay is structured in three parts, but the debate that ensued was concerned almost exclusively with the second and most novel part on civil liberty in a constitutional state. This section, for unknown reasons, carries the heading 'against Hobbes', but apart from one critical remark at the end Kant never engages with him.

Kant starts by establishing the proper relation between theory and practice. When it comes to moral questions, one must establish principles a priori, before experience, and then seek to implement them in practice. One cannot reason from *is* to *ought*; therefore one cannot very well derive morally binding principles from conventions and traditions in the manner of Möser and Burke. The a priori principle for justifying political authority is individual freedom as independence from the arbitrary choices of others. Kant's principle of right, or justice, is the following: 'The limitation of the freedom of each to the condition of its harmony with the freedom of everyone insofar as this is possible in accordance with a universal law'.[28] Freedom can be limited, but only by the rule of law and for the sake of the equal freedom of others, never by reference to public happiness, religious virtue or even moral perfection. Law is just if it could be willed by free and equal subjects, generating a rational 'general will'.[29] Kant was conscious that basing justice on individual freedom went against the traditional view of justifying authority by reference to the common good, and was careful to acknowledge his debt to the tradition even as he reinterpreted it:

> The saying *Salus publica* [*sic*] *suprema civitatis lex est* remains undiminished in its worth and authority; but the public well-being that must *first* be taken into account is precisely that lawful constitution which secures everyone his freedom by laws, whereby each remains at liberty to seek his happiness in whatever way seems best to him.[30]

24. Wittichen 1904. 25. Dietrich 1989. 26. Henrich 1967.
27. Möser 1965: 290. 28. Kant 1912b: 290. 29. Kant 1912b: 295.
30. Kant 1912b: 298. Compare Kant 1907a: 318 and 1934: 489. Mary Gregor identifies Cicero as the originator of the maxim; see her note in Kant 1996: 461.

The principle of right is the source of three a priori principles for a justified constitution. The first is 'the *freedom* of every member of the society as a human being'.[31] This is a critique of paternalistic government (*väterliche Regierung*), which with a benevolent but arbitrary will seeks to impose happiness on dependent subjects instead of giving them the freedom to pursue it in private, as in *patriotic* government (*vaterländische Regierung*). The second principle is a person's '*equality* with every other as a *subject*', which means that freedom must be equal and that 'Every member of the commonwealth must be allowed to attain any level of rank within it . . . to which his talent, his industry, and his luck can take him.' The third principle is 'the *independence* of every member of a commonwealth as a *citizen*',[32] which grants each citizen the right as co-legislator to vote for representatives. Not everyone qualifies as a citizen, however, because apart from not being a child or a woman, one must be 'one's own master (*sui iuris*)' by which Kant meant having some property. (The latter two restrictions have in different ways been singled out as contradicting Kant's universalistic presuppositions.[33]) Kant's three principles of freedom were incompatible both with the absolutist monarchy of Prussia and with the traditional institutions of the old estate society. Although he did not support a right of revolution, it was evident that *Theory and Practice* represented his rejection of the old regime. He would not have to wait long for an answer.

III

Much criticism of Kant came from students and acolytes who felt that his thoughts on politics betrayed the principles of morals he had set up in the 1780s. Radical critics argued that Kant's principles should have led him to support a right of revolution. We will return to this critique at the end. Kant's conservative critics, Gentz, Rehberg and Möser, questioned his egalitarian concept of freedom and the very idea that principles should dictate politics. The three critics were men of state with a commitment to the old regime. Gentz was a Prussian civil servant with an illustrious career ahead of him, which was to include the office of councillor to Metternich and secretary to the Congress of Vienna. Rehberg was a secretary for an aristocratic council in Hanover, where he eventually rose to the highest level. Möser, more than a generation older than the other two, went from being the secretary of the noble estate in Osnabrück in 1742 to the biggest offices of that bishopric

31. Kant 1912b: 290. 32. Kant 1912b: 290. 33. See Mendus 1992.

by the time of his death and, due to his abundant publications, to assume prominence as the most eminent German conservative voice. By 1793, all three had published essays and books against the French Revolution.

Conservatism came in a variety of types, but, as Klaus Epstein points out, it always involved a commitment to the status quo and a desire to preserve it within new circumstances.[34] Gentz and Rehberg were what Epstein calls 'reform conservatives', characterised by a willingness to engage in reform while attempting to secure 'the maximum possible historical continuity' rather than maintaining the status quo or seeking to reverse development.[35] They nonetheless exemplify two different types of conservatism. Gentz was attached to the modern view of individual freedom but disliked its intolerant and fanatical defenders and thought it must be severely limited by the state for the sake of order and stability.[36] Rehberg was less committed to freedom and more concerned with maintaining the old estate society with its guilds, churches and other intermediary associations. He justified authority by appeal to custom: the myriad agreements and traditions through which institutions grow in history. Möser made similar arguments. More than anything else, he was a defender of the old regime. He stood for the German *Kleinstaat*, its nobility and paternalistic rule, traditional beliefs and practices, and, after the Revolution in France, he decisively rejected the rights of man (*das Recht der Menschheit*).[37] His rejection of modern liberal ideas places him close to the category of a reactionary.

Gentz and Rehberg were in the peculiar position of being under the direct influence both of conservative masters and of Kant. Gentz was the translator of Burke's *Reflections on the Revolution in France*, but before that he had studied with Kant in Königsberg where he had assisted with the proofreading of the *Critique of Judgment*. Rehberg was for a period assigned to Osnabrück where he became the protégé of Möser, whom he called his 'fatherly friend'.[38] While he had not actually studied with Kant, Reinhold Jachmann, Kant's friend, described him in a letter to Kant as his 'student' in the broader meaning of that term.[39] Rehberg had studied Kant's ethics at Göttingen and had written a review of *Critique of Practical Reason*, where, some disagreements notwithstanding, he basically agreed with Kant.[40] This double commitment may have contributed to the two critics' uncomfortable

34. Epstein 1966: 7. 35. Epstein 1966: 8–9. 36. Gentz 1991: 424, 429.
37. Möser 1965. 38. Epstein 1966: 557.
39. See letter by Jachmann to Kant, 14 October 1790, in Kant 1922b: 225.
40. Rehberg 1975: 241.

attempt at combining basic Kantian principles with a defence of the old regime.

Gentz's reply to Kant appeared in *Berlinische Monatsschrift* in December.[41] Showing extreme deference (*Ehrfurcht*), he points out that he is in complete agreement with his former teacher about the freedom of the will, but that matters are a bit different in politics. While principles of human rights are necessary for political practice, they do not suffice.[42] In the construction of a constitution, one must go further and find the means for its practical realisation, and this requires empirical knowledge of people and their actual behaviour in social circumstances, which in turn can ground a new theory of implementation.[43] The purpose of this theory is to secure the stability of the state. Dieter Heinrich has argued that Gentz thereby sacrificed Kant's practical philosophy for the sake of Humean pragmatism.[44] It is not clear that Gentz's suggestion is quite so radical – Kant too accepted that constitution-building has an empirical component – but it is evident that Gentz was willing to interpret Kant's basic principles in a way that favoured the political stability of Prussia.

In this endeavour, Gentz was particularly keen to reinterpret Kant's claim that freedom entails equal rights, excluding hereditary prerogatives. He points out that Kant had required only the equality of *subjects* and that he had exempted the head of state from this equality because the sovereign has coercive rights against subjects but not vice versa. Gentz deduces that *all* prerogatives inherently connected to the government of the state must be permitted. As a consequence, the hereditary privileges of monarchs in monarchies, of senators in aristocratic states such as Venice, and of lords as in England are justified.[45] This is rather more than Kant had actually claimed. Kant's point was that, since rulers must have the right to use force, and since subjects cannot have this right, there must remain *one* juridical inequality. But this legal inequality is distinct from the many privileges of princes and nobles in the old regime and it is not hereditary. Perhaps in recognition of the weakness of this interpretation, Gentz adds that hereditary privileges prevent freedom only when they are truly exclusive. They are truly exclusive, however, only if the noble estate has been closed off to new members.[46] Nobility is perfectly just if there is equal opportunity to be chosen to join its ranks due to talent industry or luck, even when the status is passed on to descendants who did nothing to merit it.

41. Gentz 1967. 42. Gentz 1967: 101. 43. Gentz 1967: 103.
44. Henrich 1967: 105. 45. Gentz 1967: 98. 46. Gentz 1967: 99.

Rehberg's reply to Kant followed in *Berlinische Monatsschrift* in February 1794.[47] Like Gentz, he argued that a priori principles do not suffice when it comes to political practice. But he went further: empirical knowledge is necessary not just to know how to implement principles; the very principles of justice themselves are derived from the conventions of historically situated communities. The procedure of universalisation of the categorical imperative is too formal to tell us anything useful about actual conduct (a critique that G. W. F. Hegel, who read Rehberg as a *Gymnasiast*,[48] would later make famous) and the principle remains insufficient even if we add Kant's second formulation, about treating humanity in others as an end and never just as a means.[49] The reason is that according to Rehberg we are technically to respect *reason* as an end in itself and not *humanity*, because (as Kant himself had admitted) humanity involves much more than reason. In real human life reason tends to be mixed with all sorts of folly and caprice and there is no reason why the irrational and arbitrary ways individuals lead their lives should be respected or tolerated. Sometimes humans must *not* be treated as ends in themselves.[50]

Rehberg made a radical separation between having a free will (the cognitive capacity for autonomy) and having external freedom (the right to have one's choices protected by law). When humans seek to realise their freedom externally, they inevitably have to do so using material things – their own bodies and other possessions – and these must be held as private property. But property rights are not given a priori; there is no 'metaphysically free property'.[51] Humans only own their own will, and property rights arise through interpersonal contracts in history. Humans may be free as rational agents in a kingdom of ends, but as members of a real community they have to abide by the distributions of property and rights that have arisen in a society through its history. As a consequence of this dramatic reinterpretation of Kant's separation between the inner and outer domains, Rehberg revises Kant's three principles:

> The *freedom* of every member of society as *human* applies only to that which is really free in a human, that is, it applies to its will. The right to freedom does not belong to the member of the commonwealth as such, to the whole human, but only to the human *in so far as he is a rational being*.[52]

47. Rehberg 1967. 48. Hegel 2000: 224. 49. Kant 1911: 429.
50. Rehberg 1967: 119. 51. Rehberg 1967: 122. 52. Rehberg 1967: 123.

Persons do not have a right to equal civil liberty because when they act within a material world they depend on unequally distributed property. The amount of property a person has, as well as the social status of his trade, determines what estate he belongs to and membership of estates determines civil rights. Since estates are hierarchically organised, there are great differences in the 'scope and content' of rights. These differences are passed down between generations, so that a person's civil rights are inborn and contingent on his forefathers' social rank.[53]

Rehberg employed a similarly conservative and conventionalist logic with regard to citizenship. He agreed with Kant that citizenship must be limited to those who are their own masters, but becoming one's own master is not simply a matter of achieving wealth or being an industrious and skilled craftsman able to support himself. Citizenship rights are established by actual agreements among corporations and guilds; social recognition, not individual enterprise, is decisive. Echoing Möser he wrote, 'In truth, not one person in the world is completely his own master (*Herr*)' because everyone stands under laws that are historically created and express the privileges of institutions within the larger hierarchy of society.[54]

Rehberg concluded that Kant's theory of a civil society based on a priori principles 'can work only in a world where members are entirely, metaphysically free' and 'the makers of their own sphere of action'.[55] Kant had simply adopted Rousseau's principles and he should have admitted, as Rousseau had, that 'his system is fit only for a republic of gods'. If the attempt were still made to implement an a priori system of natural right among humans, anarchy would follow because perfect equality would require the sacrifice of the inherited estates that hold together every existing constitution.[56]

Möser died in 1793 before he had completed his reply to Kant's *Theory and Practice*, but in 1798 Biester published an excerpt in *Berlinische Blätter*.[57] Möser's general view was that rights depend on property, and that property is unequally distributed according to an inherited social hierarchy.[58] But in the essay Möser seeks to show that Kant's theory of justice – the hypothetical social contract – can be used to defend hereditary privileges. Möser had limited patience for philosophy, but he was a good storyteller, and in the reply he told a story about a benevolent emperor who allows his subjects in twelve different provinces to elect their duke. In the six first provinces,

53. Rehberg 1967: 125. 54. Rehberg 1967: 125.
55. Rehberg 1967: 127. 56. Rehberg 1967: 130.
57. Möser 1798. *Berlinische Blätter* was the new name for *Berlinische Monatsschrift*.
58. Knudsen 1986: 168, 179.

the people choose *not* to elect the son of the former duke and the outcome is generally quite bad. If the new ruler is elected because he is educated, he does not know local conditions; if he is not noble, he will not be respected; if the election is democratic, there will be contentiousness and civil war and so on. In the next six provinces, however, the people elect the son of the previous duke, and the outcome is very good. It is convenient that the new ruler can utilise the spectacular old castle; the son will take over the debts of his father; he is related to the nobility in the neighbouring province and can create alliances through marriage; and the subjects see the son as more legitimate because he carries on family traditions and so on. Considering these good consequences of hereditary prerogatives, Möser concludes that a people could very well choose it.

Möser's use of the social contract was not quite what Kant had in mind, and we shall return to Kant's answer to Möser. For now it is worth noting that all three conservative critics defended the existing order, partly from fear of social dissolution, and partly from a conviction that morals result from traditions and conventions. This led them to seek to show the compatibility of hereditary privileges with Kantian principles. It would have been quite an achievement for them to reveal that the principles of the great man of the *Aufklärung* could genuinely accommodate, or even justify, the cornerstone of the old regime.

IV

Kant received Rehberg's essay on 9 April 1794 and the following day he wrote a letter to Johann Erich Biester, the editor of *Berlinische Monatsschrift*, who had invited him to answer his critics.[59] In his letter to Biester, Kant took a swipe at Rehberg. Rehberg writes more like a lawyer than a philosopher, and the lawyer always defends the powers that be. He 'puts a sword onto the scales of justice to balance the side of rational grounds'.[60] Rehberg is not really applying Kant's theories to reality but just engaging in trickery, Kant writes, playing with the words application (*Praxis*) and trickery (*Praktiken*):

> In reading [Rehberg's essay], I found that, as regards the infinite disparity between rationalist and empiricist interpretations of concepts of justice the answering of his objections would take too *long*;

59. See letter from Biester to Kant on 4 March 1794, in Kant 1922b: 490–2 and letter from Kant to Johan Erich Biester, 10 April 1794, in Kant 1922b: 496–7.
60. Letter from Kant to Biester, 10 April 1794, Kant 1922b: 496.

> with regard to his principles of justice grounded on power as the highest source of legislation, the answering would be too *dangerous*; and in view of his already having decided in favour of the powers that be (as on page 122),[61] the answering would be in *vain*.

Kant concluded: 'It can hardly be expected that a man of 70 would occupy himself with tasks that are burdensome, dangerous, and in vain.'[62]

But that was not the end of the discussion. Although Kant appears never to have mentioned the names of Rehberg and Gentz in writing again, he proceeded to compose a string of political essays in which he tacitly continued the debate with his conservative critics.[63] Thus, in *Perpetual Peace* of 1795 he presents himself as a 'theoretical politician', who proceeds differently from 'practical politicians' who employ principles drawn from experience. Likewise, Kant replied swiftly to Möser as soon as the latter's critique was published in 1798. Kant undertook two tasks to meet his critics. First, he developed the explanation of the proper relation between theory and practice. Second, he showed that freedom is not merely a matter of the will but requires equal legal status in a republican state. As a result of this debate Kant developed some of the most central elements of his political theory.

Other thinkers and events also influenced Kant, in particular his views on perpetual peace.[64] But to Kant it must have been particularly important to refute Gentz's, Rehberg's and Möser's interpretations not just because they were influential contemporaries but because these critics claimed to base their reasoning on Kantian principles. They could not be brushed off as entirely on the wrong track. And, to be sure, there was something about their reasoning that might ring true to a reader of Kant both then and now. In *Critique of Pure Reason*, and in later moral writings, Kant had made much of the bifurcation between internal autonomy and external natural causality, between humans as free in a *noumenal* sense and determined in a *phenomenal* sense. It would have been easy to conclude that freedom is just a matter of inner will whereas the external world would be governed by principles drawn from historical practice.

Yet, in *Perpetual Peace* he came out even more clearly in defence of the principles of 1789. He no longer advocated 'patriotic government'; instead, for the first time he publicly endorsed republicanism, stating that 'the civil

61. Kant's page reference is to Rehberg's statement cited above in footnote 50.
62. Letter from Kant to Biester, 10 April 1794, in Kant 1922b: 497.
63. This continuity is also noted in Klemme 1993.
64. See Cavallar 1992.

constitution in every state shall be republican'.[65] The change in terminology may have been a response to Gentz, who had argued that 'patriotic government' could actually be compatible with 'paternalistic government'.[66] In his letter to Kant, Biester had pointed out just this feature of Gentz's essay as troublesome. In the 1790s 'patriotism' was an ambiguous term and could be understood both in a conservative sense, as in Möser's *Patriotische Phantasien* where it indicated adherence to the traditional corporate society, and in a radical sense, where it indicated the egalitarian ideals of the Enlightenment.[67] But 'republicanism' was unambiguously connected with civil liberty, and by switching terms Kant clarifies that paternalism is incompatible with freedom. The republican constitution is defined essentially in the same way as he had previously defined the patriotic constitution, but he now gives a more democratic dimension to his own definition of external freedom: it is 'the warrant to obey no other external laws than those to which I could have given my consent'.[68]

Gentz, Rehberg and Möser had defended different political visions but they were equally sceptical about theory dictating reality. Kant's adversary in *Perpetual Peace* is an imaginary 'practical man', who may have been an agglomerate of the three but who bears the features of Rehberg. In describing this politically prudent man, all the phrases from Kant's letter to Biester about Rehberg turn up. The practical man 'puts the sword into [the scales of justice]', dealing in 'trickery' to get his preferred outcomes.[69] The only other place in Kant's writings up to then where these phrases appear is in the letter about Rehberg (they would appear again in his reply to Möser).

The real problem with the practical man 'who frames a morals to suit the statesman's advantage' is that he is unprincipled.[70] Laws must be constructed from a formal principle and only then implemented in reality instead of letting principles be determined by whatever purposes one wishes to achieve. The practical man is 'putting the cart before the horse'.[71] One cannot hold equal freedom to be an ideal only until one discovers that inherited privileges are conducive to society's stability and prosperity. The practical man dogmatically decides that a particular social arrangement is good and reduces politics to the technical endeavour of finding the means to that outcome.

But social arrangements themselves must be based on principle, resting on the premise of a human right to freedom. Whether specific policies are

65. Kant 1912b: 349; see Dann 2002. Kant had previously used the term in a metaphorical sense to describe a spiritual community and to identify ancient republics and thinkers.
66. Gentz 1967: 97. 67. Vierhaus 2002: 26. 68. Kant 1912b: 350.
69. Kant 1912b: 369, 373. 70. Kant 1912b: 372. 71. Kant 1912b: 376.

justified can be tested by the procedure of the hypothetical original contract where citizens consider whether policies are compatible with equal liberty. Hereditary nobility is a case in point. A people could not agree to inherited rank because merit does not follow birth and 'a nobleman is not necessarily a *noble* man' (Kant adds that it would be equally absurd for the people to agree to a 'born professor').[72] This effectively disposed of Gentz's attempt to argue that Kantian principles support hereditary nobility if there is equal opportunity to seek to join it.

The same idea (and some of the wording) appears in Kant's argument against Möser, published in a pamphlet called *On Turning out Books* in 1798.[73] This would be the final essay from Kant's hand. Again, Kant's argument is that practice 'must always be arranged according to theory'.[74] Möser had attempted to show that Kant *malgré lui* must accept hereditary nobility because its salutary consequences showed that a people could indeed agree to it in a hypothetical original contract. Kant was not pleased. The idea of the original contract is not what people actually will choose, but what they ought to choose. As Kant had argued in *What Is Enlightenment?* a people can want anything including servitude. But they must choose according to the principle of right, not according to what might provide happiness. The chief requirement of right is equal civil liberty, and it is unjust to establish heritable prerogatives 'even if it might be customary and in many cases even useful to the state'.[75]

Rehberg had worried that Kant's principled defence of equal liberties would lead to the collapse of society. Kant recognises that a sudden introduction of equal rights, even if it was not through revolution, might severely weaken the state, which in most parts of Germany at the time depended on the services performed by estate owners and civil servants who were often hereditary nobles. Kant sought a principled accommodation to reality. Starting in *Perpetual Peace* he takes up the idea of 'permissive laws (*leges latae*, *lex permissiva*), which confer a provisional justice on a state even if its constitution is unjust.

> Permissive laws of reason . . . allow a situation of public right afflicted with injustice to continue until everything has either itself become ripe for a complete overthrow or has been made almost ripe by peaceful means.[76]

72. Kant 1912b: 351; 1907a: 329. 73. See Reiss 2001. 74. Kant 1912c: 435.
75. Kant 1912c: 435. 76. Kant 1912b: 327; see Brandt 1995.

Kant is keen to argue that permissive laws are not *exceptions* to laws. That was an approach that Rehberg had advocated when he wrote that, for the sake of order, rulers must very often harm the letter of law to remain faithful to its spirit.[77] But laws are universal and necessary and therefore permit no exceptions. Permissive laws, however, are internally connected to circumstances of implementation, so that feasibility constitutes a limiting condition within the law itself. This condition is that delaying putting the law into effect is permitted 'lest implementing the law prematurely counteracts its very purpose'.[78] That Kant intended permissive laws as a transition from the institutions of the old *Reich* is evident when the idea returns in the *Doctrine of Right* from 1797:

> [The state] has a provisional right to let these titled positions of dignity [hereditary privileges] continue until even in public opinion the division into sovereign, nobility, and commoners has been replaced by the only natural division into sovereign and people.[79]

Following the debate with his conservative critics, Kant for the first time makes an effort to show the connection between freedom of the will and civil liberty. In the *Doctrine of Right*, he supplies the argument lacking in *Theory and Practice* for the unity of personal autonomy and external liberty. Freedom in the 'internal' and the 'external' use both relate to the *same* human capacity for choice; this capacity is the origin of the innate right to equal external liberty and the reason why humans are responsible and can have actions imputed to them.[80] In this book he also argues that being subject to laws of which one can consider oneself the author is not really a limitation on freedom. It is just a limit on 'lawless freedom', which he (in unpublished notes) called 'Polish freedom'.[81]

Next, he shows how human freedom can be expressed through rights to property that are metaphysically grounded, that is, prior to experience. This may have been in response to Rehberg's claim that there is no 'metaphysically perfect property', which was a step in his defence of the property system of the old regime with its unequal freedoms. Although notes and lectures show that Kant had been occupied with the relation between property and freedom since the 1770s, he had not published on it before or attempted to give it a metaphysical grounding. Kant's theory begins with the argument that there can be 'intelligible possession' separated from mere 'sensible possession'.[82]

77. Rehberg 1967: 130. 78. Kant 1912b: 347. 79. Kant 1907a: 329.
80. Kant 1907a: 214, 223. 81. Kant 1912b: 354; 1907a: 316; 1923: 595.
82. Kant 1907a: 245.

This is the difference between physically occupying a house and having a *right* to the house, even if one has left it for the day. To hold on to possessions is not the same as having a right to them. The difficulty with claiming a right to possessions, however, is that ownership comes with a right to exclude others, hence limiting the scope of their freedom. But persons tend to disagree about what rightfully belongs to each, and respect for everyone's freedom therefore requires that an impartial judge must decide any conflicts over claims to property. This judge can only be conceived of as the sovereign, whom Kant calls 'the supreme proprietor'.[83] Specifically, Kant points out that the sovereign, which he conceives as the legislative assembly, may restrict the property rights of the nobility and the church. The nobility's claims to rights in Germany were based largely on holding land for generations, what Kant dismisses as mere 'sensible possession'. It is easy to see the repercussions for Rehberg's argument. For Kant, humans create their own circumstances of justice through the state so that they will not remain hostages to an arbitrary property distribution.

The most pernicious effect of the purportedly sober realism of the conservative man of practice is that he does not just respond to difficult circumstances of justice, but actually *creates* them. The practical man's central proposition is that persons are incapable of free agency, hence they must be managed. As Rehberg had written, a republic is possible only for a nation of angels. But this very propaganda makes people lose faith in their capacity for freedom and self-government.

> Such a pernicious theory itself produces the trouble it predicts, throwing human beings into one class with other living machines, which need only be aware that they are not free in order to become, in their own judgment, the most miserable of all beings in the world.[84]

He continued the argument against the practical men in *Conflict of the Faculties*, published in 1798 but written in 1795. Heavy-handedly they antagonise persons by treating them as if they have no capacity for freedom and as a result they become stubborn and uncooperative, which in turn justifies more coercion and manipulation.[85]

Kant's conservative critics had attempted to prove their points using Kantian reasoning. Kant turns the tables and seeks to prove his republican ideal by the empiricism of his opponents. He argues in Mandevillian fashion that even a nation of 'devils' would be capable of creating a republic if only

83. Kant 1907a: 323. 84. Kant 1912b: 378. 85. Kant 1912b: 80.

they have understanding.[86] Their self-seeking inclinations will naturally lead them to cooperate when facing an external threat, without morality, never mind saintliness, entering the picture.

Returning to his own idiom, he writes that when a republic that respects civil freedom is introduced, humans are also more capable of *developing* the judgement necessary for moral autonomy. Already in *Groundwork* he had written that *a priori* laws still require 'judgment sharpened by experience' for agents to know how to apply the law and to become susceptible to reason's influence.[87] In the *Doctrine of Virtue* he added that it is a duty to cultivate one's conscience.[88] This may be a matter of overall cultivation, as he wrote in *Critique of Judgment*, ranging from the appreciation of art to skills of choosing means to ends in a trade.[89] Pursuing these judgment-enhancing activities requires a domain of security, and civil liberty provides this, 'greatly facilitating' the capacity for autonomy.[90] 'It is not the case that a good state constitution is to be expected from inner morality, on the contrary, the good moral education of a people is to be expected from a good state constitution.'[91] Persons may start as rational devils, but life in the republic puts them on the path to moral freedom.

Realism produces the trouble it predicts, but idealism is equally self-fulfilling. Kant is not about to argue that, if humans were given civil liberty, their behaviour would instantly become rational and autonomous. The point is rather that, if humans are alerted to their capacity for moral autonomy, they will gain faith in it and increasingly act on it. The historical evidence of such freedom is the disinterested sympathy of the onlookers who supported the French Revolution. These onlookers must have been subject to a moral cause, the insight that a nation has a right to establish a republican constitution.[92] While there may be many setbacks in humanity's development, this event 'will never be forgotten', and it will inspire human emancipation everywhere.

Kant nevertheless rejected revolution as a legitimate means of political change and this made him a target for the scattered radicals in Germany at the time. Ludwig Heinrich von Jakob (1759–1827) and Johan Benjamin Erhard (1766–1826) were students of Kant who argued that Kant's basic principles should have led him to support a right of revolution.[93] While Kant had argued that the logic of sovereignty excludes a legal right of revolution, they thought that Kant would still be committed to a *moral* defence of it. But a

86. Kant 1912b: 366. 87. Kant 1911: 389. 88. Kant 1907a: 401, 440. 89. Kant 1913: 431.
90. Kant 1912b: 376. 91. Kant 1912b: 366. 92. Kant 1798a: 86.
93. Von Jakob 1794; Erhard 1970. Fichte had already made this claim in 1793, see Chapter 11 of this volume.

moral right of revolution makes no sense in Kant's scheme, because there is an unconditional duty to obey the state and there can be no conflicts between moral and legal duties and no exceptions from them. In this regard Kant's thinking is rigorist. But his rejection of resistence is not quite the same as a demand for absolute obedience to whoever exercises superior power in a territory. Kant never wrote that political entities that entirely fail to respect the rule of law qualify as states and impose on us a moral obligation to obey.[94] There is reason to believe that Johan Heinrich Tieftrunk (1759–1837), Kant's friend and editor, got it right in a commentary on Kant's *Rechtslehre*, published hard on the heels of the *Rechtslehre* itself:

> If a government in a state sinks so low that it perverts all right, and abolishes the human entitlements that no man can give up without losing his sense of dignity, then the civil bond is broken by the ruler himself.[95]

When the civil bond is broken, persons do not face a ruler nor are they in a state and as a consequence there is no longer an obligation to obey.

If one lives under monarchy, as Kant did, and one does not accept a right of revolution, it follows that monarchy must be legitimate at least for a transitional period. Yet, Kant is often thought to have been a staunch defender of monarchy and therefore not seriously committed to republicanism. Kant's defence of state authority was indeed vigorous, but the 'Hobbesianism' identified by Richard Tuck and others should not be taken too far. Referring to paragraph 51 of *Rechtslehre*, where Kant discusses autocracy, Tuck claims that, for Kant, 'a single-person legislator [is] quite possible and even desirable on the ground of simplicity'.[96] But Kant's view is a little different:

> It is true that, with regard to the administration of right within a state, the simplest form [autocracy] is also the best. With regard to right itself, however, this form of state is the most dangerous for a people, in view of how conducive it is to despotism.[97]

Kant adds a tacit quotation from Alexander Pope's lines 'For forms of government let fools contest / whate'er is best administer'd is best', which he rejects out of hand as false.[98] Kant associated this sentiment with the royalist and anti-revolutionary Jacques Mallet du Pan (1749–1800), who, as Kant

94. For a more extensive discussion, see Maliks 2013.
95. Tieftrunk 1798: 366. A substantially similar interpretation to that of Tieftrunk is offered by Ripstein 2009: 325–52.
96. Tuck 1999: 211; Stedman Jones 1994.
97. Kant 1907a: 339.
98. Kant 1907a: 339.

reports in *Perpetual Peace*, had taken it as his motto.[99] Incidentally, the name of the translator of Mallet du Pan was Friedrich Gentz. To be sure, republicanism to Kant is compatible with monarchy (as it was for Rousseau and for many others in the republican tradition) but he had in mind constitutional monarchy, where sovereignty remains in the elected legislature. Kant's constitutionalism was not well developed, but he evidently supported the rule of law, the separation of powers (if not checks and balances), and government accountable to citizens in elections.

Kant is often thought to have lacked realism. Fania Oz-Salzberger doubts his commitment to republicanism because he 'did put forward proposals for republics [but] did not apply them to present-day Germany'.[100] But this is like saying that Kant proposed the categorical imperative but failed to apply it to Englishmen because the English are not mentioned in *Groundwork for the Metaphysics of Morals*. Kant intended his moral principles to apply universally; like most philosophers, he did not see it as his task to specify how they should be implemented in one particular time and place. We have nonetheless seen that he was unusually sensitive to the difficulties of applying theory in practice.

V

Kant developed his philosophy in two fundamental ways during the debate with Gentz, Rehberg and Möser (and others who may have shared their views) in the aftermath of the French Revolution. First, he became more radical, endorsing republicanism for the first time and sharpening his critique of hereditary nobility. In the process, he showed that the capacity for personal autonomy entitles persons to civil liberty, in particular the rights to property, which are instrumental to the exercise of freedom. Additionally, civil liberties facilitate the development of judgement necessary for free human agency. Second, he developed his views in a more cautious direction when it came to implementation. This led him to the principle of a permissive law allowing gradual transition if implementing a law suddenly would undermine its purpose. Kant's contribution to the German debate on freedom was to provide the foundation for a liberal theory that was sensitive to its historical context of realisation.

The controversy between conservatives and progressives, between those who wished to restructure society according to a human right to freedom and

99. Kant 1796: 353. 100. Oz-Salzberger 2002: 218.

those who wanted to conserve traditional institutions, remained a source of discord in Germany for decades to come. When dusk fell on the first day of the ideological battlefield of the French Revolution, Hegel made reconciliation the task of philosophy. His *Philosophy of Right*, published in 1820 – only a few years after the Congress of Vienna – dominated the first part of the new century because it succeeded in convincing many that Kantian personal autonomy and civil rights can be preserved and sustained within traditional ethical life, complete with revived estates.

11

Freedom and state action in German late Enlightenment thought

Alexander Schmidt

In the fragment Nr. 216 of the *Athenaeum*, the leading journal of the early German Romantics, Friedrich Schlegel declared in 1798 that the French Revolution, Goethe's *Wilhelm Meister* and Fichte's *Wissenschaftslehre* were the pre-eminent tendencies (*Tendenzen*) of the time (*des Zeitalters*).[1] Schlegel's famous claim reveals a boasting self-confidence of young intellectuals around 1800 about the German contribution to human progress. It parallels a political revolution with what was perceived as a revolution in science, philosophy and aesthetics.[2] These latter revolutions are usually associated with Kantian philosophy, and German classical and romantic literature. Schlegel's fragment, however, leaves the question unanswered of how these revolutions are linked. This chapter attempts to provide this linkage, in the case of the concern with individual freedom and its relation to the state in works by Johann Gottlieb Fichte, Wilhelm von Humboldt and Friedrich Schiller, all written between 1792 and 1795. The argument will be that, in response to the problem of political transformation from the Old Regime to a new order, which became crucial in the course of the French Revolution, they developed theories of freedom which take their departure from man's capability of spontaneous self-determination driving a process of moral and aesthetic self-formation (*Bildung*). Their aim was to construct a political order that would give rise to human perfection and prepares man for the enjoyment of greater civil freedom, thus avoiding violent revolution.

To understand their answers means understanding the problems which they were trying to solve.[3] These lay at the core of modern civilisation and

I am indebted to Avi Lifschitz, Reidar Maliks, Isaac Nakhimovsky, Tilman Reitz, Quentin Skinner and James Vigus for their comments on earlier versions of this chapter.

1. Schlegel 1967: 198. 2. Cf. Moggach 2011.
3. On this complex see also the groundbreaking study by Beiser 1992.

of old regime absolutist politics in particular. Fichte, Humboldt, Schiller and a number of other German authors shared a concern with the modern bureaucratic state and its effects on human nature. In their view, despotic rule, hereditary prerogatives, the increasing division of labour and the resulting separation of human faculties constrained man's development to greater freedom.

In their unease with the external and domestic expansion of absolutist monarchy with its standing armies and levelling administration, liberal enlightened thinkers agreed with the conservative defenders of the *Staendestaat*, in which the power of the prince was balanced by the privileges of the nobility and other orders of society.[4] In contrast with conservatives like Justus Möser, Fichte, Schiller and Humboldt were also highly critical of enlightened paternalism. Paternalism had its roots in the Christian understanding of the prince as the divinely imposed authority and *pater patriae*, who should take care of religion, and the spiritual and physical well-being of his subjects. In the eighteenth century these ideas became blended with the utilitarian aim of enlightened absolutism to promote the earthly happiness of the people. Paternalism and the growing police state found their legal expression in numerous sumptuary laws and other regulations policing daily life, which in Germany were comprised under the title of *Policey-Gesetze* and taught at universities as *Policey-Wissenschaft*.[5] *Policey* also resounded with the natural law tradition. Gottfried Achenwall, whose works were used as textbooks of natural law by German academic teachers including Kant, provides a standard example. In his *Elementa iuris naturae* of 1750 he stated that it was the right of the ruler to take care of everything 'that pertains at the perfection of the subjects, be it with respect to their soul, their body, or their state in general'.[6] Achenwall deduced from this the right to found schools and universities and to prevent ideas which might harm the state.

What frustrated many German authors with paternalist ideology and its modern version of enlightened eudemism was the idea that someone else was responsible for our happiness.[7] In this respect, Fichte, Humboldt and Schiller at first viewed the French Revolution as an important historical step in the direction of a state based on human rights and principles that gave greater autonomy to the individual and abandoned inequalities based on birth. However, particularly Humboldt and Schiller were far from

4. Cf. Chapter 10 of this volume. 5. Maier 1980. 6. Achenwall 1995: §718.
7. For example, Fichte identified in 1793 the source of all current misery in the assumption that the prince had to watch over our happiness. Fichte 1964a: 171.

advocating a violent revolution. Despite their criticism of the old regime, they were convinced of the current state's ability to further reform.

Particularly public opinion was seen by authors like Immanuel Kant and Christoph Martin Wieland as a decisive means to bring about further progress and educate both subjects and rulers in order to make the former capable of greater liberty and the latter to understand the need to give up power. It would thus be misleading to overlook this German context and reduce the political and moral ideas of Fichte, Humboldt and Schiller to a simple response to the events in France. For them, the Revolution and its increasingly violent course only exemplified a central dilemma of the Enlightenment: could man become fully human and autonomous under the complex conditions of a specialised society and a potentially corrupting civilisation? What Fichte, Schiller and Humboldt here were faced with was the same problem that, according to John Zammito, lay at the core of Kant's response to Rousseau. It was 'the Rousseauian dilemma that virtue was both more necessary and less possible in our civilized condition'.[8] In the following pages I will analyse three attempts, all written between 1792 and 1795, to solve this dilemma.

I

In the summer of 1793 Fichte published *A Contribution toward Correcting the Judgment of the Public about the French Revolution* in which he applied Kantian philosophy to the current debate about the Revolution.[9] The *Contribution* was an angry pamphlet in which a little-known and destitute teacher in the household of a Prussian nobleman attacked the political and intellectual establishment. Its direct target was the just published *Investigations on the French Revolution* by the Hanoverian civil servant August Wilhelm Rehberg.[10] In this work, which comprised a number of earlier, insightful reviews of publications on the Revolution, Rehberg had criticised the events in France from the perspective of an enlightened bureaucrat committed to reform from above. Particularly, Rehberg's reviews for the *Allgemeine Literatur-Zeitung* provided the German public with a first-hand account of tracts by Edmund Burke, Thomas Paine and a number of other British and French authors before these works were translated into German. Through his critique of Rehberg, Fichte thus engaged with the most prominent texts of the debate.

8. Zammito 2002: 117.
9. Fichte 1964b: 203–404. On Fichte's revolutionary writings see La Vopa 2001: chs. 3 and 4.
10. Rehberg 1793. On Rehberg's political thought see Vogel 1972 and Chapter 10 of this volume.

Though Fichte wrote a fiery vindication of the French Revolution, he was far from getting involved in a detailed and (particularly after Louis XVI's execution) risky defence of its course in terms of day to day politics. For him, the events in France were only illustrations of universal moral and political principles. He thus cautioned his audience against reading his text as an inspiration for taking up revolutionary measures. Reform would be always preferable to a violent and potentially misguided upheaval. As Anthony La Vopa stressed, Fichte's *Contribution* could not really overcome the tensions between his preference for gradual reform and his defence of revolution.[11]

However, in his first chapter Fichte ventured to prove the legitimacy of the revolution in terms of Kant's transcendental principles. He thus fired the opening shots in the debate between Kant and his conservative disciples about the relation between theory and practice in politics ensuing the publication of his teacher's theory and practice essay in September 1793 (see ch. 10). As is well known, the legitimacy of the Revolution was a core issue in the British debate on the events in France from its very beginnings. Burke took on Richard Price's favourable comparison between the French and the Glorious Revolution in England in his *Reflections on the Revolution in France* of 1790. Against Price's human rights language, Burke rehearsed the classical Whig portrait of the Glorious Revolution as a restoration of England's ancient laws and ancient constitution. Burke created much controversy with his claim that the people had basically no right to alter a historically legitimate constitution like the English.[12] In his *The Rights of Man* Thomas Paine challenged Burke's alleged statement that the English parliament of 1688 could bind all 'posterity to the end of time'.[13] Instead, the parliament was only a delegate of the actual people, which could finally make decisions and claims about the constitution and its possible alteration.

In contrast, Rehberg's position was more complex than Burke's. Despite his advice against the translation of the *Rights of Man* he basically agreed with what he viewed as Paine's simple-minded claim that recurring constitutional changes and reform must be possible. Rehberg, however, stressed that there would be great obstacles to putting into practice a theory solely based on man's rights and reason; not least since the majority of the people were not able to act and judge reasonably.[14] In contrast, Fichte was determined to take no prisoners and treated Rehberg as being in the same camp as Burke. By discussing the constitution in terms of contract theory, Fichte

11. La Vopa 2001: 111. 12. Burke 1999: 100–12. 13. Paine 1989: 64.
14. [Rehberg] 1791: 517. The journal *Allgemeine Literatur-Zeitung* can be accessed via http://zs.thulb.uni-jena.de/content/main/journals/alz.xml.

took his point of departure from a well-established natural law tradition. For him, the question whether a constitution can be overthrown came down to whether the contracting partners were justified to make a contract in the first place.[15] In a decisive turn, however, he deviated from the well-trodden path of popular sovereignty arguments. He asked whether change could be prevented if it was part of the contract's agreement never to change the contract. According to Fichte, this would contradict man's progress towards greater freedom and thus moral law. Here, man's rational and autonomous nature is embedded in a constant process of *Bildung* and culture. Everything in the sensual world has its value only insofar as it contributes to our culture (*Kultur*). Fichte defines 'culture' as an asocial exercise concept. It is a means to use all our forces 'for the purpose of absolute freedom, i.e. complete independence of everything that is not our-self, not our pure self'.[16] The *Contribution* employed Kant's reflections on man's ultimate purpose in the *Critique of Judgment*. Having rejected happiness as man's final goal in nature, Kant argued for man's formal ability freely to set himself purposes: 'The production of the aptitude of a rational being for any ends in general (thus those of his freedom) is culture. Thus only culture can be the ultimate end that one has cause to ascribe to nature in regard to the human species.'[17]

Culture in this context comprises a positive and a negative meaning. It denotes a skill on the one hand and self-discipline on the other, by which we liberate the will from our desires. In the *Contribution* Fichte mainly refers to the latter meaning of culture as a means for the self to subject the realm of the sensuous (*Sinnlichkeit*). This includes not only physical objects like our body but also our psychic faculties like feelings, drives and intellect. In sum, everything that can be formed, trained or improved. The aim of culture is to make man autonomous, that is, solely dependent on his pure self by putting the sensual realm into his service:

> This culture to freedom is thus the only possible ultimate purpose (*Endzweck*) of man, insofar as he is part of the realm of the sensuous (*Sinnenwelt*); this highest sensuous purpose, however, cannot be the final purpose of man as such, but only the last means to achieve his higher spiritual purpose, which is the complete congruence (*Übereinstimmung*) of his will with the law of reason.[18]

In this passage, Fichte employs three concepts of liberty. One is the transcendental quality of all rational creatures, namely the condition for being

15. Fichte 1964b: 240. 16. Fichte 1964b: 241.
17. Kant 2000: 299 (§ 83), cf. Geuss 1996. 18. Fichte 1964b: 243.

rational, making decisions, following them out. The second is our capacity to be an independent cause, which is related to our being an agent within the phenomenal world, and the third is what he calls a 'cosmological' freedom, a state in which we depend solely on our pure I.[19] The last cannot be achieved by temporal beings alone but remains the aim of culture and mankind as a whole. One can surely agree with Isaiah Berlin that this threefold concept of liberty is one of self-mastery and self-realisation and thus belongs to the rather dubious camp of positive liberty.[20] Yet this would miss some of the early Fichte's central Rousseauian concerns like being free from dependence of men, particularly the arbitrary will of a (despotic) ruler.

From this point of reflection Fichte returns to politics. It is now clear that every human activity has to be judged with a view to this final purpose of an autonomous self which only abides by the self-imposed rules of reason. Thus, no constitution could be legitimate which blocks human perfection and the possibility of reform and change. The *Contribution* conceded that numerous objects for the culture and self-discipline of the individual such as schools had been granted by the established regimes in Europe. This, however, would not entitle them to require in return an absolute obedience or gratitude. The first reason is that culture or *Bildung* can never be imposed extrinsically but must be acquired autonomously in a process of self-appropriation.[21] Secondly, the 'guardians of the people', as Fichte ironically addressed Europe's princes, had granted these means only to pursue their own ends, not human freedom. Their aim was twofold: to rule absolutely at home and to enlarge the borders of their realms.[22] They had thus taught their subjects to follow the law, had trained them in the military and the sciences to enlarge their power and increase their splendour.

It should be noted that one of the topics of Fichte's *Contribution*, the replacement of an illegitimate order, had its firm place in early modern political theory in the debates on resistance. These older debates, at least in the German Lutheran context, were concerned with how to restore and return to a legitimate (good old) political order against tyrannical rule.[23] This 'conservative' core was now significantly challenged by a new concern with man's perfectibility. The aim of resistance theory became transformed into the question of installing a novel political as well as social order apt to

19. Fichte 1964b: 252*. 20. Berlin 2002: 191–7. 21. Fichte 1964b: 244.

22. Fichte 1964b: 247. Given the identical formulation, this condemnation of monarchical power politics was obviously adapted from Rousseau's account of the Abbé de Saint-Pierre's peace project. See Rousseau 1991a: 592.

23. Benert 1973: 17–36.

fit the requirements of an open future and thus human progress. Yet despite Fichte's concern with the (illegitimate) privileges of the nobility and the church, his emphasis on man's moral and transcendental nature was, as La Vopa has highlighted, rather blind to the question of material needs as a legitimate reason for revolt.[24]

Based on the absolute I as a transcendental condition of cognition and moral autonomy, Fichte developed a radically individualist approach to revolution and the social contract. He thereby significantly reformulated an argument from Kant's famous *What Is Enlightenment?* essay of 1784, with which the young philosopher must have been familiar. In this essay Kant strongly objected to the idea that a church assembly could rightly fix a religious dogma for all time, for this would deprive future generations of autonomous reasoning and enlightenment.[25] Kant's essay was written in the safe anti-orthodox religious climate of Frederick the Great's late rule.

When Fichte boldly took up the argument he did this under the much less favourable political circumstances of the Woellner era in Prussia and widespread anti-revolutionary paranoia. Nonetheless, he unearthed its political potential and launched it against any attempt permanently to fix the traditional political order. Even if the people, or any other legitimate sovereign, decide to prohibit alterations or a revolution of the constitution they will not be justified in doing so from the perspective of moral law and man's capability of freedom and self-perfection. Rousseau's *volonté général* could become implanted into a singular I. The *Contribution* went as far as to claim that any individual could leave the state and thus unilaterally abrogate the social contract if it prevented man's culture.[26]

This claim is certainly open to a number of objections. And it is no surprise that it soon provoked strongly critical responses. Karl Leonhard Reinhold, whose anonymous review of the *Contribution* for the *Allgemeine Literatur-Zeitung* appeared in May 1794 as Fichte succeeded him as professor of philosophy at Jena university, argued that this would turn the notion of a social contract upside down. Even if it might be allowed to abrogate the contract, the state would be entitled to require compensation for the security and the education (*Cultur*) it provided. Furthermore, if the state could not claim any recompense for the means of culture it bestowed, then there could have been no contract in the first place.[27]

24. La Vopa 2001: 126–7. 25. Kant 1912a, b: 38–9. 26. Fichte 1964b: 290–1.
27. [Reinhold] 1794: 351–2 and 353–4. Cf. Jens Immanuel Baggesen's similar judgement in Fuchs 1978: nr. 102.

Fichte's early concept of liberty had certainly what one might dub an anarchist and a utopian tendency. Saxe-Weimar's chief-minister, Christian Gottlob Voigt, was confronted with reports from Fichte's malicious colleagues in Jena in June 1794 stating that the young professor had declared to his students that there would be neither kings nor princes in twenty to thirty years.[28] Yet this libel had a true core. In fact, it was only logical that Fichte viewed the state as a transient means for human perfection and freedom which would be abolished after it had fulfilled its function.[29] One might even doubt whether he thought of any legitimate role for the state to play at all.

Fichte later recognised the shortcomings and incoherences of the radical individualism in his first major political work. And it was not only due to his new position as a philosophy professor at Jena, for which officials had asked him to renounce 'democratic fantasies' (Voigt), that he gave up writing the third part of the *Contribution*, which he had already announced.

II

In contrast to Fichte's *Contribution*, Humboldt's *The Limits of State Action* has become something of a classic of the liberal tradition.[30] While his call for the state to keep out of most social affairs resonated widely in nineteenth-century liberalism and its modern followers, it is often overlooked that the anthropological basis for Humboldt's theory is an aesthetic, not a utilitarian concept of human nature.

Humboldt made clear from the outset what he considered to be the value of his considerations with respect to reform and revolution. Moving the limits of state action and leaving greater freedom to the individual would help to evade revolutions and violent rebellions. In contrast to Fichte, who came from a humble social background, Humboldt had first-hand experience of the French Revolution through a visit to Paris in the summer of 1789.

Nevertheless, when he drafted *The Limits of State Action* in 1792, the twenty-five-year-old Prussian nobleman was concerned not only with the new French constitution but with the pathologies of the modern bureaucratic state in general. Through an army of excellent private teachers, Humboldt was acquainted with state-of-the-art political, economic and moral theory. As a result of his service in the Prussian department of justice, which

28. Fuchs 1978: 121 (nr. 133). 29. Fichte 1964b: 254.
30. The standard German edition is Humboldt 1903: 97–254. A modern English translation is Humboldt 1993. For a recent, thoughtful interpretation see Beiser 1992: ch. 5.

he quit out of dissatisfaction in 1791 after less than one year, he had also gained practical experience. In his view, both the French constitution of 1791 based on rational principles alone and the paternalism of the modern commercial monarchies posed a threat to individual freedom and *Bildung*.

For Humboldt, to understand the proper limits of state activity implies two interconnected questions: first, what is the end of the state and, second, what is the nature and purpose of man? Before he addresses the crucial latter question he puts the problem of liberty and the state into the well-established scheme of historical comparison between modern states and ancient republics. Humboldt here seems to anticipate Benjamin Constant's famous defence of modern liberty against a dangerous imitation of classical models in his *The Liberty of the Ancients Compared with that of the Moderns*. Constant argued that modern life consists of commerce and the peaceful enjoyment of private pleasures. In contrast, the ancients, while enjoying a greater share in government, had been slaves in their private life.[31] At first glance, *The Limits* sounds very much like this cardinal text of early liberalism:

> The ancients devoted their attention more exclusively to the harmonious development of the individual man, as man: the moderns are chiefly solicitous about his comfort, his prosperity, his productiveness. The former looked to virtue: the latter seek for happiness. And hence it follows that the restrictions imposed on freedom in the ancient states were, in some important respects, more oppressive and dangerous than those which characterize our times.[32]

Humboldt was convinced that the modern state was in many ways, such as regarding private liberty, a standard of civilisation, enlightenment and political stability, far superior to that of the ancients. In a letter to his friend Friedrich Gentz from January 1792 he also restates Montesquieu's claim that virtue is an unlikely basis for modern commercial states.[33] Yet, from a closer reading of *The Limits* it becomes clear that Humboldt was considerably less satisfied with modernity than Constant. For him, a distorted view of human nature was the basis for the extensive taxation and welfare policy of the bureaucratic state, which viewed man only in terms of utility and happiness. The moderns would hence regard 'rather what man possesses than what he really is, and that with respect to the latter they do not, like the ancients, cultivate, even to uniformity, the physical, intellectual, and moral faculties and . . . suppress those energies which are the source of every active virtue'.[34]

31. Constant 1988: 307–28, esp. 316–17 and 325. 32. Humboldt 1993: 7; 1903: 104.
33. Humboldt 1935: 54–5. Cf. Montesquieu 1989: 25–6 (I, 5). 34. Humboldt 1993: 7; 1903: 104.

Humboldt, however, made it no secret that he regarded a return to classical republicanism as misguided. In a telling letter to Schiller of December 1792 he expressed his distance from the effects of republicanism in revolutionary France:

> Generally speaking, free constitutions do not seem to be too crucial and beneficial. A tempered monarchy surely less fetters the development of the individual. However, they immensely intensify our powers, elevate the whole human being and thus, in a true sense, effect the only real good.[35]

The Limits leaves no doubt that under the conditions of modern civilisation freedom can only progress by furthering 'the development of individuals'.[36] In order to avoid the one-sidedness of both ancient and modern politics, the task was to revive some of the ancients' concern with man's moral energies and implant it into the privatised conditions of modernity.

In a next step, *The Limits* thus defines the true end of man as 'the highest and most harmonious development of his powers to a complete and consistent whole'.[37] Humboldt distils some elements of an extensive debate among German intellectuals about man's perfectibility and self-cultivation into this chapter.[38] Although this has been overlooked by modern scholarship, his definition is nearly identical to two paragraphs in Gottlieb Hufeland's *Doctrines of Natural Law* of 1790.[39] Hufeland, a young professor of law at Jena and an early follower of Kant, tries to build a system of enforceable rights and duties, including a right to resist, on the notion of human perfectibility. Our moral duty freely to cultivate ourselves and promote the perfection of mankind, Hufeland contends, justifies us in preventing by force any impairments of this capability. As long as they do not interfere with the external freedom of others there must be no limit to the development of our intellectual forces and virtues.

By contrast, Humboldt avoids any notion of collective moral perfection in terms of mankind's increasing ability to follow the precepts of the categorical imperative. Instead, he replaces notions of virtue by the morally neutral categories of energies and powers. In one passage he even claims that virtue consists in energy. This raises some questions regarding the moral limits of this concept of *Bildung*, such as whether crimes or other morally doubtful acts would be permitted as long as they serve self-cultivation. As Ursula

35. Humboldt 1962: 53. 36. Humboldt 1993: 48; 1903; 143.
37. Humboldt 1993: 10; Humboldt 1903: 106. 38. See Sauter 1989.
39. Hufeland 1790: §§ 68–70.

Vogel stresses, Humboldt formulates his ideal of human purpose or *Bildung* in 'aesthetic categories'.[40] Consequently, he seeks to complement utility and interest as basic human drives with love and disinterestedness. Only something done or performed for its own sake fits the requisite of being part of our self-appropriation of skills and experiences. At the core of this is a notion of a human personality as a fully developed work of art. With respect to this, Raymond Geuss makes Humboldt one of the champions of freedom as self-realisation in an impressive gallery of positive types of liberty.[41] This certainly does justice to the strongly intertwined character of *Bildung* and freedom. However, taking a closer look, one might ask whether this does not lump together human perfection and its condition into one. *Bildung* presupposes liberty but is not identical with it. As Humboldt states, 'freedom is but the possibility of a various and indefinite activity'.[42]

With these assumptions, Humboldt is ready to answer the question of the purpose and limits of state action. Unsurprisingly, he strongly advises against the extension of state activity beyond the care for security. The 'spirit of governing' would 'fetter the free play of individual energies'.[43] Instead of providing help, governmental measures would only take away human initiative and autonomy. 'They accustom', Humboldt continues, 'men to look for instruction, guidance, and assistance from without, rather than to rely upon their own expedients.'[44] With this Humboldt was very much in line with a growing criticism of paternalist policy in late eighteenth-century Germany. Parallels can be drawn with the political economy of (French) physiocracy, one of the most thorough critiques of mercantilism and the often concomitant paternalist policy. Borrowing the condemnation of the 'fury to govern' from the late Count Mirabeau's *Essay on Public Education* (1791) as his motto, Humboldt, from the outset, aligned his cause with physiocratic reform and the French debates about civic education. Physiocrats wanted to reduce state interference in the economy to set the natural forces of society free.

Humboldt followed this argument when he claimed that his programme would increase the forces of the nation and would thus, in the end, also make the state stronger and richer. Yet, with his call for the state to keep completely out of the economy, education and matrimony, and even refrain from taking pre-emptive measures against crime, the young Prussian nobleman went much further than the conventional criticism of paternalism and mercantilism. He thereby repudiated all plans by neo-republican authors like

40. Vogel 1982: 83. 41. Geuss and Hollis 1995: 97. 42. Humboldt 1993: 4; 1903: 100.
43. Humboldt 1993: 18; 1903: 113. 44. Humboldt 1993: 19; 1903: 115.

Rousseau to revive a public spirit through national education, national feasts and a civic religion.

To understand more precisely what Humboldt here was writing against, it is instructive to turn back to the immediate origins of Humboldt's manuscript. The text was triggered by a controversy with Carl Theodor von Dalberg about the proper limits of the state, after which Dalberg asked Humboldt to write down his ideas. Combining the roles of a Catholic cleric, member of the illuminati order (under the name of Baco de Verulam), intellectual dilettante, vice-regent and designated successor of the influential archbishop of Mainz and as such future arch-chancellor of the empire, Dalberg is an enigmatic figure in German history around 1800, not least through the role he later played as the director of Napoleon's *Rheinbund*. While Humboldt published only a few chapters, Dalberg came out in 1793 with a short tract, notably titled *On the* True *Limits of State Action*.

Dalberg claimed that the end of the state was the happiness of its members. Probably borrowing from Humboldt, he defined happiness as the development of one's own powers and their socially beneficial exercise.[45] Against Humboldt, Dalberg argued that happiness can only be increased the more everyone considers himself as part of a greater whole. To loosen the bonds of society, religion, policing and education would only make men dull and inactive like brutes.[46] Ancient states like Sparta had understood this very well. The state should thus take an active role in promoting agriculture, arts and sciences, a civil religion, and public education. Dalberg's text is interesting less because of its originality than because of its prominent author and the somewhat crude melange of paternalist Christian, enlightened eudemist and Rousseauian ideas he employed.

Humboldt was well aware of the radicalism of his theory, a fact soon to be proven by the rejection of his manuscript by a Prussian censor. The final chapter of *The Limits* thus contemplated the possibility of setting his ideals into practice. Here, Humboldt applied the model of gradual reform. The state should further and adapt to a growing ability of the citizens to be free.[47] Making itself increasingly irrelevant was hence the proper aim of the state.

III

It is instructive to turn from this to Schiller. For it is around the problem of man's ripeness for freedom that his *On the Aesthetic Education of Man in a*

45. Dalberg 1793: 3–5. 46. Dalberg 1793: 9–10. 47. Humboldt 1993: 143–4; 1903: 241.

Series of Letters (here abbreviated as *Aesthetic Letters*) of 1795 revolves. This text is also crucial because it responds to the problems broached by Fichte and Humboldt. Schiller was an avid reader of the manuscript of *The Limits* and one of Humboldt's closest friends, who moved to Jena in 1794 to spend his time with Schiller. Schiller also printed the second chapter of *The Limits* in his journal *Thalia* and assisted in finding a publisher for the whole manuscript. He moreover shared Humboldt's enthusiasm for Mirabeau's *Essay on Public Education* of 1791 and was an attentive reader of Burke's aesthetic and political writings. Being intrigued by Kant's philosophy since 1791, Schiller also took vital interest in the work of Fichte, who as his new colleague at Jena university was appointed to preach the Kantian gospel.

At first glance, Schiller's *Aesthetic Letters* were less directly concerned with politics than Fichte's *Contribution* and Humboldt's *Limits*. They should equally be read, however, as a response to the problems raised by the French Revolution. Schiller's point of departure was the idea of an intertwined and gradual progress of political and civil liberty, which had been promoted as a preferable alternative to violent revolution by a number of German *Aufklärer* since the early 1790s.

Though the first drafts of the *Aesthetic Letters* were written only one year after Humboldt's *Limits*, they were confronted with a very different historical setting. Schiller sympathised with the French Revolution but quickly became appalled by its violent course. In December 1792 he contemplated writing a vindication of Louis XVI and planned to travel to Paris to defend the king in the trial which led to Louis's execution in January 1793. In Schiller's eyes, the Terror had challenged the very principles on which both the Revolution and the project of man's enlightenment rested. In one of the letters to Friedrich Christian Duke von Holstein-Augustenburg of July 1793, which formed the basis for the later *Aesthetic Letters*, he claimed:

> The attempt of the French people to assume its sacred human rights and achieve political liberty had only revealed its inability and unworthiness and had not only thrown this miserable nation but also a considerable part of Europe and a whole century back into barbarity and slavery.[48]

According to Schiller, a corrupted generation had demonstrated that one was not ripe for political liberty if human freedom had not yet been accomplished. Schiller's criticism here resounded with Burke, who doubted

48. Schiller 1992: 262.

in a public address to François-Louis-Thibaut de Menonville in July 1791 'that France is at all ripe for liberty on any standard'.[49] Burke highlighted that men were only qualified for civil liberty as far as they could control their passions. Taking up a well-established motif of ancient moral philosophy, he declared that 'men of intemperate minds cannot be free'.[50]

In stark contrast to Burke, Schiller remained committed to the vision of a new society based on the principles of moral and political autonomy which he identified with the original intent of the French Revolution. Already in his early history lectures in Jena he had praised the constitution of Solon because it was flexible enough to allow human development and freedom. The Athenian constitution rested on the 'principle, on which all states should be based . . . to impose laws on and by oneself'.[51] In the letters to the duke von Augustenburg, Schiller leaves no doubt that freedom is 'the most sacred of all goods . . . and the centre of culture'. But, as he now saw more clearly: a free constitution must be built 'on the firm ground of ennobled character'.[52]

The third letter of the *Aesthetic Letters* lays out this political programme more precisely. Contemporary man would find himself in what Schiller describes as *Notstaat* (State of Needs) or *Naturstaat* (State of Nature), which only provides the necessary means for man's security and material needs.[53] It very much resembles the historically grown absolutist state, established to contain man's unruly physical nature. This state does not sufficiently do justice to man's moral and rational nature, and thus can be rightfully overthrown. The aim of history must be the *Vernunftstaat* (State of Reason) based on moral and egalitarian principles, where law follows the direction of the categorical imperative. However, the attempt of the French had shown the risks of radically absolving the former to attain the latter. The question was hence how to find a harmonious transition from one state to the other, which also corresponds to man's sensuous and rational nature. Help could certainly not be expected from the current state, for it was part of the problem, not part of the solution. It is thus clear why Schiller, in turning to aesthetic education and man's nature, thought that he could offer a more profound remedy for the dilemmas of modern politics.

The problem was further complicated by the fact that, as indicated above, modern man was deeply corrupted by civilisation. Following Rousseau, Schiller presents contemporary society as characterised by a materialist

49. Burke 1992: 69. 50. Burke 1992: 69. 51. Schiller 1970: 440.
52. Schiller 1992: 265. See Schmidt 2009. 53. Schiller 1962: 313–15.

and utilitarian morality, an alienating division of labour, man's intellectual faculties and personality and a mechanised bureaucracy. In this highly specialised society man could become nothing but a fragment of himself. Schiller thus challenged the prevalent enlightened faith that refinement and the (material) progress of society would naturally bring about liberty. In broad terms, Schiller addressed the question raised in the classical republican debate and later restated by Rousseau: how can a free constitution be built when citizens are already corrupted?

In contrast to the republican tradition, Schiller transferred the problem into the entirely different conceptual frame of Kantian philosophy. He thereby critically responded to Kant's and Fichte's concept of *Kultur* and *Bildung* as self-mastery of one's sensual nature. Schiller agreed that moral autonomy was the purpose of human nature. But he asked how the principle of self-governance can be implanted into us as sensuous creatures constrained by causality and nature. Schiller here picked up an issue that Kant was trying to solve in the *Critique of Judgment*. As Paul Guyer has forcefully stated, Kant's account of aesthetic judgement was deeply concerned with linking aesthetics and morality.[54] By showing that morality becomes palpable to man in his aesthetic experience, Kant aimed to bridge the gap between freedom and nature without abolishing this crucial distinction.

In his discussion of aesthetic judgement Kant described beauty as the 'symbol of morality' (§ 59). This analogy between moral and aesthetic judgement rests on a number of parallels. The important common feature, however, is that they are both free from antecedent desires for their objects and are thus not heteronomously determined.

Schiller understood this idea from the *Critique of Judgment* very well. Yet in contrast to Kant he sought to give beauty a more objective character in the sense of a certain state of personality. Against Fichte and Kant, he thereby argued that a suppression of our natural inclinations for the sake of the autonomy of our moral judgement would not make man fully free. Instead, as Frederick Beiser has recently pointed out, the *Aesthetic Letters* developed two notions of liberty.[55] One followed the Kantian notion of a free and spontaneous (moral) reasoning. But, as Schiller made very clear, this moral freedom can be prevented from fully realising its capacities in the world by our physical and sensual nature, our passions and drives. He thus proposed a second notion of freedom, in which our sensual nature is not suppressed but propitiated by our intellect.

54. Guyer 1993. 55. Beiser 2005: 150–64. Cf. Roehr 2003.

Hence, a work of art can teach our moral judgement how to tame the material and sensuous in the realm of appearance without forcing it. We can experience this equilibrium between rational 'form drive' and sensual 'material drive' in what Schiller calls the aesthetic state of our psyche, where we are determined by neither sensation nor reason. He thereby concedes to potential critics that beauty produces no particular intellectual or moral result. It cannot make us discover truths, enlighten us or prompt us to perform our duty. Aesthetic culture rather leaves man entirely indeterminate to do what he will.

> But precisely thereby something infinite is achieved. For as soon as we recall that it was precisely of this freedom that he was deprived by the one-sided constraint of nature in the field of sensation and by the exclusive authority of reason in the realm of thought, then we are bound to consider the power that is restored to him in the aesthetic mode as the highest of all bounties, as the gift of humanity itself.[56]

Thus only through this (temporary) condition of a neutral will can we realise the full capacity of our being. Equally, art and beauty are not only the symbols of this equilibrium. Human self-realisation or wholeness is itself a form of beauty which allows us fully to articulate our moral autonomy.

The parallels to Humboldt, who was a constant dinner-guest at Schiller's apartment during the gestation period of the *Aesthetic Letters*, can hardly be overstated. Schiller clearly took up Humboldt's aim to restore (temporarily) the integrated personality of the consciously idealised Greek character under modern conditions. In fact, in the sixth letter Schiller contrasted the fragmented modern man with the natural totality of the ancient Greeks.

This ideal does not, however, imply a pure interest in self-perfection and an apolitical disregard for society. It was conceived as an alternative to a utility-based sociability. To be sure, Humboldt's theory of character and Schiller's aesthetic education are morally neutral and fairly ignorant about problems of social justice. Yet they are not as asocial as Fichte's transcendental I. In accord with Humboldt, the temporal and limited character of man ensures that we all need exchange, peaceful competition and interaction with others in order to develop our powers. Particularly friendship and the partnership between the sexes are important means to become fully human. The improvement of man's social relations is certainly one of the central themes of the *Aesthetic Letters*. In the fifth letter Schiller deplores that: 'In

56. Schiller 1967: 147; 1962: 377.

the very bosom of the most refined sociality egotism has founded its system, and without ever acquiring therefrom a heart that is truly sociable, we suffer all the contagions and afflictions of society.'[57]

Schiller builds on the Mandevillian and Rousseauian notion that man by nature is not a social creature and that under the conditions of (modern) society human relations are increasingly corrupted by serving our material interests and self-liking.[58] In contrast, the disinterested state of aesthetic experience can form the basis for a free social interplay that treats others not as means for our own ends. Here, Schiller employs Kant's claim in the *Critique of Judgment* that 'the beautiful interests empirically only in society'.[59] The taste and the pleasure we take in beautiful things can only be developed within society. Reciprocally, taste further promotes our sociable inclinations. Kant, however, remained rather sceptical with regard to a transition from 'the agreeable to the good'.[60] He shared the belief, on which both Rousseau and contemporary Christian moralists agreed, that in striving for social reputation the empirical interest in beauty could also foster vain and corrupting passions (§ 41).

Schiller, who took up this Kantian criticism in the different context of his discussion of the sublime, however, emphasises the distinctively social character of the psychic experience of beauty. The final twenty-seventh letter stresses the harmony produced within individuals and between them by beauty. 'No privilege, no autocracy, of any kind, is tolerated where taste rules, and the realm of aesthetic semblance extends its sway.'[61] Taste, understood as a specific communication about beauty, somehow functions as a neutral ground where we are taught disinterested and equal exchange. Schiller thereby consciously turned the Kantian vision of a proper progress from cultured morality to good taste upside down (§ 60). For him, it was the cultivation of beauty and taste that would promote morality.

IV

Schiller left a number of questions unanswered. The *Aesthetic Letters*, notably, remain imprecise about the agents and the practical implementation of aesthetic education. This gave them a somewhat utopian character, which led later to the claim that they were not political at all. In contrast to these claims, Schiller's contemporaries like Friedrich Gentz or the young Hegel,

57. Schiller 1982: 27 (translation changed); Schiller 1962: 320. 58. See Hundert 1994.
59. Kant 2000: § 41. 60. Kant 2000: § 41. 61. Schiller 1982: 217; 1962: 411.

who welcomed the *Aesthetic Letters* as a 'masterpiece',[62] and others took the political message seriously.

Fichte immediately replied to Schiller in a text entitled *On the Spirit and the Letter in Philosophy in a Series of Letters* of 1795. He submitted the essay to the journal *Die Horen* and was baffled when Schiller, its editor, rejected it.[63] If one takes a look at the argument one can doubt that this was solely based on purely stylistic grounds as Schiller claimed. In fact, against Schiller, Fichte insisted on the priority of moral and political freedom over aesthetic education. He conceded that it was risky to grant freedom to men, who had not developed a sense for beauty. However, he equally claimed that under conditions of suppression 'the idea of elevating men through aesthetic education to be worthy of freedom, and to freedom itself, will get us into a vicious circle'. First of all, the courage had to be instilled 'to be neither the master nor the slave of anyone'.[64] Fichte here also rehearsed Rousseau's criticism of taste and the arts as corrupted under the conditions of luxury and despotic rule. In contrast to Schiller, it was not the artist but the philosopher who could offer this courage and intellectual basis for moral and political action as Fichte had tried to show in his *On the Nature of the Scholar* of 1794.

Nonetheless, this was not the last word in the debate. Despite the differences between his concepts of freedom and human drives and Schiller's, in his *System of Ethics* of 1798 Fichte discussed the duties of the fine artist (*ästhetischer Künstler*) in terms that took a remarkably Schillerian point of departure (§ 31). Fichte attributed to fine art a similarly holistic function with respect to human nature as the *Aesthetic Letters* had done. According to Fichte, fine art solely cultivates neither reason nor the heart but 'the entire unified human being'.[65] To look at the moral law as something that is not externally imposed but generated by oneself and thus beautiful means to take an aesthetic point of view. The social function of aesthetic sense in promoting the purpose of reason, that is, freedom as autonomy, is hence to prepare us for virtue.[66] Yet, in contrast to Schiller, Fichte does not derive an entire programme of social reform from this commitment. Aesthetic education sustains the cause of freedom and moral autonomy but the latter is clearly by no means dependent on it. The effect of art and the artist with respect to the progress of humanity is thus only partial and

62. Hegel 1952: 25. 63. See Wildenburg 1997.
64. Fichte 1981: 348; translation: Fichte 1984: quote 85.
65. Fichte 1977: 307; translation: Fichte 2005: 334.
66. Fichte 1977: 308; translation: Fichte 2005: 335.

neatly circumscribed within the bigger picture of the division of labour and duties.[67]

V

By way of concluding I should like to highlight the specific achievements and common features of Fichte's, Humboldt's and Schiller's notions of culture and *Bildung*. As is well known, moral perfection and culture had been recurring subjects of debate among German *Aufklärer*. Moses Mendelssohn, Johann Bernhard Basedow and other thinkers laid great stress on achieving virtue and perfection through external promotion, that is, education and teaching. In contrast, Schiller's *On the Aesthetic Education of Man* takes a different approach. While the essay prominently features *Erziehung* in its title, the term is rather misleading. In fact, Schiller manipulates and rejects its conventional meaning, arguing that aesthetic education can only be achieved from within by the individual, not through an instructor. One can now see more clearly how the early Fichte, Humboldt and Schiller took their departure from the Enlightenment's ideals but deviated from them as a result of their encounter with Kant's concept of autonomy.

In contrast to Enlightenment thinkers such as Mendelssohn or (Schiller's and Humboldt's friend) Dalberg, this clearly ruled out the state as an agent of self-perfection. Fichte, Schiller and Humboldt agreed with Kant's definition of external freedom, which allows everyone to 'seek happiness in whatever way he sees fit'.[68] They were hence deeply concerned with the Machiavellian pathologies of (monarchical) states, which pursue their own ends in terms of power politics and thereby interfere with the crucial process of *Bildung*. Their notion of *Bildung* disconnected the state from the promotion of happiness and thus imposed a limit on what politics can legitimately do. Through the education of individuals to full human beings they believed that one could achieve what Rousseau had deemed to be utterly incompatible in *Émile*: making both man and citizen. Though some of the obvious intricacies of the radical individualistic approach in German thought around 1790 later led to a positive re-evaluation of the state in Fichte and Hegel, it would be erroneous to regard the young Fichte's, Humboldt's and Schiller's projects as theoretical failures. Hegel's concept of the state should rather be seen as an attempt to integrate Schillerian insights.

67. For strongly critical comments on this restriction of aesthetics to a mere supplementary role see Hegel 1968: 60.
68. Kant 1912b: 290.

12

The political conditions of free agency: the case of Mary Wollstonecraft

Lena Halldenius

I

The focus of this chapter is the complex interplay between politics and morality in the thought of philosopher, novelist, political thinker and feminist pioneer Mary Wollstonecraft. In the decade between 1787 and her death in 1797, Wollstonecraft produced educational literature, works of political philosophy, a book about the French Revolution, an account of her travels in Scandinavia, and two novels, one of which lay unfinished when she died and was published posthumously. This was in addition to translations of religious and moral works from French and German and her day-job as book reviewer and editorial assistant to the *Analytical Review*, a journal that was started by Joseph Johnson who also became her publisher. She rose to some fame in 1790 upon the publication of *A Vindication of the Rights of Men*, which is a defence of the Revolution in France in the form of an open letter to Edmund Burke. She thoroughly established herself as a person to be reckoned with in intellectual circles in 1792 with *A Vindication of the Rights of Woman*, a scathing indictment not only of conservative politics but also of those progressive men of her own circle who saw fit to defend the rights of man as universal rights but without including women in the mankind whose rights they are. Where, she asks, does this leave women? Strangely suspended in mid-air between person and brute, women act and think, commit to and perform on duties, yet are not considered quite human enough to qualify as

I wish to thank Quentin Skinner and Martin van Gelderen for their initiative and encouragement and all participants of the symposium at the European University Institute at which an earlier version of this piece was presented. I am indebted to Åsa Burman, Ulrika Björk and Martina Reuter for insightful comments, and to Lilli Alanen and the Understanding Agency programme group at Uppsala University. The Bank of Sweden Tercentenary Foundation (Riksbankens Jubileumsfond) has provided financial support for which I am grateful.

rights-bearers. What can women be and do in a society that denies them full personhood?

It is fundamental to Wollstonecraft's moral theory that morality as a standard of rightness is derived from nature and knowable through reason. She takes this so much for granted that she hardly argues for it. The *principles* of morality are a matter of eternal, universal truth with a foundation in nature and they are the same for all. She alludes to (and needs) this unshakeable nature of morality to highlight the subversive inconsistency in calling women good while keeping them ignorant of moral duties and of holding them to duties at all while denying them rights.

Famously insisting that 'there there can be but one rule of right, if morality has an eternal foundation' and that there is no 'sex to morals',[1] she still and importantly regards the political situation of persons as prior to moral *agency*. Attending to the relation between the political circumstances of women, and other persons who live lives of dependence and subordination, and the moral principles to which they are duty-bound by nature is crucial for understanding Wollstonecraft's politics. The importance of claiming rights for women was for her not merely so that they could become citizens but, more fundamentally, so that they could be moral agents in full. Political exclusion is, ipso facto, moral exclusion.

Proceeding from an interpretation of Wollstonecraft's view of freedom and the centrality of 'independence' within it, I shall attempt an analysis of the priority of the political situation to moral agency. This priority, I argue, can be explicated in terms of three interconnected but analytically distinct relations. Two are explanatory relations. The first is causal and explains the psychological effects of oppression and submission; the other is conditional and explains processes of deliberation and reasons for action. The third relation is constitutive; it concerns the moral character of an act. I maintain that moral agency for Wollstonecraft is an exercise of freedom; moral acts are characterised by having the modality of being performed freely. An act cannot be properly classified as moral unless it is performed in circumstances where the agent is properly classified as free. Since Wollstonecraft's non-dependence approach to freedom makes freedom institution-dependent, a person who is unfree by political arrangement cannot perform acts that are moral in the proper sense. The political situation of women in Wollstonecraft's day – mere cyphers in the eyes of society[2] – made moral agency psychologically, deliberatively and inherently unavailable to them.

1. Wollstonecraft 1995b: 106. 2. Wollstonecraft 1995b: 93.

After a brief comment on the meaning and function of 'political', I shall elaborate on independence, a concept that is crucial to the explication of both freedom and virtue. I shall then proceed to the analysis of the three relations that I identify between the political and the moral: the causal, the conditional and the constitutive.[3]

II

Neither in *A Vindication of the Rights of Men* and *A Vindication of the Rights of Woman* nor in her two novels does Wollstonecraft make any extensive use of the terms 'political' or 'politics'. One rare but significant occurrence in *A Vindication of the Rights of Woman* is the remark that closes the second chapter: 'as sound politics diffuse liberty, mankind, including woman, will be more wise and virtuous'.[4] Let me explain how and why I use these terms to indicate that which is prior to moral agency. I do it via the tripartite distinction she makes – in republican spirit – between different kinds of rights, which we find in *An Historical and Moral View of the Origin and Progress of the French Revolution*.[5] Natural rights are the rights of natural morality to life, liberty and property. It is imperative for Wollstonecraft to emphasise that natural rights establish equality; distinctions not founded on reason (like hereditary wealth or the distinction between male and female virtues) are 'unnatural'.[6] Political rights are rights against oppression and are predicated on natural rights. The violation of political rights is not made up of separate instances of wrongdoing; it is a structural feature of society by which groups of people are excluded from the benefits of improvement that come with secure and stable enjoyment of natural rights. Civil rights are the rights of a people to be regarded as sovereign source of authority.

From this classification I distil a meaning of 'political' as a field of contestation concerning oppression; the question whether or not a person is oppressed is *the* political question. Arising 'out of the partial laws and customs of society'[7] oppression is a fall-out of formal institutions (like positive law) and informal institutions constituted by social norms (like socially entrenched and sanctioned expectations of female behaviour). The salient feature for our purposes is that oppression establishes relations of

3. In addition to *A Vindication of the Rights of Men* (1790) and *A Vindication of the Rights of Woman* (1792), Wollstonecraft's novels are important sources. They are *Mary, a Fiction* (1788) and the fragment *The Wrongs of Woman: or, Maria* (1798, posthumous).
4. Wollstonecraft 1995b: 108.
5. Wollstonecraft 1989a: 162, 187 and 221.
6. See for example Wollstonecraft 1995a: 8; 1995b: 93 and ch. 9.
7. Wollstonecraft 1989c: 83.

domination and a corrupting dynamic that inhibits the moral character of both oppressors and oppressed. Being oppressed is to be dependent – subjected to the will of another 'fallible being' – while submitting to the will of a perfect being (God) is the same as being independent,[8] and this dependence is sanctioned or constituted by the institutions of society. In Wollstonecraft's work this is the *political* situation not only of women but also of the poor, suffering under a system in which wealth is adulated: 'the man who lives by the sweat of his brow has no asylum from oppression . . . when was the castle of the poor sacred?'[9] Unpicking this political situation and how it stands in relation to morality requires an analysis of Wollstonecraft's theory of freedom, centred around the notion of independence.

Independence, Wollstonecraft's master value, is a merger between two complex moral concepts: freedom and virtue. It is an expression of the interplay between the political situation of a person and her individual mental states or habits of mind; it is also a vehicle for talking about moral agency.

Along with several of her contemporaries and predecessors in the republican camp, Wollstonecraft uses freedom to stand for independence in relation to others, in the sense of not being vulnerable to their whim. This applies both to an individual person in relation to others within a social union and to that social union – a people – in relation to external powers.[10] Being unfree is to be dependent on the caprice or arbitrary will of another, who by that position of dominance alone is a tyrant. Liberty is lost through dependence on the will of a master. Saying that liberty is lost is not to imply that something they once held was actually taken from them; it refers to a moral deprivation, a loss of personhood. Wollstonecraft uses 'slavery' to signify this position.[11] Unfreedom is a denial of the moral standing of your person and not directly related to what you can actually do or not do. A slave who is unrestrained is in this sense as unfree as if she were in chains, while an act that you are able to perform is nonetheless performed unfreely if you act at the mercy of another.

An implication of this, visible in both of Wollstonecraft's novels, is that the wife of a rich man is as economically dependent as a pauper begging

8. Wollstonecraft 1995b: 120. 9. Wollstonecraft 1995a: 13. See also 10 and 16.
10. Compare Price 1991. See O'Brien 2009 on Wollstonecraft's relation to her contemporary Enlightenment thinkers. See Maynor 2003, Pettit 1997, Skinner 1998 and 2008b for analyses of the republican view of freedom. See Halldenius 2003 for an interpretation of Locke along these lines.
11. See Wollstonecraft 1995b: 80, 103, 116, 117, 119, 234, 246, 248, 262, 285 and 1989b: 49, 52, 110, 232, 234. Compare Price 1991: 23 and Locke 1988: 283.

in the streets. The structure of their respective situations is the same; they have nothing they can call their own.[12] When Mary, the heroine of Wollstonecraft's first novel, is overcome by repugnance over her marriage, she exclaims: 'I will work, do anything rather than be a slave.' Being a wife is represented as slavery while working for wages as escape from servitude.[13] In fact, the importance Wollstonecraft gives to women's economic independence can hardly be overemphasised.[14]

Independence is a social phenomenon, not only because it is violated by social relations of a particular kind but because it arises as an issue only in a mode of existence which is social in character. The claim that domination constitutes a violation is predicated on the 'natural equality of man';[15] the 'birthright of man' is a degree of liberty 'compatible with the liberty of every other individual with whom he is united in a social compact'.[16] Sociality is natural, in the sense that everything that Wollstonecraft says about rights and freedom proceeds from sociality. Liberty has no point of reference outside or beyond a state of human coexistence. In isolation a person can be neither free nor unfree since the circumstances of freedom as non-dependence are not in place.[17] Unfreedom consists not only in the presence of the wrong kind of relations but also in the absence of recognition of personhood, which is not a physical absence. It is a denial of status and so makes sense only against the background of a set of social facts in relation to which status and the lack of it has meaning.

Consequently, independence can never be in contrast or opposition to social connectedness for Wollstonecraft. Indeed it is only by looking at an individual in the social context within which her life is lived that we can know whether she is independent or not. Independence is not a fact about an individual person; it is a moral position, an equal interdependence, inherently social, and bolstered by a substantive morality of equality of mutual influence between all parties who possess the capacity for reason and by virtue of that are equally endowed with natural rights. She is famous for arguing that this capacity and the endowment of natural rights (the most basic one being the right to liberty of persons) have nothing to do with sex: 'I here throw down my gauntlet, and deny the existence of sexual virtues, not excepting modesty. For man and woman, truth, if I understand the meaning of the word, must

12. Wollstonecraft 1989c: 149. 13. Wollstonecraft 1989b: 55.
14. See Wollstonecraft 1995b: 165. See also Taylor 2003: 165–75 on equality and independence in relation to property.
15. Wollstonecraft 1995a: 51. 16. Wollstonecraft 1995a: 7.
17. See Halldenius 2009 on the distinction between the meaning and circumstances of freedom.

be the same.'[18] It is necessary to her moral theory to deny that there is one set of virtues for women and another for men. If virtue and rightness were different things for different people, then morality would be relative, and she cannot have that since it would amount to founding morality on utility conceived as sheer convenience.[19] She repeatedly asserts that the reason to hold on to a unified account of virtue, the same in kind for everyone, is found in the nature of morality as an eternal standard, not in observations of what people seem to be like. The separation of standards for conduct into one set of norms for women and another for men is regarded as a direct violation of 'unchangeable morals'.[20] Wollstonecraft's account of independence is individualistic but not atomistic. It is predicated on interdependence within social coexistence, with respect for equal individual rights serving as side-constraints.

This brings us to the internal aspect of independence – independence of mind[21] – in which I trust my own reasoned judgement above any other authority. Independence of mind is a feature of freedom *and* of virtue. To be a moral agent is to be at one's own disposal, to have the power to act and speak for oneself and be held to it, to have the standing of someone to whom others can be accountable. This presupposes the recognition of a capacity or at least potential for independent thought. When Wollstonecraft talks about moral development and the acquisition of virtue (which she does a lot) this is what she has in mind: virtue as an acquired mental habit, a disposition to independent deliberation based on reason. Independence of mind is a quality of the virtuous person. She uses reason in this context for the capacity to grasp principles, form judgements and know what to do in the light of them. There is nothing mysterious about (practical) reason understood in this way; it is an acquired deliberative capacity, but more than anything it is an ongoing endeavour. Becoming a moral agent – thinking for oneself and acting rightly for moral reasons – is not the end stage of a process; it *is* the process, a constant struggle against doubt, desire and the debilitating effects of deprivation and dominance. Falling short of the eternal standard of morality is inherent to the human condition.

Virtue, then, is an attitude of the mind but also an action-guiding principle: universal rather than narrow or partial benevolence. A moral agent

18. Wollstonecraft 1995b: 124. See also Wollstonecraft 1995a: 48 and 1995b: 68, 76, 78, 87, 92, 106f, 110, 114, 132, 211, and Gunther-Canada 1996.
19. Wollstonecraft 1995b: 95 and 124.
20. Wollstonecraft 1995b: 117.
21. See Wollstonecraft 1995b: 174 and 243, and 1989a: 148 for use of this expression. See also Sapiro 1992: 62 and 80.

acts on universal benevolence because it is a moral duty to do so. A person with a dependent mind will not see beyond personal emotional ties or self-interested gratification and will act benevolently only when it serves her own interests or the narrow circle in which she moves: 'As they [women who are educated for dependence] submit without reason, they will, having no fixed rules to square their conduct by, be kind, or cruel, just as the whim of the moment directs.'[22] Part of the process of a developing mind is moving from being swayed by self-interest or personal ties to having respect for humanity as reason for one's actions.[23]

One of Wollstonecraft's major concerns is the link between independence in relation to others and independence of mind and the conviction that the process of developing an independent mind is hampered by subjection to the will or mind of others; but the link is intricate. Both the *Vindications* are filled with references to the damaging mental effects of dependence, deprivation and humiliation but also of abundance and power. The dynamic of oppression degrades master and slave alike.[24] But hard as it is to avoid, there is no determinism in this relation; it is possible but difficult – particularly for women[25] – to escape or overcome these psychologically damaging effects. So what is it like if you do? If, for some reason, you 'dare to think and act' for yourself, despite being socially dependent – if you are like one of the heroines of Wollstonecraft's novels – what kind of agent can you be?

First, though, let's stay a while with those who do not escape, those women who 'hug their chains and fawn like the spaniel'[26] to please their master, or the poor who 'quietly lick the dust'[27] without any sense of their own consequence. They, and the psychological relation between the political and the moral to which they are victim, are the main concern of *A Vindication of the Rights of Woman*.

III

In *The Rights of Woman* Wollstonecraft's argument for equality between the sexes and women's rights is expressed in this 'simple principle':

> if she [woman] be not prepared by education to become the companion of man, she will stop the progress of knowledge and virtue;

22. Wollstonecraft 1995b: 120. See also 1995a: 21.
23. See Wollstonecraft 1995b: 68, 144, 211, 221, and 1995a: 31 and 33 on moral motives for action. See also Sapiro 1992: 59–63, and Reuter 2005: 125.
24. Wollstonecraft 1995a: 39 and 61, and 1995b: 69.
25. Wollstonecraft 1995b: 234.
26. Wollstonecraft 1995b: 161.
27. Wollstonecraft 1995b: 126.

> for truth must be common to all, or it will be inefficacious with respect to its influence on general practice. And how can woman be expected to co-operate unless she know why she ought to be virtuous? unless freedom strengthen her reason till she comprehend her duty, and see in what manner it is connected with her real good?[28]

The 'simple principle' encapsulates the complexity of the political – moral relation, but most obviously it formulates the causal relation between political situation and moral development. It is worth noting that the argument is not merely that women be better educated, but that the normative context in which education of both men and women takes place be reformed. A bad education and a confined life within a set of norms according to which your main or only function is to be an inoffensive, polite ornament will foster cunning and vanity and an interest in petty, trivial things.[29] Sound judgement and magnanimity are not to be expected. This insight into the psychological improbability of intellectual robustness and moral dispositions developing in the minds of people who 'under the specious name of innocence' are kept ignorant and treated like children is an important theme of *The Rights of Woman*[30] but Wollstonecraft applies it to all people who live a hierarchically structured life within which only manners and obedience are valued: 'Soldiers, as well as women, practise the minor virtues with punctilious politeness.'[31] Taking a cue from Adam Smith's point about the 'easy price' at which the rich acquire admiration and benefits, she maintains that they 'have ceased to be men', intent as they are only on pleasure and property with nothing substantial to think about.[32] The point, of course, is that there is nothing special about women. What is special is the severity of their confinement and the systematic bombardment of humiliation to which they are subjected.

This is one way in which moral agency is politically circumstanced. That is, there is a causal relation between the political and social situation of people's lives and the development of practical reason and moral dispositions.[33] This relation is explanatory; it serves as evidence-based explanation of human behaviour. Wollstonecraft sees it as part of a male strategy: 'as blind obedience is ever sought for by power, tyrants and sensualists are in the right when

28. Wollstonecraft 1995b: 68.
29. Wollstonecraft 1995b: 89. See also Muller 1996: 55f.
30. Wollstonecraft 1995b: 87–94.
31. Wollstonecraft 1995b: 92. See also Sapiro 1992: 81–89.
32. Smith 2002: 65 and Wollstonecraft 1995a: 8.
33. See particularly Wollstonecraft 1995b: ch. 4. See also Bahar 2002: 38 and Abbey 1999, on causal relations.

they endeavour to keep women in the dark, because the former only want slaves, and the latter a play-thing'.[34]

In *Maria* the heroine observes that women's enslavement is made all the more effective by their being taught to turn their moral sentiments to partial, not universal, concerns. As Mill was later to say in *The Subjection of Women* (1869), men want women to be their *willing* slaves.[35] The strength of this social dynamic can be accounted for only by noting that women are taught not only to comply and yield, but to love it, the goal being that they obey not out of fear but out of a conviction that they should have no life of their own. Wollstonecraft's most unequivocal expression of this causality is when she says, in reference to Rousseau's *Émile*, 'Considering the length of time that women have been dependent, is it surprising that some of them hug their chains, and fawn like the spaniel?'[36]

This causal relation establishes probabilities. It is strong, but not necessarily overriding of other factors and conditions. It does not determine a person's moral and intellectual fate; the relation admits of exceptions without being falsified. It is possible but difficult ('a herculean task'[37]) for the unfree to rise above their political confinement and develop judgement and sound dispositions in spite of it. In other words, an oppressed woman is not inevitably condemned to a state of infantile stupidity. Wollstonecraft was fascinated by this possibility, but also by the frailty of it.

In *The Rights of Woman* there are merely scattered hints at this possibility, as when she says that 'whatever effect circumstances have on the abilities, every being may become virtuous by the exercise of its own reason'.[38] In the context, she seems to be making mainly a metaphysical point about human nature, bolstered by theological concerns, rather than pointing out a practical possibility. This should not surprise us. In an argument for social reform – which *The Rights of Woman* ultimately is – the important thing to convey is the harmful effects of oppression, not the chance of individual moral resistance in the face of it. The causal relation between oppression and a compliant mind is the argument of Wollstonecraft the social reformer. For the sake of progress and posterity, we need to understand the damage that is done to subjugated people who are kept in a state of infancy.

34. Wollstonecraft 1995b: 93. 35. Mill 1989b: 132. See Wollstonecraft 1989c: 145.
36. Wollstonecraft 1995b: 161. See also 115. Compare 'adaptive preferences' in Elster 1983: 110–24, Nussbaum 2000: 136–44, and Sen 1999: 62f. See Gunther-Canada 2001: 102–8 on 'denaturalising' sexual distinction.
37. Wollstonecraft 1995b: 234. See also 1995b: 154–5 on the lower classes, but compare 1995a: 15 and 1989c: ch. 5.
38. Wollstonecraft 1995b: 89.

The possibility, fragility and frustration of mental escape or resistance is discernable in *The Rights of Woman* but investigated mainly in the novels. How does a person who escapes or resists the psychological effects of oppression negotiate the trap she is in? How can your sense of self survive when the very foundation of your being as a person, your capacity for reason, is denied? Intellectually independent yet socially dependent, *what is it like to live like that?* This brings us to the other two relations between politics and morality.

IV

The conditional relation, which I shall now go on to analyse, is explanatory, but in a different way from the relation that I have just discussed. The conditional relation sets conditions for what reasons are available for deliberation. The psychological relation explains behaviour and attitudes by pointing to their causes, causes that might not figure in the deliberations of the persons affected. To exemplify, even if it is correct that oppression and ignorance are the causes that explain why a mother instructs her daughter to act sillier than she is in front of eligible men, that may tell us nothing about this woman's deliberations. The reason on which she acts will not be to perpetuate women's subordination but to secure her daughter's future in combination with the belief that men prefer silly women to clever ones.

My main interest here is how this conditional relation can operate in the case of women who have escaped the psychological effects of oppression while still being oppressed, in other words, women who have independent minds but are socially dependent. This brings us to Wollstonecraft's novels, both of which narrate the claustrophobic experience of women who find themselves trapped by and in a life that deprives them of all dignity. *Mary, a Fiction* is a quiet tale of a young woman's journey from aspiring hope to bitter disappointment. It has been described (incorrectly in my view) as introverted, self-indulgent and without politics.[39] *The Wrongs of Woman, or: Maria* can be read as a fictionalised version of *A Vindication of the Rights of Woman*. With its scathing indictment of 'the misery and oppression, peculiar to women' it is flamboyantly political.[40]

Maria, the heroine of *The Wrongs of Woman*, voluntarily marries a man whom she thought was good but who turns out to be a brute who married

39. See Todd 1991 and Johnson 2002: 199. Compare Kelly 1996: ch. 2 Conger 1994: ch. 2 and Elfenbein 2002.
40. Wollstonecraft 1989c: 83. See Kelly 1996: ch. 8 on the rhetoric of *Maria*. See Conger 1994: ch. 10 for a comparative reading of the novels.

her for money. Her married life is one of physical impediments, legal interventions and actual deprivations. When she threatens to leave her husband, he locks her in her room. When she escapes he hunts her down, takes her child and has her confined to an asylum. He takes full advantage of his legal powers as husband.

Mary, of *Mary, a Fiction*, is married against her will to a man she hardly knows, in a deal to unite two family estates. Until the last page they do not spend a single day in each other's company. At no point does he force her to do anything or deny her anything. She is plagued by the indignity 'at having been thrown away – given in with an estate'[41] but her discontent has nothing to do with the husband as a person. Let us stay with Mary for a while, since she makes an illuminating illustration of the conditional relation.

For most of the story Mary's decisions are explained by her determination not to assume the role of a wife; the humiliation of being bartered in a property deal is incompatible with her self-esteem and the notion that she could be obligated by a forced bond is incompatible with her moral convictions. She clings to the idea that she is what in fact she is not: a person whose agency is at her own disposal. But in the end she does comply, even though there is no indication that her husband would have forced her to live with him had she continued to refuse. Why does she do it? In virtue of what deliberations does she act as she does? This is what the conditional relation explains. As a thinking person her mind is not determined by the roles she is given; instead she uses them in the only moral enterprise that seems available to her.

In a curious incident in the novel, Mary is urged by a dying male friend to fulfil her 'destined course' – her marriage – and to see it as a chance to add patience to her other virtues. This follows on the heels of another incident, in which Mary calculates the pros and cons of her station as wife. One of the pros is the religious duty 'to reconcile us to the seemingly hard dispensations of providence'.[42] Virtue, we are told, is 'an active principle' which is thrown by the wayside if we simply give in to inclination. Seen in that light, the hardship of marriage appears as an opportunity to practise forbearance.

Another pro, in Mary's deliberations, is the opportunity to do good for others, which would come with her husband's fortune. These things make a case, however joyless, for the marriage, a case echoed on the last page, which is all we see of Mary the Wife. She lives for 'benevolence and religion':

41. Wollstonecraft 1989b: 34. 42. Wollstonecraft 1989b: 63.

'The latter taught her to struggle for resignation; and the former made life supportable'.[43]

Up to that point Mary's professed moral position has been a reflection of Wollstonecraft's own. On that account it is certainly true that virtue is an active principle; it is also true that no person can be duty bound (morally or religiously) to submit to unfairness. Wollstonecraft's idiosyncratic theology contains no notion of religion as a lesson in resignation. She speaks of religion as she speaks of morality; they are alternative terminologies for the same thing. Submitting to God is to submit to perfect reason, the only submission consistent with the autonomy of a moral agent.[44]

What Mary comes to realise – in an inarticulate kind of way – is that this kind of submission is not available to her. Her social entrapment is inevitable; the option to submit to nothing but reason is simply not there. But she will not give up the sense of herself as a moral being. Determined to make the situation not only tolerable but also consistent with her sense of self, she turns morality on its head by dismissing her own longing for independence as 'inclinations' and the miserable lot of a forced marriage as a duty. Knowing that this is not what her own moral convictions dictate, she whistles in the wind and acts as if it is. This is a perfectly understandable survival strategy, a rational decision not to 'fight against the stream',[45] particularly in the light of the cost for women of deviating from the norm. Both in *The Rights of Woman* and in *Maria* a point is made of the fact that a woman's reputation once lost is lost forever.[46] If you have escaped or avoided the psychological effects of oppression – and consequently do not love submission – the female 'virtues' of forbearance and complicity are still a social fact, there at the ready, easily assumable at will if there is nothing else to be had. Facing up to her lack of social independence, Mary abandons her intellectual independence in an act of will. She can see herself as a moral person only by persuading herself that resignation is now the main part of her virtuous struggle and patience her active principle.

Earlier, she had justified her resistance to honouring a forced bond by saying 'what could the world give to compensate for my own esteem?'[47] The answer is still nothing; there is no compensation in worldly approval. The only way for her to preserve her sense of self is to act, against her true

43. See Kelly 1996: 26 and 31 on the compensatory role of devotional religion and philanthropy.
44. Wollstonecraft 1995a: 27 and 34. See Taylor 2003: ch. 3 on Wollstonecraft's religious views.
45. Wollstonecraft 1995a: 57. Compare 103.
46. Wollstonecraft 1995b: 221 and 1989c: 146, 148 and 151.
47. Wollstonecraft 1989b: 47.

conviction, as if it is after all a religious (hence moral) duty to bear what the world forces upon her. Resignation *to* the fact of social dependence is the paradoxical act of an independent mind's resignation *from* true morality for the sake of a semblance to it.

V

The psychological and the conditional relations are explanatory and empirical in the sense that they serve as evidence-based explanations of human behaviour; they admit of deviations without being falsified. They can be escaped or resisted, even if it is difficult and unlikely to happen. Both Mary and Maria escape the effects of the psychological relation. Struggling against the conditioning of women's agency, Maria, contrary to Mary, resists the effects of the conditional relation when she asserts that she will not be resigned to misery and let it be 'proudly termed patience'.[48] She never deliberates herself out of her moral convictions, for reasons to which I shall return.

I now turn to the third relation between political situation and moral agency, a relation that is different in kind compared to the first two. It is not explanatory of something that is there to be observed and it cannot be escaped or resisted on the individual level. It is a constitutive relation between the political situation of a person and the moral character of her actions.

I have already noted that it is inherent in Wollstonecraft's conception of moral agency that it is an exercise of freedom.[49] Remember that her republican approach to freedom means that freedom consists in the absence of dependence on the arbitrary will of another. Freedom is not directly linked to what you can do or not do. An act that I can and do perform is performed unfreely if I act at the mercy of another, subjected to the will of someone who could restrain me with impunity if he so chose. A free act is performed by a free person, and a free person is one who is at her own, not someone else's, disposal. It is now time to examine the implications of this commitment for moral agency.

A person who is not free can act as morality dictates – she can conform in her behaviour to moral norms – but her acts will lack the moral quality of being performed freely. A moral act is a free act; in other words, moral agency is constituted by free agency. Let us look at this claim a bit more closely.

48. Wollstonecraft 1989c: 86.
49. See Brace 2000 on freedom, activity and morality. See also Sapiro 1992: 63.

First, consider the heroines of the two novels in terms of freedom from restraint and to non-restraint. Maria's husband interferes, chases after her, locks her up. He revels in his powers. Mary's shadow of a husband never forces her to do anything, never denies her anything. He takes no advantage at all of his powers, so what is the problem?

An example will help us see how this fits into Wollstonecraft's theory of freedom as non-dependence. Shortly after her marriage Mary wants to go abroad to nurse a sick friend and writes to her husband to ask his permission to go. She is determined to go whatever he says so his will is not an obstacle for her resolve. As it turns out, he has no objection, so neither is his will an obstacle for her actions. He neither interferes nor wishes to interfere; in actual fact she is perfectly free to go. But he does have the privilege to forbid her if he wants to; her actual freedom to go is conditioned on his will's continuing to be in her favour. In that sense Mary, on a packet to Lisbon, is as unfree as Maria in her asylum cell. Distinctive about Mary's situation is that she is free to go, but not to go freely. She can act, but not in the free mode.

The disgust Mary feels at having to ask her husband's permission to travel does not come from being *his* wife, but from being *a* wife, a political situation identifying her as belonging to someone empowered to control her at a distance, just as the function of property is to settle issues of ownership even if the owner is not in physical possession of the thing.[50] Mary has become property, an owned, controllable thing, the exact opposite of a rights-bearing agent.

We have already seen how Mary deals with this in her own mind, acting as if patience and endurance make up her moral project. But looked at from the outside there is a further level of moral tragedy to her situation.

Of a woman who 'acts as a woman ought to act', that is, who acts on the sex-segregated slavish norms designed for women, Wollstonecraft says that she 'be reckoned a good kind of woman. Yet in what respect can she be termed good? . . . how does she fulfil her duties?'[51] To be 'good' in the moral sense is to discharge one's duties properly, something which requires reason. But, at an even more fundamental level, it requires that one have proper duties to begin with. By proper duties I mean the duties of morality, not of polished good manners. Moral agency consists in discharging the duties of natural morality, not for the sake of vanity or any other contingent reason, but for their *own* sake.[52] Whatever the duties of morality are, it is abundantly clear

50. Compare Wollstonecraft 1989c: 106.
51. Wollstonecraft 1995b: 122.
52. Wollstonecraft 1995b: 205 and 229.

that Wollstonecraft considers such duties to be logically secondary to being granted rights.[53] A being who does not count among the rights bearers has no duties and so cannot be 'good' in the proper moral sense. When she says that women's situation 'robs the whole sex of its dignity'[54] this is regardless of whether individual women – like Mary and Maria – have managed to escape or resist the effects of one or both of the two explanatory relations that we have just looked at.

In a slightly odd passage we are told that a being who discharges its duties is independent,[55] which could be read as a paradoxical understanding of freedom to the effect that moral freedom consists in being bound by obligation. I believe, however, that the logical order is the reverse; only the being who is independent has any duties to discharge.

If you do not count as a person in your own right you have nothing; you are entitled to nothing. As Wollstonecraft puts it in a context where she is arguing for civil rights for women and legal protection against the dependence on the bounty of husbands, 'how can a being be generous who has nothing of its own? or, virtuous who is not free?'[56] This is not merely a statement about the psychological improbability of moral dispositions developing in a slavish existence; it is importantly a statement about morality itself. Moral acts, she tells us, are acts of independence, and independence is a political condition. A useful comparison can be made here with the assertion in *The Rights of Men*, that '[p]overty, shame, and even slavery, may be endured by the virtuous man – he has still a world to range in'.[57] This sounds paradoxical if freedom (the absence of slavish dependence) is a prerequisite for morality. But the implication is that for a person of moral disposition – who has escaped the psychological effects of oppression – the perception and recognition of moral obligation will provide a framework for structuring and naming thoughts and actions *as* moral (in the way that Mary did) even when political circumstance makes the truly moral, or free, mode of action unavailable.

In her life as wife, Mary acts benevolently in the only way she can, by giving handouts from an estate that is not hers. The moral failure of her gestures of goodwill is intrinsic to an act that can only mimic a universal benevolence made impossible by the institutional structure of society. You cannot be generous if you have nothing. Practising benevolence within a

53. Wollstonecraft 1995b, pp. 235–6 on the priority of rights to duties. See also Halldenius 2007. Compare Sapiro 1992: 118.
54. Wollstonecraft 1995b: 127.
55. Wollstonecraft 1995b: 235.
56. Wollstonecraft 1995b: 236. See also 288.
57. Wollstonecraft 1995a: 27.

position of complete dependence on the goodwill of another amounts to the paradoxical act of sharing what is not yours.

A situation of political subordination strips a person's agency of its moral quality; the moral mode of acting is made unavailable. This is not a matter of psychological effects, nor of any other empirical circumstance; it concerns the distinctive character of a moral act. A moral act is a free act, an act in which you dispose of, or make use of, yourself as a free person. To the extent that you live a life of bondage, dependent on the goodwill of another in circumstances that you do not control, your active self is not at your own disposal. No matter what your intellectual resources may be, you cannot act in the free mode and, by virtue of that, moral agency is not available to you.

VI

My concluding reflection revolves around a difference between the two novels. On the level of explicit narrative, political society is completely absent from *Mary*, but the political force of the novel is emphasised by this absence. Mary's life is shaped by something that she can hardly see and never talks about. She never takes on the institutions of society; she does not even seem to contemplate them. Her tactic is avoidance, and when that no longer succeeds she turns herself into the only agent she can be without losing her sense of self: the patient, devout doer of good deeds. The only thought that gives her joy is that she will soon die and come 'to that world *where there is neither marrying*, nor giving in marriage'.[58] With this wish the novel comes to an abrupt end.

In *Maria*, the society where laws are 'made by the strong to oppress the weak'[59] is glaringly visible, both to the reader and to the main characters. Maria's experiences at the hands of her husband make her do what Mary never does: she generalises from her own plight to the situation of women, the outcasts of society. Given her political awareness and her lack of religion – religion is conspicuously absent in *Maria* – it would make no sense to her to pursue a personal project through forbearance and patience. Maria is fully aware that the obstacle to her freedom is not her husband but the institutions of society and its practitioners, the 'dogs of law'.[60] In a surreal episode she pleads her case in a court of law, declaring herself free and claiming a divorce from her husband in the name of justice and

58. Wollstonecraft 1989b: 73. The same phrase appears in Wollstonecraft 1995b: 103.
59. Wollstonecraft 1989c: 180. 60. Wollstonecraft 1989c: 178.

humanity.[61] The judge is not impressed. Even though the stand she takes against the law has no constitutive power, it displays her to herself as an agent acting on what she knows is right. She will not abandon her principles; she understands them too well and identifies with them too deeply. Overwhelmed by the strength of a system of oppression that denies her the freedom she craves and strips her of all dignity, she tries to take her own life.

What we do not really know but strongly suspect is that Maria comes to understand what Mary only vaguely senses: that true moral agency is not available to women as long as the oppressive laws of society constitute for them a state of subjection. One needs to understand institutions to realise that. Freedom is institution-dependent and if the institutions make you wholly dependent on the arbitrary will of another then free agency is beyond the reach of even the most hardened individual resolve. Mary's passive death wish and Maria's attempted political suicide both illustrate how impossible the situation appears as long as it is viewed from an individualised standpoint. Liberation requires no less than a restructuring of society's institutions – breaking the constitutive relation – but those institutions remain in *Mary* as shadowy background conditions while in *Maria* they appear as an unshakeable monolith of power. For an individual person, shut out from influence over those institutions, they can be escaped only by leaving this world altogether.[62]

If you are structurally unfree and denied personhood, you may do the right thing and act as your principles direct; but you cannot act in the free mode and that particular moral quality which comes from disposing freely of one's own person will be lacking whatever you do. In this sense, the political condition is prior to moral agency for Wollstonecraft, even though the principles of morality are eternal, unwavering and founded in nature.

61. See Jordan 1997 for an analysis of the legal context. See Bahar 2002: 45–7 on the significance of Maria appearing in public.

62. Compare Kelly 1996: 38 on the fatigue over life expressed by Wollstonecraft in correspondence during the time that *Mary, a Fiction* was written.

Part III

Freedom and the limits of Europe

13

The idea of freedom in missionary writings about the New World

Catherine Ballériaux

I

In 1637, Paul Le Jeune, superior of the Jesuit mission of Quebec, commented on his work with the Huron people:

> There is nothing so difficult as to control the tribes of America. All these Barbarians have the law of wild asses, they are born, live, and die in a liberty without restraint; they do not know what is meant by bridle or bit... The Law of our Lord is far removed from this dissoluteness; it gives us boundaries and prescribes limits, outside of which we cannot step without offending God and reason. Now it is very hard to place this yoke, although it is very mild and easy, upon the necks of people who make a profession of not submitting to anything, either in heaven or upon earth.[1]

This comment illustrates European missionaries' enduring concern with liberty, discipline and control in the New World. This chapter seeks to understand how religious proselytisers addressed the idea of human liberty, and how they made sense of native societies' customs and manners within this framework. My focus is primarily on the notion of liberty in the context of theology and its relationship to the question of salvation. Liberty, I argue, was not simply considered a moral good, but envisaged both as a problem and as a potential solution in the context of conversion. The natives were thought to live in conditions either of extreme liberty or of tyranny. The converters' role was to liberate them from tyranny, or alternatively to institute rules that would limit their liberty, a liberty that could easily degenerate into licence. By doing so, they would provide the natives with access to true freedom.

1. Thwaites 1896 [hereafter *JR*]: xii, 61.

The seventeenth century was a period of intense contact with, and attempted conversion of, native peoples in America. France and England were at an early stage of the colonisation process, while Spain had been in the New World for more than a century. Nevertheless, the Spanish colonial experience in the New World had been absorbed by all those Europeans familiar with Spanish accounts of the Americas and the conversion of its peoples.[2] Moreover, if settlement was not yet the priority, English and French explorers had already encountered the natives in the sixteenth century, and discussed the necessity and possibility of converting them. Seventeenth-century colonial projects, in other words, were already a second- or third-generation experience for England and France as well as for Spain.[3]

During the same period, the three countries under study were experiencing intense movements of religious renewal, all linked to a reformative urge which took different shapes, but which stemmed from the same willingness to reform the moral climate of their country.[4] In their writings, missionaries advanced arguments about the nature of human liberty, which were in part reflective of anxieties about a European order that was itself not always comfortably ordered and for some seemed brimming with threats to their nations, to civility and to their own religious doctrines.[5] They addressed not only the moral and soteriological conflicts between Protestantism and Catholicism, but also the reformations that they thought necessary within their own nations and confessional groups. The historiography tends to neglect the relationship and interdependence of reform movements in Europe and in America, and to overlook the willingness, shared by religious reformers in all three countries, in particular Puritans and Jesuits, to experiment with new forms of piety as well as their common urge towards outward activities, such as charity, education and conversion. The European religious and intellectual climate shaped the various types of educational, social, political and religious mechanisms of control that missionaries tried to impose on native populations. But the converters' perceptions of alien political and social systems also influenced their participation in European religious and political debates, and provided them with insights, contrasts and comparisons that eluded intellectuals in the Old World.

The seventeenth century saw three major and competing European powers undertake social and political experiments with native societies. Although

2. Locke Hart 2001. 3. Fitzmaurice 2003: ch. 3; Axtell 1985: ch. 2; Hadfield 1998: ch. 2.
4. Brémond 1967: III; Scott 2000; Elliott 1989b. 5. Hadfield 1998: 80–1.

Spain had long been present in America, the early seventeenth century proved to be a period of questioning and doubt.[6] Missionaries in New Spain and Peru experienced a sense of failed conversion, combined with a willingness to harden Counter-Reformation orthodoxy in Spanish colonies.[7] Intense campaigns for the extirpation of idolatry were implemented in both New Spain and Peru, while missionaries started to venture outside well-known urban centres and were thus faced with peoples yet untouched by Christianity.[8] By the seventeenth century, a whole host of religious writers were intensely debating, discussing and grappling with the essence of conversion, the nature of paganism and the problem of coercion.[9]

The importance that the Godly placed on conversion was expressed on the seal of the Massachusetts Bay Company (created in 1630) depicting a Native American crying 'Come over and help us', echoing the Macedonians' call to Paul in a vision.[10] Despite this, and other affirmations about the necessity of conversion in the Plymouth and Massachusetts Bay colonies, little early progress was made, and little was written about the conversion of native peoples. By the 1640s, however, two men had undertaken serious missionary activities: John Eliot, Puritan minister of the Roxbury church, who began preaching to the natives and learning their language around Boston in 1646, and Thomas Mayhew, Jr., who did likewise in his father's colony of Martha's Vineyard around 1643. Following their relative success, colonists started to publish pamphlets in order to raise money in England for the conversion of New England natives.[11] This initiated a series of works known today as the *Eliot Tracts* (eleven in all), the most systematic accounts of conversion in the English colonies. In 1649, following the establishment of the English commonwealth, an act of Parliament finally established a Corporation for the promoting and propagating of the Gospel of Jesus Christ in New England.[12] This organisation continued to publish pamphlets for fund-raising until the Restoration in 1660. Despite similar views on the importance of conversion, settlers in Virginia did not undertake successful missions in the seventeenth century.[13]

By contrast, the French crown, from the time of the creation of the *Compagnie des Cent-Associés* by Richelieu in 1627, actively supported French missions to the New World. The crown granted to the venture a commercial

6. Elliott 1989a: 251. 7. Taylor 1996: 64. 8. Mills 1994: 102.
9. Mills 1994: 90. 10. Bible, Acts 16:9. 11. Clark 2003 [hereafter *Eliot Tracts*]: 1–5.
12. Firth and Rait 1911: 197–200; Winship 1920: i–lxvi.
13. Sheehan 1980: 5. The writings of the English Jesuits in Maryland will not be taken into account, given the specificity of their situation.

monopoly on the condition that it supported a missionary enterprise.[14] Those natives who converted to Catholicism would be considered French citizens. The Jesuits quickly developed a monopoly on French missions, with strong government support. The *Jesuit Relations*, published throughout the seventeenth century, consisted of a series of reports collected by the provincial of New France, and sent to the general of the society in Rome. Published annually in France, they were also used, like the *Eliot Tracts* in England, to attract investors in the missionary project.

Through their encounter with what they called heathenism, and their attempts to reform the so-called savages' minds, missionaries meditated on the human condition. In their emotional ruminations they consistently tried to evaluate the nature and extent of human liberty. This is not to say that these proselytisers proposed any coherent philosophy about the liberty and liberties of the natives as individuals or as groups. Indeed the different understandings of pagan and Christian liberty that I explore often overlapped, coexisted with and contradicted one another. This chapter is an attempt to lay out, in a comparative way, a map of the linguistic and conceptual terrain occupied by the question of liberty in missionary accounts. The study of this particular context might help further to elucidate early modern European understandings of freedom in the over-arching context of man's relationship to God. The questions that missionaries addressed in their writings had a universal bearing, and intertwined political, social, spiritual, doctrinal and, most of all, soteriological concerns.

II

French and Spanish proselytisers, when they addressed the question of pagan liberty, principally referred to a lack of constraint and to an indulgence of the passions. The term most commonly used was liberty, not licence, which was mainly applied to sexual behaviour. 'Savage liberty' in this sense meant anomie: an absence of rules and order, which allowed for excess, confusion and dissoluteness.[15] The French Jesuit Paul Le Jeune commented in 1634 on the natives' lifestyle and their undue freedom: 'With them, to conquer one's passions is considered a great joke, while to give free rein to the senses is a lofty Philosophy.'[16] Spanish writers also emphasised the negative aspects of the passions and external senses: Bernabé Cobo, a Jesuit Father preaching in Peru, thought the natives were 'easily led astray by

14. Deslandres 2003: 278–9. 15. Lalemant 1647: 141. 16. *JR* XII, 61.

passions and disordered affections', and that 'they value[d] only the visible reality which is perceived through the senses'.[17] The natives' supposed regard only for sensory experiences meant that, before the arrival of Europeans, they had been uninterested in intellectual and spiritual matters, and unable to overcome terrestrial passions, both of which conditioned access to the knowledge and true love of God, and were considered essential in Counter-Reformation Catholicism.[18]

The – supposedly nomadic – tribes' political system was also depicted within this framework of anomie. The French Jesuits tended to emphasise the natives' absence of or minimal form of government.[19] For Father Le Jeune,

> If it is a great blessing to be free from a great evil, our Savages are happy; for the two tyrants who provide hell and torture for many of our Europeans, do not reign in their great forests, I mean ambition and avarice. As they have neither political organisation, nor offices, nor dignities, nor any authority, for they only obey their Chief through good will toward him, therefore they never kill each other to acquire these honours.[20]

The perceived absence of authority implied that discipline and justice were also absent from nomadic societies. The French Jesuits particularly abhorred the native system of reparation, although they recognised its efficiency and had to respect the custom at times. According to this system, individuals were not punished for their crimes, but compensated for the wrongs they caused by gifts offered to the offended family or tribe. The French Jesuit Jérôme Lalemant, commented:

> Now although this form of justice restrains all these peoples, and seems more effectually to repress disorders than the personal punishment of criminals does in France, it is nevertheless a very mild proceeding, which leaves individuals in such a spirit of liberty that they never submit to any Laws and obey no other impulse than that of their own will. This, without doubt, is a disposition quite contrary to the spirit of the Faith, which requires us to submit not only our wills, but our minds, our judgements, and all the sentiments of man to a power unknown to our senses, to a Law that is not of earth, and that is entirely opposed to the laws and sentiments of corrupt nature.[21]

17. Cobo 1956: 23–4. 18. Arriaga 1920: 6; Delumeau 1977; Forrestal 2002; Höpfl 2004: 142.
19. Le Jeune 1634: 76, 200, 202; 1635: 102, 174, 175; 1637: 80; Biard in *JR* II, 911; du Peron in *JR* XV, 157. Compare with Hobbes 1991: 89.
20. *JR* VI, 231. Compare with Winstanley 2006: 385. 21. Lalemant in *JR* XXVIII, 51.

Although both the French and the Spaniards, when they discussed native freedom, appeared to understand it as licence, it entailed an additional dimension. Importantly voluntary, it was also what we might call hard-wired. Spanish and French authors continuously insisted that the natives would rather die than lose this liberty.[22] This quasi-obsession with freedom was codified by the absence of individual and collective discipline amongst native societies: 'I do not believe', said Father Lalemant, 'that there is any people on earth freer than they, and less able to allow the subjection of their wills to any power whatever, so much so that Fathers here have no control over their children, or Captains over their subjects, or the Laws of the country over any of them, except in so far as each is pleased to submit to them.'[23] Pagan liberty ultimately referred to human nature, and this tendency to indulge in one's passions was common to humanity as a whole. But the natives were a particular case, as they did not have the means to control their fallen nature: no religion, no civility and no political organisation. The natives' love of freedom was strongly associated with their nomadic behaviour: before the arrival of the Spaniards, said the Jesuit Alonso de Ovalle, the peoples of Chile 'were never gathered in cities, because they disliked anything that resembled any type of subjection, or constraint, they preferred to be free, and lived in the fields'.[24] In the Aristotelian tradition, living in society was a fundamental quality of the human race.[25] People in perpetual movement could not create true communities, which would allow the establishment of ordered, stable political and religious institutions.[26]

English proselytisers perceived native social and political organisation in a very similar way. The natives' nomadic lifestyle was a hindrance to both civility and religion, which were, even more so than in Catholic writings, held to be inseparable. The natives were considered 'poor, naked, ignorant *Indians*, who lately knew no civill Order', who lived 'so unfixed, confused, and ungoverned a life, uncivilized and unsubdued to labor and order'.[27] The idea that the natives had trouble avoiding their tendency to 'run wilde' implied not only bodily, but also spiritual mobility.[28] As the convert John Speene explained in his confession of 1652: 'my heart run away into the country, after our old wayes, and I did almost cast off praying to God . . . I did greatly love hunting, and hated labor.'[29] This behaviour was in

22. Le Jeune 1638: 191–2; Ovalle 1646: 85, 87–8, 97, 203; Palafox y Mendoza 1893: 28.
23. *JR* XXVIII, 49. 24. Ovalle 1646: 88. See also 103. 25. Aristotle 1932: 11–13 (1253a 1–20).
26. Pagden 1982: 195. 27. *Eliot Tracts*, 302, 159; Axtell 1985: 138, 154.
28. *Eliot Tracts*, 361, 362, 365, 366, 372, 375, 377.
29. *Eliot Tracts*, 284. On the importance of industry, see *Eliot Tracts*, 124, 266. The imperative to work is in Exodus 20:2–17 and is reasserted in Deuteronomy 5:6–21.

complete contradiction with the act of 'coming to Christ, and bearing his yoake'.[30]

Aside from the view that the natives had no or mild laws, or unregulated customs, the natives could also be thought to have arbitrary laws, and nefarious customs, which included idolatry and tyranny. This resulted from degeneracy (of human understanding or will) or corruption (of social and political practices). In Calvinist anthropology, the total depravity of man easily accounted for the natives' degenerate customs. Christianity was presented as an ancient form of knowledge among the natives, a knowledge that had disappeared because their forefathers had been 'a stubborne and rebellious children'. God had forsaken them, left them 'alone in sinne and ignorance'.[31] Now the natives were in a state of degeneracy, 'inheritors of a grievous and fearefull curse... in nearest alliance to the wild beasts that perish... so are curses entailed and come by naturall descent unto others'.[32] Offering a similar perspective, Alonso de la Peña Montenegro, bishop of Quito, commented on the natives' idolatries:

> This bad seed made so many deep roots in them, that it is as if it became their own blood and flesh... and thus, although they are born with free-will, vice comes through the blood, it feeds through the milk, and brings with it an internal empire, which tyrannises the whole republic of man... One should not be surprised that the customs of their parents and ancestors have become natural, as they are transmitted to their sons as if an inheritance; which is the main reason why the Indians are so inclined to idolatry.[33]

In 1634, Father Le Jeune lamented the difficulty of uprooting the natives' 'superstitions': 'a disease of the mind so great as is a superstition firmly established for so many centuries, and drunk in with the nurse's milk, is not eradicated in a moment'.[34]

For Calvinists, all humans were in bondage to sin. But the natives' extreme sinfulness stemmed from the fact that their forefathers had forgotten Revelation, and they themselves had no access to the Scriptures. The natives were included on a scale common to human history (as all humans were corrupt and degenerate), but were ranked low on that scale.[35] Eliot frequently characterised the natives as 'dry bones', in reference to Ezekiel 37, in which the

30. *Eliot Tracts*, 232–3. 31. *Eliot Tracts*, 89.
32. *Eliot Tracts*, 92. See also 179, 119. 33. Peña Montenegro 1726: 221.
34. *JR* VI, 221. On the power of custom, see Aristotle 1926: 630–3 (1179b30–1180a10); Vitoria 1991: 250; Bodin 1650: 147.
35. Holstun 1987: 113–14.

Lord brought the sons of Israel up out of their graves.[36] If the natives were collectively unregenerate, they needed, like all degenerate human beings, to be given a chance to become regenerate (regeneration in itself depended entirely on God's will) by instruction of the Gospel, which would give them an opportunity to repent: '*the* deepest *degeneracies*, & widest *estrangements from God, shall be no* bar *or obstacle to the* power *and freenesse of his owne grace when that* time *is come*'.[37]

Corruption could also affect the natives' political customs. Spanish writers based their accounts on José de Acosta's taxonomy. Acosta described a hierarchy of groups in native America, divided according to their political organisation: the Mexicans of New Spain and 'Ingas' of Peru, said Acosta, had a genuine form of political organisation – a monarchy, considered by the author to be the best form of government – but were tyrannical, as they treated their inferiors like beasts and wanted themselves to be treated like Gods. Acosta considered this to be an inversion of the rational order of government, which, he explained, required that 'those who are kings and nobles conform and accommodate themselves to their vassals, acknowledging that they are equal by nature, and inferior only in the sense that they have less obligation to care for the public good'.[38] A form of religious tyranny supplemented the political despotism of the Incas: the tyrants maintained their power by generating in their subjects a fear of their gods, which allowed them to reinforce their own authority.[39] The second group were the people who ruled by council, and elected a leader only in times of war. The third group of peoples were 'indians who have neither laws nor king nor fixed dwellings but go in herds like wild animals and savages'.[40] John Eliot also tended to present native political leaders as real tyrants: 'the *Sachems* of the Country . . . plainly see that Religion will make a great change among them, and cut them off from their former tyranny; for they used to hold their people in an absolute servitude . . . now they see that Religion teaches otherwise, and puts a bridle upon such usurpations'.[41]

The taste for freedom, a 'natural inclination', was held to be universal.[42] For Alonso de la Peña Montenegro, liberty was 'the most precious jewel that nature gave [men], worth more than all the treasures of the world'.[43] But this taste for liberty had to be regulated: 'if liberty is the sweetest of all the

36. Bible, Ezekiel 37:11–13. See for example: *Eliot Tracts*, 93, 99, 135, 163–7, 187, 191, 192, 291.
37. *Eliot Tracts*, 110. See also 89.
38. Acosta 2002: 346. See also Peña Montenegro 1726: 176; Cobo 1956: 29–31; Ovalle 1646: 85.
39. Pagden 1982: 174; MacCormack 2007: 97.
40. Acosta 2002: 359. On John Locke's use of Acosta's writings see Locke 1988: 335 (II, § 102).
41. *Eliot Tracts*, 202. 42. Cobo 1956: 137. 43. Peña Montenegro 1726: 311.

pleasures of human life', said Father Lalemant, 'nevertheless it can degenerate into . . . the dissolution of Savage Donkeys; it has to be regulated and submitted to the laws emanating from the eternal law'.[44] Reform and religious conversion implied both individual and collective processes, which would establish a balance between the necessary limitation of excessive liberty, and the enjoyment of a regulated freedom.

III

Reformation, if difficult amongst the natives, was nevertheless considered possible. By the early seventeenth century, many Spanish ministers realised that most natives, whom they believed had been converted, continued to practise their former religion in secret.[45] Campaigns of extirpation were implemented sporadically in New Spain and Peru over the course of the seventeenth century, and missionaries were sent to remote areas to systematically question native practices and burn their idols.[46] But extirpation went hand in hand with education.[47] Catholic soteriology emphasised human faculties in the process of conversion. As, in the Thomist tradition, moral action was considered to be willing the good apprehended by the understanding, the sincerity of conversion required both a grasp of the good and a willingness to seek it.[48] Because the natives were considered to be extremely ignorant, education was fundamental.Yet the fact that the natives had been accustomed to living for so long without morals had made them attached to their customs, even though they were made aware of their irrationality: according to Jean de Brébeuf, 'the evil is, they are so attached to their old customs that, knowing the beauty of truth, they are content to approve it without embracing it. Their usual reply is, *oniondechouten*, "Such is the custom of our country".'[49] As virtue had to be willingly embraced to be meaningful, education for Catholic authors also meant making volition virtuous.[50] For the Jesuit Matheo de Moya, the priest would 'not only enlighten understanding with doctrine, but also improve the will with fervent exhortation'.[51] The French Jesuits, like the Spaniards, thought that, in the process of conversion, 'the will must be softened and must give up its natural hardness'.[52]

44. Lalemant 1649: 156.
45. Arriaga 1920: 65; Mills 1994: 88; Lopes Don 2006: 22.
46. Mills 1997: 149, 171.
47. Mills 1997: 172.
48. See for example Peña Montenegro 1726: 136–7. See also Aquinas 2003: Qu. 3, art. 6, Rp. 2.
49. *JR* x, 19.
50. Maravall 1995: 42; Waterworth 1848: 31. On the rejection of coercion, see also Vitoria 1991: 344.
51. Matheo de Moya, in Peña Montenegro 1726, Aprobacion.
52. *JR* VIII, 273.

Both French and Spanish Jesuits conceived of conversion as helping the savages to find the 'authentic freedom of the children of God'.[53] Freedom for the Jesuits implied the complete submission of one's will and liberty to God. Indeed, a central tenet of Jesuit theology was the idea that absolute obedience was the Christian virtue *par excellence*.[54] The Jesuits knew that practice and imitation would play an important role in education, and conceived of their missions as long-term endeavours, during which the natives would be transformed 'little by little'.[55] For Le Jeune, the best way to obtain conversions would be to settle the natives down, so that, 'having received the Law of Jesus Christ, they would be called upon to put it into practice (*en faire l'exercice*), and thus, little by little, they would become accustomed to the path of truth, and in a few years this would be a consecrated people'.[56] For Father Ragueneau, 'the faith greatly enlightens a mind . . . and our Savages quite easily acquire a very blessed liberty when, having become Christians, they think that they have no more fear in this world but God and sin'.[57] Whoever sincerely repented was to be granted baptism.[58] Catholicism would thus be taught as a series of habits which would become internalised to the point where they became a second nature. Conversion in this perspective was identified with moral reformation.

In the congregational system of New England, the natives were expected to undergo the same process of examination to enter a church as anyone else.[59] They were to make a public confession, and regeneration was evaluated by a committee of elders. The natives' request to form a church was rejected once, in 1652, and it took several years for eight of them finally to be allowed to enter in a church covenant, in 1659.[60] Conversion in Puritan theology was a new birth, and an intense emotional experience.[61] The first step, accessible to all, even the reprobate, included knowledge of sin, contrition and humiliation. It implied a command of the basics of Protestant doctrines,

53. Ragueneau 1651: 133 – cf. Bible, Romans 8:21. See also Le Jeune 1662: 173; le Mercier 1667: 11; Cataldino (1614), in Valle Iberlucea 1914–21: 304.
54. Höpfl 2004: 26–30.
55. Peña Montenegro 1726: 140. See also *JR* LV, 223. On the importance of habituation in the Aristotelian–Thomist tradition, see Aristotle 1926: 631 (1179b 21–27), Aquinas 1947: IaIIae, Q97, A3; Murphy 2002: 478. On the rejection of this tradition in Calvinist soteriology, see Perkins 1606: 470; Cefalu 2004: 4–7; Herdt 2008.
56. *JR* XI, 193. On the importance of custom in Aristotle's pedagogy, see Murphy 2007.
57. *JR* XXX, 65, Le Jeune in Vimont 1641: 60.
58. See for example Torres 1596: 28. On the importance of the sacraments in Counter-Reformation Christianity, see Waterworth 1848: 33; Maravall 1995: 37–43; Evennett 1968: 37.
59. See for example *Eliot Tracts*, 268; Cotton 1645: 54. See Cohen 1986: 140–7; Morgan 1963: 34.
60. Cohen 1993: 244, 249–50.
61. Bible, John 3:3; Cohen 1993: 233–56; 1986.

and a consecutive awareness of one's sins. For John Eliot, 'our natures cannot live without Physicke, nor grace without affliction'.[62] Preparation would lead men to hate evil, and feel sorrow for their sins, triggering the cycle of justification and sanctification.[63] Conversion could only be possible when self-confidence was annihilated, and one realised one's incapacity to redeem one's sins.[64] Eliot had good hopes for the natives, as many of them were 'naturally sad and melancholly (a good servant to repentance)'.[65]

Regeneration, the reception of 'saving faith', was a free grace of God. Eliot insisted on the fact that, through human instruments, it was God who would convert the elect natives: 'It is the Lord, the Lord only who doth speak to the hearts of men.'[66] Eliot could only exhort the 'praying Indians' to 'try their hearts by the word of God to finde out what change the Lord hath wrought in their hearts'.[67] Once saving faith was imparted to man, sanctification, the radical transformation of human faculties, occurred, and the Saints would persevere in grace.[68] Eliot expected from the regenerate natives who would gather in a church as much as would be expected from any Puritan – the natives would have their own ministers, teachers and political leaders. In the first volume of this collection, Polly Ha has discussed the notion of freedom of consent in the thought of Henri Jacob, whose ideas were influential in New England.[69] Indeed, John Eliot's ecclesiology entailed both congregational and individual autonomy within the congregation, and required the approval of all members in appointments and church discipline.[70] Thus for Eliot, the natives 'must be trained up to be able to live of themselves in the ways of the Gospel of Christ'.[71] Yet, given the peculiar circumstances of native church building, the public confessions of the natives willing to establish a church had to be evaluated by the elders of neighbouring churches.

Puritans achieved few conversions. Indeed, they knew that few would be saved, which was a universal phenomenon. But beyond the Congregationalist vision of the church of Saints, Eliot emphasised the missionary role of ministers, and the duty to give access to regeneration to all (access which did not guarantee election).[72] By contrast, Catholics, because they rejected predestination and believed that everybody could be saved, worked relentlessly to convince unbelievers and include them within the church. Conversion for

62. *Eliot Tracts*, 221. 63. Cohen 1986: 76, 77, 79; *Eliot Tracts*, 88.
64. Cohen 1986: 80. 65. *Eliot Tracts*, 95. 66. *Eliot Tracts*, 151; Rooy 1965.
67. *Eliot Tracts*, 227. 68. Cohen 1986: 100. 69. Foster 1991: 63–4, 153–5.
70. Although Eliot attempted in later writings to reconcile the principles of congregationalism with a Presbyterian system of councils: Eliot 1665; Cogley 1991.
71. *Eliot Tracts*, 402. See also 93, 223; Axtell: 1985, 225–7; Cogley 1999: 61, 177.
72. See Eliot's correspondence with Richard Baxter, in Powicke 1931.

Puritans was thus a lengthy process of anguish and sorrow, culminating in saving faith for the Elect, and in the formation of, or membership in, a church. For Catholics, on the other hand, the struggle was ongoing and continued after conversion.[73] Good works and piety were apparent signs of genuine conversion, but neophytes could always relapse into their old vicious ways, and apostasy was a permanent threat.

IV

In terms of political and social organisation, the patronage of the Spanish monarchy over religious matters in the New World meant that, in Spanish colonies more than anywhere else, monarchy and religion were inextricably linked.[74] Following Acosta's taxonomy, the powerful kingdoms of America were considered tyrannies. Yet, following Francisco de Vitoria, missionaries considered that these governments, by virtue of the law of nature, had been legitimately established.[75] But men's natural right to trade and communicate with each other and to spread the Gospel provided the Spanish crown with a right to travel to those countries, and a duty to convert.[76] Thus, for Juan de Palafox y Mendoza, the conquest of the New World had been a 'just conquest and lawful action, to introduce those souls in the Church . . . and thus . . . they were brought to the sweet dominion of Your Majesty, and from sons of anger and outrage, by this means your Catholic power reduced them to the liberty of sons of the Church'.[77] Being reduced to the liberty of sons of the church meant being converted, but also being ruled by a monarch who would use reason rather than caprice to govern. This anti-voluntarist argument (a just government is based on reason rather than will) was common in early modern Spanish political thought.[78] Liberty could only be conceived within a social and political order.[79]

By the seventeenth century, the conquests of the Mexican and Incan empires belonged to history, and were no longer a central practical concern for missionaries. Nomadic groups, though, were still numerous in the mountainous and remote areas of the Spanish American empire. Only in cities could men actualise their true potential, establish hierarchical civil and religious institutions, and have rulers and magistrates who could guarantee respect

73. Waterworth 1848: 37. 74. Wright 2005: 16; Elliott 2006: 128–9; Bakewell 1995: 301.
75. Vitoria 1991: 244–6; Skinner 1978: 169–71; Pagden 1982: ch. 4, 159. See also Grotius 2009: 35–7 (pp. 6–7 of the Latin text).
76. Vitoria 1991: 278, 284. See also Grotius 2009: 29 (p. 3 of the Latin text).
77. Palafox y Mendoza 1893: 22. See also Ovalle 1646: 105.
78. See for example Madariaga 1617: 478. 79. Gil 2007: 455; Fernández Albaladejo 1997.

for established laws. In this Aristotelian vision of human communities, the mobility of non-sedentary groups meant that they were unable to develop industry, commerce and religion. Consequently, the crown demanded on many occasions that the natives be gathered – without compulsion – into 'pueblos' (or 'reducciones') where they would be peacefully converted by the religious orders, learn the art of self-government, and be isolated from the worst elements amongst Spanish settlers, 'restless, people of evil living, thieves, gamblers, dissolute and degenerate people'.[80] Missionaries also felt that the pueblos would help to isolate and protect the natives from the greed and intrusions of European settlers. The Jesuits always resisted the encomienda system (according to which the natives had to perform personal service for the Spaniards): from Paraguay, the Jesuit José Cataldino complained: 'the Spaniards hate us, because we reprove their abominable greed and we defend the liberty of the indians'.[81]

The French Jesuits depicted native social and political systems within a similar Aristotelian framework.[82] As J. H. M. Salmon has shown, the Jesuits, particularly in France, supported the idea that 'hierarchy and monarchy were essential to good order in any collective body'.[83] Yet, particularly isolated in the remote areas of New France, they had to display a great degree of adaptability and observation: 'A great step is gained when one has learned to know those with whom he has to deal, has penetrated their thoughts, has adapted himself to their language, their customs, and their manner of living; and, when necessary, has been a Barbarian with them, in order to win them over to Jesus Christ.'[84] Consequently, when they encountered semi-nomadic groups, the Jesuits recognised some positive aspects to their lifestyle, and were not necessarily willing to meddle with their political organisation. Giuseppe Bressani, a Florentine Jesuit in New France, thought that the Huron government was 'admirable in this, that, being very different from ours, and therefore to many unknown, it is nevertheless quite as effective as our own, and even more so, since there appear, amid conditions of extreme liberty, very few disorders'.[85] The Jesuits, for whom oral preaching and rhetoric were particularly significant, were usually impressed with the centrality of native eloquence.[86] Following Aristotle and Cicero, emphasising

80. *Recopilacion* 1841: 228–32; Galvan Rivera 1859: 25; Cañeque 2004: 186–7, 204–6; Pagden 1982: ch. 4.
81. Cataldino (1614), in Valle Iberlucea 1914–21: 306. On the reduction system, see Barnadas 1984: 533–4.
82. Le Jeune 1634: 76, 202; Biard 1616: 101–17. 83. Salmon 2007: 481; Höpfl 2004: 2.
84. *JR* XXIII, 207–9. See also Le Mercier 1669: 110; Le Jeune 1634: 91–2; 1635: 124, 128.
85. Bressani in *JR* XXXVIII, 265. 86. Maryks 2008: 88.

the oratorical qualities of native leaders pointed to their humanity and civility.[87] The speeches of the 'captains' were compared to classical orators, as they would 'pass in the judgment of many for one of those of Titus Livius', they spoke 'with such a delicate and sharp rhetoric that it might have come out of the schools of Aristotle or Cicero', and had 'an excellent style of narration, and great eloquence'.[88] Paul Le Jeune thought that

> he who knew their language well would be all-powerful among them, however little eloquence he might have. There is no place in the world where Rhetoric is more powerful than in Canada, and, nevertheless, it has no other garb than what nature has given it; it is entirely simple and without disguise; and yet it controls all these tribes, as the Captain is elected for his eloquence alone, and is obeyed in proportion to his use of it, for they have no other law than his word.[89]

If indeed they emphasised the importance of hierarchy, French Jesuits, as opposed to English and Spanish missionaries, did not consider it absolutely necessary to intervene in the natives' political organisation. As Jérôme Lalemant showed in his Relation of 1646, the fathers told their converted brethren that, 'as for acts of civility or of social discipline, they were free to follow their own ideas, provided they should not oppose the law of God'.[90]

Civility, in English writings, was to come before Christianity in the conversion process. The natives should 'first be Civilized, by being brought from their scattered and wild course of life, unto Civill Co-habitation and Government'.[91] The necessity of settling down before establishing a church was, for Eliot, 'according to the will of God revealed in the Scriptures'.[92] Civilising was not a secular activity separated from religious concerns, but was an injunction directly derived from the Bible: 'That which I first aymed at was to declare & deliver unto them the Law of God, to civilize them, which course the Lord took by *Moses*, to give the Law to that rude company because of transgression, *Gal.* 3.19 to convince, bridle, restrain, and civilize them, and also to humble them.' The reference to Paul's epistle to the Galatians was related to the Puritan concept of the Covenant of Law, which was to precede the Covenant of Grace.[93] The conversion experience that would make someone a visible saint was to be preceded by the establishment of a civilised space created by the foundation of a legitimate external political

87. Cicero 1949: 5–7 (I, II.2); Aristotle 1996: 13 (1253a). On this, see Pagden 1982: 70.
88. Brébeuf in Le Jeune 1637: 170; Le Jeune 1634: 129 (mispaginated 229); Bressani in *JR* XXXVIII, 261.
89. *JR* V, 195, with a reference to Cicero 1949: I.II.2.
90. *JR* XXIX: 133.
91. *Eliot Tracts*, 303. See also 268.
92. *Eliot Tracts*, 303.
93. *Eliot Tracts*, 124; Cogley 1999: 6–7.

order, and by teaching, which would prompt an attempt – and failure – to follow the law and trigger regeneration in the elect.

By the 1650s, John Eliot was convinced that the natives were one of the lost tribes of Israel, and fully integrated them in his millenarian scheme.[94] For New England millenarians, the Second Coming of Christ would be preceded by the institution on earth of a perfect form of commonwealth, ruled by divine law. Two preconditions for the middle advent were the destruction of Roman Catholicism and the conversion of the Jews. Once Eliot was convinced that the natives were Jewish, their conversion became crucial.[95] The settlers and the natives' religious and political fate went hand in hand. The coming of the English was providential for the natives, and at the same time the conversion of one of the lost tribes of Israel was a providential sign of the coming of Christ.[96] Eliot's vision of praying towns was his vision of an ideal commonwealth, where the natives were 'to be ruled by the Lord in all theire affaires civilie, makeing the Word of God theire only magna charta, for government, laws, and all conversation'.[97] For Eliot, 'Godly consciences' would not be satisfied until 'all formes and Lawes of mans invention will shake, be unsetled' and until rulers 'produce Scripture grounds for all they do'.[98] This was where freedom came into play for Puritans: being free meant choosing to live in submission to God's laws and nothing else.[99] As John Coffey has shown in volume 1 about Calvinism in general, Eliot's conception of freedom certainly did not involve liberty of conscience, but a liberty to submit to God's laws.[100] Freedom meant having the 'liberty to enjoy the holy worship of God, not according to the fantasies of man, but according to the word of God'.[101] This is what godly Protestants had been denied in England, and had gone to find in the New World. Eliot's thought by the 1650s was strongly antimonarchical. Thus, the 'glorious coming of the Lord Jesus' implied that 'that Antichristian principle for man to be above God, whether the Pope in the Church, or Monarches in the Common-wealth, is thrown to the ground'.[102]

For Eliot, the work of building an ideal commonwealth among the natives required that missionaries 'write and imprint no other but Scripture principles in the *abrasa tabula scraped board* of the naked people, that so they may be in all their principles a choice people unto the Lord'.[103] The necessity

94. Cogley 1999: 11; Maclear 1975. 95. *Eliot Tracts*, 145–6, 163–5, 410–12, 421–2.
96. On Eliot's millenarianism, see Cogley 1999: ch. 4; Maclear 1975: 223–60.
97. Eliot in Eames 1915: 7. See also *Eliot Tracts*, 191–2, 195, 257, and Eliot 1659.
98. *Eliot Tracts*, 192. 99. Davis 1992: 515.
100. See for example Eliot 1659: 35, Torrey 1674: 26. 101. *Eliot Tracts*, 423.
102. *Eliot Tracts*, 186. 103. Eliot 1660: 27 (mispaginated 23).

of returning to purity and simplicity, and of getting rid of 'human inventions' in political and religious matters was a common trope of Puritan writers.[104] The natives were particularly suited for that purpose, as they had not, as other nations had, 'been adulterate with their Antichristian or humane wisdome'.[105] Indeed, anomie was in this case an asset, as Eliot explained: 'as for these poore Indians they have no principles of their own . . . and therefore they most readily yeeld to any direction from the Lord, so that there will be no such opposition against the rising Kingdome of Jesus Christ among them'.[106] Eliot considered that the system he implemented in 'praying towns' should be applied everywhere: 'I apprehend it would be a mercy to England, if they should in this terme of lines, take up that forme of government, which is a divine institution.'[107]

V

Religious reformers sometimes presented the natives' anomie as a form of innocence, contrasting it with the excesses and degeneracy of European civilisation. When missionaries noted qualities in the natives' way of life, they often declined to recognise them as regulated practices (for example communal and nomadic lifestyles, native cults), but rather defined them as an absence of laws or religion. From this perspective, the natives were virtuous because their nature had been untouched by the pomposity and decadence of European manners. The natives would be used as examples to emulate, embodying all the virtues that came with innocence and purity, to which Europe's artificiality was contrasted. As the avant-garde of reform movements, missionaries tended to be highly critical of what they perceived as their nations' moral decay. This type of argument usually presented the manners of the natives as freer than European customs, and yet the natives as sinning less than Europeans.

Juan de Palafox y Mendoza, in his *Virtudes del Indio*, made a long list of all the virtues of the Indians in order to demonstrate that they deserved the protection of the king.[108] The natives, like all human beings, were in a fallen state, but compared to other nations they were a model of innocence and virtue.[109] Roger Williams, exiled from Massachusetts and founder of Rhode

104. Bozeman 1988: 44. 105. *Eliot Tracts*, 192.
106. *Eliot Tracts*, 195 – compare with Machiavelli 2003: 52. On this, see Greenblatt 1994: 22; Bozeman 1988: 268.
107. Eliot in Eames 1915: 7. 108. Palafox y Mendoza 1893: 8, 31.
109. Palafox y Mendoza 1893: 6, 44–5, 94.

Island, contrasted the natives' ways with Europe's: 'I could never discerne that excesse of scandalous sins amongst them, which Europe aboundeth with. Drunkennesse and gluttony, generally they know not what sinnes they be, and although they have not so much to restraine them (both in respect of knowledge of God and Lawes of Men) as the English have, yet a man shall never heare of such crimes amongst them as robberies, murthers, adulteries, &c. as amongst the English'.[110] The vices that Williams and Palafox y Mendoza enumerated were those of a decadent civilisation in which abundance had led to over-indulgence. Europe was at war because of those sins, and the natives were used as a contrastive model of purity.

Many of these comments are reminiscent of More's Utopians.[111] Pierre Biard mused on the natives' simple lifestyle: 'They are never in a hurry. Quite different from us, who can never do anything without hurry and worry; worry, I say, because our desire tyrannises over us and banishes peace from our actions.'[112] According to Father Lalemant, 'It seems as if innocence, banished from the majority of the Empires and Kingdoms of the World, had withdrawn into these great forests where these people dwell. Their nature has something, I know not what, of the goodness of the Terrestrial Paradise before sin had entered it. Their practices manifest none of the luxury, the ambition, the avarice, or the pleasures that corrupt our cities.'[113] The natives' habits were often compared with those of European peasants, and contrasted with urban settings.[114] The simplicity of the natives' lifestyle was matched by the simplicity of the landscape.[115] There, said Le Jeune, people 'come to cast themselves into our great forests as if into the bosom of peace, to live here with more piety, more immunity, and more liberty . . . how sweet is life remote from the gehenna of a thousand superfluous compliments, of the tyranny of lawsuits, of the ravages of war, and of an infinite number of other savage beasts that we do not encounter in our forests'.[116] According to Paul Ragueneau, 'The Spirit of God is everywhere holy and everywhere adorable, but it is not listened to everywhere equally. The stillness of the woods seems more adapted for the reception of its influence than the great noise of the Louvres and Palaces.'[117]

But this vision of the natives did not generally correspond to an idyllic prelapsarian view of the New World. The natives' liberty and the simplicity of their lifestyle could be used as positive rhetorical tropes to be contrasted

110. Williams 1643: 121. 111. More 2002: 67–9. 112. *JR* III, 853.
113. *JR* XXXII, 283. See also Lescarbot 1610: 33.
114. Le Jeune 1635: 101; Deslandres 2003: 79. Compare with Sorbière 1657: 80–6.
115. Davis 1981: 22. 116. *JR* IX: 139–41. See also Lalemant 1649: 112. 117. *JR* XXXVII: 191–3.

with European sinfulness despite the presence and enforcement of both divine and positive law, but most authors insisted that these apparent virtues had no moral content. Paul Le Jeune thought he had never witnessed 'one act of real moral virtue in a Savage', as the actions that seemed virtuous were only performed for personal interest or convenience.[118] What mattered was not the natives' better nature, but their isolation from the nefarious effects of corrupted culture. The natives, when they were presented as examples, were ultimately used to highlight the reformations that Europe awaited. Their absence of collective and individual discipline also suggested that they could be educated in a perfect form of civility, and that they were a blank, uncorrupted page on which both civil and Christian laws could be inscribed.

VI

This chapter has pointed to the fact that missions to the New World need to be considered as part of the history of seventeenth-century European religious reforms. At stake was salvation, not only for the convert, but also for the converter. Religious reformers felt that they had a duty to convert the pagans and the uneducated. For Catholics, good works and an exemplary life were a means to salvation.[119] For Protestants, if justification was by faith only, millenarian hopes led to the conviction that the conversion of the Jews (the natives) was an eschatological sign of the second coming of Christ. Thus, personal action for Catholics, and a collective process for Godly Protestants, would save not only the natives but also those who converted them. This reformative impulse was common to French, English and Spanish ministers, although their methods and understanding of what the reforms should entail varied radically.

For Stephen Greenblatt, the encounter of Europeans with natives was a moment 'in which a comfortably established ideology confronts unusual circumstances . . . when the moral value of a particular form of power is not merely assumed but explained'.[120] The specific encounter of missionaries perhaps further suggests that the ideology was not always so comfortably established. Their confrontation with alien forms of political and social organisation led proselytisers to contrast it with what they thought was problematic in their own culture, and to reflect on the nature of the reformations they thought should be implemented. Scholars have widely discussed European presentations of indigenous Americans as wild and irretrievable

118. Le Jeune 1635: 109. 119. Le Jeune in *JR* VIII: 176; Waterworth 1848: 37.
120. Greenblatt 1994: 28.

non-humans, or as sub-human creatures who simply required guidance and education. Missionaries presented a more nuanced and complicated picture. Their discussion was not about a radically different 'Other',[121] but about native peoples who shared their condition of fallen human beings. Paul Ragueneau complained in 1647 about the excessive zeal of some missionaries: 'It is easy to call irreligion what is merely stupidity, and to take for diabolical working something that is nothing more than human.'[122] Highly dependent on native groups for their survival, and isolated from European influences, missionaries understood that the natives were, after all, 'nothing more than human'.

Ultimately, in these writings, the pursuit of human freedom was understood not as a quest for individual autonomy, but as a search for harmony between man's nature and God's will. This harmony could be sought through political, social or educational means. Harmony in this context meant distancing oneself from one's fallen state. Decay could be caused by either civility or barbarism. Redemption, on the other hand, was a positive process. Missionaries, in their work with the 'savages', proposed visions of a future in which human freedom would coincide with an absolute respect for God's laws.

121. Pagden 1982: 5. 122. *JR* XXXIII, 145.

14

From European to cosmopolitan freedom

FONNA FORMAN

I

In *Lettres de Memmius à Cicéron* (1771) Voltaire wrote this about the Jews:

> They are, all of them, born with raging fanaticism in their hearts, just as the Bretons and the Germans are born with blond hair. I would not be in the least surprised if these people would not someday become deadly to the human race.[1]

Among the many things Voltaire famously took from his Roman heroes, apparently among them was Cicero's profound disdain for Jews. Voltaire may have overlooked the rhetorical quality of Cicero's oration *Pro Flacco* in which he spoke of the Jews as a dangerous and deceptive clique.[2] In fact he was speaking there as defence counsel in the trial of a Roman official accused of interfering with Jewish gold shipments to Jerusalem. It is at least plausible that Cicero was attempting to exonerate his client by appealing to the anti-Jewish sentiments of the jurors.[3] But whatever the case, much of what Voltaire said about Jews and Judaism, and what he claimed to have taken directly from Cicero, sits uncomfortably alongside his cosmopolitan belief in universal tolerance and is difficult to digest in the long shadow of European anti-Semitism. And of course Voltaire was often invoked in the following century for his elaborations on the corruptions of Hebrew scripture, on the parasitic nature of Jewish commercial activity, and on the fanaticism and

My thanks to Quentin Skinner and Martin van Gelderen for inviting me to present this work in Fiesole; and to Quentin additionally for his careful attention to several drafts. Thanks as well to Christian Donath, Tracy Strong, Jim Tully and members of the research group for helpful comments along the way.

1. Voltaire 1879: XXVIII, 439–40. 2. Cicero 1946. 3. See Marshall 1975.

stubborn insularity of Jewish culture.[4] Voltaire was the most severe and prolific among his French Enlightenment colleagues in his condemnation of the Jews, and his article 'Juifs' in the *Dictionnaire philosophique* stands easily among the ugliest tracts ever written about the Jewish people.[5] Depictions of the Jew by Diderot and De Jaucort in the *Encyclopédie* were far more balanced and even somewhat sympathetic. De Jaucort in 'The Jew in Ancient and Modern History' presented the Jew as an object of social injustice, a 'perpetual martyr' notable mainly for clinging steadfast to Mosaic law through centuries of persecution.[6]

There have been attempts to save Voltaire from his apparent hatred for the Jews. Hugh Trevor Roper emphasised counter-passages in Voltaire's vast *œuvre* in which he seemed to say, albeit without much sympathy, that historical persecution against the Jews went too far;[7] Peter Gay insisted that Voltaire's critique of Judaism amounted more fundamentally to a critique of Christianity at its roots, his real target, evoking Arnold Toynbee's claim that Judaism is but a fossil.[8] Others have argued that Voltaire's anti-Judaism was not biological but rather theological and cultural, and that it was thus continuous with older variants of Christian anti-Judaism, and wrongly conflated with the secular, racist anti-Semitism that would emerge in the next century.[9] Indeed, like Christians before him, Voltaire gave the Jews a way out through conversion and assimilation.

My purpose here is not to intervene on the nature of Voltaire's anti-Judaism, or its influence on later generations; but rather to explore what Voltaire's Jew reveals about the nature of his cosmopolitanism. The intransigent particularism of the eighteenth-century European Jew served as an ideal type for Voltaire, a counterpoint in every detail to his commitment to a distinctive kind of freedom that I shall explore in this chapter – a freedom that consisted in what I shall call *cosmopolitan exile*. By this I mean that freedom consisted in detaching oneself from the shackles of parochialism, superstition and immorality exemplified for Voltaire by eighteenth-century European Jews, and which served to animate his hatred for them. In 'Juifs' he wrote: 'It is certain that the Jewish nation is the most singular that the world has ever seen . . . and in a political view the most contemptible.'[10] One finds in them 'only an ignorant and barbarous people, who have long united

4. See Mitchell 2008 and Sutcliffe 2003: 231–46.
5. Voltaire 1877–95: In general, I have consulted the Besterman edition of the *Philosophical Dictionary* (Voltaire 1972), but since he did not include the article 'Juifs', I will cite Voltaire 1932.
6. Cited in Vyverberg 1989: 106.
7. Trevor-Roper 1968; but cf. Hertzberg 1968.
8. See Gay 1959 and 1964: 97–108.
9. E.g. Chisick 2000; but cf. Sutcliffe 2003: 231–46.
10. Voltaire 1877–95: II, 99.

the most sordid avarice with the most detestable superstition and the most invincible hatred for every people by whom they are tolerated and enriched'. Still, he felt compelled to add, 'we ought not to burn them'.[11] Through his very presence in European cities, the Jew flouted his intransigence, his refusal to surrender to the flow of European history – among Europe and yet not of it – and validated his parochial self-certainty with the audacious claim that he was in fact chosen by God.[12] No claim but this last one could more effectively rouse the fury of a man who elsewhere wrote:

> Woe betide the people so stupid and so barbarous as to think that there is a god for its providence alone! That is blasphemy. What! the light of the sun illuminates all eyes, and we are to believe that the light of god illuminates only a small and puny nation in a corner of the globe! What a horror and what stupidity! The divinity speaks to the hearts of all men, and the bonds of charity should unite them from one end of the universe to the other.[13]

I begin with the unfreedom of Voltaire's Jew because I want to illuminate a tension that often characterises our own twenty-first-century cosmopolitanism as well: its apparent compatibility with sometimes brutal intolerance towards wayward cultures. But my investigation aspires to be a properly historical one. I have no intention of rummaging about in history, fingering those who strike me as most culpable for the shortcomings of cosmopolitan thinking today, as if they were engaged in a grand meta-narrative and collectively plotting against the future. Instead I wish to observe what eighteenth-century cosmopolitan thinkers were doing when they articulated the view of freedom that they did. Specifically, I will argue that eighteenth-century cosmopolitans articulated an idea of freedom that fused the central claims of two inherited traditions: first the so-called tradition of negative liberty established in the previous century in which freedom was conceived as absence of interference; and second, the tradition of classical cosmopolitanism, and particularly Stoic cosmopolitanism, which helped its eighteenth-century interpreters to specify the sort of interference that most troubled them – indeed, how this modern cosmopolitan idea of interference was now to be conceived. The Stoics spoke of extirpating passionate attachment, of cultivating apathy

11. Voltaire 1877–95: II 105. The Muhammadan often fared no better for Voltaire. Voltaire's play *Mahomet* (Voltaire 1964) portrayed Muhammad as a false prophet and Islam as a barbarous sect.
12. See Sutcliffe 2003: 193–246.
13. Voltaire 1972: 94. Here Voltaire was asserting the superiority of Confucian to Christian divinity, but his more general case against fanaticism and religious particularism is evident in this passage.

towards the near and dear, and of identifying with a community of all human beings. Eighteenth-century cosmopolitans, I argue, were attracted to this formulation in both its negative and positive dimensions. They were drawn to the negative idea that freedom consisted in extracting oneself from superstition, prejudice, intolerance, fanaticism and particularism which chained the mind, defied human reason and impeded civilisational progress. But they also sought more affirmatively to cultivate a sense of broader human connectedness in the realms of knowledge, science, religion, history, morality, economics, politics and law. Two points to emphasise, which correspond to these negative and positive impulses within the cosmopolitan project. First, the eighteenth-century restoration of classical cosmopolitan thought served to orient the tradition of negative liberty towards a *spatial* conception of interference, establishing a modern cosmopolitan way of thinking about human freedom as a sort of exile. Second, I am deliberately using the positive language of virtue to characterise this eighteenth-century cosmopolitan iteration of negative liberty – that exile is best understood as the *virtue* of cosmopolitan freedom – for reasons that will become clear in due course.

II

Despite the variety of ways and the variety of national contexts in which cosmopolitan ideas flourished in the eighteenth century, it is nevertheless possible to identify an eighteenth-century tradition of cosmopolitan freedom, which serves to unify them to a very great extent. Here I violate a tenet of Enlightenment historiography in recent decades: that Enlightenments are genuinely plural, driven largely from within, and need therefore to be interpreted in national context.[14] While there is much of value in this 'national turn' in Enlightenment studies,[15] for present purposes it seemed most productive not to confine myself to one particular national context, but rather to identify prominent conceptual trends in eighteenth-century European culture, 'Enlightenment *above* national context' as John Robertson called it in his book on Scotland and Naples, in which he made a persuasive case for Enlightenment as a coherent intellectual movement.[16] Here I will often refer to eighteenth-century cosmopolitan freedom as a singular thing, and draw my examples from across national contexts. Ultimately I agree with

14. Porter and Teich 1981. For critical discussion of this late twentieth-century move, as 'refashioning the Enlightenment as a postmodern kaleidoscope of diversity and difference', see Robertson 2005: 3. Odd, however, to label as 'postmodern' a position for which J. G. A. Pocock admittedly has been the 'most powerful scholarly exponent'.
15. Robertson 2005: 27.
16. Robertson 2005.

Robertson that exploring similarities and continuities is not to devalue contextual difference.[17] It is simply the matter of continuity that most interests me here.

Identifying a unified eighteenth-century tradition of cosmopolitan freedom is further complicated by the various ways historians have tended to carve up and periodise the Enlightenment into early, middle and high. I suspect that cosmopolitanism looked very different in the early Enlightenment when the 'Science of Morals' tended to be articulated in terms of universal reason, than it did a bit further on when reason came to be seen by some as insufficient for grounding a universal morality and was supplemented by emerging interests in anthropology and moral psychology. And of course many in the later Enlightenment abandoned epistemological questions altogether and turned to utility to explain human motivation, which transformed the nature of cosmopolitan thinking further still.[18] A sensitivity to intellectual developments within the period is essential to fully understanding what eighteenth-century cosmopolitan freedom was, for indeed concepts with histories elude static definition. But again, it is beyond my purpose here of identifying continuities.

The task of identifying a coherent tradition of cosmopolitan freedom is complicated perhaps most formidably by the variety of *purposes* for which cosmopolitan ideas were employed by eighteenth-century thinkers, in debates about knowledge, religion, politics, morals, culture, law, commerce, fashion, among other things. Note some of the most predominant of these: to characterise the community of urbane intellectuals united across national, linguistic and confessional boundaries, and the international orbit of their fellowship with one another, enabled by advances in travel, printing and communication; to describe the universal, rational religion these men endorsed, a 'religion of humanity' as Thomas Paine called it, distilled from sectarian perversions, in which Jesus Christ was divested of divine substance and designated a hero of humanity alongside Socrates and Confucius, as well as Cicero, Seneca and Plutarch; to denote the universality of science and knowledge, with particular emphasis on a naturalistic 'Science of Man'; to assert the superiority of the moderns over the ancients by contrasting the ferocity and injustice of ancient virtue with modern equity and humanity; to designate the universality of the 'Rights of Man'; to denigrate parochial self-preference and expand the scope of moral concern and humanitarian action; to specify institutions that might facilitate international peace and

17. Robertson 2005: 47. 18. For discussion see Schlereth 1977: 62.

federation; to describe the legal obligations the European had to foreigners when he encountered them at home or abroad; to characterise the use of comparative anthropology to relativise European practices and prejudices, to criticise the barbarity of European exploits, particularly empire and slavery, and to defend the indigenous peoples that Europeans 'discovered' in the process; relatedly, to characterise new trends in Enlightenment historiography and literature that resisted partisan story-telling in favour of detached, unbiased accounts of distant parts of the world – notably Persia, India and China – that sought in a philosophical way to identify what David Hume called 'constant and universal principles of human nature'[19] in order to ground a universal morality, applicable as readily to Europeans as to mankind in general; to describe the spontaneous harmony that emerges when states engage freely in trade with one another; and in a critical key to describe the decline and corrupt uniformity of modern morals – as Rousseau warned the Poles:

> There are no more Frenchmen, Germans, Spaniards, or even Englishmen, nowadays, regardless of what people say; there are only Europeans. All have the same tastes, the same passions, and the same morals. All, in the same circumstances, will do the same things; all will call themselves unselfish, and be rascals; all will talk of the public welfare, and think only of themselves; all will praise moderation, and wish to be as rich as Croesus. They have no ambition but for luxury, they have no passion but for gold; sure that money will buy them all their hearts desire, they all are ready to sell themselves to the first bidder. What do they care what master they obey, under the laws of what state they live? Provided they can find money to steal and women to corrupt, they feel at home in any country.[20]

For many this homogeneity of taste reduced to an almost pathological Francophilia, with Paris firmly entrenched as the cultural capital of the cosmopolis, setting continental fashions in literature, art, cuisine, furniture and dress. Benjamin Franklin was perhaps the worst offender. He wrote to a friend:

> The time I spent in Paris and in the improving Conversation and agreeable Society of so many learned and ingenious Men seems now to me like a pleasing Dream, from which I was sorry to be awakened by finding myself again in London.[21]

19. Hume 1875: II, 68.
20. Rousseau 1997a: 184. For an account of Rousseau's alternative 'romantic cosmopolitanism' see Rosenblatt 2009.
21. In a private letter from Franklin to Thomas Francois Dalibrand, 31 January 1768, cited in Schlereth 1977: 6.

History reveals an astonishing multiplicity of purposes regarding the usage of cosmopolitan language and imagery in the eighteenth century, among proponents and critics alike; and each of these sites has produced abundant fields of scholarly investigation, which makes the task of identifying similarity and continuity 'above context' all the more daunting. But I argue that something holds these sites together, and situates them within a larger discourse. I argue that the node around which all these variants cluster is a unified eighteenth-century cosmopolitan idea of freedom. I propose that we think of these variants of eighteenth-century cosmopolitan thought – religious cosmopolitanism, moral cosmopolitanism, cultural, political, legal and commercial cosmopolitanism, and so forth – as sites of contestation. They are debates about the value and plausibility of the cosmopolitan idea of freedom that I will outline below: freedom as a sort of active exile from local constraints. Each debate turned on the extent to which a person must detach herself from a particular *sort* of constraint – self, belief, culture, language, nation – or a cluster of them. Indeed it is contestation over the extent of appropriate detachment that rendered an eighteenth-century debate a cosmopolitan one.

This is not the place to develop sites of contestation, but a few examples should serve to indicate why we might wish to re-examine essential eighteenth-century debates through the lens of cosmopolitan freedom: debates, for example, about whether one must sever all religious ties or whether religion can be accommodated to modern life and thought; debates about the proper scope of moral concern, in which there were weaker and stronger claims about the value of detaching ourselves from the local and reorienting our interests and energies towards broader circles of others; debates about international order and the extent to which nations must surrender their sovereignty to a federation of states for the security and prosperity of all, or the extent to which trade among nations adequately tempers national jealousy and stimulates tolerance and humanity; and so forth. A central feature of eighteenth-century thought concerned the extent to which we must disentangle ourselves from a dense thicket of constraints that shackle our minds, limit the free exercise of our will, and impede the progress of human civilisation. In debates about cosmopolitan freedom some advocate more detachment, others less. Only the most extreme advocate all or none. There is much work to be done here. For the moment, however, we need to establish preliminaries, and specify more exactly what this eighteenth-century cosmopolitan view of freedom consisted in.

III

The view of freedom I am considering is distinctive in its fusion of two preceding traditions: first the tradition of negative liberty in which freedom was understood as absence of interference; and second, the tradition of classical cosmopolitanism which provided the eighteenth-century with a language for specifying the type of interference that was especially vexing to them. I begin with the tradition of negative liberty which defined freedom as the absence of interference – essentially, that one is not inhibited from doing what one has a *power* to do (in the foundational Hobbesian variant), or what one has a *will* to do (in the Lockean variant).[22] Eighteenth-century cosmopolitan thought appropriated the negative impulses of the previous century, but sought more exhaustively to clear the ground of constraints, to free the will more completely than did seventeenth-century writers who were preoccupied with executive tyranny and focused primarily on state interference.[23] What the eighteenth century added, I argue, was an invocation of classical cosmopolitan thought to specify a modern cosmopolitan idea of interference. In this sense I am examining a pivot in what Quentin Skinner has called the 'genealogy' of liberty.[24]

I argue that the revival of classical cosmopolitan thought[25] served to orient the tradition of negative liberty towards a *spatial* conception of interference. My use of spatial imagery derives from the ancient Stoic idea of *oikeiōsis* which, we shall see, emerged again and again in eighteenth-century cosmopolitan thought. For the Stoic, being a cosmopolitan meant that one had disengaged from that which is familiar, *oikeion*, choosing instead to live freely in accordance with universal reason. The Stoics sought to free man not merely from the institutions that govern local life, like families, clans and nations, but more formidably from the narrow affective ties and particular habits and prejudices that characterise a life lived uncritically within these institutional boundaries.[26] Stoic thought thus illustrates why exiling oneself physically is neither a necessary nor a sufficient condition for cosmopolitan

22. My characterisation here is drawn from Skinner 2008c.
23. My thanks to Jim Tully for this point. 24. Skinner 2008c.
25. Enlightenment cosmopolitans should probably be considered 'third wave' or even 'fourth wave' cosmopolitans, for they regularly drew upon a variety of Renaissance sources, notably Erasmus and Montaigne, whose ideas were inflected quite distinctively by Stoic cosmopolitan thought. They also drew variously on Bayle, Grotius and Leibniz, seventeenth-century cosmopolites all. And so, although 'second wave' cosmopolitanism is beyond my scope here, a more adequate account of cosmopolitan influences on the eighteenth century would need to consider how the Enlightenment received and appropriated earlier inflections of the classical articulation.
26. For discussion on the radical critique of conventional belief in Stoic ethics, see Nussbaum 1994: 316–58.

freedom. Indeed, Plutarch insisted that Socrates was free as he roamed about his Athenian cage – free even as he drank the hemlock.[27] Likewise, leaving one's ancestral home is no guarantee that one will leave one's prejudices behind.

Eighteenth-century cosmopolitans regularly identified Seneca, Plutarch, Marcus Aurelius, Epictetus and especially Cicero as their classical models. Hume spoke often of his 'beloved Tully'[28] and depicted the eighteenth-century cosmopolite in his image as 'a creature whose thoughts are not limited by any narrow bounds, either of place or time'.[29] In his *Encyclopédie* article *Philosophie des Éclectiques* Diderot spoke of 'trampling underfoot prejudices, tradition, antiquity, universal assent, authority', and of 'transcend[ing] all ancient puerilities, overturn[ing] the barriers that reason never erected'.[30] Eighteenth-century philosophy was infused with classical cosmopolitan themes of detachment and transcendence.[31]

Plutarch was a hero among eighteenth-century cosmopolitans; and my use of *exile* to describe the cosmopolitan imperative of extracting oneself from local constraints derives largely from Plutarch's *De exilio* in which this thought about detachment was given perhaps its most elaborate expression in all of antiquity.[32] There Plutarch drew a distinction between the 'Cosmian' who is free and the patriot who is not, which rested on a more fundamental distinction, central to all variants of classical cosmopolitanism, Cynic and Stoic, Greek and Roman, between nature and convention. Plutarch wrote: 'Nature leaves us free and untrammeled; it is we who bind ourselves, confine ourselves, immure ourselves, herd ourselves into cramped and sordid quarters.'[33] 'Cosmians', on the other hand, are those who live closer to 'Nature' for they have freed themselves from 'the cares, distractions, and press of business that are the product of their native lands'.[34] Plutarch likened the patriot to a snail in its shell; he lives a life of contented familiarity, complacent and happy, loving his neighbours, hating his enemies, sheltered by the warmth of the city and its cosy prejudices.[35] The conventions that orient his life are of course artificial, but they take on the appearance of nature and truth to him, having insinuated themselves deeply and imperceptibly into his soul from a very young age. Such people (and Euripides was Plutarch's favourite example) cannot envisage another way, and they see

27. Plutarch 1959: 600f–601b (528–31). 28. See Gay 1966: 153.
29. Hume 1875: I, 207. 30. Cited in Schlereth 1977: 49, 10.
31. On Kant's cosmopolitan debt to the Stoics see Nussbaum 1997. 32. Plutarch 1959.
33. Plutarch 1959: 601d (533). 34. Plutarch 1959: 605c (555). 35. Plutarch 1959: 600a (525).

exile as a 'shameful calamity', 'the greatest ill' that can befall a man.[36] And is there not something to this? The idea of living one's life in exile, detached from one's past, one's family and friends, from everything familiar, can strike the imagination as incredibly sad.

In praising the exile of the Cosmian, Plutarch sought to rearrange the emotional furniture, dismissing all this sadness and alienation as pathology in need of a good dose of therapeutic *apatheia*. Indeed, he redefined exile from a 'calamity' to 'a provision granted by Fortune'.[37] Freedom – Plutarch used the Greek *eleutheria* – consisted in arriving at a certain consciousness about the artificial conventions around which we orient our lives – that our truths are partial, arbitrary, products of circumstance in a particular place in time. The person who is free will transcend these inhibiting conventions and reorient his life according to natural, universal principles. And indeed some will physically exile themselves: 'Exclusion from one city', he exuberated 'is the freedom to choose from them all.'[38] This is why, he observed: 'few men of the greatest good sense and wisdom have been buried in their own country, and that most of them, under compulsion from no one, weighed anchor of their own accord and found a new haven for their lives'.[39] It is not that a 'new haven' will be free of conventions; every place has its conventions. It is that one will not have become inured to them from childhood when one arrives. One will be free. The emancipatory possibilities were personified for Plutarch by the legions of famous exiles throughout antiquity. The pages of *De exilio* are filled with praise for Herodotus, Homer and Aeschylus, Thucydides and Xenophon, Diogenes the Cynic, Aristotle and Ariston, Zeno and Chrysippus.[40] Interesting to note here that Voltaire, Jefferson, Franklin, obsessive peripatetics all, favoured establishing open borders and formal rights of emigration, translating the 'Fortune' of classical cosmopolitan exile into a universal right of all people to move about freely and settle anywhere one chooses.

But exiling oneself did not necessitate leaving one's home. I am not, for the Stoics, constrained and thus unfree by the mere fact of being born and staying to live my life in a particular place. Indeed, we shall see that exile was far more a state of mind than the location of a body. Classical cosmopolitans were less concerned with physical place per se than they were with the affective ties and conventional norms that infuse local life in any particular place,

36. Plutarch 1959: 599d–e (521–2); 605f–606a (559–61). 37. Plutarch 1959: 605d (557).
38. Plutarch 1959: 604b (549). 39. Plutarch 1959: 604d (551).
40. Plutarch 1959: 604f–605c (553–7).

distorting the way that a local inhabitant views himself and the world, and inhibiting the free exercise of his will. Of all the expatriates Plutarch praised, remarkably enough it was Socrates who exemplified the cosmopolitan sensibility for him: Socrates who explicitly *refused* physically to exile himself even after having been unjustly condemned to death by a corrupted mob; Socrates who throughout his seventy-two years of life rarely left the city gates of Athens.[41] Socrates dwelling disputatiously as a gadfly among his fellow citizens exemplified cosmopolitan freedom for Plutarch. Without ever leaving the city, Socrates disengaged from everything that inhibited a life lived in accordance with reason and the pursuit of self-knowledge. And ever since, there have been more or less sober manifestations of this basic Socratic impulse towards critical detachment – the most extreme in antiquity, of course in Diogenes the Cynic, whom Plato reportedly described as 'Socrates gone mad',[42] choosing as he did to demonstrate his world citizenship and detachment from the arbitrariness of Athenian convention by staging public performances of various biological and sexual functions. So too the Cynics Crates and Hypparchia, the self-styled 'dog-couple' who exhibited the aptness of that designation, with apparently impressive frequency and ingenuity, on the streets of fourth-century Athens. Diderot seems to have been particularly fascinated by the audacity of Cynic world citizenship.[43]

But Socratic cosmopolitanism had its more sober adherents as well – Kant, for example, writing on cosmopolitan maturity from his Königsberg study, who also insisted he did not need to leave home to enlarge his mind. Kant's cosmopolitan description of Königsberg resonates with our perception of Socratic Athens:

> A large city such as Königsberg on the river Pregel, which is the centre of a kingdom, in which the provincial councils of the government are located, which has a university (for cultivation of the sciences), and which also has the right location for maritime commerce – a city which, by way of rivers, has the advantages of commerce both with the interior of the country and with neighboring and distant lands of different languages and customs, can well be taken as an appropriate place for broadening one's knowledge of human beings as well as of the world, where this knowledge can be acquired without even travelling.[44]

Whether one's cosmopolitan exile took the form of physical expatriation or critical detachment, however, freedom meant extracting oneself from

41. Plutarch 1959: 600f–601b (528–31). 42. Diogenes 1925: 6.54.
43. Schlereth 1977: 14. 44. Kant 2006: 4.

constraints that inhibit the free use of one's reason, that repress the possibility of self-knowledge, and bias one's judgements in sometimes very ugly ways towards oneself and one's group. Diderot summed this up in his Socratic portrait of the cosmopolite as a 'philosopher who tramples underfoot prejudices, tradition, antiquity, universal assent, authority – in a word, everything that overawes the mass of minds. He is a philosopher who dares to think for himself'.[45]

Hopefully at this point my use of exile to describe the eighteenth-century cosmopolitan inflection of negative liberty is sufficiently clear. The question now is: why characterise exile as the *virtue* of cosmopolitan freedom?

IV

I argue next that eighteenth-century cosmopolitan freedom, while a variant of negative freedom, nevertheless integrated elements of the so-called positive notion of freedom associated with Aristotle – and that this fusion of traditions ultimately produced a muddled, self-contradictory and potentially dangerous composite, still evident in cosmopolitan thinking today. There are two related ways to understand this development. The first relates to the active nature of cosmopolitan freedom, what we need *affirmatively to do* in order to be free, which I argue is a shift from the passivity of negative freedom in the originary sense. The second relates to the teleological direction in which cosmopolitan freedom was said to carry those who exercise it.

I begin with cosmopolitan freedom as an active principle. It is important to be clear that one need not actually exercise one's power or will to be free in a negative sense. You are said to be perfectly free as long as you are not constrained from doing whatever you would otherwise do, or have a will to do. If there is an agent or agency in place with power sufficient to inhibit you from doing what you have the power and will to do, you are unfree according to negative libertarians, even, some would say, in the moments when you are not acting. And thus, negative liberty, as it emerged from the natural law tradition, is compatible with passivity. Put differently, your freedom requires nothing of you; it is an enabler of action, an 'opportunity' concept, as Charles Taylor calls it, something that is either granted or prohibited by an external agency, and, most usually for early modern negative libertarians, the state.[46] Whether you choose to act, to exercise your freedom, and indeed how you choose to exercise it, is to a very great extent left up to you.

45. Schlereth 1977: 49. 46. Taylor 1979: 177.

The eighteenth-century variant of negative liberty that I am exploring here, however, takes a very different view of passivity. Cosmopolitan freedom is an active principle, one that necessitates a certain kind of vigilance. You must live mindfully, and actively work to free yourself from the various local constraints that inhibit you. Cosmopolitans, classical and modern, have always emphasised how difficult a task disengagement from the local can be, how much work is involved in exercising cosmopolitan freedom. In classical thought these ideas were perhaps best conveyed by Hierocles, a Stoic of the first and second centuries CE, in his account of *oikeiōsis*.[47] The word *oikeiōsis* derives from the Greek *oikos*, which referred in ancient life to the private realm of the household as distinct from the public realm of the *polis*. The Stoic idea *oikeiōsis* denotes the familiarity one develops over time with those who inhabit the *oikos*, with those who literally share one's physical space. Thus, the Stoics mapped our affections concentrically, arguing that they are strongest at the centre, closest and most familiar to the self, and weaken progressively as the object is removed further and further away – from family to community to nation to humanity. He wrote:

> Each of us is as it were entirely encompassed by many circles, some smaller, others larger, the latter enclosing the former on the basis of their different and unequal dispositions relative to each other. The first and closest circle is the one which a person has drawn as though around a centre, his own mind. This circle encloses the body and anything taken for the sake of the body. For it is virtually the smallest circle, and almost touches the centre itself. Next, the second one further removed from the centre but enclosing the first circle; this contains parents, siblings, wife and children. The third one has in it uncles and aunts, grandparents, nephews, nieces, and cousins. The next circle includes the other relatives, and this is followed by the circle of local residents, then the circle of fellow-tribesmen, next that of fellow-citizens, and then in the same way the circle of people from neighboring towns, and the circle of fellow-countrymen. The outermost and largest circle, which encompasses all the rest, is that of the whole human race.[48]

The point of this model was decidedly not to celebrate the diversity of our affiliations, what practitioners of identity politics today like to characterise as our multi-layered, or hybrid, or complex selves. On the contrary, the Stoics sought to dismantle the concentric structure of our identities and

47. Hierocles 1987: 1.57.G (349–50). For further discussion of modern appropriations of Stoic *oikeiōsis* see Forman-Barzilai 2010.
48. Hierocles 1987: 1.57.G (349–50).

affiliations. This was what the Stoic cosmopolitan imperative was ultimately all about – that mature individuals should cultivate apathy towards the familiar, towards those accidental facts that privilege some, degrade others, and otherwise divide humankind from one another. The Stoics thus posited the concentric model both for descriptive and for normative cosmopolitan purposes. On the one hand they offered an empirical portrait of human identity and connection – and at that level the model is rather compelling. But then they insisted that mature moral agents should work actively to overcome the pull of human affection which develops though familiarity, and collapse the circles inward, so that humanity will ultimately make the same ethical claims on the agent as those in her innermost circles. Hierocles wrote:

> Once these [circles] have all been surveyed, it is the task of a well tempered man, in his proper treatment of each group, to draw the circles together somehow towards the centre, and to keep zealously transferring those from the enclosing circles into the enclosed ones . . . It is incumbent on us to respect people from the third circle as if they were those from the second, and again to respect our other relatives as if they were those from the third circle. For although the greater distance in blood will remove some affection, we must try hard to assimilate them.[49]

Hierocles demonstrated here that cosmopolitan freedom is hard work; that it requires zealous effort, involving sacrifice and discomfort – but that the alternative of passively capitulating to concentric tendencies is to live a life that is not worth living. Living life concentrically is easy, and oriented around familiar patterns; but one surrenders one's will to *doxa*, to opinion, and thus is not free. The point of all this being that one can be perfectly free in the originary negative sense of being unimpeded from doing that which one has a power or will to do, and yet be fundamentally unfree from a cosmopolitan perspective if within that negative scheme one has been rendered unaware of one's own powers, if one has unwittingly surrendered one's will to prevailing opinions, norms and beliefs, indeed if one's mind has become the agent of one's own subjection – what Mill would later call social tyranny, and Marx false consciousness. Exile thus is the virtue of cosmopolitan freedom; it is the very action through which we become conscious of our constraints, work to emancipate ourselves from them, often against the current, inviting great opposition from those who care most about us, and move forward in a teleological sense towards our higher purposes as human beings.

49. Hierocles 1987: 1.57.G (349–50).

Which brings me to the teleology of cosmopolitan freedom. If the active nature of exile is the first reason I am using the language of virtue to characterise cosmopolitan freedom, the second relates to the direction in which cosmopolitan freedom was thought to carry those who exercise it. Aristotle claimed of course that man was *zoon politikon*, so that freedom consisted in realising one's essence through active participation in political life, through self-governance. Modern cosmopolitans, I argue, adopted this general approach to freedom, that freedom entailed realising one's highest purposes – that, as Skinner described it in his account of positive liberty, 'I am only in the fullest sense in possession of my liberty if I actually exercise the capacities and pursue the goals that serve to realise my most distinctively human purposes'[50] – but they fundamentally adjusted these capacities and goals, indeed what it meant to realise one's distinctively human purposes. They transformed Aristotle's notion of the self from the *zoon politikon* to the *zoon cosmopolitikon*, as it were, fundamentally reorienting what aspiring to our highest purpose as human beings entails – and in the process, radically altering the meaning of citizenship. In some sense, we might say that in reorienting our telos as such, modern cosmopolitans retained the political content of Aristotelean teleology but expanded its scope, globalised it. One sometimes hears political cosmopolitans today speak in such terms, as if the arena of self-government is elastic and can be expanded at will without fundamentally altering the nature and practices of democratic citizenship. Simply enlarge your stilted, parochial conception of who counts as a fellow-citizen, and you have global democracy. But from a historical perspective this is a seriously confused genre of contemporary political theory which, while noble in its aspirations, underestimates the huge gulf between a life dedicated to self-government and life as a citizen of a chimerical cosmopolis, the latter of which is perfectly compatible with local political disengagement and thus with living one's life as a slave.

V

Modern cosmopolitan freedom ultimately fused not two traditions, but three: first, the tradition of negative liberty, in which freedom was conceived as absence of interference; second, the tradition of classical cosmopolitanism which, when carried into the eighteenth century, specified the content of this interference in spatial terms and grounded a view of freedom as an act of exile or detachment; and third, the Aristotelean tradition of positive freedom

50. Skinner 1990b: 297.

which rested on a claim about what it meant to be truly human, and in which freedom consisted in realising truly human purposes – all refashioned, we might say, as *zoon cosmopolitikon*.

I am inclined to think that this fusion amounts to a very confused tradition that lives on to the present day. Something on which to reflect further is the extent to which these traditions are uncongenial towards one another, discharging implications that are highly incompatible. Recognising these incompatibilities may help us make better sense of the contradictions embedded within the cosmopolitan vision today. For one thing, I am inclined to think that cosmopolitan intolerance towards unassimilable cultures, the point on which I began this chapter, is linked with the positive cosmopolitan view of human essences, of what being truly human means. The case of Voltaire's Jew demonstrates a palpable turn from liberalism's historical impulse towards toleration, which was connected with a basic resistance to organising political life along what Isaiah Berlin characterised as monistic assertions about our highest human ends. Adam Sutcliffe observes that 'the extent of Voltaire's contempt for the Jews, and the aggressive tone in which it is often expressed, cast a problematic shadow over his commitment to universal toleration'.[51] Liberals have traditionally resisted the urge in classical and Christian thought to specify in positive terms what it means to be truly human, recognising that such claims are subject to endless contestation, and too frequently lead to intractable and bloody conflict. Liberalism historically has sought to maintain public peace by transcending fundamental contestation about human ends – by privatising its expression, cultivating a public philosophy of toleration (what Bernard Williams memorably called 'tolerating the intolerable'[52]), institutionalising negative liberty, and ultimately and usually very successfully diverting subversive energies into competitive consumption. The tradition of liberal toleration and its sublimation of fundamental conflict is, of course, very much still with us, and a target today for proponents of democratic agonism, who recognise that the repression of conflict usually works to the benefit of the powerful, and who thus seek to emancipate our differences and grievances, to air them in a more public and discursive way.

By weaving a positive teleology into the tradition of negative liberty, modern cosmopolitans invented a specious category of the 'intolerable', reserved for marginal, largely unassimilable cultures that defied what it meant to live a truly human life, cultures that resisted the flow of European

51. Sutcliffe 2003: 232. 52. Williams 1999: 65–76.

progress – exemplified by Voltaire's Jew. That Voltaire could not extend to the Jew his fascination for Chinese Confucians, say, or Indian Hindus, whom he frequently drew upon to critique European self-certainty, is a testament not only to the perfect storm of Jewish unassimilability, but perhaps more importantly to the fact that the destiny of the eighteenth-century diaspora Jew was intimately intertwined with the destiny of the European. China, India, Persia – at a distance in every sense – could remain civilisational objects of exotic fascination; no toleration was required in order to engage them. Bring them closer, into the heart of Europe, live among them, and I wonder if Voltaire's cosmopolitan fascination would have survived. It seems that Voltaire exempted himself from what is, potentially, the most compelling feature of the negative tradition he inherited. There is thus an important linkage here between the positive nature of cosmopolitan teleology, which demarcates the truly human from that which is not, and the intolerance that emerged within cosmopolitan thinking towards wayward peoples, a legacy that has endured down to the present day.

There is something of great value in Thomas Nagel's insight that no matter how hard we try to remove ourselves from our subject, something inevitably remains behind the lens and conditions what we observe.[53] But certainly the historian can be more or less reflective about this, and more or less wary, and in this spirit I have tried to proceed with a subtler orientation to relevance than the sort that erases the boundaries between history and critique, that ferrets out good evidence and discards the rest as arcane. When I suggest that the eighteenth century is 'usable' in present debates, what I have in mind is the hope that a properly historical approach will enable a richer and more active understanding of our present concepts – not only so that we know what we mean when we use a term like cosmopolitanism, which saturates moral and political discourse in the West today. My approach certainly aspires to that sort of conceptual clarity – but more ambitiously perhaps that once we grasp the ideological composition of cosmopolitan freedom (and here I am referring to the uneasy fusion of inherited traditions that sit at the centre of my interpretation, a fusion that can be grasped only through a genuinely historical engagement) I believe we are better positioned to identify contradictions within the eighteenth-century cosmopolitan project that have been carried forward. This is a perspective on cosmopolitanism that cannot be generated by a purely conceptual analysis, nor by a historical investigation that resists its own usefulness.

53. Nagel 1986.

15

Is political freedom an Islamic value?

MICHAEL COOK

I

Let me start by stating a couple of assumptions that are not, I think, particularly extravagant. The first is that most human societies are familiar with the relationship between master and slave, and the contrast it generates between being a slave and being a free person.[1] The second is that a capacity for drawing analogies is a standard part of the mental faculties of humans. Given these assumptions, we should not, I think, be surprised if we find people making analogies between slavery and freedom on the one hand and other relationships involving an asymmetrical distribution of power on the other.

One such asymmetrical relationship for many societies is that between husband and wife. Asmāʾ bint Abī Bakr, daughter of the first Caliph, is reported to have said: 'Marriage is slavery, so you should think twice to whom you enslave your daughter.'[2] The point she is making is not that a woman is *legally* the slave of her husband, but that you could think of it that way; the pay-off of doing so is that you are likely to pause before marrying off your daughter to some domestic tyrant.

I am indebted to the conference participants for their responses to the talk on which this chapter is based, and to Simon Cook, Patricia Crone, Kazuo Morimoto, Shivaji Sondhi and Qasim Zaman for their comments on an earlier draft of it. In addition to improving my argument in points of detail, they led me to rethink it at a crucial point.

1. In many societies this simple dichotomy is complicated, for example by the presence of intermediate statuses; thus in the Gortyn code, inscribed in stone on the island of Crete in the fifth century BC, the serf (*woikeus*) occupies such a position between the free man (*eleutheros*) and the slave (*dōlos*); see Willetts 1967: 10, and, for example, 40 lines 5–10 of the text. But I doubt that such complications make the contrast between a slave and a free person invisible.
2. Saʿīd ibn Manṣūr 1967: 149 no. 591 (*inna hādhā ʾl-nikāḥ riqq, fal-yanẓur aḥadukum ʿinda man yuriqqu karīmatahu*). The saying is also attributed to ʿUmar ibn al-Khaṭṭāb, ʿĀʾisha, and the Prophet himself.

Another such case would be the relationship between aristocrats and commoners. In Arabic the term *ḥurr* literally means 'free', but it can also mean 'noble'.[3] The point is not that commoners are *legally* the slaves of aristocrats, but that in some respects you could think of it that way: aristocrats behave with the full autonomy of free men, whereas commoners tend to be a bit slavish in their demeanour.

Yet another case would be the relationship between God and humans. The primary sense of the Arabic word *ʿabd* is a slave as opposed to a free man; but it can also be used of any man, free or slave, in respect of God, the idea being that he is owned (*marbūb*) by his Creator,[4] much as a slave is owned by his master. This is not to say that humans are *legally* the slaves of God, or that the law of slavery governs their relations with Him – a legal doctrine that would have some bizarre, not to say blasphemous effects. But if you think of yourself as God's slave, it could help to instill in you the humility and obedience that your relationship to your Creator requires of you. When I have occasion to refer back to this analogy, I shall follow a common usage in speaking of God's 'servants' rather than His 'slaves', but it should be remembered that we are talking about the same Arabic word.[5]

A final case, and the one that really concerns us, is the relationship between ruler and ruled. In Muslim Spain in the late ninth century a certain Ibn Ḥafṣūn led a rebellion against Arab domination; his followers were Muslims of native Spanish stock. He told them that the Arabs had enslaved them (*istaʿbadatkum*), and that he wished to deliver them from their slavery (*urīdu an . . . ukhrijakum min ʿubūdiyyatikum*).[6] Again, the point was not that

3. Rosenthal 1960: 9–11 (noting also a parallel usage in biblical Hebrew). The Persian term *āzād* likewise means both 'free' and 'noble', but here, as pointed out to me by Kazuo Morimoto, it seems that two originally distinct words have fallen together (see Nyberg 1964–74: II, 41b).

4. Lane 1863–93: 1935a; Ibn Manẓūr n.d.: III, 3:270b.6 (*al-ʿabd al-insān, ḥurran kāna aw raqīqan, yudhhabu bi-dhālika ilā annahu marbūb li-bārīhi*; *marbūb* is a synonym of *mamlūk* in the sense of slave, see Lane 1863–93: 1007b).

5. While the singular *ʿabd* carries both senses, in common usage there is a distinction in the plural: *ʿabīd* is used in relation to other humans, *ʿibād* in relation to God (Lane 1863–93: 1935a; Ibn Manẓūr n.d.: III, 271a.15). The lexicographers, however, attribute this distinction to 'the common people' (*al-ʿāmma*), no doubt because God Himself omits to observe it in the Koran: while *ʿibād* is regularly used of God's servants (as in Q2:207), there is one verse in which it clearly refers to people's slaves (Q24:32); and *ʿabīd* is used only of God's servants (as in Q3:182), possibly reflecting the exigencies of the rhyme (in all five instances the word is the last in the verse, and the last vowel of the preceding verse is an *ī*). For Koranic usage see also Ambros 2004: 181. Note that Turkish traditionally translates *ʿabd* in both senses as *kul*, slave, and that the word 'servant' itself derives from the Latin *servus*, slave.

6. Fierro 2005: 220–1; Ibn ʿIdhārī 1948–51: II, 114.17. The word *istaʿbadatkum* can also plausibly be rendered 'regard you as slaves', as in Fierro's translation.

non-Arab Muslims were literally enslaved by the Arabs, but that you could think of it that way: the Arabs were their oppressors. Note that once Ibn Ḥafṣūn had resorted to this analogy, he could perfectly well have gone on to tell his followers that his ambition was to make them free men (*aḥrār*), in other words to liberate them (*an uḥarrirakum*); but he left this implicit.

If the assumptions with which I started are valid, we should expect to come upon analogies like this from time to time. To limit ourselves to the field of politics, my hunch would be that, were we to mount a massive search, we would find such analogies to occur sporadically at different places and times in Islamic history,[7] as indeed elsewhere in human history.

What I want to do now is to raise the comparative bar. Let us make a distinction between a culture in which individuals sporadically draw analogies between slavery and subjection to political power, and a culture in which this analogy is central to the way people think and talk about politics. After telling the story of the disgraceful end of the monarchy in the first book of his history of Rome, Livy opens the second book with the statement that his task from here on is to trace the history of 'a free people, governed by annually elected officers of state and subject not to the caprice of individual men, but to the overriding authority of law'.[8] This is not a stray thought that came to Livy on the spur of the moment, but rather part of a dense and sustained tradition.[9] The existence of such a tradition in the history of Europe can be taken as a given for the purposes of the present volumes. But is it unique to Europe?

7. Thus the tenth-century philosopher Abū 'l-Ḥasan al-ʿĀmirī says that one of the trials from which Islam delivered the Persians was the fact that *all* strata of their society were oppressed through the policy of enslavement (*anna ṭabaqātihim bi-asrihim kānū muḍṭahadīn bi-siyāsat al-istiʿbād*, ʿĀmirī 1967: 175.4, 176.4, cited in Crone 2004: 315 note 1). ʿĀmirī can hardly be asserting that *all* members of Persian society were held by their rulers to be legally slaves. Thaʿālibī, a slightly later author, describes most of the Sasanian kings (*Akāsira*) as oppressive rulers who were given to enslaving free men (*yastaʿbidūna 'l-aḥrār*) and treating their subjects as hirelings and slaves (*yujrūna al-raʿāyā majrā 'l-ujarā' wa'l-ʿabīd wa'l-imā'*, Thaʿālibī 1994: 301.11); the first charge is no doubt to be understood literally, the second as analogy. Some centuries later we learn from a Persian work on statecraft that the good ruler regards his subjects (*raʿāyā*) as his sons and friends, while the bad ruler regards them as his slaves (Alam 2004: 56; for the work in question, see 51–3). Just as with Ibn Ḥafṣūn, in none of these cases is there an explicit equation of the absence of oppression with freedom (cf. Lewis 1988: 65).
8. Translation slightly adapted from Livy 1971: 105. The original uses the flexibility of Latin word-order to highlight the freedom of the Roman people: 'Liberi iam hinc populi Romani res pace belloque gestas, annuos magistratus, imperiaque legum potentiora quam hominum peragam' (Livy 1987: I, 76).
9. For illustrations of some later phases of this tradition in Rome, see Wirszubski 1950: 100–6, 159, 168.

The answer would seem to be no. Consider the people of the state of Wajo' among the Bugis of south-western Celebes.[10] According to their chronicle tradition, their state was formed by agreement – that would have been in the fifteenth century or so. But subsequently two of their rulers transgressed the freedoms of the people, and were duly killed; the people then ensured that their freedoms would be respected in future through agreements solemnly witnessed by their gods. As to what these freedoms consisted in, we are told that the people had this to say: 'To secure freedom, only three things are decisive: firstly not to interfere with people's wishes; secondly not to forbid the expression of opinions; thirdly not to prevent [people going] to the south, the north, the west, the east, upstream or downstream. These are the freedoms of the people of Wajo'.'[11] One context in which these sentiments make a strong appearance is the liberation of Wajo' from the rule of the state of Bone in 1737, a setting which leads the chronicles to record the declaration that 'the people of Wajo' are free'. The word for 'free' here is *maradeka*, a term of Sanskrit origin that was used in Malay and related languages such as Buginese in the sense of 'free' as opposed to 'slave'.[12] For the people of Wajo' the analogy would seem to have become a central feature of their political culture. As a statement attributed to the founding fathers of the polity has it, 'the people of Wajo' are free; free from birth . . . Their only master is the customary law which is agreed consensually.'[13]

So the European idea of freedom does not seem to be unique: at least one non-European culture had developed a conception of political freedom,

10. Reid 1998: 147–9; also Reid 2000: 67–8, stressing the salience of slavery in Wajo'. For the traditional political institutions of Wajo', which down to the Dutch take-over in 1906 remained faithful to a tradition of limited and decentralised government less well preserved among other states of the region, see Pelras 1971: 169–76. It is worth noting that, as Pelras's title implies, the society of Wajo' was anything but egalitarian (184–91). For the Buginese language and its literature in general, see Noorduyn 1991: 139–40, 168–98; for Buginese historical literature in particular, see Noorduyn 1965. Despite the conversion to Islam in the early seventeenth century (146–7, 148), the language is traditionally written in an Indic script. I am grateful to Thomas Gibson for bibliographical and other assistance.
11. Reid 1998: 148. Reid is translating from the chronicle published in Zainal Abidin 1985: 148. However, the editor says of this chronicle that it was 'reviewed and rewritten' by a Buginese aristocrat who died in 1969 (see 529); thus it would seem hard to exclude the possibility of some degree of contamination from Western notions of freedom. By contrast, I understand Reid's references to texts edited and translated by Noorduyn to take us to eighteenth-century sources.
12. For the etymology, see Reid 1998: 142–3 (as Reid makes clear, the Sanskrit *mahārddhika* does not mean 'free', and would seem to have acquired that sense in South-East Asia). For the use of the term in Buginese in the literal sense (free as opposed to slave), see Pelras 1971: 185, 186, 189–90; for the abstract noun *amaradekang* (freedom), see Noorduyn 1955: 41, 54.
13. Reid 1998: 148; cf. Pelras 1971: 174. Here Reid is translating Zainal Abidin 1985: v, where the text is displayed as a 'motto', and compares 115, where the text appears somewhat differently in the chronicle itself. Again, the question of contamination arises.

and had done so on the analogy of what it is to be legally free. But are such conceptions commonplace? The source from which I learnt of the case of Wajo' is a collective volume entitled *Asian Freedoms*. As the plural 'freedoms' suggests, the contributors would in general like to get away from a picture of the history of Asian political values in which the idea of political freedom is conspicuously absent until imported from the West. They are also well informed about the parts of the world they write about – mainly East and South-East Asia. This means that, if there are significant indigenous parallels to the Western idea of freedom in these regions, there is a very good chance that these contributors will tell us about them. And yet the only passable example in the entire book is the people of Wajo'.[14] Despite the limits of its geographical coverage, this suggests that convincing parallels are in fact rather rare.

At this point, perhaps somewhat perversely, I want to raise the comparative bar yet again. Let us require not just the idea of political freedom that the people of Wajo' seem indeed to have possessed, but also that the culture in question should engage in systematic reflection on its political values – what in the Western context is called political thought. To the best of my knowledge no such thing existed among the people of Wajo', which would suggest that at this level the European phenomenon may well be unique.

II

From this point on I shall be concerned mostly with the mainstream Islamic tradition. Here it will already be apparent that, so far as the metaphor of political freedom is concerned, I have nothing to offer.[15] In the previous section, I was able to cite examples in which slavery appeared as a metaphor for oppression, but none in which freedom was used concomitantly to refer to its absence. In other words, there was an idea of political slavery as a condition to be avoided, but it was not explicitly complemented by an idea of political freedom as a condition to aspire to. In this sense, political freedom is not an Islamic value. But are there relevant conceptions in the Islamic tradition that this rather narrow focus leaves aside? In what follows I shall say a little about the metaphorical use of the idea of freedom in Islamic thought, and rather

14. But for Sumatran cases where people were 'free' in the sense of not subject to a king, see Reid 1998: 145–6. This suggests that there was, or had been, a wider background to the case of Wajo' in island South-East Asia.
15. I thus find myself in much the same position as a distinguished French scholar at a comparative conference on the idea of freedom in the medieval world (Sourdel 1985, especially 123).

more about Islamic political values, though I should make it clear from the start that there is no intersection between the two before modern times.

With regard to the metaphorical use of the idea of freedom, we have already noted the worldly context that gives 'free' the sense of 'noble'. What needs to be added here is that, continuing ancient traditions, we find a comparable phenomenon on the religious side.[16] The most prominent example is the Ṣūfī concept of spiritual freedom (*ḥurriyya*). The *locus classicus* for this idea is the chapter devoted to it in the well-known handbook of Ṣūfism authored by Qushayrī (d. 1072),[17] but the range of sources he cites makes it clear that the notion was already widespread in Ṣūfī circles.[18] He himself explains the concept in these words: 'Freedom means for a human being (*ʿabd*) not to be under the yoke (*riqq*) of created things'[19] – by which we can understand such things as rank and property.[20] Less respectably and well outside the mainstream, we find the idea of freedom used in an antinomian sense: freedom from the exoteric ritual obligations of Islam. This further echo of ancient traditions is found on the margins of Ṣūfism,[21] and in extreme Shīʿite contexts. Thus an early sectarian text preserved by the Nuṣayrīs states that once a man possesses the esoteric truth, he is no longer subject to exoteric duties; he then moves from slavery (*ʿubūdiyya*, *mamlūkiyya*) to freedom (*ḥurriyya*).[22] Even leaving aside these antinomian usages, we might think that a culture already making metaphorical use of the concept of freedom in the religious sphere could easily have made the transition to applying it in the political domain; but as we have seen, premodern Islamic culture did not take this step.

16. Such metaphorical invocation of freedom is, of course, familiar from Christianity. The Christian notion of being freed from the predicament of being a slave (*doulos*) to sin (John 8:34–6, Romans 6:17–18) gives rise to the concept of 'Christian liberty', the subject of a well-known pamphlet by Martin Luther. Incidentally, John 8:31–6 shows the analogy at a point at which it is not yet part of the culture: the Jews take Jesus' reference to freeing them literally, and protest that they were 'never in bondage to any man'. Whether the idea of *mokṣa* in ancient Indian religions constitutes a further parallel is not clear to me.
17. Qushayrī 1966: 460–3; for translations of the chapter, see Rosenthal 1960: 108–13; Qushayrī 1989: 310–12; 2007: 229–32.
18. See also Rosenthal 1960: 115, 118; Crone 2004: 339.
19. This is Rosenthal's translation (Rosenthal 1960: 109). The original reads *al-ḥurriyya an lā yakūna ʾl-ʿabd taḥta riqq al-makhlūqāt* (Qushayrī 1966: 460.10); here *ʿabd* literally means 'slave' (that is, 'servant [of God]') and *riqq* is 'slavery'.
20. Cf. Rosenthal 1960: 115. A writer in the Greek ethical tradition characterises the free man as someone 'who is no longer a slave to any of his animal desires' (88, and cf. 89).
21. Rosenthal 1960: 118–19.
22. Mufaḍḍal ibn ʿUmar al-Juʿfī 1960: 45.14, and see also 100.3. For the first of these passages, see Halm 1985: 138, and 1981: 70; I owe my knowledge of the second passage and further assistance to Bella Tendler.

Turning now to Islamic political values, let me begin with a colourful story set on the southern edge of Iraq around 636.[23] By way of background, Muhammad had founded the Islamic state in Medina in 622 and died in 632 after ruling it for a decade. His successors not only maintained his state but also set about expanding it outside Arabia. This brought them into confrontation with the Persian Empire, and in a crucial battle fought around 636 at Qādisiyya the Arabs defeated the Persians and went on to conquer Iraq. Our story is about what happened on the eve of this battle. The opposing armies were camped within a few miles of each other a bit south of Najaf. The Persian general, Rustam, asked the Arabs to send him an emissary, which they did – in fact a series of emissaries. One was a scruffy bedouin called Ribʿī ibn ʿĀmir. While awaiting his arrival, the Persians discussed how best to receive him, and decided to overwhelm him with a display of Persian magnificence. Rustam accordingly sat on a throne surrounded by carpets and cushions (cushions in this culture being a sign of royal authority). But when he reached the edge of the carpets, Ribʿī rode right onto them, dismounting only when he chose to. He then advanced towards Rustam using his sharp-pointed spear as a walking-stick, jabbing holes in the carpets and cushions.[24] Another emissary, Mughīra ibn Shuʿba, made his point just as vividly: when he got to Rustam on his throne, he sat down on it beside him. This upset the Persians, and there was a scuffle, but Mughīra had his answer ready: 'we Arabs are equals' (*innā maʿshar al-ʿArab sawāʾ*), only enslaving each other in warfare. He went on to say with mock innocence that he had assumed that the Persians treated each other in the same way – how was he to know that some of them were the owners of others? The Persian audience was ominously divided in its response to this incident: the common people (*sifla*) warmed to what the Arab had said, whereas the nobles remarked that this was what their slaves had always liked to hear.[25] Once such preliminaries were over, the time had come for an exchange of views between Rustam and the emissary. Thus when Rustam asked Ribʿī what had brought the Arabs to Iraq, he replied that God had sent them to deliver those who so wished from being servants of men to being servants of God (*li-nukhrija man shāʾa min ʿibādat al-ʿibād ilā ʿibādat Allāh*).[26] Likewise another envoy summed up Islam for Rustam in a

23. The punch-lines of this story are highlighted in Crone 2004: 334. It appears in the works of several medieval historians, but in what follows I cite only the accounts given by Ṭabarī.
24. Ṭabarī 1879–1901, Series I, 2270.7 = Ṭabarī 1992: 65–7.
25. Ṭabarī 1879–1901, Series I, 2274.10 = Ṭabarī 1992: pp. 70–1.
26. Ṭabarī 1879–1901, Series I, 2271.11 = Ṭabarī 1992: 67. The wording echoes a letter from the Prophet to the people of Najrān in south-western Arabia in which he summons them from being servants of men to being servants of God (*fa-innī adʿūkum ilā ʿibādat Allāh min ʿibādat*

few basic points, among them a commitment to 'delivering men from being servants of men to being servants of God' (*ikhrāj al-ʿibād min ʿibādat al-ʿibād ilā ʿibādat Allāh*), and a belief in the full brotherhood of men, all alike descended from Adam and Eve.[27] There are further themes in these exchanges, but we can leave them aside; the outcome was a three-day truce between the two armies. When the truce was over, the battle was duly fought; the Arabs won, as they deserved, and the Persians lost, as they deserved.

What we see in this story is a vivid articulation of a rough and ready egalitarianism.[28] It comes in two distinct but mutually reinforcing idioms. One is ethnic: it is a matter of what 'we Arabs' are like – irrespective, one could say, of whatever religion the Arabs might or might not give their allegiance to. We Arabs are each other's equals, not slaves of one another. The other idiom is religious: if all men are servants of God, then they are not here to serve each other. In each case analogy is at work, and certain social and political relationships characteristic of the hierarchic society of pre-Islamic Iran are being stigmatised as *tantamount* to slavery, or as involving a subservience to men that is due only to God. Arabs and Muslims, by contrast, are self-consciously not like that; by implication, though this is not said, they are free men.

Is this just another example of the sporadic analogising I talked about earlier, or does it have a wider context?[29]

One part of the context is unquestionably the ethos of tribal Arabia. The Arabian environment was poor in resources, and this showed in the character of its tribes. Their social structures tended to be rather flat: there was a sharp division between tribesmen and anyone else, but an absence of formal stratification among the tribesmen themselves. This is revealingly illustrated by the character of the Arab genealogical tradition as it was reduced to writing in early Islamic times – it takes as its domain the entire tribal population, not just an elite.[30] It also finds expression in the unadorned forms of address characteristic of the early Arabic epistolary style.[31] At

al-ʿibād, Yaʿqūbī 1883: II, 89.18; Bayhaqī 1985: V, 385.11). Here as in the text I translate *ʿibāda* as 'being servants of'; it refers to service such as is due only to God (Lane 1863–93: 1936a; Ibn Manẓūr n.d.: III, 271a.17), and can often be translated as 'worship'.

27. Ṭabarī 1879–1901, Series I, 2268.16 = Ṭabarī 1992: 64.
28. See Marlow 1997, especially 1–6, 14–16.
29. Crone 2004: 44–6, 268. Note the statement of ʿUmar, the second Caliph, that 'I am not a king who will enslave you' (*ibid.*, 45–6).
30. It 'attempts to provide the paternal lineages of an entire nation', whereas written genealogies from other cultures 'tend to concentrate on the distinguished ancestry of one family or group' (Kennedy 1997: 531).
31. See, for example, Ṣafwat 1937: I 146.1, 152.17, 159.1, 160.3, 166.3, 167.8.

the same time political authority in the tribal society of Arabia was weak, and state-formation difficult; conversely, the level of political participation was far higher than in any modern democracy. A striking expression of the values of this society in action is to be found in an anecdote about ʿAmr ibn Kulthūm, a pre-Islamic Arab poet who killed a king; this king, ʿAmr ibn Hind, had tried unsuccessfully to trap the poet's mother into the servile act of passing a plate to his own mother.[32] The same poet, speaking for his fellow-tribesmen, boasts in a poem that 'we rebelled against the king, and would not serve him'; he asks him why we should 'be underlings to your chosen princelet' and when we were ever 'your mother's domestics'; he tells how they returned from a raid 'leading the kings in fetters', and proclaims that when kings deal with their peoples unjustly 'we refuse to allow injustice among us'.[33] The egalitarian sentiments expressed by the emissaries to the Persians fit well with this ethos. In neither case should we rely on the historicity of the details of these stories;[34] but it is eminently plausible to see them as reflecting an authentic tribal tradition going well back before the rise of Islam.[35]

Unlike the people of Wajo', however, these tribesmen did not describe their proudly anarchic society as 'free'. The Arabic term used of tribes not subject to the authority and fiscal exactions of a ruler was *laqāḥ*.[36] Thus we are told that in the generation before the rise of Islam a member of the Meccan tribe of Quraysh sought to become king of Mecca as a Byzantine client; a fellow-tribesman successfully denounced the idea, saying that 'Quraysh is *laqāḥ*, neither exercising royal power nor subject to it' (*inna Qurayshan laqāḥ, lā tamliku wa-lā tumlaku*).[37] But why the word *laqāḥ* should have had this sense is etymologically obscure.[38] One modern scholar explains the term to mean

32. Abū ʾl-Faraj al-Iṣbahānī 1927–74: xi, 53.11, translated in Nicholson 1956: 109–10.
33. Lyall 1894: 112 line 22, 117 lines 47–48, 120 line 66, 124 line 92; Arberry 1957: 204–9. I am indebted to Andras Hamori for advice on editions of the *Muʿallaqāt*.
34. My guess would be that the literary form of these and other such stories owes something to a time at which the old values were visibly being lost.
35. Compare the description of Saracen warriors given by Ammianus Marcellinus in the later fourth century: 'all alike are warriors of equal rank' (Ammianus Marcellinus 1950–6: 26 = 27).
36. *Wörterbuch* 1970–2000: ii, 1075b–1076b. Note particularly the eight instances where the word is used as an adjective modifying *ḥayy*, a common term for a tribal group, and the two where it modifies *balad*, a word meaning 'town' and here referring to Mecca.
37. Muṣʿab al-Zubayrī 1976: 210.4; Zubayr ibn Bakkār 1381: 430.8, and cf. 427.3. See Kister 1968: 154 note 2, where these and other sources are quoted.
38. The basic sense of the word *laqāḥ* is 'conception, pregnancy, gestation, fertilization'; there is no obvious transition from this meaning to the sense of 'not subject to a ruler, independent, sovereign' (these glosses are those given in *Wörterbuch* 1970–2000: ii, 1073b and 1075b respectively).

'free people who did not obey any kings or pay any taxes';[39] this is apt, but the use of the term 'free' in this context is ours, not theirs.

The other part of the context is the character of the early Islamic state as it existed under the Prophet and his immediate successors. It was a state, and as such very different from tribal anarchy; but it was an Arabian state, with its capital in the tribal oasis of Medina. It thus had its own distinctive ethos in which the tribal heritage was articulated in Islamic terms. Three features of the way this ethos is portrayed in our sources are worth picking out here. First, the ruler of this state was self-consciously not a despot. Thus Abū Bakr on his accession as Caliph in 632 told his subjects that he was now in authority over them although he was not the best of them, and that they should help him if he did right but correct him if he did wrong; he added that they had no duty to obey him should he disobey God and His Prophet.[40] Second, this state was conspicuously unpatrimonial; we might say that it was a republic in the literal sense, a *res publica*. Thus the day after becoming Caliph, Abū Bakr, who was a merchant, set out to market to sell clothes to feed his family; it was suggested to him that he could attend better to his public duties if instead he applied to the treasurer for an allowance. He did so, and the treasurer duly awarded him the allowance of one of the Prophet's Meccan Companions – not that of the best of them, nor that of the least of them – together with clothes for winter and summer. 'If you wear something out', the treasurer added, 'you bring it back and you get another instead.'[41] Third, the members of this political community were in some sense equals. The Koran famously states that 'the noblest among you in the sight of God is the most godfearing of you' (Q 49:13), and a tradition, although not one found in authoritative collections, has the Prophet say that 'people are equals like the teeth of a comb'.[42] Another tradition tells us that, on one occasion when the Prophet came out to his Companions, they showed their respect for him by rising to their feet; he responded by telling them not to stand up to honour people, as the Persians do.[43] Again the details may not be reliable,

39. Crone 2004: 268.
40. Ibn Hishām 1955: III–IV, 661.6 = Ibn Hishām 1980: 687 (Ibn Isḥāq has the anecdote from Zuhrī from Anas ibn Mālik). Note the assumption that it is for his subjects to judge the Caliph's performance of his duties.
41. Suyūṭī 1988: 59.22. Suyūṭī gives his source as Ibn Saʿd, who however has the story a little differently (Ibn Saʿd 1904–21: III, part 1, 130.19, 131.1).
42. Abū 'l-Shaykh al-Iṣbahānī 1996: 64 no. 23 (*al-nās sawāsiya ka-asnān al-mushṭ*); Ibn ʿAsākir 1995–8: X, 363.1; and see Marlow 1997: 18–19, with references to the literature on proverbs.
43. Nawawī 1988: 63.1. A further tradition relates that the Companions would not stand up when they saw the Prophet because they knew he disapproved of it (61.6). As Nawawī mentions, in the source from which he took this tradition – the collection of traditions compiled by Tirmidhī

but they fit well with the Arabian environment. Here too it would hardly be strained to think of the Muslims as a free people, in self-conscious contrast to the Persians.

Before we leave the lingering ethos of the early Muslim community behind us, let me quote some passages from a sermon which, according to our sources, was delivered in the later 740s by a sectarian rebel, the Khārijite Abū Ḥamza al-Mukhtār ibn ʿAwf.[44] He denounces the Umayyad Caliph Muʿāwiya (ruled 661–80): 'He made the servants of God slaves' (*ittakhadha ʿibād Allāh khawalan*) and the property of God 'something to be taken by turns'.[45] Likewise he says of the Marwānids, the subdynasty of the Umayyads that ruled from 684 to 750, that they 'made the servants of God slaves' (*ittakhadhū ʿibād Allāh ʿabīdan*).[46] In another passage he says of the Umayyads in general that they 'arrest on suspicion, make decrees capriciously, kill in anger, and judge by passing over crimes without punishment', and he puts into their mouths the statement: 'The land is our land, the property is our property, and the people are our slaves (*al-nās khawalunā*).'[47] A variant version of this passage includes the charge that these rulers took power and exercised it as if they had ownership (*fa-malakū 'l-amr wa-tasallaṭū fīhi tasalluṭ al-rubūbiyya*),[48] in other words as if the state were their private property. Here, then, we find the same rejection of despotism and patrimonialism that characterises the ethos of the early Caliphate, and it is combined with the familiar analogy between illegitimate power and enslavement. Once again, there is no mention of the Muslims being a free people, but the idea seems implicit in the analogy: Muslims should be treated as free men, not as slaves.

As one might expect, this sectarian attempt to roll back the tide of patrimonial despotism was a failure. The kind of state that Abū Ḥamza denounced

(d. 892) – it forms part of a chapter bringing together traditions directed against the idea that one man should stand up for another (*bāb karāhat qiyām al-rajul lil-rajul*, 61.8). Nawawī's concern, as the title of his pamphlet makes clear, is to legitimate the practice of standing up to show respect, and he is therefore at pains to neutralise this and similar traditions.

44. Crone and Hinds 1986: 129–32. For such attitudes see also Crone 2004: 52.
45. Crone and Hinds 1986: 130 §6 (the Arabic wording I quote is that of the text of the speech in Jāḥiẓ 1948–50: II, 123.8, and other versions). The phrase 'by turns' echoes Q 59:7: 'so that it be not a thing taken by turns among the rich of you' (referring to the spoils of war given by God to the Prophet).
46. Abū 'l-Faraj al-Iṣbahānī 1927–74: XXIII, 242.4 (the passage is not in the version translated by Crone and Hinds).
47. Crone and Hinds 1986: 132 §12; Izkawī n.d.: f. 274b.8 (on the authority of Haytham ibn ʿAdī).
48. Abū 'l-Faraj al-Iṣbahānī 1927–74: XXIII, 243.1; cf. the wording *sulṭānuhum sulṭān rubūbiyya*, Izkawī n.d.: f. 274b.2 (this charge is not found in the version of the passage translated by Crone and Hinds). The term *rubūbiyya* is an abstract noun from *rabb*, a word meaning lord or owner (for example of a slave) and often applied to God.

was the kind that would rule the bulk of the Islamic world into modern times. One way to think of this was in terms of a reversion to type: the states that now ruled the Muslim world were no different in character from those that had held power in the same regions before the rise of Islam.

That this was not just how it was, but how it had to be, is starkly argued in a work by Ḍiyāʾ al-Dīn Baranī, a courtier of the Delhi sultanate in fourteenth-century India.[49] He tells a story in which the ʿAbbāsid Caliph al-Maʾmūn (ruled 813–33) takes it into his head to rule in the pious manner of the first four Caliphs.[50] His vizier explains to him just how foolish a project this would be. Against the background of human history as it had been since the time of Adam and would be till the end of the world, that one generation of righteous rule was utterly exceptional. Those Caliphs lived lives of abstinence and poverty, following the practice (*sunnat*) of the Prophet in all things; they could do this only because the lifetime of the Prophet was still so close, and even they paid a heavy price through their vulnerability to assassination. No subsequent ruler should even think of exercising power in such a way; rulership, Baranī insisted, is no longer possible without 'the majesty and pomp of monarchs'. What he had in mind here becomes clear from some advice that he has Sultan Maḥmūd of Ghazna (ruled 998–1030) address to his sons.[51] Since the time of Muḥammad's immediate successors, he tells them, the Caliphs and kings of Islam have faced a grim choice. Either they can adopt the practices and way of life of the Prophet, which would issue in disaster. Or they can follow the practices and way of life of the pre-Islamic Persian kings, thereby going against those of the Prophet, which are the sum and essence of religion. It is not just that a ruler must adopt the Persian model for the selfish purpose of staying in power; if he failed to adopt it, it would not be possible for him to ensure the ascendancy of Islam and root out its opponents. The adoption of the iniquitous customs of the Persian kings – haughtiness, pride, aloofness from others, luxurious living, wearing a crown, sitting on a throne, building lofty palaces, having people prostrate themselves before one, misappropriating property, keeping a large harem – all these essentials of kingship should be seen in the same light as eating carrion: though in principle forbidden, it becomes licit when there is no other way to survive. In short, Baranī is telling us that we have to forget about Ribʿī ibn ʿĀmir and go back to doing things Rustam's way.

49. *Encyclopaedia of Islam* 1960–2009, art. 'Baranī' (P. Hardy).
50. Baranī 1972: 126.1–127.14, partially translated in Habib and Khan n.d.: 33–4, and in de Bary 1959: 471. The passage continues in the same vein.
51. Baranī 1972: 140.14–141.24; Habib and Khan n.d.: 39–40; de Bary 1959: 472–3.

It was rare for anyone to confront the dilemma as unflinchingly as Baranī did, but awareness of the profound historical discontinuity that separated the early polity from later Muslim states was widespread. At the other end of the Muslim world, in seventeenth-century Morocco, the well-known scholar Yūsī (d. 1691) wrote an epistle to the Moroccan sultan in which he took up a variant of the same theme: after the passing of the model successors of Muḥammad, the Caliphate degenerated into kingship, Muḥammad's way of ruling (*sīra*) almost disappeared, and in its place came Chosroism (*kisrawiyya*) and Caesarism (*qayṣariyya*) – the political styles of the pre-Islamic Persian and Byzantine rulers.[52] Like Baranī, Yūsī had a point. A century before his time the Ottoman sultan had acquired two new and grandiose titles on the model of the old Persian title 'King of Kings': 'Chosroes of Chosroeses' and 'Caesar of Caesars'.[53] Abū Ḥamza would not have been surprised.

And yet the anti-despotic, anti-patrimonial and egalitarian values of the early polity could never be entirely forgotten. They were part and parcel of the Islamic heritage, and they were associated with its age of paradigmatic righteousness, that of the Prophet and his immediate successors. These values occupy a conceptual space that overlaps significantly with the European idea of political freedom. But are they *equivalent* to the idea? There are three questions worth distinguishing here.

First, let us assume for the sake of argument that the Muslim values in fact occupied the same space as the European idea – not just some of it but all of it. Would it then matter that in the Islamic case there is no single concept that picks out this space? A plausible answer might be that logically it should not matter, but that in practice it might. Having a single concept that labels a given space is a convenience that can generate what might be called a bulls-eye effect: such a concept is easier to focus on, and so more readily invoked in political argument.

Second, we should ask whether the Islamic values do indeed cover – and not just overlap with – the same ground as the European idea of freedom. Here the basic point concerns the nature of the community in the Islamic vision. It is a brotherhood within which all members are equal, with rulers being more equal than others only in functional ways – someone has to give orders or all will be chaos. But this brotherhood, as the metaphor of close kinship might suggest, is not an individualist paradise; one might say that in this respect it stands closer to the Communist than to the democratic vision

52. M'daghrī 1989: 328.20. For earlier instances of this idea, see Crone 2004: 46.
53. Imber 1997: 75.

of the polity. As one of the emissaries to Rustam expressed it, 'the Muslims are like a body, parts of a whole'.[54] To put the point in a wider perspective, human societies everywhere are made up of more or less selfish individuals, and human cultures everywhere deploy resources, rhetorical and other, to rein in this selfishness for the sake of the community. Islam is no exception. What is exceptional, or at least unusual, is the emergence within European culture of a tendency to make a virtue of individualism or, as other cultures would see it, of selfishness. This individualism was to become an integral part of the European idea of freedom and at the same time is strikingly absent from the Islamic values that are its partial equivalent.

Third, we can now ask what role, if any, we should assign to the metaphor behind the European idea of freedom – a metaphor that, as we have seen, played only a limited role on the Islamic side. Obviously it would in principle be possible to have a concept that was fully equivalent to the European idea of freedom, but that arose from a quite different origin; in such a case the path that led to the concept would be of no consequence. But we do not in fact have an example of such a concept, and this suggests a certain path-dependence in its historical evolution.[55] Now it is a significant feature of the metaphor behind the European idea that it encourages a focus on the individual: it is the individual who is literally a slave or free person, either subject to the will of another or able to act as he pleases. In other words, the metaphor plays up the element of individual choice in a way that the Islamic values of limited rule and equality do not. While we should certainly not think of the metaphor as the cause of the rise of European individualism, it is surely part of the story.

III

At this point let us return to the history of the European idea of freedom. What I want to do is to divide this history into three more or less successive

54. Ṭabarī 1879–1901, Series 1, 2272.10 = Ṭabarī 1992: 68.

55. It is worth noting that when modern non-Western literary languages translate the European notion of freedom, they do not necessarily adopt the metaphor. Arabic did so: *ḥurriyya* is the traditonal word for freedom as opposed to slavery, and the modern word for political freedom, with the result that in Arabic freedom sounds like a very good thing; this in turn has prompted attempts to delimit it in such a way as to cut back on the scope it allows for individualism, seen as a bad thing. By contrast, Japanese and Chinese bypassed the metaphor: the classical Chinese term *tzŭ-yu*, which the Japanese adopted as *jiyū* to translate 'freedom' and the Chinese then borrowed back, meant doing whatever one likes, not being a free person as opposed to a slave – with the result that to this day freedom does not sound like a really good thing in Chinese (see Jenner 1998: 85, and Mackie 1998: 121).

phases. The point of this exercise in schematisation is not to tell the Europeanists anything they don't know already, but rather to generate a framework that can then be projected onto the Islamic world for heuristic purposes.

In the first phase, two things happened within a culture of city-states. First, a dense practice of thinking and talking about political freedom emerged, and second, it became the object of a tradition of systematic reflection.

In the second phase, the literary residue of the political tradition established in the first phase was preserved within the larger framework of a culture to which it no longer meant very much. The loss of meaning arose from the fact that the small-scale polities in which the idea of political freedom originally emerged had now given way to territorial monarchies. The cultural apparatus of these societies neverthless ensured the transmission of some part of the literary heritage of the city-states to posterity, and this included the idea of political freedom.[56]

In the third phase, the idea of political freedom once again became relevant against a background of rising levels of political participation. The initial context of this development was unsurprising: the re-emergence of city-states in Italy. But eventually – and much more remarkably – the process extended to the territorial states of north-western Europe.[57] This is the story of the evolution of modern politics.

So how, if at all, do these three phases map onto Islamic history? Does it make any sense to look for their counterparts there? And if we find them, will they tell us anything worth knowing? We can only try and see.

56. Note the implication that if a first phase were not to be followed by such a second phase, we would be unlikely to know about it. It is conceivable, for example, that Carthage and the tribal republics of ancient India had a first-phase tradition that has not been preserved. In the case of the Carthaginians, we have only the testimony of outsiders, and while this is enough to reveal the basic character of their polity, it does not answer the question whether they engaged in any kind of systematic reflection on their political values (cf. Warmington 1960: 134). In the Indian case, the mainstream Hindu tradition is unsympathetic towards the republican polities, and frequently ignores them (Sharma 1968: 239). The Jain and still more the Buddhist scriptures tend to be both more sympathetic to the republics and more informative about their political institutions, but they tell us nothing about their intellectual life. We learn that the Videhans had dancing girls, panegyrists and musicians (*ibid.*, 155), and we know that Mahāvīra and the Buddha stemmed from such communities. Kauṭilya mentions the occurrence of 'disputations about certain points of science (*vidyā*), arts, gambling, or sports' as occasions when dissension can be fomented in republics by spies (Kauṭilya 1919: 378.11 = Kauṭilya 1951: 407; I am indebted to Ashwini Mokashi for assistance with the original Sanskrit of this passage). But none of this tells us whether the tribal republics had political philosophers, and in any case there seems to be no indication that 'freedom' was part of their political vocabulary.

57. This development raises an issue that I will not even attempt to come to terms with, namely the ways in which the medieval evolution of north-western Europe made it peculiarly receptive to such an extension.

The first phase poses no great challenge, since we have already sketched its counterpart. What we have here is a set of values reflecting two closely related phenomena, the anarchy of tribal Arabia in pre-Islamic times and the limited character of government in the early Islamic polity. Two things, however, were not to be found here. One was philosophising; this was not a habit of the pre-Islamic Arabs, nor was it yet practised by the earliest generations of Muslims. The other, of course, was the use of the metaphor of freedom to articulate the values of this phase.

Finding a counterpart to the second phase is likewise no problem. For most of the Islamic societies that mattered down the centuries, those that had reasonably rich resource bases supporting large-scale political organisation, the values of the pre-Islamic Arabs and the early Islamic state were irrelevant. This was the age of Baranī: despotic and patrimonial states with steep social and political hierarchies were the order of the day, and radical challenges were rare. Neverthless, the cultures of these societies were well equipped to preserve a literary heritage that described an earlier and very different age, and they did so with regard to both the pre-Islamic Arabs and the early Islamic state.

But what of the third phase, that of renewed relevance? As far as the pre-Islamic heritage is concerned, there is no such phase to be found. The tribal heritage was carefully preserved by antiquarians and received an abiding measure of cultural respect; but unlike the Greek and Roman past of Europe, it carried no authority, and provided no inspiration for later generations.[58] Thus the word *laqāḥ*, for all its resonance among the pre-Islamic Arab tribes, played no part in the political vocabulary of Islamic times.

The heritage of the early Islamic state is another matter: it retained its authority even when in practice it was ignored as irrelevant. Here the outcome of our search depends on whether we are looking for an endogenous or an exogenous development.

If it has to be endogenous, we will look in vain for a *period* in which the heritage transmitted in the second phase once more became politically relevant. What we can identify instead is a geographical *fringe* of the Islamic world in which this heritage sometimes retained or regained its meaning. The effect is most obvious in sectarian environments in resource-poor tribal regions, that is to say in settings comparable with that in which the Islamic state began. Thus one Zaydī imam ruling in the mountains of northern Iran

58. Crone 2004: 268–9. A curious exception that says something about the ethnic background of al-Qāʿida is a passage in which Bin Laden tells the American Secretary of Defense about the killing of the king ʿAmr ibn Hind by the poet ʿAmr ibn Kulthūm (Shepard 2003: 537).

in the late tenth or early eleventh century would patch his own shirts,[59] and made a point of keeping his personal expenses strictly separate from the public treasury (*bayt al-māl*).[60] Once he fancied eating fish, and sent to the fishermen to cut one up for him, but they refused; he reconciled himself to a fishless dinner by praising God for the fact that his subjects were not in awe of him, but rather saw him as their equal (*annahu ʿindahum wa-raʿāyāhu sawāʾ*).[61] A century earlier the founder of the Zaydī imamate in the Yemen was just as emphatically unpatrimonial in his lifestyle,[62] and like Abū Bakr demanded only a conditional obedience from his subjects: holding up the Koran, he told them, 'this is between me and you verse by verse; if I contravene what is in it by so much as a letter, you have no duty to obey me, but rather the duty of fighting me'.[63] It is also in such environments that we encounter occasional hints of concrete constitutional arrangements for limiting power, something we do not find in the early Islamic state itself.[64] Thus in the context of the Ibāḍī imamate among the Berber tribes of North Africa in the late eighth century, we hear of a heretical doctrine to the effect that the imam could take decisions only in conjunction with some kind of assembly.[65] In the Ibāḍī imamate that ruled Oman in the late eighth and ninth centuries we find an arrangement by which the imams belonged to one tribal group but were chosen by the members of another, and came to rule from a centre located outside their own tribal homeland.[66] All these were significant articulations of political values antithetical to despotism and patrimonialism, but they were confined to the geographical fringes of the Islamic world and not specific to any one period.

If, however, the third phase can be exogenous, then we can readily equate it with the last two centuries. As a political value central to the European tradition, the idea of freedom inevitably spread to the non-European cultures with which Europe came into contact in this period, including those of the Islamic world. How far we should see the strong pull of the idea as a consequence of the prestige of European culture, and how far as a result of the spread of the same modern conditions that had made freedom so relevant to the politics of Europe, is not an issue to be debated here. We need only sketch the process by which the idea was assimilated.[67]

59. Madelung 1987: 263.10. 60. Madelung 1987: 264.13. 61. Madelung 1987: 264.4.
62. Van Arendonk 1960: 266. 63. See van Arendonk 1960: 136 and note 1.
64. Crone 2004: 59–60, 278.
65. Abū Zakariyyā 1982: 89.7; Rebstock 1983: 165, with further sources.
66. Wilkinson 1987: 9.
67. For a helpful survey, see *Encyclopaedia of Islam* 1960–2009, art. 'Ḥurriyya', section by B. Lewis.

IV

One channel through which the idea of political freedom reached the Arab core of the Islamic world was Napoleon's invasion of Egypt in 1798 and the Arabic proclamation he proceeded to issue there. In this text the foundation of the French republic was identified as 'freedom and equalisation' (*al-ḥurriyya waʾl-taswiya*).[68] To judge by the response of the contemporary Egyptian chronicler Jabartī (d. 1824/5), this concept of freedom – unlike that of equality – was not immediately transparent.[69] He explains it to mean that the French are not slaves like the Mamlūks.[70] Now a *mamlūk* is literally someone who is owned by someone else; in medieval times the Mamlūk military elite of Egypt were regularly recruited as slaves, and this was still to some exent true in Ottoman times. In other words, Jabartī seems to have understood the French to be making a claim about their *legal* status. But despite the unfamiliarity of the concept,[71] such misunderstanding did not persist. Thus the Tunisian Khayr al-Dīn Pasha (d. 1890), in a work completed in 1867, devoted a few pages to a systematic exposition of the meaning of freedom,[72] which he saw as 'the basis of the great development of knowledge and civilization in the European kingdoms'.[73] He distinguished two senses of the word. One was 'personal freedom' (*al-ḥurriyya al-shakhṣiyya*), which he defined as 'the individual's complete freedom of action over himself and his property, and the protection of his person, his honor and his wealth'. The second was 'political freedom' (*al-ḥurriyya al-siyāsiyya*), which was a matter of the participation (*tadākhul*) of the subjects in the political affairs of the state.[74] He had clearly grasped the fact that the European idea of freedom meant much more than not being a slave. He also evinces a concern to find

68. Jabartī 1975: 7.3 = 40.
69. For his treatment of the French notion of equality, see Jabartī 1975: 11.13, 12.1 = 42–3.
70. Jabartī 1975: 11.15 = 43 (*fa-qawluhum al-ḥurriyya ay laysū ariqqāʾ kaʾl-mamālīk*). Given the repeated references that the French proclamation makes to the Mamlūks as the unworthy rulers of Egypt, and the fact that the first of these references speaks of their having been imported from the Caucasus (*ibid.*, 7.8 = 40), *sc.* as slaves, it is clear that by *al-mamālīk* Jabartī intends the Mamlūk rulers of Egypt.
71. This unfamiliarity is perhaps reflected in a well-known passage in which the Egyptian Rifāʿa Rāfiʿ al-Ṭahṭāwī (d. 1873), in a work published in 1834, explains the concept by saying of the French: 'That which they call freedom (*al-ḥurriyya*) and which they crave is what we call 'justice' and 'equity', inasmuch as 'rule by freedom' means establishing equality in judgments and laws so that the ruler cannot oppress any human being' (Ṭahṭāwī n.d.: 148.20 = Ṭahṭāwī 2004: 206; and see Lewis 1982: 220, and Husry 1980: 21).
72. Khayr al-Dīn al-Tūnisī 1990–1: 222–5 = Khayr al-Din al-Tunisi 1967: 160–5.
73. Khayr al-Dīn al-Tūnisī 1990–1: 222.4 = Khayr al-Din al-Tunisi 1967: 160. Compare the response of an Ottoman diplomat to a statue of freedom at the Great Exhibition in Paris in 1878: 'all these achievements are the work of freedom' (quoted in Lewis 1964: 47).
74. Khayr al-Dīn al-Tūnisī 1990–1: 222.8 = Khayr al-Din al-Tunisi 1967: 160–1.

indigenous roots for this alien idea. Thus he makes a somewhat vague reference to freedom as a natural disposition among Muslims,[75] and cites as a parallel to political freedom a typical saying of the second Caliph: 'If one of you sees crookedness in me, he should straighten it out.'[76]

Khayr al-Dīn's focus on freedom anticipates the thinking of many Muslims in the twentieth and twenty-first centuries. This thinking can be thought of as spread out over an extended spectrum. At one end of the spectrum we have the Westerniser who adopts European political values lock, stock and barrel, without any sign of Khayr al-Dīn's concern to find indigenous roots for them; a good example of this phenomenon would be the Egyptian Aḥmad Luṭfī al-Sayyid (d. 1963) in the early twentieth century.[77] At the other end of the spectrum we have the unbending Islamist who rejects the very idea that Muslims should adopt Western political values, and insists instead that all the values Muslims need are already present in their own heritage.[78] In what follows, I will limit the discussion to the Islamists, since it is they who engage most strongly with the aspects of the heritage outlined above.

A major figure in the development of Islamism was the Indian – later Pakistani – Abū ʾl-Aʿlā Mawdūdī (d. 1979). Just as we might expect, he was excited by the anti-despotic and anti-patrimonial values that inform the accounts of the early Islamic state given in our sources. Thus he underlined the limits of the claims of the early Caliphs to authority, quoting a text we have already encountered, the accession speech of Abū Bakr.[79] He stressed that in the view of the early Muslims appointment to the Caliphate was not hereditary but elective, requiring consultation and consent;[80] he described monarchy as the very antithesis of Islam,[81] and he too referred disparagingly to 'the systems of Chosroes and Caesar'.[82] He show-cased the scrupulous attitude of the early Muslims towards public funds, telling the story of how

75. Khayr al-Dīn al-Tūnisī 1990–1: 180.11 = Khayr al-Din al-Tunisi 1967: 130.
76. Khayr al-Dīn al-Tūnisī 1990–1: 222.19 = Khayr al-Din al-Tunisi 1967: 161. For an appearance of a longer version of this saying in a pre-modern source, see Manūfī 1938: I, 99.24.
77. Albert Hourani says of him that the 'most important of the complex of ideas derived by Lutfi al-Sayyid from his western masters is that of freedom' (Hourani 1962: 173), and at the same time he remarks on 'the surprisingly small part played by Islam' in his thought (*ibid.*, 172).
78. This insistence is not, of course, to be taken at face value. In the present state of the world certain Western values are highly prestigious, and under these conditions it almost inevitably becomes an unacknowledged part of the Islamist agenda to find counterparts of these values in the Islamic heritage.
79. Mawdūdī 1977: 214.1. Since I do not read Urdu, my access to Mawdūdī's works is normally through English and Arabic translations. In citing an English translation, I give his name in the form in which it appears on the title-page.
80. Mawdūdī 1977: 212.5; see also Maudūdī 1960a: 249–53.
81. Maududi 1963: 28.
82. Mawdūdī n.d.a: 40.7 (*al-nuẓum al-Kisrawiyya wa ʾl-Qayṣariyya*).

Abū Bakr came to be paid his allowance from the treasury.[83] He dramatised the point by translating the amounts of such allowances into contemporary terms: a mere 100 or 150 rupees a month.[84] He emphasised the unrestricted access people had to the Caliph: his doors were open, and he would wander through the markets without a bodyguard.[85] This was part of the 'democratic spirit' of the Caliphate, as was the complete freedom people enjoyed in expressing their opinions.[86] So great was respect for the rule of law in this period that a Caliph could lose a lawsuit against a Christian.[87]

Mawdūdī's view of what the Islamic state should be in his own time was very much of a piece with this vision. He who rules the Muslims has no authority over them except by the command of God and His Prophet, and is not to occupy a majestic throne or dramatise any pretensions to an exalted status;[88] nor is he to erect grandiose buildings or live luxuriously.[89] In the eyes of the law he has the same status as the Muslims at large.[90] He is owed obedience only for so long as he conforms to the laws of God and His Prophet.[91] Again, anyone can take him to court.[92] In short, Mawdūdī was very successful in finding in the early Islamic state a set of features that resonate with modern political values – including freedom of speech.

All this is in the spirit of what the old sources have to tell us about the early polity. But Mawdūdī went beyond his sources in two significant ways that bear on the idea of freedom. One involved taking a very considerable liberty with the tradition. He gave his discussion a democratising twist that went beyond mere 'democratic spirit' by developing an idiosyncratic doctrine of the Caliphate of all believers. Thus for Mawdūdī, the Islamic state is ruled by 'the whole community of Muslims including the rank and file';[93] every believer is a Caliph of God (*khalīfa min Allāh*) in his individual capacity,[94] and the authority of the ruler derives simply from the fact that all Muslims delegate their Caliphate to him for administrative purposes.[95] Hence the

83. Mawdūdī 1977: 212.27. For the modest allowance of Abū Bakr's successor 'Umar (ruled 634–44), see *ibid.*, 213.11.
84. Mawdūdī n.d.a: 50.1; compare Mawdūdī 1955: 41.8.
85. Mawdūdī 1977: 218.2; see also Mawdudi 1989: 16–17, and Maudūdī 1960a: 258.
86. Mawdūdī 1977: 217.22.
87. Mawdūdī 1977: 215.23.
88. Mawdūdī n.d.a: 47.2.
89. Mawdūdī n.d.a: 47.15.
90. Maududi 1976: 44 = Mawdūdī n.d.b: 48.14; and cf. Mawdūdī n.d.a: 47.2.
91. Maududi 1976: 22, 43–4 = Mawdūdī n.d.b: 25.15, 48.10; and see Maudūdī 1960b: 192 (this work is composed of extracts from Mawdūdī's *Tafhīm al-Qur'ān* compiled and translated by the editor, see *ibid.* 163); also Maudūdī 1960c: 284–5.
92. Maududi 1976: 47 = Mawdūdī n.d.b: 51.17.
93. Maududi 1976: 24 = Mawdūdī n.d.b: 27.4.
94. Maududi 1976: 38 = Mawdūdī n.d.b: 41.10.
95. Maududi 1976: 40 = Mawdūdī n.d.b: 44.5. For this theory see also Maudūdī 1960b: 185, 196; Maudūdī 1960a: 235; Maudūdī 1960c: 277–8.

Muslims at large have the duty of strictly monitoring the ruler's exercise of power, and if he goes astray they may depose him.[96] Though he did not use the term, this is clearly a prescription for what Khayr al-Dīn had called 'political freedom'.

The second new departure was more of an elaboration of something already present in the tradition, and concerns the concept of divine sovereignty. That God is 'the true Sovereign'[97] was not in itself a novel idea. That '*the root-cause of all evil and mischief* in the world is *the domination of man over man*'[98] was an idea that, as we have seen, had a root in the tradition. From this Mawdūdī went on to claim that the aim of the prophets was to demolish man's supremacy over man,[99] so that 'man should be neither the slave (*ʿabd*) nor the master (*maʿbūd*) of his fellowbeings', but rather all should become the 'servants' (*ʿibād*) of God.[100] After quoting a number of monotheistic verses from the Koran, he commented: 'This was the proclamation that released the human soul from its fetters and set man's intellectual and material powers free from the bonds of slavery (*ghulāmī*) that held them in subjection . . . It gave them a real charter of liberty and freedom (*āzādī*).'[101] Here the term 'freedom' is conspicuously present.

As might be expected, Mawdūdī strongly endorses egalitarianism. Thus he tells us that the social organisation which the prophets sought to establish was grounded on human equality,[102] and that it was a basic principle of the early Islamic state that all were equal in the eyes of the law;[103] here Mawdūdī cites Muḥammad's condemnation of earlier communities in which lowly offenders were punished while aristocratic offenders were not.[104] In a formulation that makes very clear the link between the social and the political, he states: 'A society in which everyone is a caliph of God and an equal participant in this caliphate, cannot tolerate any class divisions based on distinctions of birth and social position. All men enjoy equal status and position in such a society.'[105] In support of this egalitarianism, he has no

96. Maududi 1976: 45 = Mawdūdī n.d.b: 49.14.
97. Maududi 1963: 20, and cf. 21.
98. Maududi 1976: 15 (italics as in the original) = Mawdūdī n.d.b: 16.13 (*ulūhiyyat al-nās ʿalā ʾl-nās*); similarly Mawdūdī n.d.a: 20.10; Maududi 1975: 247.
99. Maududi 1976: 17 = Mawdūdī n.d.b: 21.4 (*ʿubūdiyyat al-nās lil-nās*).
100. Maududi 1976: 18 = Mawdūdī n.d.b: 21.11.
101. Maududi 1976: 19 = Mawdūdī n.d.b: 22.15. In this one instance I have invoked the assistance of my colleague Qasim Zaman to check the original Urdu (Mawdūdī 1952: 21.6; 'charter' is simply the English word in Urdu transcription).
102. Maududi 1976: 18 (not matched at Mawdūdī n.d.b: 21.11).
103. Mawdūdī 1977: 202.6, and see further 202.32; also Mawdūdī n.d.a: 29.3.
104. Mawdūdī 1977: 202.21; Mawdūdī n.d.c: 32.
105. Maududi 1976: 38 = Mawdūdī n.d.b: 42.3; see also Mawdūdī 1955: 37.4. 'In the divine *darbar*, in the presence of God, all belong to one class' (Maududi 1975: 124).

problem quoting appropriate sayings of the Prophet; embedded in one of them we find the Koranic statement that 'the noblest among you in the sight of God is the most godfearing of you' (Q 49:13).[106] Mawdūdī also likes to echo the words of the expressive but less well-attested saying of the Prophet that 'people are equals like the teeth of a comb'.[107] It is this equality that uproots the tree of human sovereignty (*ḥākimiyya*).[108]

The other major figure in the development of Islamism was the Egyptian Sayyid Quṭb (d. 1966). Like Mawdūdī, he quoted the accession speech of Abū Bakr,[109] and he too was entranced by what I have called the republican as opposed to patrimonial character of the early polity; by way of contrast, he deplores the way in which the Umayyad and ʿAbbāsid kings (he does not call them Caliphs) treated the public treasury as if it were their private property.[110] Again, all this is underpinned by the basic doctrinal assertion that sovereignty (*ḥākimiyya*) belongs to God alone; Islam thus precludes men from exercising sovereignty or lordship (*siyāda*) over each other[111] – though, unlike Mawdūdī, Quṭb does not warm to the idea of democracy.[112]

Quṭb's attitude to social stratification is similar to Mawdūdī's, but emotionally more vibrant. This is one of the fields in which he gets most mileage out of his foundational texts, and the outcome is a vigorous articulation of an Islamic egalitarianism that resonates strongly with modern values. Just as with Mawdūdī, his thinking is underpinned by the principle that dominion over men belongs only to God. Islam, he tells us, was born in an age when inequality was rampant;[113] he provides details of this with respect

106. Maududi 1976: 38–9 = Mawdūdī n.d.b: 42.7; see also Mawdūdī 1977: 203.4; Mawdūdī n.d.c: 21–2; Maududi 1967: 16 note 3, and 19.
107. Mawdūdī n.d.b: 42.6, 46.9 (*sawāsiya*; the echo is not detectable in the English translation, Maududi 1976: 38, 42); Mawdūdī 1955: 37.3 (*sawāsiya*); Mawdūdī n.d.d: 39.5 (*ka-asnān al-mushṭ*); Mawdūdī n.d.a: 29.5 (*sawāsiya ka-asnān al-mushṭ*).
108. Mawdūdī 1955: 37.6.
109. Quṭb n.d.a: 178.2 = Quṭb 1996: 226. Ḥasan al-Bannā (d. 1949), the founder of the Muslim Brothers, likewise adduces this speech in affirming the right of the Islamic community to monitor the conduct of the ruler closely (Bannā 1965: 361.13, 362.2). Compare Quṭb's views that a ruler has no more rights than any other Muslim bar those specific to his exercise of public office (Quṭb n.d.a: 97.8 = Quṭb 1996: 117), and that the ruler's right to obedience derives from his enforcement of the law, so that if he departs from it he forfeits that right (Quṭb n.d.a: 95.14 = Quṭb 1996: 114; Quṭb 1952: 94.17).
110. Quṭb n.d.a: 208.18 = Quṭb 1996: 259, and see Quṭb n.d.a: 189.20 = Quṭb 1996: 239, Quṭb n.d.a: 196.2 = Quṭb 1996, p. 246.
111. Sayyid Quṭb n.d.b: 17.2 = Quṭb 1988: 16–17; see also Quṭb 1973: 8.13, 22.16 = Kutb 2005: 11, 24; Quṭb n.d.a: 36.18 = Quṭb 1996: 43; Quṭb 2003: 297–9.
112. Quṭb n.d.a: 5.14 = Quṭb 1996: 1; Quṭb n.d.a: 266.17 = Quṭb 1996: 354; and see Quṭb 1996: xlii, 108; Sivan 1990: 73.
113. Quṭb n.d.a: 50.3 = Quṭb 1996: 57.

to Iran, India and Rome.[114] Nor were the Arabs innocent: they knew that returning sovereignty to God would mean stripping away the authority of soothsayers, tribal chiefs, commanders and rulers.[115] Such was the world into which Islam emerged, and its message was absolute equality among all humanity.[116] In support, Quṭb quotes the same Koranic verse, and the same saying of the Prophet that 'people are equals like the teeth of a comb'.[117] But by far the most potent proof-text he cites, though not the most authoritative, is the story of the Arab emissaries to the Persians on the eve of the battle of Qādisiyya. As we have seen, one of these envoys tells Rustam that 'we Arabs are equal',[118] while two of them announce that the invaders have come to deliver those who so wish from being servants of men to being servants of God.[119] In one of the passages in which he quotes this announcement, Quṭb comments that in these few words are concentrated 'the fundamental principle of this creed' (*qāʿidat hādhihi ʾl-ʿaqīda*), and that in them is manifested 'the nature of the Islamic movement that arose from it'.[120] Of course this pristine Islamic equality, like so much else, was soon to prove a casualty of history: the policies of the third Caliph gave rise to a great evil, the creation of massive economic and social distinctions within Islamic society and the emergence of an idle class of aristocrats.[121] Quṭb could nevertheless make his claim that what human laws were to establish in theory only in the course of the French Revolution and its aftermath had already been realised by Islam in practice over fourteen centuries ago.[122] The central theme in all this is equality, but, as with Mawdūdī, freedom is far from absent: Quṭb regularly uses a language of 'liberation' (*taḥrīr*) in the context of the elimination of the dominion (*sulṭān*) of men over men.[123]

114. Quṭb n.d.b: 54.8 = Quṭb 1988: 55–6 (Iran): Quṭb n.d.b: 55.17 = Quṭb 1988: 57 (India); Quṭb n.d.b: 58.1 = Quṭb 1988: 59 (Rome).
115. Quṭb 1973: 22.16 = Kutb 2005: 24 (see also Quṭb 2003: 289). It may be suspected that Quṭb is anxious to deny any credit to the pre-Islamic Arabs because he wants to give it all to Islam.
116. Quṭb n.d.a: 152.13 = Quṭb 1996: 198.
117. Quṭb n.d.a: 51.19, 52.2 = Quṭb 1996: 59 and note 121; cf. Quṭb 1953: 24.10, and Quṭb 1986: 200.23.
118. Quṭb 1973: 167.17 = Kutb 2005: 144.
119. Quṭb 1973: 75.9 = Kutb 2005: 71, Quṭb 1973: 168.13 = Kutb 2005: 145; Quṭb 1962: 233.3 = Quṭb 2006: 221–2.; and cf. Quṭb 1962: 86.12 = Quṭb 2006: 75f, Quṭb 1962: 155.11 = Quṭb 2006: 142, Quṭb 1962: 231.20, 232.4 = Quṭb 2006: 220–1. For a more recent Islamist invocation of this idea, see Lawrence 2005: 217.
120. Quṭb 1962: 233.3 = Quṭb 2006: 221–2.
121. Quṭb n.d.a: 202.18 = Quṭb 1996: 254.
122. Quṭb n.d.a: 50.14 = Quṭb 1996: 57 note 112 (Quṭb's chonology is slightly off).
123. See, for example, Quṭb 1973: 73.12 = Kutb 2005: 69. The passages on jihad translated in Quṭb 2003: 299–305 are full of references to its liberating role. For the term 'freedom' (*ḥurriyya*) in this context, see, for example, Quṭb 1973: 65.1 = Kutb 2005: 62.

We see, then, that the two major Islamist thinkers of the twentieth century were alike in making a beeline for the values enshrined in the memory of the early polity, and in importing into this complex, implicitly or explicitly, the European idea of freedom. But as might be expected from the lack of sympathy for Ṣūfism among Islamists, neither Mawdūdī nor Quṭb owes anything to the Ṣūfī use of the metaphor of freedom.

V

This analysis leaves us with two clear findings. The first is that the early Islamic state is associated with a set of political values that displays a significant affinity with those of the European tradition that concerns us, and resonates powerfully with them under modern conditions. I have provided some kind of explanation for the existence of these Islamic values in terms of the nature of pre-Islamic Arabian society and its relationship to the early Islamic state. I would add here that to my knowledge no comparable set of values is to be found in the heritages of the world's other major civilisations, those of India and China. Civilisations necessarily have uncivilised origins, and their records may well preserve some recollection of those far-off times; but the antiquity that Indian and Chinese culture looked back to as normative was in relative terms a later and more sophisticated phenomenon. For Islam, by contrast, normative antiquity was identified with a time when the Islamic state was still strongly shaped by the ethos of tribal Arabia; what came later, however sophisticated, was accounted not antiquity but decadence.

The second finding is that the concept of political freedom is not the central element in this set of Islamic values. Its presence in the pre-modern Islamic context is only implicit,[124] and even in the modern context, for Islamists at least, it is rarely the centre of attention. We can end this discussion by asking why this should be so. I do not have a rigorous explanation to offer, but I can suggest some lines of thought.

One consideration relates to Islam. It may be that in some ways Islam and freedom – submission to the will of God and the right to do as one pleases – do not fit very comfortably together.[125] Describing men as owned by God is not just a rhetorical trope for denying that they are slaves of each other:

124. As Crone puts it, medieval Muslims 'did speak of political oppression as enslavement, but they did not call the opposite freedom' (Crone 2004: 315).
125. Cf. Sourdel 1985: 121.

God owns humans just as He owns the rest of His creation.[126] Is a free man then to be free to say and do ungodly things – even to apostatise from God's true religion to a false one? Of such a person it could well be said that he has 'taken his caprice to be his god' (*ittakhadha ilāhahu hawāhu*, Q 25:43, 45:23); the word here translated 'caprice' is a common and derogatory Koranic term used with regard to people who follow their own fancies (*ahwāʾ*), not the guidance of God.[127] It could likewise be asked whether a free people is to be free to overturn the law of God and put laws of their own choice in its place. No wonder Ayman al-Ẓawāhirī denounces democracy as 'a new religion that deifies the masses' and revolves around 'the whims and fancies of men'.[128] Of course few people anywhere think that freedom should be absolute licence, without any limits whatever; everyone starts to feel queasy at some point. But a case could be made for saying that, if you have internalised a mainstream form of the Islamic tradition, your threshold for queasiness will be considerably lower than that of a Western liberal.[129] It is, of course, possible to find ways to combine an uncompromising Islamic sense that 'rectitude has become clear from error' (Q 2:256) with the Western idea of freedom. Thus in presenting jihad as a selfless mission to destroy all the corrupt structures of power in the world, Quṭb clearly sees these structures as preventing people

126. As Crone says with regard to medieval Muslims, 'the choice as they saw it was not between slavery and freedom, but rather between slavery to other human beings and slavery to God' (Crone 2004: 315). One could argue that being a slave to God is no more or less constraining than being a slave to the laws. Cicero says that we are slaves to the laws in order that we can be free (quoted in Wirszubski 1950: 7), and in the same way it could be said that we are slaves to God in order that we can be free. But Muslims in pre-modern times did not talk like this, and the dominion of a personal god is arguably a more constricting idea than the dominion of impersonal laws. And even if one reduces God's dominion to that of His laws, there is still a considerable gap between laws that He imposes and laws that humans make for themselves.
127. Thus one verse asks rhetorically 'who is further astray than he who follows his caprice (*hawā*) without guidance from God?' (Q 28:50). Note also that God commands David to 'judge between men justly, and follow not caprice' (Q 38:26). The term would not be a bad translation of the pre-modern Chinese *tzŭ-yu*. My attention was drawn to its significance in the present context by Qasim Zaman.
128. Ibrahim 2007: 130, 133 (quoting Q 45:18 with its denunciation of the 'caprices (*ahwāʾ*) of those who do not know'). For the similar view held by Sayyid Imām, see Rashwan 2007: 414–15; for Bin Laden's equally negative view, see Lawrence 2005: 209.
129. For modern Muslim criticism of the excessive freedom of the West, see, for example, Cook 2000: 514–15. Such criticism has, of course, a venerable ancestry in the West itself, see, for example, Laks 2007: 142–3. It also has a precedent within the Islamic world. Badāʾūnī, an Indian Muslim scholar writing in the later sixteenth century, describes Hindūstān disapprovingly as 'a wide place, where there is an open field for all licentiousness, and no one interferes with another's business, so that everyone can do just as he pleases' (Badāʾūnī 1865–9: II, 246.13 = Badáóní 1884–1925: II, 253, cited in Alam 2004: 76).

from freely choosing their religion;[130] accordingly he speaks of 'jihad for the sake of liberation' (*al-jihād al-taḥrīrī*).[131] His assumption, of course, is that people who freely choose their religion will choose Islam, not behave like Japanese or Californians. Without that assumption, it may be that Islam and freedom have some degree of negative elective affinity for each other, and that a certain discomfort about the idea of human freedom in a world owned by God has tended to discourage Muslims from putting it centre-stage, both in the early Islamic period and in modern times. The issue this raises is, of course, what is different about Christianity. Christians too, though freed from sin, are 'enslaved to God' (Romans 6:22), and are told to live as free people (*eleutheroi*) at the same time as they are slaves (*douloi*) of God (1 Peter 2:16). I shall not attempt to go into this comparative question here, except to remark that the difference may lie less in the character of Christian norms in the abstract than in the more limited scope of their application. To give one example among many, John Milton took the view that to count as a free people we must submit only to 'such Laws as our selves shall choose'.[132] To my knowledge, this casual assertion of the legislative sovereignty of humans was not condemned by his fellow-Christians as an incitement to godless usurpation of divine authority – a response that such a remark would have invited in an Islamic context.

Another line of thought relates to the genesis of the European tradition. Here it is hard to miss the close association of the first phase with a particular kind of polity, namely the city-state. There is nothing surprising about this association. City-states typically combine two features: one is a scale of political organisation so small that against the background of the history of state-formation over the last few thousand years it is hard not to think of it as archaic;[133] the other is the possession of economic and cultural resources that may not be archaic in the least. The first is what makes possible the forms of limited, non-monarchic government that appear among city-states,[134] while the second is what makes possible a tradition of systematic reflection on

130. Quṭb n.d.b: 87.17 = Quṭb 1988: 88–9; Quṭb n.d.a: 163.10 = Quṭb 1996: 213; Quṭb 2003: 300, 302; and cf. Quṭb 1973: 63.21, 64.15 = Kutb 2005: 61–2; Quṭb 1973: 74.25 = Kutb 2005: 70.
131. Quṭb 1973: 68.23 = Kutb 2005: 65.
132. Skinner 1998: 30, citing Milton 1953–82: III, 519 (note the reference to 'Gods Law' that follows later in the same paragraph with no apparent sense of strain, *ibid.*, 520).
133. This is not to deny that city-states can be adaptive in any period: witness the case of Singapore today.
134. Summing up the results of a conference on city-states, the organiser remarks that many, perhaps most, city-states were monarchies, but that the small size of city-states led to the emergence of quite a few republics, and to similar institutions even within monarchic city states (Hansen 2000: 611–12, and the summary of the relevant data, 619 notes 81–2).

these political arrangements.[135] In the long run this combination of features is unstable: city-states occupy territory that could easily support a much larger scale of political organisation, and sooner or later it will. Thus any given cluster of city-states – and they often come in clusters – will eventually succumb to one of two fates: either one city-state will become a territorial state at the expense of the others (Athens failed in this, but Rome succeeded); or an existing territorial state will move in and take over (here Persia failed, but Macedon succeeded). Yet historically it seems quite common for fate to be sufficiently delayed to give city-states a half-life of several centuries. This package of features – the combination of the small scale of city-states with their relatively generous resources, their reasonably long life-spans, and their existence in significant numbers – helps to explain how such polities could engender a first phase of the kind we have stipulated. How then does the Arabian setting compare with that? The Arab tribes were numerous and long-lasting, but they were resource-poor, which does not go with philosophising; and even if they had been given to such musings, the fact that they were stateless would have limited them to making a contribution to anarchist thought.[136] The early Islamic polity, by contrast, was a state, and its resources increased dramatically with its conquests outside Arabia. But unlike the tribes, it was both unique and transitory, making its transition from a stateless society to a despotic and patrimonial state in a matter of decades. Thus despite the authority it enjoyed in the eyes of posterity, the experience of this state may not have been enough to generate a tradition of political thought of the kind we are looking for.

A final point, though a rather abstract one, arises from the nature of our comparative enterprise. Human history is extensive but not infinite; just as with shopping, the more elaborately we specify what we are looking for, the less likely we are to find it. In the present case, we began by looking for no more than the occasional analogy in which the relationship between master and slave is invoked to comment on that between ruler and ruled. As might be expected, stray examples did not prove too hard to find in the Islamic

135. Obviously this combination of features is not a sufficient condition for the development of a first phase. To take just one example, I am not aware that the cities of the Hansa, rich and literate societies contemporary with the Italian city-states, made any significant contribution to the evolution of modern political thought.

136. Even then, Arab tribes seem to have functioned more naturally than city-states – that is to say, with less recourse to the contrivances of political engineering that shaped and reshaped the constitution of a city like Athens; the result was that they had less to think about. One reason for this difference may be that tribes are a much older form of human collective existence than city-states, and thus more tried and tested.

context. We then proceeded to raise the comparative bar. First we required that the analogy form part of a tradition of thinking and talking about politics that was central to the political culture of the society in question. Then we added that this tradition must at the same time be the object of systematic reflection. Finally, we stipulated a long-term historical development in three phases. Taken together all this is a lot to ask, and we should not be surprised if we find it to be unique to the case from which we derived the specifications in the first place.

Postscript

This chapter was completed before the train of events that has come to be known as the 'Arab Spring' began in December 2010. The reporting on these events made it very clear that large numbers of people in the Arab world put freedom high on their list of political priorities. But it revealed little about the way people think of this value. Do they see it as one they have adopted from the West, or as one they have rediscovered in Islam, or as a universal value that in some way transcends divisions between the Islamic world and West? Or would they just shrug off the question as irrelevant or inconsequential? Would most people agree on the same response, or are they divided? There is a project in political ethnography here awaiting a researcher who is able and willing to undertake it.

Bibliography

Manuscript sources

Bodleian Library, Oxford:
MS DD All Souls c. 389
Locke, John (1681–2). 'Defence of Nonconformity', MS. Locke c. 34
British Library, London
Izkawī (n.d.) *Kashf al-ghumma*, MS. British Library, Or. 8076
Library of Trinity College Dublin
Manuscript 141 (TCD MS 141)
Biblioteca Nazionale Marciana, Venice
Querini, Antonio, MS It. VII 155 (8159): *Historia dell' scomunica fulminata da Paolo quinto ponteficii, contra la Republica di Venezia l'anno MDCV*
Staatsarchiv Zürich
Valkenier, Petrus (1693). *Copia des Schreibens an Bürgermeister, Klein- und Grossräth*, 19/29 April 1693, Staatsarchiv Zürich, B i 329, no. 147

Printed primary sources

Abū 'l-Faraj al-Iṣbahānī (1927–74). *Aghānī*, Cairo.
Abū 'l-Shaykh al-Iṣbahānī (1996). *Aḥādīth Abī 'l-Zubayr ʿan ghayr Jābir*, ed. B. ʿA. al-Badr, Riyadh.
Abū Zakariyyā (1982). *Kitāb siyar al-a'imma wa-akhbārihim*, ed. I. al-ʿArabī, Algiers.
Achenwall, Gottfried (1763). *Iuris naturalis pars posterior complectens jus familiae, jus publicum, et jus gentium*, Göttingen.
(1995). *Elementa iuris naturae (Anfangsgründe des Naturrechts)*, ed. and trans. Jan Schröder, Frankfurt.
Ackerman, Bruce (1980). *Social Justice in the Liberal State*, New Haven, CT.
Acosta, José de (2002). *Natural and Moral History of the Indies*, ed. Jane E. Mangan, trans. Frances López-Morillas, Durham, NC.
Acta of Handelingen der Nationale Synode . . . te Dordrecht in de jaren 1618 en 1619 [1885], Houten (1987).

Actio Hieronymi Laszky apud Turcam, nomine Regis Iohannis, in Matthias Bel (ed.), *Adparatus ad historiam Hvngariae: sive Collectio miscella*, Posonii (1835).
Ainsworth, Henry (1607). *The Communion of Saincts: A Treatise of the Fellowship that the Faithful Have with God, and His Angels, and One with an Other*, Amsterdam.
Akta sejmikowe województw poznańskiego i kaliskiego. Tom 1, 1572–1632 (1957), ed. Wladyslav Dworzaczek, 2 vols., vol. I, Poznań.
Albéri, Eugenio (ed.) (1844). *Relazioni degli ambasciatori veneti al senato*, vol. II, Florence.
Althusius, Johannes (1932). *Politica methodice digesta* [1603], ed. Carl Friedrich, Cambridge.
Alvinczi, Péter (1619). *Querela Hungariae. Magyarország panasza*, Kassa.
(1620). *Defensio querelarum Hungaricarum (Querelarum inclyti regni Hungariae adversus corruptelas Jesuiticas . . . defensio)*, Posonii.
Ames, William (1622). *A Reply to Dr Mortons General Defence*, Amsterdam.
(1633). *A Fresh Suit against Human Ceremonies in God's Worship*, Amsterdam.
ʿĀmirī, Abū ʾl-Ḥasan al- (1967). *al-Iʿlām bi-manāqib al-Islām*, ed. A. ʿA. Ghurāb, Cairo.
Ammianus Marcellinus (1950–6). *Res gestae*, trans. J. C. Rolfe, London and Cambridge, MA.
Amtliche Sammlung der Eidgenössischen Abschiede (EA) (1858–86). Lucerne.
Anon. (1583). *Discours verclaerende wat forme ende manier van regieringhe dat die Nederlanden voor die alderbeste ende zekerste tot desen tyden aenstellen mochten*, s.l.
(1588). *Philopolites, to iest Miłośnik Oyczyzny, albo o powinności dobrego obywatela, Oyczyźnie dobrze chcącego i oną miłującego, krótki traktat*, Cracow.
(1646). *The Parliament of Women*, London.
(1648). *A Testimony to the Truth of Jesus Christ*, London.
(1659). *The Christian Commonvvealth: or, The civil policy of the rising kingdom of Jesus Christ . . .*, London.
(1675). *L'affermissement des republiques de Hollande & de Suisse*, s.l.
(1859a). *Naprawa Rzeczypospolitej Polskiej do elekcyi nowego króla* [1573], ed. Kazimierz Turowski, Cracow.
(1859b). *Krótkie rzeczy potrzebnych z strony wolności a swobód polskich zebranie przez tego, który wszego dobrego życzy ojczyźnie swojej* [1587], ed. Kazimierz Turowski, Cracow.
(1906). *Naprawa praw i swobód i wolności naszych* [*c.* 1572] in *Pisma polityczne z czasów pierwszego bezkrólewia*, ed. Jan Czubek, Cracow, pp. 186–9.
(1918). *Libera respublica – absolutum dominium – rokosz* [1606] in *Pisma polityczne z czasów rokoszu Zebrzydowskiego 1606–1608*, 3 vols., ed. Jan Czubek, Cracow, vol. II, pp. 403–14.
(1963). *Jezuitom i inszym duchownym respons* [1606] in *Literatura antyjezuicka w Polsce 1578–1925: antologia*, ed. Janusz Tazbir, Warsaw, pp. 111–20.
(1899) 'Querelae, excusationes cum protestatione regni Hungariae, praesertim partium superiorum coram Deo et toto urbe Christiano' [1605] in *Monumenta comitialia regni Hungariae*, ed. Vilmos Fraknói and Árpád Károlyi, vol. XI, Budapest, pp. 168–84.
Aquinas, Thomas (1947). *Summa theologiae*, trans. the Dominican Fathers, New York.

(1954). *Opuscula philosophica, de regimine principum ad regem Cypri*, ed. R. Spiazzi, Turin, pp. 280–358.
(2003). *On Evil*, ed. Brian Davies, trans. Richard J. Regan, Oxford.
Arberry, A. J. (trans.) (1957). *The Seven Odes: The First Chapter in Arabic Literature*, London and New York.
Aristotle (1926). *Nicomachean Ethics*, trans. H. Rackham, Cambridge, MA.
(1932). *The Politics*, trans. H. Rackham, Cambridge, MA.
(1980). *The Nicomachean Ethics*, trans. David Ross, rev. J. L. Ackrill and J. O. Urmson, Oxford.
(1996). *The Politics and the Constitution of Athens*, ed. Stephen Everson, Cambridge.
Arminius, Jacobus (1629). 'De liberis hominis arbitrio' in *Opera theologica*, Leiden, pp. 262–6.
(1960). *Verklaring van Jacobus Arminius afgelegd in de vergadering van de Staten van Holland op 30 Oktober 1608*, ed. G. J. Hoenderdaal, Lochem.
(1986a). 'Modest Examination of Dr. Perkins's Pamphlet' [1612] in *The Works of James Arminius: The London Edition* [1875], Grand Rapids, MI, vol. III, pp. 249–484.
(1986b). 'On the Free Will of Man and Its Powers' in *The Works of James Arminius: The London Edition* [1875], Grand Rapids, MI, vol. II, pp. 189–96.
Arnisaeus, Henning (1610). *De jure majestatis libri tres*, Frankfurt.
(1651). *Doctrina politica*, Amsterdam.
Arriaga, Pablo José (1920). *Extirpación de la idolatría del Piru* [1621], Lima.
Arriaga, Rodrigo de (1644). *Disputationes theologicae in primam secundae S. Thomae, Tomus II*, Antwerp.
Arumaeus, Dominicus (ed.) (1620). *Discursus Academici de Jure Publico*, Jena.
al-Badáóní (1884–1925). *Muntakhab-ut-Tawáríkh*, trans. G. S. A. Ranking *et al.*, Calcutta.
Badāʾūnī (1865–9). *Muntakhab al-tawārīkh*, ed. W. N. Lees and Maulaví Ahmad ʿAlí, Calcutta.
al-Bannā, Ḥasan (1965). *Majmūʿat rasāʾil al-imām al-shahīd Ḥasan al-Bannā*, Beirut.
Baranī, Ḍiyāʾ al-Dīn (1972). *Fatāwā-yi jahāndārī*, ed. A. S. Khan, Lahore.
Barclay, William (1609). *De potestate papae: an & quatenus in reges & principes seculares ius & imperium habeat*, s.l.
Baronius, Cesare (1601). *Annales ecclesiastici*, Venice.
(s.d.). *Epistola Baronii Cardinalis, super excommunicatione Venetorum*, s.l.
Barozzi, Niccolò and Berchet, Guglielmo (eds.) (1871). *Relazioni degli ambasciatori e baili veneti a Constantinopoli*, Venice.
Barrow, Henry (1966). *The Writings of Henry Barrow, 1590–1591*, ed. Leland H. Carlson, London.
Bary, W. T. de (ed.) (1959). *Sources of Indian Tradition*, New York.
Baxter, Richard (1661). *Two Papers of Proposals concerning the Discipline and Ceremonies of the Church of England*, London.
Bayhaqī (1985). *Dalāʾil al-nubuwwa*, ed. ʿA. Qalʿajī, Beirut.
Becanus, Martin (1613). *Controversia anglicana de potestate pontificis et regis*, Moguntiae.
Bellarmine, Robert (1610). *Tractatus de potestate summi pontificis in rebus temporalibus. Adversus Gulielmum Barclaium*, Rome.

Bericht Iohann Hoberdanacz's an König Ferdinand I. [1529] in *Urkunden und Actenstücke zur Geschichte der Verhältnisse zwischen Österreich, Ungern und der Pforte im XVI. und XVII. Jahrhunderte*, ed. Anton von Gévay, Vienna, 1840.

Besenyei, Lajos, Géza Érszegi, and Maurizio Pedrazza Gorlero (eds.) (1999). *De bulla aurea Andreae II regis Hungariae MCCXXII*, Verona.

Besold, Christoph (1624). *Spicilegia politico-juridica de legatis; de sessionis praecedentia; de pacis jure; deque arcanis rerumpublicarum*, Strasburg.

(1625). *Dissertatio politica-juridica de majestate in genere*, Tübingen.

Beza, Theodore (1969). 'Du droit des magistrats' [1574] in *Constitutionalism and Resistance in the Sixteenth Century: Three Treatises by Hotman, Beza, and Mornay*, trans. Julian H. Franklin, New York, pp. 97–135.

Biard, Pierre (1616). *Relation de la Novvelle France, de Ses Terres, Natvrel du Pais, & de ses Habitans*, Paris.

Bielski, Marcin (1564). *Kronika, tho iesth Historya Świata na sześć wieków a cztery monarchie rozdzielona*, Cracow.

Birks, Peter and McLeod, Grant (eds.) (1987). *Justinian's Institutes*, London.

Błażewski, Marcin (1918). *Tłumacz rokoszowy powiatu ruskiego* [1607], in *Pisma polityczne z czasów rokoszu Zebrzydowskiego 1606–1608*, 3 vols., ed. Jan Czubek, Cracow, vol. I, pp. 156–77.

Bocskai, István (1992). *Levelek* (Correspondence), ed. Kálmán Benda, Budapest and Bucarest.

Bodin, Jean (1606). *The Six Bookes of a Commonweale: Written by I. Bodin a famous lawyer, and a man of great experience in matters of state. Out of the French and Latine copies, done into English, by Richard Knolles*, London.

(1650). *Methodus ad facilem historiarum cognitionem*, Amsterdam.

(1945). *Method for the Easy Comprehension of History* [1566], trans. Beatrice Reynolds, New York.

(1962). *Six Bookes of a Commonweale* [*Six Livres de la République 1576*], ed. Kenneth McRae, trans. Richard Knolles [1606], Cambridge, MA.

(1967). *Six Books of the Commonwealth*, ed. and trans. M. J. Tooley, New York.

Bohun, Edmund (1684). *The Justice of the Peace his Calling: A Moral Essay*, London.

Bornitz, Jacob (1612). *Aerarium, sive Tractatus Politicus*, Frankfurt.

Boronkai, Iván (ed.) (1987). *Vitéz János levelei és politikai beszédei* (Political Correspondence and Orations of János Vitéz), Budapest.

Botero, Giovanni (1596). *Relationi universali*, vol. IV, Venice.

Bovio, Giovanni Antonio (1606). *Risposta alle considerazioni del Padre Maestro Paolo da Venetia, sopra le censure della Santità di Papa Paolo Quinto contra la Republica di Venetia*, Rome and Bologna.

Bracton, Henry de (1968). *On the Laws and Customs of England [De legibus et consuetudinibus angliae]*, vol. II, trans. Samuel Thorne, Cambridge.

Bramhall, John (1658). *Castigations of Mr. Hobbes his last animadversions, in the case concerning liberty, and universal necessity. With an appendix concerning The catching of Leviathan or, The great whale*, London.

Brandolini, Aurelio Lippo (2009). *Republics and Kingdoms Compared*, ed. and trans. James Hankins, Cambridge, MA.

Bruni, Leonardo (1980). 'Oration on Nanni Strozzi' in *The Humanities: Cultural Roots and Continuities*, vol. I, ed. M. A. Witt *et al.*, Washington, DC, pp. 224–6.
(2001). *History of the Florentine People*, 3 vols., trans. James Hankins, Cambridge, MA.
Bullarum diplomatum et privilegiorum sanctorum romanorum pontificum (1865, 1867). Tomi IX, XI, Augustae Taurinorum.
Burges, John (1631). *An Answer Rejoyned*, London.
Burke, Edmund (1992). *Further Reflections on the Revolution in France*, ed. Daniel E. Ritchie, Indianapolis, IN.
(1999). *Select Works*, vol. II: *Reflections on the Revolution in France*, Indianapolis, IN.
Burnet, Thomas (1699). *Third Remarks upon An Essay Concerning Humane Understanding*, London.
Calasso, Francesco (1950). *I glossatori e la teoria della sovranità*, Milan.
Calvinus, Johann (1683). *Magnum lexicon juridicum*, Geneva.
Carleton, George (1610). *Iurisdiction regall, epsicopall, papall*, London.
Carré, O. (2003). *Mysticism and Politics: A Critical Reading of Fī ẓilāl al-Qur'ān by Sayyid Quṭb (1906–66)*, Leiden and Boston.
Carrerio, Alessandro (1599). *De potestate Romani Pontificis adversus impios politicos. Libri duo*, Patavij.
Cartwright, Thomas (1573). *A replye to an answere made of M. Doctor Whitgifte*, London.
Casaubon, Isaac (1607). *De libertate ecclesiastica*, s.l.
Castellio, Sebastian (1998). 'Advice to a Desolate France' [1562] in *Religious Pluralism in the West: An Anthology*, ed. David Mullan, Oxford, pp. 100–15.
Cerva, Seraphinus Maria (1977). *Bibliotheca Ragusina in qua Ragusini scriptores eorumque gesta recensetur*, vols. II and III, Zagreb.
Chemnitz, Bogislaus Philipp von (1640). *Dissertatio de ratione status in imperio nostro Romano-Germanico*, s.l.
Cheynell, Francis (1644). *Chillingworthi Novissima. Or, The Sicknesse, Heresy, Death and Buriall of William Chillingworth*, London.
Choppin, René (1605). *De domanio Franciae libri III*, Paris.
Cicero (1901). *Pro A. Cluentio oratio*, in *M. Tvlli Ciceronis orationes*, 6 vols., ed. Albert Clark, vol. I, Oxford.
(1913). *De officiis*, ed. and trans. Walter Miller, London.
(1942). *De oratore. De fato. Paradoxa stoicorum. De partitione oratoria*, trans. H. Rackham, Cambridge, MA.
(1946). *In Catilinam: Pro Murena: Pro Sulla: Pro Flacco*, trans. L. E. Lord, Cambridge, MA.
(1949). *De inventione, De optimo genere oratorum, Topica*, trans. H. M. Hubbell, Cambridge, MA.
(1991). *On Duties*, ed. M. T. Griffin and E. M. Atkins, Cambridge.
Clark, Michael P. (ed.) (2003). *The Eliot Tracts: With Letters from John Eliot to Thomas Thorowgood and Richard Baxter*, Westport, CT.
Cobo, Bernabé (1956). 'Historia del Nuevo Mundo' [1639] in *Obras del P. Bernabé Cobo*, ed. Francisco Mateos, 2 vols., Madrid.
Cocceji, Heinrich von (1695). *Juris publici prudentia compendio exhibita*, Frankfurt.

Coccejus, Johannes (1629). *Duo tituli thalmudici: Sanhedrin et Maccoth*, Amsterdam.
Cockeram, Henry (1623). *The English Dictionarie: Or an Interpreter of Hard English Words*, London.
Codex epistolaris saeculi decimi quinti (1891), 3 vols., ed. August Sokołowski, Anatol Lewicki and Józef Szujski, vol. II, Cracow.
Conciliorum oecumenicorum decreta (2002). A cura dell'Istituto per le scienze religiose, Bologna.
Condillac, Etienne Bonnot de (2001). *Essay on the Origin of Human Knowledge*, trans. Hans Aarsleff, Cambridge.
Condorcet, Jean-Marie Caritat (1955). *Sketch for a Historical Picture of the Progress of the Human Mind* [1795], ed. Isiah Berlin, Stuart Hampshire and Richard Wollheim, London.
Conring, Hermann (1643). *De origine juris Germanici*, s.l.
(2005). *Hermann Conring's New Discourse on the Roman-German Emperor [Discursus novus de imperatore Romano-Germanico]*, ed. trans. Constantin Fasolt, Tempe, AZ.
Constant, Benjamin (1988). *The Political Writings of Benjamin Constant*, ed. Biancamaria Fontana, Cambridge.
Coornhert, Dirck Volckertsz (1582). *Remonstrance oft vertooch by die van Leyden*, Leiden.
(1590). 'Van de Predestinatie, Verkiezinghe ende verwerpinghe Godes ontwarringhe' in his *Wercken*, vol. III, fols. 171–291.
(1630). *Wercken*, 3 vols., Amsterdam.
Copey eines Sendtschreibens/ welches Stephan Botschkay/ [et]c. An einen Hungarischen Herrn/ seinen Blutsverwandten/ Von jetzigem zustand und Kriegswesen in Hungarn/ gethan: Auß seiner Sprach in die Hochteutsche ubergesetzt, 1605, also in Miklós Nyakas, *Az ismeretlen szerencsi kiáltvány, Hasonmás kiadás*, Debrecen, 2006.
Corpus iuris Hungarici (CIH) (1526–1608). *Magyar törvénytár. Törvényczikkek [Acts of 1526–1608]. With Explanatory Notes by Dezső Márkus*, Budapest (1899).
(1608–1657). *Magyar törvénytár. Törvényczikkek [Acts of 1608–1657]. With Explanatory Notes by Dezső Márkus*, Budapest (1900).
Cotton, John (1645). *The vvay of the churches of Christ in New-England, or, The vvay of churches walking in brotherly equalitie, or co-ordination, without subjection of one church to another measured and examined by the golden reed of the sanctuary, containing a full declaration of the church-way in all particulars*, London.
Cousins, Norman (ed.) (1958). *In God We Trust: The Religious Ideas and Beliefs of the American Founding Fathers*, New York.
Crell, Johan (1623). *Ad librum Hugonis Grotii quem de satisfactione Christ adversus Fastum Socinum Senesem scripsit*, Rakow.
[Crell, J.] (1637). *Iuni Bruti Poloni vindiciae pro religionis libertate*, [Amsterdam].
Dalberg, Carl Theodor von (1793). *Von den wahren Grenzen der Wirksamkeit des Staats in Beziehung auf seine Mitglieder*, Leipzig.
Dante (1996). *Monarchy*, trans. P. Shaw, Cambridge.
(2007). *Four Political Letters*, trans. C. E. Honess, London.
de Diversis, Filip (2004). *Opis slavnoga grada Dubrovnika* (Description of the Glorious City of Ragusa), Zagreb.
De la Court, Johan and Pieter (1661). *Consideratien van Staat, ofte Polityke Weeg-schaal*, Amsterdam.

(1662). *Politike discoursen*, Amsterdam.
(1669). *Aanwysing der heilsame politke Gronden en Maximen van de Republike van Holland en West-Vriesland*, Leiden.
Dennison Jr, James (ed.) (2010). *Reformed Confessions of the 16th and 17th Centuries in English Translation*, vol. II: *1552–1566*, Grand Rapids, MI.
Des Maizeaux, Pierre (1725). *An Historical and Critical Account of the Life and Writings of Wm. Chillingworth*, London.
Descartes, René (1953). *Œuvres et lettres*, ed. André Bridoux, Paris.
(1984). *The Philosophical Writings of Descartes*, vol. II, trans. John Cottingham, Robert Stoothoff and Dugald Murdoch, Cambridge.
(1985). *The Philosophical Writings of Descartes*, vol. I, trans. John Cottingham, Robert Stoothoff and Dugald Murdoch, Cambridge.
(1991). *The Philosophical Writings of Descartes*, vol. III, trans. John Cottingham, Robert Stoothoff, Dugald Murdoch and Anthony Kenny, Cambridge.
(1998). *The World and Other Writings*, trans. Stephen Gaukroger, Cambridge.
Dethlefs, Gerd (ed.) (1998). *Der Frieden von Münster 1648: Der Vertragstext nach einem zeitgenössischen Druck und die Beschreibungen der Ratifikationsfeiern*, Münster.
Deusdedit (1892). 'Deusdedit presbyteri cardinalis Libellus contra invasores et symoniacos et reliquos schismaticos' in *Monumenta Germaniae Historica, Libelli de lite imperatorum et pontificum*, vol. II, ed. E. Sackur, Hanover, pp. 292–365.
Deutscher Evangelischer Kirchenausschuss (ed.) (1998). *Bekenntnischriften der evangelisch lutherischen Kirche*, Göttingen.
di Gozze, Niccolò Vito (1591). *Dello stato delle republiche secondo la mente di Aristotele con esempi moderni; giornate otto*, Venice.
Diariusz sejmu lubelskiego 1566 roku (1980), ed. Irena Kaniewska, Wrocław.
Digest of Justinian, The (1985). 4 vols., ed. Theodore Mommsen and Paul Krueger, trans. Alan Watson, Philadelphia, PA.
Digesta Iustiniani Augustii (1868), 2 vols., ed. Theodor Mommsen and Paul Krueger, vol. 1, Berlin.
[Digges, Dudley] (1642). *An Answer to a Printed Book*, London.
(1644). *The Unlawfulnesse of Subjects taking up armes against their Soveraigne*, London.
Diogenes Laertius (1925). *Lives of Eminent Philosophers*, books VI–X, trans. R. D. Hicks, Cambridge, MA.
Dod, Robert and Cleaver, John (1612). *A Godly Forme of Housholde Governement: For the Ordering of Private Families according to the directions of Gods word*, London.
Donteclock, Reginald (1609). *Tsamenspreeckinghe vande Vertaelde Theses ofte Disputatien, de eene Doct. Francisci Gomari, de andere Doct. Iacobi Arminij, aenghaende de Goddelicke Predestinatie*, Delft.
Downame, George (1609). *A Treatise Vpon John 8.36. Concerning Christian Libertie*, London.
(1611) *A Defence of the Sermon Preached at the Consecration of the L. Bishop of Bath and Welles against a Confutation Thereof by a Namelesse Author*, London.
(1635). *The Christians Freedome, Wherein is Fully Expressed the Doctrine of Christian Libertie*, Oxford.
Držić, Marin (1930). *Djela* (Works), Zagreb.

Du Moulin, Charles [Molinaeus] (1681). *Commentarius in priores titulos antiquae consuetudinis Parisiensis, omnia quae extant opera*, 5 vols., Paris.

Dworkin, Ronald (1999). *Freedom's Law: The Moral Reading of the American Constitution*, New York.

Dyaryusze i akta sejmowe r. 1591–1592 (1911), ed. Edward Barwiński, Cracow.

Dyaryusze sejmów koronnych 1548, 1553, 1570 r. (1872), ed. Józef Szujski, Cracow.

Dyaryusze sejmowe r. 1585: Ułamki dyaryusza sejmowego roku 1582. Akta sejmikowe i inne akta odnoszące się do sejmu 1585 roku (1901), ed. Aleksander Czuczyński, Cracow.

Eames, Wilberforce (ed.) (1915). *John Eliot and the Indians, 1652–1657: Being Letters Addressed to Reverend Jonathan Hanmer of Barnstaple, England*, New York.

Edwards, Thomas (1646). *Gangraena: or a Catalogue and Discovery of many Errours, Heresies, Blasphemies, and pernicious Practices of the Sectaries of this Time*, 3 vols., London.

Eliot, John (1659). *The Christian Commonvvealth: or, The civil policy of the rising kingdom of Jesus Christ*, London.

(1660). 'The Learned Conjectures of Reverend John Eliot touching the Americans' in Thomas Thorowgood, *Jews in America, or Probabilities that Those Indians Are Judaical*, London.

(1665). *The Communion of Churches: or, The Divine Management of Gospel-Churches by the Ordinance of Councils Constituted in Order according to the Scriptures. As also, The Way of bringing all Christian Parishes to be particular Reforming Congregationall Churches* . . . , Cambridge, MA.

Episcopius, Simon (1627). *Vrye Godes-dienst, of t'Samenspreeckinghe tusschen Remonstrant en Contra-Remonstrant, over de vrye Godts-dienstighe Vergaderinghen der Remonstranten*, n.p.

Episcopius, Simon *et al.* (1623). *Historisch Verhael, van t'ghene sich toeghedraeghen heeft binnen Dordrecht . . . Uytgegeven van weghen de Kercken-Dienaren Remonstranten*, n.p.

Erhard, Johann Benjamin (1970). *Über das Recht zu einer Revolution des Volkes und andere Schriften*, ed. and foreword by Hellmut G. Haasis, Munich.

Escher, Johann Caspar (2008). 'Exercitatio politica de libertate populi. Politologische Studie über die Freiheit des Volkes', *Daphnis* 37, ed. and intro. Werner Widmer, pp. 547–626.

Ferguson, Adam (1772). *Adam Fergusons Grundsätze der Moralphilosophie*, trans. Christian Garve, Leipzig.

(1995). *Ferguson: An Essay on the History of Civil Society* [1767], ed. Fania Oz-Salzberger, Cambridge.

Ferne, Henry (1643a). *Conscience Satisfied: That there is no warrant for the Armes now taken up by Subjects*, Oxford.

(1643b). *The Resolving of Conscience upon this Question, Whether . . . Subjects may take Armes and resist?* . . . , Cambridge.

Fichte, Johann Gottlieb (1964a). *Zurückforderung der Denkfreiheit von den Fürsten Europens, die sie bisher unterdrückten. Eine Rede. Heliopolis, im letzten Jahre der alten Finsternis* in *Gesamtausgabe der Bayerischen Akademie der Wissenschaften*, ed. R. Lauth, H. Jacob and H. Gliwitzky, vol. I.1, Stuttgart and Bad Cannstatt, pp. 167–92.

(1964b). *Beitrag zur Berichtigung der Urtheile des Publikums über die französische Revolution* in *Gesamtausgabe der Bayerischen Akademie der Wissenschaften*, ed. R. Lauth, H. Jacob and H. Gliwitzky, vol. I.1, Stuttgart and Bad Cannstatt, pp. 203–404.

(1977). *Das System der Sittenlehre nach den Principien der Wissenschaftslehre* in *Gesamtausgabe der Bayerischen Akademie der Wissenschaften*, ed. R. Lauth, H. Jacob and H. Gliwitzky, vol. 1.5, Stuttgart and Bad Cannstatt, pp. 21–317.

(1981). 'Ueber Geist und Buchstab in der Philosophie' in *Gesamtausgabe der Bayerischen Akademie der Wissenschaften*, ed. R. Lauth, H. Jacob and H. Gliwitzky, vol. 1.6, Stuttgart and Bad Cannstatt, pp. 313–61.

(1984). 'Fichte: On the Spirit and the Letter in Philosophy' in *German Aesthetic and Literary Criticism: Kant, Fichte, Schelling, Schopenhauer, Hegel*, ed. David Simpson, Cambridge, pp. 74–93.

(2005). *The System of Ethics*, ed. Daniel Breazeale and Günter Zöller, Cambridge.

Filelfo, Francesco (2009). *Odes*, trans. D. Robin, Cambridge, MA and London.

Filmer, Robert (1991). *Patriarcha and Other Writings*, ed. Johann P. Sommerville, Cambridge.

Firth, C. H. and Rait, R. S. (eds.) (1911). *Acts and Ordinances of the Interregnum, 1642–1660*, London.

Foner, Phillip (ed.) (1945). *Complete Writings of Thomas Paine*, New York.

Fraknói, Vilmos and Károlyi, Árpád (1874–1917). *Monumenta comitialia regni Hungariae/Magyar Országgyűlési Emlékek történeti bevezetésekkel [Souvenirs of the Hungarian Diets with Historical Introductions]*, 12 vols., Budapest.

Friedberg, Aemilius (ed.) (1955). *Corpus iuris canonici, pars prior: Decretum magistri Gratiani* [1879, Leipzig], Graz.

Fuchs, Erich (1978). *Fichte im Gespräch: Berichte der Zeitgenossen*, vol. 1, Stuttgart and Bad Cannstatt.

Gallucius, Johannes Paulus (1580). *Io. Paulli Gallucii Saloenses oratio, publicae habita in Ecclesia Cathedrali Paduae in assumptione Caputei illustris Equitis Dominici Slatarichii Simeonis F. Ragvsini*, Venice.

Galvan Rivera, Mariano (ed.) (1859). *Concilio Provincial Mexicano*, Mexico City.

Garin, Eugenio (1952). *Prosatori latini del Quattrocento*, Milan and Naples.

Garnett, George (ed.) (1994). *Vindiciae contra tyrannos*, Cambridge.

Gentz, Friedrich (1967). 'Nachtrag zu dem Räsonnement des Herrn Professor Kant über das Verhältniβ zwischen Theorie und Praxis' in *Kant, Gentz, Rehberg: Über Theorie und Praxis*, ed. Dieter Henrich, Frankfurt.

(1991). 'Über Politische Freiheit und das Verhältnis derselben zur Regierung' in *Über die Französische Revolution: Betrachtungen und Abhandlungen*, ed. Herman Klenner, Berlin.

Gerald, Joseph (1793). *A Convention the only means of saving us from ruin*, London.

Giannotti, Donato (1819). *Opere*, 3 vols., ed. G. Rosini, Pisa.

Giovanni di Conversino (1980). *Dragmalogia de eligibili vitae genere*, ed. and trans. H. Lanneau Eaker, with introduction and notes by B. G. Kohl, Cranbury, NJ and London.

Godwyn, Thomas (1685). *Moses and Aaron: Civil and Ecclesiastical Rites Used by the Ancient Hebrews*, London.

Gomarus, Franciscus (1609). *Waerschouwinghe over de Vermaninghe aen R. Donteclock*, Leiden.

(2010). 'Theological Disputation on Free Choice' [1602] in W. J. Van Asselt, J. M. Bac and R. T. Te Velde (eds.), *Reformed Thought on Freedom: The Concept of Free Choice in Early Modern Reformed Theology*, Grand Rapids, MI, pp. 128–33.

Goodman, Christopher (1558). *How Superior Powers Oght to be Obeyd of their Subiects, and Wherin they May Lawfully by Gods Worde by Disobeyed and Resisted*, Geneva.

Górnicki, Łukasz (1961). *Rozmowa Polaka z Włochem o wolnościach i prawach polskich* [1616], in Górnicki, *Pisma*, 2 vols., ed. Roman Pollak, Warsaw, vol. II, pp. 327–474.

(1997). *Droga do zupełnej wolności* [1650], ed. Wiesław Stec, Białystok.

Goślicki, Wawrzyniec (2000). *O senatorze doskonałym księgi dwie. De optimo senatore libri duo* [1568], trans. Tadeusz Bieńkowski, ed. Mirosław Korolko, Cracow.

Gouge, William (1622). *Of Domesticall Duties*, London.

Gretser, Jacob (1607). *Considerationum ad theologos Venetos libri tres, de immunitate et libertate ecclesiastica*, Ingolstad.

Greville, Fulke (1986a). 'A Dedication to Sir Philip Sidney' [1652] in *The Prose Works of Fulke Greville, Lord Brooke*, ed. J. Gouws, Oxford.

(1986b). *The Prose Works of Fulke Greville, Lord Brooke*, ed. John Gouws Oxford.

(2008). *The Complete Poems and Plays of Fulke Greville, Lord Brooke* (1554–1628). ed. G. A. Wilkes 2 vols., Lewiston, vol. I, *Caelica, Mustapha, Alaham*.

Grodziecki, Adam (1634). *Przestroga o tytułach i dignitarstwach cudzozyemskich w Polskym Królestwie y państwach do niego należących*, Cracow.

Grotius, Hugo (1622). *Oratie vanden Hooch-geleerden Voortreffelycken Meester Hugo de Groot, Raet ende Pensionaris der Stadt Rotterdam, ghedaen inde vergaderinghe der 36 Raden der Stadt Amsterdam*, Enkhuizen.

(1625). *De jure belli ac pacis*, Paris.

(1868). *De iure praedae commentarius* [1603–4], ed. H. G. Hamaker, The Hague.

(1949). *Remonstrantie nopende de ordre dije in de landen van Hollandt ende Westvrieslandt dijent gestalt op de Joden* [1615], ed. J. Meijer, Amsterdam.

(1988). *Meletius de iis quae inter Christianos conveniunt epistola* [1609], ed. H. M. Posthumus Meyjes, Leiden.

(1993). *De iure belli ac pacis*, eds. B. J. A. de Kanter and Van Hettinga Tromp, Aalen.

(1995). *Ordinum Hollandiae ac Westfrisiae pietas* [1613], ed. Edwin Rabbie, Leiden, New York and Cologne.

(2001). *De imperio summarum potestatum circa sacra* [1647], ed. Harm-Jan van Dam, two vols., Leiden.

(2005). *The Rights of War and Peace*, trans. Jean Barbeyrac, ed. Richard Tuck, 3 vols., Indianapolis, IN.

(2006). *Commentary on the Law of Prize and Booty*, ed. Martine van Ittersum, Indianapolis, IN.

(2009). *Mare liberum, 1609–2009: Original Latin Text and English Translation*, ed. Robert Feenstra, Leiden.

Guarini, Battista (1818). *Trattato della politica libertà*, Venice.

Guicciardini, Francesco (1994a). *Dialogo del reggimento di Firenze*, ed. Gian Mario Anselmi and Carlo Varotti, Turin.

(1994b). *Dialogue on the Government of Florence*, ed. Alison Brown, Cambridge.

Gundulić, Ivan (1964). *Suze sina razmetnoga. Dubravka. Ferdinandu Drugomu od Toskane* (Tears of the Prodigal Son. Letter to the Ferdinand the Second of Tuscany), Zagreb.

Habib, M. and Khan, A. U. S. (n.d.). *The Political Theory of the Delhi Sultanate*, Allahabad.

Hall [of Durham], John (1651). *Grounds and Reasons of Monarchy Considered. In A Review of the Scotch Story, gathered out of their best Authours and Records*, Edinburgh.

(1653a) *A Letter written to a Gentleman in the Country, touching the Dissolution of the late Parliament and the Reasons therof*, London.

(1653b), *A Stop to the mad Multitude, Or A Seasonable Antidote Against a dangerous Cup of Poyson, Presented in a late Scandalous Pamphlet, Entituled The Grand Politique Informer. Wherein is laid open the Hellish Plots, Designs, and Machinations, which, under the Pretence of Liberty, are now carried on for the subversion of Religion, and disturbance of the Peace of this Common-wealth. By a true Lover of his Countrey*, London.

Harrington, James (1977a). *The Political Works of James Harrington*, ed. J. G. A. Pocock, Cambridge.

(1977b). *Oceana*, in *The Political Works of James Harrington*, ed. J. G. A. Pocock, Cambridge.

Hegel, G. W. F. (1952). *Briefe von und an Hegel*, ed. Johannes Hoffmeister, vol. I, Hamburg.

(1968). 'Differenz des Fichteschen und Schellingschen Systems' in *Gesammelte Werke*, vol. IV: *Jenaer kritische Schriften*, ed. Hartmut Bucher and Otto Pöggeler, Hamburg, pp. 1–92.

(1970). *Vorlesung über die Philosophie der Geschichte* in *Werke*, ed. Eva Moldenhauer *et al.*, vol. XII, Frankfurt.

(2000). *Hegel: Vorlesungen über die Philosophie des Rechts: Berlin 1819/1820*, ed. Emil Angehrn, Hamburg.

Heidenstein, Reinhold (1672). *Rerum Polonicarum ab excessu Sigismundi Augusti libri XII*, Frankfurt.

Heineccius, Johann Gottlieb (1764). *A Methodical System of Universal Law; or The Laws of Nature and Nations*, ed. and trans. George Turnbull, London.

Herburt, Stanisław (1918). *Przyczyny wypowiedzenia posłuszeństwa Zygmuntowi, królewicowi szwedzkiemu, anno 1607 die nativitatis Joannis Baptistae*, in *Pisma polityczne z czasów rokoszu Zebrzydowskiego 1606–1608*, 3 vols., ed. Jan Czubek, Cracow, vol. III, pp. 349–57.

Herder, Johann Gottfried (2002). *Philosophical Writings*, trans. Michael N. Forster, Cambridge.

Herocles (1987). 'Fragments' in *The Hellenistic Philosophers*, 2 vols., trans. A. A. Long and D. N. Sedley, Cambridge.

Hobbes, Thomas (1969), *The Elements of Law, Natural and Politic*, ed. Ferdinand Tonnies, London.

(1996). *Leviathan*, ed. Richard Tuck, revised edition, Cambridge.

(1998). *On the Citizen*, ed. Richard Tuck and and trans. Michael Silverthorne, Cambridge.

(1999). *Elements of Law, Natural and Politic: part I, Human Nature, part II, De corpore politico, with Three Lives*, ed. John C. A. Gaskin, Oxford.

(2008). *Leviathan*, ed. Richard Tuck, Cambridge.

Hooker, Richard (1888). *Of the Laws of Ecclesiastical Polity*, in *The Works of Mr. Richard Hooker*, 3 vols., arr. John Keble, rev. R. W. Church and F. Paget, Oxford.

Hotman, François (1765). *Antitribonian* [1567], Pisa.

(1972). *Francogallia* [1573], ed. Ralph Giesey and trans. J. H. M. Salmon, Cambridge.
Huber, Ulric (1708). *De jure civitatis libri tres*, Franeker.
Hufeland, Gottlieb (1790). *Lehrsätze des Naturrechts und der damit verbundenen Wissenschaften. Zu Vorlesungen von Gottlieb Hufeland, der Welt-Weisheit und Rechte Doctor und der letztern öffentlichem Lehrer auf der Universität zu Jena*, Jena.
Humboldt, Wilhelm von (1903). 'Ideen zu einem Versuch die Grenzen der Wirksamkeit des Staats zu bestimmen' in *Wilhelm von Humboldts Gesammelte Schriften*, ed. Albert Leitzmann, vol. 1, Berlin, pp. 97–254.
(1935). 'Politische Jugendbriefe Wilhelm von Humboldts an Gentz' in *Historische Zeitschrift*, ed. Albert Leitzmann, 152, pp. 48–89.
(1962). *Der Briefwechsel zwischen Friedrich Schiller und Wilhelm von Humboldt*, ed. Siegfried Seidel, vol. 1, Berlin.
(1993). *The Limits of State Action*, ed. J. W. Burrow, 2nd edn, Indianapolis, IN.
Hume, David (1875). *Essays: Moral, Political, Literary by David Hume*, London.
(1978). *A Treatise of Human Nature*, ed. L. A. Selby-Bigge, Oxford.
(1985). *Essays Moral, Political, Literary*, Indianapolis, IN.
Hurtado de Mendoza, Petrus (1624). *Universa philosophia*, Lyons.
Ibn ʿAsākir (1995–8). *Taʾrīkh madīnat Dimashq*, ed. ʿA. Shīrī, Beirut.
Ibn Hishām (1955). *al-Sīra al-nabawiyya*, ed. M. al-Saqqā *et al.*, Cairo.
(1980). *The Life of Muhammad: A Translation of Ibn Isḥāq's Sīrat Rasūl Allāh*, trans. A. Guillaume, Karachi.
Ibn ʿIdhārī (1948–51). *al-Bayān al-mughrib*, ed. G. S. Colin and É. Lévi-Provençal, Leiden.
Ibn Manẓūr (n.d.). *Lisān al-ʿArab*, Beirut.
Ibn Saʿd (1904–21). *al-Ṭabaqāt al-kabīr*, ed. E. Sachau *et al.*, Leiden.
Ibrahim, R. (ed. and trans.) (2007). *The Al Qaeda Reader*, New York.
'Illésházy István hűtlenségi pörére vonatkozó okiratok (1600–1611)' (Documents of the Impeachment of István Illésházy), *Történelmi Tár* 1882, pp. 670–96 and 1883, pp. 306–30.
Imbonati, Carlo Giuseppe (1694). *Bibliotheca latino-hebraica; sive De scriptoribus latinis, qui ex diversis nationibus contra Iudaeos, vel de re hebraica utcumque scripsere*, Rome.
Jabartī (1975). *Al-Jabartī's Chronicle of the First Seven Months of the French Occupation of Egypt*, ed. and trans. S. Moreh, Leiden.
Jacob, Henry (1599). *A Defence of the Chvrches and Ministery of England*, Middelburg.
(1606). *A Christian and Modest Offer of a Most Indifferent Conference, or Disputation, about the Maine and Principall Controversies Betwixt the Prelats, and the Late Silenced and Deprived Ministers in England*, London.
(1610). *The Divine Beginning and Institution of Christs Church*, Leiden.
(1613). *An Attestation of Many Learned, Godly, and Famous Divines, Lightes of Religion, and Pillars of the Gospell Iustifying This Doctrine, Viz. That the Church-Governement Ought to Bee Alwayes with the Peoples Free Consent: Also This; That a True Church Vnder the Gospell Contayneth No More Ordinary Congregations but One*, Middelburg.
(1616). *A Confession and Protestation of the Faith of Certaine Christians in England Holding it Necessary to Observe, & Keepe All Christes True Substantiall Ordinances for His Church Visible and Politicall (That Is, Indued with Power of Outward Spirituall Government) under the Gospel*, Amsterdam.
Jāḥiẓ (1948–50). *al-Bayān wa'l-tabyīn*, ed. ʿA. M. Hārūn, Cairo.

Januszowski, Jan (1921). *Zwierciadło królewskie z roku 1606*, in *Sześć broszur politycznych z XVI i początku XVII stulecia*, ed. Bronisław Ulanowski, Cracow, pp. 213–80.
Kahl, Johann (1683). *Magnum lexicon juridicum*, Geneva.
Kant, Immanuel (1907a). *Die Metaphysik der Sitten*, in *Kant's gesammelte Schriften*, vol. VI, herausgegeben von der Königlich Preußischen Akademie der Wissenschaften, Berlin.
(1907b). *Der Streit der Fakultäten*, in *Kant's gesammelte Schriften*, vol. VII, herausgegeben von der Königlich Preußischen Akademie der Wissenschaften, Berlin.
(1911). *Grundlegung zur Metaphysik der Sitten*, in *Kant's gesammelte Schriften*, vol. IV, herausgegeben von der Königlich Preußischen Akademie der Wissenschaften, Berlin.
(1912a). 'Beantwortung der Frage: Was ist Aufklärung?', *Akademie-Textausgabe*, vol. VIII, Berlin, pp. 33–42.
(1912b). 'Über den Gemeinspruch: Das mag in der Theorie richtig sein, taugt aber nicht für die Praxis' in *Akademie-Textausgabe*, vol. VIII, Berlin, pp. 273–313.
(1912c). 'Über die Buchmacherei. Zwei Briefe an Herrn Friedrich Nicolai' in *Kant's gesammelte Schriften*, vol. VIII, herausgegeben von der Königlich Preußischen Akademie der Wissenschaften, Berlin.
(1912d). *Zum ewigen Frieden*, in *Kant's gesammelte Schriften*, vol. VIII, herausgegeben von der Königlich Preußischen Akademie der Wissenschaften, Berlin.
(1913). *Kritik der Urteilskraft*, in *Kant's gesammelte Schriften*, vol. V, herausgegeben von der Königlich Preußischen Akademie der Wissenschaften, Berlin.
(1922a). *Briefwechsel*, in *Kant's gesammelte Schriften*, vol. X, herausgegeben von der Königlich Preußischen Akademie der Wissenschaften, Berlin.
(1922b). *Briefwechsel*, in *Kant's gesammelte Schriften*, vol. XI, herausgegeben von der Königlich Preußischen Akademie der Wissenschaften, Berlin.
(1923). *Reflexionen zur Anthropologie*, in *Kant's gesammelte Schriften*, vol. XV.1, herausgegeben von der Königlich Preußischen Akademie der Wissenschaften, Berlin.
(1934). 'Moralphilosophie, Rechtsphilosophie und Religionsphilosophie' in *Kant's gesammelte Schriften*, vol. XIX. Berlin.
(1970). *Kant: Political Writings*, ed. Hans Reiss, trans. H. B. Nisbet, Cambridge.
(1996). *Immanuel Kant: Practical Philosophy*, ed. Mary J. Gregor, Cambridge.
(1999). *Immanuel Kant: Correspondence*, ed. Arnulf Zweig, Cambridge.
(2000). *Critique of the Power of Judgment*, ed. Paul Guyer, trans. Paul Guyer and Eric Matthews, Cambridge.
(2006). *Anthropology from a Pragmatic Point of View*, ed. R. B. Louden and M. Kuehn, Cambridge.
Kauṭilya (1919). *Kauṭilīyam Arthaśāstram*, ed. R. Shama Sastri, Mysore.
(1951). *Kauṭilya's Arthaśāstra*, trans. R. Shamasastry, Mysore.
Kern, Fritz (1911). *Acta imperii Angliae et Franciae ab anno 1267 ad annum 1313*, Tübingen.
Khayr al-Dīn al-Tūnisī (1967). *The Surest Path*, trans. L. C. Brown, Cambridge, MA.
(1990–1). *Aqwam al-masālik fī maʿrifat aḥwāl al-mamālik*, ed. M. Chenoufi, Tunis.
King James VI and I (1994). *Political Writings*, ed. Johann P. Sommerville, Cambridge.

Klonowic, Sebastian (1595). *Victoria deorum in qua continentur veri Herois educatio*, Cracow.
Knox, John (1994). *On Rebellion*, ed. Roger A. Mason, Cambridge.
Krasiński, Jan (1574). *Polonia ad serenissimum et potentissimum Henricum Primum Valesium Dei gratia utriusque Poloniae regem*, Bologna.
Kromer, Marcin (1901). *Polonia sive de situ, populis, moribus, magistratibus et Republica regni Polonici libri duo* [1578], ed. Wiktor Czermak, Cracow.
Kuczborski, Walenty (1921). *Przestroga dla króla Zygmunta z roku 1569*, in *Sześć broszur politycznych z XVI i początku XVII stulecia*, ed. Bronisław Ulanowski, Cracow, pp. 36–87.
Kurelac, Fran (1868). *Runje i pahuljice pjesni podrugljive i pastirske ponajveć dubrovačke* (Rags and Snowflakes: Satirical Poems, mostly from Ragusa), Zagreb.
Kutb, Sayyid (2005). *Milestones*, New Delhi (translation of Quṭb 1973).
Lalemant, Jérôme (1647). *Relation de ce qui s'est passé de plus remarquable és missions des pères de la Compagnie de Jésus, en la Nouvelle France, és années 1645 & 1646 envoyée au R.P. provincial de la province de France par le supérieur des missions de la mesme compagnie*, Paris.
(1649). *Relation de ce qui s'est passé de plus remarquable és missions des pères de la Compagnie de Jésus, en la Nouvelle France, es années 1647. & 1648 envoyée au R.P. provincial de la province de France par le supérieur des missions de la mesme compagnie*, Paris.
Landulfus Senior (1848). 'Historia Mediolanensis' in *Monumenta Germaniae Historiae, Scriptores*, vol. VIII, ed. L. C. Bethmann and W. Wattenbach, Hanover, pp. 32–100.
Latini, Brunetto (1863). *Li Livres dou Tresor*, ed. P. Chabaille, Paris.
Lawrence, B. (ed.) (2005). *Messages to the world: the statements of Osama Bin Laden*, London and New York.
Le Jeune, Paul (1634). *Relation de ce qui s'est passé en la Nouvelle France, en l'année 1633 envoyée au R.P. Barth. Iacquinot, provincial de la Compagnie de Jésus en la province de France par le P. Paul Le Jeune de la mesme compagnie, supérieur de la résidence de Kébec*, Paris.
(1635). *Relation de ce qui s'est passé en la Nouvelle France, en l'année 1634 envoyée au R. Père provincial de la Compagnie de Jésus, en la province de France par le P. Paul Le Jeune de la mesme compagnie, supérieur de la résidence de Kébec*, Paris.
(1637). *Relation de ce qui s'est passé en la Nouvelle France en l'année 1636 envoyée au R. Père provincial de la Compagnie de Jésus en la province de France*, Paris.
(1638). *Relation de ce qui s'est passé en la Nouvelle France en l'année 1637 envoyée au R. Père provincial de la Compagnie de Jésus en la province de France*, Rouen.
(1640). *Relation de ce qui s'est passé en la Nouvelle France en l'année 1639 envoyée au R. Père provincial de la Compagnie de Jésus en la province de France*, Paris.
(1662). *Relation de ce qui s'est passé de plus remarquable aux missions des pères de la Compagnie de Jésus, en la Nouvelle France, és années 1660 & 1661 envoyée au R.P. provincial de la province de France*, Paris.
Le Mercier, François (1667). *Relation de ce qui s'est passé de plus remarquable aux missions des pères de la Compagnie de Jésus, en la Nouvelle France, aux années mil six cent soixante cinq & mil six cent soixante six envoyée au R.P. Jacques Bordier, provincial de la province de France*, Paris.

(1669). *Relation de ce qui s'est passé de plus remarquable aux missions des pères de la Compagnie de Jésus, en la Nouvelle France, aux années mil six cens soixante-sept & mil six cens soixante-huit envoyée au R.P. Estienne Dechamps, provincial de la province de France*, Paris.

Le Petit, Jean François (1615). *Nederlantsche Republycke, bestaende inde Staten so generale, als particuliere ... geconfereert ende vergeleken met die van de Swytsersche Cantoenen ...*, Arnheim.

Leibniz, Gottfried Wilhelm (1712). *Essais de theodicée sur la bonté de dieu, la liberté de l'homme et l'origine du mal*, 2nd edn, Amsterdam.

(1963). *Politische Schriften 1677–1687*, in *Sämtliche Schriften und Briefe*, vol. IV, Berlin.

(1988). *Political Writings*, trans. Patrick Riley, Cambridge.

Lescarbot, Marc (1610). *Conversion des Sauvages*, Paris.

Leschassier, Jacques (1607). *Consulta di un Dottore Parigino intorno la controversia tra la Santità di Paolo Quinto et la Serenissima Republica Veneta. Ad un Gentilhuomo Venetiano*, Padua.

Levellers (2003). *The Levellers: Overton, Walwyn and Lilburne*, ed. James Ottenson, 5 vols., Bristol.

Liepopili, Ante (1929). 'Dopisi Marojice Kaboge vladi dubrovačkoj' (Letters of Marojica Caboga to the Ragusan Government), *Glasnik dubrovačkog učenog društva 'Sveti Vlaho'* vol. I, pp. 125–46.

Lightfoot, John (1700). *Some Genuine Remains of the Late Pious and Learned John Lightfoot, D.D.*, ed. John Strype, London.

(1824). *Journal of the Proceedings of the Assembly of Divines*, in *The Whole Works of Rev John Lightfoot*, 13 vols., ed. John Rogers Pitman, London.

Lilburne, John (1659). *Lilburne's Ghost*, London.

Lipsius, Justus (1595). *Two Bookes of Constancie, Writen in English by Justus Lipsius. Containing, principallie, a comfortable conference in common calamities ...*, trans. John Stradling, London.

(1604a). *Physiologiae Stoicorum libri tres: L. Annaeo Senecae, aliisque scriptoribus illustrandis*, Antwerp.

(1604b). *Manuductionis ad Stoicam philosophiam libri tres: L. Aenneo Senecae allisque scriptoribus illustrandis*, Antwerp.

Livy (1971). *The Early History of Rome: Books I–V of The History of Rome from Its Foundation*, trans. A. de Sélincourt, London.

(1987). *Titi Livi ab urbe condita*, ed. R. M. Ogilvie *et al.*, Oxford.

Lloyd, David (1668). *Memoires of the lives, actions, sufferings & deaths of those noble, reverend and excellent personages*, London.

Locke, John (1954). *Essays on the Law of Nature*, ed. W. von Leyden, Oxford.

(1967). *Two Tracts on Government*, ed. Philip Abrams, Cambridge.

(1968). *Epistola de tolerantia/A Letter on Toleration*, ed. Raymond Klibansky, trans. J. W. Gough, Oxford.

(1975). *An Essay Concerning Human Understanding*, ed. Peter H. Nidditch, Oxford.

(1976–89). *The Correspondence of John Locke*, ed. Esmond de Beer, 8 vols., Oxford.

(1988). *Two Treatises of Government*, ed. Peter Laslett, Cambridge.

(1989). *Some Thoughts Concerning Education*, ed. John W. and Jean S. Yolton, Oxford.

(1997). *Political Essays*, ed. Mark Goldie, Cambridge.

(1999). *The Reasonableness of Christianity*, ed. John C. Higgins-Biddle, Oxford.
(2002). *Writings on Religion*, ed. Victor Nuovo, Oxford.
London Corresponding Society (2002). *London Corresponding Society (1792–1799)*, ed. Michael T. Davis, London.
Luccari, Giacomo (1605). *Copioso ristretto degli annali di Rausa*, Venice.
Lucretius (1975). *De rerum natura*, trans. W. H. D. Rouse, ed. Martin Ferguson Smith, Cambridge, MA.
Lugo, Juan de (1633). *De incarnatione*, Lyons.
(1646). *Disputationes de iustitia et iure tomus primus*, Lyons.
Lupold von Bebenburg [Lupoldus] (1508). *De iuribus et translatione imperii*, Strasburg.
(1624). *Tractatus de juribus regni et imperii Romanorum*, Strasburg.
Luther, Martin (1883–2009). *Werke*, Weimar.
Lyall, C. J. (ed.) (1894). *A Commentary on Ten Ancient Arabic Poems*, Calcutta.
Macaulay, Catherine (1775). *An Address to the People of England, Scotland and Ireland . . .*, Bath.
Machiavelli, Niccolò (1958). *The Chief Works and Others*, 3 vols., trans. Allan Gilbert, Durham, NC and London.
(1971). *Tutte le opere*, ed. Mario Martelli, Florence.
(1988). *The Prince*, ed. Quentin Skinner and Russell Price, Cambridge.
(2001). *Discorsi sopra la prima deca di Tito Livio*, 2 vols., ed. Francesco Bausi, Rome.
(2003). *Discourses on Livy*, trans. Julia Conaway Bondanella and Peter Bondanella, Oxford.
(2006). *Il principe*, ed. Mario Martelli and Nicoletta Marcelli, Rome.
Madariaga, Juan de (1617). *Del Senado y de su Principe*, Valencia, 1617.
Madelung, W. (ed.) (1987). *Arabic Texts concerning the History of the Zaydī Imāms of Ṭabaristān, Daylamān and Gīlān*, Beirut.
Małecki, Antoni (ed.) (1860). *Wybór mów staropolskich świeckich sejmowych i innych*, Cracow.
al-Manūfī, Abū ʾl-Ḥasan ʿAlī (1938). *Kifāyat al-ṭālib al-rabbānī* in the margin of ʿAlī al-Ṣaʿīdī al-ʿAdawī, *Ḥāshiya ʿalā Kifāyat al-ṭālib al-rabbānī*, Cairo.
Mariscotti, Agesilao (1607). *Aviso sicuro contro il mal fondato aviso del Signor Antonio Quirino Senator Veneto*, Bologna.
Marnix van St. Aldegonde, Philips van (1871). 'Advys aengaende den twist in de Nederduytsche kercke tot London in Engellandt' [1568] in *Philips van Marnix van St. Aldegonde*, ed. J. J. van Toorenenbergen, vol. 1, The Hague, pp. 135–82.
Marshall, Stephen (1641). *A Peace Offering to God*, London.
(1642). *A Plea for Defensive Arms*, London.
Marsilius of Padua (2005). *The Defender of the Peace*, trans. A. Brett, Cambridge.
Maudūdī, Abul Aʿlā (1960a). 'First Principles of the Islamic State' in his *The Islamic Law and Constitution*, ed. and trans. K. Ahmad, Lahore, pp. 217–70.
(1960b). 'Political concepts of the Qurʾan' in his *The Islamic Law and Constitution*, ed. and trans. K. Ahmad, Lahore, pp. 165–213.
(1960c). 'Fundamentals of Islamic Constitution' in his *The Islamic Law and Constitution*, ed. and trans. K. Ahmad, Lahore, pp. 273–91.
(1963). *A Short History of the Revivalist Movement in Islam*, trans. Al-Ashʿari, Lahore.
(1967). *Unity of the Muslim World*, ed. K. Ahmad, Lahore.

(1975). *Fundamentals of Islam*, Lahore.
(1976). *Political Theory of Islam*, trans. K. Ahmad, Lahore.
Mawdūdī (n.d.d). *Bayn al-daʿwa al-qawmiyya wa'l-rābiṭa al-Islāmiyya*, Cairo.
Mawdūdī, Abū 'l-Aʿlā (1952). *Islām kā naẓariyya-i siyāsī*, Lahore.
(1955). *al-Islām wa'l-Jāhiliyya*, trans. Masʿūd al-Nadwī, Tripoli.
(1977). *al-Ḥukūma al-Islāmiyya*, trans. A. Idrīs, Cairo.
(n.d.a). *al-Jihād fī sabīl Allāh*, Lebanon.
Mawdudi, Abul A'la (1989). *Islam Today*, Delhi.
(n.d.c). *Human Rights in Islam*, Delhi.
Mawdūdī, al-Ustādh al- (n.d.b). *Naẓariyyat al-Islām al-siyāsiyya*, Jullundur.
Melanchthon, Philip (1834–60). *Philippi Melanthonis Opera quae supersunt omnia*, ed. Karl Bretschneider and Heinrich Bindseil, 28 vols., Halle.
Memorialia (1909–11). 'Memorialia et disquisitiones imperatori vel papae tradita' in *Monumenta Germaniae Historica, Constitutiones*, vol. IV.2, ed. J. Schwalm, pp. 1308–98.
Mendelssohn, Moses (1929–). *Gesammelte Schriften – Jubiläumsausgabe*, ed. F. Bamberger, H. Borodianski, B. Rawidowicz, B. Strauss, L. Strauss *et al.*, Berlin and Stuttgart-Bad Canstatt.
(1930). *Gesammelte Schriften, Jubiläumsausgabe*, ed. I. Elbogen, J. Guttmann and E. Mittwoch, Berlin.
(1983). *Jerusalem, or on Religious Power and Judaism*, trans. Allan Arkush, ed. Alexander Altmann, Hanover, NH.
Mikó, Imre (ed.) (1855–62). *Erdélyi Történelmi Adatok* (ETA) [Transylvanian Historical Data], 4 vols.
Mill, John Stuart (1989a). *On Liberty and Other Writings*, ed. S Collini, Cambridge.
(1989b). *The Subjection of Women*, in *On Liberty and Other Writings*, ed. Stefan Collini, Cambridge, pp. 117–218.
Milton, John (1644). *Areopagitica, or a Speech of Mr John Milton*, London.
(1931–8). *The Works of John Milton*, 18 vols., ed. F. A. Patterson, New York.
(1953–82a). *Eikonoklastes*, in *Complete Prose Works of John Milton*, 8 vols., vol. III, New Haven and London, pp. 337–601.
(1953–82b). *The Complete Prose Works of John Milton*, 8 vols. in 10, ed. Don M. Wolfe *et al.*, New Haven, CT.
(2007). *Paradise Lost*, 2nd rev. edn, ed. Alastair Fowler, London.
Modrzewski, Andrzej Frycz (1953). *Commentariorum de Republica emendada libri quinque* [1554], in Modrzewski, *Opera omnia*, 5 vols., vol. I, ed. Kazimierz Kumaniecki, Warsaw.
MOE (1874–1917). *Monumenta comitialia regni Hungariae/Magyar Országgyűlési Emlékek történeti bevezetésekkel [Documents of the Hungarian Diets with Historical Introductions]*, 12 vols. (1526–1606), ed. Vilmos Fraknói and Árpád Károlyi, Budapest.
Molina, Luis de (1614). *De iustitia et iure*, Antwerp.
Montaigne, Michel de (1958). *The Complete Essays of Montaigne*, ed. and trans. Donald Frame, Stanford, CA.
(1962). *Œuvres complètes*, ed. Maurice Rat, Paris.
(2007). *Les essais*, ed. Jean Balsamo, Michel Magnien and Catherine Magnien-Simonin, Paris.

Montesquieu, Charles Louis de Secondat (1989). *The Spirit of the Laws*, trans. and ed. Anne Cohler, Basia Carolyn Miller and Harold Samuel Stone, Cambridge.
More, Thomas (2002). *Utopia*, ed. George M. Logan and Robert M. Adams, Cambridge.
Morton, Thomas (1619). *A Defence of the Innocencie of the Three Ceremonies of the Church of England*, London.
Möser, Justus (1798). 'Über die Erblichkeit des Herrenstandes bei gewissen Familien in einem monarchischen Staate', *Berlinische Blätter*, pp. 116–25.
(1944). 'Der Begriff "Freiheit"' in *Sämtliche Werke*, Historisch-kritische Ausgabe, vol. VIII, Oldenburg.
(1965). 'Über das Recht der Menschheit, in so fern es zur Grundlage eines Staates dienen kann' in *Deutsches Staatsdenken im 18. Jahrhundert*, ed. Georg Lenz, Berlin.
Mufaḍḍal ibn ʿUmar al-Juʿfī (attrib.) (1960). *al-Haft wa'l-aẓilla*, Beirut.
Muṣʿab al-Zubayrī (1976). *Nasab Quraysh*, ed. E. Lévi-Provençal, Cairo.
Nadolski, Bronisław (ed.) (1961). *Wybór mów staropolskich*, Wrocław.
Nagel, Thomas (1991). *Equality and Partiality*, New York.
Nawawī (1988). *al-Tarkhīṣ fī 'l-ikrām bi'l-qiyām*, ed. K. M. Khalīfa, Beirut.
Neville, Henry (1647). *The Parliament of Ladies*, London.
Nodilo, Natko (ed.) (1883). *Annales Ragusini Anonymi item Nicolai de Ragnina*, Zagreb.
(ed.) (1893). *Chronica Ragusina Junii Restii item Joannis Gundulae (1451–1484)*, Zagreb.
Noorduyn, J. (1955). *Een achttiende-eeuwse kroniek van Wadjo'*, The Hague.
Oldfield, T. B. (1792). *An Entire and Complete History, political and personal of the Boroughs of Great Britain*, vol. I, London.
Orzechowski, Stanisław (1632). *Fidelis subditus sive de institutione regia ad Sigismundum Augustum libri duo* [1543], Cracow.
(1855). *Żywot i śmierć Jana Tarnowskiego, kasztelana krakowskiego i hetmana wielkiego koronnego* [1561], ed. Kazimierz Turowski, Sanok.
(1972a). *Dyalog albo rozmowa około egzekucyjej Korony Polskiej* [1563], in Orzechowski, *Wybór pism*, ed. Jerzy Starnawski, Wrocław, pp. 304–457.
(1972b). *Quincunx, to jest wzór Korony Polskiej na cynku wystawiony* [1564], in Orzechowski, *Wybór pism*, ed. Jerzy Starnawski, Wrocław, pp. 458–619.
(1984). *Policyja Królestwa Polskiego na kształt Arystotelesowych Polityk wypisana na świat dla dobra pospolitego trzema knihami wydana*, ed. Jerzy Starnawski, Przemyśl.
Orzelski, Świętosław (1856). *Mowy i pisma*, in Orzelski, *Bezkrólewia ksiąg ośmioro, czyli, Dzieje Polski od zgonu Zygmunta Augusta r. 1572 aż do r. 1576*, 4 vols., ed. Włodzimierz Spasowicz, vol. I, St Petersburg.
Otto of Freising (1912). 'Gesta Friderici imperatoris' in *Monumenta Germaniae Historica, Scriptores Rerum Germanicarum*, vol. XLVI, ed. G. Waitz, Hanover, pp. 1–161.
Ovalle, Alonso de (1646). *Historica Relacion del Reyno de Chile y de las misiones y ministerios que exercita en la Compañia de Jesus*, Rome.
Padrin, Luigi (1887). *Lupati de Lupatis, Bovetini de Bovetinis, Albertini Mussati necnon Iamboni Andreae de Fava Fuschis carmina quaedam ex codice veneto nunc primum edita*, Padua.
Paget, John (1641). *A Defence of Chvrch-Government, Exercised in Presbyteriall, Classicall, & Synodall Assemblies*, London.

Paine, Thomas (1945). 'First Principles of Government' [1795] in *Complete Writings of Thomas Paine*, ed. Phillip Foner, New York.
(1969). *The Rights of Man*, London.
(1989). 'The Rights of Man Part I [1791–2]' in *Political Writings*, ed. Bruce Kuklick, Cambridge.
Palafox y Mendoza, Juan de (1893). *Virtudes del Indio* [1650], Madrid.
Palmer, Herbert (1643). *Scripture and Reason Pleaded for Defensive Armes*, London.
Palmieri, Matteo (1982). *Della vita civile*, ed. Gino Belloni, Florence.
Palmotić, Jaketa (1878). *Dubrovnik ponovljen i Didone* (Ragusa Reborn and Didone), Dubrovnik.
Palmotić, Junije (1995). *Pavlimir*, Zagreb.
Parker, Henry (1642). *Observations upon Some of His Majesties Late Answers and Expresses*, London.
[Pastorius, Joachim] (1666). 'Vita Joannis Crellii Franci' prefixed to Johan Crell, *Opera omnia exegetica*, [Amsterdam].
Pascal, Blaise (1963). *Œuvres complètes*, ed. Louis Lafuma, Paris.
Peña Montenegro, Alonso de la (1726). *Itinerario para parochos de indios: en que se tratan las materias mas particulares, tocantes à ellos, para su buena administracion* [1668], Amberes.
Perkins, William (1598). *De Praedestinatonis modo et ordine et de amplitudine gratiae divinae Christiana et perspicua disceptatio*, Cambridge.
(1606). *The whole treatise of the cases of conscience distinguished into three bookes: the first whereof is revised and corrected in sundrie places, and the other two annexed. Taught and deliuered by M. W. Perkins in his holy-day lectures, carefully examined by his owne briefes, and now published together for the common good, by T. Pickering Bachelour of Diuinitie...*, Cambridge.
Petrarca, Francesco (1933–42). *Le familiari*, 4 vols., ed. Vittorio Rossi, Florence.
Petrycy, Sebastian (1956a). *Przydatki do Etyki Arystotelesowej* [1618], in Petrycy, *Pisma wybrane*, 2 vols., ed. Wiktor Wąsik, vol. I, Cracow.
(1956b). *Przydatki do Ekonomiki i Polityki Arystotelesowej* [1618], in Petrycy, *Pisma wybrane*, 2 vols., ed. Wiktor Wąsik, vol. II, Cracow.
Pithou, Pierre (1594). *Les Libertez de l'Eglise Gallicane*, Paris.
Plutarch (1959). *Moralia*, vol. VII, trans. P. H. De Lacy and B. Einarson, Cambridge, MA.
Polyander, Johannes, Rivetus, Andreas, Walaeus, Antonius and Thysius, Antonius (1964). *Synopsis of Overzicht van de Zuiverste Theologie* [1625], 2 vols., ed. H. Bavinck, Enschede.
Ponet, John (1556). *A shorte treatise of politike pouuer: and of the true obedience which subjectes owe to kynges and other ciuile gouernours*, Strasbourg.
Possevino, Antonio (1606). *Risposta di Teodoro Eugenio di Famagosta all'aviso mandato fuori dal Sig. Antonio Quirino Senatore Veneto*, Bologna.
Poulain de la Barre, François (1984). *De l'égalité des deux sexes*, Paris.
(2002). *Three Cartesian Feminist Treatises*, trans. Vivien Bosley, ed. Marcelle Maistre Welch, Chicago, IL.
Powicke, F. J. (ed.) (1931). 'Some Unpublished Correspondence of the Rev. Richard Baxter and the Rev. John Eliot, "the Apostle to the American Indians",

1656–1682', *Bulletin of the John Rylands University Library* 15, pp. 138–76 and 442–66.

Price, Richard (1991). 'Observations on the Nature of Civil Liberty, the Principles of Government, and the Justice and Policy of the War with America' in *Political Writings*, ed. D. O. Thomas, Cambridge, pp. 20–75.

Prynne, William (1647). *The Sword of Christian Magistracy Supported*, London.

Ptolemy of Lucca (1997). *On the Government of Rulers: De Regimine Principum*, trans. J. Blythe, Philadelphia, PA.

Pufendorf, Samuel (1703). *Of the Law of Nature and Nations*, trans. Basil Kennett, Oxford.

(1991). *On the Duty of Man and Citizens According to Natural Law*, ed. James Tully, trans. Michael Silverthorne, Cambridge.

(2007). *On the Present State of Germany* [*De statu imperii*, 1669], ed. Michael Seidler, Indianapolis, IN.

Qushayrī (1966). *Risāla*, ed. ʿA. Maḥmūd and M. Ibn al-Sharīf, Cairo.

(1989). *Das Sendschreiben al-Qušayrīs über das Sufitum*, trans. R. Gramlich, Wiesbaden.

(2007). *Al-Qushayri's Epistle on Sufism*, trans. A. D. Knysh, Reading.

Quṭb, Sayyid (1952). *Maʿrakat al-Islām wa'l-ra'simāliyya*, Cairo.

(1953). *Dirāsāt Islāmiyya*, Damascus and Cairo.

(1962). *Khaṣāʾiṣ al-taṣawwur al-Islāmī wa-muqawwimātuhu*, part 1, Cairo.

(1973). *Maʿālim fī 'l-ṭarīq*, n.p. (trans. as Kutb 2005).

(1986). *Fī ẓilāl al-Qur'ān*, Beirut and Cairo.

(1988). *Islam – The True Religion*, trans. R. A. Fidai, Karachi.

(1996). See under Shepard, *Sayyid Qutb and Islamic Activism.*

(2003). See under Carré, *Mysticism and Politics.*

(2006). *Basic Principles of the Islamic Worldview*, trans. R. David, North Haledon.

(n.d.a). *al-ʿAdāla al-ijtimāʿiyya fī 'l-Islām*, Cairo.

(n.d.b). *Hādhā 'l-dīn*, n.p.

Radawiecki, Andrzej (1614). *Prawy szlachcic w kazaniu na pogrzebie . . . Andrzeia ze Żmigroda Stadnickiego ukazany*, Cracow.

Radonić, Jovan (ed.) (1934). *Dubrovačka akta i povelje* (Ragusan Acts and Charters), book I/tomus 1, Belgrade.

(ed.) (1935). *Dubrovačka akta i povelje* (Ragusan Acts and Charters), book II/tomus 1, Belgrade.

(ed.) (1939). *Dubrovačka akta i povelje* (Ragusan Acts and Charters), book III/tomus 1, Belgrade.

Ragueneau, Paul (1651). *Relation de ce qui s'est passé en la mission des pères de la Compagnie de Jésus, aux Hursos & aux paèis plus bas de la Nouvelle France, depuis l'esté de l'année 1649 jusques à l'esté de l'année 1650 envoyée au R.P. Claude de Lingendes, provincial de la Compagnie de Jésus en la province de France*, Paris.

Rangerius (1934). 'Vita Anselmi Lucensis episcopi auctore Rangerio Lucensi' in *Monumenta Germaniae Historiae, Scriptores*, 30.2, ed. E. Sackur, G. Schwartz and B. Schmeidler, Hanover, pp. 1152–1307.

Rawls, John (1971). *A Theory of Justice*, Oxford.

(1993). *Political Liberalism*, New York.

(1999). *Collected Papers*, ed. Samuel Freeman, Cambridge, MA.
(2009). *A Brief Inquiry into the Meaning of Sin and Faith; with 'On My Religion'*, ed. Thomas Nagel, Cambridge, MA.
Razzi, Serafino (1595). *La storia di Raugia*, Lucca.
Register of Gregory VII (2002). *The Register of Pope Gregory VII, 1073–1085: An English Translation*, trans. H. E. J. Cowdrey, Oxford.
[Rehberg, August Wilhelm] (1791). [review] 'Rights of Man. Being an Answer to Mr. Burke's Attack on the French Revolution; by Thomas Payne, Secretary for Foreign Affairs to Congress in the American War, and Author of the Work intitled: Common Sense', *Allgemeine Literatur-Zeitung* 243, pp. 513–18.
(1793). *Untersuchungen über die Französische Revolution: Nebst kritischen Nachrichten von den merkwürdigsten Schriften welche darüber in Frankreich erschienen sind*, 2 vols., Hanover and Osnabrück.
(1967). 'Über das Verhältniβ der Theorie zur Praxis' in D. Henrich, *Kant, Gentz, Rehberg: Über Theorie und Praxis*, ed. Frankfurt am Main.
(1975). 'Rezension der Kritik der praktischen Vernunft' in *Rehbergs Opposition gegen Kants Ethik*, ed. E. G. Schulz, Cologne.
[Reinhold, Karl Leonhard] (1794). [review] 'Beytrag zur Berichtigung der Urtheile des Publicums über die französische Revolution. Erster Theil. Zur Beurtheilung ihrer Rechtmäßigkeit etc. (Beschluß der im vorigen Stücke abgebrochnen Recension)', *Allgemeine Literatur-Zeitung*, 154, pp. 353–60.
Reinkingk, Theodor Dietrich (1659). *Tractatus de regime seculari et ecclesiastico*, Frankfurt am Main.
Ricaut, Paul (1688). *The present State of the Ottoman Empire, in three books containing the Maxims of the Turkish Politic, their Religion, and Military Discipline*, London.
Richer, Edmond (1612). *A Treatise of Ecclesiasticall and Politike Power*, London.
Rinuccini, Alamanno (1957). 'Dialogus de libertate' in *Atti e memorie dell'Accademia Toscana di scienze e lettere la Colombaria*, vol. 22, ed. F. Adorno, pp. 265–304.
(2003). *Dialogus de libertate*, ed. Giuseppe Civati, Monza.
Robinson, Henry (1644a). *Liberty of Conscience*, London.
(1644b). *John the Baptist, Forerunner of Christ Jesus, or A Necessitie for Liberty of Conscience*, London.
Robinson, John (1610). *A Iustification of Separation from the Church of England*, Amsterdam.
Rosa, Martinus (1638). *Breve compendium nationis gloriosae totivs linguae Illyricae; in quo breviter origo ipsius Nationis ostenditur, extensio eius copiosa; Reges fidei Catholicae totius Dalmatiae, Bosnae, Seruiae, aque Rassiae, quos habuit: in fine vero sub umbra Aquilae magnarum alarum Respublica Ragusina feliciter quomodo moratur*, Madrid.
Rossi, Luigi (1898). *Dagli scritti inediti giuridico-politici di Giovanni da Legnano*, Bologna.
Rott, Jean (ed.) (1979). *Correspondance de Martin Bucer*, tome 1: *Jusqu'en 1524*, Leiden.
Rousseau, Jean-Jacques (1756). *Abhandlung von dem Ursprunge der Ungleichheit unter den Menschen und worauf sie sich gründe, ins Deutsche übersetzt mit einem Schreiben an den Herrn Magister Lessing und einem Briefe Voltairens an den Verfasser vermehret*, trans. Moses Mendelssohn, Berlin.
(1915). *The Political Writings of Jean Jacques Rousseau: Edited from the Original Manuscripts and Authentic Editions*, in 2 vols., ed. C. E. Vaughn, Cambridge.

(1966). *Two Essays on the Origin of Language: Jean-Jacques Rousseau and Johann Gottfried Herder*, trans. John H. Moran and Alexander Gode, Chicago, IL.
(1990). *Reading Rousseau in the Nuclear Age*, ed. Grace G. Roosevelt, Philadelphia, PA.
(1991a). 'Jugement sur le projet de paix perpétuelle' in *Œuvres complètes*, vol. 3, ed. Bernard Gagnebin and Marcel Raymond, Paris, pp. 591–600.
(1991b). *Rousseau on International Relations*, ed. Stanley Hoffman and David Fidler, Oxford.
(1997a). *'The Social Contract' and Other Later Political Writings*, ed. Victor Gourevitch, Cambridge.
(1997b). *The Discourses and Other Early Political Writings*, ed. Victor Gourevitch, Cambridge.
Rutherford, Samuel (1649). *A Free Disputation against Pretended Liberty of Conscience*, London.
Ṣafwat, Aḥmad Zakī (1937). *Jamharat rasāʾil al-ʿArab fī ʿuṣūr al-ʿArabiyya al-zāhira*, Cairo.
Saʿīd ibn Manṣūr (1967). *Sunan*, ed. Ḥ. al-Aʿẓamī, Malegaon.
Sallust (1920). *Sallust*, ed. and trans. J. C. Rolfe, London.
Sanderson, Robert (1661). 'The Preface to the Reader' in James Ussher, *The Power Communicated by God to the Prince, and the Obedience required of the Subject*, London.
(1689). *XXXVI Sermons*, London.
(1851). *De obligatione conscientiae praelectiones decem Oxonii in schola theologica habitae anno domini M. DC. XLVII*, ed. William Whewell, Cambridge.
Sardi, Simone (1606). *Due discorsi sopra la libertà ecclesiastica*, s.l.
Sarpi, Paolo (1940). *Istoria dell' interdetto e altri scritti editi e inediti*, ed. M. D. Busnelli and G. Gambarin, 3 vols., Bari.
(1958). *Scritti giurisdizionalistici*, ed. G. Gambarin, Bari.
(1961). *Lettere ai Gallicani*, ed. Boris Ulianich, Wiesbaden.
(1968). *Scritti scelti*, ed. Giovanni da Pozzo, Turin.
(1974). *Istoria del concilio Tridentino*, ed. Corrado Vivanti, 2 vols., Turin.
Schaff, Philip (ed.) (1877). *The Creeds of the Evangelical Protestant Churches*, London.
Schiller, Friedrich (1962). 'Ueber die ästhetische Erziehung des Menschen in einer Reihe von Briefen' in *Schillers Werke: Nationalausgabe*, vol. xx: *Philosophische Schriften Teil 1*, ed. Benno von Wiese and Helmut Koopmann, Weimar, pp. 309–412.
(1967 and 1982). *On the Aesthetic Education of Man in a Series of Letters*, ed. Elizabeth M. Wilkinson and L. A. Willoughby, Oxford.
(1970). 'Die Gesetzgebung des Lykurgus und Solon' in *Schillers Werke: Nationalausgabe*, vol. XVII: *Historische Schriften*, ed. Karl-Heinz Hahn, Weimar, pp. 414–44.
(1992). *Schillers Werke: Nationalausgabe*, vol. 26: *Briefwechsel. Schillers Briefe, 1.3.1790–17.5.1794*, ed. Edith Nahler and Horst Nahler, Weimar.
Schlegel, Friedrich (1967). *Kritische Ausgabe*, vol. I: *Charakteristiken und Kritiken I (1796–1801)*, ed. Hans Eichner, Munich, Paderborn and Vienna.
Schmitt, Carl (2008). *The Leviathan in the State Theory of Thomas Hobbes: Meaning and Failure of a Political Symbol*, trans. George Schwab and Erna Hilfstein, Chicago, IL.
Selden, John (1618). *The Historie of Tithes That is, The Practice of Payment of them, The Positiue Laws made for them, The Opinions touching the Right of them*, London.
(1640). *De iure naturali & gentium, iuxta disciplinam Ebraeorum*, London.

(1653). *De synedriis & praefecturis iuridicis veterum Ebraeorum liber*, vol. II, London.
(1726). *Opera omnia*, ed. David Wilkins, London.
Senator Anonim (1921). *Deliberacje o królu, panach radzie i urzędnikach, sejmie i bezkrólewiu, z roku 1569*, in *Sześć broszur politycznych z XVI i początku XVII stulecia*, ed. Bronisław Ulanowski, Cracow, pp. 107–96.
Seneca (1989). *Ad Lucilium epistulae morales*, ed. and trans. R. A. Gunmere, 3 vols., Cambridge, MA.
Shapiro, Lisa (ed.) (2007). *The Correspondence between Princess Elisabeth of Bohemia and René Descartes*, trans. Lisa Shapiro, Chicago, IL.
Sharp, Andrew (ed.) (1998). *The English Levellers*, Cambridge.
Shepard, W. E. (1996). *Sayyid Qutb and Islamic Activism: A Translation and Critical Analysis of Social Justice in Islam*, Leiden.
Sidney, Philip (1962). *The Defence of Poesie, Political Discourses, Correspondence, Translation*, in *The Prose Work of Philip Sidney*, 4 vols., ed. Albert Feuillerat, vol. III, Cambridge.
(1963). *The Countesse of Pembrokes Arcadia*, in *The Prose Work of Sir Philip Sidney*, 4 vols., ed. Albert Feuillerat, vol. I, Cambridge.
Simler, Josias (1576). *De republica Helvetiorum libri duo*, Zurich.
(1577). *Regiment gemeiner loblicher Eydgnoschafft*, Zurich.
Simonis de Kéza (1999). *Simon de Keza Gesta Hungarorum/Simon of Keza: The Deeds of the Hungarians*, ed. and trans. László Veszprémy and Frank Schaer, Budapest.
Skarga, Piotr (1984). *Kazania sejmowe* [1597], ed. Janusz Tazbir and Mirosław Korolko, Wrocław.
Smith, Adam (1976). *The Wealth of Nations*, ed. R. H. Campbell, A. S. Skinner and W. B. Todd, Oxford.
(1978). *Lectures on Jurisprudence*, Oxford.
(2002). *The Theory of Moral Sentiments*, ed. Knud Haakonssen, Cambridge.
Smith, Sir Thomas (1982). *De republica anglorum – A Discourse on the Commonwealth of England* [1583], ed. Mary Dewar, Cambridge.
Socinus, Faustus (*c.* 1668). *Fausti Socini Senensis Opera omnia in duos tomos distincta*, Amsterdam.
Sorbière, Samuel de (1657). *'Second Discours sceptique de Monsieur SS. sous le nom d'Alethophile, à Ariste, en faveur des bestes & du gouvernement despotique', in Michel de Marolles, Suitte des Mémoires de Michel de Marolles, Abbé de Ville-Loin. Contenant douze traitez sur divers sujets curieux . . .*, Paris.
Soto, Domingo de (1566). *De iustitia et iure*, Salamanca.
Spain (1841). *Recopilacion de leyes de los reinos de las Indias mandadas imprimir y publicar por la magestad católica del Rey Don Carlos II, nuestro señor*, 4 vols., vol. 2, Madrid.
Spelman, John (1642). *A View of the Printed Book*, Oxford.
Spence, Thomas (1989). *The Political Works of Thomas Spence*, ed. H. T. Dickinson, Newcastle.
Spenser, Benjamin (1625). *Vox Civitatis, or Londons complaint*, London.
Spinoza, Baruch de (1951). *A Theologico-political Treatise and A Political Treatise*, trans. and intro. R. H. M. Elwes, New York.
(1994a). *Theologischer-politischer Traktat – Tractatus theologico-politicus*, ed. Günther Gawlick, Hamburg.
(1994b). *Politischer Traktat – Tractatus politicus*, ed. Wolfgang Bartuschat, Hamburg.

(2002). *Complete Works*, ed. Michael L. Morgan, trans. Samuel Shirley, Indianopolis, IN.
(2007). *Theological-Political Treatise*, ed. J. Israel, Cambridge.
Stephanus, Josephus (1586). *De Potestate coactiva quam Romanus Pontifex exercet in negotia saecularia, liber primus*, Rome.
Stieve, Gottfried (1715). *Europaeisches Hof-Ceremoniel*, Leipzig.
Streater, John (1653). *A glympse of that jewel, judicial, just, preserving libertie*, London.
(1654). *Observations, Historical, Political, and Philosophical, Upon Aristotles first Book of Government: Together, With a Narrative of State-Affaires in England, Scotland, and Ireland: As also from other Parts beyond the Seas*, 11 vols., London.
(1659a). *A shield against the Parthian dart*, London.
(1659b). *Government described: viz. what monarchie, aristocracie, oligarchie, and democracie, is. Together with a brief model of the government of the common-wealth, or, free-state of Ragouse. Fit for view at this present juncture of settlement*, London.
Stryjkowski, Maciej (1846). *Goniec cnoty do prawych szlachciców* [1574], in Stryjkowski, *Kronika polska, litewska, żmódzka i wszystkiej Rusi* [1582], 2 vols., ed. Ignacy Daniłowicz and Mikołaj Malinowski, Cracow, vol. II, pp. 467–563.
Stubbe, Henry (1659). *An Essay In Defence of the Good Old Cause, or A Discourse concerning the Rise and Extent of the power of the Civil Magistrate in reference to Spiritual Affairs*, London.
Stuppa, Giovanni Battista (1680). *The Religion of the Dutch. Represented in several Letters from a Protestant Officer in the French Army to a Pastor and Professor of Divinity, at Berne to Switzerland*, London.
Stupperich, Robert (ed.) (1953). *Melanchthons Werke* in *Auswahl II: Loci praecipui theologici von 1559*, ed. Hans Engelland, vol. II, Gütersloh.
Suárez, Francisco (1619). *Defensio fidei Catholicae*, Moguntiae.
(1856). *Tractatus quinque in primam secundae Divi Thomae*, Tract. III: *De bonitate et malitia humanorum actuum*, in *Opera omnia*, vol. 4, Paris.
(1958). *De iustitia et iure* in *Die Gerechtigkeitslehre des jungen Suárez. Edition und Untersuchung seiner Römischen Vorlesungen De iustitia et iure*, ed. J. Giers, Freiburg.
(1971–81). *De legibus ac Deo legislatore*, ed. L. Pereña, Madrid.
Suetonius (1913). 'The Life of Tiberius' in *The Lives of the Twelve Caesars*, trans. J. C. Rolfe, Cambridge, MA.
Süßmilch, Johann Peter (1766). *Versuch eines Beweises, daß die erste Sprache ihren Ursprung nicht vom Menschen, sondern allein vom Schöpfer erhalten habe*, Berlin.
Suyūṭī (1988). *Ta'rīkh al-khulafā'*, Beirut.
Szilágyi, Sándor (ed.) (1878). 'Bocskay István és Illésházy István levelezése 1605 és 1606-ban [Correspondence of István Bocskai and István Illésházy, 1605–1606]', Történelmi Tár.
Ṭabarī (1879–1901). *Ta'rīkh al-rusul wa'l-mulūk*, ed. M. J. de Goeje *et al.*, Leiden.
(1992). *The History of al-Ṭabarī*, vol. 12: *The Battle of al-Qādisiyyah and the Conquest of Syria and Palestine*, trans. Y. Friedmann, Albany, NY.
Tacitus (1925). *The Histories, books I–III*, trans. Clifford H. Moore, Cambridge, MA.
Ṭahṭāwī (2004). *An Imam in Paris: Account of a Stay in France by an Egyptian Cleric (1826–1831)*, trans. D. L. Newman, London.

(n.d.). *Takhlīṣ al-ibrīz fī talkhīṣ Bārīz*, ed. M. ʿAllām *et al.*, Cairo.
Thaʿālibī (1994). *Thimār al-qulūb*, ed. I. Ṣāliḥ, Damascus.
Thale, Mary (ed.) (1983). *Selections from the Papers of the London Corresponding Society 1792–1799*, Cambridge.
Thelwall, John (1795). *The Tribune*, London.
(1995). *The Politics of English Jacobinism: Writings of John Thelwall*, ed. Gregory Claeys, Philadelphia, PA.
Thwaites, Reuben Gold (ed.) (1896). *The Jesuit Relations and Allied Documents: Travels and Explorations of the Jesuit Missionaries in New France, 1610–1791*, 71 vols., volumes 2, 3, 5, 6, 8, 9, 10, 11, 12, 15, 28, 29, 30, 32, 33, 37, 38, 55, Cleveland.
Thysius, Antonius (1964). 'Over de vrije wil' [1625] in *Synopsis of Overzicht van de Zuiverste Theologie* ed. J. Polyander *et al.*, Enschede, vol. 1, pp. 142–52.
Tieftrunk, Johann Heinrich (1798). *Philosophische Untersuchungen über das Privat- und öffentliche Recht: Erläuterung und Beurtheilung der metaphysischen Anfangsgründe der Rechtslehre vom Herrn Prof. Imm. Kant. Zweiter Theil*, Halle.
Torres, Juan de (1596). *Filosophia moral de principes para su buena crianza y gobierno y para personas de todos estados*, Burgos.
Torrey, Samuel (1674). *An exhortation unto reformation: amplified, by a discourse concerning the parts and progress of that work, according to the word of God, delivered in a sermon preached in the audience of the General Assembly of the Massachusets colony, at Boston in New-England, May 27, 1674, being the day of election there*, Cambridge, MA.
Tossignano, Giovanni da (1580). *Della perfettione della vita spirituale*, Venice.
Travers, Walter (1617). *Fvll and Plaine Declaration of Ecclesiastical Discipline Ovt of the Word of God*, Leiden.
Tschudi, Aegidius (1980). *Chronicon Helveticum*, ed. Bernhard Stettler, vol. III, Basel.
Uyttenbogaert, Johannes (1610). *Tractaet van t'Ampt ende Authoriteyt eener hoogher Christelicker Overheydt in Kerckelicke saecken*, The Hague.
Valkenier, Petrus (1677). *Das verwirrte Europa, oder politische und historische Beschreibung der in Europa, fürnehmlich in dem Vereinigten Niederlande und in dessen Nachbarschafft seither dem Jahre 1664 entstandenen . . . blutigen Kriege . . .*, Amsterdam.
(1690). *Ansprach an die Dreyzehen wie auch Zugewandete Ort der Lobl. Eydgnoßschafft in Baden versamlet, gethan den 31. Oct./10. Nov. 1690*, s.l.
Valle Iberlucea, Enrique del (ed.) (1914–21). *Documentos para la historia Argentina*, 20 vols., vol. 20: *Cartas anuas de la provincia del Paraguay, Chile y Tucumán, de la Compañía de Jesús* (1609–1614) . . . , Buenos Aires.
van Gelderen, Martin (ed.) (1993). *The Dutch Revolt*, Cambridge.
Vattel, Emer (2008a). *The Law of Nations: Or, Principles of the Law of Nature, Applied to the Conduct and Affairs of Nations and Sovereigns* [1758], ed. Béla Kapossy and Richard Whatmore, Indianapolis, IN.
(2008b). *Mélanges de littérature, de morale et de politique*, ed. Béla Kapossy and Richard Whatmore, *History of European Ideas* 34, pp. 77–103.
Vetési, László (1998). *Oratio Ad Summum Sanctissimumque Pontificem Sixtum Iiii. Pro Praestanda Obedientia Nomine Invictissimi Principis Divi Mathiae Serenissimi Hungarorum Ac Bohemorum Regis* [1475] in *Régi magyar irodalmi szöveggyűjtemény. I. Humanizmus*, ed. Pál Ács, József Jankovics and Péter Kőszeghy, Budapest.

Vigiano, Augusto (1607). *De ecclesiastica immunitate disputationes sex*, Bologna.
Vignati, Cesare (1866). *Storia diplomatica della Lega Lombarda: con XXV documenti inediti*, Milan.
Vigniero, Nicolò (1606). *Responsio ad Caesarem Baronium*, Salmuri.
Vimont, Barthélémy (1641). *Relation de ce qui s'est passé en la Nouvelle France en l'année M. DC.XL. envoyée au R.P. provincial de la Compagnie de Jésus de la province de France*, Paris.
Vitéz, Johannes (1980). *Opera quae supersunt*, ed. Iván Boronkai, Budapest.
(1987). *Vitéz János levelei és politikai beszédei (Political Correspondence and Orations of János Vitéz)*, ed. Iván Boronkai, Budapest.
Vitoria, Francisco de (1991). *Political Writings*, ed. Anthony Pagden and Jeremy Lawrance, Cambridge.
Voetius, Gijsbert (2010). 'Philosophical-theological Disputation, containing Two Questions, the Distinction of Divine Attributes and the Freedom of the Will' [1652] in *Reformed Thought on Freedom: The Concept of Free Choice in Early Modern Reformed Theology*, ed. W. J. Van Asselt, J. M. Bac and R. T. Te Velde, Grand Rapids, MI, pp. 148–52.
Vojnović, Lujo (1909). 'Depeschen des Francesco Gondola, Gesandten der Republik Ragusa bei Pius V und Gregor XIII (1570–1573)', *Archiv für Österreichische Geschichte* 98, pp. 495–645.
Voltaire (1877–95). *Œuvres complètes*, 52 vols., Paris.
(1964). *Mahomet the Prophet or Fanaticism: A Tragedy in Five Acts*, trans. Robert L. Myers, New York.
(1966). *Le siècle de Louis XIV* [1751], ed. A. Adam, Paris.
(1972). *Philosophical Dictionary*, trans. T. Besterman, London.
Volumina constitutionum, 2 vols., ed. Stanisław Grodziski, Irena Dwornicka and Wacław Uruszczak, Warsaw (1996–2008).
Volumina Legum. Prawa, konstytucye y przywileie Królestwa Polskiego, Wielkiego Xięstwa Litewskiego y wszystkich prowincyi należących (1859), 10 vols., ed. Jozafat Ohryzko *et al.*, vol. 1, Petersburg.
von Jakob, Ludwig Heinrich (1794). *Antimachiavel, oder über die Grenzen des bürgerlichen Gehorsams: Auf Veranlassung zweyer Aufsätze in der Berl. Monatsschrift (Sept. und Dec. 1793) von den Herren Kant und Genz*, Halle.
Walwyn, William (1989). *The Writings of William Walwyn*, ed. Jack R. McMichael and Barbara Taft, Athens, GA.
Warburton, William (1742). *The Divine Legation of Moses*, 2nd edn, London.
Warszewicki, Krzysztof (1588). *Paradoxa*, Prague.
(1858). *Dwie mowy pogrzebowe* [1587], ed. Kazimierz Turowski, Cracow.
(2010). *De optimo statu libertatis libri duo*, in *Krzysztofa Warszewickiego i Anonima uwagi o wolności szlacheckiej*, ed. Krzysztof Koehler, Cracow, pp. 124–256.
Waterworth, J. (ed. and trans.) (1848). *The Canons and Decrees of the Sacred and Oecumenical Council of Trent*, London.
Werbőczi, István (2005). *Tripartitum opus iuris consuetudinarii inclyti regni Hungariae per Stephanum de Werbewcz editum* [1514], ed. János M. Bak, Martyn C. Rady and Péter Banyó, Budapest.

Wesembeke (Wesembecius), Matthaeus (1611). *In pandectas iuris civilis et codicis iustinianei libros commentarii: olim paratitla dicti*, Cologne.
Wettstein, Johann Rudolf (1651). *Acta und Handlungen betreffend gemeiner Eydgnosschafft Exemption*, Basel.
Whitgift, John (1574). *The defense of the aunswere to the Admonition, against the replie of T.C.*, London.
Wicquefort, Abraham de (1719). *L'histoire des Provinces-Unies, confirmée & eclaircie par des preuves authentiques*, The Hague.
Wildman, John (1650). *London's Liberties*, London.
Willetts, R. F. (ed. and trans.) (1967). *The Law Code of Gortyn*, Berlin.
Williams, Roger (1643). *A Key into the Language of America*, London.
(1644). *The Bloudy Tenent of Persecution*, London.
(1645). *Christenings Make Not Christians*, London.
(2008). *On Religious Liberty: Selections from the Works of Roger Williams*, ed. James Calvin Davis, Cambridge, MA.
Winstanley, Gerrard (2006). *The Law of Freedom and Other Writings*, ed. Christopher Hill, Cambridge.
Wolan, Andrzej (2010). *De libertate politica seu civili. O wolności Rzeczypospolitej albo ślacheckiej*, ed. Maciej Eder and Roman Mazurkiewicz, Warsaw.
Wolff, Christian (1756). *Vernünftige Gedanken von dem Leben der Menschen und insonderheit dem gemeinen Wesen zu Beförderung der Glückseligkeit des menschlichen Geschlechts*, 2nd edn, Halle.
Wollstonecraft, Mary (1989a). *An Historical and Moral View of the Origin and Progress of the French Revolution; and the Effect It Has Produced in Europe* in *The Works of Mary Wollstonecraft*, vol. VI, ed. Janet Todd and Marilyn Butler, London.
(1989b). *Mary, a Fiction* in *The Works of Mary Wollstonecraft*, vol. I, ed. Janet Todd and Marilyn Butler, pp. 1–73, London.
(1989c). *The Wrongs of Woman, or: Maria. A Fragment* in *The Works of Mary Wollstonecraft*, vol. I, ed. Janet Todd and Marilyn Butler, London, pp. 75–184.
(1995a). *A Vindication of the Rights of Men, in a Letter to the Right Honourable Edmund Burke; Occasioned by his Reflections on the Revolution in France* in *A Vindication of the Rights of Men and A Vindication of the Rights of Woman*, ed. Sylvana Tomaselli, Cambridge, pp. 1–64.
(1995b). *A Vindication of the Rights of Woman: With Strictures on Political and Moral Subjects* in *A Vindication of the Rights of Men and A Vindication of the Rights of Woman*, ed. Sylvana Tomaselli, Cambridge, pp. 65–294.
Wood, Anthony (1815), *Athenae Oxonienses*, ed. Philip, Bliss, 4 vols., London.
Woodhouse, A. S. P. (ed.) (1938). *Puritanism and Liberty: Being the Army Debates (1647–49) from the Clarke Manuscripts*, London.
Yaʿqūbī (1883). *Taʾrīkh*, ed. M. T. Houtsma, Leiden.
Zaborowski, Stanisław (2005). *Traktat w czterech częściach o naturze praw i dóbr królewskich oraz o naprawie królestwa i o kierowaniu państwem* [1507], ed. Henryk Litwin and Jerzy Staniszewski, Cracow.
Zainal Abidin, Andi (1985). *Wajoʾ pada abad XV–XVI*, Bandung.

Zamoyski, Jan (1918). *Votum Jmci pana Zamoyskiego, hetmana i kanclerza koronnego, na sejmie warszawskim, już ostatnim za jego żywota, w r. 1605, in Pisma polityczne z czasów rokoszu Zebrzydowskiego 1606–1608*, 3 vols., ed. Jan Czubek, vol. II, pp. 85–96, Cracow.

Zubayr ibn Bakkār (1381). *Jamharat nasab Quraysh wa-akhbārihā*, ed. M. M. Shākir, vol. I, Cairo.

Printed secondary sources

Aarsleff, Hans (1982). *From Locke to Saussure: Essays on the Study of Language and Intellectual History*, London.

(2006). 'Philosophy of Language' in *The Cambridge History of Eighteenth-Century Philosophy*, 2 vols., ed. Knud Haakonssen, Cambridge, vol. I, pp. 451–95.

Abbey, Ruth (1999). 'Back to the Future: Marriage as Friendship in the Thought of Mary Wollstonecraft', *Hypatia* 14, pp. 78–95.

Abecassis, Jack I. (1995). '"Le Maire et Montaigne ont tousjours este deux, d'une separation bien claire": Public Necessity and Private Freedom in Montaigne', *Modern Language Notes* 110, pp. 1067–89.

Achinstein, Sharon (1994). 'Women on Top in the Pamphlet Literature of the English Revolution', *Women's Studies* 24, pp. 131–63.

Ahnert, Thomas (2004). 'The Soul, Natural Religion and Moral Philosophy in the Scottish Enlightenment', *Eighteenth-Century Thought* 2, pp. 233–53.

(2013). 'Natural Law, Revelation, and Toleration in the Thought of Samuel Pufendorf' in *Natural Law and Toleration in the Early Enlightenment*, ed. J. Parkin and T. Stanton, Oxford.

Ahsmann, Margreet (1990). *Collegia en Colleges: Juridisch Onderwijs aan de Leidse Universiteit, 1575–1630, in het bijzonder het disputeren*, Groningen.

Alam, M. (2004). *The Languages of Political Islam: India 1200–1800*, Chicago.

Alanen, Lilli (2003). *Descartes's Concept of Mind*, Cambridge, MA.

(2004). 'Descartes and Elisabeth: A Philosophical Dialogue?' in *Feminist Reflections on the History of Philosophy*, ed. Lilli Alanen and Charlotte Witt, Dordrecht, pp. 193–218.

Alberigo, Giuseppe (1979). 'La riforma dei principi' in *Il concilio di Trento come crocevia della politica europea*, ed. Hubert Jedin and Paolo Prodi, Bologna, pp. 161–77.

Albrecht, Michael (1982). '"Nunmehr sind Sie ein preussischer Unterthan" – Moses Mendelssohns Staatstheorie' in *Philosophie und Wissenschaft in Preußen*, ed. Friedrich Rapp and Hans-Werner Schütt, Berlin, pp. 23–47.

Altmann, Alexander (1973). *Moses Mendelssohn: A Biographical Study*, London.

(1981). 'Moses Mendelssohn on Excommunication: The Ecclesiastical Law Background' in *Essays in Jewish Intellectual History*, Hanover, NH, pp. 172–89.

(1982a). *Die trostvolle Aufklärung: Studien zur Metaphysik und politischen Theorie Moses Mendelssohns*, Stuttgart-Bad Cannstatt.

(1982b). 'The Quest for Liberty in Moses Mendelssohn's Political Philosophy' in *Humanität und Dialog: Lessing und Mendelssohn in neuer Sicht*, ed. Ehrhard Bahr, Edward P. Harris and Lawrence G. Lyon, Detroit and Munich.

Altorfer-Ong, Stefan (2008). 'Exporting, Mercenaries, Money and Mennonites. A Swiss Diplomatic Mission to the Hague, 1710–1715' in *The Republican Alternative: The Netherlands and Switzerland Compared*, ed. André Holenstein, Thomas Maissen and Maarten Prak, Amsterdam, pp. 237–58.

Ambros, A. A. (2004). *A Concise Dictionary of Koranic Arabic*, Wiesbaden.

Amussen, Susan (1988). *An Ordered Society: Gender and Class in Early Modern England*, Oxford.

Anderson, Matthew Smith (1993). *The Rise of Modern Diplomacy, 1450–1919*, London and New York.

Archer, Ian W. (1991). *Social Relations in Elizabethan London*, Cambridge.

Arendonk, C. van (1960). *Les débuts de l'imāmat zaidite au Yémen*, trans. J. Ryckmans, Leiden.

Aris, Reinhold (1936). *History of Political Thought in Germany from 1789 to 1815*, New York.

Arkush, Allan (1994). *Moses Mendelssohn and the Enlightenment*, Albany, NY.

(1999). 'The Questionable Judaism of Moses Mendelssohn', *New German Critique* 77, pp. 29–44.

Armitage, David (2002). 'Empire and Liberty: A Republican Dilemma' in *Republicanism: A Shared European Heritage*, ed. Martin Van Gelderen and Quentin Skinner, vol. II, Cambridge, pp. 29–46.

(2011). 'Globalizing Jeremy Bentham', *History of Political Thought* 32, pp. 63–82.

Assmann, Jan (1997). *Moses the Egyptian: The Memory of Egypt in Western Monotheism*, Cambridge, MA.

Axtell, James (1985). *The Invasion Within: The Contest of Cultures in Colonial North America*, New York.

Bahar, Saba (2002). *Mary Wollstonecraft's Social and Aesthetic Philosophy: 'An Eve to Please Me'*, Basingstoke.

Bahlcke, Joachim (1997). 'Calvinism and Estate Liberation Movements in Bohemia and Hungary (1570–1620)' in *The Reformation in Eastern and Central Europe*, ed. Karin Maag, London, pp. 72–91.

(1997). 'Modernization and State-building in an East-Central European Estates' System. The Example of the Confoederatio Bohemica of 1619', *Parliaments, Estates and Representation* 17, pp. 61–73.

(2005). '"Libertas"-Vorstellungen in der ständischen Gesellschaft Polens, Böhmens und Ungarns' in *Political Culture in Central Europe (10th–20th Century)*, vol. I: *Middle Ages and Early Modern Era*, ed. Halina Manikowska and Jaroslav Pánek, Prague, pp. 163–77.

(2006). 'Hungaria eliberata? Zum Zusammenstoß von altständischer Libertät und monarchischer Autorität in Ungarn an der Wende vom 17. zum 18. Jahrhundert' in *Die Habsburgermonarchie 1620 bis 1740: Leistungen und Grenzen des Absolutismus-Paradigmas*, ed. Petr Mat'a and Thomas Winkelbauer, Stuttgart.

Bahlcke, Joachim, Bömelburg, Hans-Jürgen and Kersken, Norbert (eds.) (1996). *Ständefreiheit und Staatsgestaltung in Ostmitteleuropa: Übernationale Gemeinsamkeiten in der politischen Kultur vom 16.–18. Jahrhundert*, Leipzig.

Bak, János M. (1973). *Königtum und Stände in Ungarn im 14.–16. Jahrhundert*, Wiesbaden.

(1983). 'Delinquent Lords and Forsaken Serfs: Thoughts on War and Society during the Crisis of Feudalism' in *Society in Change*, ed. S. B. Vardy and A. H. Vardy, East European Monographs, Boulder, CO, distributed by Columbia University Press, pp. 291–304.

(1994). 'The Kingship of Matthias Corvinus: A Renaissance State?' in Matthias Corvinus and the Humanism in Central Europe, vol. x ed. T. Klaniczay and J. Jankovics, Budapest, pp. 37–47.

Bak, János M., Engel, Pál and Sweeney, James Ross (eds.) (1992). *The Laws of the Medieval Kingdom of Hungary. 1301–1457. (Decreta Regni Mediaevalis Hungarie.* 1000–1526*)*, vol. II, Salt Lake City.

Bakewell, Peter (1995). 'Conquest after the Conquest: The Rise of Spanish Domination in America' in *Spain, Europe, and the Atlantic World: Essays in Honour of John H. Elliott*, ed. Richard L. Kagan and Geoffrey Parker, Cambridge, pp. 296–315.

Balázs, Mihály (1996). *Early Transylvanian Antitrinitarianism 1567–1571: From Servet to Palaeologus*, Baden-Baden.

(2009). 'Über den europäischen Kontext der siebenbürgischen Religionsgesetze des 16. Jahrhunderts' in *Humanismus und europäische Identität: Fragmenta Melanchtoniana*, vol. IV, Mainz, pp. 11–28.

Baldwin, Geoff (2001). 'Individual and Self in the Late Renaissance', *Historical Journal* 44, pp. 341–64.

Bangs, Carl (1985). *Arminius: A Study in the Dutch Reformation*, 2nd edn, Grand Rapids, MI.

Banyó, Péter and Rady, Martyn (eds.) (2010). *The Laws of the Medieval Kingdom of Hungary*, vol. IV: *1490–1526 (Decreta Regni Mediaevalis Hungariæ, Tomus IV 1490–1526)*, Budapest.

Barnadas, Joseph M. (1984). 'The Catholic Church in Colonial Latin America' in *The Cambridge History of Latin America*, 11 vols. ed. Leslie Bethell, Cambridge, vol. I, pp. 511–40.

Baron, Hans (1966). *The Crisis of the Early Italian Renaissance*, Princeton, NJ.

(1968a). *From Petrarch to Leonardo Bruni: Studies in Humanistic and Political Literature*, Chicago, IL.

(1968b). *Humanistic and Political Literature in Florence and Venice at the Beginning of the Quattrocento*, New York.

Barry, Jonathan (1990). 'Provincial Town Culture, 1640–1760: Urban or Civic?' in *Interpretation and Cultural History*, ed. J. Pittock and A. Wear, London, pp. 198–234.

(1994). 'Bourgeios Collectivism? Urban Association and the Middling Sort', in *The Middling Sort of People: Culture, Society and Politics in England, 1550–1800*, ed. Jonathan Barry and Christopher Brooks, London, pp. 84–112.

Barta, Gábor (1994). *La route qui mène à Istanbul, 1526–1528*, Budapest.

Barta, J., Jatzlauk, M. and Papp, K. (eds.) (2008). *'Einigkeit und Frieden sollen auf Seiten jeder Partei sein': Die Friedensschlüsse von Wien (23.06.1606) und Zsitvatorok (15.11.1606)*, Debrecen.

Baxter, Christopher (1973). 'Jean Bodin's Daemon and His Conversion to Judaism' in *Verhandlungen der internationalen Bodin Tagung in München*, ed. H. Denzer, Munich, pp. 1–21.

Beck, Andreas J. (2007). *Gisbertus Voetius (1589–1676): Sein Theologieverständnis und seine Gotteslehre*, Göttingen.

(2010). 'The Will as Master of Its Own Act. A Disputation Rediscovered of Gisbertus Voetius (1589–1676) on Freedom of Will', in *Reformed Thought on Freedom: The Concept of Free Choice in Early Modern Reformed Theology*, ed. W. J. Van Asselt, J. M. Bac and Te Velde R. T. Grand Rapids, MI, pp. 145–70.

Beiner, Ronald (2010). 'Three Versions of the Politics of Conscience: Hobbes, Spinoza, Locke', *San Diego Law Review* 47, pp. 1107–24.

Beiser, Frederick C. (1992). *Enlightenment, Revolution, and Romanticism: The Genesis of Modern German Political Thought, 1790–1800*, Cambridge, MA and London.

(2005). *Schiller as Philosopher: A Re-examination*, Oxford and New York.

Below, Georg von (1905). *Die Ursachen der Rezeption des römischen Rechts in Deutschland*, Munich.

Benda, Kálmán (1971). 'A kálvini tanok hatása a magyar rendi ellenállás ideológiájára (The Effect of Calvinian Ideas on the Ideology of Hungarian Estates Resistance)', *Helikon* 3–4, pp. 322–30.

(1974). 'Absolutismus und ständischer Widerstand in Ungarn am Anfang des 17. Jahrhunderts', *SOF* 33, pp. 85–124.

(1978). 'Hungary in Turmoil, 1580–1620', *European Studies Review* 8, pp. 281–304.

(1981). 'Le droit de résistance de la Bulle d'Or hongroise et le calvinisme' in *Noblesse française, noblesse hongroise, XVIe–XIXe siècles: Colloque franco-hongrois d'histoire sociale. Rennes, 11–13 juin 1975*, ed. Béla, Köpeczi and Éva H. Balázs, Budapest and Paris, pp. 155–61.

(1991). 'Habsburg Absolutism and the Resistance of the Hungarian Estates in the Sixteenth and Seventeenth Centuries' in *Crown, Church and Estates: Central European Politics in the Sixteenth and Seventeenth Centuries*, ed. R. J. W. Evans and T. V. Thomas, London, pp. 123–8.

Benedict, Philip (2002). *Christ's Churches Purely Reformed: A Social History of Calvinism*, New Haven, CT.

Benert, Richard R. (1973). 'Lutheran Resistance Theory and the Imperial Constitution', *Il Pensiero Politico* 6, pp. 17–36.

Benson, Robert (1982). 'Political Renovatio. Two Models from Roman Antiquity' in *Renaissance and Renewal in the Twelfth Century*, ed. R. Benson, G. Constable and C. Lanham, Cambridge, MA, pp. 339–86.

(1985). 'Libertas in Italy: 1152–1226' in *La notion de liberté au moyen âge: Islam, Byzance, Occident*, ed. G. Makdisi, D. Sourdel and J. Sourdel-Thomime, Paris, pp. 191–213.

Berdahl, Robert (1988). *The Politics of the Prussian Nobility: The Development of a Conservative Ideology 1770–1848*, Princeton, NJ.

Berghahn, Cord Friedrich (2001). *Moses Mendelssohns 'Jerusalem': Ein Beitrag zur Geschichte der Menschenrechte und der pluralistischen Gesellschaft in der deutschen Aufklärung*, Tübingen.

Berlin, Isaiah (1958). *Two Concepts of Liberty: An Inaugural Lecture Delivered before the University of Oxford on 31 October 1958*, Oxford.

(2002). 'Two Concepts of Liberty' in *Liberty*, ed. Henry Hardy, Oxford, pp. 166–217.

Besold, Christopher (1625). *Dissertatio politica-juridica de majestate in genere*, Tübingen.
Biberman, Matthew (1999). 'Milton, Marriage, and a Woman's Right to Divorce', *Studies in English Literature 1500–1900* 39, pp. 131–53.
Biegman, Nicolas (1967). *The Turco-Ragusan Relationship*, The Hague.
Bireley, Robert (1990). *The Counter-Reformation Prince: Anti-Machiavellianism or Catholic Statecraft in Early Modern Europe*, Chapel Hill, NC.
Bisaha, Nancy (2004). *Creating East and West: Renaissance Humanists and the Ottoman Turks*, Philadelphia.
Black, E. C. (1963). *The Association: British Extraparliamentary Political Organisation, 1769–1793*, Cambridge, MA.
Blom, Hans W. (ed.) (2009). *Property, Piracy and Punishment: Hugo Grotius on War and Booty in De iure praedae*, Leiden.
Blom, Hans W. and Wildenberg Ivo W. (eds.) (1986). *Pieter de la Court en zijn tijd (1618–1685): Aspecten van een veelzijdig publicist*, Amsterdam and Maarssen.
Blom, Hans W. and Winkel, Laurens C. (eds.) (2004). *Grotius and the Stoa*, Assen.
Blythe, James M. (2000). 'Civic Humanism and Medieval Political Thought' in *Renaissance Civic Humanism*, ed. James Hankins, Cambridge, MA, pp. 30–74.
Bödeker, Hans Erich (2002). 'The Concept of the Republic in Eighteenth Century German Thought' in *Republicanism and Liberalism in America and the German States, 1750–1850*, ed. J. Heideking and J. Henretta, Cambridge.
Bónis, György [1947]. *Hűbériség és rendiség a középkori magyar jogban* (Vassalage and Corporatism in the Medieval Legal System of Hungary), Kolozsvár.
(1965). 'The Hungarian Feudal Diet (13th–18th Centuries)', *Recueils de la Société Jean Bodin* 25, pp. 287–307.
Bonney, Richard (2006). '"God, Fatherland and Freedom": Rethinking Pluralism in Hungary in the Era of Partition and Rebellion, 1526–1711' in *Persecution and Pluralism: Calvinists and Religious Minorities in Early Modern Europe 1550–1700*, ed. Richard Bonney and D. J. B. Trim, Oxford, pp. 89–122.
Bordone, Renato (1987). *La società cittadina del regno d'Italia: formazione e sviluppo delle caratteristiche urbane nei secoli XI e XII*, Turin.
Borgeaud, Charles (n.d. 1920?). *Monument international de la Réformation à Genève – International Monument of the Calvinian Reformation – Internationales Denkmal der Genfer Reformation: Guide-Mémorial*, Geneva.
Borsay, Peter (1989). *The English Urban Renaissance: Culture and Society in the Provincial Town 1660–1770*, Oxford.
Bourel, Dominique (2004). *Moses Mendelssohn: la naissance du judaïsme moderne*, Paris.
Bouswma, William J. (1968). *Venice and the Defense of Republican Liberty: Renaissance Values in the Age of the Counter-Reformation*, Berkeley, CA.
(1988). *John Calvin: A Sixteenth-Century Portrait*, Oxford.
(1990). 'Gallicanism and the Nature of Christendom' in *A Usable Past: Essays in European Cultural History*, Berkeley, CA, pp. 308–24.
(2002). *The Waning of the Renaissance 1550–1640*, New Haven, CT.
Bowsky, William M. (1958). 'Florence and Henry of Luxemburg, King of the Romans: The Rebirth of Guelfism', *Speculum* 33, pp. 177–203.

Bozeman, Theodore Dwight (1988). *To Live Ancient Lives: The Primitivist Dimension in Puritanism*, London.
(2004). *The Precisianist Strain: Disciplinary Religion and Antinomian Backlash in Puritanism to 1638*, Chapel Hill, NC.
Božić, Ivan (1952). *Dubrovnik i Turska u XIV i XV veku* (Ragusa and the Ottoman Empire in the 14th and 15th Centuries), Belgrade.
Brace, Laura (2000). '"Not Empire, but Equality": Mary Wollstonecraft, the Marriage State and the Sexual Contract', *Journal of Political Philosophy* 8, pp. 433–55.
Brachlow, Stephen (1985). 'The Elizabethan Roots of Henry Jacob's Churchmanship: Refocusing the Historiographical Lens', *Journal of Ecclesiastical History* 36, pp. 228–54.
(1988). *The Communion of Saints: Radical Puritan and Separatist Ecclesiology, 1570–1625*, Oxford.
Brady, Thomas A. *et al.* (1985). 'Luther and Society', *Lutherjahrbuch* 52, pp. 197–238.
Brandt, Reinhard (1995). 'Das Problem der Erlaubnisgesetze im Spätwerk Kants' in *Immanuel Kant: Zum Ewigen Frieden*, ed. Otfried Höffe, Berlin.
Brecht, Martin (1986). *Martin Luther Bd. 2: Ordnung und Abgrenzung der Reformation 1521–1532*, Stuttgart.
Brémond, Henri (1967). *Histoire littéraire du sentiment religieux en France depuis la fin des guerres de religion*, 11 vols., Paris.
Brennan, Geoffrey and Pettit, Philip (1990). 'Unveiling the Vote', *British Journal of Political Science* 20, pp. 311–33.
Brennan, Theresa and Pateman, Carole (1979). '"Mere Auxiliaries to the Commonwealth": Women and the Origins of Liberalism', *Political Studies* 27, pp. 183–200.
Brett, Annabel (2011). *Changes of State: Nature and the Limits of the City in Early Modern Law*, Princeton, NJ.
Breuer, Edward (1992). 'Politics, Tradition, History: Rabbinic Judaism and the Eighteenth-Century Struggle for Civil Equality', *Harvard Theological Review* 85, pp. 357–83.
Briguglia, Gianluca (2006). *Il corpo vivente dello stato*, Milan.
Broad, Jacqueline (2002). *Women Philosophers of the Seventeenth Century*, Cambridge.
Bryce, James (1889). *The Holy Roman Empire*, London.
Buchstein, Hubertus (2000). *Öffentliche und geheime Stimmabgabe: Eine ideengeschichtliche und wahlrechtshistorische Studie*, Baden-Baden.
Buchwald-Pelcowa, Paulina (1997). *Cenzura w dawnej Polsce: Między prasą drukarską a stosem*, Warsaw.
Burgess, Glenn (1992). *The Politics of the Ancient Constitution: An Introduction to English Political Thought, 1603–42*, London.
Burgess, Glenn and Festenstein, Matthew (ed.) (2007). *English Radicalism 1550–1585*, Cambridge.
Burke, Peter (1991). 'Tacitism, Scepticism, and Reason of State' in *The Cambridge History of Political Thought, c.1450–c.1700*, ed. J. H. Burns, Cambridge, pp. 479–98.
Burns, J. H. (1992). *Lordship, Kingship, and Empire: The Idea of Monarchy, 1400–1525*, Oxford.

Burrage, Champlin (1907). 'Lost Prison Papers of Henry Jacob', *Review and Expositor* 4, pp. 489–513.

(1912). *The Early English Dissenters*, 2 vols., Cambridge.

Bushnell, Amy Turner (2004). '"None of these Wandering Nations Has Ever Been Reduced to the Faith": Missions and Mobility on the Spanish-American Frontier' in *The Spiritual Conversion of the Americas*, ed. James Muldoon, Gainesville, FL, pp. 142–68.

Cable, Lana (1995). *Carnal Rhetoric: Milton's Iconoclasm and the Poetics of Desire*, Durham, NC and London.

Campbell, Gordon and Corns, Thomas N. (2008). *John Milton: Life, Work, and Thought*, Oxford.

Cañeque, Alejandro (2004). *The King's Living Image: The Culture and Politics of Viceregal Power in Colonial Mexico*, New York.

Canning, Joseph (1987). *The Political Thought of Baldus de Ubaldis*, Cambridge.

Capp, Bernard (2004). *When Gossips Meet: Women, Family and Neighbourhood in Early Modern England*, Oxford.

Carpintero Benítez, F. (2003). 'Los escolásticos españoles en los inicios del liberalismo político y jurídico', *Revista de Estudios Histórico-Jurídicos* 25, 341–73.

Carter, Ian, Kramer, Matthew H. and Steiner, Hillel (2007). *Freedom: A Philosophical Anthology*, Oxford.

Caruso, E. (1979). *Pedro Hurtado de Mendoza e la rinascita del nominalismo nella Scolastica del Seicento*, Florence.

Cavallar, Georg (1992). *Pax Kantiana: Systematisch-historische Untersuchung des Entwurfs 'Zum ewigen Frieden' (1795) von Immanuel Kant*, Vienna.

Cave, Terence (1999). *Pré-histoires: textes troublés au seuil de la modernité*, Geneva.

Cefalu, Paul (2004). *Moral Identity in Early Modern English Literature*, Cambridge.

Chabod, Federico (1967). 'Alcune questioni di terminologia: stato, nazione, patria nel linguaggio del Cinquecento' in *Scritti sul Rinascimento*, Turin, pp. 630–61.

Chafuen, A. (2003). *Faith and Liberty: The Economic Thought of the Late Scholastics*, Lanham, MD.

Chappell, Vere (1998). 'Locke on the Freedom of the Will' in *Locke*, ed. Vere Chappell, pp. 86–105.

Cherpack, Clifton (1955). 'Warburton and the Encyclopédie', *Comparative Literature* 7, pp. 226–39.

Chiappelli, Fredi (1952). *Studi sul linguaggio del Machiavelli*, Florence.

Chisik, Harvey (2002). 'Ethics and History in Voltaire's Attitudes toward the Jews', *Eighteenth-Century Studies* 35, pp. 577–600.

Choińska-Mika, Jolanta (2002). *Między społeczeństwem szlacheckim a władzą. Problemy komunikacji: społeczności lokalne – władza w epoce Jana Kazimierza*, Warsaw.

Christie, I. R. (1962). *Wilkes, Wyvill and Reform: The Parliamentary Reform Movement in British Politics, 1760–1785*, London.

Cipriani, Giovanni (1980). *Il mito etrusco nel rinascimento fiorentino*, Florence.

Coffey, John (1997). *Politics, Religion and the British Revolutions: The Mind of Samuel Rutherford*, Cambridge.

(2006). *John Goodwin and the Puritan Revolution: Religion and Intellectual Change in Seventeenth-Century England*, Woodbridge.

(2009). 'Quentin Skinner and the Religious Dimension of Early Modern Political Thought' in *Seeing Things Their Way: Intellectual History and the Return of Religion*, ed. Alister Chapman, John Coffey and Brad Gregory, Notre Dame, IN, pp. 46–74.

Cogley, Richard W. (1991). 'John Eliot and the Millenium', *Religion and American Culture: A Journal of Interpretation* 1, pp. 227–50.

(1999). *John Eliot's Mission to the Indians before King Philip's War*, Cambridge, MA.

Cohen, Charles L. (1986). *God's Caress: The Psychology of Puritan Religious Experience*, Oxford.

(1993). 'Conversion among Puritans and Amerindians: A Theological and Cultural Perspective' in *Puritanism: Transatlantic Perspectives on a Seventeenth Century Anglo-American Faith*, ed. Francis J. Bremer, Boston, pp. 233–56.

Colclough, David (2005). *Freedom of Speech in Early Stuart England*, Cambridge.

Collinson, Patrick (1987). 'The Monarchical Republic of Queen Elizabeth I', in *Elizabethan Essays*, London, pp. 31–58.

Condren, Conal (1994). 'The Paradoxes of Recontextualization in Early Modern Intellectual History (review article)', *Historical Journal* 37, pp. 225–32.

(1997). 'Liberty of Office and its Defence in Seventeenth-Century Political Argument', *History of Political Thought* 18, pp. 460–82.

(2006). *Argument and Authority in Early Modern England: The Presupposition of Oaths and Offices*, Cambridge.

Conger, Syndy McMillen (1994). *Mary Wollstonecraft and the Language of Sensibility*, London and Toronto.

Conze, Werner *et al.* (2004). 'Freiheit' in *Geschichtliche Grundbegriffe: Historisches Lexikon zur politisch-sozialen Sprache in Deutschland. Studienausgabe*, ed. Otto Brunner, Werner Conze and Reinhard Koselleck, Stuttgart, vol. II pp. 425–542.

Cook, M. (2000). *Commanding Right and Forbidding Wrong in Islamic Thought*, Cambridge.

Cooper, John (1996). 'Eudaimonism, the Appeal to Nature and "Moral Duty" in Stoicism' in *Aristotle, Kant, and the Stoics*, ed. Stephen Engstrom and Jennifer Whiting, New York, pp. 261–84.

Cowdrey, H. J. E. (1968). 'The Papacy, the Patarenes and the Church of Milan', *Transactions of the Royal Historical Society* 18, pp. 25–48.

Cox, Rosanna (2007). 'John Milton's Politics, Republicanism and the Terms of Liberty', *Literature Compass* 4, pp. 1561–76.

(2010a). 'Neo-Roman Terms of Liberty in *Samson Agonistes*', *Milton Quarterly* 44, pp. 1–22.

(2010b). 'Milton, Marriage and the Politics of Gender' in *John Milton: Life, Writing and Reputation*, ed. Blair Worden and Paul Hammond, Oxford, pp. 125–46.

Cox, Virginia (1997). 'Machiavelli and the *Rhetorica ad Herennium:* Deliberative Rhetoric in *The Prince*', *Sixteenth Century Journal* 28, pp. 1109–41.

Cozzi, Gaetano (1995). *Venezia Barocca: conflitti di uomini e idee nella crisi del Seicento veneziano*, Venice.

Cromartie, Alan (1999). 'The Constitutionalist Revolution: The Transformation of Political Culture in Early Stuart England', *Past and Present* 163, pp. 76–120.

Crone, P. (2004). *Medieval Islamic Political Thought*, Edinburgh.

Crone, P. and Hinds, M. (1986). *God's Caliph: Religious Authority in the First Centuries of Islam*, Cambridge.

Crouzet, Denis (1999). 'Calvinism and the Uses of the Political and the Religious (France, ca. 1560–ca. 1572)' in *Reformation, Revolt and Civil War in France and the Netherlands, 1555–1585*, ed. Philip Benedict *et al.*, Amsterdam, pp. 99–113.

(2003). 'French Protestants and the Early Wars of Religion' in *Toleration and Religious Identity: The Edict of Nantes and Its Implications in France, Britain and Ireland*, ed. Ruth Whelan and Carol Baxter, Dublin, pp. 73–91.

Csepregi, Zoltán (forthcoming). *Das Widerstandsrecht bei Honter und seinen ungarischen Zeitgenossen.*

Daniel, David P. (1994). 'Calvinism in Hungary: The Theological and Ecclesiastical Transition to the Reformed Faith' in *Calvinism in Europe 1540–1620*, ed. Andrew Pettegree, Alistair Duke and Gillian Lewis, Cambridge, pp. 205–30.

Dann, Otto (2002). 'Kant's Republicanism and Its Echoes' in *Republicanism and Liberalism in America and the German States, 1750–1850*, ed. J. Heideking and J. Henretta, Cambridge.

Darwall, Stephen (1995). *The British Moralists and the Internal 'Ought': 1640–1740*, Cambridge.

Davids, Karel and Lucassen, Jan (eds.) (1995). *A Miracle Mirrored: The Dutch Republic in European Perspective*, Cambridge.

Davies, Colin (2007). 'Reassessing Radicalism in a Traditional Society' in *English Radicalism 1550–1585*, ed. Glenn Burgess and Matthew Festenstein, Cambridge, pp. 338–72.

Davis, Charles T. (1975). 'Roman Patriotism and Republican Propaganda: Ptolemy of Lucca and Pope Nicholas III', *Speculum* 50, pp. 411–33.

Davis, J. C. (1981). *Utopia and the Ideal Society: A Study of English Utopian Writing, 1516–1700*, Cambridge.

(1992). 'Religion and the Struggle for Freedom in the English Revolution', *Historical Journal* 35, pp. 507–30.

(1993). 'Against Formality: One Aspect of the English Revolution', *Transactions of the Royal Historical Society* 3, pp. 265–88.

Davis, Thomas J. (1996). 'Images of Intolerance: John Calvin in Nineteenth-Century History Textbooks', *Church History* 65, pp. 234–48.

Dawson, Hannah (2007). *Locke, Language and Early Modern Philosophy*, Cambridge.

Dawson, John (1960). *A History of Lay Judges*, Cambridge.

De Benedictis, Angela *et al.* (eds.) (2009). *Die Sprache des Politischen in actu: Zum Verhältnis von politischem Handeln und politischer Sprache von der Antike bis ins 20. Jahrhundert*, Göttingen.

de Roover, R. (1971). *La pensée économique des scolastiques*, Paris.

Decock, W. (2009a). 'Jesuit Freedom of Contract', *Tijdschrift voor Rechtsgeschiedenis* 77, 423–58.

(2009b). 'Lessius and the Breakdown of the Scholastic Paradigm', *Journal of the History of Economic Thought* 31, 57–78.

Dekker, Eef (1991). 'Wilsvrijheid volgens Coornhert in het traditie-historische licht van de scholastiek. Een kleine dieptepeiling', *Nederlands Theologisch Tijdschrift* 45, pp. 107–19.

(1993). *Rijker dan Midas: Vrijheid, genade en predestinatie in de theologie van Jacobus Arminius (1559–1609)*, Zoetermeer.

(1999). 'Theologische en filosofische vrijheid in de vroege zeventiende eeuw' in Eco Haitsma Mulier and Wyger Velema (eds.), *Vrijheid: Een geschiedenis van de vijftiende tot de twintigste eeuw*, Amsterdam, pp. 53–69.

Delumeau, Jean (1977). *Catholicism between Luther and Voltaire: A New View of the Counter-Reformation*, London.

Deslandres, Dominique (2003). *Croire et faire croire: les missions françaises au XVIIe siècle*, Paris.

Dickmann, Fritz (1977). *Der Westfälische Frieden*, 4th edn, Münster.

Dietrich, Therese (1989). 'Kant's Polemik mit dem absprechenden Ehrenmann Friedrich Gentz', in *Dialektik* 17, pp. 128–36.

Don, Patricia Lopes (2006). 'Franciscans, Indian Sorcerers, and the Inquisition in New Spain, 1536–1543', *Journal of World History* 17, pp. 27–49.

Dörries, Hermann (1970). 'Gottesgehorsam und Menschengehorsam bei Luther' in *Wort und Stunde*, Göttingen, vol. III, pp. 109–94.

Dorsten, Jan van (1986). 'The Final Year' in *Sir Philip Sidney: 1586 and the Creation of a Legend*, ed. Jan van Dorsten, D. Baker-Smith and Arthur F. Kinney, Leiden, pp. 16–23.

Doyle, J. P. (1984). 'Prolegomena to a Study of Extrinsic Denomination in the Work of Francisco Suarez, SJ', *Vivarium* 22, 121–60.

Doyle, William (1996). *Venality: The Sale of Offices in Eighteenth Century France*, Oxford.

Dreitzel, Horst (1970). *Protestantischer Aristotelismus und absoluter Staat: Die 'Politica' des Henning Arnisaeus, ca. 1575–1636*, Wiesbaden.

Duchet, Michel (1971). *Anthropologie et histoire au siècle des Lumières*, Paris.

Dunn, John (1969). *The Political Thought of John Locke: An Historical Account of the Argument of the 'Two Treatises of Government'*, Cambridge.

(1990). 'Trust and Political Agency' in *Interpreting Political Responsibility*, Oxford, pp. 26–44.

(2010). 'The Significance of Hobbes's Conception of Power', *Critical Review of International Social and Political Philosophy* 13, pp. 417–33.

Dürr, Renate (2006). *Politische Kultur in der Frühen Neuzeit: Kirchenräume in Hildesheimer Stadt- und Landgemeinden 1550–1750*, Gütersloh.

Dworetz, Steven M. (1990). *The Unvarnished Doctrine: Locke, Liberalism and the American Revolution*, Durham, NC and London.

Dzelzainis, Martin (1995). 'Milton's Classical Republicanism' in *Milton and Republicanism*, ed. David Armitage, Armand Himy and Quentin Skinner, Cambridge, pp. 3–24.

(2000). 'John Milton, *Areopagitica*' in *A Companion to Literature from Milton to Blake*, ed. David Womersley, Oxford, pp. 151–8.

(2007). 'Liberty and the Law' in *Milton, Rights and Liberties*, ed. Christophe Tournu and Neil Forsyth, Berne, pp. 57–67.

Eckhardt, Ferenc (1933). 'Bocskai és híveinek közjogi felfogása', *Károlyi Emlékkönyv*, Budapest, pp. 125–36.

Edwards, C. (2009). 'Free Yourself! Slavery, Freedom and the Self in Seneca's Letters' in *Seneca and the Self*, ed. Shadi Bartsch and David Wray, Cambridge, pp. 139–59.

Eire, Carlos (1986). *War against the Idols: The Reformation of Worship from Erasmus to Calvin*, Cambridge.

Eisen, Arnold (1990). 'Divine Legislation as "Ceremonial Script": Mendelssohn on the Commandments', *Association for Jewish Studies Review* 15, pp. 239–67.

Ekes, Janusz (2001a). *Natura – wolność – władza: studium z dziejów myśli politycznej Renesansu*, Warsaw.

(2001b). *Trójpodział władzy i zgoda wszystkich: naczelne zasady 'ustroju mieszanego' w staropolskiej refleksji politycznej*, Siedlce.

(2010). *Złota demokracja*, 2nd edn, Cracow.

Elfenbein, Andrew (2002). 'Mary Wollstonecraft and the Sexuality of Genius' in *The Cambridge Companion to Mary Wollstonecraft*, ed. Claudia L. Johnson, Cambridge, pp. 228–45.

Elliott, J. H. (1989a). *Spain and Its World, 1500–1700: Selected Essays*, New Haven, CT.

(1989b). *The Count-Duke of Olivares: The Statesman in an Age of Decline*, New Haven, CT.

(2006). *Empires of the Atlantic World: Britain and Spain in America, 1492–1830*, New Haven, CT.

Elorduy, E. (1943–45). 'La moral suareciana', *Anuario de la Asociación Francisco de Vitoria* 6, pp. 97–189.

Elster, Jon (1983). *Sour Grapes: Studies in the Subversion of Rationality*, Cambridge.

Encyclopaedia of Islam (1960–2009). 2nd edn, Leiden and London.

Enenkel, Karl A. E. and Heesakkers, C. L. (ed.) (1997). *Lipsius in Leiden: Studies in the Life and Works of a Great Humanist on the Occasion of His 450th Anniversary*, Voorthuizen.

Engel, Eva J. (1994). '"Die Freyheit der Untersuchung". Die Literaturbriefe 72–75' in *Moses Mendelssohn und die Kreise seiner Wirksamkeit*, ed. Eva J. Engel and Norbert Hinske, Tübingen, pp. 249–68.

Engel, Pál (2001). *The Realm of St. Stephen: A History of Medieval Hungary, 895–1526*, London and New York.

Epstein, Klaus (1966). *The Genesis of German Conservatism*, Princeton, NJ.

Ertman, Thomas (1997). *Birth of the Leviathan: Building States and Regimes in Medieval and Early Modern Europe*, Cambridge.

Estes, James. (2004). 'Luther and the Role of Secular Authority in the Reformation' in *The Pastoral Luther*, ed. Timothy J. Wegnert, Grand Rapids, MI and Cambridge, pp. 355–80.

(2005). *Peace, Order, and the Glory of God: Secular Authority and the Church in the Thought of Luther and Melanchthon 1518–1559*, Leiden.

Evans, R. J. W. (1973). *Rudolf II and His World: A study in Intellectual history, 1576–1612*, Oxford.

(1985). 'Calvinism in East Central Europe. Hungary and Her Neighbours' in *International Calvinism 1541–1715*, ed. Menna Prestwich, Oxford, pp. 167–96.

Evennett, Henry Outram (1968). *The Spirit of the Counter-Reformation: The Birkbeck Lectures in Ecclesiastical History given in the University of Cambridge in May 1951 by the Late H. Outram Evennett*, ed. John Bossy, Cambridge.

Ezell, Margaret J. M. (1987). *The Patriarch's Wife: Literary Evidence and the History of the Family*, Chapel Hill, NC.

Fasano Guarini, Elena (1990). 'Machiavelli and the Crisis of the Italian Republics' in G. Bock, Q. Skinner and M. Viroli (ed.), *Machiavelli and Republicanism*, Cambridge, pp. 17–41.

Fasolt, Constantin (2004). *The Limits of History*, Chicago.

Fay, Sidney Bradshaw (1911). 'The Roman Law and the German Peasant', *American Historical Review* 16, pp. 234–54.

Feenstra, Robert (1974). 'Les origines du *Dominium utile* chez les Glossateurs', *Fata Iuris Romani*, Leiden, pp. 215–59.

Feiner, Shmuel (2003). *The Jewish Enlightenment*, Philadelphia, PA.

Feldman, Karen (2001). 'Conscience and the Concealments of Metaphor in Hobbes's *Leviathan*', *Philosophy and Rhetoric* 34, pp. 21–37.

Fenton, Mary C. (2003). 'Hope, Land Ownership, and Milton's "Paradise Within"', *Studies in English Literature* 43, pp. 151–80.

Ferente, Serena (2007). 'Guelphs, Liberty and Sovereignty. Inquiries about the Quattrocento', *History of Political thought* 28, pp. 571–98.

Fernández Albaladejo, Pablo (1997). 'Católicos antes que ciudadanos: gestación de una "Política Española" en los comienzos de la edad moderna' in *Imágenes de la diversidad: el mundo urbano en la Corona de Castilla (s. XVI–XVII)*, ed. José Ignacio Fortea Pérez, Santander, pp. 103–27.

Fiedler, Joseph (ed.) (1870). *Relationen venetianischer Botschafter über Deutschland und Österreich im sechzehnten Jahrhundert*, Vienna.

Fierro, M. (2005). '*Mawālī* and *muwalladūn* in al-Andalus (second/eighth–fourth/tenth centuries' in *Patronate and Patronage in Early and Classical Islam*, ed. M. Bernards and J. Nawas, Leiden and Boston, pp. 195–245.

Fitzmaurice, Andrew (2003). *Humanism and America: An Intellectual History of English Colonisation, 1500–1625*, Cambridge.

Fonnesu, Luca (2006). 'The Problem of Theodicy' in *The Cambridge History of Eighteenth-Century Philosophy*, 2 vols., ed. Knud Haakonssen, Cambridge, vol. II pp. 749–78.

Fontana, Biancamaria (2008). *Montaigne's Politics: Authority and Governance in the 'Essais'*, Princeton, NJ.

Foretić, Vinko (1980). *Povijest Dubrovnika do 1808* (History of Dubrovnik until 1808), Zagreb.

(2001). 'Dubrovnik u doba Marina Držića' (Ragusa in the Age of Marin Držić) in Vinko Foretić, *Studije i rasprave iz hrvatske povijesti*, Split, pp. 301–21.

Forman-Barzilai, Fonna (2010). *Adam Smith and the Circles of Sympathy: Cosmopolitanism and Moral Theory*, Cambridge.

Forrestal, Alison (2002). 'Fathers, Leaders, Kings: Episcopacy and Episcopal Reform in the Seventeenth-Century French School', *Seventeenth Century* 17, pp. 24–47.

Forster, Greg (2005). *John Locke's Politics of Moral Consensus*, Cambridge.

Foster, Stephen (1991). *The Long Argument: English Puritanism and the Shaping of New England Culture, 1570–1770*, Chapel Hill, NC and London.

Foucault, Michel (1984). *Le souci de soi: histoire de la sexualité*, 3 vols., Paris.

Fournel, Jean-Louise and Zancarini, Jean-Claude (2004). '"Les mots propres et naturels et les termes d'état". Lexique de l'action et syntaxe de la conviction dans *Le prince*' in *Langues et écritures de la République et de la guerre: études sur Machiavel*, ed. Alessandro Fontana *et al.*, Genoa, pp. 51–86.

Foxley, Rachel (2004). 'John Lilburne and the Citizenship of "Free-Born Englishmen"', *Historical Journal* 47, pp. 849–74.

Frame, Donald (1965). *Montaigne: A Biography*, London.

Franklin, Julian (1963). *Jean Bodin and the Sixteenth Century Revolution in the Methodology of Law and History*, New York.

(1991). 'Sovereignty and the Mixed Constitution: Bodin and His Critics' in *The Cambridge History of Political Thought, 1450–1700*, ed. J. H. Burns and Mark Goldie, Cambridge.

Frede, Michael (2011). *A Free Will: Origins of the Notion in Ancient Thought*, ed. A. A. Long, Berkeley.

Friedeburg Robert von (2005). 'Magdeburger Argumentationen zum Recht auf Widerstand gegen die Durchsetzung des Interims (1550–1551) und ihre Stellung in der Geschichte des Widerstandsrechts im Reich 1523–1626' in *Das Interim 1548/50: Herrschaftskrise und Glaubenskonflikt*, ed. Luise Schorn-Schütte, Gütersloh, pp. 389–437.

(2008). 'Church and State in Lutheran Lands, 1550–1675' in *Lutheran Ecclesiastical Culture 1550–1675*, ed. Robert Kolb, Leiden and Boston, MA, pp. 361–410.

Friedeburg, Robert von and Seidler, Michael (2007). 'The Holy Roman Empire of the German Nation' in *European Political Thought, 1450–1700: Religion, Law and Philosophy*, ed. Howell Lloyd, Glen Burgess, and Simon Hodson, New Haven, CT, pp. 103–72.

Friedrich, Karin (2007). 'Polish-Lithuanian Political Thought, 1450–1700' in *European Political Throught, 1450–1700: Religion, Law and Philosophy*, ed. Howell Lloyd, Glenn Burgess and Simon Hodson, Cambridge, pp. 409–47.

Frier, Bruce W. and McGinn, Thomas A. J. (2004). *A Casebook on Roman Family Law*, Oxford.

Fröschl, Thomas (1981). '*Die frühneuzeitliche Republik: Verfassungsform, Selbstverständnis und Selbstdarstellung der europäischen "Ausnahme" vom 16. zum 18. Jahrhundert*' (unpublished Ph.D. thesis), Vienna.

(ed.) (1994). *Föderationsmodelle und Unionsstrukturen: Über Staatenverbindungen in der frühen Neuzeit vom 15. zum 18. Jahrhundert*, Vienna and Munich.

Frugoni, Arnaldo (1950). 'Sulla renovatio senatus del 1143 e l'ordo equestris', *Bullettino dell'Istituto Storico Italiano per il Medio Evo* 62, pp. 159–74.

Funkenstein, Amos (1993). *Perceptions of Jewish History*, Berkeley, CA.

Gabel, Helmut (1999). 'Die Niederlande und das Heilige Römische Reich. Zur politischen und perzeptionellen Konfiguration einer Beziehung' in *Onder den Oranje boom. Textband: Dynastie in der Republik das Haus Oranien-Nassau als Vermittler niederländischer Kultur in deutschen Territorien im 17. und 18. Jahrhundert*, ed. Horst Lademacher, Munich, pp. 27–42.

Gamboni, Dario and Germann, Georg with de Capitani, François (eds.) (1991). *Zeichen der Freiheit: Das Bild der Republik in der Kunst des 16. bis 20. Jahrhunderts*, Berne.

Garnsey, Peter (1970). *Social Status and Legal Privilege in the Roman Empire*, Oxford.

(2007). *Thinking about Property: From Antiquity to the Age of Revolution*, Cambridge.

Gauss, Julia and Stöcklin, Alfred (1953). *Bürgermeister Wettstein: Der Mann – Das Werk – Die Zeit*, Basel and Geneva.
Gay, Peter (1959). *Voltaire's Politics*, Princeton, NJ.
(1964). *Party of Humanity: Essays in the French Enlightenment*, New York.
(1966). *The Enlightenment: The Rise of Modern Paganism*, New York.
Gemmeke, E. (1965). *Die Metaphysik des sittlich Guten bei Franz Suarez*, Freiburg.
Gerics, József (1987). *A korai rendiség Európában és Magyarországon*, Budapest.
Gerrish, B. A. (2006). 'Natural and Revealed Religion' in *The Cambridge History of Eighteenth-Century Philosophy*, 2 vols., ed. Knud Haakonssen, Cambridge, vol. II, pp. 641–65.
Geuna, Marco (2006). 'Skinner, Pre-humanist Culture and Machiavelli' in *Rethinking the Foundations of Modern Political Thought*, ed. Annabel Brett and James Tully, Cambridge, pp. 50–72.
Geuss, Raymond (1996). 'Kultur, Bildung, Geist', *History and Theory* 35, pp. 151–64.
Geuss, Raymond and Hollis, Martin (1995). 'Freedom as an Ideal', *Proceedings of the Aristotelian Society, Supplementary Volumes* 69, pp. 87–112.
Giesey, Ralph (1961). *Juristic Basis of Dynastic Right to the French Throne*, Philadelphia, PA.
Gil, Xavier (2007). 'Spain and Portugal' in *European Political Thought, 1400–1700: Religion, Law and Philosophy*, ed. Howell A. Lloyd, Glenn Burgess and Simon Hodson, New Haven, CT, pp. 416–57.
Gill, C. (2006). *The Structured Self in Hellenistic and Roman Thought*, Oxford.
Gilmore, Myron Piper (1941). *Argument from Roman Law in Political Thought, 1200–1600*, Cambridge.
Glavina, Mladen (2009). '17. *Yüzyıl Başında Osmanlı İmparatorluğu ile Dubrovnik Cumhuriyeti İlişkileri*' (The Relationship between the Ottoman Empire and Ragusan Republic at the Beginning of the Seventeenth Century), MA thesis, University of Ankara.
Glover, Samuel Denis (1999). 'The Putney Debates: Popular vs Elitist Republicanism', *Past and Present* 164, pp. 47–80.
Goetschel, Willi (2004). *Spinoza's Modernity: Mendelssohn, Lessing, Heine*, Madison, WI.
(2007). 'Mendelssohn and the State', *Modern Language Notes* 122, pp. 472–92.
Goldenbaum, Ursula (2000). 'Einführung' in Jean-Jacques Rousseau, *Abhandlung von dem Ursprunge der Ungleichheit unter den Menschen*, trans. Moses Mendelssohn, ed. Ursula Goldenbaum, Weimar, pp. 1–63.
Goldie, Mark (2001). 'The Unacknowledged Republic: Officeholding in Early Modern England' in *The Politics of the Excluded, c1500–1850*, ed. Tim Harris, Basingstoke, pp. 153–94.
(1997). 'Introduction', in *Locke: Political Essays*, Cambridge, pp. xi–xxvii.
Gómez Camacho, F. (1998). 'Later Scholastics: Spanish Economic Thought in the XVIth and XVIIth Centuries' in *Ancient and Medieval Economic Ideas and Concepts of Social Justice*, ed. S. T. Lowry and B. Gordon Leiden, pp. 503–61.
Gooch, G. P. (1966). *Germany and the French Revolution*, New York.
Goodwin, Albert (1979). *The Friends of Liberty: The English Democratic Movement in the Age of the French Revolution*, London.

Gorski, Philip S. (2001). 'Calvinism and Revolution: The Walzer Thesis Reconsidered' in *Meaning and Modernity: Religion, Polity, and Self*, ed. Richard Madsen *et al.*, Berkeley, CA, pp. 78–104.

Graf, Friedrich Wilhelm (2007). 'Der Protestantismus' in *Säkularisierung und die Weltreligionen*, ed. Hans Joas and Klaus Wiegandt, Frankfurt, pp. 78–124.

Graham, Michael F. (2008). *The Blasphemies of Thomas Aikenhead: Boundaries of Belief on the Eve of the Enlightenment*, Edinburgh.

Green, Janet (2000). 'Queen Elizabeth I's Latin Reply to the Polish Ambassador', *Sixteenth Century Journal* 31, pp. 987–1008.

Green, Kenneth Hart (1992). 'Moses Mendelssohn's Opposition to the *Herem*: The First Step toward Denominationalism?', *Modern Judaism* 12, pp. 39–60.

Greenblatt, Stephen (1994). 'Invisible Bullets: Renaissance Authority and Its Subversion, Henry IV and Henry V' in *Political Shakespeare: Essays in Cultural Materialism*, ed. Jonathan Dollimore and Alan Sinfield, 2nd edn, Manchester, pp. 18–47.

Griffiths, Gordon (1970). 'Humanists and Representative Government in the Sixteenth Century: Bodin, Marnix, and the Invitation to the Duke of Anjou to Become Ruler of the Low Countries' in *Representative Institutions in Theory and Practice: Historical Papers Read at Bryn Mawr College April 1968 (Études présentées à la commission internationale pour l'histoire des assemblées d'états*, vol. XXXIX), Brussels, pp. 59–83.

Grunert, F. and Seelmann, K. (eds.) (1997). *Die Ordnung der Praxis: Neue Studien zur Spanischen Spätscholastik*, Tübingen.

Gruppelaar, Jaap and Verwey, Gerlof (eds.) (2010). *D. V. Coonhert (1522–1590): Polemist and Vredezoeker*, Amsterdam.

Grześkowiak-Krwawicz, Anna (2006). *Regina libertas: wolność w polskiej myśli politycznej XVIII wieku*, Gdańsk.

Guggisberg, Hans R. (2003). *Sebastian Castellio, 1515–1563: Humanist and Defender of Religious Toleration in a Confessional Age*, trans. Bruce Gordon, Aldershot.

Gunn, John A. W. (1969). *Politics and the Public Interest in the Seventeenth Century*, Toronto.

Gunther-Canada, Wendy (1996). 'Mary Wollstonecraft's "Wild Wish": Confounding Sex in the Discourse on Political Rights' in *Feminist Interpretations of Mary Wollstonecraft*, ed. M. J. Falco, University Park, PA, pp. 61–83.

(2001). *Rebel Writer: Mary Wollstonecraft and Enlightenment Politics*, DeKalb, IL.

Guttmann, Julius (1981). 'Mendelssohn's *Jerusalem* and Spinoza's *Theologico-Political Treatise*' in *Studies in Jewish Thought: An Anthology of German Jewish Scholarship*, ed. Alfred Jospe, Detroit, MI, pp. 361–86.

Guy, John (2002). 'Monarchy and Counsel' in *The Sixteenth Century*, ed. Patrick Collinson, Cambridge, pp. 1485–1603.

Guyer, Paul (1993). *Kant and the Experience of Freedom*, Cambridge.

Ha, Polly (2011). *English Presbyterianism, 1590–1640*. Palo Alto, CA.

Haakonssen, Knud (1996). *Natural Law and Moral Philosophy: From Grotius to the Scottish Enlightenment*, Cambridge.

(1998). 'Divine/Natural Law Theories in Ethics' in *The Cambridge History of Seventeenth-Century Philosophy*, 2 vols., ed. Daniel Garber and Michael Ayers, Cambridge, vol. II, pp. 1317–57.

Hadfield, Andrew (1998). *Literature, Travel, and Colonial Writing in the English Renaissance, 1545–1625*, Oxford.

Hadot, Pierre (2000). *Exercices spirituels et philosophie antique*, Paris.

Haitsma Mulier and Eco Oste Gaspard (1980). *The Myth of Venice and Dutch Republican Thought in the Seventeenth Century*, Assen.

(1987). 'The Language of Seventeenth-Century Republicanism in the United Provinces: Dutch or European?' in *The Languages of Political Theory in Early-Modern Europe*, ed. Anthony R. Pagden, Cambridge, pp. 179–95.

Haitsma Mulier, Eco Oste Gaspard and Velema, Wyger R. E. (eds.) (1999). *Vrijheid: een geschiedenis van de vijftiende tot de twintigste eeuw*, Amsterdam.

Halldenius, Lena (2003). 'Locke and the Non-Arbitrary', *European Journal of Political Theory* 2, pp. 261–79.

(2007). 'The Primacy of Right. On the Triad of Liberty, Equality, and Virtue in Wollstonecraft's Political Thought', *British Journal for the History of Philosophy* 15, pp. 75–99.

(2009). 'Liberty and Its Circumstances: A Functional Approach' in *New Waves in Political Philosophy*, ed. B. de Bruin and C. F. Curn, Basingstoke, pp. 19–39.

Halm, H. (1981). 'Das "Buch der Schatten"', *Der Islam* 58, pp. 15–86.

(1985). 'Courants et mouvements antinomistes dans l'islam médiéval' in *La notion de liberté au Moyen Age: Islam, Byzance, Occident*, ed. G. Makdisi *et al.*, Paris, pp. 135–41.

Hampsher-Monk, Iain (1976). 'The Political Theory of the Levellers: Putney, Property and Professor Macpherson', *Political Studies* 24, pp. 397–422.

Hampton, Jean (1986). *Hobbes and the Social Contract Tradition*, Cambridge.

Hankins, James (1995). 'The "Baron Thesis" after Forty Years and Some Recent Studies of Leonardo Bruni', *Journal of the History of Ideas* 56, pp. 309–30.

(ed.) (2000a). *Renaissance Civic Humanism: Reappraisals and Reflections*, Cambridge, MA.

(2000b). 'Rhetoric, History, and Ideology: The Civic Panegyrics of Leonardo Bruni' in *Renaissance Civic Humanism: Reappraisals and Reflections*, ed. James Hankins, Cambridge, MA, pp. 143–78.

Hansen, M. H. (2000). 'Conclusion: The Impact of City-state Cultures on World History' in *A Comparative Study of Thirty City-state Cultures*, ed. M. H. Hansen, Copenhagen, pp. 597–623.

Harding, Alan (1980). 'Political Liberty in the Middle Ages', *Speculum* 55, pp. 423–43.

Harline, Graig E. (1987). *Pamphlets, Printing, and Political Culture in the Early Dutch Republic*, Dordrecht, Boston and Lancaster.

Harnack, Carl Gustav Adolf von (1900). *Geschichte der Königlich Preußischen Akademie der Wissenschaften zu Berlin*, Berlin.

Harris, Ian (2000). 'Locke on Justice' in *English Philosophy in the Age of Locke*, ed. M. A. Stewart, Oxford, pp. 49–85.

(2002). 'Tolérance, église et état chez Locke' in *Les fondements philosophiques de la tolérance*, 3 vols., ed. Yves-Charles Zarka, Franck Lessay and G. A. J. Rogers, Paris, vol. I, pp. 175–218.

(2008). 'Toleration and its Place: A Study of Pierre Bayle in his *Commentaire Philosophique*' in *Studies on Locke: Sources, Contemporaries, and Legacy*, ed. Sarah Hutton and Paul Schuurman, Dordrecht, pp. 225–43.
Harris, James A. (2005). *Of Liberty and Necessity: The Free Will Debate in Eighteenth-Century British Philosophy*, Oxford.
Harris, Robin (2003). *Dubrovnik: A History*, London.
Harris, Seymour F. (ed.) (1899). *The Elements of Roman Law Summarised: A Concise Digest of the Institutes of Gaius and Justinian*, etc., 3rd edn revised, London.
Harris, Tim (2001). *The Politics of the Excluded, c1500–1850*, Basingstoke.
Harrison, John and Laslett, Peter (eds.) (1965). *The Library of John Locke*, 2nd edn, Oxford.
Hart, H. L. A. (1994). *The Concept of Law*, Oxford.
(2001). *Representing the New World: The English and French Uses of the Example of Spain*, New York.
Harth, Erica (1992). *Cartesian Women: Versions and Subversions of Rational Discourse in the Old Regime*, Ithaca, NY.
Harvey, Warren Zev (1998). 'Mendelssohn's Heavenly Politics' in *Perspectives on Jewish Thought and Mysticism*, ed. Allan Arkush, Alfred Ivry and Elliot Wolfson, Amsterdam, pp. 403–12.
Haskin, Dayton (1994). *Milton's Burden of Interpretation*, Philadelphia, PA.
Hatcher, John (1981). 'English Society and Villeinage: Towards a Reassessment', *Past and Present* 90, pp. 3–39.
Hausknecht, Gina (2005). 'The Gender of Civic Virtue' in *Milton and Gender*, ed. Catherine Gimelli Martin, Cambridge, pp. 19–33.
Heinämaa, S. and Reuter, M. (eds.) (2009). *Psychology and Philosophy*, Dordrecht.
Helmrath, J. (2000). 'Pius II. und die Turken' in *Europa und die Türken in der Renaissance*, ed. Bodo Guthümüller and Wilhelm Kühlmann, Tübingen.
Henderson, Ernest (ed.) (1903). *Select Historical Documents of the Middle Ages*, London.
Henrich, Dieter (1967), 'Über den Sinn vernünftigen Handelns im Staat' in *Kant, Gentz, Rehberg: Über Theorie und Praxis*, ed. Henrich, Frankfurt am Main.
Herdt, Jennifer A. (2008). *Putting on Virtue: The Legacy of the Splendid Vices*, Chicago.
Heringa, Jan (1961). *De eer en hoogheid von de staat: over de plaats der Verenigde Nederlanden in het diplomatieke leven van de Zeventiende eeuw*, Groningen.
Hertzberg, Arthur (1968). 'The Chosen People', *New York Review of Books* (October 24).
Hexter, J. H. (1973). 'The Predatory Vision: Niccolò Machiavelli. *Il Principe* and *lo Stato*' in Hexter, *The Vision of Politics on the Eve of the Reformation: More, Machiavelli, Seyssel*, New York, pp. 150–75.
Hilfrich, Carola (2000). *Lebendige Schrift: Repräsentation und Idolatrie in Moses Mendelssohns Philosophie und Exegese des Judentums*, Munich.
Hilton, R. (1965). 'Freedom and Villeinage in England', *Past and Present* 3, pp. 3–19.
Hindess, Barry (1996). *Discourses of Power: From Hobbes to Foucault*, Oxford.
Hinton, R. W. K. (1967). 'Husbands, Fathers and Conquerors', *Political Studies* 15, pp. 291–300.
Hirst, Derek (1975). *Representative of the People? Voters and Voting in England under the Early Stuarts*, Cambridge.
Hochstrasser, Tim (2000). *Natural Law Theories in the Early Enlightenment*, Cambridge.

Höfert, Almut (2003). *Den Feind beschreiben: 'Türkengefahr' und europäisches Wissen über das Osmanische Reich 1450–1600*, Frankfurt am Main.
Hoffmann, George (1998). *Montaigne's Career*, Oxford.
Hogson, Peter C. (2009). 'Luther and Freedom' in *The Global Luther*, ed. Christine Helmer, Minneapolis, MN, pp. 32–48.
Hohfeld, Wesley Newcomb (1919). *Fundamental Legal Conceptions as Applied in Judicial Reasoning*, ed. Walter Wheeler Cook, New Haven, CT.
Hoke, Rudolf (1968). *Die Reichsstaatsrechtslehre des Johannes Limnaeus: Ein Beitrag zur Geschichte der Deutschen Staatsrechtswissenschaft im 17. Jahrhundert*, Aalen.
Holenstein, André, Maissen, Thomas and Prak, Maarten (eds.) (2008). *The Republican Alternative: The Netherlands and Switzerland Compared*, Amsterdam.
Holmes, Stephen (1990). 'The Secret History of Self-interest' in *Beyond Self-interest*, ed. Jane J. Mansbridge, Chicago, IL, pp. 267–86.
Holstun, James (1987). *A Rational Millennium: Puritan Utopias of Seventeenth-Century England and America*, Oxford.
Holt, J. C. (1992). *Magna Carta*, Cambridge.
Höpfl, Harro (1991). *Luther and Calvin: On Secular Authority*, Cambridge.
(2004). *Jesuit Political Thought: The Society of Jesus and the State, c. 1540–1630*, Cambridge.
Höpfl, Harro and Thompson, Martyn P. (1979). 'The History of Contract as a Motif in Political Thought', *American Historical Review* 84, pp. 919–44.
Hopp, Lajos (1992). *Az 'antemurale' és 'conformitas' humanista eszméje a magyar-lengyel hagyományban*, Budapest.
Hörnqvist, Mikael (2000). 'Two Myths of Civic Humanism' in *Renaissance Civic Humanism: Reappraisals and Reflections*, ed. James Hankins, Cambridge, MA, pp. 105–42.
Hotson, Howard (1999). 'Rudolf II' in *Encyclopedia of the Renaissance*, vol. v, ed. Paul Grendler, New York.
Houlbrooke, Ralph (1984). *The English Family, 1450–1700*, London and New York.
Hourani, A. (1962). *Arabic Thought in the Liberal Age, 1798–1939*, London.
Hsia, R. Po-Chia and Nierop, Henk van (eds.) (2002). *Calvinism and Religious Toleration in the Dutch Golden Age*, Cambridge.
Hughes, Ann (1995). 'Gender Politics and Leveller Literature' in *Political Culture and Cultural Politics in Early Modern England*, ed. David Underdown, Susan Dwyer Amussen and Mark A. Kishlansky, Manchester, pp. 162–88.
Hundert, E. J. (1994). *The Enlightenment's Fable: Bernard Mandeville and the Discovery of Society*, Cambridge.
Hunter, Ian (2001). *Rival Enlightenments: Civil and Metaphysical Philosophy in Early Modern Germany*, Cambridge.
al-Husry, K. S. (1980). *Origins of Modern Arab Political Thought*, Delmar.
Illés, József (1931). *A Quadripartitum közjogi interpolátiói* (The public law interpolations of the Quadripartitum), Budapest.
Imber, C. (1997). *Ebu's-su'ud: The Islamic Legal Tradition*, Edinburgh.
Imre, Mihály (2004). 'Der ungarische Türkenkrieg als rhetorisches Thema in der Frühen Neuzeit' in *Deutschland und Ungarn in ihren Bildungs- und Wissenschaftsbeziehungen*

während der Renaissance, ed. Wilhelm Kühlmann and Anton Schindling, Stuttgart, pp. 93–107.

Israel, Jonathan I. (1994). 'Toleration in Seventeenth-Century Dutch and English Thought' in *Britain and the Netherlands*, vol. XI, ed. S. Groenveld and M. Wintle, pp. 13–30.

(1995). *The Dutch Republic: Its Rise, Greatness and Fall, 1477–1806*, Cambridge.

(1997). 'The Intellectual Debate about Toleration in the Dutch Republic' in *The Emergence of Tolerance in the Dutch Republic*, ed. Christiane Berkvens-Steelinck *et al.*, Leiden, pp. 3–36.

(1999). 'Locke, Spinoza and the Philosophical Debate concerning Toleration in the Early Enlightenment (c. 1650–c. 1750)', *Medelingen van de Afdeling Letterkunde. Royal Netherlands Academy of Sciences. New Series* 62, pp. 5–19.

(2000). 'Spinoza, Locke and the Enlightenment Battle for Toleration' in *Toleration in Enlightenment Europe*, ed. Ole Peter Grell and Roy Porter, Cambridge, pp. 102–13.

(2001). *Radical Enlightenment: Philosophy and the Making of Modernity, 1650–1750*, Oxford.

Jacobi, Thorsten (1997). *Christen heißen Freie: Luthers Freiheitsaussagen in den Jahren 1515–1519*, Tübingen.

James, Susan (1997). *Passion and Action: The Emotions in Seventeenth-Century Philosophy*, Oxford.

Janicki, Marek (2004). 'Wolność i równość w języku prawno-politycznym oraz ideologii szlachty polskiej (od XIV do początku XVII wieku)' in *Łacina jako język elit*, ed. Jerzy Axer, Warsaw, pp. 73–107.

Jenner, W. J. F. (1998). 'China and Freedom' in *Asian Freedoms: The Idea of Freedom in East and Southeast Asia*, ed. D. Kelly and A. Reid, Cambridge, pp. 65–92.

Jobert, Ambroise (1974). *De Luther à Mohila: la Pologne dans la crise de la chrétienté, 1517–1648*, Paris.

Johnson, Claudia L. (2002). 'Mary Wollstonecraft's Novels' in *The Cambridge Companion to Mary Wollstonecraft*, ed. Claudia L. Johnson, Cambridge, pp. 189–208.

Jolley, Nicholas (1999). *Locke: His Philosophical Thought*, Oxford.

Jordan, Constance (1993). 'The Household and the State: Transformations in the Representation of an Analogy from Aristotle to James I', *Modern Language Quarterly* 54, pp. 307–26.

(2003). 'Montaigne on Property, Public Service and Political Servitude', *Renaissance Quarterly* 56, pp. 408–35.

Jordan, Elaine (1997). 'Criminal Conversation: Mary Wollstonecraft's *The Wrongs of Woman*', *Women's Writing* 4, pp. 221–34.

Kahn, Victoria (2004). *Wayward Contracts: The Crisis of Political Obligation in England, 1640–1674*, Princeton, NJ.

Kantorowicz, Ernst (1985). *The King's Two Bodies: A Study in Mediaeval Political Theology*, Princeton, NJ.

Kaplan, Benjamin (1994). '"Remnants of the Papal Yoke": Apathy and Opposition in the Dutch Reformation', *Sixteenth Century Journal* 25, pp. 653–69.

Kapossy, Béla (2006). *Iselin contra Rousseau: Sociable Patriotism and the History of Mankind*, Basel.

Kármán, Gábor (2005). 'Transylvania between the Ottoman and Habsburg Empires' in *Statehood before and beyond Ethnicity: Minor States in Northern and Eastern Europe, 1600–2000*, ed. Linas Eriksonas and Leos Müller, Brussels, pp. 151–8.

(2010). 'An Ally of Limited Acceptability: Johannes Bocatius and the Image of the Turk in Hungary' in *Perspectives on Ottoman Studies: Papers from the 18th Symposium of the International Committee of Pre-Ottoman and Ottoman Studies*, ed. Ekrem Čauševi, Nenad Moačanin and Vjeran Kursar, Berlin, pp. 971–80.

Kaufmann, M. (2007). 'Luis de Molina über subjektive Rechte, Herrschaft und Sklaverei' in *Politische Metaphysik*, ed. M. Kaufmann and R. Schnepf, Frankfurt, pp. 205–26.

Kaufmann, M. and Schnepf, R. (eds.) (2007). *Politische Metaphysik*, Frankfurt.

Kaufmann, Thomas (1998). *Dreißigjähriger Krieg und Westfälischer Frieden: Kirchengeschichtliche Studien zur lutherischen Konfessionskultur*, Tübingen.

(2003). *Das Ende der Reformation: Magdeburgs 'Herrgotts Kanzlei' 1540–1551/2*, Tübingen.

(2004). 'Luther zwischen den Wissenschaftskulturen – Ernst Troeltschs Lutherdeutung in der englischsprachigen Welt und in Deutschland' in *Luther zwischen den Kulturen*, ed. Hans Medick and Peer Schmidt, Göttingen, pp. 455–81.

(2006). *Konfession und Kultur*, Tübingen.

(2007). 'Evangelische Reformationsgeschichtsforschung nach 1945', *Zeitschrift für Theologie und Kirche* 104, pp. 404–54.

(2008a). *'Türckenbüchlein': Zur christlichen Wahrnehmung 'türkischer Religion' in Spätmittelalter und Reformation*, Göttingen.

(2008b). 'Das Bekenntnis im Luthertum des konfessionellen Zeitalters', *Zeitschrift für Theologie und Kirche* 105, pp. 281–314.

(2010a). *Geschichte der Reformation*, Berlin.

(2010b). '"History Is Good at Confounding and Confessing Labelers" – "Die Geschichte versteht es meisterlich, Schlagwortexperten zu irritieren und zu verwirren". Zu Diarmaid MacCullochs "Reformation"', *Archive for Reformation History* 101, pp. 305–20.

(2012). 'Theokratische Konzeptionen in der spätmittelalterlichen Reformliteratur und in der Radikalen Reformation' in *Der Anfang der Reformation: Studien zur Kontextualität der Theologie, Publizistik und Inszenierung Luthers, und der reformatorischen Bewegung*, Tübingen.

Keller-Escher, Carl (1885). *Geschichte der Familie Escher vom Glas, 1320–1885. 1. Teil: Geschichtliche Darstellung und biographische Schilderungen*, Zurich.

Kelley, Donald (1964). 'De Origine Feudorum: The Beginnings of an Historical Problem', *Speculum* 39, pp. 207–28.

(1970). *Foundations of Modern Historical Scholarship: Language, Law and History in the French Renaissance*, New York.

(1981). 'Civil Science in the Renaissance: Jurisprudence in the French Manner', *History of European Ideas* 2, pp. 261–76.

(1988). 'The Theory of History' in *The Cambridge History of Renaissance Philosophy*, ed. C. B. Schmitt and Q. Skinner, Cambridge.

(1990). *The Human Measure: Social Thought in the Western Legal Tradition*, Cambridge.

Kelly, Gary (1996). *Revolutionary Feminism: The Mind and Career of Mary Wollstonecraft*, New York.
Kennedy, H. (1997). 'From Oral Tradition to Written Record in Arabic Genealogy', *Arabica* 44, pp. 531–44.
Keohane, Nannerl O. (1977). 'Montaigne's Individualism', *Political Theory* 5, pp. 363–90.
(1985). *Philosophy and the State in France: The Renaissance to the Enlightenment*, Princeton, NJ.
Kessler, Wolfgang (1995). 'Stände und Herrschaft in Ungarn und seinen Nebenländern im 18. und frühen 19. Jahrhundert' in *Stände und Landesherrschaft in Ostmitteleuropa in der frühen Neuzeit*, ed. Hugo Weczerka, Marburg, pp. 171–91.
King, Margaret (1986). *Venetian Humanism in an Age of Patrician Dominance*, Princeton, NJ.
Kishlansky, Mark (1986). *Parliamentary Selection: Social and Political Choice in Early Modern England*, Cambridge.
Kiss, Gábor Farkas (2007). '1523 – Nagyszombati Márton: Magyarország előkelőihez, A törökellenes irodalom retorikája' in *A magyar irodalom történetei*, vol. 1., ed. László Jankovits and Géza Orlovszky, Budapest, pp. 185–95.
Kister, M. J. (1968). 'Al-Ḥīra: Some Notes on Its Relations with Arabia', *Arabica* 15, pp. 143–69.
Klapisch-Zuber, Christiane (2011). *Retour à la cité: les magnats de Florence 1340–1440*, Paris.
Kleingeld, Pauline (1999). 'Six Varieties of Cosmopoliotanism in Late Eighteenth-Century Germany', *Journal of the History of Ideas* 60, pp. 505–24.
Klemme, Heiner F. (1993). 'Einleitung' in *Über den Gemeinspruch: Das mag in der Theorie richtig sein, taugt aber nicht für die Praxis*, ed. Heiner F. Klemme, Hamburg.
Klinger, Andreas (2006). 'Die "deutsche Freiheit" im Revolutionsjahrzehnt 1789–1799' in *Kollektive Freiheitsvorstellungen im frühneuzeitlichen Europa (1400–1850)*, ed. Georg Schmidt, Martin van Gelderen, and Christopher Snigula, Frankfurt am Main, pp. 447–71.
Klippel, Diethelm (1976). 'Der politische Freiheitsbegriff im modernen Naturrecht' in *Geschichtliche Grundbegriffe: Historisches Lexikon zur politisch-sozialen Sprache in Deutschland*, ed. Otto Brunner, Werner Conze and Reinhart Koselleck, Stuttgart.
Kloczkowski, Jacek (ed.) (2008). *Wolność i jej granice: polskie dylematy*, Cracow.
Knebel, S. (2000). *Wille, Würfel und Wahrscheinlichkeit: Das System der moralischen Notwendigkeit in der Jesuitenscholastik 1550–1700*, Hamburg.
Knoppers, Laura Lunger (2008). 'Consuming Nations: Milton and Luxury' in *Early Modern Nationalism and Milton's England*, ed. David Loewenstein and Paul Stevens, Toronto and London, pp. 331–55.
Knudsen, Jonathan B. (1986). *Justus Möser and the German Enlightenment*, Cambridge.
Kobusch, T. (1993). *Die Entdeckung der Person. Metaphysik der Freiheit und modernes Menschenbild*, Freiburg.
Koenigsberger, Helmut G. (1986). 'Dominium Regale or Dominium Politicum et Regale. Monarchies and Parliaments in Early Modern Europe' in Helmut Koenigsberger, *Politicians and Virtuosi: Essays in Early Modern History*, London, pp. 1–26.

(1991). 'Epilogue: Central and Western Europe' in *Crown, Church and Estates: Central European Politics in the Sixteenth and Seventeenth Centuries*, ed. R. J. W. Evans and T. V. Thomas, London, pp. 300–10.

(1997). 'Republicanism, Monarchism and Liberty' in *Royal and Republican Sovereignty in Early Modern Europe*, ed. G. C. Gibb, Robert Oresko and H. M. Scott, Cambridge, pp. 43–74.

(2001). *Monarchies, States Generals and Parliaments: The Netherlands in the Fifteenth and Sixteenth Centuries*, Cambridge.

Kohler, Alfred (2001). *Karl V. 1500–1558: Eine Biographie*, Munich.

Kolb, Robert (ed.) (2008). *Lutheran Ecclesiastical Culture, 1550–1675*, Leiden and Boston, MA.

Kontler, László and Trencsényi, Balázs (2007). 'Hungary' in *European Political Thought 1450–1700: Religion, Law and Philosophy*, ed. Howell A. Lloyd, Glenn Burgess and Simon Hodson, New Haven, CT, pp. 176–207.

Korolko, Mirosław (1974). *Klejnot swobodnego sumienia: polemika wokół konfederacji warszawskiej w latach 1573–1658*, Warsaw.

Koschaker, Paul (1947). *Europa und das Römische Recht*, Munich.

Koselleck, Reinhart (1985). 'The Historical-Political Semantics of Asymmetric Counterconcepts' in *Futures Past: On the Semantics of Historical Time*, Cambridge and London, pp. 159–97.

(1988). *Critique and Crisis: Enlightenment and the Pathogenesis of Modern Society*, Cambridge, MA.

(2004). 'Bund, Bündnis, Föderalismus, Bundesstaat' in *Geschichtliche Grundbegriffe: Historisches Lexikon zur politisch-sozialen Sprache in Deutschland. Studienausgabe*, ed. Otto Brunner, Werner Conze and Reinhard Koselleck, Stuttgart, vol. 1, pp. 582–671.

Kossmann, Ernst Heinrich (1960a). *Politieke theorie in het zeventiende-eeuwse Nederland (Verhandelingen der Koninklijke Nederlandse Akademie van Wetenschappen, afd. Letterkunde*, Bd. 67, 2), Amsterdam; English trans. 'The Course of Dutch Political Thought in the Seventeenth Century' in E. H. Kossmann, *Political Thought in the Dutch Republic: Three Studies*, Amsterdam (2000), pp. 25–129.

(1960b). 'The Development of Dutch Political Theory in the Seventeenth Century' in *Britain and the Netherlands*, ed. J. S. Bromley and Ernst Heinrich Kossmann, London, pp. 91–110.

(1985). 'Dutch Republicanism' in *L'età dei lumi: studi storici sul settecento europeo in onore di Franco Venturi*, vol. 1, Naples, pp. 455–86; also in E. H. Kossmann, *Political Thought in the Dutch Republic: Three Studies*, Amsterdam, (2000), pp. 169–93.

(1991). 'Freedom in Seventeenth-Century Dutch Thought and Practice' in *The Anglo-Dutch Moment*, ed. Jonathan Israel, Cambridge, pp. 281–98.

(2000a). *Political Thought in the Dutch Republic: Three Studies*, Amsterdam.

(2000b). 'Popular Sovereignty at the Beginning of the Dutch Ancien Régime' in *Political Thought in the Dutch Republic: Three Studies*, Amsterdam, pp. 144–6.

Kot, Stanisław (1957). *Socinianism in Poland: The Social and Political Ideas of the Polish Antitrinitarians in the Sixteenth and Seventeenth Centuries*, trans. Earl Morse Wilbur, Boston.

Kraye, Jill and Stone, M. W. F. (2000). *Humanism and Early Modern Philosophy*, London.

Krekić, Bariša (1972). *Dubrovnik in the 14th and 15th Centuries: A City between East and West*, Norman, OK.

Krzyżanowski, Julian (1975). *Mądrej głowie dość dwie słowie: pięć centuryj przysłów polskich i diabelski tuzin z hakiem*, 3 vols., vol. II, Warsaw.

Kubinyi, András (1998). *König und Volk im spätmittelalterlichen Ungarn: Städteentwicklung, Alltagsleben und Regierung im mittelalterlichen Königreich Ungarn*, Studien zur Geschichte Ungarns 1, Herne.

(1999). 'István Werbőczy als Politiker in der Zeit vor Mohács (1526)' in *The Man of Many Devices Who Wandered Full Many Ways... Festschrift in Honor of János M. Bak*, ed. Balázs Nagy and Marcell Sebők, Budapest and New York, pp. 558–82.

(2006). 'Az 1505. évi rákosi országgyűlés és a szittya ideológia', *Századok* 140, pp. 361–74.

La Vopa, Anthony J. (2001). *Fichte: The Self and the Calling of Philosophy 1762–1799*, Cambridge.

Laborde, Cécile and Maynor, John (eds.) (2008). *Republicanism and Political Theory*, Oxford.

Lagrée, Jaqueline (1994). *Juste Lipse la restauration du stoicisme: étude et traduction de divers traités stoiciens*, Paris.

(1999). 'Juste Lipse: l'âme et la vertu' in *Iustus Lipsius, Europae Lumen et Columen. Proceedings of the International Colloquium, Leuven, 17–19 September 1997*, ed. Gilles Tournoy, Jeanine de Landtsheer and Jan Papy, Leuven, pp. 90–106.

Laks, A. (2007). 'Freedom, Liberality, and Liberty in Plato's *Laws*' in *Freedom, Reason, and the Polis: Essays in Ancient Greek Political Philosophy*, ed. D. Keyt and F. D. Miller, Cambridge, pp. 130–52.

Lamont, William (1969). *Godly Rule: Politics and Religion, 1603–1660*, London.

Lane, E. W. (1863–93). *An Arabic–English Lexicon*, London.

Lang, Daniel George (1985). *Foreign Policy in the Early Republic: The Law of Nations and the Balance of Power*, Baton Rouge, LA.

Larmore, Charles (1998). 'Scepticism' in *The Cambridge History of Seventeenth-Century Philosophy*, ed. Daniel Garber and Michael Ayers, 2 vols., Cambridge, vol. II, pp. 1145–92.

Laureys, Marc (ed.) (1998). *The World of Justus Lipsius: Contributions towards His Intellectual Biography*, Turnhout.

Le Maire, André Alexandre (1974). 'O Dubrovniku i Dubrovčanima 1766' (On Ragusa and Ragusans in 1766), *Dubrovnik* 6, pp. 9–65.

Lecler, Joseph (1960). *Toleration and the Reformation*, 2 vols., London.

Lee, Daniel (2011). 'Popular Liberty, Princely Government, and the Roman Law in Hugo Grotius's *De Jure Belli ac Pacis*', *Journal of the History of Ideas* 72, pp. 371–92.

Leppin, Volker (1999). *Antichrist und Jüngster Tag: Das Profil apokalyptischer Flugschriftenpublizistik im Deutschen Luthertum 1548–1618*, Gütersloh.

(2006). 'Freiheit als Zentralbegriff der frühen reformatorischen Bewegung. Ein Beitrag zur Frage "Luther und die Bauern"' in *Kollektive Freiheitsvorstellungen im frühneuzeitlichen Europa (1400–1850)*, ed. Georg Schmidt, Martin van Gelderen and Christopher Snigula, Frankfurt am Main, pp. 317–27.

(2008). 'Streit um Luther? Gerne!', *Luther* 79, pp. 49–52.
Lewalski, Barbara (2002). *The Life of John Milton: A Critical Biography*, revised edn, Oxford.
Lewis, B. (1964). *The Middle East and the West*, London.
(1982). *The Muslim Discovery of Europe*, New York and London.
(1988). *The Political Language of Islam*, Chicago, IL and London.
Leyser, Karl (1994). *Communications and Power in Medieval Europe: The Gregorian Revolution and Beyond*, trans. T. Reuter, Cambridge.
Lifschitz, Avi (2007). 'From the Corruption of French to the Cultural Distinctiveness of German: The Controversy over Prémontval's *Préservatif* (1759)', *Studies on Voltaire and the Eighteenth Century* 6, pp. 265–90.
(2009). 'The Enlightenment Revival of the Epicurean History of Language and Civilisation' in *Epicurus in the Enlightenment*, ed. Neven Leddy and Avi Lifschitz, Oxford, pp. 207–26.
(2012a). 'The Arbitrariness of the Linguistic Sign: Variations on an Enlightenment Theme', *Journal of the History of Ideas* 73 (4), pp. 537–55.
(2012b). *Language and Enlightenment: The Berlin Debates of the Eighteenth Century*, Oxford.
Lloyd, S. A. (1992). *Ideals as Interests in Hobbes's Leviathan*, Cambridge.
Lobenstein-Reichmann, Anja (1998). *Freiheit bei Martin Luther: Lexikographische Textanalyse als Methode historischer Semantik*, Berlin and New York.
Lobingier, Charles Sumner (1916). 'The Reception of Roman Law in Germany', *Michigan Law Review* 14, pp. 562–9.
Long, A. A. (2003). 'Stoicism in the Philosophical Tradition: Spinoza, Lipsius, Butler' in *The Cambridge Companion to the Stoics*, ed. Brad Inwood, Cambridge.
Long, A. A. and Sedley, D. N. (1987). *The Hellenistic Philosophers*, vol. 1, Cambridge.
Lovett, Frank (2010). *A General Theory of Domination and Justice*, Oxford.
Lowry, S. T. and Gordon, B. (eds.) (1998). *Ancient and Medieval Economic Ideas and Concepts of Social Justice*, Leiden.
Luhmann, Niklas (2000). 'Familiarity, Confidence, Trust: Problems and Alternatives' in *Trust: Making and Breaking Cooperative Relations*, ed. Diego Gambetta, Oxford, pp. 94–107.
Łukowski, George (1991). *Liberty's Folly: The Polish-Lithuanian Commonwealth in the Eighteenth Century*, London.
(2010). *Disorderly Liberty: The Political Culture of the Polish-Lithuanian Commonwealth in the Eighteenth Century*, London.
Luxon, Thomas H. (2005). *Single Imperfection: Milton, Marriage and Friendship*, Pittsburgh, PA.
al-M'daghrī, Abd al-Kabīr al-ʿAlawī (1989). *al-Faqīh Abū ʿAlī al-Yūsī: numūdhaj min al-fikr al-Maghribī fī fajr al-dawla al-ʿAlawiyya*, n.p.
MacCormack, Sabine (2007). *On the Wings of Time: Rome, the Incas, Spain, and Peru*, Princeton, NJ.
McCormick, John P. (2011). *Machiavellian Democracy*, Cambridge.
McCoy, Richard (1979). *Sir Philip Sidney: Rebellion in Arcadia*, Hassocks.
McCrea, Adriana (1997). *Constant Minds: Political Virtue and the Lipsian Paradigm in England, 1584–1650*, Toronto.

MacCulloch, Diarmaid (2004). *The Reformation*, London, New York and Toronto.
McDiarmid, John F. (ed.) (2007). *The Monarchical Republic of Early Modern England: Essays in Response to Patrick Collinson*, Aldershot.
McDonnell, Myles (2006). *Roman Manliness: Virtus and the Roman Republic*, Cambridge.
McGrath, Alister (1986). *Iustitia Dei: A History of the Christian Doctrine of Justification*, 2 vols., Cambridge.
Maciszewski, Jarema (1986). *Szlachta polska i jej państwo*, 2nd edn, Warsaw.
Mackie, V. (1998). 'Freedom and the Family: Gendering Meiji Political Thought' in *Asian Freedoms: The Idea of Freedom in East and Southeast Asia*, ed. D. Kelly and A. Reid, Cambridge, pp. 121–40.
McLachlan, Herbert John (1951). *Socinianism in Seventeenth-Century England*, London.
Maclear, J. F. (1975). 'New England and the Fifth Monarchy: The Quest for the Millennium in Early American Puritanism', *William and Mary Quarterly*, Third Series, 32, pp. 223–60.
Magnien, Marcel (1998). 'Aut peregrinator, aut sapiens: Montaigne vs Lipse' in *The World of Justus Lipsius: Contributions towards his Intellectual Biography*, ed. Marc Laureys, Turnhout, pp. 209–32.
Mährle, Wolfgang (2000). *Academia Norica: Wissenschaft und Bildung an der Nürnberger Hohen Schule in Altdorf (1575–1623)*, Stuttgart.
Maier, Hans (1980). *Die ältere Deutsche Staats- und Verwaltungslehre*, Munich.
Maissen, Thomas (2006). *Die Geburt der Republic: Staatsverständnis und Repräsentation in der frühneuzeitlichen Eidgenossenschaft*, Göttingen.
(2008). 'Inventing the Sovereign Republic. Imperial Structures, French Challenges, Dutch Models, and the Early Modern Swiss Confederation' in *The Republican Alternative: The Netherlands and Switzerland Compared*, ed. André Holenstein, Thomas Maissen and Maarten Prak, Amsterdam, pp. 125–50.
Maitland, F.W. (1898). *Township and Borough*, Cambridge.
Maitland, F.W. (ed.) (1895). *Select Passages from the Works of Bracton and Azo*, London.
Major, J. Russell (1994). *From Renaissance Monarchy to Absolute Monarchy: French Kings, Nobles and Estates*, Baltimore, MD.
Mäkinen, V. and Korkmann, P. (eds.). (2006). *Transformations in Medieval and Early-Modern Rights Discourse*, Dordrecht.
Makkai, László (1974a). 'A Habsburgok és a magyar rendiség a Bocskai-felkelés előestéjén', *Történelmi Szemle* 1–2, pp. 155–82.
(1974b). 'Bocskai és európai kortársai', *Történelmi Szemle* 4, pp. 483–94.
Malcolm, Noel (2003). *Aspects of Hobbes*, Oxford.
(2007). *Reason of State, Propaganda, and the Thirty Years' War: An Unknown Translation by Thomas Hobbes*, Oxford.
Maliks, Reidar (2013). 'Kant, the State, and Revolution', forthcoming in *Kantian Review* 18 (1).
Mályusz, Elemér (1942). 'A magyar köznemesség kialakulása.' [The Development of the Hungarian Lesser Nobility], *Századok*, pp. 272–305 and 407–34.
(2005). *A konstanzi zsinat és a magyar főkegyúri jog*, Gödöllő.
Manetsch, Scott (2000). *Theodore Beza and the Quest for Peace in France, 1562–1598*, Leiden.

Manin, Bernard (1997). *The Principles of Representative Government*, Cambridge.
Mansfield, Harvey C. (1983). 'On the Impersonality of the Modern State: A Comment on Machiavelli's Use of *Stato*', *American Political Science Review* 77, pp. 849–57.
Mantey, Volker (2005). *Zwei Schwerter – Zwei Reiche: Martin Luthers Zwei-Reiche-Lehre vor ihrem spätmittelalterlichen Hintergrund*, Tübingen.
Maravall, José-Antonio (1995). *La philosophie politique espagnole au XVIIe siècle, dans ses rapports avec l'esprit de la contre-réforme*, Paris.
Marchwicki, Wojciech (2006). 'Pojęcie wolności w opinii szlachty Rzeczypospolitej XVII wieku', *Scripta Minora* 4, pp. 315–401.
Marlow, L. (1997). *Hierarchy and Egalitarianism in Islamic Thought*, Cambridge.
Marshall, Anthony J. (1975). 'Flaccus and the Jews of Asia (Cicero Pro Flacco 28.67–69), *Phoenix* 29, pp. 139–54.
Marshall, John (1994). *John Locke: Resistance, Religion, and Responsibility*, Cambridge.
(2000). 'Locke, Socinianism, "Socinianism", and Unitarianism' in *English Philosophy in the Age of Locke*, ed. M. A. Stewart, Oxford, pp. 111–82.
(2006). *John Locke, Toleration and the Early Enlightenment*, Cambridge.
Marshall, John (1998). *Descartes's Moral Theory*, Ithaca, NY.
Martin, John Jeffries (1997). 'Inventing Sincerity, Refashioning Prudence: The Discovery of the Individual in Renaissance Europe', *American Historical Review* 102, pp. 1309–42.
Martinich, A. P. (1992). *The Two Gods of Leviathan: Thomas Hobbes on Religion and Politics*, Cambridge.
Maryks, Robert Aleksander (2008). *Saint Cicero and the Jesuits: The Influence of the Liberal Arts on the Adoption of Moral Probabilism*, Aldershot.
Maurer, Wilhelm (1949). *Von der Freiheit eines Christenmenschen*, Göttingen.
Mautner, Thomas (2005). 'Grotius and the Skeptics', *Journal of the History of Ideas* 66, pp. 577–601.
Maynor, John (2003). *Republicanism in the Modern World*, Cambridge.
Mendus, Susan (1992). 'Kant: "An Honest but Narrow-Minded Bourgeois"?' in *Essays on Kant's Political Philosophy*, ed. Howard Williams, Chicago.
Meyer, Hermann (ed.) (1926). *Verzeichniss der auserlesenen Büchersammlung des seeligen Herrn Moses Mendelssohn*, Berlin.
Meynial, E. (1907). 'Notes sur la formation de la théorie du domaine divisé' in *Mélanges Fitting*, 2 vols., Montpellier.
Miller, Perry (1970). *Orthodoxy in Massachusetts, 1630–1650*, New York.
Mills, Kenneth (1994). 'The Limits of Religious Coercion in Mid-Colonial Peru', *Past and Present* 145, pp. 84–121.
(1997). *Idolatry and Its Enemies: Colonial Andean Religion and Extirpation, 1640–1750*, Princeton, NJ.
Milton, Anthony (ed.) (2005). *The British Delegation and the Synod of Dort (1618–1619)*, Woodbridge.
Miović, Vesna (2003). *Dubrovačka diplomacija u Istambulu (Ragusan Diplomacy in Istanbul)*, Dubrovnik and Zagreb.
(2005). *Dubrovačka Republika u spisima osmanskih sultana* (Ragusan Republic in the Documents Issued by the Ottoman Sultans), Dubrovnik.

Mitchell, Annie C. (2004). 'A *Liberal* Republican "Cato"', *American Journal of Political Science* 48, pp. 588–603.
Mitchell, Harvey (2008). *Voltaire's Jews and Modern Jewish Identity: Rethinking the Enlightenment*, London.
Mitchell, Joshua (1990). 'John Locke and the Theological Foundations of Liberal Toleration: A Christian Dialectic of History', *Review of Politics* 52, pp. 64–83.
Mitić, Ilija (2004). *Dubrovačka država u međunarodnoj zajednici* (Ragusan State within the International Community), Zagreb.
Moeller, Bernd (2001). 'Klerus und Antiklerikalismus in Luthers Schrift "An den christlichen Adel deutscher Nation" von 1520' in his *Luther-Rezeption*, Göttingen, pp. 108–20.
Moggach, Douglas (2011). 'Aesthetics and Politics' in *The Cambridge History of Nineteenth-Century Political Thought*, ed. Gareth Stedman Jones and Gregory Claeys, Cambridge, pp. 479–520.
Monserrat, Gilles D. (1984). *Light from the Porch: Stoicism and English Renaissance Literature*, Paris.
Monti, Gennaro Maria (1940). 'La dottrina anti-imperiale dei angioini di Napoli: i loro vicariati imperiali e Bartolomeo di Capua' in *Studi in onore di A. Solmi*, Milan, vol. II, pp. 11–57.
Morford, Mark (1991). *Stoics and Neostoics: Rubens and the Circle of Lipsius*, Princeton, NJ.
Morgan, Edmund S. (1963). *Visible Saints: The History of a Puritan Idea*, Ithaca, NY and London.
Morgan, Michael (1989). 'Liberalism in Mendelssohn's *Jerusalem*', *History of Political Thought* 10, pp. 281–94.
Moritz, Anja (2009). *Interim und Apokalypse: Die religiösen Vereinheitlichungsversuche Karls V. im Spiegel der magdeburgischen Publizistik*, Tübingen.
Mörke, Olaf (1999). 'Der "schwache" Staat als Erfolgsrezept? Die Niederländische Republik und die Schweizer Eidgenossenschaft' in *Quantität und Struktur: Festschrift für Kersten Krüger zum 60. Geburtstag*, ed. Werner Buchholz and Stefan Kroll, Rostock, pp. 45–62.
Mortimer, Sarah (2009). 'Human Liberty and Human Nature in the Works of Faustus Socinus and His Readers', *Journal of the History of Ideas* 70, pp. 191–211.
(2010). *Reason and Religion in the English Revolution: The Challenge of Socinianism*, Cambridge.
Mortimer, Sarah and Robertson, John (2012). 'Nature, Revelation and History' in *The Intellectual Consequences of Religious Heterodoxy 1600–1750*, ed. Sarah Mortimer and John Robertson, Leiden, pp. 1–40.
Mout, Nicolette (1988). 'Ideales Muster oder erfundene Eigenart. Republikanische Theorien während des niederländischen Aufstands' in *Republiken und Republikanismus im Europa der Frühen Neuzeit* (Schriften des Historischen Kollegs. Kolloquien 11), ed. Helmut Koenigsberger, Munich, pp. 169–94.
Muller, Richard A. (1991). *God, Creation, and Providence in the Thought of Jacob Arminius: Sources and Directions of Scholastic Protestantism in the Era of Early Orthodoxy*, Grand Rapids, MI.

Muller, Virginia J. (1996). 'What Can Liberals Learn from Mary Wollstonecraft?' in *Feminist Interpretations of Mary Wollstonecraft*, ed. M. J. Falco, University Park, PA, pp. 47–60.
Murdock, Graeme (2000). *Calvinism on the Frontier 1600–1650*, Oxford.
(2003). 'Freely Elected in Fear: Princely Elections and Political Power in Early Modern Transylvania', *Journal of Early Modern History* 7, pp. 213–44.
Murphy, James Bernard (2002). 'Nature, Custom, and Reason as the Explanatory and Practical Principles of Aristotelian Political Science', *Review of Politics* 64, pp. 469–95.
(2007). 'Habit and Convention at the Foundation of Custom' in *The Nature of Customary Law*, ed. Amanda Perreau-Saussine and James Bernard Murphy, Cambridge, pp. 53–78.
Nagel, Thomas (1986). *The View from Nowhere*, New York.
Nagy, László (ed.) (2005). *Iratok Bocskai István és kora történetéhez* (Documents for the History of István Bocskai and his Age), Debrecen.
Najemy, John (2000). 'Civic Humanism and Florentine Politics' in *Renaissance Civic Humanism: Reappraisals and Reflections*, ed. J. Hankins, Cambridge, pp. 75–104.
(2006). *A History of Florence 1200–1575*, Oxford.
Nauta, Lodi (2002). 'Hobbes on Religion and the Church between *The Elements of Law* and *Leviathan*: A Dramatic Change of Direction?', *Journal of the History of Ideas* 63, pp. 577–98.
Nederman, Cary (2003). 'Commercial Society and Republican Government in the Latin Middle Ages', *Political Theory* 31, pp. 644–63.
Nellen, Henk (2007). *Hugo de Groot: een leven in strijd om de vrede, 1583–1645*, Amsterdam.
Nellen, Henk and Rabbie, Edwin (eds.) (1994). *Hugo Grotius Theologian: Essays in Honour of G. H. M. Posthumus Meyjes*, Leiden.
Nelson, Eric (2001). ' "True Liberty": Isocrates and Milton's *Areopagitica*', *Milton Studies* 40, pp. 201–21.
(2004). *The Greek Tradition in Republican Thought*, Cambridge.
(2010). *The Hebrew Republic: Jewish Sources and the Transformation of European Political Thought*, Cambridge, MA.
Ng, Su Fang (2007). *Literature and the Politics of the Family*, Cambridge.
Nicholson, R. A. (1956). *A Literary History of the Arabs*, Cambridge.
Noorduyn, J. (1965). 'Origins of South Celebes Historical Writing' in *An Introduction to Indonesian Historiography*, ed. Soedjatmoko *et al.*, Ithaca, NY, pp. 137–55.
(1991). *A Critical Survey of Studies on the Languages of Sulawesi*, Leiden.
Norbrook, David (1988). *Writing the English Republic: Poetry, Rhetoric and Politics 1627–1660*, Cambridge.
Nowak, Kurt (1981). 'Zweireichelehre. Anmerkungen zum Entstehungsprozeß einer umstrittenen Begriffsprägung und kontroversen Lehre', *Zeitschrift für Theologie und Kirche* 78, pp. 105–27.
Nussbaum, Martha (1994). *The Therapy of Desire: Theory and Practice in Hellenistic Ethics*, Princeton, NJ.
(1996). *For Love of Country: Debating the Limits of Patriotism*, Boston, MA.

(1997). 'Kant and Cosmopolitanism' in *Perpetual Peace: Essays on Kant's Cosmopolitcal Ideal*, ed. J. Bohman and M. Lutz-Bachmann, Cambridge, MA.
(2000). *Women and Human Development: The Capabilities Approach*, Cambridge.
Nyberg, H. S. (1964–74). *A Manual of Pahlavi*, Wiesbaden.
O'Brien, Karen (2009). *Women and Enlightenment in Eighteenth-Century Britain*, Cambridge.
O'Neill, Eileen (1999). 'Women Cartesians, "Feminine Philosophy," and Historical Exclusion' in *Feminist Interpretations of René Descartes*, ed. Susan Bordo, University Park, PA, pp. 232–57.
Oakeshott, Michael (1975). *Hobbes on Civil Association*, Oxford.
Oakley, Francis (1999). 'Legitimation by Consent: The Question of the Medieval Roots' in *Politics and Eternity: Studies in the History of Medieval and Early Modern Political Thought*, ed. Francis Oakley, Leiden, pp. 96–137.
Oberman, Heiko A. (1986). 'Martin Luther: Vorläufer der Reformation' in his *Die Reformation: Von Wittenberg nach Genf*, Göttingen, pp. 162–88.
Oborni, Teréz (2004). 'From Province to Principality. Continuity and Change in Transylvania in the First Half of the Sixteenth Century' in *Fight against the Turk in Central-Europe in the First Half of the 16th Century*, ed. István Zombori, Budapest, pp. 165–79.
Ochmann-Staniszewska, Stefania (1990). 'Rzeczpospolita jako *monarchia mixta* – dylematy władzy i wolności' in *Kultura, polityka, dyplomacja: studia ofiarowane Profesorowi Jaremie Maciszewskiemu w sześćdziesiątą rocznicę Jego urodzin*, ed. Andrzej Bartnicki *et al.*, Warsaw, pp. 264–78.
Oestreich, Gerhard (1982). *Neostoicism and the Early Modern State*, Cambridge.
(1989). *Antiker Geist und moderner Staat bei Justus Lipsius (1547–1604): Der Neostoizismus als politische Bewegung*, Göttingen.
Oldfield, Paul (2007). 'Urban Government in Southern Italy c.1085–c.1127', *English Historical Review* 122, pp. 579–608.
Onuf, Nicholas (1998). *The Republican Legacy in International Thought*, Cambridge.
Opaliński, Edward (1995). *Kultura polityczna szlachty polskiej w latach 1587–1652: system parlamentarny a społeczeństwo obywatelskie*, Warsaw.
Osmond, Patricia J. and Ulery, Robert W. (2003). 'Sallustius Crispus, Gaius' in *Catalogus translationum et commentariorum: Medieval and Renaissance Latin Translations and Commentaries*, ed. V. Brown, associate J. Hankins and R. A. Kaster, vol. VIII, Washington, DC, pp. 183–208.
Oxford English Dictionary (1971). Oxford.
Oz-Salzberger, Fania (1995). *Translating the Enlightenment: Scottish Civic Discourse in Eighteenth-Century Germany*, Oxford.
(2002). 'Scots, Germans, Republic and Commerce' in *Republicanism: A Shared European Heritage*, vol. II: *The Values of Republicanism in Early Modern Europe*, ed. Martin van Gelderen and Quentin Skinner, Cambridge, pp. 197–226.
Pagden, Anthony (1982). *The Fall of Natural Man: The American Indian and the Origins of Comparative Ethnology*, Cambridge.
(2002). *The Idea of Europe: From Antiquity to the European Union*, Cambridge.

Pajorin, Klára (2005). 'Antiturcica negli anni quaranta del '400: le epistole di Francesco Filelfo, di Poggio Bracciolini e di János Vitéz', *Camoenae Hungaricae* 2, pp. 17–28.

Pálffy, Géza (2006). 'Zentralisierung und Lokalverwaltung. Die Schwierigkeiten des Absolutismus in Ungarn von 1526 bis zur Mitte des 17. Jahrhunderts' in *Die Habsburgermonarchie 1620 bis 1740: Leistungen und Grenzen des Absolutismus-Paradigmas*, ed. Petr Mat'a and Thomas Winkelbauer, Stuttgart.

(2010a). 'Bündnispartner und Konkurrenten der Krone: Die Ungarischen Stände, Stefan Bocskai und Erzherzog Matthias 1604–1608' in *Ein Bruderzwist im Hause Habsburg (1608–1611)*, ed. Václav Bužek, Budweis, pp. 363–99.

(2010b). *The Kingdom of Hungary and the Habsburg Monarchy in the Sixteenth Century*, New York.

Panaite, Viorel (2000). *The Ottoman Law of War and Peace: The Ottoman Empire and Tribute Payers*, Boulder, CO.

Pánek, Jaroslav (1996). 'The Question of Tolerance in Bohemia and Moravia in the Age of the Reformation' in *Tolerance and Intolerance in the European Reformation*, ed. Ole Peter Grell and Robert Scribner, Cambridge, pp. 231–48.

Papp, Sándor (2003). *Die Verleihungs-, Bekräftigungs- und Vertragsurkunden der Osmanen für Ungarn und Siebenbürgen: Eine quellenkritische Untersuchung*, Vienna.

(2004). 'Hungary and the Ottoman Empire (from the Beginning to 1540)' in *Fight against the Turk in Central-Europe in the First Half of the 16th Century*, ed. István Zombori, Budapest, pp. 37–90.

Papy, Jan (2004). 'Lipsius' Neostoicism: Constancy between Christian Faith and Stoic Virtue' in *Grotius and the Stoa*, ed. Hans Blom and Laurens te Winkel, Assen.

Parkin, Jon (2007). *Taming the Leviathan: The Reception of the Political and Religious Ideas of Thomas Hobbes in England, 1640–1700*, Cambridge.

Parrish, John Michael (1997). 'A New Source for More's *Utopia*', *Historical Journal* 40, pp. 493–8.

Parssinen, T. M. (1973). 'Association, Convention and Anti-Parliament in British Radical Politics 1771–1848', *English Historical Review* 88, pp. 504–33.

Pateman, Carole (1988). *The Sexual Contract*, Oxford.

Pelras, C. (1971). 'Hiérarchie et pouvoirs traditionnels en pays Wadjo'', *Archipel* 1, pp. 169–91.

Peltonen, Markku (1995). *Classical Humanism and Republicanism in English Political Thought 1570–1640*, Cambridge.

(2002). 'Elizabethan England' in *Republicanism: A Shared European heritage*, vol. 1, ed. Martin Van Gelderen and Quentin Skinner, Cambridge, pp. 85–106.

Pennington, Kenneth (1993). *Prince and the Law: Sovereignty and Rights in the Western Legal Tradition*, Berkeley, CA.

Perry, Ruth (1999). 'Radical Doubt and the Liberation of Women' in *Feminist Interpretations of René Descartes*, ed. Susan Bordo, University Park, PA, pp. 169–89.

Péter, Katalin (1994). 'Hungary' in *The Reformation in National Context*, ed. Bob Scribner, Roy Porter and Mikulás Teich, Cambridge, pp. 155–67.

(1996). 'Tolerance and Intolerance in Sixteenth-ccentury Hungary' in *Tolerance and Intolerance in the European Reformation*, ed. Ole Peter Grell and Bob Scribner, Cambridge, pp. 249–61.

(2008a). 'Illésházy Istvánról', *Publicationes Universitatis Miskolciensis*, Sectio philosophica. (tom. 13) fasc. 2, pp. 127–65.

(2008b). 'Religionsangelegenheiten auf den Wiener Friedensverhandlungen' in *'Einigkeit und Frieden sollen auf seiten jeder Partei sein': Die Friedensschlüsse von Wien (23.06.1606) und Zsitvatorok (15.11.1606)*, ed. J. Barta, M. Jatzlauk and K. Papp, Debrecen, pp. 151–6.

Péter, László (1995). 'Montesquieu's Paradox on Freedom and Hungary's Constitutions 1790–1990', *History of Political Thought* 16, pp. 77–104.

(2003). 'The Holy Crown of Hungary, Visible and Invisible', *SEER* 81, pp. 421–510.

Peterson, Luther D. (1990). 'Justus Menius, Philipp Melanchthon and the 1547 Treatise Von der Notwehr Unterricht', *Archive for Reformation History* 81, pp. 138–57.

Pettegree, Andrew (1996). 'The Politics of Toleration in the Free Netherlands, 1572–1620' in *Tolerance and Intolerance in the European Reformation*, ed. Ole Peter Grell and Robert Scribner, Cambridge, pp. 182–98.

Pettit, Philip (1989). 'A Definition of Negative Liberty', *Ratio* 2, pp. 153–68.

(1993a). 'Negative Liberty, Liberal and Republican', *European Journal of Philosophy* 1, pp. 15–38.

(1993b). 'Liberalism and Republicanism', *Australasian Journal of Political Science* 28, pp. 162–89.

(1997). *Republicanism: A Theory of Freedom and Government*, Oxford.

(2002). 'Keeping Republicanism Simple: On a Difference with Quentin Skinner', *Political Theory* 30, pp. 339–56.

(2005). 'Rawls' Political Ontology', *Politics, Philosophy, & Economics* 4.2, pp. 157–74.

(2008). *Made with Words: Hobbes on Language, Mind and Politics*, Princeton, NJ.

Piergiovanni, Vito (1985). 'Diritto e potere a Genova alla fine del Trecento: a proposito di tre "consigli" di Baldo degli Ubaldi' in *La storia dei genovesi*, vol. v, pp. 42–65.

Pink, T. (2003). 'Suárez, Hobbes, and the Scholastic Tradition in Action Theory' in *The Will and Human Action: From Antiquity to the Present Day*, ed. T. Pink and M. Stone, London, pp. 127–53.

(2009). 'Natural Law and the Theory of Moral Obligation' in *Psychology and Philosophy*, ed. S. Heinamåa and M. Reuter, Dordrecht, pp. 97–115.

Pink, T. and Stone, M. (eds.) (2003). *The Will and Human Action: From Antiquity to the Present Day*, London.

Płaza, Stanisław (1984). *Sejmiki i zjazdy szlacheckie województw poznańskiego i kaliskiego: ustrój i funkcjonowanie, 1572–1632*, Cracow.

Pocock, J. G. A. (1967). *The Ancient Constitution and the Feudal Law: A Study of English Historical Thought in the 17th Century*, New York.

(1975). *The Machiavellian Moment: Florentine Political Thought and the Atlantic Republican Tradition*, Princeton, NJ.

(2002). 'Some Europes in Their History,' in *The Idea of Europe: From Antiquity to the European Union*, ed. Anthony Pagden, Cambridge.

(2006). 'Foundations and Moments' in *Rethinking the Foundations of Modern Political Thought*, ed. Annabel Brett and James Tully, Cambridge, pp. 37–49.
Pollok, Anne (2010). *Facetten des Menschen: Zur Anthropologie Moses Mendelssohns*, Hamburg.
Porter, Roy S. and Teich, Mikulás (eds.) (1981). *Enlightenment in National Context*, Cambridge.
Pross, Wolfgang (1987). Epilogue to Herder, *Werke*, vol. II: *Herder und die Anthropologie der Aufklärung*, ed. W. Pross, Munich.
(2006). 'Naturalism, Anthropology and Culture' in *The Cambridge History of Eighteenth-Century Political Thought*, ed. Mark Goldie and Robert Wokler, Cambridge, pp. 218–47.
Rady, Martyn (2000). *Nobility, Land and Service in Medieval Hungary*, Basingstoke.
Rady, Martyn (2005). 'Rethinking Jagiello Hungary (1490–1526)', *Central Europe* (London) 3 (1), pp. 3–18.
(2008). 'Bocskai, Rebellion and Resistance in Early Modern Hungary' in *Resistance, Rebellion and Revolution in Hungary and Central Europe: Commemorating 1956*, ed. László Péter and Martyn Rady, London, pp. 57–66.
Rady, Martyn (ed.) (2003). *Custom and Law in Central Europe*, Cambridge.
Rahe, Paul (1994). 'Antiquity Surpassed: The Repudiation of Classical Republicanism' in *Republicanism, Liberty and Commercial Society, 1649–1776*, ed. David Wootton, Stanford, pp. 233–69.
(2008). *Against Throne and Altar: Machiavelli and Political Theory under the English Republic*, Cambridge.
Rashwan, D. (ed.) (2007). *The Spectrum of Islamist Movements*, Berlin.
Rebstock, U. (1983). *Die Ibāḍiten im Maġrib (2./8.–4./10. Jh.): Die Geschichte einer Berberbewegung im Gewand des Islam*, Berlin.
Regosin, Richard L. (1977). *'The Matter of my Book': Montaigne's Essais as a Book of the Self*, Berkeley, CA.
Reid, A. (1998). 'Merdeka: The Concept of Freedom in Indonesia' in *Asian Freedoms: The Idea of Freedom in East and Southeast Asia*, ed. D. Kelly and A. Reid, Cambridge, pp. 141–60.
(2000). 'Pluralism and Progress in Seventeenth-Century Makassar' in *Authority and Enterprise among the Peoples of South Sulawesi*, ed. R. Tol *et al.*, Leiden, pp. 55–71.
Rein, Nathan (2008). *The Chancery of God: Protestant Print, Polemic and Propaganda against the Empire, Magdeburg 1546–1551*, Aldershot.
Reiss, Hans (2001). 'Kant, Möser und Nicolai' in *Möser-Forum XXXXIII*, 3, pp. 15–35.
Reuter, Martina (1999). 'Questions of Sexual Difference and Equality in Descartes' Philosophy' in *Norms and Modes of Thinking in Descartes*, ed. Tuomo Aho and Mikko Yrjönsuuri, Helsinki, pp. 183–208.
(2000). *'Questions of Body, Sexual Difference and Equality in Cartesian Philosophy'*, doctoral dissertation, Helsinki.
(2002). 'Descartes on the Body, Sexual Difference, and the Passions' in *Bios, Eros and Thanatos in Ancient and Early Modern Philosophy*, ed. Vigdis Songe-Møller and Vibeke A. Tellmann, Bergen, pp. 109–32.

(2005). 'Mary Wollstonecraft on Love and Friendship' in *Philosophical Aspects on Emotions*, ed. Å. Carlson, Stockholm, pp. 119–39.
Richards, Jennifer (2003). *Rhetoric and Courtliness in Early Modern Literature*, Cambridge.
Ricken, Ulrich (2000). 'Mendelssohn und die Sprachtheorien der Aufklärung' in *Moses Mendelssohn im Spannungsfeld der Aufklärung*, ed. Michael Albrecht and Eva J. Engel, Stuttgart and Bad Cannstatt, pp. 195–241.
Rieger, Reinhold (2007). *Von der Freiheit eines Christenmenschen: De libertate christiana*, Tübingen.
Riesenberg, Peter (1956). *Inalienability of Sovereignty in Medieval Political Thought*, New York.
Riley, Patrick (1976). 'Three 17th Century German Theorists of Federalism: Althusius, Hugo and Leibniz', *Publius: The Journal of Federalism* 6, pp. 7–41.
(2007). 'Kant against Hobbes in *Theory and Practice*', *Journal of Moral Philosophy* 4, pp. 194–206.
Ripstein, Arthur (2009). *Force and Freedom: Kant's Legal and Political Philosophy*, Cambridge, MA.
Robertson, John (2005). *The Case for the Enlightenment: Scotland and Naples, 1680–1760*, Cambridge.
Roehr, Sabine (2003). 'Freedom and Autonomy in Schiller', *Journal of the History of Ideas* 64, pp. 119–34.
Rogers, G. A. J. (1992). 'Locke and the Latitude-Men: Ignorance as a Ground of Toleration' in *Philosophy, Science and Religion in England 1640–1700*, ed. Richard Kroll, Richard Ashcraft and Perez Zagorin, Cambridge, pp. 230–52.
Roobol, M. (2005). *Landszaken: de godsdienstgesprekken tussen gereformeerde predikanten en D.V. Coornhert onder leiding van de Staten van Holland (1577–1583)*, Amsterdam.
Roosen, William James (1980). 'Early Modern Diplomatic Ceremonial: A Systems Approach', *Journal of Modern History* 52, pp. 452–76.
Rooy, Sidney H. (1965). *The Theology of Missions in the Puritan Tradition*, Grand Rapids, MI.
Rosand, David (2001). *The Myths of Venice: The Figuration of the State*, Chapel Hill, NC.
Rose, Jacqueline (2005). 'John Locke, "Matters Indifferent", and the Restoration Church of England', *Historical Journal* 48, pp. 601–21.
Rosenberg, Hans (1966). *Bureaucracy, Aristocracy, and Autocracy: The Prussian Experience, 1660–1815*, Cambridge, MA.
Rosenblatt, Helena (2009). 'Rousseau, the Anticosmopolitan?', *Daedalus* 137, pp. 59–67.
Rosenblatt, Jason (2004). 'John Selden's *De Jure Naturali . . . Juxta Disciplinam Ebraeorum* and Religious Toleration' in *Hebraica Veritas? Christian Hebraists and the Study of Judaism in Early Modern Europe*, ed. Allison Coudert and Jeffrey Shoulson, Philadelphia, PA, pp. 102–24.
(2006). *John Selden: Renaissance England's Chief Rabbi*, Oxford.
Rosenbloom, Noah H. (1972). 'Mendelssohn's Redefinition of Judaism – Tension and Solution', *Judaism* 21, pp. 477–89.
Rosenthal, F. (1960). *The Muslim Concept of Freedom Prior to the Nineteenth Century*, Leiden.

Rossi, Paolo (1984). *The Dark Abyss of Time: The History of the Earth and the History of Nations from Hooke to Vico*, trans. Lydia G. Cochrane, Chicago.
Rotenstreich, Nathan (1966). 'On Mendelssohn's Political Philosophy', *Leo Baeck Institute Yearbook* 11, pp. 28–41.
Roth, John D. and Stayer, James M. (ed.) (2007). *A Companion to Anabaptism and Spiritualism 1521–1700*, Leiden.
Rowen, Herbert H. (ed.) (1972). *The Low Countries in Early Modern Times*, London.
Rubinstein, Nicolai (1971). 'Notes on the Word *Stato* in Florence before Machiavelli' in *Florilegium Historiale*, ed. J. G. Rowe and W. H. Stockdale, Toronto, pp. 313–26.
Rubinstein, Nicolai and Ciappelli, Giovanni (2004). *Studies in Italian History in the Middle Ages and the Renaissance*, vol. I: *Political Thought and the Language of Politics: Art and Politics*, Rome.
Russell, Paul (1995). *Freedom and Moral Sentiment: Hume's Way of Naturalizing Responsibility*, Oxford.
Ryan, Alan (1983). 'Hobbes, Toleration, and the Inner Life' in *The Nature of Political Theory*, ed. David Miller and Larry Siedentop, Oxford, pp. 197–218.
Ryan, Magnus (2000). 'Bartolus of Saxoferrato and Free Cities', *Transactions of the Royal Historical Society*, Sixth Series, 10, pp. 65–89.
Salmon, J. H. M. (1959). *The French Religious Wars in English Political Thought*, Oxford.
(1991). 'Seneca and Tacitus in Jacobean England' in *The Mental World of the Jacobean Court*, ed. Linda Levy Peck, Cambridge, pp. 169–88.
(1996). 'The Legacy of Jean Bodin: Absolutism, Populism, or Constitutionalism?', *History of Political Thought* 17, pp. 500–22.
(2007). 'France' in *European Political Thought 1450–1700: Religion, Law and Philosophy*, ed. Howell A. Lloyd, Glenn Burgess and Simon Hodson, London, pp. 458–97.
Sanderson, John (1989). *'But the People's Creatures': The Philosophical Basis of the English Civil War*, Manchester.
Sapiro, Virginia (1992). *A Vindication of Political Virtue: The Political Theory of Mary Wollstonecraft*, Chicago.
Sauter, Christina M. (1989). *Humboldt und die deutsche Aufklärung*, Berlin.
Savigni, Raffaele (1996). *Episcopato e società cittadina a Lucca da Anselmo 2. (+1086) a Roberto (+1225)*, Lucca.
Scattola, Mario (1999). *Das Naturrecht vor dem Naturrecht: Zur Geschichte des 'ius naturae' im 16. Jahrhundert*, Tübingen.
Schaefer, David Lewis (1990). *The Political Philosophy of Montaigne*, Ithaca, NY.
Schama, Simon (1987). *The Embarrassment of Riches: An Interpretation of Dutch Culture in the Golden Age*, London.
Schatz, Andrea (2009). *Sprache in der Zerstreuung: Die Säkularisierung des Hebräischen im 18. Jahrhundert*, Göttingen.
Scheible, Heinz (ed.) (1969). *Das Widerstansrecht als Problem der Deutschen Protestanten 1523–1546*, Gütersloh.
Schilling, Heinz (2008). *Early Modern European Civilisation and Its Political and Cultural Dynamism*, Lebanon, NH.
Schilling, Heinz (ed.) (2007). *Konfessioneller Fundamentalismus: Religion als Politischer Faktor im Europäischen Mächtesystem um 1600*, Munich.

Schilling, Heinz and Smolinsky, Heribert (eds.) (2007). *Der Augsburger Religionsfrieden 1555*, Gütersloh.
Schlereth, Thomas (1977). *The Cosmopolitan Ideal in Enlightenment Thought*, Notre Dame, IN.
Schlumbohm, Jürgen (1975). *Freiheit: Die Anfänge der bürgerlichen Emanzipationsbewegung in Deutschland im Spiegel ihres Leitwortes (ca. 1760–ca. 1800)*, Düsseldorf.
Schmid, Carl Christian Erhard (1809). *Adiaphora: Wissenschaftlich und Historisch Untersucht*, Leipzig.
Schmidt, Alexander (2009). 'The Liberty of the Ancients? Friedrich Schiller and Aesthetic Republicanism', *History of Political Thought* 30, pp. 286–314.
Schmidt, Georg (1998). 'Luther und die frühe Reformation – ein nationales Ereignis?' in *Die frühe Reformation*, ed. Bernd Moeller, Gütersloh, pp. 54–75.
(1999). *Geschichte des Alten Reiches*, Munich.
(2006). 'Die Idee "deutsche Freiheit". Eine Leitvorstellung der politischen Kultur des Alten Reiches' in *Kollektive Freiheitsvorstellungen im frühneuzeitlichen Europa (1400–1850)*, ed. Georg Schmidt, Martin van Gelderen and Christopher Snigula, Frankfurt am Main.
(2009). *Wandel durch Vernunft: Deutsche Geschichte im 18. Jahrhundert*, Munich.
(2010). 'Luthers Freiheitsvorstellungen in ihrem sozialen und politischen Kontext' in *Martin Luther – Biographie und Theologie*, Marburg, pp. 9–30.
Schmidt, Georg, van Gelderen, Martin and Snigula, Christopher (2006). *Kollektive Freiheitsvorstellungen im Früneuzeitlichen Europa (1400–1850)*, Frankfurt am Main.
Schneewind, J. B. (1998). *The Invention of Autonomy: A History of Modern Moral Philosophy*, Cambridge.
Schochet, Gordon (1975). *Patriarchalism in Political Thought*, Oxford.
Schorn-Schütte, Luise (1998). 'Die Dreiständelehre im reformatorischen Umbruch' in *Die frühe Reformation in Deutschland als Umbruch*, ed. Bernd Moeller, Gütersloh, pp. 435–61.
(2004). 'Obrigkeitskritik und Widerstandsrecht. Die Politica Christiana als Legitimationsgrundlage' in *Aspekte der politischen Kommunikation im Europa des 16. und 17. Jahrhunderts*, ed. Luise Schorn-Schütte, Munich, pp. 195–232.
(2006). *Historische Politikforschung: Eine Einführung*, Munich.
Schreiner, Klaus (1991). 'Iura et libertates. Wahrnehmungsformen und Ausprägungen "bürgerlicher Freyheiten" in Städten des Hohen und Späten Mittelalters' in *Bürger in der Gesellschaft der Neuzeit: Wirtschaft – Politik – Kultur (Bürgertum*, vol. 1), ed. Hans-Jürgen Puhle, Göttingen, pp. 59–105.
Schröder, Peter (1999). 'The Constitution of the Holy Roman Empire after 1648: Samuel Pufendorf's Assessment in His *Monzambano*', *Historical Journal* 42, pp. 961–83.
Schubert, Anselm, Driedger, Michael and von Schlachta, Astrid (eds.) (2009). *Grenzen des Täufertums / Boundaries of Anabaptism*, Gütersloh.
Schüssler, R. (2006). 'Moral Self-ownership and *ius possessionis* in Late Scholastics' in *Transformations in Medieval and Early-Modern Rights Discourse*, ed. V. Mäkinen and P. Korkmann, Dordrecht, pp. 149–72.

(2007). 'Locke, Kasuistik und die Wurzeln des Liberalismus' in *Politische Metaphysik*, ed. M. Kaufmann and R. Schnepf, Frankfurt, pp. 257–84.
Schultze, Johanna (1925). *Die Auseinandersetzung zwischen Adel und Bürgertum in den deutschen Zeitschriften der letzten drei Jahrzehnte des 18. Jahrhunderts (1773–1806)*, Berlin.
Schulze, Manfred (1993). 'Onus ecclesiae: Last der Kirche – Reformation der Kirche' in *Anticlericalism in Late Medieval and Early Modern Europe*, ed. Peter A. Dykema and Heiko A. Oberman, Leiden, pp. 317–42.
Schulze, W. (1991). 'Armed Conflict in East-Central Europe: Protestant Noble Opposition and Catholic Royalist Factions, 1604–20' in *Crown, Church and Estates: Central European Politics in the Sixteenth and Seventeenth Centuries*, ed. R. J. W. Evans and T. V. Thomas, London, pp. 123–8.
Sciacca, Enzo (2005). *Principati e repubbliche*, Florence.
Scott, Jonathan (1992). 'The English Republican Imagination' in *Revolution and Restoration in England in the 1650s*, ed. J. S. Morill, London, pp. 35–54.
(1993). 'The Rapture of Motion: James Harrington's Republicanism' in *Political Discourse in Early Modern Britain*, ed. Nicholas Phillipson and Quentin Skinner, Cambridge, pp. 139–63.
(2000). *England's Troubles: Seventeenth-Century English Political Instability in European Context*, Cambridge.
(2002). 'Classical Republicanism in Seventeenth Century England and the Netherlands' in *Republicanism: A Shared European Heritage*, vol. 1, ed. Martin van Gelderen and Quentin Skinner, Cambridge, pp. 61–84.
(2004). *Commonwealth Principles*, Cambridge.
Seaward, Paul (2004). 'Edward Hyde, First Earl of Clarendon (1609–1674)' in *Oxford Dictionary of National Biography*, Oxford.
Secretan, Catherine (1990). *Les privilèges berceau de la liberté. La Révolte des Pays-Bas: aux sources de la pensée politique moderne (1566–1619)*, Paris.
Seelmann, K. (2007). 'Selbstherrschaft, Herrschaft über die Dinge, und individuelle Rechte in der Spanischen Spätscholastik' in *Politische Metaphysik*, ed. M. Kaufmann, and R. Schnepf, Frankfurt, pp. 43–59.
Seidler, M. J. (1990). 'Introduction' in *Samuel Pufendorf's On the Natural State of Men*, Lewiston, IL, pp. 1–53.
Sen, Amartya (1999). *Development as Freedom*, Oxford.
Serjeantson, Richard (2009). 'Samson Agonistes and "Single Rebellion"' in *The Oxford Handbook of Milton*, ed. Nicholas McDowell and Nigel Smith, Oxford, pp. 613–31.
Severino, Gabriella (1992). 'La Vita metrica di Anselmo da Lucca scritta da Rangerio: ideologia e genere letterario' in *Sant'Anselmo Vescovo di Lucca (1073–1086)*, ed. C. Violante, Rome, pp. 223–71.
Shaffer, Gina Victoria (2004). 'The Missing Wives of Leviathan', *Seventeenth Century* 19, pp. 53–68.
Shagan, Ethan (2007). 'The Two Republics: Conflicting Views of Participatory Local Government in Early Tudor England' in *The Monarchical Republic of Early Modern England: Essays in Response to Patrick Collinson*, ed. John McDiarmaid, Aldershot, pp. 19–37.

Shanley, Mary (1979). 'Marriage Contract and Social Contract in Seventeenth Century English Political Thought', *Western Political Quarterly* 32, pp. 79–91.

Shapiro, Lisa (1999a). 'Princess Elisabeth and Descartes: The Union of Soul and Body and the Practice of Philosophy', *British Journal for the History of Philosophy* 7, pp. 503–20.

(1999b). 'Cartesian Generosity' in *Norms and Modes of Thinking in Descartes*, ed. Tuomo Aho and Mikko Yrjönsuuri, Helsinki, pp. 249–75.

(2007). 'Volume Editor's Introduction' in *The Correspondence between Princess Elisabeth of Bohemia and René Descartes*, ed. and trans. Lisa Shapiro, Chicago, pp. 1–51.

Sharma, J. P. (1968). *Republics in Ancient India c. 1500 B.C.–500 B.C.*, Leiden.

Sharpe, Kevin (1989). 'A Commonwealth of Meanings: Language, Analogues, Ideas and Politics' in *Politics and Ideas in Early Stuart England: Essays and Studies*, ed. Kevin Sharpe, London, pp. 3–71.

Sheehan, Bernard (1980). *Savagism and Civility: Indians and Englishmen in Colonial Virginia*, Cambridge.

Sheehan, James (1989). *German History 1770–1866*, Oxford.

Shepard, W. E. (2003). 'Sayyid Qutb's doctrine of *Jāhiliyya*', *International Journal of Middle East Studies* 35, pp. 521–45.

Shepherd, Alexandra (2000). 'Manhood, Credit and Patriarchy in Early Modern England c. 1580–1640', *Past and Present* 167, pp. 75–106.

Shuger, Debora (2006). *Censorship and Cultural Sensibility: The Regulation of Language in Tudor-Stuart England*, Philadelphia, PA.

Sivan, E. (1990). *Radical Islam: Medieval Theology and Modern Politics*, New Haven, CT and London.

Skinner, Quentin (1978). *The Foundations of Modern Political Thought*, 2 vols., Cambridge.

(1984). 'The Idea of Negative Liberty: Philosophical and Historical Perspectives' in *Philosophy in History*, ed. Richard Rorty, J. B. Schneewind and Quentin Skinner, Cambridge, pp. 193–221.

(1990a). 'Machiavelli's *Discorsi* and the Pre-humanist Origins of Republican Ideas' in *Machiavelli and Republicanism*, ed. G. Bock, Q. Skinner and M. Viroli, Cambridge, pp. 121–41.

(1990b). 'The Republican Ideal of Political Liberty' in *Machiavelli and Republicanism*, ed. G. Bock, Q. Skinner and M. Viroli, Cambridge, pp. 293–309.

(1996). *Reason and Rhetoric in the Philosophy of Hobbes*, Cambridge.

(1998). *Liberty before Liberalism*, Cambridge.

(2002a). 'John Milton and the Politics of Slavery' in *Visions of Politics*, vol. II: *Renaissance Virtues*, Cambridge, pp. 286–307.

(2002b). 'Classical Liberty and the Coming of the English Civil War' in *Republicanism: A Shared European Heritage*, 2 vols., ed. Martin van Gelderen and Quentin Skinner, Cambridge, vol. II, pp. 1–28.

(2002c). *Visions of Politics*, 3 vols., Cambridge.

(2002d). 'The Idea of Negative Liberty: Machiavellian and Modern Perspectives' in *Visions of Politics*, vol. II: *Renaissance Virtues*, Cambridge, pp. 186–212.

(2002e). 'Classical Liberty, Renaissance Translation and the English Civil War' in *Visions of Politics*, vol. II: *Renaissance Virtues*, Cambridge, pp. 308–43.

(2002f). 'A Third Concept of Liberty', *Proceedings of the British Academy* 117, pp. 237–68.

(2002g). 'Thomas More's *Utopia* and the Virtue of True Nobility' in *Visions of Politics*, vol. II: *Renaissance Virtues*, Cambridge, pp. 213–44.

(2005). 'Hobbes on Representation', *European Journal of Philosophy* 13, pp. 155–84.

(2006). 'Rethinking Political Liberty', *History Workshop Journal* 61, pp. 156–70.

(2008a). *Hobbes and Republican Liberty*, Cambridge.

(2008b). 'Freedom as the Absence of Arbitrary Power' in *Republicanism and Political Theory*, ed. Cécile Laborde and John Maynor, Oxford, pp. 83–101.

(2008c). 'A Genealogy of Liberty' (unpublished lecture) Berkeley, CA, 15 September.

(2009a). 'A Genealogy of the Modern State', *Proceedings of the British Academy* 162, pp. 325–70.

(2009b). 'On the Slogans of Republican Political Theory', *European Journal of Political Theory* 9, pp. 1–8.

Skurla, Stijepo (1871). *Sveti Vlaho: biskup i mučenik od Sevasta* (Saint Blaise. Bishop and Martyr of Sebasta), Dubrovnik.

Sleigh Jr, Robert, Chappell, Vere and Della Rocca, Michael (1998). 'Determinism and Human Freedom' in *The Cambridge History of Seventeenth-Century Philosophy*, 2 vols., ed. Daniel Garber and Michael Ayers, Cambridge, vol. II, pp. 1195–1278.

Smuts, Malcolm (1994). 'Court-Centered Politics and the Uses of the Roman Historians, c. 1590–1630' in *Culture and Politics in Early Stuart England*, ed. Peter Lake and Kevin Sharpe, London, pp. 21–43.

Sobieski, Wacław (1922). '"Si non jurabis, non regnabis . . . ". Spór o przysięgę królewską', *Reformacja w Polsce* 2, pp. 54–70.

Sommerville, J. P. (1999). *Royalists and Patriots: Politics and Ideology in England 1603–1640*, London and New York.

(2000). 'Hobbes, Selden, Erastianism, and the History of the Jews' in *Hobbes and History*, ed. G. A. J. Rogers and Tom Sorell, New York, pp. 160–88.

(2001). 'Selden, Grotius and the Seventeenth Century Intellectual Revolution in Moral and Political Theory' in *Rhetoric and Law in Early Modern Europe*, ed. Victoria Kahn and Lorna Hutson, New Haven, CT, pp. 318–44.

(2004). 'Conscience, Law, and Things Indifferent: Arguments on Toleration from the Vestiarian Controversy to Hobbes and Locke' in *Contexts of Conscience in Early Modern Europe, 1500–1700*, ed. Harold Braun and Edward Vallance, Houndmills, pp. 166–79.

Sorabji, Richard (2000). *Emotion and Peace of Mind: From Stoic Agitation to Christian Temptation*, Oxford.

Sorkin, David (1996). *Moses Mendelssohn and the Religious Enlightenment*, Berkeley, CA.

(2008). *The Religious Enlightenment: Protestants, Jews, and Catholics from London to Vienna*, Princeton, NJ.

Sourdel, D. (1985). 'Peut-on parler de liberté dans la société de l'islam medieval?' in *La notion de liberté au Moyen Age: Islam, Byzance, Occident*, ed. G. Makdisi *et al.*, Paris, pp. 119–33.

Sreedhar, Susanne (2010). *Hobbes on Resistance: Defying the Leviathan*, Cambridge.

Stacey, Peter (2007). *Roman Monarchy and the Renaissance Prince*, Cambridge.

Stanton, Timothy (2008). 'Hobbes and Locke on Natural Law and Jesus Christ', *History of Political Thought* 29, pp. 65–88.

(2011a). 'Authority and Freedom in the Interpretation of Locke's Political Theory', *Political Theory* 39, pp. 6–30.

(2011b). 'Hobbes and Schmitt', *History of European Ideas* 37, pp. 160–7.

Starobinski, Jean (1985). *Montaigne in Motion*, trans. Arthur Goldhammer, Chicago, IL.

Stedman Jones, Gareth (1994). 'Kant, the French Revolution and the Definition of the Republic' in *The Invention of the Modern Republic*, ed. Biancamaria Fontana, Cambridge, pp. 154–72.

Stein, Peter (1999). *Roman Law in European History*, Cambridge.

Stettler, Bernhard (2001). *Tschudi-Vademecum: Annäherungen an Aegidius Tschudi und sein 'Chronicon Helveticum'*, Basel.

Stewart, M. A. (2003). 'Religion and Rational Theology' in *The Cambridge Companion to the Scottish Enlightenment*, ed. Alexander Broadie, Cambridge, pp. 31–59.

(2006a). 'Revealed Religion: The British Debate' in *The Cambridge History of Eighteenth-Century Philosophy*, 2 vols., ed. Knud Haakonssen, vol. II, pp. 683–709.

(2006b). 'Arguments for the Existence of God: The British Debate' in *The Cambridge History of Eighteenth-Century Philosophy*, 2 vols., ed. Knud Haakonssen, vol. II, pp. 710–30.

Stintzing, Roderich (1880). *Geschichte der Deutschen Rechtswissenschaft*, Vol. I, Munich.

Stolleis, Michael (1972). *Staatsraison, Recht und Moral in philosophischen Texten des späten 18. Jahrhunderts*, Meisenheim am Glan.

(1988). *Geschichte des Öffentlichen Rechts in Deutschland*, vol. I: *Reichspublizistik und Policeywissenschaft, 1600–1800*, Munich.

Stone, Lawrence (1977). *The Family, Sex, and Marriage in England 1500–1800*, New York.

Strauss, Gerald (1986). *Law, Resistance and the State: The Opposition to Roman Law in Reformation Germany*, Princeton, NJ.

Strohm, Christoph (2000). 'Zugänge zum Naturrecht bei Melanchthon' in *Der Theologe Melanchthon*, ed. Günter Frank, Stuttgart, pp. 339–56.

Stubbs, William (1905). *Select Charters and Other Illustrations of English Constitutional History: From the Earliest Times to the Reign of Edward the First*, Oxford.

Stuurman, Siep (2004). *François Poulain de la Barre and the Invention of Modern Equality*, Cambridge, MA.

Sucheni-Grabowska, Anna (2009). *Wolność i prawo w staropolskiej koncepcji państwa*, Warsaw.

Suda, Max Josef (2006). *Die Ethik Martin Luthers*, Göttingen.

Sutcliffe, Adam (2003). *Judaism and Enlightenment*, Cambridge.

Sweet, Rosemary (1998). 'Freemen and Independence in English Borough Politics c. 1770–1830', *Past and Present* 161, pp. 84–115.

Świderska-Włodarczyk, Urszula (2003). *Mentalność szlachty polskiej w XVI i XVII wieku*, Poznań.

Szabó, András Péter (2010). 'Inhalt und Bedeutung der Widerstandslehre im Bocskai-Aufstand' in *Calvin und Reformiertentum in Ungarn und Siebenbürgen: Helvetisches Bekenntnis, Ethnie und Politik vom 16. Jahrhundert bis 1918*, ed. Márta Fata and Anton Schindling, Münster, pp. 317–40.

Szabó, János B. and Erdősi, Péter (2003). 'Ceremonies Marking the Transfer of Power in the Principality of Transylvania in East European Context', *Majestas* 11, pp. 111–60.
Szabò-Bechstein, Brigitte (1985). *Libertas Ecclesiae: Ein Schlüsselbegriff des Investiturstreits und seine Vorgeschichte*, Studi Gregoriani XII, Rome.
Szigeti, Jenő (1984). 'Luther és Werbőczi találkozója' (The Encounter between Luther and Werbőczi) in *Tanulmányok a Lutheri reformáció történetéből*, ed. Tibor Fabiny, Budapest, pp. 195–208.
Szijártó, István M. (2007). 'The Diet: The Estates and the Parliament of Hungary, 1708–1792' in *Bündnispartner und Konkurrenten des Landesfürsten? Die Stände in der Habsburgermonarchie*, ed. Gerhard Ammerer, William D. Godsey Jr, Martin Scheutz, Peter Urbanitsch and Alfred Stefan Weiss, Vienna, pp. 151–71.
(2010). 'Die Reformierten und die Frage des ständischen Widerstands im Königreich Ungarn im 18. Jahrhundert' in *Calvin und Reformiertentum in Ungarn und Siebenbürgen: Helvetische Bekenntnis, Ethnie und Politik vom 16. Jahrhundert bis 1918*, ed. Márta Fata and Anton Schindling, Münster, pp. 341–55.
Szűcs, Jenő (1983). 'The Three Historical Regions of Europe: An Outline', *Acta Historica Academiae Scientiarum Hungariae* 29, pp. 131–84.
Tadić, Jorjo (1939). *Promet putnika u starom Dubrovniku* (The Traffic of Travellers in the Old Ragusa), Dubrovnik.
Taylor, Barbara (2003). *Mary Wollstonecraft and the Feminist Imagination*, Cambridge.
Taylor, Charles (1979). 'What's Wrong with Negative Liberty?' in *The Idea of Freedom*, ed. Alan Ryan, Oxford, pp. 175–93.
Taylor, William B. (1996). *Magistrates of the Sacred: Priests and Parishioners in Eighteenth-Century Mexico*, Stanford, CA.
Taźbierski, Zdzisław (1981). 'Misja Pawła Działyńskiego do Hagi i Londynu w 1597 roku na tle stosunków gospodarczych polsko-angielskich za panowania Elżbiety Tudor (w świetle źródeł)', *Zeszyty Naukowe WSP w Opolu* 1, pp. 89–108.
Tazbir, Janusz (1986). *Myśl polska w nowożytnej kulturze europejskiej*, Warsaw.
(1993). *Reformacja w Polsce: szkice o ludziach i doktrynie*, Warsaw.
(1998). *Kultura szlachecka w Polsce. Rozkwit, upadek, relikty*, 4th edn, Poznań.
Tellenbach, Gerd (1991). *Church, State and Christian Society at the Time of the Investiture Contest*, Toronto.
(1993). *The Church in Western Europe from the Tenth to the Early Twelfth Century*, trans. T. Reuter, Cambridge.
Teszelszky, Kees (2009). *Az ismeretlen korona: jelentések, szimbólumok és nemzeti identitás*, Pannonhalma.
Thomson, Judith Jarvis (1990). *The Realm of Rights*, Cambridge.
Tierney, B. (2006). 'Dominion of Self and Natural Rights before Locke and After' in *Transformations in Medieval and Early-Modern Rights Discourse*, ed. V. Mäkinen and P. Korkmann, Dordrecht, pp. 173–208.
Tilmouth, Christopher (2007). *Passions's Triumph over Reason: A History of the Moral Imagination from Spenser to Rochester*, Oxford.
Todd, Janet (1991). 'Introduction' in *Mary Wollstonecraft's Mary and Maria; Mary Shelley's Matilda*, ed. Janet Todd, London, pp. vii–xxviii.

Tolmie, Murray (1977). *The Triumph of the Saints: The Separate Churches of London, 1616–1649*, Cambridge.

Toomer, Gerald (2009). *John Selden: A Life in Scholarship*, 2 vols., Oxford.

Topolska, Barbara (2002). *Społeczeństwo i kultura w Wielkim Księstwie Litewskim od XV do XVIII wieku*, Poznań.

Tóth, István György (2005). 'The Political Culture in Hungary: One Kingdom in Two World Empires (16th–17th Centuries)' in *Political Culture in Central Europe (10th–20th Century)*, vol. 1: *Middle Ages and Early Modern Era*, ed. Halina Manikowska, Jaroslav Pánek and Martin Holy, Prague.

Tournoy, Gilles, De Landsheer, Jeanine and Papy, Jan (eds.) (1999). *Iustus Lipsius Europae Lumen et Columen: Proceedings of the International Colloquium, Leuven, 17–19 September 1997*, Leuven.

Tralau, Johan (2011). 'Hobbes contra Liberty of Conscience', *Political Theory* 39, pp. 58–84.

Trevor-Roper, Hugh (1967). *Religion, The reformation and Social Change*, London.

(1968). 'Some of My Best Friends Are Philosophes', *New York Review of Books* (22 August).

(1987). 'The Great Tew Circle' in *Catholics, Anglicans and Puritans: Seventeenth Century Essays*, pp. 166–230, Chicago, IL.

Troeltsch, Ernst (2001). *Kritische Gesamtausgabe*, Bd. 8: *Schriften zur Bedeutung des Protestantismus für die Entstehung der modernen Welt (1906–1913)*, ed. Trutz Rendtorff and Stefan Pautler, Berlin and New York.

Tuck, Richard (1979). *Natural Rights Theories: Their Origin and Development*, Cambridge.

(1993). *Philosophy and Government 1572–1651*, Cambridge.

(1999). *The Rights of War and Peace: Political Thought and the International Order from Grotius to Kant*, Oxford.

Tully, James (1991). 'Introduction' in *On the Duty of Man and Citizens According to Natural Law*, ed. James Tully, trans. Michael Silverthorne, Cambridge, pp. xiv–xxxvii.

(1993). *An Approach to Political Philosophy: Locke in Contexts*, Cambridge.

Turner, James G. (1994). *One Flesh: Paradisal Marriage and Sexual Relations in the Age of Milton*, Oxford.

Uleman, Jennifer K. (2004). 'External Freedom in Kant's Rechtslehre: Political, Metaphysical', *Philosophy and Phenomenological Research* 68, pp. 578–601.

Ullmann, Walter (1949). 'Development of the Medieval Idea of Sovereignty', *English Historical Review* 64, pp. 1–33.

Urwanowicz, Jerzy (1994). 'Ideologia a działalność polityczna szlachty w czasach Zygmunta III. Wokół wartości ustrojowych' in *Między monarchią a demokracją: studia z dziejów Polski XV–XVIII wieku*, ed. Anna Sucheni-Grabowska and Małgorzata Żaryn, Warsaw, pp. 170–90.

Valensi, Lucette (1993). *The Birth of the Despot: Venice and the Sublime Porte*, Ithaca, NY and London.

Valjavec, Fritz (1951). *Die Entstehung der politischen Strömungen in Deutschland 1770–1815*, Munich.

van Asselt, Willem J., Bac, J. Martin and Te Velde, Roelf T. (2010). *Reformed Thought on Freedom: The Concept of Free Choice in Early Modern Reformed Theology*, Grand Rapids, MI.

van Asselt, Willem J. and Dekker, Eef (eds.) (1995). *De scholastieke Voetius: een luisteroefening aan de hand van Voetius' 'Disputationes Selectae'*, Zoetermeer.

van Gelderen, Martin (1992). *The Political Thought of the Dutch Revolt, 1555–1590*, Cambridge.

(1996a). *De vrijheid van conscientie: het vrijheidsideaal van de Nederlandse Opstand, 1555–1610*, Gouda.

(1996b). 'Liberty, Civic Rights, and Duties in Sixteenth-Century Europe and the Rise of the Dutch Republic' in *The Individual in Political Theory and Practice*, ed. Janet Coleman, Oxford, pp. 99–122.

(2002). 'Aristotelians, Monarchomachs, and Republicans: Sovereignty and *Respublica Mixta* in Dutch and German Political Thought' in *Republicanism: A Shared European Heritage*, vol. 1, ed. Martin van Gelderen and Quentin Skinner, Cambridge, pp. 195–218.

(2006). '"So meerly humane": Theories of Resistance in Early Modern Europe' in *Rethinking the Foundations of Modern Political Thought*, ed. Annabel Brett and James Tully, Cambridge, pp. 149–70.

(2008). 'Turning Swiss? Discord in the Dutch Debates' in *The Republican Alternative: The Netherlands and Switzerland Compared*, ed. André Holenstein, Thomas Maissen and Maarten Prak, Amsterdam, pp. 171–89.

(2009). '"Hot Protestantism". Die Rhetorik und politische Sprache der Englischen und Niederländischen Calvinisten', in Ansgar Reiss and Sabine Witt (eds.), *Calvinismus: Die Reformierten in Deutchland und Europa*, Dresden, pp. 189–95.

(2011). 'Freedom Fighters: The Act of Abjuration, Hugo Grotius and Dutch Debates on Liberty' in *The Act of Abjuration: Inspired and Inspirational*, ed. Paul Brood and Raymond Kubben, Nijmegen, pp. 155–72.

van Gelderen, Martin and Skinner, Quentin (eds.) (2002). *Republicanism: A Shared European Heritage*, 2 vols., Cambridge.

van Ittersum, Martin (2006). *Profit and Principle: Hugo Grotius, Natural Rights Theories and the Rise of Dutch Power in the East Indies (1595–1615)*, Leiden and Boston.

van Oort, J. (ed.) (1989). *De onbekende Voetius*, Kampen.

van Ruler, Han (1995). *The Crisis of Causality: Voetius and Descartes on God, Nature and Change*, Leiden.

van Schelven, Aart Arnout (1947). 'De Staatsvorm van het Zwitsersche Eedgenootschap den Nederlanden ter navolging aanbevolen', *Miscellanea historica in honorem Leonis van der Essen*, Brussels, pp. 747–56.

van Veen, Mirjam (2001). *'Verschooninghe van de roomsche afgoderye': de polemiek van Calvijn met Nicodemieten, in het bijzonder met Coornhert*, Houten.

Van't Spijker, W. *et al.* (1994). *De Dordtse synode van 1618–1619*, Houten.

Varga, Benedek (2004). 'The Term Libertas in 17–18th c. Hungary', *Studia Caroliensia* 3–4, pp. 309–13.

(2006). 'Szempontok a Bocskai-felkelés ideológiájának európai kontextusához' (Remarks on the European Context of the Ideology of the Bocskai Revolt), *Studia Caroliensa* 1, pp. 29–41.
(2010). 'Political Humanism and the Corporate Theory of State: Nation, Patria and Virtue in Hungarian Political Thought of the Sixteenth Century' in *Whose Love of Which Country? Composite States, National Histories and Patriotic Discourses in Early Modern East Central Europe*, ed. Balázs Trencsényi and Márton Zászkaliczky, Leiden, pp. 285–313.
Varga, J. János (2006). 'Heiducken und Heiduckenstädte in Ungarn' in *Kollektive Freiheitsvorstellungen im frühneuzeitlichen Europa (1400 bis 1800)*, ed. Georg Schmidt, Martin van Gelderen and Christopher Snigula, Frankfurt am Main.
Várkonyi, R. Ágnes (2007). 'Die internationalen Hintergründe des Bocskai-Freiheitskampfes (Die ungarische Feschichte aus europäischer Perspektive)' in *'Einigkeit und Frieden sollen auf Seiten jeder Partei sein': Die Friedenschlüssen von Wien (23.06.1606) und Zsitvatorok (15.11.1606)*, ed. J. Barta, M. Jatzlauk and K. Papp, Debrecen, pp. 13–29.
Vatter, Miguel (2000). *Between Form and Event*, Dordrecht.
Veen, T. J. (1976). *Recht en nut: studiën over en naar aanleiding van Ulrik Huber (1636–1694)*, Zwolle.
Velema, Wyger R. E. (2007). *Republicans: Essays on Eighteenth-Century Dutch Political Thought*, Leiden and Boston, MA.
Venásch, Eszter (2007). 'Homonnai Drugeth Bálint hadinaplójának kiadatlan része', *Lymbus*, pp. 19–46.
Ventura, Angelo (1981). 'Scrittori politici e scritture di governo' in *Storia della cultura Veneta*, ed. G. Amaldi and M. Pastore, Vicenza, pp. 513–663.
Verbeek, Theo (1992). *Descartes and the Dutch*, Carbondale, IL.
Verboom, W. (2005). *De belijdenis van een gebroken kerk*, Zoetermeer.
Verkamp, Bernard (1977). *The Indifferent Mean: Adiaphorism in the English Reformation to 1554*, Athens, OH.
Veszprémy, László and Schaer, Frank (eds. and trans.) (1999). *Simon de Keza Gesta Hungarorum / Simon of Keza: The Deeds of the Hungarians*, Budapest.
Vickers, Brian (1990). 'Leisure and Idleness: The Ambivalence of *Otium*', *Renaissance Studies* 4, pp. 1–37 and 107–54.
Vierhaus, Rudolf (1967). 'Politisches Bewusstsein in Deutschland vor 1789', *Der Staat* 6, pp. 175–96.
(2002). 'Wir nennen's Gemeinsinn' in *Republicanism and Liberalism in America and the German States, 1750–1850*, ed. J. Heideking and J. Henretta, Cambridge.
Vinogradoff, Paul (1929). *Roman Law in Medieval Europe*, Oxford.
Violante, Cinzio (1955). *La pataria Milanese e la riforma ecclesiastica*, Rome.
Viroli, Maurizio (1992). *From Politics to Reason of State: The Acquisition and Transformation of the Language of Politics*, Cambridge.
(2002). *Republicanism*, trans. Antony Shugaar, New York.
Visentin, Stefano (1998). 'Assolutismo e libertà. L'orizzonte repubblicano nel pensiero politico olandese del XVII secolo', *Filosofia Politica* 12, pp. 67–85.

Vivanti, Corrado (2006). *Guerre civile et paix religieuse dans la France d'Henri IV*, Paris.
(2007). 'Note intorno al termine "stato" in Machiavelli' in *Storia sociale e politica: omaggio a Rosario Villari*, ed. Alberto Merola *et al.*, Milan, pp. 79–98.
Vogel, Ursula (1972). *Konservative Kritik an der bürgerlichen Revolution: August Wilhelm Rehberg*, Darmstadt and Neuwied.
(1982). 'Liberty Is Beautiful: Von Humboldt's Gift to Liberalism', *History of Political Thought* 3, pp. 77–101.
Volkmar, Christoph (2007). *Reform statt Reformation*, Tübingen.
von Albertini, Rudolf (1970), *Firenze dalla repubblica al principato: storia e coscienza politica*, trans. C. Cristofolini, Turin.
von Leyden, W. (1991). 'John Locke and the Natural Law' in *John Locke: Critical Assessments*, 4 vols., ed. Richard Ashcraft, London, vol. II, pp. 3–15.
Vyverberg, Henry (1989). *Human Nature, Cultural Diversity and the French Enlightenment*, Oxford.
Waldron, Jeremy (2008). 'Hobbes on Public Worship' in *Toleration and its Limits*, ed. Melissa S. Williams and Jeremy Waldron, New York, pp. 31–53.
Wallace, Robert (1850). *Antitrinitarian Biography*, 3 vols., London.
Walzer, Michael (1977). *Just and Unjust Wars: A Moral Argument with Historical Illustrations*, New York.
Wandycz, Piotr S. (2001). *The Price of Freedom: A History of East Central Europe from the Middle Ages to the Present*, London.
Ward, Lee (2010). *John Locke and Modern Life*, Cambridge.
Warmington, B. H. (1960). *Carthage*, London.
Wartenberg, Günther (1999). 'Theologischer Ratschlag in Zeiten politischen Umbruchs: Die Wittenberger Theologen und ihre Landesherrn 1546/7' in *Religionspolitik in Deutschland: Von der Frühen Neuzeit bis zur Gegenwart*, ed. Anselm Doering-Manteuffel and Kurt Nowak, Stuttgart, pp. 37–47.
Wartenberg, Thomas E. (1999). 'Descartes's Mood: The Question of Feminism in the Correspondence with Elisabeth' in *Feminist Interpretations of René Descartes*, ed. Susan Bordo, University Park, PA, pp. 190–212.
Webb, R. K. (1996). 'The Emergence of Rational Dissent' in *Enlightenment and Religion: Rational Dissent in Eighteenth-Century Britain*, ed. Knud Haakonssen, Cambridge, pp. 12–41.
Weber, Hermann (1979). 'L'accettazione in Francia del Concilio di Trento' in *Il Concilio di Trento come crocevia della politica europea*, ed. Hubert Jedin and Paolo Prodi, Bologna, pp. 85–107.
Weiden Boyd, Barbara (1987). '*Virtus Effeminata* and Sallust's Sempronia', *Transactions of the American Philological Society* 117, pp. 183–201.
Weinmann, Barbara (2002). *Eine andere Bürgergesellschaft: Klassischer Republikanismus und Kommunalismus im Kanton Zürich im späten 18. und 19. Jahrhundert*, Göttingen.
Weisser, Michael (1979). *Crime and Punishment in Early Modern Europe*, Atlantic Highlands, NJ.
Welch, Marcelle Maistre (2002). 'Introduction' in François Poullain de la Barre, *Three Cartesian Feminist Treatises*, trans. Vivien Bosley, ed. Marcelle Maistre Welch, Chicago, IL, pp. 125–37.

Wende, Peter (1974). '"Liberty" und "Property" in der politicshen Theorie der Levellers', *Zeitschrift für Historische Forschung* 1, pp. 147–73.

Whatmore, Richard (2009). '"Neither Masters nor Slaves": Small States and Empire in the Long Eighteenth Century' in *Lineages of Empire: The Historical Roots of British Imperial Thought*, ed. Duncan Kelly, Oxford, pp. 53–81.

White, B. R. (1971). *The English Separatist Tradition: From the Marian Martyrs to the Pilgrim Fathers*, Oxford.

Whitman, James (1990). *The Legacy of Roman Law in the German Romantic Era: Historical Vision and Legal Change*, Princeton, NJ.

Wieacker, Franz (1995). *A History of Private Law in Europe, with Particular Reference to Germany*, trans. Tony Weir, Oxford.

Wilbur, Earl Morse (1946). *A History of Unitarianism: Socinianism and Its Antecedents*, Cambridge, MA.

Wildenburg, Dorothea (1997). '"Aneinander vorbei": Zum Horenstreit zwischen Fichte und Schiller', *Fichte-Studien* 12, pp. 25–41.

Wilkinson, J. C. (1987). *The Imamate Tradition of Oman*, Cambridge.

Wilks, Michael (1963). *The Problem of Sovereignty in the Later Middle Ages: The Papal Monarchy with Augustinus Triumphus and the Publicists*, Cambridge.

Williams, Bernard (1999). 'Tolerating the Intolerable' in *The Politics of Toleration: Tolerance and Intolerance in Modern Life*, ed. Susan Mendus, Edinburgh, pp. 65–76.

Williams, Howard (2003). *Kant's Critique of Hobbes: Sovereignty and Cosmopolitanism*, Cardiff.

Wilson, Peter (2004). *From Reich to Revolution: German History, 1558–1806*, New York.

(2006). 'Still a Monstrosity? Some Reflections on Early Modern German Statehood', *Historical Journal* 49, pp. 565–76.

Winship, George Parker (1920). *The New England Company of 1649 and John Eliot*, Boston, MA.

Wirszubski, C. (1950). *Libertas as a Political Idea at Rome during the Late Republic and Early Principate*, Cambridge.

Withington, Phillip (2001). 'Two Renaissances: Urban Political Culture in Post-Reformation England', *Historical Journal* 44, pp. 239–67.

Witt, Ronald (1971). 'The Rebirth of the Concept of Republican Liberty in Italy' in *Renaissance Studies in Honor of Hans Baron*, ed. A. Molho and J. Tedeschi, Florence, pp. 173–99.

(2000). *In the Footsteps of the Ancients: The Origins of Humanism from Lovato to Bruni*, Leiden.

Witte Jr, John (2007). *The Reformation of Rights: Law, Religion and Human Rights in Early Modern Calvinism*, Cambridge.

Wittichen, Paul (1904). 'Kant und Burke', *Historische Zeitschrift* 93, pp. 253–5.

Witusik, Adam (1978). *O Zamoyskich, Zamościu i Akademii Zamojskiej*, Lublin.

Wolgast, Eike (1977). *Die Wittenberger Theologie und die Politik der evangelischen Stände*, Gütersloh.

(1980). *Die Religionsfrage als Problem des Widerstandsrechts im 16. Jahrhundert*, Heidelberg.

Wood, Neal (1988). *Cicero's Social and Political Thought*, Berkeley and Los Angeles, CA.

Woods, Susanne (1988). 'How Free Are Milton's Women?' in *Milton and the Idea of Woman*, ed. Julia M. Walker, Chicago, IL, pp. 15–31.
Woolf, Cecil S. (1913). *Bartolus of Sassoferrato: His Position in the History of Political Thought*, Cambridge.
Worden, Blair (1984). 'Toleration and the Cromwellian Protectorate' in *Persecution and Toleration*, ed. W. J. Shiels, Oxford, pp. 199–233.
(1995). 'Milton and Marchamont Nedham' in *Milton and Republicanism*, ed. David Armitage, Armand Himy and Quentin Skinner, Cambridge, pp. 156–80.
(1996). *The Sound of Virtue: Philip Sidney's Arcadia and Elizabethan Politics*, New Haven, CT.
(2002). 'Republicanism, Regicide and Republic: The English Experience' in *Republicanism: A Shared European heritage*, vol. 1, ed. Martin van Gelderen and Quentin Skinner, Cambridge, pp. 307–28.
(2007). *Literature and Politics in Cromwellian England: John Milton, Andrew Marvell, Marchamont Nedham*, Oxford.
(2011). 'Oliver Cromwell and the Cause of Civil and Religious Liberty' in *England's Wars of Religion, Revisited*, ed. Charles Prior and Glenn Burgess, Farnham, pp. 231–51.
Wörterbuch der klassischen arabischen Sprache (1970–2000), Wiesbaden.
Wright, Anthony D. (2005). *The Counter-Reformation: Catholic Europe and the Non-Christian World*, Aldershot.
Wyss, David (1790). *Lebensgeschichte Johann Kaspar Eschers Bürgermeister der Republik Zürich*, Zurich.
Yaffe, Gideon (2000). *Liberty Worth the Name: Locke on Free Agency*, Princeton, NJ.
Zager, Werner (ed.) (2010). *Martin Luther und die Freiheit*, Darmstadt.
Zajączkowski, Andrzej (1993). *Szlachta polska: kultura i struktura*, Warsaw.
Zammito, John H. (2002). *Kant, Herder, and the Birth of Anthropology*, Chicago, IL and London.
Zedelmaier, Helmut (2003). *Der Anfang der Geschichte: Studien zur Ursprungsdebatte im 18. Jahrhundert*, Hamburg.
Zernack, Klaus (1995). 'Staatsmacht und Ständefreiheit. Politik und Gesellschaft in der Geschichte des östlichen Mitteleuropa' in *Stände und Landesherrschaft in Ostmitteleuropa in der frühen Neuzeit*, ed. Hugo Weczerka, Marburg, pp. 1–10.
Zweig, Stefan (1936). *The Right to Heresy: Calvin against Castellio*, London.

Index of names

Numbers in italic type refer to this volume

Index of subjects

Numbers in italic type refer to this volume

Lightning Source UK Ltd.
Milton Keynes UK
UKHW032142160820
368285UK00004B/12

9 781108 817783